CAPITALISTS AGAINST MARKETS

Capitalists against Markets

*The Making of Labor Markets
and Welfare States
in the United States and Sweden*

Peter A. Swenson

OXFORD
UNIVERSITY PRESS

2002

OXFORD
UNIVERSITY PRESS

Oxford   New York

Auckland   Bangkok   Buenos Aires   Cape Town   Chennai
Dar es Salaam   Delhi   Hong Kong   Istanbul   Karachi   Kolkata
Kuala Lumpur   Madrid   Melbourne   Mexico City   Mumbai   Nairobi
São Paulo   Shanghai   Singapore   Taipei   Tokyo   Toronto

and an associated company in Berlin

Published by Oxford University Press, Inc.
198 Madison Avenue, New York, New York 10016

www.oup.com

Oxford is a registered trademark of Oxford University Press

Library of Congress Cataloging-in-Publication Data
Swenson, Peter A.
Capitalists against markets : the making of labor markets and welfare states
in the United States and Sweden / Peter A. Swenson.
p.   cm.
Includes bibliographical references and index.
ISBN 0-19-514296-9   ISBN 0-19-514297-7 (pbk.)
1. Labor policy—United States—History—20th century. 2. Labor policy—
Sweden—History—20th century. 3. Labor market—United States—History—
20th century. 4. Labor market—Sweden—History—20th century. 5. Capitalism—United
States—History—20th century. 6. Capitalism—Sweden—History—20th century. 7. United
States—Social policy. 8. Sweden—Social policy. 9. Public welfare—United States—
History—20th century. 10. Public welfare—Sweden—History—20th century.
11. New Deal, 1933–1939. 12. Welfare state. I. Title.
HD8072. S92 2002
331.12'09485—dc21   2001036133

2 4 6 8 9 7 5 3 1

Printed in the United States of America
on acid-free paper

Ultimately . . . it is the relation of a class to society as a whole which maps out its part in the drama; and its success is determined by the breadth and variety of the interests, other than its own, which it is able to serve. Indeed, no policy of a narrow class interest can safeguard even that interest well.

Karl Polanyi, *The Great Transformation* (1944)

PREFACE

In the politics of work and welfare in capitalist democracies, capitalists invariably play a conservative role according to most historical, sociological, and political analysis. Projecting onto them a cold disinterest in almost everything except market action for their exclusive material gain, this scholarly consensus, I believe, underestimates capitalists' contributions toward the passage of egalitarian and protective social reform. By attributing the many reforms that take place exclusively to other political forces, it also tends to underestimate the power of capitalists in capitalist society.

These errors are probably a consequence in part of the politics of those who study labor and social policy. For most of them, capitalism is something we probably have to live with, and perhaps even should live with, but not without trying to modify and improve it. Thus, it stands to reason, if capitalism needs reform, then capitalists—with perhaps a few politically irrelevant exceptions—are the main obstacle. When reform is imposed, they accept it, supposedly, only in begrudging recognition of a shift in the balance of power against them.

While I also hold strong progressive sentiments for reform, I have come to disagree with the idea of capitalists as invariant and unregenerate opponents. This book explains why. It looks in depth at capitalists' interests in the shaping of labor markets and social policy making over the course of a century in the United States and Sweden. Within the broad category of economically advanced capitalist democracies, these two countries differ radically in the character of their industrial relations systems and social policy regimes. Capitalists' interests there have also differed in the same measure. My analysis of these variations across the countries, and over time within them, shows that the political weakness of Swedish capital gives a less than persuasive explanation for the extraordinary successes of the social democratic labor movement relative to what labor and liberals have accomplished in the United States. It also shows that the ebbing of capitalists' relative power cannot adequately account for when and why these societies imposed some measure of equity and security on the arbitrariness and uncertainty of markets.

The economic, historical, and political analysis indicates that some of the error in conventional thinking arises not just from ideology but from our difficulties as outside observers in seeing through the deceptive game of politics. In that game, capitalists' strategic positions may obscure their real wants. Their wants or preferences may not quickly and faithfully adjust to the complex workings of real, underlying, and changing interests over time. Thus, economic theory about capitalists' varying interests and in-depth comparative historical research on their evolving wants and strategies are the means used here to develop an alternative and, I hope, more penetrating understanding of capitalists and reform.

Private sector employers and their organizations are the analytical and research focus. I chose to study them not because I believe they are the only important agents of social policy reform. Nothing could be further from the truth. Most initiative takers come from outside the ranks of capitalists and many of the most vocal opponents step forth from among them. I selected this focus because most literature neglects employers in the investigation of other agents of change: party politicians, for example, who appeal to popular, especially working-class interests, or policy intellectuals and bureaucrats with their potentially "autonomous" agendas. Therefore, I make no claim that impersonal capitalist mechanisms frictionlessly or even clankingly drive political systems. Nor do I claim that capitalist elites pull all the strings attached to puppet-like actors on the political stage. Instead, the politics of reform, I argue, is usually the result of a pragmatic and strategic search by noncapitalists for policy founded on *cross-class alliances of interest.* In this building of bridges, the interests of neither capitalists nor of other groups exclusively determine who gets what from the two-way traffic in benefits.

Some readers may be disappointed to find no formal elaborations and quantitative testing of theory. Here I follow a tradition of qualitative work in comparative political economy, hoping to achieve another kind of rigor through the gathering and analysis of historical evidence. In this tradition, slippery metaphors like "the balance of power between labor and capital" appear with frustrating frequency, without clear definition, and never face the criticism that similar notions about power among nation-states endlessly suffer in the international relations literature. My notion of cross-class alliances may not be an enormous improvement in precision. I do not even think it can account for all reform. Indeed, "class compromise" resulting from changing power balances between social classes—or better, shared recognition that the costs of continued conflict exceed the costs of compromise—no doubt accounts for some progressive change at the margin. I believe, however, that the cross-class alliance analysis has more traction for pulling together the facts about the labor and social politics of capitalist democracies into a realistic argument.

Although class compromise does take place, I have concluded that cross-class alliances are the real foundation for *enduring systems* of equity and social protection. In cross-class alliances, there are often losers on both sides of the class divide, and it is they who have to do most of the compromising.

Also, in this qualitative literature, the interests of political actors identified in causal narratives are often left conceptually indistinct from their strategic positions and real preferences. That all these things vary significantly across and within many levels of aggregation in heterogeneous social structures and complex hierarchical organizations is barely hinted at. Though this book shares some of that inevitable imprecision, my hope is that it improves on the tradition and partially clears the conceptual fog. Hopefully it will inspire further clarifying research and debate.

These shortcomings, and all others, are not the responsibility in any way of the many people who helped me along the way, in many ways, in my research and writing. Some read and commented critically and almost always encouragingly on pieces and versions of this work as it progressed; others helped immeasurably in my investigations; some just helped with their friendly and generous hospitality during my visits to Sweden. They are Klas Åmark, Måns and Lolita Arborelius, Edward Berkowitz, Svala Bjorgvinsdottir, Fred Block, Lennart Bratt, Youssef Cohen, Hans De Geer, Bill Domhoff, Per Gunnar Edebalk, Nils Elvander, Gøsta Esping-Andersen, Karl-Olof Faxén, Curt-Steffan Giesecke, Colin Gordon, Jacob Hacker, Peter Hall, Ann-Britt Hellmark, Torben Iversen, Sandy Jacoby, Michael Katz, Baldur Kristiansson, Matts Bergom Larsson, Philip Manow, Jeff Manza, Andy Martin, Cathie Jo Martin, Rudolf Meidner, Stig Nilsson, Ben Page, Åke Nordlander, Paul Pierson, Jonas Pontusson, Bo Rothstein, Ben Schneider, Ian Shapiro, Kicki Sjöquist, Sven-Anders Söderpalm, David Soskice, Kjell Treslow, and Robert Wiebe. Kathy Thelen and Michael Wallerstein, my friends and colleagues at Northwestern, deserve a separate and special thanks for their enthusiastic interest in my work and ideas for improving it.

I am of course grateful to a number of institutions that made my research and writing possible with financial assistance and the temporary release from teaching responsibilities. These are the German Marshall Fund of the United States; the Hagley Museum and Library in Wilmington, Delaware; Northwestern University and its Institute for Policy Research; the American-Scandinavian Foundation; and the University of Pennsylvania. Much of the material in chapters 9 and 10 appeared earlier in "Arranged Alliance: Business Interests in the New Deal," *Politics and Society* 25:1 (March 1997); its revised presentation here benefitted from the reactions the article received. I am especially grateful to the Swedish Employers' Confederation (SAF) and the Swedish Engineering Employers' Association in Stockholm for granting me permission to use voluminous minutes and other documents from their archives. Warm and special thanks must go to Margareta Englund, Vivi-Ann Melander, Björn Holmberg, and Susanne Palmer at SAF for their generous good will and enormous help in locating and retrieving hundreds of documents from vaults and basements.

Thanks also to the late Bertil Kugelberg for agreeing to let me use extensive notes he recorded from his many meetings and conversations with key figures in Swedish labor relations and politics during his years at SAF.

Loving and laughing thanks also to my wife, Pauline, and my sons, Mattias, Samuel, and Diego. They teased me mercilessly about how slow I was in finishing this book. That was their most direct contribution to the long-delayed outcome, though time has told that it didn't work all that well. Finally, it is dedicated with loving memory to my mother, Shirley Taylor, for all she gave.

A NOTE ON SOURCES

This book draws on many primary and secondary sources. Of greatest importance for the discussion on the United States is the vast secondary literature in history, political science, sociology, and economics. The scale and resources of the country's system of research universities has made available a rich supply of information to draw on without direct recourse to primary sources. Of course the best of the secondary literature brought a wealth of archival evidence to light for use in the analysis. The Hagley Museum and Library in Wilmington, Delaware, houses a few of the archives directly consulted, especially the collection of the National Association of Manufacturers. Box and file designations for the NAM documents cited may have changed, for, unfortunately, the entire collection has undergone reorganization. Use was also made of transcribed interviews with Marion Folsom, Arthur Altmeyer, and Herbert Lehman housed at the Columbia University Oral History Collection, Columbia University, New York. Newspapers, especially the *New York Times,* and other periodical literature also proved invaluable.

By contrast, the research on Sweden relies heavily on archival sources, although I also draw on practically all the secondary research available. Most valuable by far were minutes transcribed from meetings of the board of directors (*styrelsen*) of SAF (*Svenska Arbetsgivareföreningen*), the Swedish Employers' Confederation, and of its directors' conferences (*ombudsmannakonferenser;* later *förbundsdirektörskonferenser*). The former consisted of full-time company executives and owners, usually prominent ones, elected by the confederation's membership. The latter included the full-time executive leadership of SAF and of its sectoral affiliates. Other important collections consulted at SAF were those of former executive director Bertil Kugelberg, who granted me permission to consult his extensive notes from conversations (*minnesanteckningar*) and other documents. I also consulted minutes of meetings at VF (*Verkstads-*

föreningen), the Swedish Engineering Employers' Association, and archives of other SAF sectoral affiliates housed at their respective headquarters. (SAF has since been reorganized into *Svenskt Näringsliv,* or the Confederation of Swedish Enterprise, and VF into *Verkstadsindustrier,* the Association of Swedish Engineering Industries.)

Other valuable sources were from the Swedish National Archives (*Riksarkivet*) in Stockholm. In particular, J. Sigfrid Edström's collection, including extensive correspondence, and that of his Directors' Club (*Direktörsklubben*) of executives from the country's five top engineering firms, were indispensable. Finally, the collection of Finnish employer confederation leader Axel Palmgren, at the library of Åbo Akademi, Åbo, Finland, contained much illuminating correspondence with Swedish employer officials.

Full citations for any secondary work referred to in any chapter in abbreviated form can be found earlier on in that chapter's endnotes. A bibliography of secondary sources will be made available upon request to the author.

CONTENTS

ABBREVIATIONS

United States

ACWA	Amalgamated Clothing Workers of America
AFL	American Federation of Labor
AGC	Associated General Contractors of America
AIC	Associated Industries of Cleveland
BAC	Business Advisory Council
CCF	Central Competitive Field
CES	Committee on Economic Security
CIO	Congress of Industrial Organizations
EAD	Employers' Association of Detroit
FLSA	Fair Labor Standards Act
IAM	International Association of Machinists
ILGWU	International Ladies' Garment Workers' Union
IMU	International Molders' Union
IRC	Industrial Relations Counselors
NAM	National Association of Manufacturers
NCF	National Civic Federation
NEA	National Erectors' Association
NFA	National Founders' Association
NICB	National Industrial Conference Board
NIRA	National Industrial Recovery Act
NLRA	National Labor Relations Act
NMTA	National Metal Trades Association
NRA	National Recovery Administration

NWLB	National War Labor Board
OAI	Old Age Insurance
SCC	Special Conference Committee
SFNDA	Stove Founders' National Defense Association
SSA	Social Security Act
SSRC	Social Science Research Council
UAW	United Auto Workers' Union
UI	Unemployment Insurance
UMW	United Mine Workers' Union
USW	United Steel Workers' Union
WIC	Wisconsin Industrial Commission
WLPB	War Labor Policies Board
WMA	Wisconsin Manufacturers' Association

Sweden

AMS	Arbetsmarknadsstyrelsen (The Swedish Labor Market Board)
ATP	Allmänna Tillägspensionen (General Supplementary Pension)
BIF	Byggnadsindustriförbundet (The Swedish Building Industry Employers' Association)
BMF	Byggmästareförbundet (The Swedish Building Masters' Association)
JBF	Järnbruksförbundet (The Swedish Iron and Steel Industry Employers' Association
LO	Landsorganisationen i Sverige (The Swedish Confederation of Labor)
Metall	Metallindustriarbetareförbundet (The Swedish Metalworkers' Union)
PBF	Pappersbruksförbundet (The Swedish Paper Industry Employers' Association)
PMF	Pappersmasseförbundet (The Swedish Paper Pulp Industry Employers' Association)
SAF	Svenska Arbetsgivareföreningen (The Swedish Employers' Confederation)
SPIAF	Svenska Pappersindustriarbetareförbundet (The Swedish Paper Industry Workers' Union)
TCO	Tjänstemännens Centralorganisation (The Swedish Confederation of Salaried Workers' Unions)
TIF	Textilindustriförbundet (The Swedish Textile Industry Employers' Association)
VF	Verkstadsföreningen (The Swedish Engineering Employers' Association)

Part I

History and Theory

1

A HISTORICAL PUZZLE

The odds that a child born in America today will lead a life of extraordinary material comfort and benefit from all manner of expensive medical wonders are higher, it is fair to say, than anywhere else in the world. Born in a country like Sweden, with an economy at a roughly equal level of development, that child would start with different, and in a way, better odds: less chance of luxury, but also less chance of misery. In other words, a Swedish child is more likely to reach old age without ever having to face economic privation and an avoidable or surmountable medical catastrophe. For those reasons, quite possibly, even the prospects of surviving infancy and growing old in Sweden are higher.[1]

Across the world, large differences in labor markets and welfare states account for most of people's uneven life chances as they go from cradle to grave. Today, for example, Swedish employers pay about the most egalitarian wages and salaries in the world. The Swedish government also enjoys, or suffers, a reputation as a vanguard among welfare states. It is hardly surpassed in the generosity of its monetary benefits and supply of services for people needing them because of childbearing, child rearing, unemployment, sickness, disability, and old age. America, by contrast, stands out among affluent capitalist societies with its highly unequal distribution of pay and benefits, including private health insurance, attached to gainful employment. Likewise, its welfare state, though important for keeping many out of poverty, is rather meager. For example, it is the only wealthy nation where vast numbers of people, roughly 40 million at current count, have no health insurance and therefore often miss out on timely, high quality medical care—that is to say, if they get any care at all.

That market-generated inequalities are high in the United States is well known. It is also beyond dispute that the American welfare state deserves to be characterized as laggard or limited in comparison to other affluent societies.

People continue to research and argue about why there are differences—many of them perhaps harboring the hope of discovering what is politically possible in the way of improvement, especially in the United States. Their research on labor markets identifies a number of causes of relative inequalities. The relative centralization of wage determination appears to be the strongest. Decentralized pay setting in the United States creates inequalities; centralization of collective bargaining in Sweden compresses them. Research on comparative levels and forms of social security frequently finds, not surprisingly, the ideological agendas of partisan governments to be most important. America, lacking strong Social Democratic or Christian Democratic parties, falls well behind Sweden, Germany, and the Netherlands, for example.[2]

Two intuitively plausible theories about underlying causes commonly figure in these comparative analyses. One, a "power resources" or "political class struggle" argument, points logically to differences in the clout of reform-oriented political forces, which in the case of Swedish Social Democracy include the large and unified labor unions allied with the party. This kind of argument attributes America's limited welfare state in part to weak labor unions and the absence of a labor party that could assert their power, together with electoral pressures, in the legislative process.[3] The same power factors implicitly or explicitly figure in varying explanations of wage and salary inequalities because of their causal link to the centralization of collective bargaining.[4] Recent welfare analysis turns its attention to Catholic or Christian Democratic power resources, arguing they are of equal significance in some countries in the allocation of comforts and miseries within nations through institutionalized pay setting and redistributive social policy.[5]

Another influential but somewhat less obvious line of analysis, focusing on America's "exceptionalism," blames the country's inequalities on its decentralized and fragmented political institutions. In this view, hopeful movements for progressive and egalitarian reform in America lose energy and cohesiveness as they scrape and fracture on the rough terrain (the "veto points") spread out across this vast country's complex political system. "There is an excessive friction in the American system, a waste of force in the strife of various bodies and persons created to check and balance one another," British observer James Bryce noted in 1893. "Power is so much subdivided that it is hard at a given moment to concentrate it for prompt and effective action."[6] Later, state-centric "institutionalist" reasoning of this nature also comes into service to help explain the failure to develop centralized labor market institutions and therefore relatively uneven wages. Recent comparative analysis argues implicitly that in Europe, constitutional differences combined with the power resources of both Christian Democratic and Social Democratic movements effectively overcome capitalist resistance.[7] A good summation of this point of view identifies the American institutional terrain as particularly biased in favor of capitalists and their power resources, even as they obstruct the accumulation of power resources in "large cohesive labor unions and parties."[8]

The Welfare State: A Question
of Timing

Compelling or even downright obvious though they may sound, power re-source and institutionalist arguments strain to make clear sense of historical facts about the timing of twentieth-century welfare state development, at least in the United States and Sweden. What is puzzling from the standpoint of these theories is that the United States experienced a "big bang" in develop-ment of modern welfare before Sweden did, but without electorally and orga-nizationally strong labor or Christian Democratic movements. With social leg-islation passed by a Democratic Party, representing both labor and farm interests even as it drew on substantial funding from capitalists, America's New Deal dramatically departed from the past and gave the country a progres-sive head start on Sweden.[9] Swedish Social Democrats, ruling in a similar sort of alliance with agricultural interests, introduced little change in the 1930s. Though both countries had unchanging institutions in place over the period in question, the Swedish welfare state evolved rather slowly at first and started to accelerate past America's only in the 1940s and 1950s. Invariant institu-tions and power balances seem to have generated highly variant results.

To be more specific: in Sweden, during the 1930s, the Social Democrats only barely improved on earlier and limited government benefits passed by centrist and conservative parties. Although they were self-professed socialists almost exclusively dependent on labor for outside financing, their reforms in 1935 and 1937 of the existing public pension scheme they had inherited were so mod-est that the employer support they enjoyed hardly demands an explanation. Their unemployment insurance legislation of 1934 did encounter business hostility, but it was actually inferior, as explained later, to what business-financed New Deal Democrats installed as part of America's Social Security Act of 1935.

So it is not surprising that when journalist Marquis Childs elevated Swedish Social Democracy to celebrity status among liberals in Depression-era Amer-ica as a "middle way" between capitalism and socialism, it was not because he found much to write home about in its social legislation. Instead, his books ex-tolled the country's consumer and producer cooperatives, limited but robust state enterprise, and "a strong, all-inclusive labor movement" for making cap-italism work "in a reasonable way for the greatest good of the whole nation."[10] If there were advantages to a strong labor movement, it was not its ability to force through the kind of social insurance legislation that would be passed as part of the New Deal—much less to bring capitalism to ruin as the more hys-terical among American businessmen and their ideologues seemed to fear.

Confirming Childs's observations on the Swedish welfare state, a recent study of the American case found that, in 1938, "American performance outpaced the efforts of Sweden, today's world leader in social spending."[11] Peter Flora's and Jens Alber's broad comparative analysis of welfare state development informs us that to the limited extent Sweden stood out before the 1970s, it had already done so by 1913 when the Social Democrats' parliamentary power was still limited and its unions still enfeebled by the severe thrashing employers meted them in the gigantic conflict of 1909. Because of Sweden's low level of industrial development relative to other European countries at the time, its backwardness relative to the United States in the 1930s can be of only limited value in explaining its lagging performance then.[12]

Later, through the 1930s and 1940s, according to Flora and Alber, other European countries under varying kinds of political control narrowed the gap, even though Social Democrats, easily boasting the best-organized labor force in the world, dominated Swedish politics and government. Ultimately, other than some innovative family welfare policies, practically all of Sweden's major improvements had to wait until the mid-1940s and beyond, despite the labor movement's firm grip in national politics since 1932.[13] The Social Democratic minister of social affairs was even able to invoke Sweden's relative laggardness in 1953 to justify improvements in social insurance.[14] As one prominent Scandinavian expert puts it, "by international standards Sweden was a rather average welfare state in 1960." In sum, according to another author, "welfare expenditure in Sweden lagged far behind what one might have expected after thirty years of social-democratic hegemony."[15]

It should be granted, however, that in terms of form or structure, not expenditure levels, the Swedish welfare state had begun to assume some exceptional features by 1960. According to the eminent comparative social policy expert Gøsta Esping-Andersen, "the cornerstones of the contemporary welfare state [in Sweden] were set during the 1940s and 1950s."[16] Those comprehensive health and pension reforms that were eventually to put Sweden way ahead in terms of "decommodification" (the use of social policy to "emancipate individuals from market dependence") came in 1955 and 1959. But even on this dimension, Swedish progress was still modest. Social Democrats in fact did very poorly with their unemployment insurance scheme in 1934, which covered barely one third of the labor force by 1950, only increasing to over 80 percent in the 1980s. By his measurements of decommodification, Esping-Andersen even finds that, as late as 1980, Swedish unemployment insurance ranked exactly at the mean among 18 affluent countries. Alongside Sweden, but slightly above the mean, was the United States.[17]

Because Sweden's labor unions had somewhat amazingly grown in membership rather than declined as in the rest of the world during the 1920s, and maintained a clear lead ever after, these comparisons probably come as something of a surprise. Here more than elsewhere, one would think, the Left should have been quickly able to overcome powerful forces of resistance to social insurance, whatever their source. Instead, their success came much later and more in the realms of health and retirement security than in unemployment insurance. But employers—our usual suspects rounded up to explain the resistance—were less than terribly inconvenienced in these areas. The reforms, after all, spared mostly the sick and elderly, rather than the able-bodied unemployed, from the labor market's rod.

The health and pension reforms actually left employers feeling, on the whole, well cared for. The same holds for "active labor market policy" of the 1950s and onward. This policy, according to Esping-Andersen, "was only possible due to the extraordinary labor market powers of the union movement."[18] But such an assessment is hard to square with the fact that labor market intervention was designed to equip workers with the most up-to-date and marketable industrial skills and move them about the country to meet employers' needs. In other words, it promoted commodification, at least in the sense of keeping workers circulating in the labor market and away from their fishing spots, gardens, pubs, and sofas. Development and expansion of day care starting in the 1960s had a similar employer-friendly purpose. The public sector hired female labor to free up female labor, a net gain for the private sector. Getting potential workers away from domestic, labor-intensive kitchens or bedsides and onto factory production lines was a service Social Democrats helped provide employers with their rapid expansion of public child care. Having pleaded for government action in the 1950s, manufacturing employers welcomed the Social Democratic initiatives of the 1960s and participated actively in government commissions that designed day care policies.[19] Later analysis in this book will explain why.

The Equivalency Premise

Two plausible assumptions fully consistent with the conventional thinking are what make these facts about the timing of welfare state development in the two countries so puzzling. The first is a specific historical one already mentioned in passing: that the relevant political institutions in the two countries did not change over the period in question. Sweden remained a relatively centralized parliamentary system with strong parties and therefore a limited number of veto points. The United States remained a federal and presidential system with weak parties, strong committees in a bicameral legislature, Senate filibusters, and an independent Supreme Court exercising powers of judicial review. The countries' different coefficients of institutional friction then are hard-pressed, by themselves at least, to explain the fact that Sweden lagged behind the United States in the 1930s and then sped up in the 1940s and 1950s to pass it on the left. Other variables are needed, it seems, possibly related to the changing interests or power of groups like labor and capital, and possibly interacting somehow with the fixed institutions.

The second conventional assumption that makes a puzzle out of historical facts deals directly with these interests. It maintains that labor and capital in Sweden and the United States held consistently opposing interests regarding the welfare state in both countries over time. This assumption applies a broader premise about enduring class interests in all national settings. As Esping-

Andersen, a leading proponent of the labor power argument, puts it, "Employers have always opposed decommodification." Likewise, in his view, labor's interests across countries are roughly equivalent. For labor movements, decommodification "has always been a priority" and therefore, presumably because of capital's perennial opposition, it is a "hugely contested issue" within countries.[20] In short, there is a practical equivalence of interests among like classes in different countries, and equivalence of conflict across their respective class divides. By this *equivalency premise*, the stronger Swedish labor movement, with backing from a socialist party in government entirely independent of funding from business, should not have been outclassed by the New Deal. After all, that was the project of a Democratic Party relying on considerable financial support from business and backed by a divided labor movement that was struggling to get back on its feet.

Revealing the equivalency premise as the source of puzzlement points to the need for comparative empirical validation of the premise itself—not just a resumption of the search for new interactive variables. In general, comparative research tends simply to accept the premise on faith and then look for factors other than variations in interests that might explain national variations in welfare states. In practice, this actually goes for institutionalists and power theorists alike—although that, to be sure, is not logically required by either approach. Institutionalists, one critique points out, tend in practice to start from unexamined assumptions about broad structural or economic similarities across countries, including class interests, in order then to identify institutional variations that explain different historical outcomes.[21] An influential model of this tendency is Theda Skocpol's comparative analysis of social revolutions. She assumed outright that peasant exploitation was virtually equivalent across old-regime agrarian societies, only some of which experienced social revolutions. What therefore endowed only some peasant classes with revolutionary potential were particular state-related institutional structures that, in some countries and not others, facilitated the translation of objective exploitation into subjectively and collectively perceived grievances and then facilitated collective action.[22]

Institutionalists are usually not this extreme, or at least this explicit. Recent institutionalist work on the welfare state, most notably that of Kathleen Thelen, even avoids the problems entirely. Indeed, she astutely shows how capitalist interests can coincide with those of labor regarding market intervention in the realm of skill formation. Thus the problem lies not in institutionalism as an approach, but only in applications of it that assume too much about capitalists' interests against reform.[23] But typical analyses of health care reform by comparative-historical institutionalists, for example, implicitly treat the variable, and therefore potentially pivotal, interests of capitalists as exclusively oppositional. Ellen Immergut comes very close to the equivalency position in explaining why Swedish employers "seemed ready to acquiesce to national health insurance," a description that understates their profound amenability. In her view, it was only in their strategic, not immediate interests, for they wanted to preserve good will in their dealings with an extraordinarily well-organized and politically muscular labor movement in other policy realms. Thus, she attaches no particular causal importance to variable business interests; the conventional argument about the unusual power of Swedish labor suffices. Consequently, she leaves unexamined the possibility that if French or Swiss capitalists had been equally favorable, then constitutional factors delaying or limiting reform in those places may have proved less important.[24]

Those who look elsewhere than institutions seem even more unambiguously inclined to tie themselves down to an unexamined equivalency premise about fixed class interests, and in particular capitalist interests against reform. Doing so allows if not requires them to turn to variations in the power of the working class against capital for their causal logic. The variable and changeable "balance of class power," as it is sometimes put, explains important variations in social and labor policies. In Fred Block's influential analysis, for example, changes over time can be accounted for by changes in the balance, as when capital's "structural power" against reform is neutralized or disabled by war or depression.[25]

Others, like Esping-Andersen, find evidence in cross-national quantitative analysis of data from recent decades for the role of "working class power mobilization" in welfare state formation. Power mobilization in this "political class struggle" perspective is measured, for example, by legislative and cabinet seat shares for left-wing or labor parties. All in all, Esping-Andersen finds the power of the Left in the postwar era explains a substantial amount of variation in the structure (though not, interestingly, size) of welfare states in advanced industrial countries. Left power correlates strongly with universalism (lack of demeaning means-testing) and degrees of decommodification (e.g., measured as short waiting periods, long benefit periods, and high income-replacement rates for sick pay and unemployment benefits).[26] In Sweden specifically, Esping-Andersen argues that the power of the Left "is the key to the evolution of Sweden's postwar political economy." More than in any other European nation, he asserts, the "working class has been capable of initiating and imposing its policy preferences." In sum, the "evolution of Swedish state policies is therefore largely a reflection of their labor market strategies and powers to tame the private economy via the state."[27] Even an institutionalist like Skocpol, in turning from social revolutions to comparative social policy, resorts to this conventional brand of power analysis, and therefore unambiguously adopts the equivalency premise. "The political class struggle between workers and capital," she says, "helps to explain why the United States has not developed a comprehensive full-employment welfare state along postwar Scandinavian lines." In other words, the political dominance of the Social Democrats "induced business to come to terms . . . with the emerging Swedish welfare state."[28]

Though measures of working-class power mobilization may well statistically vary with welfare state development in the late twentieth century, as Esping-Andersen and others show, the correlation does not prove causation was at work. This skepticism is bolstered by the historical puzzle of the early to mid-twentieth century. Again, confidence about causality requires independent empirical substantiation of the initial equivalency premise. If further investigation were to reveal that employer interests regarding social policy are strikingly more positive where labor is "strong" according to the typical measures, then the conceptual treads in the causal analysis would lose all traction. The same would hold for employer interests regarding equalization of results in labor markets, another central subject of this book. For example, a recent attempt to demonstrate how labor's power (measured by union organization levels) compresses wages in various countries fails to control for variable capitalist interests for or against wage equalization. It therefore implicitly adopts the equivalency premise as an operational assumption. To put it another way, it fails to consider the possibility that union strength and employer interests in equalization may partially coincide. To the extent they coincide, no conclusions about the use of union power to achieve equalization can confidently be drawn from the study's results.[29]

In short, empirical analysis of labor's power over things that capitalists care about—labor markets and welfare states—must step back and either prove the equivalency premise or control for measured variations in employer interests before reaching causal conclusions. Though not acknowledging the challenge formulated exactly in this way, Esping-Andersen does, somewhat cryptically, wrap up his analysis of the welfare state and the capitalist power structure with an appropriately skeptical question: "[I]s political power a decisive or only spurious historical variable?"[30] The answer offered here is that the political power of labor, measured conventionally, is indeed spurious if conceived exclusively as "power against capital and its interests." But as the cross-class alliance analysis indicates, the power of labor, otherwise conceived, is indeed decisive. It can be used against capitalist interests or for them, and the choice makes a big difference for the durability of reform.

Labor Brings Capital In: Reformer Initiative and Cross-Class Alliance Making

Empirical evidence about employer interests presented later in this book shows beyond a doubt that the equivalency premise is a shaky one. This conclusion holds for both wage compression and social policy. Some of the most astonishing evidence shows that the Swedish Employers' Confederation was remarkably eager to create a more level structure of wages across firms and industries, well before the unions unified behind a "solidaristic wage policy" in the 1950s onward. The power of well-organized unions helped employers achieve results that their organization could not achieve on its own in the face of market forces.

In the realm of social policy, history shows that Swedish employers were anything but foot draggers when it came to the belated post–New Deal reforms of the 1940s and 1950s and were, in some cases, even more generous reformers than the Social Democrats themselves. With the one exception of a pension reform in 1959, their confederation favored legislation over no legislation. Even after the 1959 reform, however, they decisively intervened to muzzle the Conservative Party when it called for dismantling the reform once it passed. In the debate leading to the 1946 pension reform, the employers' organization rejected a cheap "means-tested" version of legislation (targeted to poorer applicants who could demonstrate need) initially favored by leading Social Democrats. Employers favored the more expensive "universalistic" (nontargeted) proposal up for discussion, which is what the Social Democrats ultimately chose. In the case of health insurance in 1953, employers preferred the legislation's expensive sick-pay linked to previous earnings over a cheaper flat-rate system and were glad to jettison company provision of health benefits. After coming around to the employers' view, the Social Democrats discarded the flat-rate system they had passed in 1946, but not yet implemented, having once intended to leave ample room for American-style supplementary private benefits provided by individual employers.

And in 1947 organized employers eagerly signed on to the idea of "active" labor market policy measures, which were rolled out in large quantity the following decade. Active labor market policy, possibly more than any single piece of the welfare state, makes Sweden famous among social and labor policy experts as what Skocpol calls a "comprehensive full-employment welfare state" coherently integrating economic and social policy. Employers warmly endorsed activist training and mobility measures even before the labor confederation included them as the centerpiece of their plan for economic stabilization and industrial development (the "Rehn-Meidner Model"). This cross-class consensus emerged well before Social Democratic government leaders abandoned their incredulity about the plan's economic logic and reluctance to dig into taxpayers' pockets to finance it. As in the other cases, the interests that employers expressed in active labor market policy were not, as one might suppose, the "strategic" preferences of a capitalist class that was, at heart, antagonistic to social and labor market legislation. Organized employers were not merely resigned to hegemonic Social Democrats and hoping to appease them for special consideration on particular details, for nicer treatment in other domains, or to avoid public disfavor. They knew what they wanted. Sometimes they liked best what they got and got what they liked best.

Intriguing historical details like these presented throughout this book indicate the need for an entirely different kind of comparative argument—one that rejects the equivalency premise common, though by no means logically necessary, in existing power and institutionalist analyses of the welfare state. In broad strokes, the analysis developed in this book builds on a *contingency premise*, backed by theoretical analysis of how employer interests in wage distribution and social policies derive from their variable strategies and institutions in labor markets. In other words, capitalists and workers sometimes agree, and sometimes do not agree, about egalitarian policies. As economic actors in labor market formation, or political actors in welfare state development, Swedish employers were nothing like American employers.

Elaboration of theory about how employer interests in social policy vary with their labor market strategies and institutions will have to wait until the next chapter. It will suffice to say here that there is usually a *regulatory logic* to their interests, and therefore the support they show, before and after, in varying ways. Capitalists often like government regulation when they see a net benefit and little risk. Like a powerful solvent, interests often quickly dissolve ideological sentiments against advantageous government regulation. Welfare policies can provide just such intervention. To say that capitalists have interests in reform is not, however, to say that they always act according to those interests as opposed to competing ones, institutional constraints, free-market liberalism, or just plain stick-in-the-mudism. For many, the road from interests to action is a long and rocky one, and their means of transportation often fail.[31]

The comparative historical argument maintains that, because of these obstacles and handicaps, reformers with considerable organizational distance from the capitalist world (mostly liberal Democrats in the United States and Social Democrats in Sweden) were usually responsible for taking the political initiative. Responding eagerly to popular pressures "from below," they of course exercised autonomous power and put their own stamp on legislation. But they also took into account variable capitalist interests, about which they were usually quite knowledgeable, regarding the regulatory value of social and labor policy. They usually hesitated, it seems, to take full advantage of electoral and parliamentary opportunities to roll over these interests in the shaping and timing of their legislation.

Even the exceptional cases examined here, where capitalist opposition seemed monolithic and positive signals about favorable interests weak, are few and ambiguous. In the United States the major exception was the 1935 National Labor Relations Act; in Sweden the exceptions were unemployment insurance in 1934 and the 1959 pension reform. The Sweden-U.S. comparison suggests that reformers tended to proffer their major initiatives when clear signals of interest emanated from important circles in the capitalist camp. In the United States, those signals came through with considerable strength during the interwar depression; in Sweden, they came through during the postwar period of vigorous growth. The differences in timing derived from profound differences in employers' regulatory interests.

Political survival instincts told the reformers that opportunistic initiatives founded solely on episodic and unstable mass electoral support could be undermined after passage due to the anticipated ability of capital to regroup and shift the sands of electoral and parliamentary support under their feet. New York's Senator Robert Wagner, the legislative pilot of the New Deal, was well aware from Progressive-era experiences in his state that, according to his biographer, "passage of a measure [did not] mean that it was permanently secure." Businessmen of all sorts had "maintained powerful lobbies at Albany and could always find lawmakers who were willing to sponsor bills that would repeal, or amend into insignificance, the Factory Commission laws." And as leading New Dealer and "cautious reformer" Edwin Witte saw it, the Roosevelt administration could have shrugged off concerns about business or labor support for the Social Security bill "and still force a measure through Congress." But a major objective was robust legislation, anchored in a cross-class alliance, capable of weathering future challenges. "The violent opposition of either group is likely to mean trouble hereafter," Witte wrote as the debates raged.[32]

"Interested" employers were rarely the initiating or driving force, especially on a collective level. There were good reasons for this de facto political division of labor. In the United States, especially, major employer organizations like the National Association of Manufacturers had long been dominated by antilabor ideologues whose suspicions spilled over onto social reform. The majority of manufacturers were not members, especially the union-friendly ones, and many moderates quite possibly voted with their feet and stayed out. Of course, individual capitalists had to consider the entirely avoidable business or social costs of taking progressive political stands for their relations with buyers, suppliers, stockholders, and fellow country club members when reactionary organizations set the tone of debate. Most, of course, had neither the time nor inclination to devote resources to studying the advantages or disadvantages of social legislation. Furthermore, proposing social legislation was simply not in the mandate for the organizations or in the job description of their staff experts. Even if it had been, business leaders could not take or maintain the initiative in social reform because of the high and certain cost of internal divisiveness and uncertain payoff from success. Moderate leaders who did go over the line into progressivism were vulnerable to activist ideologues ready to take power from them, something that actually happened in the U.S. Chamber of Commerce in 1935.

For those businessmen with progressive tendencies, therefore, it was probably better to lie low and wait for outside forces to push for change. The added advantage was that they could blame a *force majeure* for the reformist course of events they supported once reform was under way and justify their participation by saying that if they did not go along, worse things could happen. At that point, prominent business supporters of reform could help push things in regulatory directions they favored, sometimes surprisingly progressive in character. Sometimes they even put the brake on reactionary movement. The same logic probably applied to conservative parties strongly dependent on business support and paralyzed by the need to shun highly divisive positions on social policy questions. This syndrome of left-wing reform happiness and right-wing inhibition no doubt helps explain the usual statistical correlations found between leftist and Christian Democratic control of government and social legislation across economically advanced democracies in general. Thus the distribution of parliamentary or cabinet seats among various parties says relatively little about the zero-sum distribution of power between capital on the one side and various heterogeneous social forces on the other.[33]

As research on the United States and Sweden shows, though reformers from outside the capitalist camp took the initiative, their sensitivity to capitalist interests left its stamp on the reform. This probably helps explain the subsequent weakness or absence of reactionary pressures. Reformers tended to act in prudent anticipation of delayed reactions from capital, hoping to design reforms that maximized supportive reactions and minimized backlash. Analysis of the reformer initiative in pulling together cross-class alliances behind major legislation reform suggests that, by favoring a part of the capitalist class with regulatory assistance (necessarily at the expense of others), they guaranteed themselves post facto support for their initiatives. More important for them than overt prior support was anticipation of tacit support after passage. Electoral advantage may have been enough, as Witte argued, to win the day for a time—but probably not over the long haul.

In examining the two countries over a period from the beginning of the twentieth century, this book first analyzes their dramatically different labor market systems. It then reveals the effect of their labor markets on welfare state development, mediated by the political process.[34] As economists might put it in their peculiar way, welfare states are at least in part endogenous to labor market systems. Therefore, it appears as no accident that America's limited welfare state today is causally related, via a political process sensitive to employer interests, to higher levels of inequality in the labor market. However, despite the strong interaction, there is unlikely to be a certain "welfare regime" for any given "labor market regime." The relationship is, after all, only partial. For in principle the analysis is political, not economically deterministic. It upholds the essential role of noncapitalists with their own agendas in shaping labor markets and welfare states, enlisting capitalists into broad cross-class alliances. In the process, reformers leave their own distinctive stamp, as well as that of capitalists, on both systems. In the end, politics, and therefore choice within a range of opportunities, matters immeasurably. Even political institutions are likely to matter, as institutionalists rightly claim, in shaping values and interests and structuring coalitional opportunities and strategies.

Nevertheless, to compensate for neglect of employers in the literature to date, most of the analysis in this book focuses on them, not powerful labor leaders, politicians, and institutions. The next chapter begins with a theoretical analysis, drawing partly from an important school of thought in labor economics, of three important systems of labor market governance: *cartelism*, *segmentalism*, and *solidarism*. These, as later chapters demonstrate, characterize varying kinds of labor market governance that radically differentiate the United States and Sweden. The analysis introduces economic reasoning behind differences and changes in employer interests arising from those different systems with regard to the socialization of welfare tasks. By explaining changes in interests over time and identifying when capitalists are likely to signal amenability to welfare legislation, it helps solve the historical puzzle about Sweden's delayed welfare state.

Chapters 3 and 7 examine the evolution, location, and logic of segmentalism and cartelism in the United States. Chapters 4 through 6 do the same for solidarism in Sweden. Along the way, the discussion presents reasons why and how employers helped shape the different systems. Their choices had weighty consequences for later welfare state formation. One dramatic and politically consequential difference is the diametric contrast in interests between employers in the two countries with regard to pay inequality across firms. Big American employers individually sought to establish and maintain wage inequalities (within limits) across the labor market, while large Swedish ones collectively sought pay compression. Related to that contrast, another was American employers' whole-hearted promotion of company-based social benefits ("welfare capitalism") and their Swedish counterparts' collective or solidaristic efforts to suppress and eliminate the same practices. A third is the dramatic differences in unionization and centralization in the two countries, in part a result of employer strategies. In the United States, employer hostility to unionism, except in some sectors, effectively hindered its growth. In Sweden, a powerful employers' confederation helped create the world's most powerful social democratic labor movement and had minimal regrets about doing so.

At times, the discussion in these chapters shifts back and forth between the two countries to explain other intriguing differences between them arising from differences in employers' labor market strategies. These differences have had important economic and political consequences. Among them are the remarkable and hitherto unexplained differences between the two countries in the prevalence of pay-for-performance schemes ("piece work") and their radically different incidence of corruption and labor racketeering. An even more important part of the comparative analysis shows how the varying levels of overt hostility between capital and labor in America and Sweden resulted in part from the opportunities for cross-class alliances that employers' differing strategies in labor markets provided. In particular, a burning issue in both countries for major employers in the 1920s and 1930s was the problem of intersectoral wage differentials, especially between manufacturing and construction enterprises. In Sweden, a cross-class alliance with organized labor and Social Democrats helped solve the problem and thereby helps explain the politics of consensus in the interwar period and beyond—despite the socialist ideology inspiring its labor movement. In the United States, similar problems exacerbated hostilities toward labor among major employers in the same period because a cross-class alliance to deal with it was not in the offing.

The next four chapters then direct the analysis to employers' roles in the New Deal in the United States in the 1930s and Social Democratic legislation from the 1930s through the 1950s. Here the formative effect of labor market systems on the development of welfare states comes into focus. The argument and evidence incorporate the role of reformers as cross-class alliance makers in designing their initiatives to deal with employers' regulatory problems arising from their labor market practices. The evidence suggests that, all in all, reformers acted in response to a favorable alignment of employer interests with those of the reformers themselves. They did not, it seems, take advantage of a shifting balance of power against capital.

In these final chapters, I subject competing historical arguments about specific developments and reforms in the two countries to a critique based on evidence more consistent with my theoretical perspective. Chapter 10 in particular examines evidence against Theda Skocpol's "state-centric" institutionalist analysis of the New Deal. Studies by her and collaborators merit detailed attention, I think, because of their explicit and contentious aim of proving the irrelevance of capitalists in the American reform process—and because of the considerable influence that her arguments continue to have. Chapter 12, on the Swedish welfare state, focuses the critique on influential authors whose understanding of Sweden has been, I believe, skewed by both theory and mythology about the power of the Swedish labor movement, fortified in a sense by the relative paucity of research on Swedish employers and their labor market interests.

The conclusion, chapter 13, looks at developments since the 1960s. Among other things, it examines the variable importance of international market forces in the recasting of alliances and thus changes in labor market organization and welfare. It also looks at the role of strategic choice and mistakes in the use of power by labor in response to social and economic changes of the 1960s and 1970s, especially in Sweden. It suggests, for example, that Social Democrats and labor leaders fell victim to illusions about the role of labor's power in the country's remarkable labor market and welfare state accomplishments of an earlier time. As a result they used their power in risky initiatives without cross-class foundations and, therefore, invited a costly capitalist reaction. It analyzes the rise and abandonment of efforts in the 1990s to install a national health insurance system in the United States as a failed attempt to forge a cross-class reform alliance. Thus, in turning to these and other developments in the two countries, it looks at recent events through the lens of theoretically informed analysis of the more distant past.

2

SOLIDARITY, SEGMENTATION, AND MARKET CONTROL

In conversations with management expert Peter Drucker, during Drucker's time at General Motors in the 1940s and 1950s, GM President Charles E. Wilson once made a peculiar and extravagant boast. Wilson claimed, as Drucker recalled, "We have the union relations *I* designed . . . and they are right for our industry and our union."

> We lose fewer days to strikes than any other major company in this country or in any other unionized country. We have greater continuity of union leadership. And both the union and we get the things the country, the company, and the union need: high discipline, high productivity, high wages, and high employment security. A union is a political organization and needs adversary relations and victorious battles. And a company is an economic organization and needs productivity and discipline. At GM we get both— and to get both we need the union relations we have.[1]

To illustrate unions' need for adversary relations and victorious battles, Wilson pointed to circumstances leading up to the company's collectively bargained Supplementary Unemployment Benefits (SUB). GM began paying these benefits in 1955 to complement the limited unemployment support provided by twenty-year-old New Deal legislation. The plan for the company welfare scheme was, Wilson said, worked out under his and board chairman Alfred Sloan's watch, not by the United Auto Workers (UAW). Instead, the union had long called for a "guaranteed annual wage" connected to work sharing during production downturns. GM had formulated its SUB scheme, probably early in 1947, as a good place to put some of the auto industry's increased earnings instead of wages.[2]

Intrigued, Drucker asked Wilson when he planned to introduce the SUB scheme. Wilson responded, "*I* am never going to put it into effect. . . . I grudgingly yield to a union demand for it when I have to." The reason: the union leaders "won't go along unless it's a 'demand' we resist and they 'win.'. . . . No union can believe that what management offers can be anything but harmful to the union and its members as well. Sure, I'll plant the idea—I know enough UAW people. But we'll yield to them, after a great show of reluctance, only when it's worth something to them. The time will come."[3]

Sure enough, the time came in 1955, eight years later, when the UAW geared up for militant action. Ford, which the union reportedly believed to be even more amenable in principle than GM, was chosen as the target of the first strike threat. Ford settled quickly and favorably, and GM simply followed suit, agreeing to supplement statutory unemployment insurance so that auto workers would receive roughly 60 percent of take-home pay for 26 weeks of joblessness.[4] Over the next twelve years, SUB plus regular unemployment insurance would be increased to 95 percent for 52 weeks of unemployment. A similar procedure, Wilson said, had already worked for introducing company pensions to supplement Social Security, in 1950. According to Drucker, Wilson had favored improving company pensions, but "waited until employee pensions became a union demand."[5]

For the American blue-collar industrial worker, the auto industry's wages and benefits were about the best thing going, even if the work pace was grueling. The UAW's president, Walter Reuther, got a great deal of credit, complete with his portrait on the cover of *Time*. That probably suited Wilson just fine. Privately, Wilson regarded Reuther as "the ablest man in American industry"; Reuther, in turn, regarded Wilson as "a very decent, genuine human being."[6] But the gulf between Reuther and Wilson was probably broad and deep with regard to Wilson's hope and apparent belief that his union's vanguard actions would pave the way to more generous material benefits for the entire working class. In historian Nelson Lichtenstein's assessment, "by 1955 Reuther thought collective bargaining with the Big Three automakers might well generate in the United States the kind of classwide settlement that was characteristic of industry-labor relationships in northern Europe." He reasoned that the UAW's unusual leverage at the bargaining table "could be used to pry open the doors long closed to government expansion of the welfare state." Big employers, went the political logic, would respond to the proliferation of collectively bargained benefits "by seeking government assumption of the costs." Union power would neutralize capital's opposition to an expansion of the welfare state.[7]

Employers, however, did not follow Reuther's script. Events showed that GM and other major employers making benefit "concessions" to unions were easily able to pay for their premium pension, health, and unemployment benefits with higher product prices in the well-insulated national market. More important, as Lichtenstein put it, "managers recognized that company-specific benefits built employee loyalty, and at some level they understood that a low social wage [a limited welfare state] was advantageous to their class interest, even if their own firm had to bear additional costs as a consequence. Ironically, it was the UAW's own commitment to an expansion of the welfare state that began to flag." And it is not hard to see why union pressure subsided. As Jill Quadagno argues, the expansion of the welfare state was impeded because "independent negotiations for private pensions reduced whatever incentive they might have had to support Social Security benefit increases."[8] This was exactly the interpretation of Marion Folsom, former Kodak executive and "corporate liberal." Folsom noted on the eve of the limited Medicare and Medicaid reform of 1965 that "there's nothing like the pressure among the labor unions for compulsory health insurance for the laboring population that there used to be. . . . They lost a lot of their enthusiasm when they began to get all those fringe benefit contracts."[9] Medicare and Medicaid, of course, did not cover the "laboring population" Folsom spoke of. In other words, millions of working Americans were left uninsured, while employment-based benefits that others received were left, as Folsom wanted, intact.

Eventually Reuther would lower his social reform expectations to realistic levels suiting employer figures like Folsom and Wilson. Wilson wanted a broad old age security system but only "on a minimum basis," so he told a gathering of corporate executives in 1950.[10] Reuther's earlier hopes for better things to come had possibly been inflated by knowledge of northern European conditions, Swedish ones in particular. He was a close friend of Arne Geijer, the leader of the Swedish Metalworkers' Union, and beginning in 1956, head of the country's entire blue-collar labor confederation.[11] In Sweden, the 1950s brought highly centralized multi-employer, multi-industry collective bargaining, a system capable of and used for negotiating an increasingly egalitarian structure of pay across firms and industries. It was also the decade when major compulsory health insurance and sick pay reform was looming. Employers in Sweden, as Geijer would have known, were collectively favorable to the idea of reform, for they had struggled for decades to eliminate the practice of company benefits.[12]

Perhaps illusions about the Swedish labor movement's power, and employers' interests, fed Reuther's optimism about employers' readiness to accept social democracy in America. Sweden's Social Democratic labor leaders may have been unable to disabuse him of those hopes, for they probably had no more than a dim understanding of the huge differences between Swedish and American employers. As different as they were, however, there is reason to think that business leaders on both sides of the Atlantic shared a similar understanding about the psychology of organized labor and how to work with it for their distinctive ends. For example, in 1955, when the Swedish Confederation of Labor (LO, or *Landsorganisationen*) had begun heavily promoting its famous egalitarian "solidaristic wage policy" (*solidarisk lönepolitik*), Hans Söderlund, a staff economist with the negotiation division of the Swedish Employers' Confederation (SAF), found nothing particularly objectionable. After all, the unions' ideas about wage compression were quite similar to organized employers' own for standardization of remuneration across firms and industries. However, in a remarkable internal memorandum, he echoed GM's Wilson, recommending that employers should hold their cards close to the chest.

If the employer confederation openly promotes wage policy goals whose general purpose is so closely related to solidaristic wage policy, we cannot exclude the possibility that the unions might strike off in a different direction. Unity among workers and confidence in their organizations' leadership depends of course to a large extent on members feeling that the organization has some impact on results in the area of wage policy that otherwise would not have been achieved [without the union]. The feeling that this is happening can be weakened of course if the distance narrows between [employers and the unions] with regard to their conceptions about the "correct" wage structure.[13]

In this, the young Hans Söderlund, 33 years old, was probably speaking less from direct experience than from what he had learned from his father. Gustaf Söderlund had been executive director of SAF from 1931 to 1939 and 1943 to 1945 and was currently one of the country's most powerful bankers. His lesson was identical to the one Wilson conveyed to Drucker about the need for adversarial relations: union leaders may be more willing and able to push harder for something both sides want if employers disguise or conceal their interests in it.

Twenty years earlier, in a 1935 SAF board meeting, Gustaf had advocated official silence about rules changes that LO leaders were seeking for more power over its affiliates, and through them, over militants in the membership who frequently overturned central agreements in membership referenda. The centralization of union authority was something SAF looked forward to with quiet glee.[14] "If the . . . revision is carried out, employers' wishes are likely to be satisfied as much as we can desire," the elder Söderlund predicted. Now that the revision was under way, a pronouncement in favor "would only cast suspicion on LO and obstruct a solution of the problem."[15] To clam up about a cause it had long advocated, and so help preserve unity within the union confederation, was good for employers. Unity behind a more secure and powerful leadership was not going to be a source of power against them. With SAF's silence, the LO leadership was better able to represent the reform, which it finally passed in 1941, as necessary for union solidarity against employers. Radical critics knew better, that it was "in the spirit of class collaboration" (i klasssamarbetets anda).[16]

In the realm of social legislation, in contrast with collective bargaining, Swedish employers adopted a quietly favorable position. However, they routinely waited for the Social Democratic labor movement to take the initiative. This division of political labor probably influences how, in retrospect, we measure the forces of change. Our understanding of what happened is probably also skewed by employers' abstinence from claiming credit after the fact. In any event, they more or less played the role that the UAW's Reuther had wrongly anticipated for American employers. For example, compulsory health insurance, complete with generous sick pay, was passed in 1953, to take effect in 1955, with only minimal employer opposition to various details of the legislation. Overall, leading Swedish employers, for reasons discussed later, welcomed the chance to hand over the role of providing insurance and health services to the Swedish state.

These major events in the history of labor markets and the welfare state during the 1950s, when labor unions in the United States and Sweden took both the initiative and the credit, but mostly kicked in doors left open by leading employers, give reason to ask the following question: how much illusion and myth lies behind our understanding of the role of labor's power in the shaping of industrial relations systems and welfare states? If the grandiosity of Wilson's boast invites some skepticism, the similarity of the two Söderlunds' statements lends it credibility. If true, at least in these important instances, organized labor's ability to achieve something of value to workers had more to do with capital's friendliness than its relative weakness.

To develop an argument about the causally interdependent interests of capitalists in market governance and social policy making, the remainder of this chapter moves to an analysis of what employers want to accomplish in and with labor markets, and sketches out three different means of achieving them: (1) *cartelism*, a collective multi-employer strategy for enforcing wage and benefit floors; (2) *segmentalism*, a decentralized firm-level strategy of providing higher wages and benefits than other firms; and (3) *solidarism*, another collective strategy, whose main purpose is to enforce ceilings, not floors, on wages and benefits. As indicated later, the three practices are not entirely mutually exclusive, and various admixtures can be found in practice. Nevertheless, in the two countries and period studied here, cartelism and segmentalism strongly characterizes distinct parts of the American labor market, while solidarism gives the Swedish labor market its striking distinction.

The analysis draws on theory from labor economics, which helps identify a number of explanations, though not all possible ones, about when and why employers will favor social legislation in support of their labor market strategies. These reasons thus explain why employers may become partners of sorts in *cross-class alliances* that support social legislation in active and tacit ways. The chapter's conclusion summarizes the comparative historical argument developed in the rest of the book. The evidence throughout reveals the important role—and often a progressive one—that capitalists in both countries played, together with liberals and labor, in the interactive development of labor markets and welfare states. The following theoretical analysis helps to make sense of the evidence.

Employers against Markets

Employer dispositions, both positive and negative, toward collective bargaining and social legislation originate to a great but not exclusive extent from strategies pursued to secure their interests in labor markets, and through labor market control, in their product markets. The strategies employers choose to pursue depend no doubt on established organizational practice and hospitable or compelling economic, cultural, political, and legal conditions for adapting organization toward those strategic ends. By that token, current politics and institutional and ideological legacies of the past, and feedback from current strategies on later developments probably matter too and would have to be included in a broader and deeper analysis. So, too, would the vagaries of leadership decisions about different options, no matter how constrained the environment. The consequence of including all this, however, would be an even larger book than this one or, probably because of the amount of research necessary, no book at all.

What mostly concerns this analysis are employers' immediate interests in managing and shaping labor markets for their larger objectives in market competition. In the search for high and secure profits, employers endeavor to structure the price of labor, to create incentives promoting labor productivity, and to secure a reliable supply of labor with an appropriate mix of skills. Here, wages influence the supply of labor, both in the sense of bringing bodies and minds in contact with capital that can employ them and inducing physical and mental exertion. Employers also want to manipulate the overall level of wages, both for themselves and for competitors, to influence prices of their goods or services in shared markets. They may also recognize the role of high and stable wage levels as a source of demand for the goods and services they sell. Employers can try to achieve these related but varied and often contradictory objectives with different devices, both individually and collectively. Inevitably, distinctive benefits and complications arise from each particular strategy. Their choices will in turn pattern their interests in welfare state development, to which this chapter turns at the end.

Cartelism

Businesses often try to collude with each other to set product prices and restrict competitive entry into their markets. The familiar argument goes as follows. Whenever possible, firms pursue independent monopoly strategies to maximize and stabilize profits in product market competition, carving out secure niches with strategic location, advanced technology, product patents, and consumer loyalty. Some sectors of an economy, however, lack the technological or other bases for individual firms to achieve stable "monopoly rent." Labor-intensive sectors, with small-sized firms producing uniform and easily transported goods, requiring only quickly learned skills, and using inexpensive and simple machinery, are among them. These factors allow easy entry to competitors, who trigger intense and often ruinous price competition. Slim, unstable, and sometimes nonexistent profits result. This was often the case, historically, in the American coal mining, building, and garment industries, for example, as well as in services like retailing, transportation, and others.

In addition to other problems, intense competition among capitalists in their sales markets can set off bruising conflict between classes, as both employers and workers try to protect their incomes at the other's expense when prices for their products and services sag. Low morale and effort, high turn-over, absenteeism, theft, and other costly manifestations of worker discontent become endemic. For purely pragmatic and profit-seeking reasons, and proba-bly often humanitarian ones, employers regret that market competition com-pels them to shift hardships onto their workers. As Samuel Gompers, head of the American Federation of Labor, wrote in 1897, "Is there . . . an employer who is at all inclined to be fair to his employees, who has not felt the awful and degenerating influence which some of his unscrupulous—commonly known as "cut throat"—competitors have wrought . . . by contemptible methods of hiring the lowest priced labor and demanding the longest hours of labor?"[17]

In the absence of government protection from competition through price and entry regulations, and where the law allows, firms' remaining chance of increasing and stabilizing profits is to band together in a collusive cartel against competitive price reductions. However, because of cheating by cartel mem-bers, and new entrants to the market, the difficulties of maintaining such an arrangement are enormous, even where the practices are legal. When cartelist collusion is effectively illegal or unenforceable, firms may yet have another op-tion. They can turn to labor unions as a useful enforcement mechanism against cheaters and new entrants.[18] All unions may have to do to stabilize competition is to impose a floor under wages paid by competing firms. Minimum wage stan-dards can prevent the destabilization of product market competition caused by wage "chiseling." Low-wage entrants to the trade are blockaded. Even exit by firms with unusually high nonlabor costs may be accelerated, a loss to the in-dustry that other firms will more likely celebrate than mourn. Here, the union performs a function similar to that of the purchasing pool in cornering the supply of a key input or factor of production, or of a monopolistic supplier or financier, who might be willing to cooperate in choking off competitive en-trants and punishing violators.[19]

Capitalists' desire to regulate product market competition is among the most widely understood of employer motivations for organizing and engaging in collective bargaining with unions strong enough to police competition effectively. Existing literature, in fact, focuses almost exclusively on this as the primary regulatory motive for bargaining on what is often called a multi-employer, or centralized, basis with unions. In this arrangement, usually in the small-scale, easy-entry industrial or service sectors, organized labor steps in as an ally in a regulatory cross-class alliance.[20] In short, this *negotiated car-telism*, sometimes called "bilateral monopoly" by economists, substitutes for government protection or unilateral cartelism. It can stabilize and pacify rela-tions at unionized workplaces by displacing their distributional conflict onto other employers and workers, whose higher wages are not affordable. Conflict is also displaced onto relations between a cross-class alliance of producers with the consumers who pay higher prices for their products. Consumers do not necessarily lose, however, because negotiated cartelism does not eliminate all price competition. It only moves it to other dimensions. As it is sometimes put, negotiated cartelism "takes wages out competition." In taking only wages out of play, it probably displaces entrepreneurial and managerial energies into a more intensive search for efficient labor-saving technology. Both innovators and consumers may benefit: first, the innovators, who in the short run can capture a larger market share, and then consumers in the long run by paying lower prices.

Ironically, a successful unilateral cartel may make unions superfluous as a source of entry control, price maintenance, and stable workplace relations. Employers in that case are probably more inclined to play the role usually expected of them in fighting off unions, especially because of the challenge they represent to managerial sovereignty. German heavy industrialists' powerful cartels early in the twentieth century are probably a good case in point. *Unilateral cartelism* thereby eliminates a main source of union strength, that is to say, "employer recognition."[21] But where employers cannot solve the problem unilaterally, unions can undergo a remarkable transformation from menace to savior—as long as they become strong enough to be an effective police force. Firms favoring control of competition but unable to bring it about on their own may therefore even find it in their interest to subsidize the union, usually indirectly (by the check-off system, or automatic enrollment of their workers and deduction of union dues from their pay).[22]

The cross-class alliance underlying negotiated cartelism does not eliminate class conflict. Strikes are, of course, the union's mechanism of enforcement on recalcitrant employers. This conflict can be intense, violent, and even murderous. Conflict on a broader scale between the union and employers' associations does not disappear either. Unions may still choose to use the power conferred upon them by the arrangement or by other circumstances to impose and maintain wage standards higher than the bulk of employers wish to go. They might use their power to impose constraints on managerial rights. Large-scale strikes and lockouts do not necessarily become obsolete, in other words, even if they decline in quantity. Unions may take such advantage of their power position that they create a climate of open and permanent hostility. But chilly and conflictual relations do not imply the absence of an alliance, just as permanent conflict in a marriage does not always mean divorce. The labor union may, of course, recklessly use a short-term power advantage to push relations to the breaking point. After that comes the strong likelihood of a long-term loss of power with the loss of employer recognition. Many employers will share a loss with workers from the decline in their union's power. But pragmatic union leaders do not often let things get so out of hand.

Segmentalism

Firms in less competitive product markets than the ones just described have dramatically different problems and options with regard to managing their affairs in labor markets. Often they prefer to deal with their workers without the intermediation of outsiders like union leaders. When they deal with unions, they are likely to prefer negotiating agreements about wages and other conditions of employment tailored only to the company, not to the industry as a whole. Nonregulated or decentralized arrangements with workers have a dramatic and distinctive effect on the structure of income in labor markets. To understand how and why they do so requires first an introduction to concepts from labor economics, especially from the literature on "efficiency wages."

The core assumption of a number of efficiency wage models about employer behavior in labor markets is that, in some firms at least, workers' efficiency may be a positive function of their wage relative to wages paid in alternative employment and relative to other sources of income attached to unemployment. The better employer gets better workers, in a nutshell. "Where wages are high," Adam Smith wrote, "we shall always find the workmen more active, diligent, and expeditious."[23] Various efficiency wage models work from distinct but noncontradictory angles about this *wage-productivity nexus*, though policy implications of the distinct models vary.[24] All, however, focus on reasons some employers might *voluntarily* pay higher wages than others, or more than appears necessary in the face of surplus labor or unemployment. High wages do not always require coercive intervention of powerful outsiders like unions or governments.

Early theory along these lines, coming out of development economics, stressed the productivity advantages to employers of income-related improvements to workers' nutrition and vitality.[25] Later theory focused on "information asymmetries" leading to the "selection" or "sorting" effects of high wages. This theory says firms with supracompetitive wages attract more able workers, which spares the employer some costs of discerning who should be chosen, even as they enlarge the pool from which to choose.[26] Another current in the literature focuses on the behavior of workers once employed by the firm. High wages, for example, it is supposed, reduce quit propensity, or turnover, which is especially costly for some firms, and therefore reduce expenditures on recruiting and training good new workers.[27] Behavior on the job is also the subject of important "shirking models" in the literature, which stress the incentive effect of high wages on worker effort. For example, the possibility of getting caught loafing and being fired, and forced into unemployment or a job with lower pay, induces effort levels that could otherwise be generated only with more authoritarian and, in terms of worker morale and money, costly "monitoring" (what labor historians call the "drive" system).[28]

An important variant invokes "sociological" or normative motivations behind workers' efforts. These motivations are inconsistent with most economists' simplistic and monotonous assumptions about workers' preferences (e.g., for indolence over exertion, or for daydreaming over problem solving). For example, emloyers may offer a gratuity or "gift" of high wages in excess of what would be necessary to attract enough workers or to make current workers indifferent to the job with respect to outside options. The superior wages may therefore generate good will and a normative obligation (i.e., an endogenously created preference for working over shirking) to reciprocate with more than minimum effort. Employers spend less on monitoring and discipline. In this variant, efficiency wages elicit greater effort by cultivating norms, enforced by peer influence, of what constitutes a fair and respectable day's work for their employers' generosity.[29] Norms of pay equity and the dynamics of group cooperation may transmit upward pressure on wages within firms from occupations where the wage-productivity nexus is present to occupations where it is not.[30]

The most important and consistent implication of this theoretical literature—whether it is built on biological fundamentals, rational maximizing behavior based on exogenous preferences for shirking over working, or endogenous normative motivations favoring working over shirking—is that it helps us explain a certain kind of unemployment. In short, if enough firms voluntarily pay supracompetitive wages, they can cause *involuntary unemployment at equilibrium.*[31] The theory makes sense of the commonly observed fact that employers often do not cut wages when faced with an excess supply of labor. Instead, with the high pay they offer, they voluntarily cause "queues," figuratively or literally speaking, to form at the factory gates, and then "ration" jobs among the surplus of workers available. Reducing wages would cause some applicants to turn on their heels and make the queue disappear. Some current workers would also leave, and probably the better ones at that. Thus, regardless of aggregate demand levels, labor markets will not always clear at the micro-economic level. Involuntary unemployment created by efficiency wages may be therefore structurally part of the "natural" rate of unemployment.[32] It is therefore beyond the reach of Keynesian demand manipulation, except at the risk of accelerating inflation.

The second major implication of efficiency wage theory concerns the existence of labor market segmentation. Segmentation refers to "dual" and "internal" labor markets, where *wage levels and managerial practices differ markedly across firms or sectors* in ways that cannot be accounted for by worker or job attributes, as in traditional neo-classical models. Those models predict far more uniformity for similar workers and jobs, regardless of employer or industry. In some sectors (primary labor markets, in dual systems), efficiency wage theory says, in contrast, there will be voluntary payment of wages exceeding market-clearing levels, whereas in others (secondary labor markets), we are likely to see lower and more flexible wages of the neo-classical, market-clearing variety.[33] Some models also predict intrafirm wage differentiation and related administrative or managerial practices (so-called internal labor markets) that are not explicable in terms of worker quality, task difficulty, and the operation of external labor markets. Among these are wages rising with seniority without regard to individual workers' specific ability and effort. Young workers are not attracted away by higher wages elsewhere, expecting large deferred rewards. Older workers are not discarded despite availability of more productive replacements willing to accept a lower wage.[34] One thing likely to explain such differentiation of pay practices across firms and sectors is heterogeneity in capital/labor ratios. Some firms utilize sophisticated, expensive, and secret technology, where shirking, quitting, absenteeism, low ability, and worker ill-will (leading to sabotage, theft, and spying) are extra costly. These firms will find payment of supracompetitive efficiency wages advisable. Also, some firms' product market power, and therefore high operating profits or value added per worker, makes "rent sharing" (or profit sharing) in the form of high wages especially affordable.[35]

Firms choosing to pay an efficiency premium, voluntarily and for profit-maximizing reasons, need not put the money into cash wages alone, though the labor economics literature seems without exception to theorize and test only in those terms. The firm may pay a premium in the form of free vocational training in needed skills, while later even sharing the firm's returns to the skills thus acquired in the form of pay increases. Naturally, in the desire to reduce costly turnover, it is likely to concentrate training expenditures on firm-specific skills, that is, specific to its own technology, so as to reduce the risk of losing the investment, a risk that increases if the investment is in more general-purpose "human capital" of value to many other employers. A competing employer may even be able and prepared to offer higher wages for those skills, having not had to finance their creation. Retaining skilled workers by the firm that trains them is also aided by promises of internal promotion up the career ladders associated with internal labor markets.

Most important, firms may find it expedient to offer nonwage benefits and services associated with "welfare capitalism"—health, pension, unemployment, and other kinds of insurance, and sports, cultural, and entertainment facilities available only to employees (and very often their dependents). Even expenses put into better lighting, heating and air-conditioning, ventilation, noise, and safety conditions may have efficiency payoffs for the employer. Large employers are especially likely to provide an efficiency premium in the form of insurance benefits. Their per capita costs, given underwriting and other administrative economies of scale and their larger and therefore less risky pool of beneficiaries, will be lower than for smaller firms. Also, paying higher wages may attract a larger pool of applicants from which to select healthier workers. Depending on workers' preferences, such benefits, perceived as a kind of "gift," may provide productivity benefits in excess of what could be achieved from paying the same costs in cash wages.[36]

In the case of these and other paternalistic practices, attitudes, and emotions about what constitutes a fair day's work for a fair day's pay—again what economists call "sociological" causes of a "fairness-productivity nexus"—might sometimes play a more powerful efficiency role than mere cash benefits. Sometimes insurance-type benefits, like pensions, take the form of "deferred wages," further inhibiting turnover by inducing workers to stay long enough to qualify for and then receive them. The efficiency differentials might also come in the form of "implicit contracts" that partially protect workers from wage cuts or layoffs when prices and profits decline. Naturally, only some kinds of firms will believe they have the necessary "reserves" to shoulder these risks and offer the insurance benefit.[37]

For the remainder of this book, the payment of efficiency wages or benefits in various forms will be called *segmentalism,* and employers paying them *segmentalists.* Unfortunately, the term may have the raw sound, as John Kenneth Galbraith once put it, of a newly coined word. But the limited meaning of "welfare capitalism" and the ungainliness of any alternative incorporating the phrase "efficiency wages and benefits" recommend this choice. It is suggested, of course, by the efficiency wage literature dealing with labor market segmentation. Segmentalist strategies can be used, as in early twentieth century America, to ward off unionization, not just promote efficiency. But *unilateral segmentalism* is not the only possibility. It can also be pursued in collaboration with unions. A firm's workers, whether unionized or not, favor extra wages and benefits. Unions will be hard put to reject the extras and will instead endeavor to take credit for them. Segmentalist employers may (as did GM's Charlie Wilson) not mind letting them take credit. One way or another, a kind of cross-class alliance operates between the segmentalist firm and its employees. Where employers and unions engage in joint regulation of segmentalist practices, we can call this *negotiated segmentalism.* (Occasionally, as in the case of negotiated cartelism, for the sake of variety, the interchangeable terms *joint* and *bilateral* are also used.)

As in joint cartelism, class conflict does not vanish in the presence of the cross-class segmentalist alliance. Some of it may be ritualized and manipulatively channeled—to use the Wilson example again. Some of it may be a manifestation of real conflict over the terms of segmentalism, and unions might use their situational power to push wages and benefits beyond the efficiency range. Being decentralized, collective bargaining may give unions better opportunity than in centralized multi-employer bargaining to wrest some control over managerial matters, not just wages and benefits. (For practical and strategic reasons, union negotiators largely confine themselves to industry-wide, not shop-floor issues, in centralized bargaining.) Conflict in the context of bilateral segmentalism takes place, in other words, over the terms and at the perimeters of segmentalism. Pragmatic union leaders may want and need to vent off militant pressures building up from below in their unions. But they know full well that they should not bite too hard and fast into the employer hand that feeds them.

Segmentalism, as a decentralized system of labor pricing, is closely approximated by both unilateral and negotiated practices in the United States, where efficiency wage theory has considerable appeal among economists. In other countries, the same kind of large employer—the kind not requiring the protection of joint cartelism—often finds itself in centralized bargaining nevertheless. Efficiency wage theory poses the following question therefore: if the same employers who see a benefit in the segmentalist strategy were, for some reason, able to overcome obstacles to joining together in a collective strategy, might they do things differently? If they chose to do things differently, what would be the effects on unemployment and the wage structure, and how might they deal with the problems of labor supply, turnover, and effort? What circumstances would make it possible for employers to make and stand by the collective choice? Finally, what difference would a collective, as opposed to the segmentalist, strategy make for employer interests and behavior in the politics of industrial relations and welfare?

Solidarism

An interesting offshoot of the efficiency wage literature deals with centralized pay setting and therefore helps answer some of these questions. The analysis originates in Norway, a country with a history of highly centralized pay setting and related political developments much like Sweden's. Its answers shed light on why Swedish employers, coordinated by a powerful confederation and affiliated sectoral associations, have behaved in a radically different way from their American counterparts in labor market governance and social politics.

Beginning with the usual efficiency wage assumption about a wage-productivity nexus in many firms, models of centralized pay setting by a highly disciplined association of employers, with or without union cooperation, indicate that wages would be set lower than in the typical decentralized efficiency wage model. This is also what the standard monopsony model would predict for a buyers' cartel of employers. But in stark contrast to the monopsony model, employment would be higher, which helps explain why unions might cooperate.[38] For employers, according to the efficiency wage model, the gain from lower overall wage levels (inhibitions on individual firms' attempts to achieve an efficiency advantage with higher relative wages) outweigh the loss from reduced worker effort associated with lower unemployment. Total profits, therefore, would exceed those achieved in the decentralized equilibrium.[39]

The unorthodox equilibrium in the centralized model is one where many firms offer wages below market-clearing levels, not above, as with segmentalism. In other words, the marginal revenue to a firm from hiring one additional worker exceeds the wage the firm has agreed to offer under the terms of the centralized arrangement. In that sense, centralization creates for many firms a *scarcity of labor:* there will be a shortage of workers willing to take work at the going rate. To put it another way, there will be a "queue" of employers seeking to hire more workers at the given wage. Many firms, in this case, would actually prefer to raise wages to reduce resignations or shirking on the job, expand employment and production, or otherwise improve productivity and profits. But this would only work if others abstained or could be prevented from following suit.

Because cheating the arrangement by raising wages would be profitable for individual firms, centralized wage setting presupposes some mechanism for monitoring adherence and punishing violations by would-be segmentalists. Normative support for a policing arrangement is a natural possibility, a short logical step from the disapproval widely, if not always, accorded to employers who, in American parlance, "poach" workers from each other by offering higher wages. That is to say, norms of support for a policing agency follow logically from disapproval of the moral equivalent of trespassing and theft. In

Sweden, employers sometimes referred to this illicit behavior as "disloyal recruitment" (*illojal värvning*) through the use of "black-market wages" (*svartabörslöner*). Full exercise of freedom in an unregulated labor market was not a capitalist virtue.

In this centralized equilibrium, there is, in a sense, "involuntary" underpricing of labor by the individual employer under centralization and a scarcity of labor. In segmentalism, the opposite prevails: voluntary overpricing and surplus labor. Another way to look at the contrast between segmentalism and the centralized alternative is this: in the decentralized equilibrium, with involuntary unemployment, workers who are not employed at a firm paying efficiency wages may offer to work for lower wages than those enjoyed by the currently employed. But the voluntary and rational actions of individual firms will mean they decline the apparently attractive offer. (Workers willing to take lower wages are powerless to force the employer to hire them, so no external agency is needed to prevent them from underbidding.) Segmentalism is therefore self-enforcing. In the centralized case, however, external enforcement of behavior by individual firms must be applied to make it possible to speak of any kind of equilibrium. This is an artificial equilibrium in a strict economic sense, for individual firms facing scarcity have an unambiguous interest in eliminating it. Workers will only too gladly help out by offering their work at higher wages.[40]

In short, while centralized or administered pricing of labor may seem collectively rational to employers, their individual behavior in labor markets is likely to undermine it. It follows then that an association of employers in the position to summon the relatively easy initial agreement to set low wages is likely to seek authority for the tricky task of coercive enforcement. Consequently, it will seek to legitimate its authority with appeals to norms of fair competition in the marketplace. As effective as these may be, there will be limits. Individual employers will not gladly suffer highly intrusive policing and restrictions on their entrepreneurial and managerial autonomy, even if imposed by other employers and not workers or the state. Thus, the association is also likely to promote policies that accomplish the same ends as efficiency wages with different means, and therefore reduce the individual employer's incentive to raise wages.

This mix of supportive and coercive policies for centralized labor market governance will be called *solidarism*, a term borrowed from Swedish parlance (i.e., from *solidarisk lönepolitik* or solidaristic wage policy).[41] For reasons to be elaborated, solidaristic governance of labor markets supplements the setting of wages at subequilibrium levels with collective measures to

> Facilitate compliance with wage restraint and reduce turnover through interfirm and intersectoral standardization, backed by norms of fair competition over labor. In practice, this may mean discouraging the use of pay forms that are hard to monitor and measure, like social benefits.

> Induce worker effort by promoting and regulating the use of individualized pay-for-performance schemes ("piece work").

Manage and ration labor supply with coordinated recruitment and training practices, including restrictions on advertising and poaching, promoting the formation and use of labor exchanges for mobilization and deployment of idle workers and skills, and regulating or collectivizing vocational skill formation.

Work with organized labor to legitimate and co-administer solidaristic policies.

Later chapters will show how well these measures describe much of the ambitions and activity of the Swedish employers' confederation.[42] In the meantime, the following discussion elaborates in general why the measures logically follow from the centralized efficiency wage model.

Collective Turnover Control through Wage Standardization   While the efficiency wage literature on centralization of wage setting predicts higher employment levels and labor scarcity by comparison to the decentralized model, it is so far silent on the question of the structure of wages. But recall that a major result of efficiency wage theory in the decentralized context was wage differentiation that could not be accounted for in traditional neo-classical models. Thus, ironically, one might expect to find that if firms employed a highly centralized system to administer the pricing of labor, the result would be a pay structure that more closely approximates the neo-classical model of unfettered decentralized markets with perfect information and mobility, that is, a standardization of wages across firms and industries.[43]

A good reason to expect this result lies in the fact that centralization requires a regime for monitoring compliance and sanctioning violations of collective efforts to hold wages below the market-clearing equilibrium. In this context, "sociological" factors regarding equity or fairness introduced in some efficiency wage models of decentralized firm behavior with respect to employees, and employees' relationships with each other, come into play. But in the centralized case they do so in the relationships among firms and between firms and employers' associations. In principle, centralized wage regulation might mean no more than forcing unequal wages down across the board without altering their structure. But firms paying the lower wages are unlikely, on the grounds of fairness, to recognize and obey the employer authorities trying to enforce restraint.[44] For they will now be experiencing enormous disadvantages (higher turnover, difficulty attracting good workers to expand production), with respect to higher paying firms in the tighter labor market.

Disobedience among low-pay employers is especially likely because their workers will at the same time push for increases on equity grounds (because of interfirm disparities) and take advantage of tight labor markets to strike for those ends. It would be wishful thinking to expect obedience of the association's orders in rejecting worker demands that are identical to the firm's own micro-economic interests. To complicate matters, standing up to a strike for such selfless ends would mean losing customers and profits, a cost that could be externalized only at great expense to the employers' association in the form of strike support. The association, simply put, would be squeezed between the rock of membership discontent and the hard place of costly strike support, requiring high membership fees from other firms. This dilemma can be avoided to a large extent by combining interfirm standardization with repression of wages.

An added advantage of solidaristic wage standardization for the employer association is its ability to promote and defend the policy as a means to reduce turnover, which is likely to be high in a tight labor market created by centralized wage repression. This is rather ironic, for wage differentiation, the opposite, was the strategy of individual firms in the segmentalist system for reducing *their* costly turnover. In short, decentralization brings differentiation to reduce turnover, causing unemployment. Centralization brings low unemployment, which increases turnover. So now the problem of turnover control is externalized or displaced as a collective service that has to be to fulfilled by the employers' association.

By definition, a well-enforced system of wage standardization reduces individual firms' ability to raise wages to attract workers from other firms when they are highly motivated to do so in tight labor markets with wages set at subequilibrium levels. Many firms are likely to regard solidaristic wage policy with special favor if it reduces one of their workers' main reasons for changing jobs. In sum, solidaristic standardization helps serve one of the central purposes of segmentalism: control of turnover. It is therefore an important condition for making centralized wage restraint a viable institutional equilibrium that will not degenerate into the decentralized market equilibrium of segmentalism.

Productivity through Performance Pay   The efficiency wage literature sees centralized wage restraint and the resulting tight labor markets as having a cost, albeit a compensated one, in terms of reduced effort or discipline that might result from low levels of unemployment. Solidaristic standardization of wages, as a way of making centralization institutionally viable, also tends to eliminate the wage differentiation between high-pay firms that can induce workers to repay their blessings with greater effort. It is therefore likely that an employers' association trying to maintain centralization will seek to support and promote policies that reduce individual firms' incentives to cheat and raise wages unilaterally to improve productivity. One way to do that would be to promote, where practicable, the shift from straight time wages (hourly wages for example) to incentive pay arrangements, such as piece work. These arrangements would take collectively imposed standard hourly wage rates as the base or standard from which to calculate individual workers' output-linked premiums above the base.

In principle, therefore, incentive pay can maintain something like an average effort-earnings parity across firms, while promoting, for the sake of individual effort, individually differentiated earnings within firms. However, collaborative design and monitoring of incentive pay administration will also be required to prevent the illicit use of incentive pay to spirit efficiency wage differentials in again through the back door. That is to say, pay relative to that of other employers must be prevented from rising surreptitiously because of loose management of piece rates. For example an employer desiring to attract more labor may neglect to revise rates per piece downward when new machinery rather than intensified worker effort generates output increases. Therefore, external supervision of incentive practices will be called for. Collective efforts to design incentive pay systems transferable from firm to firm and monitoring piece work earnings trends in firms are likely to become part of the complicated solidaristic agenda. Violation of regulation begets new regulation.

To the inevitable extent that incentive earnings drift upward in firms evading fully effective solidaristic correction, such pay systems may have an added productivity and growth advantage under solidarism. The lag time in the correction process introduces a strong incentive for workers to accept the introduction of new technology that reduces labor time per unit of output, thus increasing their hourly earnings. Meanwhile, solidarism injects an unusually powerful incentive for employers to search for and introduce this new labor-saving technology. Lacking the easy ability to hire additional labor by raising wages to meet increased demand, solidarists may more actively seek new technology and retrain existing labor.[45] Segmentalists, in stark contrast, can easily hire more labor to go with current technology. They may not even need to raise wages, but they are in any case freer to do so.

The labor economics literature on performance pay predicts variations in piece work usage associated with differences between industries, occupations, and the heterogeneity of workers within them. The efficiency wage literature barely mentions piece work. But when it does, it speculates that efficiency wages and piece work may be substitutes whose usage varies across occupations and industries. Efficiency wages, for example, may be an effective alternative in occupations where piece rates are impractical because "monitoring is too costly or too inaccurate."[46] By contrast, the argument here indicates that large variations that cannot be accounted for by industry, occupational, or labor force characteristics should also be expected across countries because of their different systems of labor market governance.

Labor Supply In segmentalism, employers individually ration scarce jobs among a surplus of needy workers; in solidarism, they collectively ration scarce labor among a surplus of needy employers. By creating scarcity, solidarism in wage setting generates interests in regulatory machinery that finds, creates, and allocates labor. For example, solidaristic employers are likely to see labor exchanges (employment offices), combined with restrictions on job advertising, as an important means for nonmarket rationing of available workers, be they idled by layoffs or newly entering the labor market.

Labor exchanges combined with advertising restrictions assist solidarism in a number of ways. Employer organizations can point to the existence of exchanges in their efforts to discourage firms from using wage or benefit increases to attract additional labor from other workplaces when growing demand calls for expanding production. An exchange gives firms a legitimate place to turn to find available workers ready to fill job openings at regulated levels without advertising. Restriction of advertising, be it general or targeted, protects the lower-paying employer against the higher-paying violators of solidarism, by making their deviations less effective. Advertising restrictions also protect employers who invest in training from the one who free rides by raiding them for their skilled labor.

Labor exchanges are especially important in administratively rationing available workers with expensive skills. Skilled labor tends to be in chronically short supply in all labor markets because of employers' underinvestment in training. Because employers have no property title to their investments in the "human capital" assets or brain power of mobile workers in free labor markets, workers can abscond with those assets and share the dividends between themselves and new employers. Thus, skills are suboptimally provided where labor is highly mobile because employers discount the anticipated payoff of investments in training by the probability of the workers leaving.[47] In the solidaristic context, because of subequilibrium wages, competition among employers over skilled labor can be especially intense.

Solidaristic employers may therefore seek to regulate or collectivize training. They may impose obligations on each other to spend a certain amount on training, or keep some percentage of their workforce in apprenticeships. With legitimate machinery of quantitative regulation in place, regulators may take the next logical step to make regulation more invasive, forcing employers to provide training in general rather than narrow, company-specific skills (versatile, more knowledge-based rather than rote skills dedicated to the specific production and managerial technology of the firm). Then, if the company that provides the training must shed employees, other employers can quickly absorb and make good use of them. A potential alternative, or at least complement, is to set up collectively funded training facilities outside the firm. The feeding of trainees from these training institutions into labor exchanges set up to ration them on an equitable and rational basis will be the natural consequence.[48]

Cross-Class Solidarism   Solidarism, in principle, can be pursued unilaterally by employers acting on an organized basis. Because it prioritizes wage repression, one might be surprised to see anything else. On the other hand, capitalists do not gladly give away power over their managerial affairs to anyone, including other employers or their representatives. They are also powerfully tempted by the rewards of defecting from solidaristic wage restraint because of the resulting labor scarcity. Thus, the viability of unilateral solidarism is questionable.

A cross-class alliance with organized labor on a solidaristic basis remains a distinct possibility, the theory suggests, because of higher employment levels and more egalitarian pay. These may compensate for the costs paid by high-wage members whose abstention allows for "excess profits" in many firms.[49]

The Swedish case of *negotiated solidarism* suggests, indeed, that it may be necessary. Only in the crucible of conflict with unions did the cohesive norms and organizational apparatus of broad-based employer solidarism evolve in Sweden. Where worker militants in the context of unilateral solidarism take advantage of labor scarcity to raise wages and impose limits on managerial rights, unionism can play into the hands of employer leaders trying to build the resources and solidaristic authority of the association. Other employers, now pressured by the militancy of their workers seeking similar victories, but less able and willing to concede them, may seek protection from a powerful association that can stiffen employer resolve across the board. The association can then use the unifying pretext of controlling labor militancy to strengthen its ability to establish control over employer as well as union behavior.

Strike and lockout insurance, financed by dues to the association, can then be applied to defeat local militancy and make unions' decentralized tactics too expensive. The mere existence of such insurance gives employer leaders the right to establish rules of behavior so individual employers do not engage in risky behavior leading to the waste of insurance funds. Prudential regulation of pay practices is required, according to insurance-speak, to mitigate this "moral hazard." Forced to the centralized bargaining table, unions then can become collaborators in solidaristic labor market governance because their concerns for pay equity harmonize well with organized employers' self-interest in pay standardization. The centralized agreements hammered out then become the law invoked by employer organizations in policing their members. In solidarism, collective agreements imply an obligation of employers to each other not to pay above contract ceilings, just as joint cartelism imposes a pact of solidarity among workers not to "scab" for wages under contract floors.

Centralized governance of labor markets may win the approval and participation of organized labor because it strengthens the insecure hierarchical control of union leaders over their membership and subunits. Union leaders can promote the solidaristic policies as their own and likewise participate in their design and implementation, while employers may actually let them take credit. Egalitarian wage results can be presented as a very good deal for the price of wage restraint. Union leaders may also enjoy credit for the higher employment that results. In the course of time, an institutional equilibrium may be reached in the mutually supportive relations between centralized labor market organizations. This institutional equilibrium may be necessary for maintaining the micro-economic disequilibrium of solidaristic wages. Equilibrium does not mean the absence of conflict, though, it should be emphasized. Unions are still likely to use their power in the relationship to challenge employers on the details and limits of solidarism. The pragmatic application of union power, and employers' response, may promote the evolution of stable solidarism. Likewise, the imprudent use of power can set in motion the employer response that destabilizes or destroys it.

The Incidence and Admixture
of the Three Systems

Counterintuitive as it might seem, in practice, cartelism, segmentalism, and solidarism appear in mixed or hybrid forms. To understand why, one must keep in mind that employers, especially manufacturers, often compete in two distinct and only partially overlapping markets. They compete over customers in product markets of a large, even international scope. But they compete over workers in labor markets that tend to be much smaller geographically. Of course, the reason for the market differences lies in the easy transportability of merchandise and the strong ties between workers and their communities. Moreover, the advantages and disadvantages of cartelism, segmentalism, and solidarism will likely change, depending on macro-economic conditions. Over time, complex institutional mixes evolve, varying by country.

Take negotiated cartelism, for example. By holding wages up at a level appropriate for stabilizing competition in far-flung product markets, a company operating in a more localized labor market may reap an efficiency or segmentalist's advantage. The cartelist wage may be higher than normal for local employers producing other goods and services but drawing on the same local labor pool. Because of the high wage, the employer will have the pick of better workers, and those workers may work harder than otherwise. Under such circumstances, joint cartelism can have a subsidiary or incidental segmentalist function.[50] In times of rapid growth and high demand, when labor markets tighten, cartelism may also have a solidaristic side benefit. Restricting collective bargaining to the multi-employer level at infrequent intervals may reduce the upward pull of wages to levels beyond what is necessary to stabilize product market competition. Union leaders with an eye on the horizon may even participate in restraining workers from taking advantage of the situation, knowing full well that when the economy cycles down, the elevated wages may do injury to the industry's profit and employment levels. Evidence from the garment industry in the United States illustrates this phenomenon.

Segmentalists may also enjoy side benefits of solidarism and cartelism if they can in some way coordinate their policies. If they compete with other segmentalists over the same local labor supply, coordination among them, especially in a business upturn, will reduce upward pressures on wages and benefits beyond the point necessary for an efficiency advantage relative to lower pay employers in the rest of the labor market. In Japan, for example, the traditional role of leading banks and interlocking ownership has probably facilitated this kind of coordination, preventing big employers from poaching labor from each other and engaging in other opportunistic practices. They could offer very low entry-level wages in order to pay for high seniority-based wage increases. Other big employers would not bid up those entry-level wages, for, because of coordination, they also structured their segmentalist pay on a similar seniority basis. Hence, a system of "integrated segmentation," according to one astute analysis.[51]

Unions can help coordinate segmentalists. In doing so, they can supply a cartelist side benefit. Through "pattern bargaining," or imposing similar wage and benefit conditions across a product market dominated by segmentalists, unions can prevent certain employers from taking advantage of semi-insular labor markets, where wages are lower, to reduce product prices at competitors' expense. The role of the UAW in the American auto industry comes to mind here, where pattern bargaining probably helped stabilize relations with the "Big Three" automakers. They did so by depriving the smaller "independents" of any advantage they could capture with lower wages and benefits.

In the United States and Sweden, at least, different patterns have clearly dominated others. Whether that is the case in other countries is a matter for future research and analysis. In the United States, cartelism gave way to segmentalism in some product sectors at the beginning of the century and continued to develop in others. A kind of institutional "dualism" emerged, with both coexisting side by side. Only in extraordinary periods of labor scarcity brought on by two world wars did solidarism emerge as a strong but uneven tendency and it only took hold with state intervention. It receded afterward. In Sweden, solidarism over time reigned supreme across the entire labor market, especially after the 1930s. Employers' solidaristic agenda was aggressively anti-segmentalist. Also, by creating endemic scarcity, it rendered cartelism superfluous. Wages did not need to be propped up by unions to inhibit low-wage low-price competition, for labor scarcity did the job by itself.

Labor Market Governance and the Welfare State

Despite inevitable tensions and conflicts across and within classes, the three systems described can achieve a more or less stable state. Segmentalism is a self-enforcing micro-economic equilibrium. Cartelism and solidarism are socio-institutional equilibria with collective enforcement tools for neutralizing the forces of breakdown arising from the micro-economic disequilibria they create. However, they all suffer strains and vulnerabilities associated with cyclical swings and other exogenous pressures or shocks. How these forces affect employers depends on the institutions and practices they use to manage their labor markets.

Welfare policies can mediate the disruptive effect of economic disturbances, depending on the labor market regime. Hence, variable economic institutions and managerial practices strongly influence the nature of employer interests in the welfare state. Politicians and other reformers take those interests into account in planning their major reform initiatives. While responding to popular pressures and electoral opportunities, they also seek employer support, and therefore broad cross-class alliances as the foundation for durable reform.

Segmentalism and Cartelism: Market
Security through Social Security

Segmentalists, one might think, would have no interests in public systems of welfare, being private providers of welfare in their own economic interests. Economic analysis of wage rigidities even in unregulated or highly decentralized labor markets suggests reasons to think otherwise. As the following analysis shows, segmentalists are highly reluctant to reduce wages and benefits in a recession or depression. If they are less able to do so than some product market competitors, they might welcome welfare state initiatives. They would so for the simple reason that the welfare state imposes new and costly rigidities on their competitors, thus staving off at least some injurious price competition.

Efficiency wage theory accounts for the empirically observed fact of downward wage rigidity even under conditions of labor surplus or unemployment. After all, some unemployment is caused by efficiency wages. Historical observation also indicates that wages are inertial in a recession, that is, even in the face of exogenously increased unemployment, a phenomenon central to Keynes's theory and policy argument.[52] Some theory in labor economics, assimilable with efficiency wage theory or at least consistent with some variants of it, also claims to explain why some employers would react sluggishly in response to cyclical changes in the economy.

Related phenomena are features of "Okun's Law," which says, among other things, that high-pay employers' share of employment, production, and profits increases during cyclical upturns. Arthur Okun had argued that high-standard employers, in economic upturns, are in the enviable position of being able to increase output and profits in response to increased demand by hiring more labor even without immediately raising wages or benefits. As Okun put it, "Because of the typical queue of applicants at their hiring gates, [wage rates at high-paying firms] need not rise to permit increased employment." More important for this discussion is Okun's proposition that in the weak labor market of cyclical downturns, by contrast, "they cannot be cut—perhaps not even readily slowed down," because of implicit promises not only of pay stability, but even regular "equitable" increases.[53]

The existence of long-term "implicit contracts" that Okun alludes to here can, according to George Akerlof and Janet Yellen, two leading proponents of efficiency wage theory, easily be incorporated in an efficiency wage model. In their model, implicit contracts, together with efficiency wage models, "jointly explain Okun's Law and involuntary unemployment."[54] Though skeptical of implicit contract theory, like most economists today, Truman Bewley finds empirical reason to think that Okun's version is at least partially consistent with reality, as are the efficiency wage arguments of Akerlof and Robert Solow. His exhaustive and penetrating survey of American employers during the early 1990s recession finds that employers' desire to preserve worker morale and inhibit turnover explain wage inertia in recessions. The desire to attract good workers and reduce turnover explains why some employers pay high wages.

Keeping them there, at least at the existing nominal level, is motivated by their fear of declining productivity and rising labor costs.[55] In short, during economic downturns, efficiency wage and kindred theories, along with empirical evidence, indicate that many segmentalist employers abstain from playing employees off against the unemployed, even if applicants are available and ready to underbid current employees. With their "invisible handshakes," "gift exchanges," "fair wage-effort" bargains, or "reciprocal fairness"—or simply their solicitousness of employee morale—segmentalist employers make strenuous efforts not to take advantage of downturns and reduce wages and benefits.[56]

The trouble comes, of course, when the bill arrives and segmentalists have to honor their part of the bargain as demand, prices, and profits start to decline. They may absorb some of the shock in profit cuts and pass some along in layoffs. In a severe recession or depression, these measures may be inadequate, especially in product markets where technology and therefore the labor process is heterogeneous. That is to say, segmentalists may compete at the margin with viable competitors who extract productivity with the "drive system" instead of softer inducements. These competitors may more indifferently shed labor and rehire on the external "spot market," in effect bidding down wages when demand is slack and joblessness is high. Finally, new entrants appear, hiring the eager unemployed at bargain wages.

To follow suit, welfare capitalists would be required, at considerable cost in terms of workplace morale and efficiency, to violate their company-based moral economy. In other words, being tied up in long-term trust transactions with their workers, they have expensive relationship-specific investments to protect.[57] Because their micro-level social contracts account for much of their market and managerial advantages, segmentalists will be tempted to look for alternatives to wage, benefit, and job reductions. One alternative may be offered to them on a silver platter by outsiders: government taxation of their competitors, associated with compulsory social insurance. Segmentalists who lack or are able to see around conventional ideological blinders may appreciate in this a potential for regulating product market competition and therefore compensating them for segmentalism's vulnerability under conditions of depression, deflation, and high unemployment.

For all their profound differences, joint cartelism may have the identical effect as segmentalism on employer attitudes toward the welfare state in hard times. The reason for this lies in the fact that employers in both systems can be undercut by low-wage, low-benefit competitors when low-price competition roils their highly permeable product markets. Cartelists, tending to be smaller and more labor-intensive, are probably even more vulnerable than segmentalists to competition from new entrants to the sector who can hire unemployed workers at wages below those negotiated between unions and employer associations. These fly-by-night competitors are also likely to manage without providing any social benefits that might be included in multi-employer union contracts.

Thus, because of the powerful insult effect on worker morale, joint cartelists have the same motivation to avoid wage and benefit reductions in recessions. Furthermore, union contracts with distant expiration dates prohibit wage cuts in prompt response to competitors' prices. Strong and pragmatic union leaders may make negotiated cuts possible, though quite probably not adequate ones. Not all union leaders enjoy the ability to persuade a heterogeneous and fractious membership of the need for cuts, and efforts to do so may cause severe damage to the union and the viability of whatever regulatory protection, welcomed by employers, they still provide. Imposing cost increases on competitors therefore seems a less messy alternative to imposing cost reductions on workers.

Cartelists are likely to be especially enthusiastic about minimum wage legislation. Wage floors inhibit low-wage competition from employers who for one reason or another do not fall under union control. Cartelists may even perceive an advantage in legislation that strengthens organized labor's ability to extend its reach. Employers in this camp who have overcome ideological and other blocks to entering a cross-class alliance with unions in centralized bargaining are especially likely to welcome, as an extension of the alliance, government help in regulating competition in these ways. Joining with liberal segmentalists, they may signal their interests to politicians and reformers, emboldening them to initiate major expansions and innovations in social and labor policy. The resulting cross-class alliance embraces both the interests of mass electoral constituencies in social security and capitalist interests in market security. Like segmentalists, cartelists are likely to be foul weather friends of the welfare state. When good times resume, support will subside.

Solidarism and the Regulatory Welfare State

Solidarism, by contrast, turns employers into fair weather friends of the welfare state. The economic conditions likely to open solidarists' minds to the advantages of welfare legislation—growing demand, tightening labor markets, and inflation—are, not surprisingly, exactly the opposite of those that can turn segmentalist and cartelists into social liberals. Under solidarism, buoyant demand creates powerful incentives for individual employers to expand production, and therefore recruit additional labor. Collectively raising wages is unlikely, however, to appreciably increase the total labor supply. Individually raising wages at the expense of other employers is not allowed, though the impulse to cheat will be strong. Individual firms are therefore likely to seek any allowable substitute or undetectable outlet to fulfill their need for labor. Above all, they will be tempted to resort to social benefits as a device to attract and keep labor, and thereby come out from under centralized control of money wages.

The political receptivity of a solidaristic community of employers to compulsory social welfare legislation arises from this urgent profit-driven tendency to supplement wages with benefits. Creators of a solidaristic regime are likely, from the beginning, to have encouraged employers to stick largely, if not exclusively, to the use of hourly wages and piece rates to remunerate workers. From the standpoint of economies of scale, administration of social benefits is likely to be inefficient when practiced equally across the board, but only on a company-by-company basis. Once social benefits creep in, solidarism might logically entail efforts to standardize benefits. The disadvantage here is that measuring, monitoring, and enforcing standardization of benefits might even be more difficult than for wages. Also, forging agreement among a highly diverse collection of employers about the design of benefit systems will be fraught with problems because of their highly unequal impacts.

By contrast, compulsory social legislation in the form of pension and health insurance paid in whole or in part by employers may offer scale economies as well as assistance to the employers' association in its efforts to manage the labor market on a solidaristic basis. For one thing, social legislation can reduce worker pressure from below on individual employers all too eager to offer social benefits in violation of the spirit if not letter of solidarism. Acceptance of the state's legitimate role in this realm will also lend extra moral force to the association's dictates against company benefits, and so disarm companies that might try to argue, in self-defense, the urge to offer humanitarian assistance to workers in need. Social legislation takes company benefits off the labor market agenda, to the employer association's relief. Government efforts in the realm of "labor market policy" will also be welcome. Unable to increase the size of the suitably trained workforce with wage increases, employers will welcome systematic training efforts to better match the supply of skills to rapidly evolving employer needs. Geographic mobilization subsidized and administered through centralized labor exchanges can sensibly ration idle labor to strategically important sectors that labor and employer organizations can reach cross-class agreement on.

As in the case of segmentalism and cartelism, the task of initiating legislation will probably fall largely to reformers outside of the organized capitalist community. Anti-government ideology quite suited to normal business and political conditions obstructs employers from taking on the role themselves. Leaders of employer organizations lack the mandate to promote legislation, and the staff they hire are likely to lack the ideological predilection, if not the requisite expertise. They are also likely to be hobbled by traditional and personal loyalties to conservative parties and party officials who also lack the mandate and staff dedicated to government interventionism. This is not to say that astute and cautious reformers are not responding to clear signals from employers about their interests.

Conclusion

The peculiar strategic and policy thinking of GM's Charles Wilson in the United States and the Söderlunds of the Swedish Employer Confederation make perfect sense when seen in the light of analysis about variable systems of labor market governance. Wilson sought to solidify union control over workers and channel union demands in the direction of welfare capitalist benefits particular to big firms in the auto industry. The arrangement, combined with a minimalist welfare state, would distance GM from most of the labor market through a system of negotiated segmentalism. The Söderlunds likewise understood the advantage of employer actions that would solidify the leadership of a centralized union movement that it could nudge in directions that went with the grain of solidarism, the country's radically different brand of labor market governance and class relations.

The remainder of this book will bring to light many other profound and sometimes astonishing differences in employer behavior in politics and markets in America and Sweden. The most intriguing difference is in the progressive social policy inclinations of a small if articulate minority of politically significant large employers during the 1930s in the United States, when New Deal legislation was passed, and the absence of the same in Sweden at the same time. The roles reversed in the 1940s and 1950s, however, when Swedish employers gave their stamp of approval to the core reforms of the social democratic welfare state. During this period, even the most progressive of American corporate executives resisted major expansion of social policy and instead promoted company-level social benefits, both with and without union input. Swedish employers, in contrast, participated gladly in the liquidation of company-based and even some collectively bargained social benefits and replacement of them with legislation.

To account for the dramatic differences between the two countries, and solve the historical puzzle of the previous chapter, the narrative integrates theory from this chapter with considerable historical evidence. The comparative argument, in broad strokes, goes as follows. Beginning early in this century, leading manufacturing employers in Sweden and the United States pursued diametrically opposite strategies with regard to labor markets and labor unions. In the United States, after the failure of joint cartelism in steel, machine, and foundry production, leading manufacturers set off on a distinctive individualistic and decentralized course of action. Technological change, shortages of skilled labor, and, above all, employers' inability to disabuse unions of skilled workers of their militant ambitions to control managerial decisions through collective bargaining were responsible. Employers' collective action would now be dedicated primarily to crushing rather than negotiating with unions.

For many employers, the decentralized strategy involved offering higher wages than necessary to fill their workplaces (efficiency wages) and, as part of that strategy, relatively generous social benefits (welfare capitalism). Both were designed to achieve the mixed but consonant purposes of warding off unionization, reducing turnover costs, and securing flexibility and efficiencies in the labor process. Employers in other sectors, by contrast, continued to work with unions on a cartelist basis, most importantly in the coal, clothing, and construction industries, where technological and competitive conditions made it more attractive.

The segmentalist and cartelist strategies had a major disadvantage. They left employers vulnerable to the macro-economic shock of the Great Depression, a fact well understood by New Deal reformers. Slack demand and high unemployment exposed these firms to extremely injurious competition from low-wage and low-benefit product market competitors. Taxation for compulsory social insurance, and minimum wages, promised to "uplift" competitive conditions. The interests signaled by employers emboldened the New Dealers to initiate dramatic innovations in social policy and guided the design of their reforms to satisfy important capitalist interests simultaneously with those of their mass constituencies.

In Sweden, by contrast, employers organized effectively, starting early in the century, in pursuit of a radically different strategy of collectively repressing wages (as opposed to individually raising them) and compressing rather than differentiating pay across firms and industries. The employers' associations and their confederation also tried to suppress and drive out the use of welfare capitalist company benefits instead of promote them, as did every major American business organization. Massive general and sympathy lockouts, a tool not available to their American counterparts, had effectively rooted out all union ambitions to impose the closed shop and to control managerial decisions, thus making them attractive partners in joint labor market governance of a solidaristic nature.

Employers' strategy of negotiated solidarism, evolving from 1905 onward, achieved phenomenal success in the 1940s and 1950s. For big employers solidarism represented, as a politico-institutional equilibrium with a cross-class foundation, at least as favorable a solution as the market equilibrium of segmentalism. However, the vulnerability of the institutional arrangement was radically different. Conditions of robust demand from postwar international trade made widespread cheating against collectively administered pricing of labor by individual employers too tempting to be fully controlled. Cheating, even by firms that supported the system in principle, often took the form of company-based welfare benefits, which could not be easily monitored, measured, and regulated by the employers' confederation. Thus, private welfare benefits experienced explosive, and from the employer organizations' standpoint, disturbing growth in the 1940s and early 1950s. At this time Social Democrats in Sweden introduced their dramatic reforms, support for which was openly signaled by the employers' confederation. Putting welfare on the legislative agenda would help them manage the labor market on a solidaristic basis by reducing pressure from below on individual employers all too eager to offer concessions. Solidaristic interests left a distinctive and even a progressive stamp on the design of reforms.

With strong growth in the postwar period, then, Swedish employers took their feet off the brake on the welfare state and even occasionally stepped on the accelerator, allowing social democracy to pass American developments on the left. Under the same economic circumstances, by contrast, America gave way to a reascendant welfare capitalism. Now, because of the Wagner

Act, the revival of unions, and Supreme Court rulings, unilateral gave way to negotiated segmentalism, while expansion and innovation in compulsory, universal social insurance slowed considerably relative to Sweden. To understand the reasons for these dramatic differences, one must trace these events and circumstances from the beginning of the twentieth century, when employers in the two countries started developing their different systems of labor market governance.

Part II

Labor Markets

3

MANAGERIAL CONTROL

The Origins of American Segmentalism

According to historian Howell Harris, in his illuminating study of major American employers and during the 1940s, "the roots of the modern American industrial relations system were more likely to be found outside the labor movement than within it." Labor, he concluded, "looked more like a reactive than an initiating force in the process of social change: a weak institution in a powerfully organized, pervasively capitalist society." In America, "the business community was the dynamic force."[1] Even though many major employers only begrudgingly accepted collective bargaining under pressure from the state during the New Deal and the political exigencies of war, executives like Charles Wilson of General Motors ultimately accommodated it only on their own terms.

In other words, unionism shaped itself into an existing segmentalist mold, the system of high-wage and company welfare practices of the period before World War II. Militant pressures, of course, influenced the practices significantly in the process. In any case, as Harris argues,

> bargained fringe benefits continued to serve many of the old purposes of stabilizing the employee population of the plant and increasing its attachment, if not to the work, then at least to the job. Reducing labor turnover of prime adult males, and increasing the seriousness of the threat of disciplinary discharge (which came to mean loss of accrued seniority and welfare entitlements), increased management's control over the workforce.

In sum, "Unions, as well as firms, tried to strengthen the ties which bound plant communities together."[2]

Thus, even where American unions seemed to exercise so much power over management—in the realm of seniority rights, for example—they did so by building on a principle that management, not labor, had introduced. So concluded historian Ronald Schatz, writing on General Electric (GE).[3] In other words, a system of *negotiated segmentalism* emerged, largely displacing the earlier unilateral version. To be sure, profound tensions remained because unions never shed all their ambitions to capture more control over managerial practices. At most, what they achieved was "job control unionism" limited to regulation of individual workers' movement through internal labor markets according to highly detailed job classification systems and intricately spelled-out promotion rules, bumping rights, shift preferences, and the like.[4] Unions worked their way into the management of segmentalism, reaping credit from a relatively privileged stratum of American workers, even if their employers benefitted too.

Historian Sanford Jacoby shows that negotiated segmentalism coexisted alongside a smaller part of the American labor market where workers took home similar and sometimes even better wages and benefits even without the help of powerful national unions. Big manufacturing companies like Du Pont, Kodak, IBM, Procter and Gamble, S. C. Johnson, and Thompson Products (later TRW) succeeded in preserving a unilateral form of welfare capitalism, or a variety incorporating relatively tame "independent" unions. Some, like Union Carbide, maintained similar practices for both unionized and nonunion facilities. Jacoby thus portrays "separate but overlapping" systems, where major unionized and nonunionized employers influenced each other within a common segmentalist framework. Overlapping features resulted from "capture" and "spillover": unions appropriated early welfare capitalist practices like benefit systems and seniority preferences in layoffs, and nonunion companies often followed (though sometimes led) collectively bargained wage and benefit expansions. Nonunionized welfare capitalists, or those with company unions, zealously maintained separation because they enjoyed less rigid layoff, seniority, pay, and promotion rules.[5]

The viability of this rocky marriage of unionism and segmentalism had a lot to do with the overall success, documented by Harris, of employer militancy against union control ambitions in the late 1940s. GE's "Boulwarism," named after its vice president Lemuel Boulware, is well known as a rather extreme example of the militant campaign by major employers to recover managerial control lost during World War II. Boulware's harnessing of collective bargaining to segmentalism was less subtle than Charlie Wilson's approach at GM, described in the previous chapter, but it achieved similar results.[6] As Wilson's colleague Alfred Sloan put it in 1963, "on the whole, we have retained all the basic powers to manage."[7]

The rest of this chapter traces the origins and consequences of segmentalism in the United States in the period leading up to the Great Depression. Major employers' desire to secure managerial domination helps explain the development of their unilateral version. It began as a strategy designed in part to destroy and ward off a brand of unionism that could not be shaken of its militant designs on managerial control. The analysis, some of it covering territory familiar to specialists in American industrial relations history, illuminates the stage for the following chapter, which traces the concurrent emergence of centralized solidaristic industrial relations in Sweden. There, employers were far more successful, earlier on, in persuading unions to give up virtually all ambitions to control management and confine themselves largely to more negotiable wage issues.

The Ruins of Negotiated Cartelism

Deep-seated antagonism and overwhelming power with respect to unions early in the century do not really explain why major American employers turned to decentralized wage setting without union input early in the twentieth century. A better explanation lies in their organizational weakness and thus their inability to impose joint governance of markets on terms they favored. At the turn of the century, multi-employer bargaining was actually more developed in this country than in Sweden: about 19 employers' associations and 16 unions had negotiated no fewer than 26 national or large district agreements between 1895 and 1905.[8] In the latter year, centralized bargaining in Sweden was only just taking off. In the American iron industry, multi-employer collective bargaining with a union of skilled iron workers and related craftsmen had already been in existence more than a quarter of a century. The auspicious start for national collective bargaining for foundries producing iron stoves in 1891 inspired similar efforts in 1899 and 1900 in engineering, where foundries and machine shops produced metal goods and machinery for America's expanding farming, manufacturing, and consuming economy.[9]

Manufacturers' desire for market control of chaotic price competition underlay practically all multi-employer bargaining in force in 1900. Union-enforced wage floors across an industry inhibited the outbreak of disruptive price wars. The benefits of joint cartelism also motivated employers' continuing attempts to expand centralized bargaining, led by the National Civic Federation (NCF), an organization uniting capitalists and workers behind the cause.[10] But by 1905, all hopes had been dashed in the heart of American manufacturing industry. Employers gave up on a militant labor movement unable or unwilling to carry out the role they needed to perform in durable cross-class alliance for joint cartelism. Meanwhile, with their "great merger movement" of 1895 to 1904, large numbers found horizontally and vertically integrated combines to be a fairly effective substitute for unilateral cartelism, which was often unstable, to check ruinous competition.[11] Most major employers and their associations thus retooled for battle against unions that were becoming superfluous at best and dangerous at worst. In that largely successful battle, they developed the ideology and practices of segmentalism. Along the way, if not always from the very start, they also acquired a belief in its efficiency logic.

The Steel Industry

The first deep injury to the future prospects of centralized bargaining was inflicted in the steel industry in 1892, even as joint cartelism elsewhere showed robust signs of life. At the time, unionists in the Amalgamated Association of Iron, Steel, and Tin Workers proved unwilling and unable to adjust their behavior to the demands of the rising steel industry. Here, employers' desires to capture large profits and expanded markets from large investments in rapid technological advances clashed with the particular terms of well-established joint cartelism in the older iron industry. In iron production, chaotic competitive conditions and more uniform, crafts-based technology had given rise to a mutually agreeable solution involving centralized bargaining on the basis of a complex system of standard rates, sliding up and down with price fluctuations, for uniform jobs.

The famous coup came at the Homestead Works of Carnegie Steel, which led the way in its strategy of capital intensive modernization. A frontal collision with the union resulted, where "the decisive issue was wages," according to historian David Brody. The Amalgamated refused to accept company-specific cuts in piece (tonnage) rates that would be deep enough to align the company's workers' earnings with what workers at Homestead's competitors, using less advanced machinery, were receiving. (In the past, given more uniform technology, standardized tonnage rates brought uniform earnings; now, to regularize earnings, rates had to differ.)[12] In a deeper sense, the issue was the union's foot-dragging response toward rapid technological change in the industry. Had the union submitted quickly to the principle of uniform earnings rather than demanding a share of the profits from Carnegie's investments in improved machinery (seen by the company as "a tax on improvements"), it could have negotiated a new lease on life. When it refused, other companies, including every steel plant of consequence in Western Pennsylvania, followed suit in banishing the union.

As late as 1901, no less a figure than financier J. P. Morgan, the most powerful figure inside the newly formed U.S. Steel Corporation, apparently remained open to an alliance with unionism for product market control. To be sure, most of the steel executives now assembled together in the corporation, which was constructed out of Carnegie Steel and roughly half of the entire country's industry, were fiercely opposed. They were rankled above all by the union's obstruction of the profitable use of new technology. Nevertheless, in the first year of the corporation's existence, Morgan agreed to accept unionism in subsidiaries where it was already established and gave assurance according to the AFL's Samuel Gompers, from information conveyed to him by U.S. Steel's Charles Schwab, "that in course of time, perhaps two years, the company would be ready to sign for all its constituent plants." Morgan may have simply been buying time for the new and politically unpopular giant. On the other hand, he was "almost obsessed with the idea of stability" and viewed competition as a "destructive, inefficient force."[13] Thus, his reassurance to the union may have genuinely reflected a perception that the union might step in as a stabilizing force against predatory price cutting that continued to bedevil the steel industry—despite his efforts to still it with the formation of the corporate behemoth.

The union's executive committee recklessly spurned Morgan's offer. Instead, it called a general strike against the corporation to force immediate agreements on its entire tin plate, sheet steel, and steel hoop operations, thus breaking current agreements at some of them. By antagonizing even those in the industry who could see a redeeming regulatory value in unionism—especially the bankers—this impatient action played into the hands of the "steel men," the many belligerent union opponents within the corporation.[14] Accepting the union's sweeping demands would have left U.S. Steel vulnerable to "independents" still free to operate without union contracts and therefore able to charge lower prices. The corporation broke the strike, leaving the union in shambles. By 1909, when the finishing blow was delivered to the crippled union, U.S. Steel, led by Morgan's choice, Elbert Gary, was busy working on a substitute scheme: unilateral cartelism through price collusion with the independents.[15]

Engineering: Foundries and Machine Shops

In the engineering (machinery) industry, as in steel, employers' struggle to capture or recover the "right to manage" largely explains the failure of centralized bargaining. The move to centralization in the foundry industry was inspired by the resounding success of nationally centralized collective bargaining in its smaller stove-making segment. There, since 1891, employers in the Stove Founders' National Defense Association (SFNDA) and the International Molders' Union (IMU) had worked together in a mutually rewarding cartelist setup. As enforcer of the joint cartel, the IMU effectively imposed SFNDA rates on manufacturers who refused to join in the collective process.

Over time, from 1886 when the first 62 employers joined the SFNDA to counter the union threat, to the years after the first central agreement in 1891, many stove manufacturers grew to value the union's services. The floor it laid blocked competitive burrowing into the profits and market shares of better-paying employers and insulated them from the destructive effects of wage cutting on worker morale. In the preceding years, a combination of excess capacity and stagnant demand (as alternative heating and cooking equipment gained popularity) had brought ruinous price-cutting, at the expense of both profits and wages. In other words, according to economist Bauder's analysis, "The industry needed the Union to protect it from the demoralization of cutthroat competition."[16] Likewise, the union got what it had longed for: an association of employers that would help in jointly eradicating "unfair employers" or "chiselers" from the trade. The same logic had moved Samuel Gompers in 1903, as head of the American Federation of Labor, to welcome the formation of employers' associations. Union statesmen of his nature did not reflexively fear the organizational concentration of capitalist power.[17]

The rest of the foundry sector, producing a far more heterogeneous mix of castings, especially for machinery components, tried to follow suit in introducing joint cartelism. Leadership in their efforts was assumed by William Pfahler, an important figure in the union-friendly SFNDA. Pfahler, who helped establish the National Founders' Association (NFA) in 1898, speculated that "if all manufacturers were on an equal basis" in the realm of labor costs, "how much would it lessen the strain of that awful competition that is sapping the life of our business, tending to increase the commercial depression and retarding the return of prosperity?"[18] The constitution of the association identified its purpose as that of adopting "a uniform basis for just and equitable dealings between the members and their employees."[19] In national-level negotiations with the union over wages in Cleveland in 1901, the NFA welcomed the union's argument for minimum wages, for it would place "manufacturers on an equitable basis as to labor cost."[20] The next year, at the annual convention of the NFA, the organization again endorsed the idea of "obtaining stable conditions by minimizing uncertainty as to the wage rate."[21]

Ultimately, centralization of collective bargaining in the expanding foundry industry shipwrecked on control issues like apprenticeship regulations, work rules, the use of machinery, and piece work. It also broke up on the matter of how to structure minimum wage standards, which, at its core, was also a managerial control issue. The union, and especially local militants, refused to accept the employers' demand for a three-tier system of minimum rates for various skill levels. It insisted instead on one flat and high minimum rate for all molders, despite skill levels and jobs performed, even for a relatively unskilled worker tending the advanced molding machinery now rapidly appearing in the industry. A differential rate would have allowed manufacturers to amortize their investment in labor-saving machinery more quickly, which was necessary to take advantage of expanding markets with larger scale production under conditions of an enduring scarcity of skilled labor.[22]

The impatient union also pushed too fast for national uniformity across regions, while employers were still too divided on the matter. Even a geographically differentiated but centrally regulated structure could have helped employers stabilize competition over these expanding markets. A more patient union might actually have enjoyed a better fate had it bided its time and cultivated an alliance with employers in the organization who agreed about national uniformity. That there was such a faction is not in doubt. Even after the employers' association had given up on the IMU and abrogated its arbitration agreement in 1904, NFA President Isaac Frank continued to challenge the principle of regional differentiation of wages, saying that "this country is small enough that each founder producing a similar grade of work is a competitor, whether he be located in hamlet, town or city, and therefore in equity should pay the same rate in his class." Hinting that all was not forever lost for the idea of an alliance, Frank still favored establishing a common rate "either with or without the consent of the Iron Molders' Union."[23] That is to say, cartelism was his main goal, one way or another, be it unilateral or bilateral.

Local militancy and intransigence, which the national union leadership had been unable to control, on the minimum wage question, apprenticeship, work rules, machinery use, also contributed directly to failure. Local militants frequently resorted to wildcat strikes to enforce the closed shop and numerous encroachments on managerial autonomy, violating the spirit of the IMU leadership's promises of flexibility. When the radical element took over leadership of the IMU in 1903, most of the NFA leaders, unlike Isaac Frank, threw up their hands in disgust, giving up forever on making the union ever accept "equitable conditions" in the realm of managerial control.[24]

In machine making, as in the foundry sector of the engineering industry, the union leadership was also unable to control local militancy and designs on managerial control. Had it done so, it might have secured union recognition and centralized bargaining over wages and working hours in exchange for acceptance of managerial absolutism. In optimistic anticipation of such a deal, the NFA's Pfahler encouraged machine shops to organize on a national basis in 1899. In fact, all participants in the administrative council of the National Metal Trade Association (NMTA), formed that year, had NFA affiliations. Most of them, therefore, were likely to share its cartelist ambitions. Hence, the following year in New York City, the NMTA signed the so-called "Murray Hill" conciliation and working-hour agreement with the International Association of Machinists (IAM). NMTA leader H. F. Devens touted as one of its advantages "that a uniform standard has been adopted for all members of the Metal Trades Association."[25]

At Murray Hill, employers conceded a reduction of the normal working day from 10 to 9 hours for all machinists in NMTA shops. Unfortunately, complications arose from the union's inability to persuade all NMTA employers to grant a 12.5% across-the-board increase in wages to compensate for working time reduction (and therefore to maintain weekly earnings at earlier levels). The resulting nationwide strike backfired, bringing a quick and permanent end to centralization. The NMTA, the impatient union said, violated the centralizing spirit of Murray Hill by refusing to negotiate a uniform increase. The employers' association accused the union of violating, directly, the letter of the agreement by impatiently calling strikes instead of bringing demands for increases to central arbitration on a case-by-case basis.[26] In response to the strike wave, the employers abrogated the Murray Hill agreement and declared war on the union.[27]

In time, employers would probably have accepted uniformity, and many of them would have welcomed it. They slammed the door shut for all time, however, because union militants used the strikes to impose the closed shop (employment of union members only) and rules prohibiting men from operating more than one machine at a time, working for piece rates, and instructing unskilled workers.[28] The national IAM leadership did not officially sanction or even approve of these objectives. However, credible information available to

the outraged employers indicates that the union leadership studiously neglected to inform the rank-and-file of the commitments made at Murray Hill to
respect the open shop (no discrimination for or against union members) and
management's right to manage. The insecure leadership feared antagonizing
local militants and hoped to buy time for centralization by not intervening.[29]
On the occasions when IAM president James O'Connell would inform militants
that they should not put down their tools to challenge management rights, a
typical response was that of some steamship machinists who "simply laughed
at him" and advised him to "go to the dickens."[30] Not surprisingly, the combined effect of O'Connell's inaction and the rank-and-file challenges to management convinced the NMTA of unionism's unrepentant "treachery."

Thus in engineering, as in steel, centralized multi-employer bargaining failed
miserably because union militants would not be averted from their mission to
take control over crucial managerial matters, not because centralized bargaining chafed against the grain of dominant culture, ideology, law, or institutions.
The viability of joint cartelism in other sectors, discussed in chapter 7, indicates
as much. When it became clear that unions could not be tamed, employer associations like the NFA and NMTA turned quickly around and became the nation's most powerful and belligerent anti-union employers' associations. Violating their own nondiscriminatory open shop principles, these employers fired
and blacklisted unionists. Smaller belligerents often relied on their organizations to procure spies, guards, and strikebreakers to fight off unions and their
strikes. Large corporations often provided for themselves, sometimes creating
their own anti-union police forces and arsenals. They also enjoyed the decisive
ability to move production from units facing strikes to other sites, thereby suffo-
cating the revival of unionism at its isolated points of origin. Participants on
both sides in this depressing American story engaged in various deceitful, corrupt, illegal, racist, and violent acts. How employers and unions were deformed
in the bitter conflict has been told before and need not detain us here.[31]

The Rise of Segmentalism

There was also a kinder, gentler war against organized labor. Most historians
of early twentieth-century industrial relations in America argue that employers put great stock in "welfare capitalism," the provision of company-based
social benefits and services, to innoculate themselves from the disease of radical unionism. High wages also served the same purpose, often in combination
with benefits linked to employment. Smaller employers, especially in engineering where union re-entry was an ever-present threat, lacked the scale necessary to make the administrative costs of welfare work bearable. They were
therefore more or less limited to the high wage devices of segmentalism. By
improving morale, both strategies, employers concluded, served another purpose—to improve efficiency. Out of the ruins of cartelism, therefore, rose
American segmentalism.

Welfare Capitalism

In pursuit of their strategy to mollify workers and attach them physically and emotionally to their companies, many employers sought to elevate themselves above other firms in the labor market by providing paternalistic extras like housing, recreational, educational, and cultural services. In company towns, employers doubled as municipal governments providing necessary services. Less overbearingly paternalist were vacation time, profit sharing payments, and insurance benefits for retirement, illness, disability, and unemployment. "Welfare capitalists" often introduced more professional management practices to replace the mean and capricious authoritarianism of foremen. Often they endeavored to "regularize" employment. Things like careful production and inventory planning to cope with seasonal and cyclical variations in demand increased workers' annual earnings beyond prevailing standards. In all probability, these practices generated some good will and weakened the union impulse. Of course the company's ability to withdraw benefits could be powerful a sanction against inveterate malcontents still tempted by unionism.[32]

According to Jacoby, benefit programs covered "no more than" 14 percent of American industrial workers in 1929. But this was still a sizeable and in many ways the most important piece of America's vast labor market.[33] Huge companies like Armour, AT&T (and its subsidiary Westinghouse), Bethlehem Steel, Du Pont, Filene's, General Electric, Goodyear, IBM, Leeds and Northrup, National Cash Register, Otis Elevator, Packard, Sears Roebuck, Studebaker, and U.S. Rubber—like many others—began offering at various times, starting in the late nineteenth century, some mix of welfare benefits. The practices were also quite stable. While Jacoby offers convincing evidence that progressive managerial practices suffered considerably during the 1920s, there is little reason to think that welfare capitalism declined along with it.[34] Tight labor markets and high turnover associated with the war years, combined with government pressure, had given professional personnel management a boost. Unemployment, deflation, and the pressure to drive forth greater productivity after the war knocked them back a few notches at many places, though not all. However, for welfare capitalism the period was one of continued growth, according to Sumner Slichter, one of the period's most eminent labor economists, not retrogression. A big move came for example in 1928, when General Motors signed a contract with Metropolitan to cover 180,000 workers in a group disability insurance plan.[35] A 1932 study of industrial pensions showed that at least 131 new plans were established between 1921 and 1929, and only a handful of those folded before 1929. Those remaining represented 32 percent of the 397 in operation in 1929. By 1932, "relatively few of the largest companies [were] without pension plans." At worst, the trend was stagnant, as Jacoby concludes on the basis of welfare spending's share of total payroll costs.[36]

Whatever role the fight against the labor movement played in its development and stability, other motivations for welfare work also mattered. According to a GE manager in 1904, welfare work "is a cold business proposition." At National Cash Register (NCR) the same year, labor costs had been reduced between 23 and 49 percent by welfare measures, at least according to the man responsible for setting them up. Altruism, sympathy, and union fighting were not the main point. "It pays," said NCR President John Patterson. Jacoby concludes that Eastman Kodak pursued welfare capitalism not simply because of, and even quite independently of, a labor threat, though probably much of the time the two were practically indistinct as motives. In 1929 economist Sumner Slichter saw employers using welfare benefits as a way to avoid labor trouble but also because of their perceptions about "the relation between morale and efficiency of labor."[37] In short, fear of unions and labor unrest, and the desire for greater efficiencies in the use of labor, worked hand-in-hand to promote and sustain welfare capitalism, a main pillar of segmentalism.

Every major national employer organization promoted these policies from the turn of the century onward. The National Civic Federation (NCF) advocated welfare work even as it promoted joint cartelism and continued to do so after that mission failed. The fact that top officials of the American labor movement cooperated with the NCR's activities in this area adds evidence that company welfare measures were not exclusively introduced as weapons against organized labor.[38] Open-shop bastions like the NMTA and the NFA, rising to overshadow the NCF, also promoted welfare work and progressive management practices. So did the National Association of Manufacturers (NAM), which engineering employers dominated.[39] In the 1920s and 1930s, the NAM promoted things like company housing, which, by "reducing turnover and providing loyal and understanding workers, make greatly for increased and cheaper production." The NAM also encouraged production planning for "employment stabilization" and provided a forum for promoting company pensions. In the case of elderly workers, whom employers hesitated to fire for morale and public opinion considerations, an influential speaker invited by NAM declared that "as human machinery they have depreciated to a point where their continued employment is unprofitable if not actually hazardous." Therefore, company pension plans "if wisely drawn up and prudently administered, may be an actual economy rather than an expense."[40]

Of great importance in organized advocacy of welfare capitalist strategies, especially in the 1920s, was a network of groups, associations, and consulting outfits, starting with the National Industrial Conference Board (NICB). The NICB was created in 1916 for research and dissemination of information about best management practices by a number of trade and employer associations (including the NAM). In 1925, for example, the NICB published a favorable evaluation of company pensions. Its president in the 1920s, Magnus Alexander, was an executive at GE. His company was also a member of a "Special Conference Committee" (SCC) of big employers formed in 1919 to work out and coordinate their labor policies, including wage setting.[41] With the Rockefeller industrial interests at its center, the secretive SCC also included Standard Oil of New Jersey, Bethlehem Steel, Du Pont, General Motors, Goodyear, International Harvester, Irving National Bank, U.S. Rubber, and Westinghouse

(AT&T and U.S. Steel joined in 1925 and 1934). Promoting "employee representation" or pliant company unions to stave off the militant labor movement and realize a hypothesized fundamental harmony between capital and labor was apparently its main purpose. But the group also discussed their welfare measures, especially the more modern, less paternalistic variety like pensions, paid vacations, and group insurance.[42]

The American Management Association (AMA), started in 1923, became the leading exponent of the SCC's views about personnel management. Also of considerable importance was the consulting and research outfit called Industrial Relations Counselors (IRC), established in 1926. Because of its funding and personnel, it was, like the SCC, part of what G. William Domhoff calls the "Rockefeller network." Its board of directors included the chairmen of SCC members U.S. Steel and Jersey Standard. The IRC, which conducted an exhaustive study of industrial pensions, concluded in 1932 that there was a clear advantage in the form of worker morale and "payroll relief."[43] The author of the study, Murray Latimer, was later recruited by the presidential administration of Franklin Roosevelt to help craft Social Security legislation that would harmonize with, not supplant, welfare capitalism.

Efficiency Wages

Welfare benefits were, of course, a form of wage payment. Because welfare capitalists also tended to pay high money wages, their benefits clearly served the efficiency and profitability purposes of what labor economists call efficiency wages—remuneration exceeding what is necessary to supply a firm with a sufficient number of workers.[44] Employers enjoying some sort of monopoly in technology, product patents, customer loyalty, or other sources of economic rent, were those most likely to be able to afford high money wages as well as benefits. Efficiency wages were probably also well-advised to protect high returns on their expensive investments in advanced machinery from the inexperience, indifference, indiscipline, and ill-will of footloose and disloyal workers. Finally, as the president of the American Management Association noted in 1935, a 15 percent wage differential could yield a gain of 25 percent or more in productivity. It may, he thought, also serve as part of the big corporation's immune system against outside unionism. Company unions or works councils would only work, he argued, "where the employer has adopted the fixed policy of maintaining his wage levels on a plane distinctly above the current market wages for the locality in which he operates."[45]

The Ford strategy of doubling wages in the winter of 1913 and 1914, according to varying accounts, was based on a mix of such motives. As Henry Ford famously summed it up, his extraordinary five-dollar day "was one of the finest cost cutting moves we ever made." The six-dollar day, introduced later, was "cheaper than the five." In Ford's own words, high wages were for "efficiency engineering," bringing greater productivity, peace, and lower turnover and absenteeism. More prosaically, he said, "When you pay men well, you can talk to them"—where talking probably meant telling them what needs to be done without shouting any more than was necessary to be heard over the noise of machinery. As Ford manager John R. Lee put it, foremen once learned to say "hurry up" in forty or fifty languages and dialects. After the five-dollar day, he said (still stretching the truth, for sure), it was "rarely, if ever, heard."[46]

Evidence supports the efficiency wage motive for Ford's dramatic increase in wages, as opposed to more conventional labor market theory, which would expect them to have fallen in response to the workings of supply and demand in the labor market. It took place, after all, during a deep recession. All its effects, including a huge influx of labor to Detroit (an immense "queue"—or better, throng—of workers camped outside the River Rouge plant), are entirely consistent with efficiency wage theory. Even other Detroit employers seemed to benefit from the flood of labor into the city that Ford's new policy attracted, counteracting any upward wage pressure that his high wages might have caused them had the city's supply of labor been inelastic in response to Ford's move.[47]

Other big, technologically advanced, mass production companies did not seek such drastic differentiation with the rest of the labor market, but nevertheless sought to keep wages consistently and noticeably above standards. U.S. Steel was somewhat of a vanguard in its wage levels and welfare work since its early union-busting days, backing its anti-unionism with "good, liberal wages" relative to the rest of steel and therefore well above the average for the industrial labor market.[48] At International Harvester, directives coming down from top management called for wage increases to maintain differentials, closely following U.S. Steel's wages. Executives wanted to prove to workers that their wages were about the most favorable in the country (and four times better than what their German counterparts got). In the 1920s, the company's industrial relations department kept close tabs on wages paid in neighboring plants and on union rates. Not surprisingly, Harvester wages always stayed ahead of the rest of manufacturing. In the first years of the Great Depression, between 1929 and 1933, their advantage increased between 1929 and 1933, and because of deflation, their real hourly earnings actually rose by almost 6 percent.[49]

The same strategy was followed in far-flung reaches of manufacturing, and probably in every branch from oil refining and electrical engineering to shoe manufacturing and plumbing fixtures. At Standard Oil of New Jersey, Clarence Hicks (who had apprenticed in his industrial relations career at International Harvester) introduced industrial relations policies he helped develop first for John D. Rockefeller, Sr., after Rockefeller's shocked reaction to his Colorado Fuel and Iron Company's murderous response to the 1913–1914 miners' strike. At Jersey Standard, an official policy statement printed and distributed to all employees promised "at least the prevailing scale of wages for similar work in the community"; in practice, the company boasted later that its wages had been "the highest in the industry."[50] In the 1920s, the policies of Gerard Swope and Owen Young at General Electric were the same: to pay well above community standards to get lower costs of production. By 1935, after a period of cutbacks, GE 's wages were raised to 5 percent above their 1929 levels; by 1937, they were higher than ever.[51]

Mass producing employers in consumer goods industries behaved similarly. At Procter and Gamble in the 1920s, base wages were kept fairly close to the standard, but "profit sharing" dividends, received by the three-quarters of the workforce with enough seniority to qualify, added ten to twenty percent.[52] A central component ("efficiency expense") of major shoe manufacturer Endicott Johnson's paternalistic "Square Deal" policy was payment of wages that were high in comparison with other shoe firms. This policy originated in response to tight labor market and union militancy conditions of World War I, but was maintained into the era of slack labor markets and weak unionism. Even a union critic of the company had to concede that the nonunion firm "for many years . . . continued to maintain an hours-and-wages schedule which compared very favorably with those in the more-or-less unionized centers of Rochester . . . and New York City."[53]

Rochester's Eastman Kodak also pursued supracompetitive wage policies. Kodak's wages, in the 1920s for example, were, according to Jacoby, "above average for similar work in Rochester, in keeping with the firm's obvious ability to pay." It even set up its own building division, which "matched or exceeded union wages and working conditions."[54] At Kohler, a major nonunion manufacturer of plumbing fixtures in Wisconsin, wages were fixed at the levels of major unionized competitors paying higher wages due to skill-based craft production, despite Kohler's location in a small town where going wages were lower. Many competitors paid half as much, and during the Depression some paid only a third. As at Ford, the high wages for semi-skilled operatives had helped Kohler to demand a grueling work tempo from the many recent immigrants who formed the core of its unskilled work force. Mass production and high demand from the residential building sector between 1922 and 1928 enabled Kohler to afford its high wages. They also enabled it to afford some additional but limited paternalistic benefits like home finance, a group life insurance program, and a "Kohler Benefit Association."[55] The presence of these extra company benefits at Kohler, just as at many others, alongside high wages indicates, clearly, the close relationship between welfare capitalism and efficiency wages as common features of segmentalism.

Many employers who stood outside the welfare capitalist camp probably also paid their workers supracompetitive wages alone, without welfare benefits and progressive personnel practices. Unfortunately, evidence for this conjecture is not readily available. That many smaller employers, who have not received the same attention from historians as the larger ones, would have done so is all the more probable considering that the per capita overhead and administrative costs of nonwage benefits provided by the bigger welfare capitalists were prohibitive.[56] Also, in providing insurance benefits, the bigger employers' benefitted from a much larger "risk pool" of beneficiaries. Thus, their risks of costly default on their moral commitments were much lower than for smaller employers. If only another 10 percent or so also received efficiency wages exclusively in the form of cash benefits on top of Jacoby's figure of 14 percent of workers enjoying some form of welfare benefit, the number of workers directly affected by segmentalism was large indeed.

The Unintended Consequences of Segmentalism

For all its virtues, segmentalism was not without disadvantages. Two unintended consequences were deeply disturbing for its practitioners. One was in the realm of labor relations, the other in product market competition. These unintended consequences gave rise to a response that at first glance seems contradictory with segmentalism: segmentalists often leveled harsh criticism at low-standard employers and exhorted the larger employer community to resist opportunistic lowering of standards. In short, segmentalists benefitted from carefully measured efforts to rise above the crowd. But they also suffered when the crowd lowered itself in complete disregard for segmentalists' interests. Ironically, by sharing some responsibility for creating unemployment—if efficiency wage theory is correct—and for weakening unionism, segmentalists paved the low road that other employers traveled.

Concern about low-life employers was strong in the belligerent associations like the NFA, NMTA, and NAM. These anti-union organizations were probably dominated by high standard employers in the engineering trades, which their promotion of welfare work indicates. Unfortunately, historical data are not readily available to establish this fact with full certainty. To the extent that they followed the most rudimentary pay principles of Frederick Winslow Taylor's "scientific management," written with the engineering industry very much in mind, they paid efficiency wages. Taylor did not have a system for driving more work out for low or even standard wages. Instead, he advocated "coupling high wages with low labor costs." His system was supposed to get workers up to maximum speed "providing they are paid from 30 to 100 per cent more than the average of their trade." Management, he testified before Congress, should "deliberately treat their employees far better than the employees of their competitors are treated." If they persist long enough in this, "invariably the workmen respond by giving them their real initiative, by working hard and faithfully, [and] by using their ingenuity to see how they can turn out as much work as possible."[57]

Over time, as research by Howell Harris shows, the NMTA came to be increasingly dominated by very large employers, who tended, it seems, to pay the best wages. The usual picture of it as dominated by "little businessmen" is simply wrong. By the 1920s, and 1930s, in fact, "its agenda was set, and the bulk of its resources provided, by companies which were large by any criterion." Its Philadelphia affiliate, the Metal Manufacturers' Association, was dominated by what he calls "progressives"—larger firms "creating their own internal labour markets, which involved paying the best rates in the Philadelphia area . . . in order to give themselves the pick of the bunch." Finding out what it took to pay the best rates was serious business. The NMTA's municipal branches began conducting systematic surveys of area wages as early as 1914.[58]

One problem for the progressives was the flame of labor militancy kept burning by skinflint employers who opened themselves to successful union attack. Being successful, this brush fire militancy could spread, especially if fanned by negative public sentiment projected indiscriminately onto all employers, not just the bad ones. In an address before the Iowa State Manufacturers' Association in June 1907, NAM President James W. Van Cleave declared it a mistake to think "that the blame for labor disturbances is always on one side." Often the problem was "dishonest and oppressive employers." Fighting labor meant "fighting these employers by all the legitimate weapons on which we can lay our hands. And, with these weapons, we will continue the fight while any of these offenders remain."[59] In *American Industries*, a NAM journal, Van Cleave on at least two occasions around that time wrote of the "oppressive," "greedy and tyrannical," and "recreant" employers whose "pernicious activity" had inflicted "damage to the rest of the members of his calling and also done more damage to the country than we are apt to realize." "We are just as much opposed to such men as any labor unionists can possibly be," Van Cleave said [60]

Similar sentiments were expressed repeatedly to audiences made up exclusively of employers throughout the anti-union employers' movement. Walter Drew of the ferocious National Erectors' Association (NEA) expressed the same view in private letters to individual employers. Heading U.S. Steel's main weapon against sallies into the steel industry from unionism's bridgehead in construction, he repeatedly warned that when wages and other working conditions are left entirely up to individual employers' discretion, some take advantage of unemployment and union weakness "to drive a better bargain with their men" than their competitors could. Drew therefore endeavored to bring up wage standards in the industry, for among other things, substandard wages would bring the open shop into disrepute and stimulate union organization. Drew identified "the mean and unprincipled employer" as one of the chief causes of industrial conflict. According to historian Sidney Fine, Drew believed "if employers took advantage of the open shop to pay their structural iron workers less than mechanics received in comparable jobs in other building trades, this would increase support for the ironworkers among the other building trades."[61] The NEA, in line with its policy of recommending wage increases "and so remove conditions that would in part justify union agitation," even claimed in 1912 "not to have reduced wages, but to have increased them for individuals with superior merit or skill," and "that in some localities it ha[d] advanced wages because they were below those paid elsewhere."[62]

The NEA's views were shared by the two leading open-shop associations in engineering, the NMTA and the NFA. As the NMTA's Declaration of Principles put it, "In the conduct of our business and in the payment of wages, by whatever system, this Association will not countenance any condition or any rates of compensation which are not reasonable and just or which will not allow a workman a proper wage in proportion to his efficiency and productiveness." In general, the NMTA "always urged its members to pay the *highest* prevailing wages commensurate with skill and productivity" (my italics). Members of its affiliate in Detroit felt pressure from above to fight only the closed shop and so apparently "could concede almost anything in the way of hours and wages," according to a contemporary observer. The NFA used the same "will not countenance" language regarding low wages. In 1905, retiring NFA president Antonio Pessano, in parting words to the association's members, admonished them to "pay your skilled men all you can possibly afford to pay them."[63]

During the 1920s, the line stayed the same. Sometime in the early 1920s, probably 1921, NAM leader Noel Sargent cautioned employers against reducing wages to take advantage of unemployment, saying they

> now have it in their power in many cases to squeeze the very life blood from the workers. In short, they have the same opportunity to abuse power which the unions possessed but a short time ago. The consequences of abuse would be as harmful to the employers as . . . the uneconomic practices of the closed shop unions. It is the duty of all industrial organizations to most seriously caution their members against the abuse or even the seeming abuse of the power now possessed.[64]

Local open-shop associations echoed the argument. The Merchants and Manufacturers' Association of Los Angeles, "a strong open shop community," wrote members in 1921 urging that

> no wage reduction should be made without due consideration of living conditions. . . . By taking an undue advantage of a surplus of labor you lower American shop standards. Such action is a boomerang—part of a vicious cycle—that keeps boiling the pot of unrest and antagonism. It is the cause of many costly industrial evils. As a well informed employer you cannot afford to be a party to it.[65]

At the local level, as in major cities like Indianapolis and Cleveland, powerful open-shop associations borrowed language verbatim from the NMTA and NFA. The Declaration of Principles, for example, of the highly belligerent Associated Employers of Indianapolis declared that "We shall not countenance any employer who does not pay a fair day's wage for a fair day's work."[66]

Identical sentiment prevailed during the Depression, now with special urgency. In 1935, American manufacturers assembled at the annual meeting of the NAM to discuss strategy for dealing with the new pro-union labor law. A panel consisting of three of the country's top employer officials—Homer D. Sayre (chief executive of the NMTA), John C. Gall (NAM Counsel), and John L. Lovett (General Manager of the Michigan Manufacturers' Association)—discussed ways for manufacturers to arrest unionization without running afoul of the new law. Unions and elected politicians were by no means the only villains, according to their "Wagner Bill Clinic."[67] A good part of their discussion pilloried fellow employers. Action against the most cutthroat and miserly of them was as much a "community responsibility" as collective defense against unions. Solidarity against labor was violated most by the ever-present employers "who operated on low standards," according to Lovett, not the high standard employers like much of the NAM membership. The duty of "decent employers" in a community was to "talk 'turkey' to Poorpay, Shiftless and Chisel," those substandard employers whose low pay not only allowed them to undercut their competitors with lower prices but who stoked the fires of unionism with their miserly and badly administered wages and working conditions. The objective of the organized community of employers with respect to the wage cutters was therefore to "emphasize that they are going to be quite unpopular in this town if they don't get in line both as to wages and working conditions." NMTA Commissioner Sayre added, "Of course, it's not going to be pleasant to tell that fellow, Chisel, that he's got to clean up."[68]

With their reference to "chiselers," the NAM leaders flagged a closely related problem experienced by high standard employers. Chiseling was their favorite name for low-price competition made possible by imprudent and shabby practices, one of them being squeezing labor too hard. The problem was severe for some segmentalists. Because of it, in 1926, GE's Gerard Swope, probably together with fellow executive Owen Young, was even able to imagine something still quite repugnant to most other segmentalists: bringing unionism into a hybrid mix of joint cartelism and segmentalism. An industry-wide union could jointly negotiate segmentalist wages and benefits benefitting big firms like GE and Westinghouse in their local labor markets. Meanwhile they could enforce similar conditions on chiselers who took advantage of lower wages and benefits in their local labor markets, possibly in combination with drive methods and less advanced technology. Swope therefore invited the American Federation of Labor's William Green to organize a new industrial, not craft, union, one without ambitions to control management, that the company could work with. Green could not oblige him.[69]

During the year preceding the Wagner Clinic, in fact, a controlling element of the NAM actually favored government intervention for stabilization of competition in the form of the National Industrial Recovery Act. What they liked most was the aim of setting minimum wage and hour standards by government agencies they could exercise some direct control over.[70] That such a view prevailed would have been no surprise to someone like the NEA's Walter Drew, who explicitly decried substandard wages as a source of unfair competition, not just an incitement to the dreaded unionism.[71] The NFA, the NEA's comrade in arms against unions, actually made its official vow of intolerance toward substandard wages, logically enough, while it was still trying to establish union-friendly joint cartelism. The vow of intolerance remained in force even after the organization turned belligerent.

The question remains whether organized employers' desire for better general standards was all talk and no action. All the NAM's Van Cleave could come up with in 1907 was to fight mean and unprincipled employers "by education, by precept, and by example."[72] The report of the Senate committee investigating employers' organized violations of workers' rights to speak, assemble, and organize freely in the first years after passage of the Wagner Act concluded that the NMTA had no power to correct any deviations from acceptable standards of wages, pursuant to the "will not countenance" language in its Declaration of Principles. The most the organization ever did, according to the LaFollette committee's report, was to "bring the matter to the attention of the member" if he deviated. Likewise, the report concluded that the paragraph of the NMTA constitution about securing and preserving "equitable conditions in the work shops of members for the protection of both employer and employee" was in practice no more than a commitment to "uniform conditions, particularly in the maintenance of the open shop."[73]

But belligerent employers' associations may not have been entirely hypocritical or toothless in these endeavors. NMTA Commissioner Sayre testified that when an employer applied for membership, the NMTA would "make an investigation of his financial condition, labor condition, what his policy is toward employees," sometimes even sending association spies ("undercover men" or "special operatives") to get the real story before granting admission.[74] Thus, "fair" wages may have been included along with membership dues in the price of admission. Other actions were taken, at least on an irregular basis. NMTA Commissioner (chief executive) E. F. Du Brul reported in 1904 that he had resorted to "much vigorous language, some of which was unfit for publication" in an attempt to persuade a plant superintendent in Cincinnati, where his own company was located, to rescind an injudicious piece-rate cut. "His cut of a time limit was in violation of the guarantee that had been made to all the machinists of Cincinnati by the associated manufacturers, and his cut would have wrecked the system, not only in his own shop, but in all the others. If his ideas had been carried out the result would have been a rejuvenation of the walking delegate [the despised union agent], with whom we have not been bothered for some years."[75]

In recommendations to member firms, the NMTA called for "constant and continuing attention" so as to "prevent the unfortunate situation arising of the unions making demands for increases which are justified, and which, under these conditions, can only be granted with an increased prestige for the union." Although the recommendations explicitly recognized "the impossibility of naming rates of wages which shall be fair and equitable for different classes of work and for different localities," the NMTA did prepare statistical tables of wages for its own use and for members, and according to Bonnett, in 1922, refused to "combat a strike where the demand is purely for wages which are not considered excessive." Members were to "avoid the embarrassing situation of finding that increases should be made" and being denied assistance.[76]

As a condition for assisting against a strike, once under way, the NFA and the NMTA could require members to place the matter in the charge of the association and bind themselves "to carry out any decision made by the Administrative Council or those acting under its authority." Failure to comply could bring expulsion, according to the NFA constitution.[77] The NMTA required its members to notify the association about potential or ongoing strikes, and the local branch secretary or national commissioner then advised the member what steps to take. Constitutionally, the NMTA "reserved the right to settle all strikes in the plant of a member" if it provided any assistance; in practice, however, the association sent officials "in an advisory capacity rather than in a capacity of dictating the policy."[78]

Similarly, the leadership of the Associated Industries of Cleveland, whose members and leaders overlapped with the Cleveland branch of the NMTA, actively undertook to remove grievances in member plants that might lead to strikes or union organization. William Frew Long of the Cleveland organization, who kept in close touch with the NMTA and the NFA, warned employers not to give union organizers a "wage incentive." Wages that were way out of line were inviting trouble, he would tell them. It was also his "invariable procedure to examine conditions of employment including wage rates, in the plants of members who anticipated strikes." Then the association would advise the employer to make the necessary adjustments in his wages or the management of his plant. Because it also exercised the discretionary authority to offer or refuse the expensive "strike services" of scabs and guards, it was also in position at the time of strikes to influence wages in an upward direction.[79] The Associated Employers of Indianapolis likewise regularly provided strikebreaking services, but mostly against the closed shop and other encroachments on management, not primarily against wage increases. It claimed "no sympathy whatever with unwise employers who . . . force wages down below a consistent average level."[80] In short, these organizations had the authority and resources to influence members' wages in the direction their policies dictated.

In all probability, however, the direct effect was limited, in part because membership levels, especially in the national organizations, were very uneven and low. The NMTA only had 952 manufacturing plants as members by 1937, for example, and these were mainly located east of the Mississippi River and north of the Mason-Dixon line.[81] Of course, much anti-union activity was organized at the municipal level, about which little is really known. At most, active intervention in members' wage policies was limited and unsystematic. There was one exception at least: the "most class conscious and belligerent" NEA. This association actually unilaterally imposed minimum wages on its members.[82]

Wages and the Depression

When President Herbert Hoover entreated a conference of leading American businessmen not to cut wages after the stock market crash of 1929, his plea fell on sympathetic ears. The fact that newsreel cameras were present probably helped hold them to their promise to maintain wage rates. Some interpretations of their remarkably restrained behavior in the first two years of the depression, consistent with Hoover's plea, attribute it to business understanding of the macro-logic of maintaining workers' "buying power" by holding up wages. Henry Ford, maintaining his position, as *Time* put it, "as Most Original U.S. businessman," dramatically announced an increase, to a seven-dollar day. He wanted to start "a movement to increase the general wage level." In 1926, he had espoused what historian Irving Bernstein calls "the Doctrine of High Wages," one of whose tenets was the purchasing power argument.[83]

Other major companies were not so bold, but they did wait a surprisingly long time in the face of declining demand, prices, and profits, to lower wages. For example, U.S. Steel maintained its rates for common labor until October 1931. Firms like International Harvester, which patterned its wages on U.S. Steel's, acted during the economic collapse after 1929 "as if they were carrying the economic system on their shoulders," according to Harvester's historian Robert Ozanne. Not surprisingly considering the main market for its products, Harvester's President Alexander Legge served as chairman of President Hoover's Federal Farm Board, energetically joining government efforts against the devastating effects of sinking purchasing power and deflation on the rural economy.[84] Myron Taylor of U.S. Steel, Owen Young of GE, Walter Teagle of Standard Oil of New Jersey, Alfred Sloan of GM, and Pierre du Pont apparently needed no White House prodding; in fact, according to Brody, "Wage maintenance had become part of the doctrine of 'stability' that governed the oligopolistic industries." Meetings of the secret Special Conference Committee (SCC) provided a forum for mutual exhortation not to cut wages. General Motors reported in 1931 to a meeting of the SCC that it was still opposed to any downward adjustment in wages. Hence, NICB data indicate that, overall, manufacturing wages had declined by only about 2 percent by January 1931, 17 months into the depression.[85]

Explaining Wage Rigidity

The purchasing power argument for wage maintenance appears as early as an article in 1897 in *The Engineering Magazine*, according to which "statistics prove that a reduction in wages is always followed by an immediate reduction in consumption" and that "increases of wages and increase of consumption go hand-in-hand, and a period of high wages is synonymous with a period of great prosperity." Supposedly, "enlightened manufacturers" were already beginning to take a broader view of the subject at the time, rejecting the "fallacious argument . . . advanced to show that high wages are the effect, and not in any respect the cause, of prosperity."[86] The same views reappear with increasing regularity in the 1920s. According to a 1928 article in *Factory and Industrial Management*, "managements urge[d] their fellow employers to maintain high wage rates." In 1931, *Iron Age* reported the existence of a widespread school of thought among manufacturers that it was best to keep wages high to maintain purchasing power rather than, as before, to immediately cut them in periods of depression.[87]

Knowledgeable people saw a dramatic change in employer behavior in the course of the 1920s. In a 1926 address, Herbert Hoover noted it was "not so many years ago that the employer considered it was in his interest to use the opportunities of unemployment and immigration to lower wages irrespective of other considerations." The following year the NICB reported that, whereas employers now cut wages only as a last resort, they once used wages as "the first point of attack upon high costs"—as in the depression of 1920–1921 when the generalized wage deflation "paralyzed the domestic market." Statistical evidence seems to confirm the change in behavior: unusual wage rigidity at the beginning of the Depression contrasts distinctly with greater downward flexibility in previous contractions from 1890 to 1924.[88]

It is not clear, however, that employers' unusual behavior can be fully explained by a growing consensus about purchasing power, bolstered by earlier experience, and backed by mutual exhortation and political pressure to act upon it. For one thing, one employer, no matter how large, could have had very little effect on aggregate demand, and even all the SCC firms combined was not enough. Therefore, part of the logic for increasing employer restraint may well have to be segmentalist. Segmentalism may even have helped sensitize employers to purchasing power arguments, for slumps in demand set in motion the employer practices that segmentalists found so repugnant. Thus, in 1929, economist Slichter saw a "growing realization by managers of the close relationship between industrial morale and efficiency," and therefore nervousness about the effects of reducing wages. In fact, instead of cutting wages to meet price reductions, they wanted to reduce unit labor costs by making workers more efficient. Reluctance to resort to excessive "driving," or authoritarian and punitive methods, left only one option, which was widely adopted, "to increase efficiency by developing a stable force and by winning the good will and cooperation of the men." Thus, on the eve of the Depression, Slichter attributed the increasing reluctance he saw between 1923 and 1927 to make wages follow prices downward "to the fear that wage cuts would destroy the good will which has been built up at considerable trouble and expense." In short, "when a fall in prices reduces the marginal worth of labor, it is not necessarily advantageous to reduce money wages—to do so might still further diminish the worth of labor by provoking a withholding of efficiency."[89]

Ozanne's penetrating historical research on International Harvester supports Slichter's conjecture. Harvester, according to Ozanne, abstained from wage cuts in the two years of high unemployment after October 1929 "from the standpoint of employee morale rather than short-run profits."[90] Thus, Slichter's argument about the growing significance of segmentalism over time probably helps explain the puzzling finding that wage rigidity from 1929 to 1931 was far greater than during earlier slumps. In all probability, both forces were at work: segmentalism as an increasingly important micro-rational motive, and purchasing power maintenance, backed by coordination and political pressure to enforce collective rationality.[91]

The Exaggerated Death
of Welfare Capitalism

In late 1931, however, the plug had to be pulled on wages. Even Ford joined in wage cutting, abandoning the seven-dollar day a few weeks after U.S. Steel and International Harvester cut their wages. He eventually brought the minimum down to four dollars by November 1932, following another U.S. Steel cut earlier in the spring of that year. As Bethlehem Steel executive Charles Schwab put it, try as we might, "None of us can escape the inexorable law of the balance sheet." America's managerial elite took no pleasure in the reductions. In 1935 M. C. Rorty, president of the American Management Association, bemoaned "the evils of excessive wage reductions" in the preceding years.[92]

But wages were not the only thing cut. Welfare capitalism came under stress, too. According to Stuart Brandes, "welfare companies drew their belts ever tighter and reduced or eliminated expenditures on a variety of welfare activities," and thus "the growth of welfare capitalism was . . . arrested for all practical purposes." Brandes, without much evidence, even concludes that "the Great Depression terminated the movement as it had existed," in part because of the Wagner Act and collective bargaining, which "spelled the end of employee representation and, indirectly, of the whole array of welfare practices." Welfare capitalism, Brody agrees, collapsed in the face of depression and the rise of organized labor and the welfare state. This is a view that continues to be shared by some historians.[93]

The truth of the matter, contra Brody and Brandes, is that welfare capitalism probably did not collapse as much as sag somewhat, in some places, and probably not even as much as wages did. Employers were simply too reluctant to cut benefits. Frank Dobbin's careful research based on NICB data overwhelms the sparse evidence cited by Brody and Brandes, showing net growth not declining in company pensions and health insurance between 1928 and 1935. Only 7 percent of all pension and health insurance existing at the onset of the Depression, he shows, was canceled by 1935. These findings are consistent with Murray Latimer's IRC report published in 1933 that "the period from mid-1929 to the spring of 1932 witnessed an almost unprecedented activity in the establishment of industrial pension systems." "In sum," Dobbin concludes, "Depression-era industrial conditions do not seem to have put an end to welfare work or retarded the growth of employment-related insurance."[94]

The fact that the Depression did not strike all companies evenly accounts for some of the stability of welfare capitalism, despite the stresses it experienced. Jacoby finds that it was often the "vanguard" companies with the best wages and benefits, such as AT&T, Du Pont, IBM, Procter and Gamble, that escaped the full fury of the Depression and therefore did not respond to the same pressures to cut wages and benefits, much less jump at the golden opportunity. For example, because of Eastman Kodak's domination of an expanding market for photographic goods, Depression conditions did not make themselves felt on its workers' remuneration until 1933. Only then did Kodak finally reduce its "wage dividend," a substantial profit-sharing bonus that most employees benefitted from and which added to the earnings differential with the rest of the labor market. Likewise, Latimer noted that a substantial number of the new pension plans established between 1929 and 1932 were in industries "relatively little affected by the [D]epression." Companies like these, especially the vanguards who had a tradition of the most generous benefits, Jacoby persuades us, were also much more successful in standing up to the onslaught of unionism in the 1930s and later, preserving a form of nonunionized or unilateral segmentalism.[95]

Dobbin's aggregate figures no doubt obscure the signs of stress at places like Goodyear, which according to Jacoby, in vain "tried to preserve jobs and welfare benefits," despite its severe slump in sales after 1929. Its valiant efforts, and good previous record, paid off in the form of "a huge reservoir of goodwill to draw upon" and a large number of "company loyalists" among workers who kept the rubber workers' union hold on the company weak well into the 1940s. Likewise, at Endicott Johnson, wages reluctantly cut by 20 percent in 1920 and other cuts in the 1930s to cope with price and demand reductions met with strains but not rebellion—as it did at its competitor, Amoskeag in Manchester, New Hampshire. At Endicott, the "paternalistic balance" had not been upset—perhaps because it had so successfully established itself "as the most generous employer in the region."[96] By contrast, hit hard by the Depression's decline in new construction, Kohler, another welfare capitalist, was forced to make big cuts in hours, wages, benefits, and employment, which plunged it into the thirty years of bitter labor conflict that followed.[97]

Jacoby probably sums up the complex situation well when he concludes that it was mostly the "laggard companies" in industries like autos, rubber, and steel that got themselves in most trouble. These were companies that, because of their unstable markets in the 1920s, had introduced only relatively meager and inconsistent welfare benefits alongside rather too extravagant claims about the security and benevolence being provided. When the Depression forced drastic cuts in wages, employment, and benefits, it was often in these companies that "workers turned to unions in the 1930s not to reinstate moral capitalism but to transform employers' overblown rhetoric into reality." In other words, "workers did turn to national unions when their employers failed to keep promises—but not all employers reneged, and among those who did, half-hearted promises angered workers more than sincere but failed attempts."[98] Having pursued a segmentalist strategy of high wages and at least the promise, if not reality, of secure welfare benefits, some endeavored strenuously and sincerely, though not always successfully, to honor the deal they had with their workers.

Conclusion: Toward a New Deal

Before the Depression, large numbers of important manufacturers experienced disturbing but unintended effects of their anti-union segmentalism. By weakening unions, and by helping generate unemployment (as efficiency wage theory suggests), segmentalists made it possible for other employers to engage in shabby and reckless labor practices. These "mean and unprincipled" employers kept the torch of unionism alive, a flame that might spread at any moment back into the segmentalist's workplace. They aroused anti-employer public opinion, bringing costly political consequences. The effects of segmentalists' practices also allowed "chiselers" to undercut them, especially during hard economic times, by charging lower prices based on lower wages. Out of fear of damaging worker morale and aggregate purchasing power, better employers did not quickly and gladly join competitors down that low road.

Attempts to maintain wages in the face of the Depression, and preserve and even expand welfare commitments, show how deeply rooted segmentalism had become in important parts of the American labor market. The winds of Depression-era competition pulled at segmentalist employers as they dug in and clutched the soil the best they could. Then politicians stepped in with the New Deal. The evidence, examined in a later chapter, indicates that the reformers did not mean to dig up the roots of segmentalism and plant another system for stabilizing an American economy and society in turmoil, as the arguments of Brody and Brandes suggest. Their aim was to still the winds pulling at those roots. The final postwar result, a system of negotiated segmentalism not unlike what GE's Gerard Swope envisaged, and a limited welfare state that complemented it, conformed with this aim.

4

EMPLOYERS UNITE

Swedish Solidarism in the Making

By the 1930s, a consensus among most large employers in America had formed around a segmentalist system of decentralized wage setting. Promoting efficiency and combatting unionism, they chose to provide above-standard wages and a widening variety of social benefits. The Great Depression's sagging prices and wages disturbed the stability of their system, and big employers tried to coordinate efforts to hold wages up. In Sweden, meanwhile, things could hardly have been more different. There, leading employers had long since chosen a centralized system of wage setting in which labor unions exercised valued influence. Nonnegotiated company benefits were common, as in America. But employers collectively sought to eliminate them. And during the Depression, high wages, not sagging ones, occasioned alarm.

Militant coordination was necessary to bring wages down. In April 1932, ten leading Swedish industrialists and employer leaders assembled in a conference room at the Stockholm Opera Restaurant to discuss the crisis. Called by the chairman of the Swedish Employers' Confederation (*Svenska Arbetsgivareföreningen*, or SAF), the meeting had as its main issue a massive lockout. Of utmost importance at the moment was to persuade all employers to close ranks behind this multi-industry attack to force down wages in one sector, the paper pulp industry. A weak link in the solidaristic chain was independent, high-pay, high-standard welfare capitalists who refused to join in. The disreputable employers, in other words, were the generous paternalists—not "Poor-pay, Shiftless, and Chisel," the troublemakers among American employers according to the NAM's Wagner Bill Clinic in 1935.[1]

Case in point was Carl Kempe of MoDo (Mo & Domsjö), a large producer and exporter of lumber and paper pulp. Kempe, from a family of a very successful rural-industrial factory masters (*brukspatroner*), was invited to the meeting though he had steadfastly refused to join the employers' confederation from its inception in 1902. At the meeting, the patriarch proved deaf to efforts to change his mind, insisting on the value of treating workers "along softer lines." Together with good pay, his welfare capitalism—worker home ownership and other social benefits—gave him exactly the labor relations he wanted. His disinclination to cooperate was complicating efforts to persuade other industrialists to commit to joining the lockouts.[2]

"Pure abdication," SAF's executive director Gustaf Söderlund called Kempe's stance in a letter to J. Sigfrid Edström, Sweden's preeminent industrialist and employer statesman. Chairman of both SAF and its most important affiliate, the Swedish Engineering Employers' Association, this prodigious organizer also ran ASEA, Sweden's "General Electric." Despite his 1893–1897 apprenticeship as a young engineer at Westinghouse in Pittsburgh and GE in Schenectady, New York, he had become as much a model of solidarism as GE's Gerard Swope was of American segmentalism. He had nothing good to say, for example, about Henry Ford's and other Americans' "theory of high wages" and instead wanted to dissuade as many fellow employers as possible against it.[3] According to Söderlund, if Kempe's approach were pursued by everyone, the collective struggle to hold wages down would be impossible. If only one or a handful of employers followed Kempe's course, "they may well get decent conditions, but hardly thanks to their own efforts and only because the organized part of industry shouldered the burden." Kempe's beneficence to workers was after all a relative thing—measured against the harder terms that other employers conveniently set across the rest of the labor market. Did Kempe merit any respect, Söderlund fumed, profiting as he did "from others' efforts and troubles?"[4]

Solidarism's evolution in Sweden, as promoted by employer leaders like Edström and Söderlund, reached its pinnacle in the 1950s and 1960s. By that time, the Kempe family's company had finally joined the fold (brought in by the next generation, in 1949).[5] Pay determination was now centralized, at organized employers' behest, to a degree hardly matched in any other country of the world. Wage differentials across firms and industries were low, and with employers' blessing, still declining. Company welfare capitalism was mostly a thing of the past. The contrast with the American labor market was stark. Table 4.1 shows the dramatic differences achieved by the end of the 1960s. By leaving out company-based benefits concentrated in high-pay industries dominated by large American firms, but relatively absent across Swedish industries, it actually understates them. Economists, examining America-Sweden differences in the 1980s, conclude that centralized pay setting was the main cause.[6]

In short, Sweden distinguishes itself as a system with a highly egalitarian structure of wages and a well-developed welfare state in which individual employers have no significant role in providing social insurance and other benefits. Most observers think this must be the work of Sweden's exceptionally well-organized labor movement against capitalist forces and their standard inegalitarian, anti-government interests. The reality, however, is more complicated, and even more interesting. For events and trends earlier in the twentieth century, long before Social Democrats came to power, were already pointing in social democracy's direction and away from patterns of labor market governance that the United States developed. This chapter begins the argument with evidence indicating that core institutions and policies associated

TABLE 4.1. Relative Hourly Earnings
for Manual Workers, Various Sectors, 1970
(Average for All Industry in Each Country = 100)

	Sweden	United States
Clothing	79	71
Textiles	85	73
Shoes	87	73
Leather products	90	78
Beverages	94	109
Food processing	95	93
Wood products	96	86
Chemicals, oil, and plastics	96	113
Rubber	97	96
Quarries	101	101
Pulp, paper, and paper products	101	103
Engineering	103	110
Iron and steel	105	121
Auto industry[a]	110	126
Publishing	112	117
Mining and minerals	120	115
Building and construction	131	157

[a]The automobile industry is a subset of engineering.

Source: Ingvar Ohlsson, "Den solidariska lönepolitikens resultat," in Lönepolitik och solidaritet—Debattinlägg vid Meidnerseminariet den 21–22 February 1980
(Stockholm: LO, 1980).

with Swedish social democracy were built on a foundation of support from
powerful capitalists. The interests underlying their support derived from the
solidaristic system of labor market regulation they built in cross-class alliance
with organized labor. The first steps, however, required the exercise of enormous coercive power, with the lockout, against a union movement still optimistic, like American ones, about capturing managerial control.

The Mass, Multi-Employer Lockout

The lockout was employers' single most powerful tool used in the building of
Swedish solidarism. Their draconian multi-employer and even multi-industry
lockouts had no equal in the American drama of industrial strife. Lockouts
were to Swedish developments what strikebreaking and blacklisting was to the
American ones. They gave organized capital in Sweden the ability to hammer
unions into a shape that made them useful as partners in centralized regulation of labor markets. The leadership of the unions, closely tied to the Social
Democratic party, was by no means fully resistant to movement in the direction employers wanted to go. What stood in their way was lack of control over

decentralized militancy in the ranks. Consequently, evidence in this chapter indicates, labor leaders may have sometimes welcomed lockouts, or threats thereof. The rattling of employers' mighty sword gave them an ideologically respectable pretext to intervene against disruptive rank-and-file militancy.

The first effective use of the multi-employer lockout in building the Swedish system took place, as discussed later, in 1905. Statistics recorded on the practice, starting about a decade later, give a clear picture of its importance. Although Swedish workers of the 1920s and 1930s once acquired a reputation in some analyses as about the most militant in the entire world (because of the number of days lost to industrial conflict), much of the militancy appearing in the statistics on labor disputes actually belongs to employers. On average each year between 1919 and 1938, fully one third of workers involved in disputes were either locked out by employers, or else drawn into "mixed disputes"— where responsibility was hard to establish. (Often small strikes in one or more bargaining sectors brought sweeping lockouts for a whole or many industries.) In six of those years, the figures climbed to over 50 percent. In the 1920s, the years with the biggest disputes tended also to be those with the most locked out workers (see table 4.2).[7]

The multi-employer lockout dragged hosts of employers and their workers into nonviolent confrontation, usually when the immediate cause of the dispute was far removed from their own workplaces. In other words, they were "sympathy" lockouts imposed by organized employers on members not party to the original disputes. Sectoral employer associations representing different industries, often under pressure from SAF and other sectoral affiliates, forced member companies (who risked fines and expulsion if they disobeyed) to lock out their workers. In these mostly orderly affairs, workers simply stayed away from their workplaces and picked up lockout pay from their unions. Often firms requested exemption, pleading special circumstances. Usually their requests were denied.[8] Naturally, firms often regretted having to cease production and lose sales, especially when their workers were prepared to continue under existing wage and working conditions. No wonder, then, that the fiercely independent Kempe of MoDo would refuse to join an employers' organization, only to be ordered to cease production and lock out his own loyal and satisfied workers. No wonder too that other employers resented him, when his prices and sales would improve because they were idled by lockouts.

The multi-employer sympathy lockout's chief purpose was simple: a quick and massive bloodletting of union strike funds. Large union treasuries could comfortably fund a small number of strikes indefinitely. These cheap pressure-point tactics could be extraordinarily effective in whipsawing employers, picking them off one at a time (*lönesaxning*). Employers' best retaliatory defense was the massive sympathy lockout, which threatened workers' financial support, and shut down alternative places of employment. It inflicted huge financial damage on the unions because they were required by their rules to pay out support to every last member locked out. Organized employers prized the device so highly that they opposed anti-union legislation in 1911 on the

TABLE 4.2. Worker Involvement in Industrial Conflict, 1919–1949

Year	Workers involved	Percent locked out (a)	Percent in mixed disputes (b)	Percent combined (a + b)
1919	81,041	0.9	12.7	13.6
1920	139,039	27.3	42.0	69.3
1921	49,712	1.5	9.9	11.4
1922	75,679	0.4	42.1	42.5
1923	102,896	20.9	37.3	58.2
1924	23,976	6.4	12.2	1.9
1925	145,778	80.1	5.2	85.3
1926	52,891	45.6	1.4	47.0
1927	9,477	12.1	7.4	19.5
1928	71,461	68.2	6.5	74.7
1929	12,676	1.1	2.9	4.0
1930	20,751	1.3	3.9	5.2
1931	40,899	0.9	0.6	1.5
1932	50,147	0.2	4.5	4.7
1933	31,980	0.2	13.6	13.8
1934	13,588	0	0	0
1935	17,189	0.2	30.6	30.8
1936	3,474	1.4	0.9	2.3
1937	30,904	0	78.2	78.2
1938	28,951	44.6	35.4	80.0
1939	2,194	0	2.9	2.9
1940	3,936	2.0	0.1	2.1
1941	1,929	0.7	0	0.7
1942	1,337	0	0	0
1943	6,926	0	0	0
1944	7,021	0	10.1	10.1
1945	133,171	0	0	0
1946	1,277	0.4	0	0.4
1947	56,851	0	0	0
1948	6,061	0	0	0
1949	1,008	0	0	0

Source: Statistiska Centralbyrån, Statistisk årsbok (Stockholm: SCB, various years).

grounds that restricting unions' ability to use boycotts, blockades, and sympathetic strikes, which also hit innocent third parties, would undermine the legitimacy of lockouts.[9]

Locking out entirely innocent workers was in fact SAF policy. The ramifications were enormous. As early as 1912, SAF's Hjalmar von Sydow, serving as both chairman and executive director, advocated indiscriminate lockouts. Non-striking workers were to be taken out whether they were union members or not. Sometime between then and 1920, this became standard practice. Earlier it had been normal to keep operations going with the unorganized workforce. But that proved untenable because, during a lockout, some members could maintain output and steal customers from others fully idled by the conflict. Therefore, SAF went over to "shutting all mills and factories completely." The confederation also justified the practice with the argument that it was hard to know who was organized or not. Secretly organized workers could continue to pay into union strike funds to support other striking and locked out workers.[10]

Because of indiscriminate lockouts, many Swedish workers probably ran for cover by joining unions. Their dues served as premiums for lockout insurance.[11] They found the purchase of lockout insurance with union membership all the more advisable because idleness due to lockouts disqualified them from all public unemployment relief measures. Thus by 1923, practically all unions in the largest manufacturing and construction sectors dominated by SAF had comfortably cleared the 50 percent mark, some of them reaching over 80 percent (see table 4.3). Sweden was in fact a glowing exception to the downward international trend of the 1920s and witnessed a steady growth in union density (percent of manual workers organized) from 41 percent in 1920 to 63 percent in 1930. Stagnation or decline prevailed practically everywhere else. Even at the peak of their development in later years, very few union movements anywhere in the world would ever match levels that Swedish unions reached in 1930. A big part of the explanation has to be the Swedish lockout.[12]

Union strength, measured by organization levels, was not the same as employer weakness. In the late 1920s SAF's Axel Brunius judged the Swedish confederation to be "one of the most powerful combinations of industrial employers the world over."[13] Thus, if strong employers helped create strong unions, then Swedish union density can not simplistically be equated or confused with what many analyses call their "working class strength" or "power resources." As later discussion shows, organized capital in Sweden wanted strong unions, and when they got them, they did not regret the consequences—a strong ally in the building of solidarism.

TABLE 4.3. Union Density, 1923

Union (sector)	Workers employed	Percent organized
Book printing	15,620	68.6
Building and construction	30,000	67.0
Chemicals	50,787	47.1
Clothing	14,777	55.3
Electrical installation	4,500	70.2
Food processing	15,356	76.3
Lumber	44,200	53.6
Metal working	78,506	74.5
Painting	3,747	88.0
Pulp and paper	29,003	71.2
Shoe and leather	13,560	80.0
Textiles	30,866	53.6
Transportation	15,850	75.2

Source: Sigfrid Hansson, *Den svenska fackföreningsrörelsen* (Stockholm: Tiden, 1927), 170–71.

International Market Pressures and
the Need for Managerial Control

Why did employers in Sweden resort to such draconian devices, and with them, begin forging the solidaristic system? What enabled them to do so? The answers to these questions lie in Sweden's size and vulnerability in international markets. The story of solidarism begins with manufacturing employers' collective efforts to improve their position in two international markets: the market for internationally mobile labor and the market for internationally traded goods. Balancing conflicting interests in these two markets was devilishly complicated. On the one hand, and in the very short run, manufacturers needed to hold wages low enough to keep the prices of Swedish goods competitive in international product markets. On the other hand, they needed wages to rise so that they could hold their own in international competition over Sweden's mobile labor force.

Reconciling the two objectives, or increasing wages without raising prices, had only one solution: rapid managerial and technological improvements to reduce unit labor costs. The productivity problem was severe. In 1900, Swedish labor productivity, measured as GDP per man hour, was as low as in France and Italy, and only 40 percent of American levels. American employers' advantage enabled them to pay far higher wages and attract large numbers of immigrants, an alarming number of Swedes among them. Not surprisingly, urban as well as rural-industrial areas of Sweden suffered continuous net outmigration to foriegn lands in the first decade of the twentieth century. About 12,000 of almost 17,000 emigrants from Stockholm went to the United States in that decade; most of the rest settled somewhere in Europe.[14]

Swedish manufacturers also competed with Americans in shared product markets, on a price as well as quality basis. Austrians, Belgians, Germans, Dutch, Swiss, and British manufacturers were also threats. They too enjoyed significantly higher levels of productivity. British workers, for example, required only half the time to produce the same quantity of merchandise.[15] Thus, Swedish employers, especially in engineering, recognized the acute need to increase both productivity and wages to become competitive internationally. An important Riksdag motion submitted in 1904, which led to the formation of a commission to investigate government solutions to the emigration problem, explicitly recognized the interrelated problems of emigration, low productivity, low wages, and international competition.[16]

Employers did not wait for help from government measures being contemplated by the commission, which reported in 1913. Their first move, in 1905, was a mass lockout. Sweden's small size and the relative cohesiveness of its capitalist class made it practical for employers to organize and communicate effectively enough to carry out this and subsequent measures. Lockouts served two purposes. First, they neutralized unions' powerful whipsaw strike tactic to drive wages up under conditions of localized or general labor shortages. Second, they punished unions for promoting or supporting worker resistance to employers' frenetic drive for higher labor productivity.

Employers regarded the lockout as a device to tame unions, not destroy them. For one thing, there was not much labor available to replace unionists, as there might have been if Sweden had been a site of in-migration like the United States. Making virtue out of necessity, employers saw in national unions a potential ally in securing managerial absolutism. With clauses guaranteeing managerial absolutism and strike-free operations for the duration of agreements, unions would in effect enforce management's ability to achieve their goal of lower unit labor costs. Indeed, the lockout's effectiveness in ridding the labor movement of its radical designs on managerial control, as will be seen, was predicated on the existence of strong unions with an officialdom that preferred to hoard rather than spend down their strike resources fighting losing battles over managerial issues.

In the United States, the mass lockout could hardly have been seriously considered, given the country's vast size, rapid formation of new enterprises, and consequent difficulties in coordination. Nor did employers need the lockout. Unlike conditions in Sweden, their high wages and therefore massive inflow of labor into the country allowed them to replace militant skilled craftsmen with machines manned by unskilled strikebreakers. Success with strikebreaking, unlike the multi-employer lockout, was not predicated on the continued existence of unions. Instead, strikebreaking was especially suited to destroying them. Whereas Swedish circumstances made virtue out of necessity with regard to unions, they made evil out of impossibility as far as strikebreaking was concerned. To SAF's von Sydow, a fervent lockout advocate, there was something repellant about the idea of moving workers about like so many "pieces on a chess board."[17] But repellant as it may have been, SAF did not completely abstain from strikebreaking. As chapter 5 shows, employers relied on it only in sectors where the lockout was useless—usually in sectors where the Social Democratic unions were weak.

The 1905 Engineering Lockout

In 1902, engineering employers assembled on a national basis in the Swedish Engineering Employers' Association (*Verkstadsföreningen*, or VF). Within three years, their association carried out a large multi-employer lockout against the Swedish Metal Workers' Union (*Metallindustriarbetareförbundet*, or Metall, for short). Metall had been supporting about 4,000 workers on strike at 23 machine shops and shipyards. VF responded by locking out 83 member firms. All in all, roughly 13,800 workers were idled, voluntarily or involuntarily, directly and indirectly, including 7,784 union members. Employer solidarity was extraordinary: only two VF firms refused to obey the lockout order, forfeited their membership bonds, and lost their membership. Conflict led to agreement, the first industry-wide multi-employer wage settlement for any industry in the country.[18]

The VF-Metall agreement of 1905 was the first important step toward negotiated solidarism in Sweden. Of utmost importance to engineering employers was their decisive victory on the question of managerial control. The agreement allowed no restrictions on managerial rights regarding the introduction and manning of machinery or hiring of unskilled workers and apprentices. Also in the spirit of promoting productivity, the union even graciously agreed that employers were free to introduce piece work wherever it was "possible to implement." Finally, the union agreed to an open shop clause, thereby eliminating any residual possibility of imposing restrictive work rules by controlling the supply of labor. These, of course, were the underlying issues on which the American foundry and machinist unions would not, or could not, compromise—with consequences as devastating to American unions as the 1905 agreement was auspicious for the Swedish ones.

All in all, the 1905 agreement was a resounding success for employers. American machine shop and foundry owners would have sorely envied their Swedish counterparts' success. Militant skilled craftsmen in the IAM and IMU would have regarded the deal with dismay and disgust. For example, the agreement created a multi-tier and regionally segmented system of minimum wages, with one set for skilled workers 21 years or older with 4 years' experience in the trade and one for unskilled workers having reached the age of 21.[19] Firms could hire unskilled workers under 21 in whatever quantity and for whatever price the external labor market allowed. Because of their untrammeled rights to introduce new machinery and hire cheaper unskilled labor to operate it, the graduated minimum wage system was perfectly designed to favor rapid technological change. Such a system was exactly what the IMU had militantly—and self-destructively—spurned.

Metall did not come away completely empty-handed, however. The union's leaders could now boast of securing minimum wages for most metalworkers across the country, a first for any industry.[20] Employer recognition of the union vastly improved union activists' shaky prospects of a prestigious and stable professional career with relatively high income. Despite the agreement, not all major employers in VF abandoned hopes of crushing the union. About the most aggressive among them was VF chairman John Bernström of AB Separator, a mass producer of dairy machinery with a successful nonunion American subsidiary. The industrial patriarch only went begrudgingly along with the lockout and subsequent agreement. His nemesis, J. Sigfrid Edström, director of ASEA, a producer of power generating and transmission equipment, elevators, and electrical railroad equipment, led the faction seeking centralized collective bargaining with a strong union. The happy results of 1905 settled the matter on the side of the employer statesman, just as the fiasco following the Murray Hill Agreement of 1900 in the United States threw the victory to the belligerents. Edström would later replace Bernström as VF chairman, and then, as SAF chairman, proceed in the forging of the Swedish model.

Strong economic growth in the period after 1905 brought high demand for the industry's products. The freeze on centrally negotiated wage increases held wages below market-clearing equilibrium levels. Prima facie evidence indicates this in the form of acute labor shortage, rampant poaching of labor, and upward wage drift. In February of 1907, less than a year and a half after the agreement, one leading employer wrote to Edström complaining about "the most cutthroat and worst sort of competition when . . . people drive up wages by outbidding each other." Unfortunately, he added, "by competing with each other and driving up wages we cannot create more men."[21] The union was not the problem. Despite the labor scarcity, Metall honored its agreement and offered no opposition to the introduction of apprentices or labor saving and de-skilling machinery to deal with the flood of orders. A real problem was emigration from urban and rural industrial Sweden. Because of good times in America, outmigration was peaking and far outstripping return migration.

As an increasingly active figure in VF, Edström responded to the labor supply problem by pushing for solidaristic resources to help manage recruitment practices. A first step in this direction was the creation of a "statistical department," one of whose main purposes was to identify and discourage the hiring of job-hoppers (*flyttfåglar*), who drove up wages in tight labor markets. (It was not, however, to be a blacklisting device against union members.) In the spirit of mobilizing more labor, since raising wages would be counterproductive, Edström also championed the idea of setting up a bureau with the mandate and resources to encourage emigrated Swedish workers to return from America. VF also shortly began encouraging its members to make "the greatest possible" use of municipal labor exchanges rather than steal labor from each other.[22] Over the next decade, with Edström at the helm, VF would take more such measures to manage the labor market according to the logic of solidarism.

The December Compromise and Multi-Industry Lockouts

The year after the groundbreaking events of 1905 in engineering, the Swedish Employers' Confederation resolved to unleash an unprecedented *multi-industry* general lockout. Nothing less than a halt to the country's entire manufacturing activity was in sight. SAF threatened this huge action in reprisal against only eight firm-level strikes outside the engineering sector. Despite some grumbling from within the ranks, SAF and its sectoral associations confidently asserted a right to enjoin (*påbjuda*) lockouts on individual members despite contracts they may have signed with unions, and despite the fact that the unions were currently respecting their contracts.[23]

All eight disputes involved worker challenges to employers' managerial prerogatives. One of them involved union pressure on a copper producer in Hälsingborg. Because it employed its own bricklayers, the company was being pressured to join a bilateral monopoly (closed shop combined with union boycott of unorganized employers) between the municipal builders and the city local of the Mason's Union. But joining would violate SAF's rules, in particular its famous "paragraph 23," which prohibited members from entering into closed-shop agreements. Paragraph 23 also prohibited members from conceding union control over any managerial decisions involving hiring, firing, and supervising work. In the other seven disputes, unions were also challenging firms to disobey SAF's supreme command.[24]

Passed in 1905, and amended in 1906, paragraph 23 required SAF members to include an iron-clad managerial rights clause in all collective agreements made with workers at any level. It also required members to submit all agreements to SAF's executive leadership for advance approval before signing. In exchange for handing over bonds (*garantiförbindelser*), membership fees, and bargaining autonomy to SAF, the members guaranteed themselves substantial payments out of strike insurance funds, and possibly even sympathy lockouts. Stiff fines (forfeiture of bonds) and expulsion were the consequences of failure to join in the mission.

Seeing a big lockout on the horizon, the LO leadership, which had just spent considerable funds in the metalworkers' conflict the year before, willingly accepted SAF's invitations to discuss the eight disputes. The result was the so-called "December Compromise" of 1906. In it, LO agreed in full to employers' rights to manage exactly as SAF conceived them. In exchange, LO extracted from SAF a formal recognition of workers' right to join unions. SAF had already demonstrated goodwill in this regard when it intervened earlier in the year against Mackmyra, a sulfite producer, which had locked out and evicted workers for their union membership and activities.[25] By signing, LO signaled its intention to refuse money to workers locked out over managerial disputes. Unions wishing to defy SAF were now on their own.

LO also made another remarkable and fateful concession in the December Compromise, one that is often overlooked. The labor confederation begrudgingly agreed, at SAF's insistence, that sympathy lockouts of workers were "not to be regarded as violations of currently valid contracts." Of course, workers were likewise free to join in sympathy strikes if sanctioned by their national union. But so far, sympathy strikes were fairly rare and unimportant. Therefore, according to historian Ragnar Casparsson, LO regarded the demand "with coolness and marked suspicion." But SAF's von Sydow maintained flatly that "without the right to sympathy lockouts, employer organizations might as well cease to exist."[26] To achieve managerial absolutism required sympathy lockouts.

LO's acceptance of the terms of the December compromise did not end the eight disputes, however. LO affiliates were still free to spend their own funds on the strikers, who in the meantime could take other jobs, which were plentiful. What happened next seems bizarre, though procedurally it was entirely in order. Despite LO's formal rejection of the workers' demands, SAF turned around and announced plans for a mass sympathy lockout against it. The December Compromise, after all, had just given it permission. The lockout would force LO's hand, requiring it to choose between bankrupting itself by providing support to locked-out members, or finding a way to end the disputes. One can only speculate about how indignantly or calmly, surprised or unsurprised,

LO reacted. SAF historian Hans De Geer conjectures that SAF may have threatened the lockout to "support" LO, which was trying to persuade the workers to submit to employers.[27] By that token, LO may have been neither particularly astonished nor outraged. In any event, SAF's threat worked. LO now intervened compellingly, resolving the disputes to SAF's satisfaction. The threat alone of a mass lockout proved sufficient.

The passage of two years brought a repeat performance. SAF once again raised its mighty weapon against the entire labor confederation in order to enforce paragraph 23 across the entire Swedish labor market—except for engineering, whose association had not yet joined SAF. The immediate and primary objective was to break the efforts of the Transport Workers' Union (Transport) to make firms prioritize union members in the hiring and firing of longshoremen. When supplying English strikebreakers and strike insurance to companies in Northern Sweden failed to settle the matter, SAF once again aimed a general lockout threat against LO. Unwilling to spend funds on a cause it had explicitly rejected, LO joined forces with the government in pressuring Transport to submit to paragraph 23.[28] Had Transport succeeded in its aims, it would then have been free to use its supremely efficient sympathy actions to help other unions overthrow managerial absolutism. A crucial sector of the Swedish export-based manufacturing economy was now under control, making unionism safe for rapid technological progress.

Solidarism Ascendant: Suppressing Welfare Capitalism, Leveling Wages, Reviving Unionism

In the course of time, organized capital in Sweden acquired a distinct liking for the Social Democratic labor movement, at least in comparison to the alternatives, including no unions at all. Centralized collective bargaining with unions that had shed all ambitions to control management proved highly convenient for achieving two basic solidaristic objectives: suppression of welfare capitalism and compression of pay. In fact, it was probably easier to accomplish these ends with unions rather than without them. Lockouts served as powerful tools for achieving employer objectives only if there were unions that minded being locked out.

From the beginning, suppressing what Americans call welfare capitalism was one of the projects associated with SAF's use of the lockout and its push for centralization. Substituting centralized governance of the labor market for welfare capitalism was decidedly the preference of R.F. Berg, director of the large Skånska Cement works in Malmö. Early in the century he "ceased being a benevolent patriarch," as he put it himself, so that "people can help themselves" with strong unions and the wages they negotiated. Berg for one played an important role in imbuing SAF with its mission of imposing centralized bargaining over wages, while sweeping social benefits along with managerial control off the bargaining table.[29]

Eliminating company benefits had been a desideratum of the Paper Industry Employers' Association from its inception in 1907, along with other rural based industries.[30] The Iron and Steel Industry Employers' Association (JBF, or *Järnbruksförbundet*), took the first successful step however in 1908. To bring about a national-level agreement similar to the one achieved in 1905 in engineering, the association called a multi-employer lockout in response to a few isolated actions by Metall, which also organized iron and steel. To the union's surprise—and displeasure—JBF also announced its intentions to sweep all remuneration with in-kind goods and services out of the industry.[31]

Iron and steel employers had agreed among themselves to use the conflict to eliminate completely all free housing, physician and hospital services, firewood, and "potato land." In exchange, hourly workers were to get guaranteed minimum wages to pay for such necessities. Negotiations ran aground on this and other issues. Once again, menaced by the threat of a costly multi-industry lockout, LO applied all necessary pressure on its metalworkers' union to sign an agreement. Metall conceded most of the iron and steel manufacturers' wishes. In return, it was able to retain existing company medical benefits (but not other company-provided goods and services). It also obtained a guaranteed floor on piece work earnings, which was not, apparently, a big hurdle for employers.[32]

JBF also drove through the SAF's demand that sympathy actions be recognized as fully legitimate in the national iron and steel agreement. Local ironworkers' representatives could only "rub their eyes" in disbelief when confronted with this outrageous notion, according to LO chairman Herman Lindqvist. The flabbergasted unionists declared they themselves had little use for sympathy strikes.[33] Employers, by contrast, had plans. Before the year was out, JBF extended lockout backing for VF's efforts to prolong its two-year old agreement from 1905. The two associations, one inside SAF and the other still outside, threatened to lock out all steel and engineering workers, both organized by Metall. Against this imposing array of forces, Metall accepted extension of the 1905 engineering agreement. Only one important change was added: the sympathy clause. With it now in place, VF was very soon able to repay JBF in kind.[34]

The advance of centralization and solidarism proceeded on another industrial front in 1908. In the sawmill industry, SAF's multi-industry lockout threat and LO intervention once again pressured a reluctant union to fall in line and relinquish the tactical advantages it enjoyed in decentralization and whipsawing. The result was the industry's first national-level agreement, with distinct solidaristic elements, including a downward leveling of wages across the industry (reductions only for higher pay firms), and uniform general working conditions. The Sawmill Employers' Association (*Sågverksförbundet*) also sought, against many workers' misgivings, liquidation of in-kind company benefits. The end result was a limited success. The union (*Sågverksindustriarbetarförbundet*) now accepted the principle of cash remuneration only. Workers were now on their own in their efforts to hold on to company benefits should the employers' association prevail on firms to drop them.[35]

The following year brought disaster for LO. To employers' regret, the labor confederation's rout in the general strike of 1909 arrested the forward march of centralization and solidarism. The debacle started when SAF threatened to unleash, in five stages of escalation, a multi-industry lockout of 82,000 workers in response to only ten disputes involving 2,500 strikers. With this retaliatory sympathy lockout, employers planned to impose national agreements in sectors not yet covered, and with them, force through wage reductions because of the severe international recession.[36] Even more ambitiously, SAF also wanted to force LO to the multi-industry bargaining table for a basic agreement that formally committed all of its affiliates to managerial absolutism. The December Compromise had only committed LO not to defend its affiliates' violations of managerial rights.[37]

In retrospect, it seems, SAF pushed too hard and fast with its impatient and overweening ambitions, squeezing LO against left-wing Social Democrats and other splinter groups inside and outside the LO unions. The radicals were fired up by the idea of a mass strike, temporarily the rage of left-wing socialists throughout Europe. In order to save face among militant workers, the conservative LO leadership threw caution to the winds and declared a general strike. Lasting several months, the conflict bankrupted the young labor movement and cut its membership almost in half. For a number of years after the fiasco, the leadership of LO and its affiliated unions could hardly show their faces at central bargaining tables to forge national agreements in several industrial sectors where employers still desired them. To sign anything that employers found acceptable look like a sellout of worker interests.

Oddly enough, one might think, the SAF leadership willingly passed up the opportunity to crush the Social Democratic labor movement when it was down. It could have done so "without difficulty," as SAF's von Sydow recalled twenty or so years after the debacle. He did not mourn the missed opportunity.[38] The reason was quite simple. In 1912, while the unions were still nursing their wounds, von Sydow advised employers that eliminating the Social Democratic unions would only mean having to deal with Syndicalist organizations waiting in the wings. That would be highly regrettable, he said, because "against syndicalist strikes one cannot readily resort to the weapon that . . . has proven to be very effective for employers, namely the lockout." Because the Syndicalist movement collected no funds and distributed no strike or lockout support, it was not possible to "disable it economically." In short, "it is hard to declare a lockout when there is nobody to declare a lockout against."[39] Anyone who witnessed the recent successes of 1905, 1906, and 1908 knew exactly what he was talking about.

Employers in the Textile Industry Employers' Association (*Textilindustriförbundet*, or TIF), for example, were not at all eager to kick their union when it was down. On the contrary, dominant ones actually looked forward to its revival. They were the first SAF employers to bring the trend toward centralized solidaristic labor market governance back to life in 1914. A national agreement with the union had been a core objective (*hjärtesak*) for TIF, since around 1909 if not earlier.[40] With it, they fully expected to revive the textile workers' union. To be sure, some textile employers voiced regret that a national agreement "would ineluctably result in the revival of the union, which in effect has ceased to exist." However, theirs was not the prevailing sentiment.

When the time was ripe, the employers' association rattled its swords in preparation for conflict. The leadership resolved, however, to proceed delicately so as not to undermine the fragile union's leadership. Wheeling the convalescing union to the centralized bargaining table for a fixed wage agreement would, they hoped, help neutralize the revival of decentralized pressure for wage increases as the economy improved. Labor scarcities were becoming worrisome, creating upward wage pressures. Freely mobile labor, more than localized strikes and Syndicalist inroads, was the problem. In general, textile employers feared that some firms would give in, forcing others to follow suit at the expense of profits, because, simply, "workers will not stay put."[41]

The national agreement of 1914—and the anticipated revival of the union—was thus largely employers' doing. "No other employer organization has so completely pushed through its demands as we have done," the leadership boasted. First of all, the association accomplished a more or less "full equalization of working and wage conditions in the textile industry." In the spirit of solidarism, the agreement required individual employers to eliminate in-kind benefits like worker housing (replacing them with individually grandfathered monetary premiums above the standard rates). Physician services and accident benefits were retained for the time being, though standardized across the industry. TIF even imposed a new measure of solidarism in the agreement by eliminating seniority wage practices, common in segmentalism, wherein "wages rose illogically (*principlöst*) with length of employment."[42]

Most remarkably, the agreement introduced a rigidly fixed system of "normal wages" (*normallöner*) for unskilled operatives, not just minimum wage scales as introduced in the engineering and steel agreements of 1905 and 1908. This solidaristic innovation fully standardized wages by imposing ceilings as well as floors on wages. With "maximum wages," the national agreement empowered the association to control employers' disloyal behavior toward each other, not just control worker militancy—just as minimum wages committed workers not to betray the cause by accepting pay below a contractual floor.[43]

The next big steps in the development of solidarism occurred six years later, in 1920, when three more sectors joined engineering, steel, sawmills, and textiles.[44] That year employers in the Wood Industry Employers' Association (*Träindustriförbundet*) unleashed a four-month long industry-wide lockout in response to limited strike actions. The woodworkers' union was struggling to preserve local autonomy in wage setting. SAF's intervention broke the impasse in employers' favor. The confederation announced that industry-wide lockouts currently in progress in engineering and steel would remain in force as sympathy measures, even after resolution of the disputes in those sectors, until the woodworkers caved in. At that point, the union finally accepted a national wage agreement, and according to the association's history, "it became no longer possible for the workers to whipsaw their way to higher wages." As in the engineering agreement, the industry agreement set minimum wages, differentiated by region and skill level, and granted that piece rates were to be paid whenever technically feasible.[45]

The Paper Industry Employers' Association (*Pappersbruksförbundet*, or PBF) and the Building Masters' Association (*Byggmästareforbundet*, BMF) followed suit the same year. By introducing the industry's first nationwide wage agreement, paper producers bought off company welfare benefits with wage increases. PBF had wanted to do this since its inception in 1907. Also, it introduced a schedule of normal or minimum-maximum wages, following the textile industry's solidaristic innovation.[46] In construction, likewise, an eight-month industry-wide lockout brought into being a national agreement in November 1920, complete with normal wages, as favored by SAF. Now members who paid higher than contractual wages in efforts to attract labor stood to forfeit bonds they were newly required to submit.[47] The lockout was backed by the cement and brick industry, which refused building materials to the many unorganized contractors willing to build on the strikers' terms. Behind them in turn was SAF, which spent an unprecedented 5 million crowns on the conflict, much of it to compensate the building materials industry for its foregone earnings.[48]

The Paper Pulp Industry Employers' Association (*Pappersmasseförbundet*, PMF), and the newly formed, organizationally fragile Paper Industry Workers' Union (*Svenska Pappersindustriarbetareförbundet*, SPIAF) took the next step toward solidarism in 1921. Though desired by many employers, a lockout was never formally planned and indeed proved unnecessary. Strike insurance benefits from SAF proved adequate to deal with the strikes under way. After a month, the union settled at the central level for wage reductions of 15 percent across the board and interfirm leveling according to the increasingly common normal wage system.[49] With centralization in the paper pulp industry complete, the most important sectors of Swedish industry were now corralled into the institutions of solidaristic regulation. Except on this one occasion, SAF-sponsored multi-employer lockouts, or threats thereof, were involved. Other sectors continued pushing in the same direction. In 1925, for example, garment industry leaders continued the push for centralized wage setting. The executive director of the Clothing Industry Employers' Association (*Sveriges Konfektions-industriförbund*) justified his efforts with the unabashedly solidaristic argument that "the foremost task for an employers' organization naturally must be to try and neutralize competition among employers over manpower."[50]

Swedish garment producers wanted what other employers in SAF had achieved, in other words. According to SAF historian, Carl Hallendorff, writing around the same time, SAF's project involved "the tricky [*vansklig*] but important task" not of destroying unions, but of "leading or forcing the labor movement's defiantly swelling tide into channels where it could be to the benefit of industry in everyone's common interest." One direction employers pushed the unions toward was "a certain uniformity in working conditions and especially in wage rates." As Hallendorff put it, desire to move in this egalitarian direction "can just as well arise among businessmen as from workers." That, indeed, is what von Sydow had looked ahead to in 1912, listing "uniform labor costs," along with managerial absolutism, among the supreme objectives of an employers' association.[51]

The Evolution of Solidaristic Authority in Engineering

SAF predicated its mission of bringing unions into solidaristic labor market governance on thoroughly disabusing them of their ambitions to control management. But solidarism came at a cost for owners and managers, too. In short, they had to surrender precious autonomy to their own organizations. When, for example, the Paper Industry Employers' Association proposed to impose the minimum-maximum wage system in 1920, some members protested the loss of upward "freedom of movement" in wage setting.[52] The association, however, was not apologetic. The collective agreement with unions was not merely a system for controlling workers. As SAF's yearly report for the following year put it, "it also mutually binds employers." They can, it went on, "claim no right to go above the contract's wage level without approval of their association." Without centralized multi-employer contracts, employers would behave "exclusively according to selfish principles and cause a considerable disruption in the uniform wage levels that every organized branch of industry desires."[53] Negotiated solidarism was to be defended; unions therefore were good things, not bad.

The problem of imposing associational control was probably more difficult in engineering than any other sector, even though the industry had spearheaded the movement toward negotiated solidarism in 1905. Their agreement that year had occasioned the immediate and wholesale dismantling of physician, credit, and accident insurance benefits by at least one major shipbuilding firm, Lindholmen in Göteborg. At Munktell's large machine making works, social benefits as a proportion of total remuneration dropped after peaking in the 1905–1909 period when the engineering agreement was sinking its institutional roots. In 1939, looking back, Hugo Hammar—another leading employer leader from shipbuilding—recalled 1905 as a clean and welcome break with paternalism.[54]

But these moves were voluntary. In the forced elimination of company benefits and imposition of anything like normal wages, engineering lagged behind other sectors. The process began in 1919. VF had just achieved a favorably low central agreement after its chairman, Sigfrid Edström, helped broker the last important constitutional change toward full political democratization in Sweden (female suffrage and one person, one vote in elections for communal government, which in turn elected the upper chamber of the Riksdag chamber). Possibly one of Edström's motives, historian Sven Anders Söderpalm speculates, was to smooth the way to a favorable central agreement in his sector.[55]

The new political circumstances brought passage of the eight-hour workday in September 1919. The shorter working day made already acute labor short-ages worse, as employers saw it, and therefore indirectly pushed events in a sol-idaristic direction. Poaching of workers, often by means of openly advertised wage increases, became rampant. VF's minimum wage system gave members complete license to raise wages far above the negotiated minimums to compete over labor. Arguments raged inside VF about countermeasures. In the end, VF gained the power to monitor and veto company wage increases on an ad hoc basis. It also acquired the power to restrict and approve all advertising for man-power. This new power to control advertising lasted for the next five decades.[56]

Discussion also turned to the idea of using centralized bargaining with unions to force a downward leveling of actual wages closer to the negotiated minimum. Deviations above them would then be monitored and limited strictly according to skill and local living costs rather than the company's ability to pay. With the onset of a sharp recession late in 1920, engineering employers easily agreed the time was surely ripe for downward leveling. However, the newly elected and untested leader of the metalworkers' union refused to submit to re-ductions after the current contract expired. Now, for the first time since 1905, no central wage agreement was in force. Individual firms could freely raise or lower wages as they pleased. Workers in individual firms could also strike at will. The haphazard results were likely to be decidedly unsolidaristic and diffi-cult to cleanse out of later centralized agreements. Consequently, Edström and the rest of the VF board sought emergency powers. VF, they thought, should be empowered to promulgate binding directives against excessive pay levels and to fine and expel firms for violations. With powers of unilateral solidarism, they hoped VF could keep uneven increases resulting from renewed competi-tion over labor when the economy picked up again.[57]

Emergency powers were easier proposed than passed. Expecting objections, the board dropped the idea of seeking permanent authority. Gunnar Jacobs-son of Atlas Diesel led the fierce protest against even a temporary arrange-ment. An industrial manager's freedom of action in our days, he said, was so circumscribed by laws and regulations (he did not mention unions) that noth-ing much was left. Now "those small remains" were supposed to be handed over to an employers' association, he fumed. Preserving flexibility, he argued, required "paying qualified people well" and because "competition with other firms often compelled wage increases." Hugo Hammar, Edström's friend and ally, and like him a leading champion of friendly centralized relations with unions, countered that at least firms would be handing over freedom of action to an authority under their own direct control.[58]

Jacobsson spoke for over one fourth of the votes exercised by industrialists assembled, many of them small ones, which was enough to deprive Edström of the qualified majority he needed. In what must have been a tense drama, Ed-ström and the rest of the board then tendered their resignation. After retiring to fashion a compromise, they returned with a proposal requiring preliminary consultations with regional groups and a qualified majority in the board for approval of binding directives. In his statement before the vote on the compromise, Edström warned that the life of the organization was at stake. Receiving a vote of confidence with the passage of the proposal, he resumed leadership of the engineering association.[59]

Now the association's leadership could unilaterally dictate the structure of wage reductions across the industry, without the help of centralized bargaining. In addition to imposing a downward leveling of wages across firms, and eliminating coffee breaks, washup time, and like concessions, VF leaders seized the opportunity to do the kind of thing other sectors accomplished through collective bargaining: order member firms to eliminate all in-kind company benefits, such as free medicine, free or subsidized housing, and other "necessities."[60] Any firms that had instituted profit sharing were possibly told to give it up. Two years earlier, in 1919, VF and SAF's von Sydow had jointly declared their disapproval of profit sharing, which "in reality is simply an augmentation of wages" in violation of solidarism.[61]

Centralized bargaining relations in engineering resumed the following year, helped along with a lockout threat backed by SAF. VF's emergency authority to issue solidaristic directives was suspended. To some extent, it no longer needed them, because now the association could simply veto company-level agreements that deviated substantially from the central VF-Metall agreement. Nevertheless, in following years, VF gradually accumulated more unilateral powers to monitor and control its members. A new rule taking effect in 1922 no longer allowed any local negotiations to take place without a VF representative present. VF also acquired the power to issue directives "concerning both the implementation of contracts and wage and working conditions that are not regulated in such contracts." Furthermore, it acquired the new right to regulate "recruitment of manpower." Most notably, in 1929, VF legislated against "disloyal measures" like poaching (recruiting workers employed at other firms) or advertising without VF's approval. Finally, it strongly encouraged the use of public labor exchanges, whose primary task was to place workers not currently employed elsewhere.[62]

VF introduced its most important and innovative solidaristic measure in 1923, a functional though only partial substitute for the normal wage system, introduced first in textiles and recently appearing in other sectors, to put a lid on upward wage drift. That year, VF negotiated more than the usual adjustments to minimum wage scales, which many firms exceeded in practice. It also negotiated across-the-board increments to whatever "current" (utgående) wages were being paid above the minimums in individual firms. These new levels were now to constitute fixed maximums, frozen throughout the contract period. Firms could only raise (or lower) these current wages by entering a formal "voluntary agreement" with the union. But, of course, the VF representative whose presence was required at company negotiations would advise against it. Furthermore, the association's rules gave VF veto power over any such agreement before it could take effect. Advance approval was not a likely event.

This new system for capping wages was not wildly popular in the VF ranks. At a plenary meeting, attended by SAF's von Sydow who spoke on behalf of the new procedure, a majority of VF firms voted against it. The measure passed only because votes were allocated according to the size of a company's workforce. Thus, a minority of 76 firms, on average larger ones, casting 294 votes, prevailed over 77 members casting together only 215 votes.[63] From then on, firms that raised pay beyond those allowed in central agreements were vulnerable to highly intrusive investigations and fines or expulsion by the association. Within a few years, VF was forced to make a clear example out of a company whose executive actually sat on the board of the association. AB Pumpseparator was fined 25,000 crowns in 1926 when its larger competitor (AB Separator) submitted a blistering complaint about the smaller company's pay bonus.[64]

In another instance, many years later, Volvo and Saab-Scania were fined 200,000 and 100,000 crowns respectively for similar unauthorized pay increases.[65] This spectacular event took place, in 1978, when solidarism was undergoing decay, and if the truth be known, helped speed up the process. It was only possible because of associational authority acquired during an equally uncertain period of change in the 1920s. Solidarism in the engineering industry evolved successfully until then, in part, because it was so successful in protecting managerial rights. However, it ended up costing employers a large loss of freedom to their own associations. Collectively, sometimes only begrudgingly, they came to accept the principle that their self-interested individual behavior in competition over labor under conditions of labor scarcity needed heavy mutual oversight and control.

From Intersectoral Conflict
to Cross-Class Alliance:
The 1920s

Tense relations plagued the engineering employers' association during the building of solidarism. Difficulties were, if anything, even greater across industrial sectors. Disunity in the 1920s and early 1930s brought SAF to the brink of fracture at its sectoral joints. In 1932, while SAF struggled with the worst crisis of its existence, it was the Social Democratic labor movement that stepped in to redeem employers' faith in the lockout and hold their solidaristic project together. Its friendly intervention, triggered by an ostensibly hostile lockout threat, boded well for relations between capital and labor for many years to come.

The Intersectoral Problem

By the early 1920s, centralized and increasingly uniform wage determination for Sweden's industrial labor force had taken root at the national level within all major industries. It did not however, bridge across industrial sectors, and that was a disturbing flaw. Solidarism—restrained leveling of wages—within one industry could be destabilized by large disparities in wages and other working conditions across industry lines. Employers in the same product markets often faced different labor market constraints across the vast geographical expanse of Sweden. Labor mobility and the spread of militant worker demands for equalization within regions threatened uniform conditions and internal relations within sectoral associations. Employers in shared labor markets, in turn, faced profoundly different problems in their separate product markets. Resulting conflicts of interests between and within sectoral associations made unity within SAF about when, where, and even why to spend scarce resources on lockouts anything but easy to generate.

In 1920, for example, textile employer leader Wilhelm Paues hotly criticized engineering employers for letting their wages drift too far above VF's negotiated minimums. His and other industries, unfortunately, "were forced to follow along in order to retain their workers." Because of "mutual competition among employers over labor," SAF chief von Sydow agreed, "the minimum wage principle had been abused" in engineering. VF had not yet discovered a way to cap wage movement like the normal wage system that Paues had helped introduce in his sector. Engineering employers defended themselves, claiming that normal wages in their sector would require an excessively complicated array of distinct wage groups.[66]

Engineering employers also claimed injuries from abusive wage setting in other sectors. Their main grievance, of long standing, was of course not against lower paying textile employers. The biggest thorn in their sides was the high, uneven, unstable pay in building and construction. Within a year after Edström took control of the engineering employers' association in 1916, he finally arranged for VF to join SAF. As a firm believer in SAF's role of imposing order across sectors, he hoped to use his large association's influence in the confederation to get control over builders' wages. It was no coincidence then that within a year, in 1918, SAF incorporated the heretofore independent association of building contractors, the Central Employers' Association (*Centrala Arbetsgifvareförbundet*). There was no question about the purpose of the move. Wage policy was now to be "planned in full concordance among the spokesmen of industry as far as possible and within the limits set by the different industries' particular conditions." Without coordination, the risk was too great "that wages are driven up excessively within one sector, whereupon it is difficult to prevent the spread of increases to the others."[67]

SAF's exorbitant intervention in the 1920 conflict in the building trades followed, bringing normal wages to the sector. But a rapid shift away from standardized time wages to piece work brought runaway earnings and dashed all hopes that normal wages could solve the problem. In 1921, VF representatives pleaded the "indisputable necessity" of bringing construction wages down in "greater uniformity with wages in other industries." Meat processing was another problem; like the building trades, it was sheltered from the international price competition engineering had to face head on.[68] VF, in other words, wanted SAF to coordinate a downward leveling of wages across industries while trying to accomplish the same within its own. VF's pleas were repeated by a multi-industry group of industrialists in fifteen mining, forest products, engineering, and chemical companies. For them, lumber producers were also a nuisance, along with the building trades. They had been untouched by the international depression for the same reason that the building trades were paying so well—the postwar building boom.[69]

During a discussion of the issue at the November 1921 meeting of the SAF board, Axel Ivar Swartling of the steel industry went so far as to call for "leveling out the wage differences in different industries" and "maintaining a fully uniform wage level." But von Sydow would only endorse the more realistic hope of "balancing the wages in different industries more uniformly than is the case under current conditions."[70] Even that was a bit overoptimistic, because SAF lacked effective authority to force entire associations into lockouts against their will, which would have been necessary to bring a quick end to the problem. A lockout lacking broad support in an industry was sure to result in mass resignations. Such was the case in construction, where contractors faced little market discipline and saw little reason to lower wages.

Thus, in the 1920s consensus around a goal of downward wage leveling across industries was forming, especially among manufacturers. Therefore, SAF's resources were best spent restraining and reducing wages in sectors like building and construction. By necessity, this meant letting upward leveling occur when labor market and union pressures so dictated, for SAF was reluctant to spend scarce money and membership goodwill in support of lockouts to help low-wage sectors stay low. In 1922, when the Building Materials Association (*Byggnadsämnesförbundet*) requested permission and support for an industry-wide lockout to maintain the status quo on wages, SAF turned it down. Wages in the sector, SAF argued, were already very low relative to the rest of industry.[71] In 1928, a few years later, von Sydow rebuffed steel employers' request for SAF's help in enforcing restraint on wage increases in the sawmill industry, which were threatening to pull up wages in steel. Wages at sawmills, he said, did not exceed the median wage level in industry as a whole.[72] SAF needed to apply pressure at the other end of the wage spectrum.

Beyond Solidarism's Reach: Iron Ore Mining

One problem area was iron ore mining, where wages seemed to know no limit. In 1925, the vast Grängesberg mining operations conceded astonishingly large wage increases on the order of 18.2 percent in its northern mines and between 8 and 10 percent in central Sweden. Before that, Grängesberg's wages were already high—well over 20 percent higher than other miners' wages in central Sweden, for example. Howls of employer outrage followed Grängesberg's act of "crass selfishness." The deal had been made "behind SAF's back," that is, in willful violation of the confederation's rules, dating back to 1906, requiring its "collaboration and approval" in the negotiation of all contracts.[73] Grängesberg was fined and resigned from SAF.

Only the year before, iron mine operators had forced through an 8 percent reduction in wages for miners—to take place in January 1925. The shutdown of the German steel industry and cancellation of orders for Swedish ore when France occupied the Ruhr had justified the reductions. In the meantime, however, France withdrew and demand for iron ore rose dramatically. Militant miners now extracted not only a reprieve from the reduction but a stunning increase. In its defense, Grängesberg pleaded, its export operations brought in more than 10 million crowns a month in foreign currency. A long strike or lockout would have been a disaster for the entire country. Also, SAF could not have come close to providing sufficient lockout support. Normal strike insurance payments to Grängesberg, calculated on the basis of the number of workers employed in the company, would have been minuscule compared to the sums the company would lose should it try to hold out alone. Extra help was not possible, for SAF had just spent huge sums in a successful multi-industry lockout in March 1925, the biggest and most expensive mass lockout of the entire decade, to help freeze wages in engineering and other export sectors. They had been under market and union pressure spilling over from the building trades.[74]

Punitive action against Grängesberg was in order, for notice had to be served to other employers who might consider similar opportunistic action down the road. But its fine of 500,000 crowns had to be reduced to 275,000 crowns to entice it back into SAF. Other more surprising concessions were offered. Because of its peculiar importance in export trade, unlike the other mining operations, the Grängesberg concern was allowed to form its own "association" (*Grängesbergskoncernens Gruvförbund*) for three of its four subsidiaries, formally equal in status to other SAF associations like VF that encompassed entire sectors.[75] As an association in its own right, the firm was also to enjoy unprecedented privileges, like an informal promise from SAF to refrain from ordering it into all except general sympathy lockouts for other associations whose interests were overlapping, including other mines in central Sweden. Defending this extraordinary exemption, SAF pointed out that it had actually never forced whole associations into sympathy actions (an impracticality sure to result in mass defections), though individual companies within associations agreeing to a sympathy action could be forced to participate. In lieu of participation in sympathy lockouts, Grängesberg was to be assessed 5 crowns a day for every one of its workers who remained employed during sympathy lockouts, up to a certain limit.[76]

Of greatest interest here was Grängesberg's formal carte blanche to pursue whatever wage strategy it wished—in other words, pay as much as it pleased in order to avoid a conflict—on the sole condition that it do so in constant consultation with SAF. In fact, the company's high wages were not to be brought down to the vicinity of normal levels until the late 1960s, which contributed to the famous wildcat strike at the LKAB mines and a crisis for LO in 1969, which had fully sanctioned their downward leveling. Possibly because SAF desired to keep as many rank-and-file employer members as possible in the dark about the Grängesberg's strange privileges, the press, according to the agreement, was to be informed only about the fine and readmission. No other company or association in SAF, in the end, ever sought or achieved such privileges.[77]

SAF in Crisis: Fractious Politics in Forest Products

In the summer and fall of 1931, SAF faced another, more serious crisis. Dismemberment of the organization was under way and hopes of maintaining the solidarity necessary for overarching intersectoral wage control were rapidly fading. In August, Christian Storjohann, an important pillar of the unified employer community, pulled his large paper and pulp company, Billerud, out of its sectoral association and therefore out of the confederation. Once a fiercely independent and autocratic employer, Storjohann transformed into one of Sweden's leading advocates of employer solidarity and strong authority in SAF to forge centralized and friendly relations with unions. He was instrumental in negotiating the compromise with Grängesberg.[78] Now he was returning to the ranks of the independents, vexed by difficulties past and present in lining up support from other firms and sectors for defense of his company's and sector's interests. Among the remaining independents were a number of other major pulp producers, the Kempe (M.D.), Versteegh, and Hedberg concerns, led by unrepentant foes of negotiated solidarism. These were the firms that had sorely tested Storjohann's previous solidarity with SAF, taking opportunistic advantage of employer solidarity by continuing production and sales during lockouts.[79]

Other problems in achieving unity in the sector arose from the organizational division of the forest products industries into three independent associations for each of its main segments. Sharing labor markets, they operated under highly varying constraints, determined by their distinct product markets, on their efforts to deal with wage problems.[80] Lumber and pulp producers, for example, were price makers in world markets and could therefore recover some costs of big lockouts by cashing in on the higher prices generated by resulting shortages. Paper manufacturers, facing far more competition abroad, were price takers. Also, in 1931, pulp producers more eagerly than others in forest products joined a lockout, for they had committed themselves to reduce output by 30 percent over the course of 1932 in an international cartel agreement with Finnish, Norwegian, German, Austrian, and Czech producers.[81] Another equally severe problem arose from the fact that wages were relatively low in much of the forest products sector. Therefore, tt was not a priority for SAF's efforts. For example, while engineering employers would concede that the pulp industry was about the most in need of reductions early in the depression, they believed its workers to be, as one put it, among "the worst paid." Other sectors should get priority if VF were to make such sacrifices.[82]

Despite all these complications, SAF began discussing a multi-industry sympathy lockout on behalf of the pulp industry in summer 1931. In response to strikes, it had locked out pulp workers since February 23, almost five months. But Storjohann predicted that lack of unity would prevent SAF from taking the immediate and resolute sympathy actions necessary to accomplish any reductions that Billerud could benefit from. For this and other reasons, he decided to disobey the lockout and go back into production.[83] Insufficient solidarity from SAF had already been his experience three years earlier, in 1928, when SAF only begrudgingly, it seemed, extended itself in a sympathy action. For the industry as a whole, to be sure, some good things had resulted on that occasion. Most of all, it had helped weed out growing "excrescencies" (*utväxter*) in piece rates, especially in the northern parts of the country, and therefore accomplished some significant downward leveling. Extreme irregularities in wages "for roughly equal performance at different factories," a deplorable state of affairs in SAF's view, had been planed off. Some welcome reductions and standardization of company benefits, like paid vacations and medical care, were accomplished.[84]

The 1928 results had been bought, however, in exchange for some upward leveling, most notably at the expense of Storjohann's central Sweden, where wages were lower. SAF calculated the wage reductions to have been worth about 700,000 crowns a year, while the increases amounted to only 50,000.[85] Storjohann blamed lack of solidarity in SAF for the need to accept this upward compression. His efforts to drum up early and strong support for the lockout had been met with annoyance by other employers who were seeing better times ahead and looking forward to peaceful and acceptable settlements with their unions. Those included engineering and steel employers; VF and JBF had stalled throughout.[86] Now, expecting the same lack of sympathy once again, he broke with SAF in 1931.

SAF reacted with intense alarm. Textiles leader Bergengren warned of SAF's demise if many other employers acted so selfishly. In more diplomatic tones, Edström wrote to his friend Storjohann warning him gingerly that "in the long run we don't win by breaking off."[87] Within a day or so, Storjohann's predictions of deficient solidarity received confirmation when Carl Wahren, an SAF board member, gave notice of his plans to pull Holmen Bruk, a paper company, out of SAF and PBF. Wahren's move was ostensibly in protest against a mutual insurance agreement among the three forest product industry associations to supplement SAF's assistance. Ironically, this arrangement was one of Storjohann's earlier accomplishments on behalf of solidarity. Two more paper companies gave similar notice, both run by another SAF board member, hoping to persuade Wahren to stay. Protracted crisis negotiations ensued, but failed to remedy the damage. Instead, a landslide of other paper firms followed, constituting close to 85 percent of PBF's combined workforce.[88]

With the forest products sector crumbling, engineering employers were not likely to rise in enthusiastic solidarity with the paper pulp producers. VF board member Georg Ahlrot, director of the Kockums shipbuilding firm, argued that SAF was "demanding too much of VF." Like steel, engineering was working things out quite nicely with Metall. Therefore, SAF, he felt, "could not demand that these employers go into a lockout for the others."[89] The prospects for getting VF to join in multi-industry solidarity darkened further in late September 1931, less than two months after Storjohann's resignation, when Sweden followed Britain off the gold standard. The depreciation of the crown reduced effective wage costs in those industries from about the highest of their international competitors to lower than the majority—more or less what they wanted to accomplish by joining in a lockout for a simultaneous reduction across industries.[90] Self-interest spoke clearly for letting the pulp industry go it alone. Unity in SAF was coming apart at its sectoral seams.

The Labor Confederation
to SAF's Rescue

In 1928, three years before he resigned his leadership posts and took Billerud out of PMF and SAF, Christian Storjohann made a remarkable claim—and in that context, a strange proposal. LO, along with the Social Democratic Party, he claimed, was "on our side." They too were bothered by militant Communists who mobilized workers to vote against acceptable wage agreements hammered out at the bargaining table with SPIAF, LO's Paper Workers' Union. Billerud's older workers and their representatives would also "greet Communism's destruction with the greatest pleasure," or so he heard from the top LO leadership. But LO was not yet ready to come out publicly with such a stand. It was actually obligated to find support for pulp workers locked out for vetoing contracts and continuing strikes.[91]

Then came the strange proposal. Storjohann called for an immediate and massive expansion of the lockout to include another 107,000 workers, mostly in steel, engineering, and textiles.[92] In the same breath he praised LO as an ally and then advocated a frontal assault against it. The logic was simple, however: attack a friend to give it the pretext to intervene against a common enemy. But the argument did not persuade. SAF leader Hjalmar von Sydow, growing increasingly pessimistic about lockouts, worried that LO was gaining an alarming amount of financial clout by recruiting workers in the public sector. The additional membership dues strengthened their ability to hold out during lockouts in the private sector. A case in point was the railroad workers' union, which "never occasioned expenses and only brought income." Von Sydow rejected Storjohann's plan for an immediate and broad-scale assault, arguing that LO and public opinion would only be inflamed and provoked into supporting pulp workers against SAF if it widened the conflict. SAF therefore escalated slowly, only in small increments, bringing the extremely disappointing results that provoked Storjohann's later resignation.[93]

Storjohann's idea of rolling out the big cannon in expectation of an immediate and favorable result, probably without even having to fire it off, was not unprecedented. SAF had leveled threats of massive lockouts against LO in 1906 after the December Compromise and again in 1908, even though the labor confederation had discouraged the very actions against employer absolutism that triggered the threats. Indeed, the lockouts did not have to be executed in either instance, because LO subsequently intervened to SAF's satisfaction. That is what Storjohann seemed to expect again in 1928. Ironically, SAF finally resorted to the Storjohann strategy in 1932, shortly after Storjohann himself left the confederation in despair of it ever acting so resolutely again. In the interim, von Sydow, simultaneously chairman and executive director of SAF until 1931, had retired. Sigfrid Edström took over the chairmanship, with Gustaf Söderlund as executive director. Perhaps it was a new, more optimistic leadership that made the difference. Another irony is that Storjohann had been responsible for suggesting Söderlund in response to Edström's inquiries in 1930 about a suitable replacement. Edström, Storjohann knew, wanted someone who was liked and trusted by leaders of the labor movement for better communication across classes.[94]

Through such trusting communication with LO, Söderlund came to believe a big lockout would only have to be threatened, not executed. LO chairman Edvard Johansson, it seems, signaled clearly that the conflict would be brought to an end immediately after a lockout materialized, according to a report from Söderlund to PMF. In other words, LO would quickly intervene against the paper workers' union in order, we can assume, to save money. If intervention did not work right away, LO would extend the symbolic support to workers in the paper mills, though continuing to withhold it from pulp workers. SAF was not going to regard this as a hostile action. Thus, in a memo from SAF to its sectoral associations, Söderlund argued that the threat alone would be enough. On those grounds, the iron and steel association, for one, was able to agree to the lockout plan.[95]

In the end, SAF managed to gather agreement in 1932 behind a large and rapidly escalating multi-industry sympathy lockout threat to support paper pulp manufacturers. The official plan called for taking out all paper mills first, and within four weeks, all saw mills, engineering firms, and steel mills. Finally, if this proved insufficient, textile manufacturers were to follow shortly, and then some further unspecified sectors. As expected, the threat worked. Only three days passed before the pulp workers abandoned their five-month long battle.[96]

Söderlund had good reason to trust LO's signals. The labor confederation's leadership had done nothing but openly disapprove of the pulp workers' actions. It had consistently refused to extend financial support, even a loan, for the locked out pulp workers (a choice LO could exercise having withheld official approval for the initial strike actions that triggered the lockout). It had pressured the union to concede wage reductions. It had backed the Transport Workers' Union in rejecting a request from pulp workers for sympathy action in the form of a refusal to handle pulp stockpiles that were making their way onto the market. Transport actually expelled a number of members who boycotted pulp shipments.[97] Even much of SPIAF's leadership had been reluctant to sanction the strikes, but buckled under pressure building up from intense Communist agitation among the ranks of SPIAF members. Internal SAF discussions warmly acknowledged LO's restraint and efforts to persuade SPIAF to settle and cautioned against doing anything to antagonize the confederation.[98]

In short, the mass lockout was aimed directly at a labor confederation that had, from the beginning, in its very own words, "tried with all means to prevent the outbreak [of the dispute], and likewise once it broke out, took pains to make it go away."[99] The threat gave LO the ideologically respectable pretext of capitalists' overwhelming power display to intervene. Under LO's pressure, SPIAF leaders assumed dictatorial authority explicitly denied to it by members voting in three contract referenda and finally brought the strike to an end. Wages were reduced across the board by 7 percent, a result that even Billerud would feel. Incentive pay rates were adjusted where earnings had risen too high so as to create a more even, solidaristic pay structure across firms. Pulp employers also hailed another victory for "an old demand" of theirs—substantial elimination of costly company benefits in the form of rent subsidies and free housing.[100] Solidarism prevailed, welfare capitalism suffered another major setback, and a cross-class alliance did the work.

Conclusion

In the half-decade or so before the Social Democratic Party's rise to power in 1932, organized employers in Sweden experienced alarming difficulties generating and maintaining unity behind a policy of intersectoral wage control. By and large, the policy meant controlling sectors where wages were high. This targeted strategy meant, at times, letting low wages rise. The policy had evolved as the next necessary step following extraordinary successes in imposing managerial absolutism, of eliminating paternalistic company benefits, and of compressing wages within sectors. The multi-industry sympathy lockout proved essential in the process. The problem now was to maintain the requisite organizational unity for imposing control across industries, especially to force through wage reductions mandated by low prices for internationally traded goods in the late 1920s and early 1930s. The too-frequent resort to lockout in order to reduce and level wages across the economy exhausted employers' resources and sorely tested patience with SAF's crucial weapon—indeed, its very reason for existence in von Sydow's view.

Less than two months short of the formation of a Social Democratic government on September 24, 1932, the employers' confederation's stunning lockout victory cleared the air of much pessimism and dissension. Unity behind the official lockout threat, directed at a friendly LO, was possible because the union leadership signaled that the threat alone would achieve the mutually desired effect. With this victory, pulp employers got significant wage reductions and elimination of social benefits in the paper pulp industry, a dangerously weak link in SAF's chain. This would not be the last time the lockout was put to this strange but effective use—to attack a Social Democratic labor confederation whose favorable attitude to SAF's solidaristic mission was abundantly clear.

5

CROSS-CLASS ALLIANCE

The Social Democratic Breakthrough

When the Social Democrats came to power in September 1932, it was anyone's guess what repercussions would follow for relations in the Swedish labor market. That the government lacked a majority in the Riksdag boded well for employers, though disunity across the bourgeois camp remained a problem. Would the government seize its chances to manipulate divisions among employers and the three parties to the right of the Social Democrats? Would it take advantage of creeping doubts in the bourgeois ranks about the benefits of wage reductions and lockouts? Would social democracy divide and rule?

Social Democratic control of the cabinet certainly did not make employers lockout-shy in any case. Within a year, SAF threatened a gigantic sympathy action, bringing a quick end to a protracted 10-month conflict in the building and construction trades. Gratified by a 1934 editorial in *Dagens Nyheter,* a leading Liberal newspaper, SAF's executive director Söderlund noted that lockouts were not as unpopular as "we had reason to fear earlier." Employer leaders excitedly congratulated each other on their most important solidaristic victory ever—a dramatic downward leveling of wages in the building trades, and in the process, between that sector and manufacturing. As building activity resumed, SAF's vice director Ivar Larson marveled to the leader of the Finnish employers' confederation that the lockout weapon "has not been blunted," but rather "still has its old edge." Two years later, Larson glowed with satisfaction that SAF had been extremely successful in controlling wages and that other basic contract terms had in no way been "softened up." They were "if anything even sharpened." In sum, despite social democracy, "the Swedish employer is still lord of his manor" (*herre i sitt eget hus*), he boasted to his Finnish correspondent. Thus, SAF remained, in its own estimation, "one of the most powerful industrial employers' organizations the world over."[1]

The Building Trades Conflict, 1933–1934

High wages and worker militancy in building and construction deeply disturbed virtually all other employer groups in SAF for the last three decades. As intersectoral problems went, similar conditions in iron ore mining paled in comparison. Ironically, employers had to wait until the Social Democratic Party's rise to power to put an end to the misery. Did success come despite or because of social democracy's advances? The answer, all evidence indicates, is that the new political conditions actually improved employers' chances, for the simple reason that the Social Democratic labor movement shared interests in bringing the building trades to heel. By intervening forcefully to do so, it assisted employers in achieving their most valued solidaristic goal ever.

But first employers had to prod it into action, and in a big way. Christian Storjohann's logic of attacking a friendly LO to force it into action against a common foe, proposed in 1928 and applied effectively in 1932, proved stunningly useful once again in 1934. LO had shown nothing but chilly indifference, if not outright hostility, to strikes in the building trades, which started where contractors began imposing wage reductions after expiration of the previous contract. When building contractors retaliated with a sector-wide lockout, lasting 45 weeks in all, the labor confederation made sincere but unsuccessful efforts to persuade its building trades unions to settle on terms acceptable to SAF. In the end, after considerable difficulty in summoning agreement, the employers' confederation finally declared its plans to escalate by shutting down virtually all the remaining private sector economy—that is, to administer a good therapeutic "bleeding" (*åderlåtning*) of LO's funds.[2]

As in 1932, all SAF had to do was rattle its mighty sword to get its way. The smaller lockout, so far confined to the building trades, was finally brought to an end on February 14, 1934. LO responded predictably and appropriately to the threat of escalation. "Normal" hourly wages, which applied to only a small proportion of construction workers, were reduced between 6 and 12 percent. More important, because most building tradesmen now worked for piece rates, LO forced Stockholm workers to accept drastic reduction of their rates by 30 percent; lesser "excrescencies" elsewhere were cut between about 12 and 16 percent. Even more important for the long run, the industry's "chaotic," "degenerate," and "grotesque" system of piece rate setting was thoroughly reformed and highly centralized. From now on, it was going to be impossible for militant sit-down strikes at the building site to rebuild the sharp peaks in the comparatively high and uneven pay structure. Wages that had reached 115 percent of their 1922 level in 1932 now fell below that level in 1934. Furthermore, disputes about contract interpretation were now, as in other sectors, to be settled not by private arbitration but by the Labor Court, where other industries' interests were directly represented. Best of all for SAF as a whole, the highly invasive surgery on wage practices within the sector brought a more compressed, solidaristic pay structure across industry lines.[3]

The Intersectoral Problem

The outcome represented a monumental breakthrough for employers and a watershed in the evolution of Swedish solidarism. Among the most jubilant were those in Sweden's dynamic export-oriented engineering industry, SAF and VF chairman J. Sigfrid Edström among them. Not always particularly eager to take decisive action in support of Storjohann and the lower-pay forest products industry, he was probably among the most insistent advocates of multi-industry action in 1934. As head of Sweden's most important electrical engineering firm, and like other employers in engineering, he had long recommended using SAF to impose control across sectoral lines between export industry and trade-sheltered sectors like food processing and construction. He had helped ensure that wages in engineering rose to only 155 percent of their 1913 level by 1929. By contrast, wages at building sites and in other sectors sheltered from international competition had increased between 185 percent and 210 percent. In 1930, while other industries suffered from the worldwide depression, "uncommonly lively" building activity brought more wage increases, putting salt in engineering employers' wounds.[4]

In 1926 the engineering employers' journal *Verkstäderna* published an essay by the young economist Bertil Ohlin, a future Liberal Party leader and Nobel Prize winner, identifying the divergence in wages between manufacturers in internationally traded goods and trade-sheltered construction as one of the most important economic problems facing all industrial countries in the 1920s, not just Sweden. Georg Styrman, VF's executive director (under chairman Edström), explained five years later that Sweden was more afflicted than the rest, according to data he collected on wage differentials between engineering and the building trades in European countries. In Stockholm, he found, carpenters were paid over 190 percent and bricklayers 216 percent of what skilled metalworkers received; in Berlin, where the differentials were the next highest of the capital cities he looked at, they received only about 156 percent.[5]

One reason for the huge differentials probably lay in the long nordic winters, when low temperatures and short daylight hours made construction slow and often prohibitively costly. According to American estimates from the 1940s, mixing, placing, and curing mortar and concrete at freezing temperatures and after an early nightfall required extra heating, lighting, shelter, and up to a fivefold increase in labor hours for concrete work. To compensate for winters with little or no pay when construction ceased, and a feverish work pace during the short building season, workers in the trade demanded high wages. Contractors often quickly caved under the pressure, badgered as they were on the other side by anxious financiers and manufacturers eager to see their residential, commercial, and industrial properties finished on schedule. Some contractors, in painting, for example, were more or less indifferent about the wages they paid, so easy was it for them to pass on the costs.[6]

Though relatively unprotected from nature, this and other home market industries enjoyed shelter from import competition and its price discipline and could therefore more easily pass on high wages to other parties in higher prices. This phenomenon was repeatedly bemoaned in internal SAF and VF discussions. The problem became especially acute in the early 1920s, when construction boomed and the supply of skilled craftsmen dried up. Both were a result of the World War I period, when residential building stopped, and with it the training of apprentices. Feverish public sector building activity after the war made things worse by offering high pace-setting wages, contributing to skill shortages, and strengthening the unions by providing jobs to workers locked out in actions by private sector employers. Thus, although SAF was successful in holding down wages in internationally traded goods sectors, in "home market industries" according to SAF's year-end report for 1924, "the association has not been able to prevent significant wage increases." These trends were especially regrettable, for they further widened "the great gulf" between home market and export sector wages.[7]

High wages and militancy in construction hiked production costs and caused infuriating delays for manufacturers exposed to merciless international competition. Leading employers in SAF knew the problem intimately. As early as 1918, Edström complained to von Sydow about the constant rise of building costs for his company, ASEA. Particularly irritating was the need to enlist contractors whose laborers, organized by Syndicalists, received higher wages than skilled metalworkers. ASEA's office building, under construction for two years, had ground to a halt for the third time. Elsewhere, unfinished engineering facilities worth millions "stand idle month after month." Over a decade later, the problem remained. Erik August Forsberg of AB Separator (a leading exporter of dairy and other food processing machinery), complained that high wages in home market industries resulted in higher production costs than his competitors had to pay, especially in the building of industrial plant. In 1930, construction militancy delayed completion of steelmaking capacity at Hofors, which belonged to and supplied SKF, a big exporter of ball bearings, as well as at other steel companies.[8]

High wages and, therefore, prices in the building and food trades reduced manufacturing workers' living standards. Consequently, manufacturing employers hoped that restraining high rent and food costs rather than raising wages might soften demands for wage increases. Thus, manufacturers in engineering, whose wages were higher in the 1920s and 1930s than those of most competitors in Europe, believed that compressing the large intersectoral gap in wages would vent off wage pressures building up from below. In 1922, production at ASEA was at least once disrupted by wildcat actions against high rent charged workers by the company for use of its housing. The same housing, visited later in the 1930s by a delegation of Belgians studying friendly industrial relations in Swedish manufacturing, was an embarrassment to Edström. When a Belgian unionist expressed his astonishment that "big sprawling Sweden had such tiny hovels for worker housing," calling ASEA's workers "real cave dwellers," he was quickly informed of the reason—"enormous building costs."[9]

ASEA, like many major manufacturers, insisted on an "ancient right to have its own construction team" for extensive housing and other construction "in house" (*i egen regi*), often using regular production workers and paying them the lower wages of the engineering agreement. The practice helped remedy, at relatively low cost, the critical housing shortages toward the end of World War I. In forest products and steel, especially, in-house projects helped employers hoard workers during slack seasons, keeping them available later when orders picked up.[10]

By the late 1920s, however, complications intruded into in-house building operations. Metall, the metalworkers' union, came under steady pressure from building craftsmen to force engineering employers either to pay regular building trades wages for in-house work or to enlist properly paying outside contractors. Building craftsmen had accepted the principle of industrial unionism resolutely advocated by Metall and VF, relinquishing claims in the early 1920s on laborers, carpenters, electricians, plumbers, steamfitters, sheet metal workers, painters, and masons permanently employed in engineering. However, in exchange, Metall reluctantly promised to insist on outside contracting for larger projects involving housing, industrial plant, or major installation work. For this reason, decisions by the labor court put manufacturers' in-house work under threat. In the meantime, building craftsmen waged guerilla warfare against rural manufacturers, using secondary boycotts and other militant actions to gain or regain turf. Increasingly unable to use in-house jobs to circumvent payment of contract wages negotiated in construction, manufacturers became all the more determined to take the offensive against the source of the problem—the contracts themselves.[11]

Finally, high wages in the building trades spread pressures for wage increases across sectoral lines. Metalworkers, for example, set their sights on wages earned in the building sector, often craftsmen brought in to replace in-house work or to do major building and installation work. Metall's leadership took the heat, making it difficult for them to counsel restraint on behalf of export firms' interests. Wage pressures from building and construction were also transmitted through unmediated free market forces. Manufacturing employers had to compete in the same labor markets for workers moving back and forth across sectors, and the risk of spill-over was high if the differentials got out of hand, especially when labor markets were tight.[12]

An Arduous Search for Solutions

As early as 1907, the problem was already of such magnitude that it prompted discussion about cross-Scandinavian, not just cross-sectoral collaboration. That year, when Danish, Swedish, and Norwegian employers met to discuss common problems, one of the few substantive resolutions they made was to "keep earnings in the building trades roughly in line with earnings in other industries." The very same year, rising VF leader Edström apparently saw entry of his association into the employers' confederation as a first step in this direction. But he conditioned his participation in negotiations about VF's subordination inside SAF on the simultaneous participation of building contractors. At the time, they too remained outside SAF, in CAF (*Centrala Arbetsgivareförbundet*). The VF-SAF negotiations failed because of personal incompatibilities between VF chairman John Bernström and SAF's Hjalmar von Sydow. In 1917, shortly after Edström assumed the VF chairmanship, he quickly brought the engineering industry into SAF. Not coincidentally, building contractors were folded into the confederation the following year in the new Building Masters' Association (*Byggmästareförbundet*, or BMF).[13]

Organizational consolidation brought some action, limited results, and occasionally bitter intersectoral animosities. During the expensive 1920 lockout, contractors accused manufacturers of employing some 4,000 locked out building workers. They angrily entreated manufacturers to join BMF and pay dues for that proportion of their labor force engaged in in-house construction. In any event, they insisted, all in-house work should cease for the duration. "We have had our fill of fighting battles for manufacturing," according to a handful of Göteborg builders not particularly enthusiastic about the lockout. "Had we followed our own selfish interests we would immediately have accepted the workers' demands, for our work is free of foreign competition," they said. They were particularly furious about Grängesberg, which allegedly arranged a special train in order to employ striking building tradesmen in their Oxelösund iron mining operations.[14]

The 1920 action brought success in the form of the first national agreement, complete with centrally determined normal wages. But the success was temporary, for in subsequent years builders shifted workers from the new, highly restrictive normal wages into piece work, where rates and earnings could freely drift upward in a highly decentralized process. Then, in 1924, manufacturers stood helplessly by as alarmingly high wage increases appeared in that year's building trades agreements. Feverish building activity and labor shortages made it impossible for BMF and other specialist contractors' associations to maintain solidarity during the disputes leading to the agreements. Unorganized employers paid higher wages than those affiliated with SAF and ruthlessly stole jobs away from the loyalists. The profusion of organized contractors added to severe problems of dissension, indiscipline, and defections experienced by BMF in surrounding years.[15]

Manufacturers in SAF resorted to a huge lockout in 1925 in a holding action against wage pressures spilling over from the building trades. With this mammoth and expensive action, taking out engineering, paper, pulp, lumber, and textile, the employers' confederation also made LO pay dearly for some of its members' excesses. A very small dispute, measured by the number of workers and employers involved, triggered the massive escalation, which lasted 11 working days and idled about 130,000 workers in all. The initial conflict involved the two sides in electrical installation—the Electrical Employers' Association (*Elektriska Arbetsgivareförbundet*, EAF) and LO's Electricians' Union (*Elektriska Arbetareförbundet*). Electrical installation of heavy engineering products, generators and hoisting machinery, for example, was a bridge across engineering and building. Its ownership and labor force overlapped that of the engineering industry. Skilled electricians worked side by side with machinists in mixed production and installation work at the big electrical engineering firms ASEA and LM Ericsson, as also in shipbuilding and the steel industry. Edström's ASEA, in fact, maintained subsidiaries in the business, members of EAF, to carry out some assembly and installation of ASEA's products. Questions about which wages to pay bedeviled relations both within and between classes.[16]

The 11-day mass lockout, ending on March 30, 1925, succeeded temporarily in blocking the spread of wage increases from construction to manufacturing via electrical installation. It did practically nothing to relieve wage pressures emanating from their point of origin. The long-term problem was that organized employers employed only about a third of workers in building and construction. In residential construction, for example, where many builders were not members of BMF, unorganized employers often paid wages exceeding contract levels. The large majority of workers were union members, by contrast. During lockouts, new contractors would, according to SAF's yearly report for 1924, "shoot up like mushrooms from the earth and offer their services," making solidarity impossible. In manufacturing, by contrast, there was little risk that new entrants could so suddenly materialize.[17]

Among some SAF board members, defeatism reigned toward the end of the 1920s and early 1930s. Carl Wahren of the forest products industry claimed that "industry has continuously been injured by the association's membership in SAF" and therefore wished simply to expel BMF and wash their hands of troubles with the industry. The same sentiments were uttered by at least one leading figure in VF. Edström, now chairing both VF and SAF, fired back that excluding construction from SAF would be "reprehensible" (*förkastlig*) and called instead for better coordination and new solutions. For example, he had been an eager advocate of raising SAF's fees to increase support in the case of strikes and lockouts, which helped electrical installation to hold out as long as it did in 1925. That year he assumed his first leadership position in SAF and began agitating for measures to force unorganized contractors into SAF. Thus, he promoted the idea of contracting exclusively with organized firms, or supplying them with credit and materials at discounted rates, the costs of which would surely be lower than subsidization of construction's open conflicts.[18]

It was possibly Edström's initiative that led to SAF's offer in 1926 to subsidize the training of bricklayers, who were in scarce supply, an unprecedented solidaristic venture for SAF, which had always left vocational issues to its branch associations. Later he advanced the idea of hiring a special recruitment agent and "propaganda minister" whose sole task was to monitor solidarity and imprint "the idea of unity . . . in every member's inner self," so that members would "favor the whole above our individual selves." To encourage firms in their mutual dealings to discriminate in favor of other SAF members, he stood behind the introduction of a special SAF insignia to be printed on members' letterhead, advertisements, and brochures.[19]

Replacing von Sydow; Enlisting the Banks

In May 1929, Edström set in motion highly discreet efforts to find a replacement for the chairman and executive director von Sydow, who was nearing 70 years of age. One reason may have been that around that time, von Sydow had been blocking Edström's efforts to bring leading industrialists with close ties to big finance onto SAF's board of directors. Skandinaviska Banken, especially, needed representation. Von Sydow favored allocating available seats to smaller industrial sectors currently not well represented and of less interest to big bankers.[20]

Evidence suggests that Edström's efforts to take control of the succession process, to strengthen ties with the banking world, and to advance engineering's interests had a common purpose. With them, it seems, Edström was intent on firming up SAF's commitment to doing battle against wages in the building trades. In 1928, von Sydow had shown less than deep concern for engineering's interests by ignoring its urgent need for a representative intimately familiar with the sector in the new Labor Court. In this same year, von Sydow began expressing pessimism about the lockout, which Edström regarded as indispensable for employers' solidaristic mission. Even as Edström was busy looking for a replacement, new problems with the old leader surfaced, possibly reflecting past ones. Edström found "particularly repugnant" (*synnerligen motbjudande*) von Sydow's meddling in 1930 in engineering's affairs with regard to the sticky matter of wage setting in construction-related installation work. In 1931, von Sydow revealed that he had come under the influence of the idea of workers' "purchasing power" as a reason for thinking twice about too forceful measures for wage reductions. Edström, around the same time, sought to exorcize American businessmen's "theory of high wages" from the Swedish debate, for fear perhaps that it would reinforce the pessimism von Sydow had been expressing about lockouts.[21]

Until the early 1930s, bank cooperation with SAF appears to have consisted exclusively of large lines of credit for lockout support, with members' bonds as collateral. In the early 1920s, von Sydow seemed not to expect much else. That was to change under Edström's watch. In July 1930, well before SAF's official search committee for a new executive director was formed, Edström and a few close associates had already settled on Gustaf Söderlund. It was possibly no accident that the candidate had, as Stockholm city treasurer, close ties to the banking world. Banker Marcus Wallenberg, Sr., was directly involved in the decisive phases, and he even intervened to stop Edström from recruiting his favorite candidate, Vilhelm Lundvik. Wallenberg preferred to keep Lundvik at the head of *Industriförbundet*, the Swedish Trade Federation. Completely shut out of the decision making about his replacement, von Sydow left "not without some bitterness," as von Sydow's vice director Ivar Larson, an Edström antagonist, put it. Larson had seen himself as the rightful heir to von Sydow's throne.[22]

Söderlund's appointment as executive director in 1931 thus brought closer integration of SAF with the commanding heights of Swedish banking. That he moved into one of the three top positions in the Swedish banking world after leaving SAF in 1946, at Handelsbanken, is telling. This was the same kind of integration Edström had already created with VF, dominated as it was by export-oriented firms closely tied to the leading banks. Enskilda Banken, controlled by the Wallenberg banking dynasty, had long been ASEA's main bank connection, and relations between Edström and Marcus Wallenberg were close. In 1930, for example, Wallenberg bought a large share of ASEA to protect it from General Electric's international campaign to capture a stake in all major electrical engineering firms.[23]

During the 1920s, an uncontrolled supply of building credit for speculative purposes by banks and materials suppliers had made it possible for unorganized contractors to continue to build during lockouts. This money often went into the pockets as wages for workers locked out by BMF loyalists. With the conflict of 1933–1934, however, things changed. For the first time, SAF enlisted banks to impose a moratorium on building loans. Edström also set up a special emergency credit fund for builders under financial duress and therefore all too eager to appease unions to expedite their projects.[24] Big banks were now fully engaged in SAF's most important solidaristic project ever, brought into the picture by the country's preeminent engineering employer.

Forced Aid: The Threat of an Escalated Lockout

But bringing the big banks into the picture, and therefore harnessing the supply of credit, was not enough to alter the balance of power in building and construction to solidarism's advantage. For one thing, the moratorium on lending to builders was undercut by the extension of credit by disloyal materials suppliers. Vastly more important in the end was SAF's declaration of intentions to unleash a mass sympathy lockout against over 200,000 LO workers. About the only significant element of the economy to be excepted from the lockout was iron mining at Grängesberg.[25]

As the construction conflict dragged on through the winter of 1933, Edström and Söderlund firmed up SAF's plans for expanding the lockout, which so far had been confined to the building trades. Some groups, especially in forest products, fretted about what it would cost them to join a sympathy action. SAF leaders soothed their jitters with the same argument used in 1932—that the threat alone would probably suffice. In meetings on December 15 and 16, 1933, Söderlund and Edström announced their expectations that, in response to an enlarged lockout, the Social Democrats would move to impose a settlement via compulsory arbitration (*obligatorisk skiljedom*). The settlement, they were sure, would be better than what construction employers, losing patience, would gladly concede in the near future if left to their own devices.[26]

But Söderlund and Edström also hinted strongly at an even better possibility—that the threat of government intervention, made in response to the giant lockout threat, would push LO into action to forestall arbitration. But again, even in this case, a big lockout threat was necessary, for only a lockout could force the Social Democrats to take the first step, according to Söderlund. That eventuality, Edström implied, was a very good one, for the unions were "at least as strong opponents of compulsory arbitration as employers" and would step in for that reason.[27] Either way, threatening a big lockout was a winning strategy, in part because it would not even have to be executed.

In short, SAF would be targeting a friendly LO to force it to choose between intervention against its own unions and one of two worse options: compulsory arbitration, or a massive financial bleeding if the government did not impose arbitration. All things pointed in the direction of friendly intervention. SAF leaders had well-founded knowledge about highly paid building tradesmen's unpopularity. Three years earlier Edström had noted "criticism from other worker groups" as clear testimony that building wages were "out of line." Discussion of attitudes like these was not at all unusual at union and LO congresses in the 1920s and 1930s, where aversion to construction workers' tactics and ill will toward their high wages were openly expressed. SAF saw the current conflict as "unpopular among workers" and moderate LO leaders as tacit allies who also held Communists and Syndicalists responsible as prime instigators of the building conflict, especially in agitating for building craftsmen to vote against mediated contract proposals.[28]

Tensions within the labor movement about the economic advantages of workers in sheltered home-market industries expressed themselves in other ways known to SAF. One was in rank-and-file refusal to honor boycotts, as in the celebrated 1925 Skromberga bakers' conflict. Coal miners, whose wages were half those being demanded by union bakers, refused to boycott the cheap bread coming from bakeries able to continue producing. The Skromberga conflict, among other things, gave rise to an intensive debate within LO about the need to centralize power in LO to better serve the interests of low-pay unions, especially in sectors involved in international competition. Union clashed with union about low-pay workers' wages finding their way into the pockets of high-paid workers in the building and food trades. Leadership in this debate about using LO to establish centralized control was seized by Metall's section in Stockholm, where wage differentials between sheltered and traded good sectors were greatest. On the issue of wage compression across industries, its members apparently shared much in common with their employers organized in VF.[29]

LO's press statements beginning in May 1933, and then a statement by Minister of Social Affairs Gustaf Möller at a union congress two months later, strongly validated SAF's perceptions about building trade workers' unpopularity. Both attacked the striking workers for their crass selfishness and "guild mentality." Möller had recently eliminated rules so hated by the labor movement that withheld unemployment benefits or relief jobs to workers indirectly idled by strikes or lockouts—but kept them in force for workers in "seasonal industries," mostly populated by building trades workers.[30] These events no doubt emboldened SAF to reject a disappointing mediation proposal from no less than Per-Albin Hansson, the prime minister, in September 1933. Subsequent mediation proposals suited employers much better, but were rejected in the building workers' referenda. Finally, on February 1, SAF finally announced its plans for an expanded multi-industry lockout. Edström telephoned the prime minister around midnight to inform him of SAF's resolve to unleash the big lockout on schedule. At a meeting the next morning, he repeated the threat in person to Hansson and a number of cabinet members. This "evidently resulted in the government now using its influence to pressure the recalcitrant carpenters' and bricklayers' unions to give up their resistance," Edström concluded.[31] The pressure took the form, as SAF expected, of an announcement on the following day that compulsory arbitration legislation was ready for passage through the Riksdag.

In the following days, things proceeded as expected. A lead article in *Socialdemokraten*, a party mouthpiece, declared on February 8 that it was unreasonable to imagine that 200,000 workers suffering from a lockout should line up in solidarity with the building workers who put them in that undeserved situation. Pushed by impending government intervention it abhorred, and pulled by a convenient and popular pretext to fix things on its own, LO finally stepped in. Applying severe pressure through 14 February, LO persuaded the construction union leaders to agree to the third and final mediation proposal that SAF favored and workers had rejected. Ultimately the LO leadership even had to browbeat the chairman of the mason's union to violate his union's constitution and sign a contract—under a formal protest he inserted in writing.[32]

In short, as Söderlund put it as early as June 1933, although SAF's aims were not unpopular in much of LO, it could not count on any intervention from the labor confederation until sympathy measures targeted "quite a large number of workers."[33] That meant, of course, targeting LO as a whole and its finances in particular. Once again, as in 1932, the implicit and rather peculiar logic in the strategy was that SAF needed to launch a broad frontal assault on an ally to force it to turn on a common foe who was out of SAF's reach. The lockout would then hand LO leaders an ideologically respectable and popular pretext for shutting the building conflict down and letting employers have their way with deep wage reductions.

All in all, SAF spent over 6,000,000 crowns supporting the long lockout confined to the building trades and had in theory been prepared to spend much more on an escalated lockout. Jubilant with the success, Söderlund attributed it in part "to the political situation, which forced LO to accept and with all means try to drive home the settlement proposed by the mediation commission and to avoid compulsory arbitration legislation." However, he added, what really decided things was SAF's lockout decision, which moved first the Social Democratic government and then LO into action.[34]

The "Cow Trade" and
the Crisis Program

With his reference to the "political situation," Söderlund implied that building trades workers' high wages were not the only reason that the Social Democratic labor movement so willingly intervened to end the building trades conflict on solidaristic terms. Of greater immediate urgency was the political bind the minority Social Democratic government found itself in, trying to pass majoritarian measures to deal with depression levels of unemployment. The Agrarian Party (*Bondeförbundet*) was prepared to help, but declared it would withhold its pivotal votes for the government's large job creation program until the building conflict was settled. If the money were to be released before resolution, the argument went, building employers' brittle unity would pulverize as they scrambled to grab the contracts for roughly 100,000,000 crowns' worth of publicly financed building and construction projects.[35]

Employers had strongly criticized details of the program when it was proposed. But after the Social Democratic government and LO intervened, as the farmers insisted, imposing large wage reductions and reforming the woefully chaotic system of piece rate setting, material cause for objection vanished. For reasons explained later, the changes imposed had the effect of detoxifying the program and thus eliminated employers' reasons to fear damage to their solidaristic interests. In short, resolution of the building trades conflict, crucial to passage of the crisis program, brought employers into the heart of the coalition of interests usually regarded as an exclusive coalition of farmers and workers. Dominant employers in SAF came out winners too.

A watershed event in modern Swedish history, the deal with farmers followed a dramatic back-bench revolt against their current leader. Under new leadership, the Agrarian party promised to support the creation of large numbers of "emergency" jobs (*beredskapsarbeten*). Using a broad mix of building trades skills, the jobs would be contracted out to the private sector. About half would be in road works, and the remainder would mostly involve the construction and improvement of railroad crossings, bridges, waterways, excavations, and buildings. There would also be a number of more traditional "reserve jobs" (*reservarbeten*) involving unskilled labor in simpler projects. About 40 million was to be spent on cash assistance. Both borrowing and increased taxes would pay for the projects. To pay for farmers' support, the Social Democrats offered various protectionist measures for agricultural products.[36]

Employers had two main objections to the crisis program when it was first proposed in early 1933–before resolution of the building trades conflict. They feared that implementation of the program would make it utterly impossible to implement a lockout in the sector, a first step before moving on to the multi-industry sympathy lockout, should it prove necessary. There would simply be too much work for eager and disloyal contractors to pass up. The building employers' association, now called the Building Industry Association (*Byggnads-*

industriförbundet, BIF) insisted therefore that the proposed emergency works not get underway until new agreements were established for the building industry.[37]

Another chief complaint was that the program called for payment of high union wages for work on the older style reserve projects, as well as on the new emergency jobs. The old system of reserve jobs in the 1920s until the early 1930s provided wages below those negotiated by building trades and public sector unions for unskilled laborers. This was a deeper and potentially more long-term problem. It united employers in industry with those in rural enterprise, including farmers. All foresaw a loss of manpower and ruinous upward wage pressure if union wages were now to be paid for reserve jobs.

Saw and pulp mills, for example, worried about a drift of unemployed workers from the forest product industry into reserve jobs in other areas. They would then "find scarce reason to return to a job in the forest products, should one become available." In northern Sweden, union-negotiated piece rates for skilled carpenters in road and bridge works brought earnings of about 2.5 crowns per hour. In the six hours of an unskilled reserve job, at this rate, a carpenter would earn 15 crowns. By contrast, a full eight hours' work at a sawmill would not even yield 8 crowns. On hourly wages, a lumberjack earning 6 to 7 crowns in a 9-hour day would no doubt seek a reserve job on road works where he could earn 9 crowns a day or more in a 6-hour reserve job.[38]

Urban industries were nervous too. Stockholm building workers in 1931 received average hourly earnings of 2.89 crowns per hour, whereas adult male workers in the metal trades achieved an average wage of only 1.45 crowns. Engineering employers complained about having to compete for unskilled manual labor even with the earlier, more miserly reserve system, which did not pay union wages. In part, because of the free travel, housing, and sometimes health assistance attached to its jobs, reserve jobs brought earnings virtually equal to what was available in the regular labor market. Furthermore, because of negligent control of piece rates, and therefore lower work intensity required to reach targeted earnings, "actual wages relative to tasks performed," or unit labor costs, were not infrequently higher than in the regular labor market.[39]

Employers saw a long-term risk in the program's exacerbation of unemployment, the very problem it was supposed to solve. By holding private sector wages up, the job measures would hinder the adjustment of wages in other sectors to internationally competitive levels and reduce unemployment, according to E. W. Paues, the textile industry leader. Employers in forest products and engineering sounded the same alarm about "a pull of manpower from our export industries, where the wage levels, as is well known, are . . . far lower than in . . . the construction industry in the home market, a sector which would be especially favored in terms of subsidies." Paper pulp employers worried about losing their skilled electricians, mechanics, masons, carpenters, and others to the construction industry, with the ultimate effect of raising their own wage costs and perpetuating the problems of competing with low-wage countries like Finland. Engineering employers feared that high-paying emergency works would further aggravate the problem of "wages in home-market firms relative to export industry." Their workers would have every reason to be "tempted to look for some pretext to get these advantageous emergency jobs."[40]

SAF's executive director Gustaf Söderlund summarized these concerns in SAF's official response to the government about the proposed jobs program. He highlighted in particular the aggravating effect the program would have on the skewed wage differentials between different sectors. It would, he said, "cause private industry increased difficulties in their efforts to bring about the necessary leveling of the different wages." Söderlund also devoted painstaking detail to the wage-inflationary consequences of careless administration of piece rates in the construction sector, which were now proposed for emergency works. The "grotesque conditions" associated with piece rates in the building trades frustrated manufacturers in export industry more than they did contractors.[41]

By intervening as they did, Social Democratic party and union leaders eliminated problems in the design of the crisis program. Refusing to relax the requirement that union wages be paid, *they simply lowered the union wages instead.* In Stockholm, where the problem was by far the worst, building trades workers saw piece rates reduced by no less than 30 percent; elsewhere rates fell between about 12 and 16 percent. Because it also centralized piece rate setting in order to keep the rates down, it promised a long-term fix. Thus, the result for employers, in the long run, was actually better than simply relaxing the union standards provision.[42]

Furthermore, employers were actually unenthusiastic about substandard pay in the case of the new emergency projects, which, unlike the older reserve projects, required skilled building trade workers. They and conservative politicians, it seems, had been coming around to the view that paying less than standard wages made no economic sense for these essential public works, which the engineering and steel industries directly benefitted from. Hugo Hammar, a member of VF and SAF boards—and fervent peacemaker in class relations—noted in 1933 that "railroad facilities constructed in recent years at contract wage levels were cheaper than those that had been built as reserve jobs at lower wages." In the end, paying standard union wages for the new emergency works seems to have been practically uncontroversial; parties to the right of the Social Democrats only questioned the policy in the case of the old, unskilled reserve job system. Given that paying lower than standard wages on emergency jobs was inefficient, the optimal solution, which SAF got, was to lower the standards. [43]

Conventional discussions of the famous "cow trade" (*kohandeln*) of May 1933 between the Agrarian and Social Democratic parties ignore or glance over the labor movement's intervention in the building trades. Therefore, they characterize the deal, at least implicitly, as a "red-green" or labor-farmer coalition at capitalists' expense. But the intervention was as much an element of the deal as were the jobs program and agrarian protectionism. It was crucial to closing the deal. Manufacturing employers may have been unenthusiastic in principle about public works jobs programs—though many directly benefitted. But even assuming opposition (for the sake of argument), what they gave up was richly rewarded with reductions in building trades wages. "Logrolling," or giving up something of relatively little importance in exchange for something valuable, characterized the cow trade of the farmer-labor alliance of the 1930s. By that token, the cow trade and the cross-class alliance included capital and its solidaristic interests too.

Fortifying the Solidaristic Alliance: The Basic Agreement of 1938

In 1936, LO and SAF began negotiations producing the famous Basic Agreement (*Huvudavtalet*) of 1938 in Saltsjöbaden, a pleasant resort town in the Stockholm archipelago. Sometimes called the Saltsjöbaden Agreement, it is widely regarded as an important contributor to extraordinarily peaceful relations between labor and capital in Sweden for the next three decades. The most important provisions in the agreement between LO and SAF called for centralized mediation of disputes over the interpretation of contracts, elimination of certain conflict practices aimed at neutral "third parties," and special procedures for preventing the outbreak of "socially dangerous conflicts."

The principal reason both sides gave for this mostly procedural agreement was a mutual desire to head off legislative moves to regulate labor conflict. Both LO and SAF wished the parties in the Riksdag to halt the process moving rapidly in the direction of legislation. (The same logic had inspired LO's intervention in 1934 against building trade militants, when the Social Democratic government threatened compulsory arbitration in response to SAF's titanic lockout threat.) By and large, the Basic Agreement of 1938 restrained workers, not employers. About the only thing of substance that LO extracted in exchange was a one-week guaranteed notice before layoffs—as a rule—for workers with one year's employment. This was an exceedingly minor trimming of the absolute right to manage that employers had so forcefully carved out for themselves. By 1938, big firms in engineering were already experiencing renewed labor shortages, and the concession on layoffs would have cost very little. In fact, Edström had already floated the same idea to fellow industrialists two years earlier as something employers could offer workers in the way of economic security.[44]

Experts in Sweden today wonder why so much significance has been attributed to the Basic Agreement. Historian Klas Åmark, for one, rightly questions the causal importance of the actual details in the text of the Basic Agreement for long-term labor peace or cross-class consensus (*samförstånd*). Puzzling about the mythology surrounding the agreement, he speculates that the peace may have been secured not by the agreement itself but by a set of implicit and ultimately more important understandings that evolved simultaneously between the two confederations during the years leading to the formal agreement. In other words, simultaneous gentlemen's agreements, rather than the Basic Agreement itself, probably explain the prevailing harmony in labor market and political relations between capital and labor after the mid-1930s. One of the side agreements in this speculative unwritten "secret protocol" was a solidaristic one, Åmark says: both sides agreed that export industry should play the role of the "wage leader," while building wages should be held back. Thus, LO earned enormous good will from employers with its "brutal public rebuke," as Åmark puts it, of renewed militancy in the building trades in 1937—as the Saltsjöbaden negotiations proceeded.[45]

Secondary Strikes, Boycotts, and Strikebreaking

In his conjecture about solidarism and labor peace, Åmark is fundamentally correct, as the circumstances around the 1933–1934 building trades conflict indicate. But the cross-class solidaristic understanding was probably central, rather than peripheral, to important and explicit details in the Basic Agreement. One of the issues it was supposed to resolve was the use of secondary strikes and boycotts against "neutral" third parties—for example, of materials suppliers, transporters, lenders, and nonunion workers. Often these tactics were used in jurisdictional raiding or to force employers to hire only union members. Anathema to LO as well as SAF, the tactics were practically nonexistent in engineering and other important sectors. Because they appeared by and large in the trade-sheltered building and food industries, measures against them were measures against their high wages. Cross-class agreement to end them was, therefore, it stands to reason, solidaristic in nature.[46]

For the building trades unions, the particularly offending parts of the agreement were the prohibition of jurisdictional disputes and closed-shop tactics they used to force workers into unions or prevent them from quitting. Also, they objected to exclusion of their members from the guaranteed one-week notice before layoffs. It was not to apply to "seasonal trades," meaning, most significantly, building and construction. The unions' leaders, tellingly, had no input in its drafting. As late as 1989, more than fifty years later, they had still not signed the agreement, unlike other constituent unions of LO. The unions that did sign, along with LO, bound themselves to withhold all support for workers locked out in retaliation, rendering the protest ineffectual.[47]

The signatories did not, however, extract any controls on SAF's sympathy lockouts in exchange. These too, in a certain sense, were often directed at "neutral"—even friendly—third parties. Employers had possibly entered the Saltsjöbaden negotiations so eagerly to head off legislative precedents that might lead to restrictions on their most important weapon. Edström, for one, was fully familiar with how conservative parties had saddled Norwegian employers, their supposed allies, with legislative restrictions on lockouts.[48] Thus, LO tacitly acknowledged, by not even raising the issue, the value of sympathy lockouts for the emerging alliance. They, after all, had given the labor confederation the ideologically respectable pretext to assert solidaristic control where it was sorely lacking.

Åmark posits that a peripheral agreement in his speculative "secret protocol" might have called for SAF to suspend its use of strikebreakers and shut down strikebreaking organizations. Here Åmark takes his lead from a consensus among Swedish historians about an apparent disappearance of strikebreaking. Specifically, he argues, the disappearance of strikebreaking organizations might have been bought by LO's commitment to control Communists and Syndicalists. But any such deal, if it happened, would have predated Saltsjöbaden by several years. According to a history of LO by a long-time insider in the organization, Ragnar Casparsson, a tragedy at Ådalen in 1931, where the military killed five protesters and bystanders in a demonstration against strikebreakers, had brought "an end to the disturbing recruitment of strikebreakers during open conflicts." That may indeed have been SAF's official line. It was, in any case, what President Roosevelt's commission sent to study Swedish industrial relations heard in 1938, the year of the Saltsjöbaden Agreement. "We were told by officers of the employers Federation that this so shocked the people that no such attempt would again be made to use strike-breakers," the commission's report read.[49]

The strange truth is that strikebreaking did not disappear in the 1930s. SAF did not cut off funding for strikebreaking operations. In the two years after Ådalen, discussions proceeded unabashedly inside SAF about when and how to use strikebreakers—as if the Ådalen tragedy had never occurred. The main problem was that strikebreaking was hard to organize, and available workers were often "less-than-desirable elements."[50]

Instead of suspending support, SAF proceeded, albeit secretly and on a fairly small scale, through 1938 and beyond. Through the 1940s, SAF coordinated fund-raising efforts for strikebreaking organizations and contributed up to 17,000 crowns per year of its own money. For example, a certain V. Boyton received 5,000 crowns in overhead from SAF in 1944 for his "labor bureau." *Boytons Arbetsbyrå* was the private outfit that delivered strikebreakers to Ådalen for loading paper pulp in 1931. It had also been active in the construction branch, helping out, for example, in 1926 with a major bridge project. *Arbetets Frihet*, a private agency that proved especially useful in forest products and the building trades, received 5,000 crowns yearly from the confederation through most of the 1940s. SAF came to its rescue in 1943 when the agency, financially strapped, lacked the overhead for procurement efforts on behalf of an important rural construction project. The confederation reinstated its earlier contribution of 5,000 crowns, after having reduced it to 4,000 the year before. It also persuaded paper pulp employers to reconsider the withdrawal of their usual support of 2,000 crowns and endeavored to round up new support from associations inside and outside of SAF. SAF continued to contribute to *Arbetets Frihet* through the 1940s, finally phasing out its support in 1951.[51]

Indeed, it would have been reckless for SAF to swear off strikebreaking. Suspension of the activity would have undermined its own solidaristic goals.

Strikebreaking in the building sector, more than anywhere else, had proved an indispensable tool. In this sector, the lockout proved worthless for controlling many militant workers and their special tactics. As von Sydow pointed out, the lockout had leverage only when and where workers depended on strike funds and their unions wanted to economize on their expenditure. That was not so much the case in the building trades. Ingemar Flink's data show, therefore, that between 1926 and 1935, strikebreakers were deployed to deal with as many as 120 strikes in building and construction. In all the lumber and forest products industries, they were used in only 75, and across the metal industries, where strikebreaking was regarded as practically useless, only 11. Syndicalists and Communists led many strikes in these sectors, and because LO could not control them, it would have been foolhardy to drop strikebreaking and count on LO alone, as Åmark speculates, to clean up matters.[52]

If indeed SAF and LO came to a secret side agreement at some point in the 1930s, consistent with the evolving solidaristic alliance, it would have committed LO to desist from exposure and criticism of SAF's continuing strikebreaking activities. By serving shared solidaristic interests, LO would serve its own organizational ones. SAF's strikebreaking helped strengthen the reformist labor movement, as Ivar Larson planned to remind LO in 1933. By targeting the measure at Syndicalists and Communists, the confederation cleared the way for LO to assert better control over the building trades. In the mid-1920s, SAF had concluded that strikebreakers were to be removed after successful actions. Thus, LO would have a good shot at replacing them, leaving the strikebreakers available for actions elsewhere. However, even in the Depression year of 1933, executive directors Söderlund from SAF, Karl Wistrand from the steel industry, and Georg Styrman from engineering all bemoaned the LO unions' inability to "procure sufficient manpower" to substitute for strikebreakers. "We, through our actions against Syndicalists, are fighting LO's battle," said Ivar Larson, SAF's assistant executive director. But LO, he complained, proved unable, if not unwilling, to round up enough workers.[53]

Thus, LO leaders had good reason to suppress its criticism of SAF's strikebreaking, despite the tragic mistake at Ådalen, and little reason to ask SAF to stop the activity. That Swedish historians have been under the impression that SAF stopped supporting strikebreaking in the 1930s is the fact that needs explaining, not the cessation of strikebreaking. Their mistaken impression might be explained by a secret commitment on the part of LO to do a better job delivering labor after Syndicalist and other wildcat actions and to keep quiet about employers' efforts to do it themselves.[54]

Eliminating Contract Votes and Strengthening LO's Authority

Despite his misses on some matters of detail, Åmark is probably fundamentally on the mark in suspecting that unwritten understandings of the 1930s, more than the explicit terms of the Basic Agreement, explain the prevailing harmony in labor market and political relations between capital and labor after the mid-1930s.[55] If so, one of these understandings probably concerned taking away union members' power to vote down centrally negotiated contracts. Getting rid of contract referenda (*medlemsomröstningar*) had been high on SAF's wish list throughout the 1920s and early 1930s. Called for in a small number of LO unions' constitutions, they were the cause of enormous grief for employers, especially in the pulp and paper industry and in the building trades.[56]

Because LO hoped to head off legislation, including the matter in the Basic Agreement would have made sense. Indeed, it was initially discussed at Saltsjöbaden, but was quietly dropped and ignored in the written agreement. In 1935, a year before the negotiations had started, SAF's executive director Gustaf Söderlund had already thought it best to fall silent about the matter. It was his understanding that LO was busy trying to eliminate the practice with a revision of its constitution. "A *démarche* from employers while this revision is in process," he said, "would only cast suspicion on LO and stand in the way of the issue's resolution." He added that, if the revision succeeded, employers' wishes would be satisfied "as much as one could possibly desire."[57]

In contrast to some unions, leaders of SAF's sectoral associations enjoyed standing authority to sign "at the table," only on the condition that they look upward to the SAF board, not down to members, for approval. Unions requiring referenda were bound to honor the voting outcomes, despite disastrous collisions with lockouts, bankruptcy of conflict funds, unemployment, and membership losses. Frequently, as employers pointed out in exasperation, voting turnout was only moderate, in which case the combined vote of abstainers and supporters of compromise settlements outnumbered the highly motivated and organized—and therefore victorious—militants. These binding membership referenda bedeviled many efforts by SAF and LO leaders to regulate wage matters on a centralized basis. They became a favorite subject in many internal, joint, and public discussions—including a conference in 1928 between top union and employer leaders about how to achieve labor peace.[58]

SAF leaders had every reason to think that the labor confederation might eventually satisfy them. After all, contract votes often put LO in the expensive line of fire from SAF's sympathy lockouts. In 1928 LO successfully exhorted the paper union's leaders to violate their own union's constitution and settle "at the table" with PMF, after a third membership veto of a contract. The same had just happened in 1934, ending the building trades conflict. In 1933, almost unanimously, LO's executive board (*representantskap*) had almost unanimously approved a "model" constitution (*normalstadgar*) that allowed only for advisory, not binding votes. (But LO unions were still free to adopt or reject the model for their affairs.)[59]

In 1935, Social Democrats called for an end to binding referenda in a 1935 government-appointed commission investigating legislative and other ways to promote "the people's welfare and labor peace." Finally, at the 1936 LO congress, the metalworkers' union, which did not call referenda, submitted a motion prepared by a wider coalition calling for centralization of decision making. It included August Lindberg, head of the sawmill workers union, whose bargaining relations were not steered by membership votes. Lindberg was elected chairman of LO and was the key figure at the Saltsjöbaden negotiations that year, where the matter of referenda was dropped.[60] Better, it seemed, to adopt the change unilaterally to make it appear as something valuable in its own right, not a concession to employer desires.

Söderlund's silence proved golden for SAF, for LO did not disappoint. The new rules, passed in 1941, fortified the solidaristic alliance by disallowing the infamous membership referenda on contract proposals. LO also gained veto rights over strikes involving more than 3 percent of an affiliate's members, along with the right to propose settlements, whose rejection by the affiliate could disqualify it from strike and lockout support. As called for by Metall, the reform directives issued by the congress in 1936 looked for organizational changes that would facilitate a "solidarity-oriented wage policy" led by an LO executive with "greater influence on wage movements." In the meantime, while the Saltsjöbaden negotiations were underway, LO economist Albin Lind wrote a celebrated 1938 article entitled "Solidaristic Wage Policy." It recommended restraint by high-pay groups "in order to create the conditions for a transfer of purchasing power from one industry to another." Ultimately, the 1941 report explicitly rejected the idea that centralized wage policy could bring low wages up, as many called for in 1936. It did not, however, explicitly reject Lind's transfer concept, which could not have resonated more harmoniously with export employers' own solidaristic views, especially about getting and keeping wages in home-market sectors, particularly in the building trades, under control.[61]

Enlarging SAF's Central Authority

By fortifying the confederation's authority against the building trades, LO's leadership shift and internal reforms gave backbone to the emergent cross-class solidaristic alliance. SAF itself also saw some auspicious internal changes in the 1930s. To start with, in replacing von Sydow, Edström scouted around for someone with "a sense of pragmatism and humor" and "calmness and dignified bearing." A more agreeable man than Ivar Larson, von Sydow's second in command, was needed to tap into the enormous potential for cross-class agreement around wage distributional issues. (Later, Edström would also have disagreements with Larson about dealing with the building trades.) Edström thus went out of his way, through discreet go-betweens, to sound out what Social Democratic politicians thought of Söderlund, who was treasurer for the city of Stockholm at the time. What he found out was most reassuring: Söderlund was "used to wrestling with the Soshies" (sossarna). Nevertheless, "the Social Democratic leadership in the city government value Commissioner Söderlund highly." Once in place, Söderlund wrote to Edström of his "energetic hope that our work can be carried out in the spirit of consensus for the betterment of all" (*till allas båtnad*).[62]

Early on, Söderlund dropped initial plans to seek extra powers for the SAF board to command lockouts after the Social Democrats and LO so agreeably intervened in 1934. Within a few months, however, SAF took the unusual step of hiring and paying for an inspector (*kontrollant*) for the building trades to "prosecute deviancy and other disorders [*beivra oarter och andra missförhållanden*] that creep into workplaces" because of organized contractors' weakness, neglect, and indifference. Normally such tasks fell to the officialdom of sectoral associations. But SAF needed to establish such a prefectoral apparatus, its own solidaristic backbone, because the problems so quickly spread across organizational lines within and beyond the building trades.[63]

Construction employers accepted SAF's assumption of this unprecedented role in 1934 without major protest. (By contrast, both the Saltsjöbaden agreement of 1938 and the 1941 constitutional changes in LO were openly opposed by construction and other high-pay, home-market workers.) This quiescence was assured, no doubt, because the leadership of any potential opposition had already split off from SAF during the 1933–1934 conflict. SAF's command of the battle had so outraged BIF leader Nils Dahlqvist that he angrily resigned his chairmanship, which as founder he had held since 1918, along with his seat on SAF's board. First, Dahlqvist had objected to SAF's pragmatic exemption of the separate plumbing contractors' organization from the lockout. He was then infuriated when SAF exempted, for public relations reasons, Skånska Cementgjuteriet for an important hospital renovation project in Oskarshamn. In addition to being Sweden's biggest cement producer and exporter, the southern Swedish company was the largest general contractor. Dispensation for Skånska Cement was the last straw for Dahlqvist, who resented SAF's favoritism toward big firms and nursed an "old grudge" against this one in particular. Many small firms had been eager to end the conflict on terms unacceptable to SAF and return to work. Now they had to obey the lockout order while Skånska Cement continued with its profitable project.[64]

Subsequently, in 1935, SAF prevailed on BIF to adjust its constitution to SAF's strictures. Dahlqvist's Malmö-based affiliate refused to adjust its own rules in line with the national organization's and was therefore expelled from BIF and SAF.[65] Skånska Cement and about twenty other SAF loyalists, especially larger contractors responsible for about 37 percent of all work in Malmö, formed a new local unit in order to rejoin BIF and SAF. SAF then coordinated a boycott of members of Dahlqvist's recalcitrant association, who lost all lucrative work contracted out by large manufacturers, including Edström's ASEA.[66] Economically banished from the respectable employer community, their association was doomed to marginality. Like LO, SAF resolutely consolidated its central authority with measures like these in the years immediately following the huge building trades conflict. The two confederations could now count on each other to keep control of unsolidaristic tendencies arising in their respective ranks and dragging the two friendly giants into expensive conflicts.

Conclusion

A crucial phase in the evolution of solidaristic management of the Swedish labor market was accomplished by a complex cross-class alliance of capitalist and labor forces in the 1930s. This alliance advanced the distributional and control interests, above all, of firms in the engineering industry like ASEA. SAF and VF chairman J. Sigfrid Edström chose Gustav Söderlund, it seems, for the very purpose of building bridges between his export interests and the worlds of finance and labor. The alliance leaned hard against the interests of militant workers in industries like building and construction, whose high wages came out of the pockets of capitalists and workers alike. It also tightly constrained building contractors' freedom of entrepreneurial and managerial action.

Completion of the joint solidaristic project, about as far as it could go, would come in the 1950s and 1960s. In the meantime, events during World War II, marked by severe labor shortages and emergency control of wage setting, continued to serve the cross-class coalition against the building trades and other sectors sheltered from international competition. Home-market employers complained of exclusion from SAF's decision making. SAF even exercised its right to scotch a wage agreement offering high increases that food industry employers were more than willing to accept. Construction wages were reduced by the terms of emergency wartime central agreements between LO and SAF, while wages for other sectors were merely frozen at current levels. (Iron-ore miners' unusually high wages at Grängesberg were also reduced.) Also, during the war, cost-of-living increases were distributed, as employers recommended, disproportionately to low-pay workers and therefore industrial sectors. Above all, SAF leaders strove to maintain as much uniformity as possible across firms and sectors despite wildly divergent market and union pressures in different sectors.[67]

On a few occasions in their wartime internal discussions, employers referred to their wage regulation objectives as *solidarisk lönepolitik*—solidaristic wage policy. As Söderlund's successor Fritiof Söderbäck put it in 1940, "solidaristic wage policy is looking difficult to implement," even though the LO chairman and Saltsjöbaden signatory August Lindberg favored it. Nevertheless, he added, "as far as I am concerned, it is necessary." After the war, in 1947, the executive director for both the textile and garment associations anticipated developments of the 1950s analyzed in the next chapter. He called for centralization, or at least a tight coordination of contract negotiations across sectors, to hold wages down in high-pay sectors. Centralization, he argued, "would be a good platform for solidaristic wage policy."[68]

6

EGALITARIAN EMPLOYERS

Behind Swedish Wage Equality

A powerful labor movement, a centralized, multi-industry bargaining system, a solidaristic wage policy—hence a compressed income structure. According to virtually all scholarly accounts of the development of labor market governance in the 1950s and 1960s in Sweden, these things followed almost as inevitably as the seasons of the year. Thus, convention has it that employers had to pay a price to get the powerful, egalitarian labor confederation to submit to pressure for wage restraint at the national level. "The price for getting LO to go along," according to one historian's typical view, "was to negotiate about solidaristic wage policy." Organizational unity and tight labor markets gave the Social Democratic labor movement enormous leverage to impose its egalitarian agenda. LO would sacrifice wage militancy in exchange for intersectoral equality and "employers were forced into discussions about the fairness of wage differentials." The wage discourse was, quite simply, "conducted on Social Democracy's terms."[1]

To be sure, the term solidaristic wage policy belonged to the labor confederation, popularized by LO economist Albin Lind in his famous essay published in 1938, the year of the Basic Agreement at Saltsjöbaden. Employers did not appropriate and use it themselves, at least openly. Nor did they challenge the idea until the 1970s, when the labor confederation began invoking it for more radical purposes than before. When it still denoted the initial purpose attached to it by the labor movement—equal pay for equal work across firms and industries—employers went along contentedly.[2]

In practice, moving in the direction of equal pay for equal work was acheived in different ways by LO and SAF negotiators in the 1950s and 1960s. Usually it took the form of a floor on wage increases for any particular multi-employer contract unit and at times extra increases for female workers. In effect, the "differentiated" structure of contractual increases consistently gave low-pay sectors faster wage growth than others. It logically entailed, as intended, restraint at the high end. "Wage drift," or extra-contractual wage growth associated with competition over labor in tight labor markets, usually undid some of the compression, but not entirely. The fact that between the late 1950s and the early 1970s wage differentials across Swedish industries in the private sector declined steadily indicates considerable success for the policy. For example, wages in the garment industry, dominated by women, increased from 74 percent to 79 percent of the manufacturing average between 1960 and 1970. By contrast, men in the troublesome building industry saw their wages fall precipitously from a high of about 146 percent of the manufacturing industry average in 1960 to 131 percent in 1970 (and further down to a modest 116 percent in 1975). Workers in the auto industry saw their already modest advantage decline from 116 percent to 110 percent between 1960 and 1970 (and further to 103 percent in 1975). Overall, the relative position of high pay industries declined, while average pay in low-pay sectors moved toward the middle (see fig. 6.1).[3]

In glaring contrast to the conventional account, historical evidence examined later shows incontrovertibly that employers favored the solidaristic wage policy of the 1950s and 1960s. It also shows that they chose, for strategic reasons, to conceal the fact. The policy was not forced upon them, and it was not a concession. To be sure, they did not force it on unions, either. Instead, the policy took root in a powerful cross-class alignment of interests behind a central component of a larger solidaristic system of labor market governance employers strived for. Analysis of the evidence is followed by discussion of two

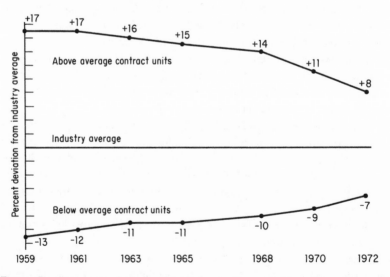

Figure 6.1. Intersectoral wage compression, 1959–1972. Note: Upper line combines all higher pay LO:SAF bargaining units, showing the deviation between their average wages and the average for all industry. Lower line combines all lower pay units. Source: Rudolf Meidner, *Samordning och solidarisk lönepolitik* (Stockholm: LO/Prisma, 1974), 52.

closely related solidaristic objectives: continued suppression of "welfare capitalist" or company social benefits, and overarching regulation of incentive pay (piece work) practices, whose usage in Sweden probably outstripped that of any other country in the world.

Tail Wags Dog? The Real Origins of Centralized Solidaristic Wage Policy

The conventional perspective on solidaristic wage policy understands that employers drove developments forward toward the multi-industrial centralization of collective bargaining in 1952 and, after a brief hiatus, from 1956 onward. This centralized bargaining was superimposed over sector-level bargaining, whose main purpose henceforth was to interpret and implement the terms of restrained but egalitarian peak agreements. Conventional analyses tend to identify three forces behind the egalitarian element of the deal, all of them originating from the labor movement: (1) the Social Democratic labor movement's egalitarian ideals, (2) the bargaining power of low-pay unions, and, finally, (3) a model of dynamic economic development, authored by LO economists, in which economic growth under full employment could be facilitated rather than obstructed by wage compression across firms and industries (the "Rehn-Meidner model"). In short, multi-industry bargaining created an institutional setting where it was administratively feasible to pursue a wage policy with an industrial development as well as egalitarian purpose, and gave low-pay unions the decisive leverage to extract distributive concessions from employers in exchange for overall wage restraint.[4]

Silence Is Golden

In 1951 LO's yearly congress approved a report, *The Trade Union Movement under Full Employment,* containing the wage and economic policy ideas of its economists Gösta Rehn and Rudolf Meidner. Complete silence was SAF's response to, among other things, the labor confederation's official call for systematic pursuit of wage equality. No publications or official statements were issued. Public reticence, however, reflected neither indifference nor a judgment that LO's formulation of an official policy was without practical significance. In fact, in October 1952, SAF commissioned a special, modestly titled "wage committee" of top SAF economists and officials, including its chairman Sven Schwartz and executive director Bertil Kugelberg, to discuss how employers should respond.[5]

If anything like a consensus took shape in the course of the committee's deliberations between 1953 and 1956, it was agreement with LO on broad principles. The tendency emerged early and frictionlessly. In a discussion in

December 1953, Lennart Bratt, executive director of SAF's General Group (organizing diverse and often low-pay manufacturers and processors of chemicals, petroleum, plastics, and other nonmetallic goods) stated flatly that export industry's ability to pay should set the overall norm and that otherwise SAF's policy "must have a leveling effect, upwards and downwards" (*den måste bli en utjämnare uppåt och nedåt*). Chairman Schwartz thought there was much to be said for the principle of equal pay for equal work, especially across sectors. Furthermore, "from the standpoint of fairness the correct thing is to pay for the same work the same way everywhere." There was no major disagreement on these things. Only Sven Dahlberg from the building industry, sitting as he said "on the benches for the defense" (*på de anklagades bänk*), mildly defended high and differentiated piece-work earnings in his sector. Otherwise, there were only quibbles about how rigidly any such policies could be in the face of heterogeneous and shifting market constraints.[6]

In the wage committee discussions the following year, SAF economist and negotiator Hans Söderlund made the cross-class agreement explicit. His lengthy April 1955 discussion paper strongly advocated standardization of wages across the labor market, noting that LO's solidaristic wage policy "for the most part . . . agrees with the standard wage principle." SAF, he said, arguing on grounds he had been examining for several months, could not really apply the "ability to pay principle" (*bärkraftsprincipen*) that it occasionally invoked as its official position. For one thing, it would unjustifiably let wages in the building trades loose. Also, arguing along the same lines as labor union economists Rehn and Meidner, if not directly drawing from them, he argued that setting wages according to ability to pay would allow low wages to subsidize inefficient industry and therefore deprive other sectors of capital and labor necessary for expansion.[7]

Discussing Söderlund's paper and presentation, director Kugelberg noted that different firms' or sectors' "ability to pay" had actually been only one among other more important principles guiding SAF. Otherwise, "we would have produced a 'jaggedness' [*taggighet*] in wages that we have opposed in reality." Export industry's ability to pay was the real guiding concern. Overall, the tone of the meeting's minutes suggests general agreement among the employer committee members with the labor movement's new official line—and deep skepticism about the ability to pay idea. There was only disagreement about the possibility of producing and applying a complicated job evaluation system (*arbetsvärderingssystem*) envisioned by Rehn and Meidner to measure and rank the quality of jobs across the economy to achieve systematic equity in pay. Kaj Åberg, director of the textile industry association, supported the idea, knowing full well that it would mean raising his industry's wages relative to the rest.[8]

Remarkably, Söderlund's paper advised only outward silence, not a public celebration of cross-class solidarity. Silence would pay off because exposing agreement might cause the various unions, which he noted were by no means strongly unified about the policy, "to move off in a different direction."

Some might, for example, demand higher wages in more profitable firms, invoking ability to pay. He reasoned that "solidarity among workers and confidence in their organizations' leadership rely, of course, to a great extent on members' feeling that the organization does a service in wage setting." The unions cannot be made to look superfluous, in other words. In short, confidence in strong union leadership supporting wage solidarity would suffer "if the distance narrows between [employers and the union] with regard to their conception about the 'correct' wage structure." The identical psychology, no doubt, had guided his father's counsel of silence in 1936 about SAF's desire to ban unions' contract referenda—once it was clear that LO was moving resolutely in SAF's direction.[9]

SAF chairman Schwartz concluded the discussion about Söderlund's analysis in complete agreement with his strategy of silence, interpreting it to mean SAF should adopt a "passive policy" and only gingerly "apply the brakes in various ways" in response to LO's policy. In effect, SAF would send signals that could more easily be interpreted as disagreement than agreement. Hence, only on the rarest of occasions did SAF ever expose the inside truth. In a talk to a December 1955 meeting of the Swedish Economics Association, SAF director Bertil Kugelberg informed the economists that, "as astonishing as it might seem," regarding the general economic logic behind solidaristic wage policy, "you will find that in certain regards it runs parallel with the principles underlying employer thinking." Eight years later, once solidaristic wage policy had become deeply rooted in the labor confederation, Schwartz abandoned his policy of passivity, arguing in an employer publication that employers and unions now needed to make a "serious attempt" to develop a job evaluation system that could be applied within and across all industries (*ett genomgående arbetsvärderingssystem*)—exactly what Rehn and Meidner had advocated a decade earlier in the service of equal pay for equal work.[10]

Most astonishing in light of all that has been said and written since were the views advanced by SAF economist Karl-Olof Faxén in his 1956 contribution to the wage policy committee's deliberations. A solidaristic policy, he maintained, was above all the most practical one, being "more easily administered" than a policy based on ability to pay. In other words, it was easier to generate agreement on among employers. Further, he argued, a precondition for administering a solidaristic wage policy was not a strong labor confederation, but rather a "*very strong* employer organization" (his emphasis). Otherwise, certain worker groups could take advantage of labor scarcities and the lack of other market constraints to raise their wages above those with similar qualifications in other sectors. Finally, he said, with bland, matter-of-fact certainty, "it is employers' policy that determines those of wage earners' organizations." In other words, "they must adapt themselves to the wage policy that employer organizations accept and carry out." LO's policy thinking, he seemed to say, was drafting behind an extraordinarily powerful SAF already moving in that direction. He added, probably in allusion to Söderlund's golden silence policy, that unions had greater need than employer organizations to "verbalize their wage policy principles."[11] No wonder, then, that history gives labor full credit.

To what extent other people in the confederation agreed with Faxén's eccentric and counterintuitive perspective is not clear. It did not disqualify him from becoming SAF's chief economist later. In that position, in 1977 and 1978, Faxén published two papers for largely academic audiences in which he developed the same remarkable points he had made two decades earlier. Solidaristic wage policy, he wrote in an industrial relations journal, had historically meant equal pay for equal work. The ability to pursue it had been "based upon the existence of a strong and centralised employers' organisation." Had employers been divided, "a trade union in a branch of industry experiencing favourable economic conditions would have been able to strike and obtain a more favourable settlement than the rest of LO, without LO being able to do anything about it." For unions to promote wage solidarity, "withdrawal of support in the case of conflict with employers" was their most "efficient weapon." Anyone familiar with Sweden would see the militant, high-pay workers in the building trades as an implicit case in point. Solidaristic wage policy, in sum, "did not develop independently of employer policy" and "must to a very large extent be seen as an answer to the tactics and bargaining practices developed by the Swedish Employers' Confederation."[12]

In conclusion, at least in Faxén's eccentric account, capital's solidarism begat labor's solidaristic wage policy. The tail had started the dog wagging. If the truth be known, both wagged each other once the whole thing got going. A completely balanced view fitting both the reality and other employers' perceptions suggests that shared interests, arrived at independently, explain both the origins and maintenance of the policy. Axel Brunius, editor and author of many SAF publications over the years, argued presciently in 1947 that the labor movement buttressed the solidaristic edifice under construction. In that time of great labor scarcity, "planned management" (*planhushållning*) of wages was necessary. "An employers' association that understands its task is a planning agency: it should try to brake or overcome wage anomalies, check local invasions at others' expense, strengthen wage levels against slippage and ruin, in short, impose order and logic in pay setting." But, he added, an employers' association cannot manage this "gigantic task" alone. Working at its side it must have organized labor, which, he added incidentally, "calls the plan 'solidaristic wage policy.'"[13]

While an effective solidaristic wage policy required a cross-class alliance with a strong labor movement, having an egalitarian Social Democratic Party in control of government was neither help nor hindrance. Certainly LO and SAF received no encouragement from the government. In 1955 a confidant of SAF's Kugelberg overheard Prime Minister Tage Erlander tell the cental bank chief that the unions' idea of achieving pay equity across the labor market was "the damndest of all existing lunacies" (*den djävligaste av alla existerande galenskaper*). Around the same time, Finance Minister Per-Evin Sköld saw raising the textile industry's wages relative to others as pointless. It would be a good thing if its workers drifted over to more dynamic export industry for its higher wages, Sköld believed.[14] Textile employers had a rather different view, and engineering employers would, as argued later, be well compensated.

Multi-Industry Solidarism: The Evolution and Practice of Peak-Level Centralization

Sweden's employer and labor confederations took their first step toward multi-industrial solidaristic wage policy in 1952, when they negotiated the first peak agreement of the peacetime period. Both sides had regarded wartime wage regulation and its solidaristic components as temporary, emergency phenomena. They even saw the 1952 agreement as an experiment. The second experimental step toward multi-industrial solidarism came in 1956. Defying the pessimists, that step inaugurated an uninterrupted 26-year stretch of peak-level wage regulation.

SAF's strategic decision around this time not to reveal its interest in solidaristic wage policy (as recommended by Söderlund and Schwartz), and LO's greater need to "verbalize its wage policy principles" (as Faxén put it), make it necessary to reexamine conventional narrative accounts about what happened. In contrast to employers, according to these accounts, there was not much of a consensus among the LO unions behind either centralization or egalitarian wage policy principles—despite the report accepted by the 1951 LO congress. Rudolf Meidner and Axel Hadenius make this abundantly clear in their historical accounts based on minutes from LO deliberations. The unions were, in fact, extremely divided. Even the metalworkers' union, which had carried the banner for solidaristic wage policy in the 1930s, had lost passion for the cause now that the building trades were more or less under control and the food industry transformed from a crafts-based into a low-pay mass production industry.[15]

In light of this division, but still convinced that the power of an egalitarian labor movement made the difference, Hadenius imparts an institutionalist spin to the conventional argument, maintaining that solidaristic agreements "were a consequence of the new position of power that the low-pay unions assumed under central negotiations." They were institutionally empowered, in other words, against a rather broad array of employers and unions. SAF offered "hard resistance" to the solidaristic structure of LO's demands in 1956 to upward leveling of wages, according to Hadenius's reading of the minutes of LO deliberations, and rests his case for employer opposition on that single year. Thus, SAF conceded the solidaristic result only in exchange for overall restraint provided for in a highly centralized process, which the low-pay unions could have refused to join.[16]

Hadenius does not clarify, however, what could possibly have lent credibility to the low-pay unions' threat not to cooperate. Would they have been able to inflict significant costs on other unions and employers while sparing them-selves by refusing to go along with centralization? Only under some such im-probable circumstance would they have been able to impose their interests, as a condition for centralization, on the opponents of solidarism. Of course, the assumption that employers were among those opponents has to fall. With it falls the argument that centralization transformed low-pay unions into a new power factor in the Swedish labor market.

Compression from Below Strategic discussions in SAF's wage policy commit-tee in 1955 put what Hadenius calls SAF's "hard resistance" in 1956 in entirely new light. Perhaps it was exactly the subterfuge Chairman Schwartz implied when he recommended "putting on the brakes." Strategic distortion of one's position is, of course, standard fare in all bargaining and was probably noth-ing new and extraordinary in the history of solidarism. It was not confined to the top SAF leadership. In 1954, Gunnar Larsson, the director of the paper in-dustry's association, had already proposed the clever idea of formulating a "differentiated" line for wage increases and then "confidentially secure accept-ance of it by the LO leadership." Presumably then, LO could present it as a de-mand that SAF could resist and then reluctantly concede.[17]

Other bargaining strategy sessions at meetings in the 1950s fully demolish any thought that low-pay unions could somehow have been extraordinarily empowered by centralization against resolutely inegalitarian employers. In fall 1951, contemplating confederation-level centralized negotiations for the first time since the emergency World War II and Korean War wage freezes, director Kugelberg announced that if centralized negotiations proved necessary to pre-vent a long, drawn-out wage round due to inflationary wage rivalry among nu-merous unions, "we must try to set wage increases in absolute terms [*i örestal*] instead of percentages, so that high-wage groups are not unreasonably fa-vored." Various industries' representatives voiced support for such "differenti-ation" in favor of low-pay sectors. In January of the next year, SAF signed the first of the famous centralized solidaristic agreements.[18]

In 1954, during multi-industrial bargaining's three-year hiatus, a remark-able outpouring of support for solidaristic leveling occurred. In internal dis-cussions, employers from low-pay industries now expressed alarm at widening wage differentials across sectoral lines. Things were moving away from the direction desired. Rapid wage drift (*löneglidning*), that is, earnings growth ex-ceeding contractual increases, had recently produced more than two thirds of all wage increases across industry, especially in high-pay sectors. Wage drift, according to Nils Holmström (Kockums shipyard, and VF), resulted from "a lack of balance between demand and supply in the labor market." As SAF board member Ernst Wehtje (from Skånska Cement, and chairman of the building materials employers) put it, there was a "disturbing degree of competition over labor among companies." The relatively moderate increases negotiated the two previous years on a decentralized basis and the subsequent heavy demand for

Swedish goods, labor shortages, and high inflation had produced what Wehtje called "overfull employment" and these telltale symptoms of solidaristic disequilibrium.[19]

Low-pay employers were losing their workers to high-pay sectors with strong upward drift. Einar Hallström, speaking for shoe, leather, and clothing industries, argued that because of wage drift they needed to grant extra high increases now and "would rather run their companies at a significant loss than empty the factories of skilled workers." As his colleague Wilhelm Bahrke said, "however bad the situation is for the clothing industry, it must follow if wages in other areas are being pulled up. It cannot let go of its workers." Fellow clothing representative J. P. Bager reported labor hoarding: "People are so worried about their workers that they let them sit in the factories and give them wages even if there is no work for them."[20]

T. C. Bergh, from the textile employers' association, pointed out that part of the textile industry's problem was that "[s]ince there are no manpower reserves, a wage increase could also result in a movement of labor from one sector to another." The industry "could afford neither to raise wages nor to lose workers." As things got worse, he changed his mind a month later, however, saying now wage increases were necessary to keep workers from leaving. In the low-pay trucking sector, the situation was also alarming. Its association's director, Erik Elmstedt, warned that wage drift in some, mostly higher pay sectors, had so overwhelmed contractual increases that "bankruptcy for the bargaining system" was on its way unless it could provide compensatory or "differentiated" increases for low-pay sectors.[21]

Speaking for the food industry, which because of advancing mechanization and mass production had long since lost its high-pay status and was losing workers, William Björnemann asked plaintively for help from a strong SAF. "What possibilities does SAF have to let low-wage groups approach high-wage groups?" Excessive wage drift in high-pay sectors was making the situation "insufferable." In short, "What is going to happen to those of us who are down at the bottom? How can we avoid being crushed by those on top?" Gösta Wahlstedt, chairman of the trucking employers' association, proposed the answer: high-pay employers should freeze their wages so that trucking could catch up. In other words, extra increases at the low end had to be matched by restraint at the high end for the sake of economic balance and monetary stability, and this is where SAF's strength was necessary. As Carl Andersson, also from food processing, put it, "We must keep up to retain our people." Therefore, "SAF's major task is to hold back wage developments in engineering and other high-pay sectors." Finally, speaking on behalf of shoe, leather, and garment industries, Bahrke put it similarly: "With regard to the current shortage of labor, the high-wage associations should observe restraint. . . . Just as workers plead for better pay conditions for the worst paid, so should SAF promote the welfare of the worst-off sectors from the employers' standpoint."[22]

In the context of this alarming situation, Gunnar Larsson proposed, as mentioned before, for SAF to draft a plan for differentiated increases which LO could present as its own and then be "conceded" by SAF in a multi-industry agreement. Nothing ultimately came of his suggestion, for in 1955, the following year, negotiations remained decentralized at the industry level. What ultimately transpired, however, without centralization, was the most remarkably differentiated set of sector-level agreements ever, giving workers in low-pay sectors average increases of between 12 and 14 percent (trucking, busing, meat packing and food processing, bakeries, dairies, flour milling) and increases of only 2 to 3 percent for high-pay sectors (road and bridge construction, electrical installation).[23] Low-pay unions did not need institutionally conditioned empowerment through peak centralization, contrary to what Hadenius argues.

The overall magnitude of the raises resulting from the decentralized whipsawing process of 1955 persuaded SAF to push hard for centralization in 1956. To a limited but unsatisfactory extent, it had steered the previous year's agreements from the center, threatening a jumbo multi-industry lockout of about 500,000 LO members when the paperworkers' union gave notice of intentions to take around 4,000 workers out on strike. The disturbance inside LO set off by SAF's threat possibly helped the labor confederation's leaders pull the unions together behind centralized bargaining in 1956.[24]

SAF's oppositional stance in 1956 to compression from below, the only opposition Hadenius notes for any year, may actually have been real rather than feigned. Very high agreements that low-pay employers had signed in the decentralized process to recover ground relative to higher pay groups were now causing them problems in meeting hardening international competition. Thus they were much more resistant to extra high increases than in the year earlier. Nevertheless "conceding" wage compression after hard resistance was also, in all probability, partly a ploy to make it look like employers also sacrificed something in exchange for unions' sacrifice of high wage increases. Thus, SAF made sure LO would stand on firm ideological ground in order to sell restraint. It had to have something to show for being entrusted with high command of the class struggle. By coming out openly in favor of solidaristic wage policy, as Söderlund said, SAF would have robbed the labor confederation of that possibility.

The restrained peak agreement of 1956 brought new labor market disequilibria, complete with renewed wage drift. Internal discussions echoed earlier ones, and low-pay employers' support for leveling picked up again. This time it was Kaj Åberg, representing textiles, who recommended a new bargaining ploy. SAF should initiate negotiations for 1957 with a call for a freeze in wages and "then as a concession"—as if it were beneficial to workers alone—"offer a certain degree of differentiation." In light of this sequence of events, it appears that if SAF had already managed to push LO into peak-level centralization in 1955 as it wanted, it would possibly have produced a more restrained agreement overall and redistribution within a more "restricted framework," as Kugelberg put it.[25] In that case, SAF's position in 1956 would probably have been less aggressively resistant to the peak-level negotiation of differentiated increases, and Hadenius would not have been able to cite its unusually hard opposition of that year as evidence for principled objection to solidarism.

Leveling from Above   All the while, before centralization was fully accomplished, SAF continued successfully to pursue a policy of wage solidarism by leveling from above. In spring 1954, this kind of leveling ran a course familiar from the 1930s. It was motivated, as usual, by tensions between producers of internationally traded goods and home-market sectors. Though the engineering industry, a modestly high pay sector with much internal differentiation, was currently leaching workers away from the low-pay industries, it was also troubled by similar problems spilling over from one of the highest pay sectors, construction. As in the past, engineering still competed in the same labor markets as construction, especially, but not exclusively, over unskilled workers. Now, booming investment by both public and private sectors, and in single-family home construction recently liberated from countercyclical regulation, was stealing too many workers away.[26]

In 1954, these conditions encouraged construction workers to demand higher wages. Even more alarmingly from employers' point of view, they insisted on free summer Saturdays, or the five-day week during the busy summer season. Steel industry employers, according to Hjalmar Åselius, were especially sensitive about resulting increases in building costs and workers' protests about higher rent. Building workers' success would make it virtually impossible for engineering employers to hold the line in their sector. As in the 1930s, SAF could not wait for informal or formal joint regulation with LO and had to proceed unilaterally. The confederation succeeded, though against considerable opposition, in mobilizing its member associations to meet the demand with the threat of a jumbo multi-industry lockout. The threat alone brought a victory, though only a short-lived one, against the spread of free summer Saturdays across and therefore out of the building industry.[27]

As in 1934 and on other occasions, SAF leaders operated in full confidence that having Social Democrats in government would not make a giant lockout for a solidaristic purpose like this one politically dangerous. Economist and Liberal Party leader Bertil Ohlin conveyed to Kugelberg his belief that a lockout against construction would not "be exploited politically" by the government. Conservative leader Jarl Hjalmarsson concurred, in part because "building workers were certainly not especially popular among their comrades." Minutes of SAF meetings reveal employers' confidence that LO would, by withholding support, play the solidaristic role that Faxén saw for it. Building trades workers were still rather unpopular, even though wage growth in the sector had already been held to a slower pace than other industries in the postwar period. Therefore, a mass lockout would bring "a very quick result," and a favorable one at that.[28]

Things changed little during the 1960s, when industrial peace reigned around what had become a fairly routinized system of centralized bargaining and solidaristic wage policy. Remarkably similar attitudes reaffirming employer support for the leveling of wages from below and above reappear in SAF meetings. An interesting case is that of the employers' association in the low-pay flour-mill industry (*Kvarnindustriförbundet*). Its executive director, Per Osvald, considered the low-pay question "fundamental," pointing out in 1965 that "a lower spread of wages and a concentration of them toward the middle" would be to his low-pay sector's advantage. He was optimistic that something could be done along these lines. After all, the great spread of wages "no doubt are the result, for the most part, of traditions and prejudices." When LO economist Per Holmberg criticized the labor confederation the same year for being too timid in its redistributive efforts, saying that employers' distributional interests were "quite fluid," he was absolutely correct. LO's inhibitions were probably as much internal as external.[29]

Curt-Steffan Giesecke, SAF's executive director, suggested, in response to complaints like Osvald's, a meeting of low-pay industry representatives to work out solutions to the "low-wage problem." Lennart Bratt of the General Group seconded the idea. As a participant in the earlier wage policy committee meetings 12 years earlier, he had proposed both upward and downward compression. Now he favored the same, hoping only that raises at the low end "to employers' advantage" would not add more than 1 percent to the entire package. In other words, low wages were to be brought up at the expense of holding wages at the high end back, just as LO's own solidaristic wage policy dictated.[30]

The building trades remained a problem in the mid-1960s, as they had been from the beginning of the century, despite much progress on that front. Contemplating the sector's high earnings and wage drift, executive director Giesecke, Kugelberg's protege and soon-to-be successor, suggested a "mirror-image demand" for counterbalancing LO's prioritization of leveling from below, resulting "in a compression of differentials that exist between the general pay level and the level in certain high-pay industries." With views like these uttered in internal employer discussions, it is no surprise, then, that LO's chairman Arne Geijer could boast of achieving, in 1966, the "best low-wage agreement ever."[31] Now, as before in the 1950s, employers stood silently by while the unions took credit.

The entire system probably pivoted on the support of export-oriented employers, especially in engineering, who ever since the 1930s dominated SAF. Unlike Finance Minister Sköld, they did not worry about the labor supply problems it might cause, and therefore never voiced disagreement with compression from below. Either way, they stood to gain. If wages remained low in sectors like textiles, garments, leather, trucking, and mass food processing, they would benefit from the leakage of labor across sectoral lines. If, however, solidaristic wage policy had the effect, not entirely unintended, of throwing the least productive firms in such sectors into bankruptcy, or imposing labor-saving rationalization on them, engineering employers also gained from the shedding of their labor. Because the better, more productive firms dominated the low-pay employer associations, they could tolerate the raises and could even benefit from the transfer of labor.[32]

Engineering employers, on the other hand, unambiguously benefitted from and openly favored leveling from above, or the wage restraint that solidaristic wage policy imposed on the even higher pay building and construction sectors. This restraint held down their building costs, limited the spillover of wage demands, and stemmed the outward flow of labor. All the while, generally restrained wages kept the prices of Swedish goods in check and thus facilitated export-based development of the Swedish economy. For engineering employers, the arrangement thus largely reconciled the principle of equal pay for equal work with their "ability to pay," the two competing principles debated in SAF's wage policy committee.

Managing the Managers: Unilateral Suppression of Segmentalism

To a considerable extent, the employers' confederation had to continue relying on its own devices, not union help in collective bargaining, to pursue its solidaristic mission. This applied in particular to SAF's perpetual struggle against company social benefits, or what Americans call welfare capitalism. Thus, despite the political ascendance of social democracy in Sweden in the 1930s, organized capital unilaterally fought trends that might have helped strengthen the bond between employer and worker at the workplace and thereby loosen the bonds of solidarity to the wider labor movement.

In other words, SAF continued energetically to suppress the temptation of employers competing over labor made scarce by solidaristic wage restraint to spirit segmentalist practices in through the back door. One such practice was "year-end bonuses." They were first discussed and roundly frowned upon in 1937, when, despite the Depression, and because of wage restraint, labor markets in the export sector began to tighten up. It had come to SAF's attention that firms on the upbeat in the steel industry had decided to give bonuses worth one month's wages. Under yet tighter labor market conditions, nine years later, SAF went to battle again. In a 1946 circular to members, it argued that while firms justify year-end bonuses as a way of sharing the fruits of good years with their workers, "in fact however this motive is often combined with another: bonuses give the company an advantage in [intense] competition over labor, which increasingly characterizes our labor market." On behalf of SAF's executive committee, director Kugelberg wrote to Patrick Rydbeck of SKF, the internationally dominant producer of ball bearings, insisting that SKF cancel its planned bonus. "If such a pace-setting [tongivande] company as SKF were also to set off in this direction," Kugelberg wrote, "then it would endanger SAF's ability to maintain the sanctity of centralized, contractually controlled wages."

Much peeved, Rydbeck asked Kugelberg to withdraw his letter, but Kugelberg refused.[33]

SAF tried to channel the urge to share good times with scarce workers into less disruptive practices. The best it could come up with was "welfare facilities"—nicer cafeterias and sanitary facilities, high-quality childcare, vacation, and sports facilities, and so on. Individual employers, of course, usually needed little prompting. A study around this time found that the tight hold on wages immediately after the war resulted in intense competition over workers and therefore "more and more luxurious washrooms and more flowers in the workshops." Probably because of the industry's particularly vulnerable position, the textile employers' association went to unusual lengths agitating on the "comfort issue" (*trivselfrågan*), promoting the use of relatively cheap amenities to help make up for low wages and, therefore, high turnover, absenteeism, and departures. Meanwhile, SAF issued even sharper warnings against bonuses in 1947, insisting that firms comply with the previous year's directives. The confederation claimed to have more than employers' interests in mind. "Disloyal overpayments" were also, for workers, a "demeaning form of compensation" for their efforts.[34]

Profit sharing, another common segmentalist practice, produced a similar response. In 1945 Alrik Björklund, director of the metal trades association (*Mekanförbundet*, VF's sister organization for dealing with the sector's non-labor market trade and lobbying affairs), wrote a plan for profit sharing as a wonder drug against worker militancy, low productivity, and disloyalty. His plan included company-based profit sharing in the form of individual cash benefits, and partly in the form of "collective" benefits—vacation spots, day-care for children, medical services, and housing. With this, Björklund naively stepped out of line, which he was to learn at a meeting of the "Directors' Club." This was an elite group of five big, export-oriented engineering firms, all VF members, founded by VF and SAF chairman, Sigfrid Edström. Indicating the gravity of the problem, SAF director Söderlund appeared as a guest. Profit sharing, he said, should not be left up to individual employers. If absolutely necessary, it should be negotiated centrally between the employer and labor confederations. The problem was that profit sharing could be used as a device for gaining separate advantage in the intense competition over labor. Others present urged strict secrecy about the idea, fearing that opposition parties to the Social Democrats might latch on to the idea, propagate it in the contest over votes, and plant it in the minds of disloyal employers.[35]

Six years later, the issue came up again in the context of agitation outside SAF for profit sharing, including a visit and lecture to a wholesalers' group outside SAF by Professor Robert Hartman, the dilettantish chairman of the American Council of Profit Sharing Industries (and a translator of August Strindberg's autobiography). Again, according to Kugelberg, profit sharing was not something appropriate for Swedish conditions, and there was "no reason for SAF to alter its standing rejection." In SAF's wage policy committee deliberations in 1953, SAF chairman Sven Schwartz once again vigorously criticized profit sharing, declaring that any firm desiring to pursue it did not belong in the organization. Future director Curt-Steffan Giesecke also argued against it, considering its potential for abuse in competition over labor.[36]

Both year-end bonuses and profit sharing, in segmentalist practice, tend to be distributed to longer-term employees as a form of "deferred compensation," in part to reduce costly turnover. In the immediate postwar period, when extremely tight labor markets and therefore "excess labor mobility" (high turnover) were at their worst, SAF worked to hold the line against introducing other seniority-linked deferred benefits. In 1947, director Kugelberg warned against seniority wage premiums, invoking a current consensus. Meanwhile the LO leadership was currently inspired by the idea, and the metalworkers' union was pressuring heavily for it in negotiations with VF. Pleading innocence on account of duress—to prevent a conflict with metalworkers' union—VF conceded a premium for workers over 24 years of age with four years in the same firm. In the post mortem, the publishing industry had nothing positive to say about their experiences with similar arrangements, having found that the seniority differentials were impossible to maintain against erosion from below caused by external labor market competition and union pressure.[37]

In 1950, the seniority idea reappeared on the SAF agenda, once again put there by union interest. LO's chief economist Gösta Rehn had suggested introducing seniority-based wage supplements among other forms of individual differentiation (to get away from the current "rigid contracts"). Employer leaders from the export sector flatly rejected the idea, arguing that "due to weak resistance among employers" in tight labor markets, increments for certain groups would very quickly bring the same for others who technically were not entitled. According to paper industry association director Gunnar Larsson, "Rehn's project" would be the "death blow to the cartel that employer organizations constituted."[38] The solidaristic cartel called for uniformity; greater flexibility to differentiate wages meant greater freedom to cheat.

In 1954, when textile employers caved to union pressure for holiday wages after four years of employment in a firm, other employers rose in indignation. Similar demands, they feared, would quickly spread across industry lines. Defending his association, Kaj Åberg explained that textile workers had completely spurned an alternative wage increase that far exceeded the cost of the holiday pay. Although they showed some grudging sympathy for introducing the seniority incentive, employer officials from other industries found it inexcusable that the textile employers had failed to observe SAF's rule requiring its prior approval. VF director Matts Larsson declared to other sectors' directors that VF's policy was strictly one of "wages only for time worked." In the end, the SAF board voted reluctantly for retroactive approval of the textile agreement. Rejecting it now would be too confrontational.[39]

In the end, SAF issued only a declaration that special compensation for holidays, with or without seniority conditions, "was not a suitable pay form." For these solidaristic employers, only "piece work or hourly wages were the natural payment form." Problems with turnover would have to be dealt with by means other than deferred compensation. Among the legitimate means in the solidaristic context were stiff sanctions for poaching workers. VF, in particular, continued to pursue a stringent policy introduced in 1920 of forbidding firms to advertise for labor without VF permission and directly approaching workers employed at other firms. Among firms singled out for criticism, if not always fines, for their practices over the years were Volvo, SKF, LM Ericsson, and Husqvarna. Engineering firms were not even allowed to discuss the prospect of employment with workers who could not show a certificate (*betyg*) documenting that they had left their previous jobs.[40]

Regulating Performance Pay, or Solidarity in Pieces

By collectively suppressing segmentalist practices, Swedish employers created a new problem while solving another. In segmentalism, paying wages or providing benefits markedly above the standard in other firms helps recruit better workers and promote their productivity once hired. Therefore, it is not surprising that, in the search for productivity, employers in Sweden turned with a vengeance to incentive or performance pay ("piece rates"), a "natural payment form" suited to the solidaristic system. There was a condition, however: performance pay had to be heavily regulated from above and not entrusted entirely to individual firms, their engineers, and their foremen.

As early as 1932, SAF director Hjalmar von Sydow observed that piece work (*ackord*) "is probably used in Sweden more than in any other country in the world." The Swedish Federation of Industries (*Industriförbundet*) confirmed that view the following year. Von Sydow regarded Sweden's extensive use of incentive pay "as one of the reasons that Swedish industry has been able to carry on and flourish even in times when wages were disproportionately high in comparison with other countries." Indeed, during the periods from 1913 to 1950, and then from 1950 to 1973, Sweden, Norway, and Switzerland were the only advanced capitalist countries to consistently narrow the productivity gap with the United States, with Sweden closing the gap the fastest. From 1929 through 1938, 1938 to 1950, and 1950 to 1973, only Sweden under social democracy consistently narrowed the gap, a performance that must be explained, at least in part, by solidaristic employers' extraordinary reliance, with practically no worker resistance, on performance pay. Surely, as asserted by historian Maths Isacson, the role of incentive pay is a "clearly overlooked factor in the debate" about technical change and productivity growth in Sweden.[41]

Little changed in the thirty years after von Sydow's international comparison. In 1962, SAF director Kugelberg noted that the productivity-stimulating effect of incentive pay had become "an article of faith." Chairman Schwartz noted that Swedish industry's piece work volume "stood out as extremely high" in international comparisons, an observation confirmed by ILO and OECD studies around the same time. In engineering, approximately 65 percent of total hours were worked on incentive schemes in the mid-to-late 1940s. Pay-for-performance usage increased to about 71 percent for men and 74 percent for women by 1961. Piece-work volume in Swedish shipbuilding was the highest in the world in the 1960s. In building and construction piece rates were also unusually common by world standards (65.4 percent for above ground work, 85 percent for underground work in 1961). The centralization of rate setting imposed in 1934 produced a voluminous number of rates for specific tasks published in a fat book known in the industry as "the Bible." German contractors, who themselves shied away from performance pay, beheld the book with horrified amazement.[42]

Swedish employers clearly saw piece work as way to promote productivity under conditions of labor scarcity. During the confederation's wage policy committee deliberations, in which piece work came up, SAF's top representative from the building industry explained American contractors' ability to use hourly wages for practically all work by the fact that workers could be fired "at the drop of a hat" (*hur som helst*). Similarly, in 1957, a representative of the Swedish paper pulp industry attributed the ongoing decline in pay for performance in the United States to its employers' "access to manpower." Even union leaders understood the phenomenon. Arne Geijer of the metalworkers' union easily explained to his friend Walter Reuther of the UAW why auto manufacturers in America could manage without piece work. They could simply study how many wheels should be mounted in an hour, and if a worker is unable to maintain the pace, "he loses his job." In short, more inclined to hoard scarce labor than let it go, Swedish employers naturally turned to incentive pay as a productivity carrot.[43]

One of the peculiar blessings of incentive pay under labor scarcity was the disappearance at the workplace of collusion among workers to collusively set ceilings on each others' output. For example, in 1957 Wilhelm Ekman of VF (from shipbuilding) mused over the welcome fact that workers' "tendency to maintain [output] ceilings has increasingly disappeared in our country." Collusive "soldiering" by workers had been a major impetus for Frederick Winslow Taylor's "principles of scientific management," which called for highly intrusive managerial study and supervision of the labor process. Coordinated slow-downs occurred when workers feared their extra effort would yield only temporary increases in piece-work earnings. Management would then intervene and revise rates downward. Workers would then have to work at the faster rate to maintain their old earning levels—or surrender the work to other job seekers in ready supply. Because now the same quantity could be produced with fewer workers, there would be layoffs.[44] But under labor scarcity, Swedish employers did not eagerly revise piece rates downward. Because of that, though, they did not need such intrusive management. The downward stickiness of rates, and therefore upward drift of earnings, helps explain Swedish workers' high work tempo. It also helps explain their notable agreeability to technical improvements and automation, which could increase their piece work earnings without requiring greater effort.[45]

But while promoting greater effort without collusive output restriction and reducing worker resistance to technological innovation, this welcome aspect of piece work presented a severe drawback for solidarism. Individual employers' routine neglect in revising rates often amounted in practice to cheating on solidaristic wage restraint. In the most extreme cases, workers could pocket practically all the direct benefits of productivity increases. Consumers would not benefit from price reductions, and owners gained only a short-term advantage in competition over labor in exchange for foregoing an increase in profits.

Thus, by collectively promoting piece work, Swedish employers also subjected themselves to perpetual frustration with unsolidaristic wage drift. The natural response, then, was collective regulation of the practice to keep cheating under control. One way to do so, VF recognized early on, was to discourage negotiation of rates at shop level, where managers lacked the backbone—that is, the incentive—to enforce stringency. Their incentive was the opposite. In the 1940s, the engineering industry struggled mightily with the problems of controlling drift emanating from piece work under conditions of acute labor shortage. VF led an attack against the Engineering Science Academy (IVA, or *Ingenjörsvetenskapsakademin*), which recklessly proselytized about the high wages piece work could bring à la F. W. Taylor. Its "false doctrine" of progressive Taylorism encouraged workers to think that earnings should eat up all productivity increases. Worse yet, the IVA was training a whole generation of industrial engineers responsible for time studies and rate setting to think the same. VF experienced the same problem with foremen trained at an SAF-funded training institute (*Arbetsledareinstitutet*) and dealt with it by setting up its own instruction facilities.[46]

Meanwhile, at the peak level, SAF and LO worked together solidaristically on the problem. The Labor Court, with judges nominated by both, ruled in 1944 that piece rates should be set "objectively" according to time-and-motion study principles applicable across firms. Four years later, in that spirit, the two confederations forged a central agreement giving firms not only the right but the obligation to do time and motion studies. The 1948 LO-SAF Time Study Agreement (*Arbetsstudieavtalet*) gave rise to the mass and uniform education of an army of industrial engineers to impose "correct" piece work times across Swedish industry. Their job was to break down the country's highly heterogeneous jobs into standard time units for normal performance. Formulas combining those times with standardized pay rates negotiated centrally would generate standardized earnings. In the spirit of that agreement, VF and Metall jointly sponsored the implementation of the MTM (Methods-Time-Measurement) system in 1955. To put it simply and insightfully, as does expert Eric Giertz, the "objective" system was a "linchpin" (*grundbult*) of the Swedish model." Pointing straight in its direction was "LO's demand for a 'solidaristic wage policy,'" in which "equal pay for equal work was the basic idea."[47] Giertz misses the fact, of course, that the idea was as much SAF's as it was LO's. How else could one explain employers' enormous enthusiasm for centralized micromanagement?

Despite valiant efforts to impose overarching multi-industrial control, acute exasperation within SAF about the problem of wage drift, much of it attributable to piece work earnings, exploded in intensity after the introduction of centralized, solidaristic collective bargaining in the 1950s. By restraining wages overall, but especially at the high end where piece work was particularly common (engineering and the building trades, for example), the centralized solidarism of the 1950s created powerful incentives for individual employers to let piece work earnings drift upward. Labor scarcity, created by solidaristic restraint, was the problem (see fig. 6.2). For example, in 1957, actual wages rose significantly beyond what was centrally negotiated. An unprecedentedly feverish level of study and debate about what was going on ensued.

LO collaborated in SAF's study of the wage drift problem. Its expert Nils Kellgren was invited, for example, to participate in a 1957 meeting of executive directors of SAF affiliates, an unusual event. The same year, in private conversation with Kugelberg, LO chief Arne Geier complained that employers often used too much piece work in order to "camouflage" earning increases. This collaboration behind restraint at the top was matched by collusion for largesse below. In sectors like the sawmill industry, operating on a normal wage basis, the employer association pursued a "very hard policy" against sur-

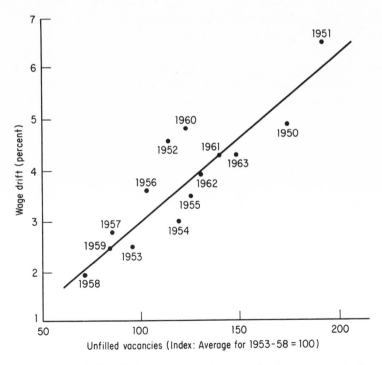

Figure 6.2. Wage drift and labor market conditions in Sweden, 1950–1963. Source: Axel Schwartz, "Löneglidning och arbetsmarknadsläge," *Arbetsgivaren* 14 (August 1964), 4.

reptitious wage increases. Member firms were therefore tempted to convert to incentive pay, which was harder to monitor. They were not particularly interested in its effects on productivity, but rather wanted to liberate wages from centralized control. For the same reason, there was a movement afoot among flour millers in 1965 to introduce performance pay and thus undermine its normal wage system, even though piece work was technically ill suited to the industry's process technology. SAF's new director Giesecke advised against incentive pay in favor of a negotiated solidaristic raise for the industry. A centralized adjustment, in other words, was a more legitimate way to solve the industry's acute "low-wage problem."[48]

By the 1960s, the SAF leadership reached near consensus that the combination of intense competition in tight labor markets and careless use of incentive pay were root and branch of the wage drift phenomenon. Because of infectious wage drift spreading across sectors, negotiated wage increases amounted to a disturbingly small share, less than 25 percent, of total wage cost increases in 1964.[49] Hostile attention focused yet again, though not exclusively, on the building trades, whose infectious drift spread into engineering. Recalling conditions back in the 1920s and 1930s, new "degenerate varieties" (*avarter*) of piece work practices in the construction industry were spreading. The rigidity of centrally negotiated piece rates for the entire country's building and construction sector (resulting from the settlement of 1934 and compiled in "the Bible") had once solved the problem of decentralized and undisciplined piece-rate setting. But now, because of a brisk pace of rationalization, the rigidly centralized system of rate setting perversely allowed earnings to shoot rapidly upward. Construction workers' earnings reached a peak at 148 percent of manufacturing earnings for workers in 1964 and 1965. This alarming result could be attributed largely to piece work.[50]

Collaborative cross-class efforts ensued to reform the setting of piece rates along the "objective" lines strived for in other sectors, sometimes involving the central union and employer officialdom in on-site monitoring of rate setting. Full success in controlling wage drift coming out of the building sector remained perpetually elusive, aided as it was by recurring labor scarcities and rapid change in building techniques.[51] This was, however, only to be expected in the solidaristic system, which imposed on the employers' confederation a permanent role as manager of managers.

Looking Ahead: From Solidarism to the Welfare State

The march of solidarism, which commenced early in the century, did not skip a beat during a generation or so of Social Democratic political domination in Swedish politics since 1932. Despite the fact that wage restraint, interfirm and intersectoral wage compression, suppression of welfare capitalism, and promotion and regulation of piece work were employer objectives, the labor movement lent welcome assistance on repeated occasions and in various ways. Employers were most grateful for help immediately after the party came to power in controlling wages and militancy in the high-pay building trades, solidarism's bête noire. By agreeing to centralized multi-industry bargaining, responsible for wage freezes during World War II and a redistributionist "solidaristic wage policy" in the 1950s onward, unions acted as allies, not enemies, of employer objectives. Despite the underlying agreement, employers continued to find the mass lockout useful in the process of forging solidarism with labor's support. Although supposedly aimed at the union confederation as a whole, the lockout was designed to give LO the pretext to intervene against high-pay militants without losing face ideologically.

Despite the fact that a solid cross-class alliance promoted the development of a dynamic solidaristic system, relying heavily on incentive pay systems to promote efficiency and reduce worker opposition to technical change, the system suffered chronic problems. Wage compression and restraint created large pockets of labor scarcity. In other words, the administered pricing of labor meant wages below market-clearing levels for individual employers. Hence, the system operated in a state of perpetual market instability. A national cross-class alliance created an institutional equilibrium around policies that generated pervasive micro-economic disequilibrium.

Chronic wage drift, or wage increases above negotiated solidaristic levels, resulting from tight labor markets and intense competition over labor, provides telltale evidence of the disequilibrium. Piece work, a practice supported by the national-level cross-class alliance, offered individual employers, in firm-level collusion with their own workers against solidaristic restraint, an easy outlet for "disloyal competition" over scarce labor. The result was, in employers' own words, highly infectious "overpayment" (överbetalning) "black market wages" (svartabörslöner) or "illicit wage drift" (okynneslöneglidning).[52] Firms also spent money, as later chapters show, on segmentalist-style company pension and medical benefits to come out from under solidaristic control. From a collective standpoint, however, employers regarded these practices as disruptive and self-defeating.

The labor confederation and its unions were not well equipped to help employers police such behavior. The best they could do was withhold support for union activists taking excessive advantage of tight labor markets. The labor movement's ideological mission after all was to demand more, not less, for the Swedish working class. However, the labor movement was able to give assistance—through the legislative process—the subject of the second half of the book, in the 1940s and 1950s. Landmark "active labor market policy" would aid employers by better mobilizing available manpower in tight labor markets, reducing the need for disloyalty in the form of upward wage and benefit drift. Compulsory national social insurance would also help by taking company benefits off the labor market agenda. Having collaborated in setting up the solidaristic system, they would now—with the welfare state—collaborate in managing it.

7

CARTELISM AND MARKET CONTROL

The United States in Comparison

To almost all big employers in twentieth-century America, the Swedish system of industrial relations would have seemed a strange and oppressive way to manage their affairs, be it with workers or with one another. It certainly appeared that way to Ivan Willis, an industrial relations executive from Standard Oil of New Jersey, in 1939. From what he knew, the Swedish system

> closes the door to any employer doing more for his employees than his competitors, even though his company is in a favorable position and willing and anxious to pass some of the benefits on to its workers. Even if the unions did not object, his fellow members in the employers' federation would block his setting a precedent that the union might use to club the rest of the industry into line.

On this, Willis had the complete agreement of Homer Sayre, commissioner of the strikebreaking, union-busting National Metal Trades Association (NMTA). As far as Sayre was concerned, the problem for his association, unlike the Swedish Engineering Employers' association, was getting employers to improve their standards, not hold them back.[1]

A national debate on industry-wide bargaining occasioned this critique. The year before, a group commissioned by President Franklin Roosevelt reported their findings from visits to Sweden and Britain about centralized bargaining practices across the Atlantic. Front-page material in the *New York Times*, the report on Sweden found nothing to fault in the country's system of multi-employer bargaining.[2] The report did not, however, go deeply into the reasons for its success and why big business in Sweden was warming up to social democracy. The warming trend was most evident in the engineering sector, the NMTA's territory, because of the control now being exercised over the building and construction trades. By 1941, the Social Democratic leadership had so proven its merit that SAF and VF chairman J. Sigfrid Edström decided to cut off financial life support from ASEA, the big engineering firm he led, to numerous small conservative newspapers. Exasperated at the "badly managed" newspapers' unending requests for handouts, Edström justified the move saying, probably half-facetiously, "for that matter, the Soshies [*sossarna*] are becoming conservatives themselves."[3]

In the 1930s, of course, anything like Sweden's cross-class political concord was practically unimaginable in the United States. The dominance of unilateral, anti-union segmentalism across most of the manufacturing economy made sure of it. Earlier in the century, however, a politically fortified cross-class alliance based on shared interests in labor market control was not only imaginable, it was a work in progress. The chief architect was Ohio Senator Marcus Alonzo Hanna, a supremely successful industrialist, shipper, and banker, with business interests radiating out from the mining and transport of coal and iron. Boss of his state's Republican Party machine, and chairman of the National Committee of the Republican Party—in other words, the party's most powerful national figure—Hanna masterminded Ohio Governor William McKinley's rise to the presidency in 1896. At the same time, he was emerging as the nation's foremost employer statesman. Next to John Mitchell of the United Mine Workers' Union, he stood as one of the main pillars of the National Civic Federation (NCF), a progressive cross-class industrial and political reform association dedicated to all forms of collective bargaining. Hanna served as NCF president for the two years before his death in 1904, Mitchell between 1908 and 1911. Other active employer figures in the NCF during Hanna's time came from the foundry industry, where industry-wide bargaining struggled to take root. The association was also trying to promote the same for the country's engineering firms before being eclipsed by anti-union belligerents like the NMTA and the NAM.

Hanna's friendliness to unionism and collective bargaining predated but also coincided with his phenomenal success as boss of a national Republican Party machine in the making. A pioneer among employer statesmen, he cofounded and led an association of Ohio coal operators in the mid-1870s. Its purpose was to stabilize the anarchically competitive industry with the help of a fledgling union. For his promotion of multi-employer collective bargaining, he was lauded by the secretary of the Miners' National Association as "the first mining operator in the bituminous fields of the United States to recognize the cardinal principle of arbitration in the settlement of wages, [and] disputes." In light of Hanna's career linking industry, finance, and labor market regulation to control competitive anarchy, speculation about J. P. Morgan's open-mindedness about unions and collective bargaining around the time seems all the more plausible.[4]

Hanna's death in 1904 came three years after the failure of industry-wide bargaining to take root in engineering, the same year that industry-wide bargaining collapsed in the foundry sector, and five years before all hope for unionism seemed to be dying in steel. From then on, anti-unionism became a dominant though not all-vanquishing factor inside and outside the Republican Party. But despite all political and legal handicaps commonly blamed for unionism's weakness in the United States, collective bargaining on a multi-employer basis as promoted by the NCF survived and even thrived in a number of important and politically significant sectors. One of them was coal mining, where Hanna began as an employer statesman. The home that unions found here in centralized bargaining was not built on the foundations of employer solidarism, however, as in Sweden, but in cartelism. In short, multi-employer collective bargaining in the United States and Sweden evolved as an entirely different species, in an entirely different market environment, with entirely different political implications.

Negotiated Cartelism: American Unionism's Market Niche

An American industrial relations theorist, drawing exclusively on observations about employers' behavior in United States, once dismissed outright the possibility that employers might organize to pursue the advantages of "monopsony" (a buyer's monopoly or cartel) in labor markets. Because he lacked knowledge of Sweden or other countries characterized by solidarism, his omission was hardly surprising and probably typical. Employers' only market control motive for organizing, he thought, was to inhibit product market competition through joint enforcement of a floor on wages, and therefore prevention of predatory price cutting.[5]

Indeed, employer organization for pursuit of negotiated cartelism marks a good deal of American industrial relations history, especially outside manufacturing. Where employers organized for these purposes, unions did well. In 1934, private sector unions in trades or industries where an association of employers usually, or at least frequently, assumed the responsibility for negotiations accounted for about 77 percent of the entire organized labor movement's membership. Most strikingly, a handful of unions in only three sectors accounted for no less than 51 percent of all union members. In those three sectors—coal mining, clothing, and building and construction—bargaining was virtually always multi-employer in character. Their share remained fairly stable over the first third of the twentieth century, hovering around the figure of 48.5 percent reached in 1915.[6] Union density (the unionized share of the work force) in the three sectors was unusually high, as table 7.1 indicates, while in critical sectors dominated by segmentalism (like steel and engineering) unions remained weak and consistently weaker than in manufacturing as a whole.

Only joint cartelism can explain the exceptional vitality of unionism in these sectors during the period of American history leading to the New Deal, as the following discussion will show. The patchy spread of unionism, where political jurisdiction mattered less than sectoral differences, raises thorny questions about the role of political repression as opposed to variable employer

TABLE 7.1. Union Density and Collective Bargaining in Four Sectors, 1920–1933

Sector	Multi-employer bargaining	Percent unionized					
		1923[a]	1925	1927	1929	1931[a]	1933
Coal mining	Prevalent	57.1	55.4	49.0	37.4	48.2	61.5
Clothing	Prevalent	54.6	55.8	47.1	35.5	44.2	69.1
Building trades	Prevalent						
Masons, tile layers		50.0	—	—	—	49.4	—
Carpenters, joiners		40.5				32.3	
Iron, steel, metalworking	Absent	10.8	10.2	10.1	9.4	12.8	13.9
All manufacturing[b]	Rare	12.7	12.4	12.1	10.9	14.1	16.2

[a]Figures for the buliding trades group are from 1920 and 1930.

[b]Includes major sectors like chemicals, meat packing, oil, rubber, and textiles, where collective bargaining was virtually absent.

Sources: Leo Wolman, *Ebb and Flow in Trade Unionism* (New York: NBER, 1936), index, tables 6 and 7, and Wolman, *The Growth of American Trade Unions 1880–1923* (New York: NBER, 1924), index, table 8.

interests in explaining the broad sweep of American developments. Analysis of differences in employer interests shared with labor—not variations in their power against labor—helps to make better sense of the diversity. Comparative reflection on the Swedish case, where powerful employers welcomed and helped cultivate strong, centralized, and well-organized unions across all sectors—even in engineering—lends great plausibility to this conclusion.

In the Shadow of Segmentalism: Coal, Clothing, and Construction

Historically, the highly variegated American industrial relations practices included decentralized segmentalism, initially "belligerent" with respect to unions, and a collective "negotiatory" stance among organized employers in other sectors dedicated to joint cartelism.[7] Economic theory offers reasons for variation. Efficiency wage theory suggests that, in a decentralized labor market, certain kinds of firms are especially likely to pursue the high-wage, high-benefit segmentalist policy: firms where monitoring of effort is expensive and ineffective and turnover is costly, for example, or firms enjoying monopoly advantages that make competitive entry into their markets difficult, and therefore where premium wages and benefits can be paid for out of monopoly profits or rent. By that token, the theory suggests that firms in sectors where competitive entry is fast and cheap will operate on a different basis—in the shadow of segmentalists. In these sectors, monitoring and "driving" of worker performance may be relatively more cost-effective, skills may be fairly quickly acquired, and therefore the costs of turnover (partly resulting from low wages, partly from disciplinary firing) may be more easily borne.

Efficiency wages, the theory goes, can help explain the existence of voluntary unemployment at equilibrium. This unemployment may help create a pool of excess labor available to employers in the nonsegmentalist sector, facilitating cheap and easy competitive entry. Furthermore, high wages and benefits offered by segmentalists are quite possibly responsible for the leaching of surplus labor from distant, including foreign, labor markets where wages are lower. Hence, many migrants may be willing to venture the price of travel to the vicinity of segmentalist jobs, a virtual lottery ticket for a gamble at high pay and good benefits. Meanwhile, they can bide their time moving about in the nonsegmentalistic sector as they, figuratively speaking, queue up for the more exclusive and secure jobs. This theoretical scenario makes sense of the American experience. Thus, before the partial closing of American doors to immigration in the 1920s, millions of immigrants—including many Swedes— eagerly shouldered the emotional and economic costs of passage in hopes of finding a job with wages only to be dreamed about in the old country. Afterward, the movement of labor from rural America, exceeding what could be absorbed by a high-wage segmentalist sector, probably added to the pool of unemployed feeding and destabilizing competition in the nonsegmentalist sectors.[8]

In these parts of the economy, multi-employer bargaining was most likely to emerge and endure. Where it did, unions gained greatest vitality. Until politics and state power turned against belligerent employers in the 1930s and 1940s, therefore, bargaining with well-organized multi-employer units offered the most nourishing and sheltering institutional niche unions could find. The reason, to be sure, was not employer weakness but employer interest in enlisting unions as the enforcers of a jointly managed cartel.

Cross-Class Struggle: Cartelism in Bituminous Coal Mining

In terms of history, extensiveness, and economic and political consequences, multi-employer bargaining in the American bituminous coal industry towers over all others. The first interstate multi-employer agreement with the National Federation of Miners and Mine Laborers, covering fields in six states, including Hanna's Ohio, was made in 1886. It preceded by five years the important cartelist arrangement between the Stove Founders and the International Molders Union in 1891 mentioned in chapter 3. The same logic was at work. As economist Bauder put it for stove foundries, "The industry needed the Union to protect it from the demoralization of cut-throat competition."[9] The arrangement in coal broke apart by 1889 when West Virginia operators withdrew, followed by those in Illinois, Indiana, and Iowa. Not ready to give up, Ohio and western Pennsylvania operators continued with separate multi-employer district agreements. The United Mine Workers of America formed shortly thereafter, uniting the old federation with groups from the Knights of

Labor, who had competed with, undercut, and weakened the earlier miners' organization. In 1898, interstate bargaining resumed in the "Central Competitive Field" (CCF), which encompassed bituminous fields in Illinois, Indiana, Ohio, and Pennsylvania. The UMW and various state operators' associations, meeting at periodic Joint Interstate Conferences, enjoyed a continuous, if at times rocky relationship of joint control over the industry, lasting for twenty-five years.[10]

The surfeit of labor available for price cutting and low-wage entry into competition made the UMW's services desirable. Although economists, speaking of relative factor endowments, and noting relative wages and net migratory inflows of labor, characterize the United States at the time as a "labor-scarce" economy, the coal mining community saw a different reality. Easy entry made possible by relatively simple machinery and a ready labor supply gave rise to excess capacity and production. Bituminous coal operators recognized that labor was in such great supply that, under untrammeled competition, the price of overproduced coal was "not sufficient to pay a living price for the labor employed in its production." In the Pittsburgh district, for example, one year before the 1898 interstate agreement, a state legislative investigation found that "there are at least two miners engaged . . . for every one man's work."[11]

The dramatic growth of the UMW that followed the 1898 agreement occasioned the joke by John Mitchell, an early leader recruited for his statesmanship in relations with militant workers and suspicious employers, that he was "seriously contemplating the absorption of the American Federation of Labor." The union was aided immeasurably of course by the "check-off" system, a provision of the agreement calling for employers to automatically deduct fees from workers' pay. It can hardly be said that this "union shop" system was forced down the throats of unwilling operators. As *Black Diamond*, a mining trade journal reported, the 1897 strike preceding the agreement had "with few exceptions, the sympathy and moral support of the operators, especially in Indiana and Illinois, who wish them success."[12]

The operators hoped that the strike would allow them to sell off excessive inventory and so drive depressed prices upward. They also anticipated a long-run benefit from forcing recalcitrant employers into a regulated system of wage setting. Their regulatory objective, of course, was to impose a floor on wages and other working conditions affecting production costs and choke off entry by the low-wage, low-price competition. When centralized bargaining proved flexible to fluctuations in demand for coal, things went best, as when Mitchell negotiated a reduction in wages during the recession of 1904. When the union exploited its power to refuse reductions in the 1920s, it proved highly costly to relations with the operators and therefore the union's organization levels.[13] The hiatus in bargaining relations of the late 1920s that resulted was even mourned by employers who hated the disruptively wild swings in output and prices that ensued.

Low-wage, low-cost competition from the South continuously bedeviled centralized, multi-employer bargaining with the CCF operators, which had helped stabilize East-West competition across most of the bituminous industry. This competition, which the union proved unable to control, guaranteed that there would be intense class conflict between CCF operators and workers over how high wages should be. Competition from unorganized coal mines in West Virginia and eastern Kentucky caused the breakdown in the 1920s. Both sides blamed the other for failure. When Mitchell inquired why the operators could not bring their West Virginian counterparts with them to the bargaining table in 1906, the operators shot back: "Why don't you bring them? If it was not for the check-off system granted you by the operators of these four states your organization would not last two years. We are giving your organization its strength here today. It is not you, . . . it is the gentlemen seated on this side of the hall that are making your organization what it is."[14]

Thus, over the principle of organized, centralized regulation there seemed to be cross-class agreement. Intense conflict between capital and labor confined itself largely to what constituted tolerable leveling and structuring of wages in the face of cheap nonunion competition and great heterogeneity among organized operators. On these issues, there was also intense division within classes. Hence, the terms and therefore the factional leadership of the rocky cross-class alliance that underpinned centralized bargaining shifted over time. By the 1950s, for example, the miners' wage policy entirely favored operators using advanced mining machinery. But initially, under Mitchell, central agreements discriminated against them. Thus, piece-rate scales were set high for mines whose thick seams gave access to bulky machinery. In effect, by setting unequal wages, collective bargaining equalized total production costs, leveling the competitive playing field across an industry with heterogeneous technology and productivity.[15]

For example, in Illinois around 1901, the UMW negotiated a "machine differential" of seven cents a ton (49 cents for pick-mined and 42 cents for machine-mined coal). Miners using machinery therefore achieved higher earnings than others and absorbed a large share of the returns on capital investment. This was explicitly calculated "to prevent machines from suppressing the output of non-machine mines." Enough members of the Illinois Coal Operators' Association agreed to outvote others in establishing differentials; thereafter, the size of the differentials, and their uniformity across district and state lines, became furiously disputed items in the association. At least one major Illinois operator changed sides on the issue after investing in machinery. Where coal veins tended to be thicker, as in southern Illinois, some operators bucked the negotiated scales, setting off bloody disputes with union militants.[16] Vicious class warfare accompanied solid alliances in capital-labor relations—not as anomalous, episodic, and localized contradictions to be explained independently of each other, but as two sides of the same coin.

By the 1930s, the lines of alliance had fully shifted, uniting the union and major mechanized mine operators in Northern states against low-wage operators in West Virginia and Kentucky. Promotion of further mechanization of northern mines was designed in part to offset the low-wage advantage of nonunion mines in the South. The legendary John L. Lewis was instrumental in recasting the alliance, eliminating scaled rates despite "rumbling from the ranks." He also served the northern operators' cause with demands for uniform national wage rates, seeking the assistance of FDR's National Recovery Administration.[17]

Lewis stepped up modernizing efforts in the 1950s, financing many a large coal company's mechanization out of its own sizable health and welfare funds. Cyrus Eaton, a coal, steel, rail, and utilities magnate, masterminded the union's financial dealings in exchange for sweetheart treatment of his own mining operations. He also received loans of at least $35 million for his innovative leveraging techniques to gain control, often shared with the UMW, of various utilities that bought coal in large quantities. Lewis negotiated the welfare funds, the source of these finances, with his cross-class collaborator, employer statesman George Love of the Bituminous Coal Operators' Association (BCOA). Together with Lewis, Love dominated the coal industry during the 1950s, from his position of president of BCOA and of the Pittsburgh Consolidation Coal Company (Consol), the world's largest producer of bituminous coal. Love even joined forces with the union to lobby for stricter mine safety law, whose "covert aim was to force small companies out of business by imposing on them the same expensive safety standards required of larger producers."[18]

Thus, according to biographers Dubofsky and Van Tine, "No twentieth-century American labor leader preached class struggle more loudly than John L. Lewis—nor practiced class collaboration more cunningly." There was no contradiction in Lewis's thunderous rhetoric of class conflict, calculated to mobilize militancy in service of negotiated cartelism. Nor was the use of violence against low-wage nonunion mines in the South, about which northern operators perpetually complained, a contradiction. In service of the cross-class alliance, he delegated the "rough stuff" to the infamous William Anthony "Tony" Boyle, whose reign of violent guerilla warfare stretched from the late 1940s well into the 1950s.[19] Vicious class warfare was neither contradiction nor exception to the cross-class alliance, but rather a logical complement.

Another peculiar phenomenon characterizes the special cross-class alliance in American coal mining: upward mobility from union leadership into the ranks of employers and their organizations. Early in the century Mitchell's successor Tom Lewis (not related to John L. Lewis) became a well-paid official of a West Virginia mine owners' association. By the time John L. Lewis was elected UMW president in 1921, "nearly every top UMW official had eventually entered the employ of the coal operators as a labor relations executive with a high salary." This was not at all a traitorous act—more a mundane career move from seller to purchaser in some line of business. There is evidence to think that in 1926 Lewis prevailed on the Peabody Coal Company, the largest operator in Illinois, to hire a bothersome rival for the leadership of his union. The rival sold his chances at replacing Lewis for a salary five times his current one and three times Lewis's own. Most astonishingly, Lewis himself was approached by some unionized operators in 1924 as the best man to head a powerful new mine owners' association, an honor he declined. Meanwhile Lewis would find other ways to get rich and confound naive notions of what class relations under joint cartelism can be about. While still UMW boss, and under Cyrus Eaton's tutelage, he acquired ownership of one the nation's ten largest coal mining operations.[20]

If organized business in coal mining could join labor in such amicable bargaining and other arrangements, it is also not surprising that the network of mutually rewarding relations branched into the higher reaches of politics. For example, William Lewis, the older brother of Tom Lewis, became a close political lieutenant of national Republican Party boss Marcus Hanna after serving as labor commissioner in the state of Ohio under Governor William McKinley, Marcus Hanna's friend and protege. Perhaps given the number of miners in the Ohio electorate and elsewhere in the country, and the ability of mining strikes to upset Republicans' claim to most ably rule the country, it was important for Hanna to find ways to please the UMW. Giving the union a foothold in collective bargaining was one way of helping; providing political patronage jobs for upwardly mobile union officials in government was probably another.[21] But there was more going on here than buying votes, as indicated by Hanna's pre-political career in joint cartelist regulation of the coal industry, and his later work for the NCF.

At the turn of the century, the NCFs' most important mission was to promote industrial arbitration and collective bargaining. It successfully volunteered the services of its Industrial Arbitration Department across the country in promoting "trade agreements"—that is, collective bargaining on both a single and a multi-employer basis. Many active figures in the Industrial Department were employers and unionists from the shoe, typographical, waterfront, and foundry industries, where multi-employer bargaining for bilateral product market control was making considerable inroads. The NCF could also claim at least partial credit for bringing negotiated cartelism to fruition in these and other areas like breweries, entertainment, boiler making, trucking, and clothing.[22]

Friendly relations between the miners' and other unions and the Republican party continued after the passing of Hanna and McKinley from the scene. Mitchell and Theodore Roosevelt continued with a "personal and direct" working relationship. John L. Lewis, a Republican himself, maintained a very friendly but not always smooth relationship with Herbert Hoover. An expert mining engineer, Hoover had reached the conclusion by 1909 that, according to his *Principles of Mining*, unions were "normal and proper antidotes for unlimited capitalistic organization." As secretary of commerce in 1924, Hoover had welcomed the UMW's Jacksonville Agreement for the stabilization it promised for the riotously competitive mining industry. Though Hoover and Lewis would come to disagree strongly about the implementation of the agreement, Hoover publicly admired Lewis for his "sound conception of statesmanship of long-view interest to the people and the industry he serves." Lewis would later serve as the head of the labor committee in Hoover's presidential campaign. The Republican Party's protectionism possibly also helped bring miners and operators together politically, closing off foreign competition that might undercut coal prices resting on the floor laid through centralized collective bargaining.[23]

Everything about early centralized multi-employer bargaining in American coal mining, from formative labor market conditions to its political foundations and consequences, differed enormously from the Swedish version. If an excess of labor was a key formative factor in mining, the opposite was the case in Sweden. In 1911, according to confederation leader von Sydow, Swedish industry had, "until only very recently suffered a labor shortage, while in America, as is well known, a surplus obtains." Coal mining in Sweden, both because of its size, and because of its radically different labor market problems, could never have played such a prominent role in the politics of labor relations as in the American case. In Sweden, coal mining was a tiny industry employing only about 1,600 men (in 1929). Because of tighter labor supply conditions and restricted entry possibilities in Sweden's small fields, these miners' yearly earnings were not much lower than those in steel and paper.[24]

Of course, the mining of iron ore was by far more important in the Swedish economy and industrial relations, though still employing only something over 8,000 miners in 1929. In central Sweden, wages earned by iron miners were slightly above average for all manual workers, but because of geological conditions and limited labor supply, wages in the important northern mines above the Arctic circle (at Grängesberg, for example) were at least 50 percent above the industrial average.[25] Mining companies in both cases did not suffer from easy entry by low-wage fly-by-night operators taking advantage of destitute miners, but more from upward wage pressures originating from big firms suffering little competition and therefore enjoying the freedom to pay premium wages. If anything, because of their monopoly position, their natural labor market strategy was a segmentalist one. They therefore proved close to impossible for SAF to bring under control (see chapter 4).

The varying role of labor and employer militancy—strikes and strikebreaking—reveals the radical difference between the solidaristic and cartelist alliances. Fierce and sometimes violent class conflict never served the solidaristic alliance as it sometimes did the joint cartel in bituminous mining. In Sweden, the real militants—Syndicalists and Communists—played their conventional role in defiance of cross-class collaboration. Their actions were often directed at organized employers and their strikebreakers. Employers used strikebreaking with the known and welcome effect, if not purpose, of assisting collaborative unions at the expense of the radicals. By contrast, American coal operators, outsiders to the alliance, were the ones who used strikebreakers, playing the conventional role of smashing collaborative unionism. In sum, American unionists friendly to employers and collective bargaining were the source of intense militancy to impose and enforce the terms of joint cartelism on low-pay employers. In Sweden, the Social Democratic unions never aimed strikes at employers who defied and destabilized its terms with high wages and benefits.

Finally, the political implications of the two systems were dramatically different. In Sweden, the socialist origins of Swedish unions and their leaders probably inhibited the sort of upward mobility of unionists into the ranks of employers common in American coal mining, channeling it strictly up through a promising career in the larger labor movement and into the Social Democratic Party. Because of the more clear-cut ideological separation of labor market and political careers, business interests could not easily have recruited union leaders into the bourgeois partisan camp the way Marcus Hanna and the Republican Party did. But it was perhaps also in the peculiar nature of union assistance to employers in joint cartelism, helping to fight competitors about whom they had inside knowledge, that the ranks of employer organizations opened to union officials.

The lack of ideological division between labor and capital in the United States did not, however, in the end, help much in smoothing the way toward consensual cross-class relations in national politics as in Sweden. Ironically, more political harmony prevailed there despite the labor movement's more clear-cut socialist ideology. A major obstacle to cross-class harmony in the United States, after all, was the deep divide running through the American capitalist class, with belligerent anti-union segmentalists politically ascendant. Their domination, ultimately even in the NCF, but especially in associations like the NMTA and the NAM, did not allow for a variety of labor inclusion that Marcus Hanna welcomed. To recall, the National Association of Manufacturers did not include employers from coal mining and the building trades, major sectors engaged in joint cartelism, which were not involved in manufacturing. It also did not include the garment industry, the site of peculiarly friendly cross-class relations and still an important part of American manufacturing economy.

The Clothing Industry:
A "Strange Alignment"

Next to bituminous coal, garment manufacturing was the most important sector in American history to experience multi-employer bargaining. Just as in coal mining, unions served employer interests in regulating competition and thereby enjoyed a relatively secure existence. Over time employers realized that only collective bargaining and regulatory unionism could quell the competitive war of all against all and uplift the moral and material standards of their ferociously competitive world. Politicians could help out, combining idealistic with electoral motives. In 1929, for example, New York Governor Franklin Roosevelt appointed future governor Herbert H. Lehman to represent the state as chairman of a board of conciliation for the women's garment industry. One of Lehman's roles was to help employers promote better organization of the industry. The year before, leading manufacturers had complained in 1928 about the "union's failure to bring about complete unionization," and sought measures to remedy the situation. Roosevelt agreed, advocating the consolidation of "strong and comprehensive organizations of both employers and workers," and exhorting them to "work together heartily to spread such enlightened industrial standards into the less fair and progressive portions of the industry."[26] What could be better politically than favoring labor and capital simultaneously? Republicans had done it for coal mining; Democrats could do it just as well for the clothing industry.

Early in the century, the "rock-bottom question" disturbing the industry, according to New York employer statesman Julius H. Cohen, was how to make it possible for manufacturers to "put the industry on a higher plane," or rid it of cut-throat competition on a low-wage, sweat-shop basis. Only then could "legitimate" employers earn a respectable living and at the same time treat workers humanely. Competition was bitter warfare that dragged "inside" manufacturers (larger, often better paying manufacturers combining all phases of production) into battle with all sorts of small outside contractors. There was also the problem, in Cohen's eyes, of "unfair competition . . . among the employees" when they scrambled over one another for starvation wages offered by employers in their own struggle for survival. As Jesse Carpenter put it in his encyclopedic and penetrating analysis of the needle trades, market competition provoked a "war of labor against labor." Intraclass struggle over jobs between the experienced and unskilled, natives and immigrants, organized and unorganized, facilitated and enabled intraclass struggle among manufacturers over markets. Brutal competition "demoralized" the entire chaotic industry, giving rise to acrimonious shop-level disputes, bitter ideological divisions, and greedy racketeering.[27] As any realistic observer could see, no broad interests other than those of consumers, perhaps, were being served.

Frenetic competitive warfare was possible because of the relatively small amount of capital needed to enter the business and an abundant supply of immigrant labor, especially from central and southern Europe. Competitive entry was so easy that workers would often become contractors and employers themselves, as in the building trades, hoping that way to escape their misery. In doing so, they often inadvertently added to the travails of other workers and employers, fighting over precarious and paper-thin profit margins by squeezing wages. As in coal, but unlike in the building trades, however, intense competition was interregional. Transportation costs constituted only a minimal portion of retail prices; even coal operators enjoyed more regional insulation. "So footloose is the industry and so significant is any change in labor cost that even a minor wage differential may result in a shift from one market to another," according to one analysis.[28]

Only a class-intersecting, cross-class alliance of broad geographic scope could remedy these ills, it seemed. Collective bargaining with a strong union, many employers recognized early on, could sanitize the industry by "taking wages out of competition." Initial distrust of unions' control ambitions, however, and especially of their desire for the closed shop, obstructed communication. Gradually, however, a critical mass of employers came to see unions less as menace and more as a source of redemption, or at least necessary evil.

Before finally reaching that conclusion, as one large manufacturer put it, he had as much desire for external regulation by unions "as the devil had for holy water."[29]

An important event in the evolution of negotiated cartelism took place in 1910, when the progressive Boston department store owner Lincoln Filene persuaded Louis Brandeis, the nationally prominent lawyer and civic reformer, to step in and mediate during a strike in New York City. Major strikes disrupted Filene's business, and he refused on principle to undermine strikes by placing orders with recalcitrant employers or to pass the costs of interrupted business onto his own workers. With AFL President Samuel Gompers's backing, Brandeis prevailed on the union to drop its demand for the closed shop and presided over a series of conferences leading to the famous "Protocol of Peace" between Julius Cohen's Cloak, Shirt and Skirt Manufacturers' Protective Association and nine locals of the International Ladies' Garment Workers' Union (ILGWU).[30]

The Protocol Agreement prohibited strikes and lockouts, setting up arbitration procedures instead to deal with wages and other issues not regulated in the document. It also called for the creation of a joint Board of Arbitration, the prototype of "Impartial Machinery" installed elsewhere in the garment industry. Brandeis, the future New Dealer and Supreme Court justice, was chosen as the industry's first "Impartial Chairman." These agencies of cross-class industrial self-governance, initially intended simply as a quasi-judicial device, would often acquire considerable autonomous authority to set industry standards (without formal union and employer association ratification), monitor and investigate compliance, and sanction violations. At times, impartial chairmen "became virtual dictators of labor-management policy for their industries," according to Carpenter. During the 1920s, however, this autonomous regime began to give way to more direct and ongoing negotiation of rules and their implementation by union and employer officials.[31]

Rocky and uneven, the development of multi-employer bargaining across the garment trades never encompassed more than one municipal area at a time until the 1930s. The men's garment industry followed the New York Agreement when the AFL's United Garment Workers (UGW), starting in 1913, established collective multi-employer bargaining in New York City, Rochester, and Boston for skilled workers. The UGW was later eclipsed by Sidney Hillman's secessionist Amalgamated Clothing Workers of America (ACWA), a rival union dedicated to organizing unskilled as well as skilled workers. The ACWA signed its first citywide agreements in New York, Baltimore, Boston, Chicago, and Rochester between 1915 and 1919 and Philadelphia in 1929. Because of intercity competition, and because the union could achieve only partial success in organizing each city's labor force, the agreements were fragile and prone to breakdown. Philadelphia and Baltimore, the troublemakers, were to the heart of the garment industry in New York City what West Virginia was to coal mining in and around western Pennsylvania.[32]

The ACWA aimed in the long run to bring about a nationwide standardization of wage costs, undertaking therefore to restrain wages somewhat in New York City and elevate conditions in other garment centers for New York's competitive survival. The weakness of employer associations and therefore confinement of bargaining to the metropolitan level obstructed the process. President Roosevelt's National Recovery Administration (NRA) experiments in joint corporatist regulation of the clothing industry on a nationwide basis proved comparatively successful and nonconflictual, imposed on an industry with a strong core of support, if not yet organizational infrastructure, for the idea. Among other things, the NRA code for the industry included national wage minimums, a source of protection for New York workers and employers. In 1937, two years after the NRA was declared unconstitutional, the Clothing Manufacturers' Association of the United States, formed in 1933 to help formulate the code, entered into national-level collective bargaining with the ACWA as a substitute means of regulating competition in men's clothing.[33]

In the late 1930s and onward, the ACWA ambitiously tried to equalize labor costs across the entire country, in part in response to complaints from manufacturers. The idea was to impose a detailed classification system for different "grades" of men's garments produced in various cities, depending on the complexity and skill required in their making. Then a standard labor cost would be fixed to each grade. Reversing the pattern observed in coal mining, Hillman hired a former manufacturing executive as director of the union's "Stabilization Plan" of 1939, which no doubt helped him to persuade manufacturers across the country of its wisdom and workability. He also instituted a stabilization department of full-time inspectors "to police the industry and prevent chiseling."[34]

In the women's garment industry, citywide bargaining patterns developed for separate garment categories, the most important categories being coats/suits and dresses/blouses. National-level bargaining never developed as in the men's sector, except in hosiery in 1929.[35] The ILGWU played the coordinating and leveling role across city markets. The division of bargaining labor by product category made practical sense for both employers and unions in their attempts to equalize labor costs for piece-work production of similar garments in the same segment of the product market. In the words of the ILGWU's most powerful official, general secretary-treasurer John A. Dyche, it was "as much in the interest of the legitimate manufacturer to have the costs of labor standardized as it is in the interest of the union." Following a career trajectory common to the coal industry, the dynamic and enterprising Dyche later became a manufacturer himself. But he continued to insist that equality in labor costs must be the first objective of collective bargaining.[36]

Employer associations and unions needed to reinforce and protect each other, the better to enforce discipline in the name of equalization. Some contracts required employers to keep their doors unlocked at all times, subject to penalties, so agents of the impartial boards could "enter the premises undetected and undisturbed." These "deputy clerks" would investigate wages and working conditions and, to help the unions, look into the books to nab employers who subcontracted work to nonunion shops. Unions, according to Carpenter, endeavored to drive reluctant employers into the open arms of their associations so that they could more effectively see to the uplift of the industry. They would, for example, direct unorganized employers to join the association as a condition for ending a strike. Alternatively, they would demand cash bonds for contract performance or exact "fines" to cover strike costs as punishment for refusal to join the favored employers' association. They would occasionally even prohibit unionists from working for nonmembers. When failing to force employers to join, unions often abided by "most favored employer" clauses, refusing to settle on better terms with independents without extending the same terms to the employer organization. The employers' associations then assumed partial responsibility for investigating and prosecuting violations of union agreements with reprimands and fines, including forfeiture of cash securities, suspension, and expulsion.[37]

But primary reliance on the union as enforcer was necessary because, in the absence of a strong union, expulsion of a chiseling employer from the association was akin to teaching Peter Rabbit a lesson by tossing him into the briar patch. Employer associations learned over time that they could best strengthen their own authority by strengthening unions. The gradual advance of the closed shop resulted, therefore, not from any increasing strength of the unions against employers but of their increasing appeal to the more respectable ones, Carpenter concludes. It was in the logic of the situation, ultimately, that unions should play judge, jury, and hangman against employer rebels rejecting "government of the industry." Early on, even if the closed shop was still too much to swallow, employer statesman Julius Cohen sought in the union "one of the strongest means by which to prevent the inexorable law of competition." In contracts, the ILGWU would solemnly promise Cohen's organization to extend its reach over as much of the competition as possible. On one occasion, employers even hauled the union before the impartial machinery for neglecting its express "duty of organizing the industry." Employers often did what they could to help the union, for example, pushing exclusive reliance on union-controlled labor exchanges, punishing firms that discriminated against unionists, and trying to enforce rules against contracting work to nonunion employers.[38]

Obeying the logical dictates of the arrangement, organized employers welcomed strikes, the ultimate enforcement tool against their competitors. In negotiated cartelism, strikes are often directed against employers individually, and not always collectively. Organized employers would refuse to do work on contract for struck firms. Not infrequently, they even assisted in the financing of strikes. In their contract language, they explicitly exempted general organizing strikes from no-strike clauses. Ironically, they would even collude in the planning of general strikes. For show only, the general strike might shut down member firms for a couple of days. Unorganized employers would, however, remain shut down until they capitulated and accepted union wages. Sometimes unions even forced them to apply for membership in the employers' association.[39]

In addition to strikes, organized employers also logically welcomed the active violation of the principles of entrepreneurial and managerial autonomy so ferociously defended elsewhere in the manufacturing economy. Thus, the collective bargaining agenda regularly included issues involving investment, accounting, and pricing. For example, impartial boards prescribed uniform bookkeeping and accounting practices that the unions were obliged to enforce on independent employers. "Bad management practices," among them "ignorance of the principles of cost calculations,"often led manufacturers to underprice their product, and so tighten the screws on prices and wages elsewhere. Through collective bargaining, unions and employers also sought to root out unnecessary and inefficient overhead costs, because of their depressive effect on wages. In at least one case, the United Cloth Hat, Cap and Millinery Workers Union demanded a stop to the production of unprofitable items and even struck against "employers who didn't allow for a fair profit on the sale price of their products."[40]

Joint cartelism even more seriously encroached on entrepreneurial prerogatives with its intrusive regulation of subcontracting. The 1910 Protocol of Peace began by prohibiting internal subcontracting, a practice that turned a firm's workers into employers of cheaper labor. Increasingly elaborate regulations evolved through the 1920s and 1930s. "Inside" manufacturers were often held responsible for their contractors' wages should they vanish without paying. In many cases, subcontractors had to register with the impartial machinery to receive orders. In some cases, the impartial machinery actually acted as a kind of hiring hall, assigning acceptable subcontractors to manufacturers seeking to give out work. In 1913, the ILGWU agreement for women's coats and suits prohibited manufacturers from taking on new contractors they had not registered at the beginning of the season unless all original ones were fully supplied with work, and none could be discharged without cause. This was to prevent the playing of subcontractors off against each other to drive prices and wages down. Unions acted as gatekeepers and police in the subcontracting process. According to Carpenter, employers' associations often showed "far more enthusiasm" for this kind of restriction on their entrepreneurial freedom than "for enforcement of most other provisions in their collective agreements."[41]

Garment employers also affirmed unions' role in enforcing deeply invasive regulation of managerial practices, especially in the realm of piece work. Both sides agreed on the need to prevent the setting of fraudulently low standard times per piece at shop level, and therefore the earning of substandard wages for normal output levels. Sometimes the root of the problem was corrupt unionists making low-rate sweetheart deals that hard-up workers were forced to accept. Sometimes workers made collusive "shop allegiances" to steal work and jobs from other employers. For both unions and employers, according to Carpenter, it was "less a question of how to prevent inequities in wages and standards of living among workers than . . . of how to maintain equality in labor costs among manufacturers." They therefore set up "wage scale boards" and other elaborate joint machinery for centralized monitoring, analysis, and arbitrating of local piece-work practices throughout the industry.[42]

For a brief period in the 1920s, the major unions in the garment industry tried to stop piece work abuse by imposing straight time wages. But in recognition of employers' dual imperative of lowering as well as equalizing unit labor costs, they willingly shouldered the strange burden of defining and enforcing high and uniform "standards of production" to replace the effort-inducing effects of piece work. In short, the union served employer interests in market control through upward leveling of productivity and therefore downward leveling of unit labor costs. Not surprisingly, this peculiar experiment did not last long. In one case, impartial arbitrator William Leiserson, future chairman of the National Labor Relations Board, summarily transferred 7,000 workers, or 55 percent of the Rochester men's clothing industry, back to piece work.[43] The norm, therefore, was piece work, "the sinew of the industry's wage structure," according to one valuable study. Garment unions' acceptance of piece work, and centralized collaboration with employers in regulating it so individual employers would not use it to depress earnings, helps explain their friendly relations with "scientific management" and collaboration in the liberalized Taylor Society of the 1920s and 1930s.[44]

In sum, garment employers organized in the United States to create, as Carpenter puts it, a "strange alignment" with unions "against those who bowed to the law of the lowest bidder" in order to "maintain a floor under competition." The American cross-class alliance was entirely guided by the fundamental concept of "creating and maintaining minimum standards of employment, below which no union member would be allowed to work."[45] Because of identical technological conditions in the Swedish garment industry, one would perhaps expect to find the same employer motivations behind multiemployer sectoral bargaining there. But the facts, consistent with solidarism, indicate otherwise.

During the 1920s, despite considerable unemployment and unstable markets, the Clothing Industry Association (*Sveriges Konfektionsindustriförbund*), sought, for the first time, a nationwide agreement for the men's clothing industry. According to the group's executive director, the purpose was solidaristic. "The foremost task for an employers' organization naturally must be to try and neutralize competition among employers over the labor force." American manufacturers and unions alike would have been astonished that he neglected to mention competition among them over bargain-hungry buyers.[46] Neutralizing competition on a low-wage, low-price basis over buyers was apparently not needed, for the statement was made in the context of a recruitment appeal to unorganized employers. Many of them were disrupting the labor market with their upwardly deviant pay policies. In the United States, unorganized manufacturers were notorious for the exact opposite.[47]

Even in 1931, a Depression year, the Clothing Industry Association deliberated measures to control poaching and advertising for labor. Responding to complaints about disloyal recruitment by fellow members as well as unorganized firms, the executive board sent out a membership circular with stern warnings against wage-inflationary recruitment practices and exhortations to train rather than poach for skilled labor. The following year, when the issue of renegotiating contracts came up, only those sectors in the clothing industry facing stiff competition from abroad called for wage reductions. Home market competition from low-wage, unorganized employers paying substandard wages was evidently not a threat.[48]

Economist Bertil Ohlin, heading a Swedish royal commission studying cartels in the 1930s, substantiated the conclusion that unions and collective bargaining in garments did not function primarily, if ever, as agents and instruments of joint cartels. According to his commission's report, union collaboration in such actions as "intervention to hinder their members from taking work from outsiders" had not played any significant role. Only "to a certain extent" had smaller firms working with unorganized workers been able to count on lower wages. Ohlin found, however, that in the absence of anti-trust controls in Sweden, unilateral cartel arrangements among textile and garment manufacturers, wholesalers, and retailers were partially successful.[49] This success may have rendered unions superfluous as a device to check product market competition. By contrast, stringent anti-trust law in the United States handed this job by default to unions.[50]

Another dramatic contrast between multi-employer arrangements in the two countries involved managerial and entrepreneurial rights. In Sweden, organized employers defiantly blocked all union efforts to put entrepreneurial and managerial issues on the bargaining agenda. With their superficially similar system of centralized bargaining in the United States, organized clothing manufacturers willingly put such issues front and center, as in other areas like stove foundries, where uniform work and apprenticeship rules helped level the competitive playing field.

Profound systemic differences and only superficial similarity characterize joint regulation of one managerial issue—piece work. Collaboration in the U.S. garment industry culminated in the 1930s and 1940s with the centralized imposition of the "unit system"—a "standard data" technique, like MTM, that replaced messy shop-by-shop procedures requiring on-site observation of real workers. "Objectivity" was promoted from the top to prevent the downward erosion of wages. The unions were the chief innovators and enforcers of the system. In Sweden, by contrast, the unions collaborated with employers on centralized regulation to restrain the upward drift of wages, not their downward slippage. Logically then, it was up to officials from the employers' associations to fill the role as primary innovators and enforcers, not unions.[51]

Finally, an intriguing contrast between Swedish solidarism and American can be seen in the role of strikes and lockouts. In Sweden, employers' lockouts, backed to some extent by strike insurance, served as the most powerful enforcement mechanism, keeping localized union militancy in check to enforce a ceiling on wages. It probably also assisted unions in organizing workers, offering as they did "lockout insurance" in exchange for membership fees. In the

U.S. garment industry, the strike was the chief enforcement tool for centralized market regulation, maintaining a floor on wages and helping employer associations by driving unorganized manufacturers into their arms.

Cartelism in Building and Construction: Regulators, Policemen, and Racketeers

In 1931, a national convention of the country's largest building contractors, organized in the Associated General Contractors of America (AGC), attacked "irresponsible" contractors across the land who were taking advantage of Depression unemployment to undercut going wage rates and appealed to politicians for help. In particular, they felt, the government should make sure that its building projects paid "living wages" to construction workers. Congress obliged later that year with the Davis-Bacon Act, which required the payment of prevailing local wages, therefore usually union wages, on all federal projects. The AGC leadership objected only to an administrative detail in the legislation, not the principle behind it. That detail was corrected in 1935, at the height of the New Deal, so that wages would be fixed for the duration of building projects even if prevailing wages changed. The AGC membership gave the law unanimous approval. Their only regret was that it proved ineffective in regulating wages of all unskilled laborers, as opposed to skilled craftsmen. For this reason, as the organization's historian reported, all contractors were still not entirely "on an equal footing in wage competition."[52]

It is probably little known today that the Davis-Bacon Act was a Republican job, sponsored by Pennsylvania and New York Republicans and signed into law by Republican President Herbert Hoover. In the words of Pennsylvania representative Robert Bacon, one of the main problems he wanted to solve was the importing of a "cheap, bootleg labor supply" (often blacks and recent immigrants) by unscrupulous contractors who nabbed prized contracts on the basis of low bids and then dumped the cheap labor, "stranded as derelicts," into an "already demoralized labor market at the expense wholly of the local workman, his family, and his community." President Hoover, who earlier had exhorted businessmen not to lower wages, strongly favored the legislation. (Much later he would look back on the New Deal's minimum wage legislation as one of its "good actions," a remedy for "sweated labor," which was "ruinous to industry everywhere.") So did all the major departments responsible for Hoover's "gigantic building program" ($600 million), which was supposed to help relieve, not exploit mass unemployment. The Davis-Bacon Act was also, of course, supported by the AFL, dominated by people like carpenter union boss William Hutcheson, the "trade union Republican" who headed its building trades division. It is no surprise, therefore, that the measure passed the Senate unanimously and the House by a two-thirds majority.[53]

On the wage issue, if not quite on the relative scale of their building and jobs program, the Republicans got a good head start on Swedish Social Democrats and their celebrated crisis program of 1934. This puts the Swedes' accomplishments in a new and, it must be said, less heroic light. One of the most celebrated aspects of the Swedish crisis program was the new rule, like the Davis-Bacon Act's, requiring payment of union wages on government projects. It was probably also about the most politically controversial. Thus, what Social Democrats had to purchase by propping up food prices at farmers' insistence, organized labor in the United States got from Republicans at no extra charge, and three years earlier. This jarring contrast can be explained only by the cross-class, bipartisan foundations of negotiated cartelism in America's building and construction trades.

Friendly, negotiatory relations between labor and capital in American construction developed according to the same regulatory logic as in coal and clothing through much of the twentieth century. Multi-employer bargaining developed on a piecemeal basis, by craft and by municipality. It stopped at city boundaries because of the immobility of the product assembled, and therefore the highly localized nature of competitive problems in the product market. According to foremost expert William Haber, large numbers of builders in the United States looked favorably upon the union "as a policeman to equalize and regulate competition by enforcing uniform labor and wage standards upon non-association employers." Employers endangered by small unorganized contractors willingly paid the police force "and profited by its operations."[54]

Just as in coal and clothing, an abundant supply of highly mobile labor seeking the relatively high wages possible in the sector made competitive entry on a substandard basis relatively easy. Well organized co-regulation of the construction industry by organized employers and unions developed first in Chicago in 1900, in New York in 1903, and in many other major cities in the following years. Labor organization preceded capitalist organization, and unions were more likely to welcome than fear contractor unity.[55] In many cases, local contractors' associations and union locals negotiated forty to fifty agreements, one for each trade. Sometimes multi-craft bargaining over general terms of employment and procedural agreements took place on a municipal basis.

Very often, unions successfully imposed the closed shop without substantial resistance from employers. Once in place, many initial opponents among employers came to like the arrangement, recognizing how it fortified the union in its task of imposing standard wages, hours, and working conditions of fly-by-night, substandard, and unorganized competitors. Sometimes unions returned the favor, allowing members to work only for organized employers in formal bilateral monopoly arrangements. Employer receptiveness to joint cartelist regulation and the closed shop allowed the sector to become, even more than coal mining, the backbone of the American Federation of Labor and a bridgehead into other industries. It provided almost a third of AFL membership in the 1920s as unionism hobbled along elsewhere, especially in manufacturing.[56]

The vacuum formed by the elimination, in 1921, of union control from the San Francisco building industry illustrates how and why many contractors valued the unions' regulatory role. Before 1921, under union leader Frank Murphy, the Building Trades Council unilaterally legislated conditions of employment for employers, whose organizations pursued trade matters, not collective bargaining. Murphy's "dictatorship" ended, however, when bankers and manufacturers in the city prevailed on reluctant contractors, using a citywide lockout and other devices, to eliminate the closed shop and impose unilateral control of their own.[57]

Within a short time San Francisco building trades employers missed some of the things the union once accomplished for them. Through the San Francisco Industrial Association, they set up an "Impartial Wage Board" as a surrogate for union control. The board's task was to legislate uniform wage scales and pressure contractors to comply with them. Unilateral control by one side supplanted unilateral control by the other. The Industrial Association also took over other questions regarding working conditions, hours, and even restriction of output. Beholding the arrangement, according to Haber, union men were apparently "somewhat bewildered by the apparent effort to be fair."[58]

Labor leaders' bewilderment was probably heightened by fear that they might find themselves permanently out of business. But as it turned out, the employer organization discovered its corps of inspectors lacked the sure means to keep contractors in line. The unions kindly came to the rescue with "job stewards," who would monitor the trades and inform the association of violations. The association would then "chastize" the wayward employer. Then, according to Haber, if an employer persisted in violating the standards, "the Industrial Association sanctioned a strike against him." By 1931, shaky unilateralism had completely given way to a fully bilateral system of control when the Industrial Association invited the unions to place a representative on a revamped Impartial Wage Board. Despite the Depression, big employers argued before the new board that wage cuts were not warranted; some even proposed increases.[59]

The natural working relationship of employers and unions in the building trades gave rise to the same blurring of lines between careers that unionists and employers experienced in coal and garments. A notorious and somewhat exotic case in point is that of Theodore Brandle, a banker who in the 1920s was able simultaneously to serve as president of an association of employers, the Hudson County (N.J.) Building Trades Council, and as the top union official in a local of the Bridge and Structural Iron Workers' Union. As late as the 1980s, employers rented office space in union buildings and even relied on unions to collect their dues—an interesting twist on the practice in coal mining and clothing, where employers collected dues for the unions.[60]

Interlocking employer and union interests in regulating highly competitive industries could therefore sometimes breed the localized germ of corruption and racketeering. This was especially true in the highly decentralized building trades, and less so in the other two sectors already discussed. According to Harold Seidman's historical account, almost every corrupt "labor czar" he examined, mostly from the building trades, "actively collaborated with employers to inflate prices and monopolize the markets in their particular industries." Unions and employers would sometimes also collude in the rigging of competitive bidding processes, where union officials punished low bidders by directing strikes and violence in their direction. Frequently corruption of the joint regulatory process included negotiation of kickbacks for "sweetheart" deals, which gave favored contractors abatements or exemptions from standard terms of employment. Unions would also shake down employers for "strike insurance" payments, an extortionary protection racket enforced by punitive strikes, a choke-hold on the supply of building materials (via control of the transport sector), and sometimes preparedness to inflict injury on people and property if payments did not flow.[61]

The first big labor czars, New York City's Sam Parks and Chicago's "Skinny" Madden, at the turn of the century, were among the most notorious practitioners of these corruptions of regulatory unionism. The successful prosecution in 1921 of New York labor czar Robert Brindell, head of an AFL-affiliated Building Trades Council and backed by both Tammany Hall and the monopoly-oriented leadership of New York City's Building Trades Employers' Association, cleared the way for penetration by a new and more ruthless breed of racketeer, the mafioso. Thus, in recent history much of New York construction has been regulated by "Cosa Nostra" networks—the Gambino, Genovese, Lucchese, Colombo, and Bonanno families—who enjoyed interlocking control of unions and employers' associations. For all its ugliness, many builders welcomed the system for the services it provided, not free of charge, in the form of stability and profitability. "Union corruption flourishes," Seidman wrote, "because certain employers want it."[62]

Criminality in American construction labor, the subject of much historical and government investigation, has also come under the attention of economists interested in the market conditions congenial to it. John Hutchinson argues, for example, that "small business units, high proportional labor costs, intensive competition, small profit margins, relative ease of entry, and a considerable rate of business failures" best explain the construction sector's vulnerability to labor racketeering. Of course, exactly such industries are often hospitable to negotiated cartelism and the "union as a policeman" to enforce its terms.[63] And where there is a policeman, there is also the possibility of graft, shakedowns, and protection racketeering.

In light of Hutchinson's analysis of how market structure correlates with corruption, it is something of a puzzle that Swedish building and construction exhibit the same structural characteristics but not the corruption he described for America. For all the irritation Swedish building trades unions caused employers, their confederation never tried to expose corruption in union practices or discussed it in the voluminous recorded minutes in its archives. The lack of academic or governmental investigation and exposure also indicates that labor racketeering in the building trades or, for that matter, anywhere else in the labor market, has been close to nonexistent. As Marquis Childs concluded during his research in Sweden in the 1930s, American-style labor rack-eteering was "unheard of" and even "incomprehensible" in Sweden.[64]

This absence of corruption may simply mean that other factors affected the supply of thieves and stood between them and their opportunities in Sweden. Cultural or ideological differences may have reduced the pool of would-be thieves and a more efficient criminal justice system, or different anti-monopoly laws, may have radically altered the opportunity structure.[65] But the virtual absence of labor racketeering in Sweden may also mean that Hutchinson, drawing exclusively from American observations, may have missed an impor-tant market-based explanation for variations in corruption.

Solidarism suggests a possible economic factor. In the solidaristic context, unions do not police and prosecute "chiseling"—because underbidding in the labor market hardly happens. Organized building employers in Sweden wor-ried little about the builder paying unorganized workers substandard wages and working conditions. Most of the mischief was caused by the fly-by-nighter in Sweden who offered more, not less, than what unions had agreed to in order to attract scarce labor. If anything, unions were allies, albeit reluctant and ineffective ones, for maintaining a ceiling on wages. Union officials, there-fore, were in no position to enrich themselves with sweetheart deals and pro-tection racketeering. No opportunity, no thieves.

Dramatic differences in the use of piece work also distinguish the American and Swedish building and construction trades. Early on, unions in the build-ing trades in America fought to eliminate payment by measurable unit of out-put instead of hours worked. Contractors did not energetically challenge them on the matter, for they had their own qualms about the practice. The reason was that piece-work practices gave individual firms considerable freedom to chisel, or drive competitive wages and prices down. Surplus labor allowed them to do so by many means, coercive and collusive. Thus, early leaders of the Brotherhood of Carpenters "believed that the legitimate contractor had as much to lose to the pieceworker as did the carpenter." In New York and Brook-lyn, mass meetings held in 1882 between unionists and "genuine contractors" generated joint pledges to eliminate piece work, "which led to intense competi-tion injurious to both contractor and carpenter." Around the same time, Chicago employers conditioned their willingness to engage in collective bar-gaining on the ability of the carpenters' union to "control piecework and pre-vent the overwhelming majority of carpenters from accepting work at below union scale."[66] In short, as Haber put it, "fear of undermining the standard rate" motivated the opposition to piece work—a fear shared by unions and employers alike.

Another supposed reason for the relative rarity of piece work was that it was not possible on a large scale in the building trades. As the typical argu-ments go, individual performance in largely team-based construction work is difficult to define, measure, monitor, and therefore separately reward. Also, a practicable and equitable piece-work system requires uniformity of product. These views are belied, of course, by the extensive use of piece work in

Swedish building trades—also noted by Childs—where workers, union leaders, and employers all favored the practice. Piece work gave workers an opportunity to push earnings upward above centrally negotiated rates, often in tacit collusion with individual contractors eager to finish their jobs or compete over scarce labor. Collectively, employers recognized this drawback but would not part with piece work for its productivity advantages, preferring instead to try and regulate its administration centrally.[67]

Intriguingly, the institutions of cartelism in the building trades assumed—episodically and exceptionally—the functions of solidarism, even if the motive for creating those institutions was different. As Haber notes, building trade unions occasionally resisted worker pressures to exploit cyclical phases of labor scarcity to drive up wages, for fear that they would attract an influx of workers to the area and complicate the task of maintaining existing wage floors later. In an unusual case, a union even agreed to a solidaristic "anti-snowballing clause" during the building boom of 1923 to 1926. The unusual machinery of unilateral cartelism proved particularly useful for solidaristic purposes in San Francisco during this period. The minimum rates set unilaterally by the Impartial Wage Board served as solidaristic maximum rates, so between 1922 and 1926 employers were able to keep the city's building wages down despite the building boom across the country and increases in other cities.[68] Carpenter also mentions a similar cyclical phenomenon in the garment industry, indicating the solidaristic potential in institutions created for bilateral cartelism. Maintaining a "ceiling over competition," unions counteracted individual employers "who deliberately bid up wages in a competitive orgy of labor pirating."[69] As in the building industry, this role was only episodic, largely peripheral to collective bargaining's main purpose.

Conclusion

Taking note of the unusual success of unionism in the American needle trades, American labor historian David Brody once argued that structural conditions faced by unions in other sectors gave their employers a greater advantage in their "battle against labor." In other sectors, "corporate employers had grown too large and powerful" and the skilled crafts had "weakened too much" in the face of these sectors' technological advances. These big corporations were also "too unyielding in defense of managerial prerogatives"[70]

The allure of broad-stroke comparative analysis of this nature, focusing on the competing power resources of capital and labor, fades rapidly in the light of knowledge about how joint cartelism operates. Smallness among employers in sectors like clothing, coal, and the building trades, a function of their technological simplicity and, therefore, minimal capital requirements, did not so much make them weak against unions as against each other in product market competition. Smallness, at least sometimes, was probably an advantage in opposition to unions, for with low fixed costs employers could more easily move about, shut down operations, or take other evasive actions. Larger employers tended often to be more friendly to collective bargaining than small, chiseling subcontractors.

Also, employers—in garments especially—were willing to surrender managerial prerogatives when it served their collective interests in market government. In that sense, Brody is right in suggesting they were not as "unyielding" in their defense. But "yielding" incorrectly suggests passive surrender against a hostile and coercive force. It does not suggest what really happened: open praise for the stabilization and uplift that unions could offer by imposing uniform managerial standards in an anarchic and demoralizing competitive environment. Finally, craft leverage as a factor in power distribution explains very little of unions' success. In the mining and garment industries, if not the building trades, a great deal of the work could be learned in a very short time.

In short, Brody comes close to endorsing what Jesse Carpenter called a "one-way street" theory of collective bargaining, which makes little sense of the enthusiasm with which employers in the needle trades greeted it. "Organized manufacturers compelled to accept one-way dictation at the bargaining table," he argues, "would hardly have shown so much concern for a rigid enforcement of their contracts." Hence, in contemplating the peculiar nature of industrial relations in the American clothing industry, John Kenneth Galbraith had to cite its unions, along with the miners' union, as a glaring exception to his own broad-ranging "theory of countervailing power." The theory, he believed, explained the emergence and robustness of most interest organizations, including unions like the United Auto Workers, as a product of conflicts between large monopoly forces and numerous small economic actors. "Unions have another explanation," he wrote, "in the modern bituminous coal-mining and more clearly in the clothing industry." There they emerged in the face of employer weakness and lack of monopoly, assuming "price- and market-regulating functions that are the normal functions of managements."[71] Labor stepped in to help capital, advanced interests shared across class lines, and thereby achieved its early and distinguishing success.

8

WORLD WAR AND CLASS POLITICS

Solidarism and Intersectoral Control in the United States

In summer 1918, 36-year-old Felix Frankfurter embarked on a project whose scope was nothing short of stupendous, the word chosen by a contemporary observer and later by Frankfurter's biographer. An assistant to President Woodrow Wilson's secretary of labor, he assumed the chairmanship of the new War Labor Policies Board (WLPB) to deal with problems associated with America's growing involvement in the war in Europe. He then asked his mentor and wealthy patron Louis Brandeis to persuade President Wilson of his plan's necessity and to take a leave of absence from the Supreme Court to lead the effort, should the president desire it. But Wilson preferred to keep Brandeis where he was and instead chose Frankfurter himself.[1]

What the future New Dealer and Supreme Court justice set out to accomplish was a nationwide standardization of wages within and across industries in the vast number of manufacturing companies now producing for the war effort. Order had to be imposed on an anarchic wartime labor market producing highly irregular wage increases. In some cases, according to one analysis, they were "wildly incredible ones."[2] Franklin Delano Roosevelt, the assistant secretary of the Navy, had already begun imposing wage controls in the same spirit, through the Navy's Emergency Fleet Corporation and the Shipbuilding Labor Adjustment Board (SLAB), as were other top military procurement officials within their respective sectors. A prodigious administrative reformer bent on better economies and more speed in the procurement process, Roosevelt asserted control over the numerous contractors building ships for the war effort. An acute problem he experienced in the context of wartime labor scarcity was "contractors who paid more than the standard rates in order to attract the employees of other shipbuilding plants." By summer 1918, when Frankfurter was ready to proceed, it was already "settled policy" in shipbuilding—a solidaristic one—to prevent payment of higher than standard rates to any considerable portion of men in any particular craft. Now Roosevelt, also 36 years old, fully supported Frankfurter's more comprehensive project.[3]

Later, as governor of New York in the 1920s, Roosevelt would, as we have seen, sponsor efforts to promote negotiated cartelism in the state's important garment industry. By then, wartime labor scarcity had turned into surplus. Even worse unemployment during the following decade of the Depression would prompt Frankfurter to help the Roosevelt administration in the drafting of the New Deal's minimum wage and maximum hours law. Frankfurter had been introduced to the arguments for minimum wage regulation by Brandeis, cross-class alliance maker for the New York City women's garment industry.[4] After the Depression, the pendulum swung once again as America's full industrial and military engagement in World War II once again replaced unemployment with labor scarcity. State-imposed solidarism returned as the order of the day. Representatives of capital and labor would join in its pursuit, hammering down wage ceilings instead of floors through special "tri-partite" or corporatist boards.

Through all these experiences, Roosevelt and other prominent American reformers schooled themselves in reasons why American employers might sometimes willingly work with organized labor and the state to disable the normal market mechanisms of wage formation. But unlike in Sweden, their chances of forging and institutionalizing an enduring regulatory alliance of unions and employers in America were slim. The roots of unilateral segmentalism had sunk too deep in some places and negotiated cartelism in others. Thus, employers' interests were too deeply divided about centralized labor market governance under normal peacetime conditions. This division among capitalists helped ensure that American politics would remain torn over organized labor and collective bargaining through the rest of the century. Much of the divisiveness concerned, as the following discussion will show, wages in the building trades. Difficulties there were very similar to the ones whose resolution united labor and capital on a national level in Sweden. Thus, the unruliness and embitterment of class politics far outstripped what Swedes experienced—even though socialist ideology permeated their labor movement and should have, one might think, infected its politics with far worse class conflict.

State-Imposed Wartime Solidarism

In the first half of the twentieth century, organized American employers pursued two different and largely contradictory strategies with respect to governing markets. In some sectors, they fought collective bargaining tooth and nail in the pursuit of unilateral segmentalism. In others, they eagerly promoted collective bargaining with unions on a multi-employer basis for the purposes of joint cartelism. Solidarism, however, had no promising career except under wartime conditions. War brought severe labor shortages, making cartelism (to stop chiseling) superfluous, and segmentalism (for attracting more labor) disruptive and self-defeating.

Labor supply bottlenecks and overall scarcities resulted directly from explosive expansion of war-related industry and the military draft. In this context, anti-inflationary wage freezes held wages well below equilibrium for most employers. Labor scarcity and resulting pathologies applied especially to military contractors operating on a "cost-plus" basis. Their government contracts ensured enough income to leave a profit after payment of all bills, including wages. Thus, their powerful micro-economic interest lay in raising wages, by all means fair and foul, to attract more labor. When about the only labor available was already employed, this meant poaching from other firms. Getting ahead in this way was self-defeating, however. High wartime labor turnover and mobility would immediately transmit the pressure on other employers to raise their own wages and give the wage-wage spiral one more spin.

World War I: Solidarism Writ Large

During the scarce labor and high turnover conditions of World War I, employers responded to the strong micro-economic impulse to attract and retain the best workers available by introducing more professional and enlightened managerial practices and a smattering of new company welfare benefits. Any resulting tendency toward greater differentiation across firms in their benefits and working conditions was simultaneously countered by overarching collective pressures for compression of wages. The countervailing pressures emerged, it seems, mostly out of the ranks of wartime government officials responsible for procuring military equipment and supplies.

In effect, when military contractors poached workers from each other, they turned military bureaucrats into competitors trying, at each other's expense, to meet their procurement quotas on time. As the U.S. Employment Service put it, "the recent uncoordinated activities of Government contractors in the matter of hiring labor for war industry," made rational coordination of war production impossible. The lack of coordination, in turn, "resulted in competitive bidding by one contractor against another for the available labor at any scale deemed expedient for the occasion, which has resulted in producing restlessness and wasteful movement of labor from one industry to another." The increasingly manifest idiocy of this game culminated in the formation of Frankfurter's WLPB shortly before the armistice. Its Committee on Standardization was set up in June 1918 to create standardized scales, in consultation with employer and labor representations.[5]

In Frankfurter's own words, the "notoriously wasteful" labor turnover and "competition for the labor supply" necessitated fixing "standards to be determined for all industries in a given section of the country." Standardizing wage conditions across sectors would help eliminate "the incentive for workers to leave one industry and go to another." Because many sectors competed over the same classes of labor (for example, shipbuilding with construction, machinery, munitions railroads, and others), often the wage and recruitment policies of one agency wreaked havoc in the other. Procurement officials had to some extent succeeded in standardizing conditions within industries, but now intersectoral standardization was necessary. In short, Frankfurter said, "Under decisions of the board on this score it will be impossible for one industry to draw the labor supply from another unless it has been regularly determined that the first industry has a higher claim upon the supply on the basis of a more pressing Government need than the industry from which it would draw the workers."[6]

Employers were no doubt ambivalent about the government's gigantic ambition. But its purposes resonated with interests they recognized as their own—the need to check other employers' strong impulses to poach and trigger expensive and ineffective countermeasures. Equilibrium peacetime differentials associated with higher unemployment could not be maintained. This is what W. A. Grieves discovered as an executive at Jeffrey Manufacturing in Columbus, Ohio, a major engineering firm producing elevating and conveying machinery, especially for coal mining and electric locomotives. In a personnel magazine article entitled "Organizing the Labor Market," Grieves criticized "unstandardized rates of wages" and the profusion of federal, state, and local wartime agencies, private job agencies, and employer advertising for causing anarchy in the labor market. "Immediate action on the part of the government is needed," he asserted. Standardization, he argued, would "see that justice prevails between industrial plants, between government departments seeking men, between the men and women seeking work."[7]

To put it another way, Frankfurter's and Roosevelt's designs did not come entirely out of the thin air of ambitious policy intellectuals and the autonomous interests of state institution builders. It was also grounded in a reality experienced by Walter Stearns, an industrial relations executive at Westinghouse in East Pittsburgh, Pennsylvania. At his plant, he had helped set up an elaborate system of job evaluation to standardize pay for its 20,000 workers and reduce turnover across divisions. There was more to be done though, because of "job shopping" between firms, industries, and regions. "The real labor problem," he said, is "the difficulty in keeping men with any one concern long enough for them to become trained and to absorb the spirit of their employer and feel that they are part of the organization." Employers' associations should therefore try to work out encompassing plans for wage standardization within districts. But because the problem was now of stupendous magnitude, "the ultimate aim should be such standardization for the whole country." He therefore asked, "Wouldn't the gains be sufficient and isn't this work important enough, to be taken up by the United States Department of Labor?"[8]

An employer-friendly figure in the wartime administration, former president William Howard Taft, was antagonistic, however. Behind his opposition lay personal animosities developed toward Felix Frankfurter during Frankfurter's time as an advisor to the Taft administration, and probably conflict over administrative turf. Taft headed the already existing National War Labor Board (NWLB), which had been set up to mediate in labor disputes with the encouragement and heavy representation of the employers' National Industrial Conference Board. Now Taft and the NWLB would have to take its cues on settlement of wage disputes from Frankfurter's WLPB. Therefore, we should not take Taft's antagonism as representative of employer consensus. After all, the WLPB included two important employer leaders willing to cooperate, Herbert F. Perkins from International Harvester and Charles Pietz from Link Belt and the Illinois Manufacturers' Association.[9]

At the local level, important employer associations did not unilaterally take up Stearns's suggestions, but they did take measures to try and check "destructive labor recruiting"—what Swedes called "disloyal competition over labor." Solidaristic efforts to limit local and intercity poaching, through advertising for example, was a subsidiary function that became central only in wartime. The Employers' Association of Detroit (EAD) mediated an agreement among companies to cease advertising for labor in an effort to stop wages from spiraling out of control. Ford, initially a member of the EAD, actually quit in 1917, shortly before his solidaristic cooperation was most needed. Detroit employers in the EAD also pressured for a "War Loafing Ordinance." Passed on October 8, 1918, it would have required all workers between the ages of 16 and 60 to carry and, if asked by the police, produce "work cards," documents enabling authorities to catch job hoppers. They even obtained support from the Detroit Federation of Labor for the measure. Had the war not ended the following month, in mid-November, workers would then have been fined $100 or sentenced to up to thirty days in jail for job hopping. Lobbying by the Associated Employers of Indianapolis also led to passage of a local "war loafer" ordinance.[10]

The armistice also put an end to plans for interindustry standardization a few months after it was announced. Frankfurter had managed in the meantime, however, to organize joint labor-management boards for the metal and building trades to fix regional wage standards for both government and private industry. But highly intrusive government-imposed solidarism left no traces in employer institutions and policies after the war and possibly only helped discredit collective bargaining further. Government intervention inevitably meant input from manufacturing unions, which had not abandoned their closed-shop and workplace control ambitions. Union leaders demonstrated little will or ability to force militant members to honor no-strike agreements and abstain from encroachment on managerial rights. Thus, unlike the Swedish unions, they did not trade in their workplace control ambitions for centralized institutions that could produce highly egalitarian distributional rewards over time. They therefore guaranteed themselves a hostile employer attitude toward union input at all levels after the war.[11]

World War II: From Great Depression to Great Compression

A predictably similar story can be told about World War II, when typical labor scarcities and bottlenecks once again triggered massive efforts to impose solidaristic governance. Again, government initiated the process, bringing unions and employers into tripartite boards at all levels to craft policy and promote compliance. Employers resisted government control to some extent, depending on the issue. Their resistance to vigorous and unprecedented government promotion of multi-employer bargaining with unions for the standardization it brought was "not unequivocal," according to Howell Harris. At least those participating vehemently defended the tripartist or corporatist arrangements established to regulate wages. For example, all eight employer members of the tripartite NWLB praised the principle of direct labor and management representation when a *New York Times* editorial in 1943 attacked the board for its lack of "statutory existence" or congressional authorization of any sort—and for its corporatist design, whereby private interests were "vested with the public power to dictate wages."[12]

During this war, ambitions to standardize never reached the breathtaking levels of 1918. The wartime formation of particularistic military-industrial alliances (between the "dollar-a-year men" recruited from industry and various military procurement agencies) obstructed pressures from people like Senator Harry Truman and the UAW's Walter Reuther toward more centralized and rationalized coordination of the war economy.[13] Mere "stabilization" of wages was the government's initial and more modest objective early after America entered the war in Europe. The first steps taken were to freeze existing wages across the board. Then, in July 1942, the NWLB allowed firms to augment wages by up to a 15 percent if they had not already done so between January 1941 and May 1942 (the "Little Steel Formula"). The official justification was to compensate for inflation; an unofficial reason was to reinstate differentials between the majority of workers who had already gained those increases and those who had not. For the rest of the war, direct employer and union participation was enlisted to craft a set of common law principles, to be implemented by regional war labor boards, for approving wage increases on a case-by-case basis. These, almost exclusively, were to allow for correction of "intra-plant and inter-plant inequities." Wasteful poaching, turnover, industrial strife, and upward wage drift were thereby to be reduced. Interplant inequities in fact accounted for more than 60 percent of all approvals for wage increases. In practice, however, the boards sometimes granted wage increases less for equity reasons than in response to acute labor needs of firms and sectors crucial to the war effort.[14]

Only in certain regions and industries did the government, with employer and union collaboration, actively impose solidaristic interfirm standardization in a manner pursued during World War I. In 1941 the National Defense Advisory Committee (predecessor to the NWLB) organized management and labor in shipbuilding to hammer out common standards concerning wages, hours, and shift work in order to prevent employers from pirating workers by offering better terms. In June 1942, the NWLB worked out with building trades unions a nationwide standardization of wages and working conditions, which apparently "had the same effect as the shipbuilding stabilization plan: drastically reducing turnover and wage competition." In 1943, the NWLB ordered the west coast airframe industry to draw up a uniform multi-employer job evaluation scheme for classifying occupations and assigning standard wages. Here, according to Clark Kerr, the pressure for uniformity emanated from employers as well as unions and the government. Other industry-wide standardization of intraplant wage differentials, often through common job evaluation schemes, was introduced in basic steel, meat packing, and cotton textiles.[15]

The most invasive of all the government actions taken against free labor markets did not involve imposing standardized pay administration. It involved restricting the freedom of labor to move freely from one employer to another. By 1943, the War Manpower Commission (WMC) implemented 78 multi-employer, multi-industry plans in labor-scarce municipalities to inhibit job hopping and at least partially neutralize employers' incentive to poach and retain workers by raising wages. Under this system, pioneered in Baltimore in 1942, workers were not allowed to leave their jobs without permission (a "certificate of separation") issued by the U.S. Employment Service (USES), which was under control of the War Production Board (WPB). If they did, they were then subject to the military draft. This was highly reminiscent of the Detroit War Loafing Ordinance mentioned before, which seems to have been largely an employer invention. Employers, likewise, were not allowed to hire workers locally without such certificates. Experience in Baltimore led the WMC to develop a similar program for nonferrous metals mining, milling, smelting and refining, and logging and lumbering in twelve western states experiencing an exodus of labor because wages were still low. Step by step, authorities pieced together a nationwide "command labor market" where the WPB, the WMC, the USES, and the Selective Service (with its "work or fight" policy) all collaborated with employers and unions in tying labor to the firm in labor-scarce areas, forcing it out of nonessential sectors, and rationing surplus labor, instead of relying solely on administrative pricing of labor.[16]

The similarities in labor market practices associated with wartime in the United States and peacetime conditions in Sweden after World War II are striking. For example, in the 1950s, Sweden's VF did not allow its engineering firms to discuss the prospect of employment to workers who could not produce a certificate attesting that they had separated from their previous employers. Uniform job evaluation systems in the United States, designed to make similar work pay more equal wages within sectors, resembled those in Sweden, where even the idea of imposing the system on a multi-industry basis enjoyed cross-class appeal. Also, the expanded use of incentive pay in heavy manufacturing during World War II confirms the strong affinity observed in Sweden between systemic labor scarcity—generated by tight centralized control on wages–and piece work.

For example, the auto industry responded to wage controls, acute labor shortages, and the need for greater productivity in 1941 by resorting to increased use of incentive schemes. Piece work had declined on the whole during the Great Depression. The revival was encouraged from above by President Roosevelt and the War Production Board. The latter cautiously promoted incentive pay under conditions considered inadvisable during peacetime, that is, when individual output was impossible to measure and, therefore, group incentives had to be used. But there were drawbacks. Predictably, as the Swedish experience tells us, excessive wage drift due to intentional "loose timing" of incentive work, and "crude and poorly developed incentive plans" would become a major preoccupation of the NWLB. The board, regarding the problem as "of very high order," frequently stepped in to correct abuses. But like the Swedish Employers' Confederation, it was ultimately unable to impose effective control. After the war, incentive pay once again suffered a decline in the American auto industry in the late 1940s and through the 1950s, as well as among major segmentalists in other sectors, it appears. By the mid-1950s, for example, GE had declared all out war against the system. Crude comparative data suggest that between the end of the war and the late 1950s the share of workers under incentive plans dropped in the aircraft industry from about 20 to 4 percent. No such trend appeared in Sweden, where systemic labor scarcity endured.[17]

Solidarism during World War II, unlike the earlier war, had plenty of time to bring about a dramatic leveling of wages across the economy—a "Great Compression" according to economic historians. Though the machinery of solidaristic wage control was state-imposed, much of the compression came at the behest of employers, especially in low-pay sectors, making uncommon cross-class alliance with unions. Normal prewar differentials "suddenly became serious inequities to both management and labor," according to John Parrish's illuminating post mortem. Thus, the powerful interindustry "leveling up" effect of the NWLB's initial equity rules was so strong and disruptive that they had to be modified.[18]

Low-wage textile employers became proponents of solidaristic wage policy just as in Sweden the following decade. Their goal was to stop Rosie from becoming a riveter, to hold on to a female labor force drifting away for higher pay. Of course, textiles were essential to the war effort, so the NWLB agreed to their urgent requests for increases. The same applied to groups like coal miners and lumber workers. Even cafeteria and laundry workers could be, according to Parrish, "as important as riveters in a bomber plant." Laundries became an essential service in the Pacific Northwest, where in summer 1943 workers would not show up at crucial airplane plants. The reason, understandable perhaps, though probably not to American ground troops abroad, was that "their laundry was not available."[19]

Solidarism quickly fell by the wayside in the United States after World War II. No doubt it chafed against the leading employers' ingrained segmentalism. Perhaps it also snagged against the grain of American ideology and culture. But that may not be an easy case to make. A special breed of employer-initiated solidarism thrives today even in the most American of settings—in professional baseball and basketball, where a scarce and inelastic supply of enormously profitable skilled athletic labor prevails. With a typical solidaristic agenda covering restriction of labor mobility, capping of salaries, and limiting differentials, it is accompanied, characteristically, by multi-employer industry-wide lockouts.[20] In any event, emergency state-imposed solidarism gave way in the postwar period to a dual system of negotiated segmentalism, to be analyzed later, and joint cartelism. Both evolved out of practices from earlier in the century. To understand the peculiar class politics of the postwar period associated with these practices, one must first step back in time and look at intersectoral relations and class politics of the interwar period.

Class Politics and Intersectoral Control in the Interwar Period

Between the two wars, Cleveland, Ohio, was a municipal battleground, among many others, of a class war waged at home. During the 1920s, the Associated Industries of Cleveland (AIC) mobilized an "open shop drive" against the building trade unions. The organization was not led or controlled by building contractors. Metal product manufacturers and bankers were the ones to organize and finance the fight, just as in Sweden, where the same groups dominated efforts to bring the sheltered sectors' wages and workers under control. Thus, the AIC, like other city-level organizations across the country, operated according to the realization that contractors' interests in joint cartelism made them reluctant and unreliable allies at best. Hence they "could not be depended upon to fight the building trades unions," and "the business men in the collective sense in any community are responsible if the contractors fail to operate on the Open Shop."[21]

The Cleveland campaign was led by William Frew Long, who through his far-flung activities personally connected it with belligerent metal trades manufacturers organized nationally in the NAM, the NMTA, and the NFA. They in turn supported similar municipal actions around the country. Though a municipal effort, the Cleveland battle reverberated in national politics. Long blamed Robert LaFollette's majority in the Cleveland area in the presidential campaign of 1924 on the "radicals who are fed and nurtured in our building-trades unions." Later in the 1930s LaFollette would single out the AIC among other possible city organizations for his Senate committee's in-depth investigations of various employer associations and their violations of the rights of labor.[22]

In the United States, unlike Sweden, organized capital never received assistance from labor in controlling the building trades. Therefore, the intersectoral struggle was exclusively a unilateral one, largely fought on a municipal battleground. By the 1930s, in Sweden, organized capital and dominant elements in organized labor united behind a goal of controlling the building trades. Had a similar alliance been possible in the United States, it might have appeased the more belligerent among employers and, as in Sweden, pacified the country's particularly ugly and unruly class politics.

Belligerent Outsiders Seek Control
of the Building Trades

The first open-shop crusade, during the twentieth century's first decade, was in many ways a mission led by engineering and steel employers in order to extend their victory into the building trades. For example, as Thomas Klug writes, in 1904, metal manufacturers in Detroit coordinated the charge on the new front, accepting the risk of temporarily weakening their flank against the machinists' union. The reason was that members of the Employers' Association of Detroit (EAD), according to Klug, "considered the open shop in the building trades a precondition of anti-unionism in the metal trades." Therefore, metal trades employers dominating the EAD did not wait for contractors to bring a Builders' Association of Detroit into the world. For this, they borrowed John Whirl, the EAD's dynamic Labor Bureau chief, to conduct a fight that building contractors would never have pursued on their own.[23]

In many cities the campaign failed—Chicago, for example. The same year that the EAD began its battle in Detroit, Chicago's International Harvester had to give up its fight with the building trade unions in order to concentrate efforts on the continuing fight against unionization of its metalworkers. In exchange for the separate peace, the Chicago Federation of Labor, dominated by the building trades, turned its back on the company's metalworkers, thereby allowing Harvester's McCormick plant to avert a successful strike and organizational victory. For this favor, the city labor federation extracted a promise from the company to put up new buildings only on union terms. This demonstration of weakness at the municipal level persuaded manufacturers that they needed to coordinate the attack on a nationwide basis. Clarence Bonnett reports that in 1907 the NAM, representing manufacturers, promised large sums of seed money to San Francisco businessmen if they would gather additional funding for a general lockout of the union federation in that city, dominated as it was by the building tradesmen. In 1910, employers far and wide helped in the San Francisco fight, including city organizations like the Metal Manufacturers' Association of Philadelphia and the highly belligerent National Erectors' Association.[24]

The more abundant literature on the open-shop crusade of the 1920s regularly recognizes that manufacturers were the chief belligerents and the building trades the neutral territory to be occupied and controlled. Manufacturers and the organizations they dominated intensified and perfected their efforts against construction in the 1920s after a temporary lull imposed by the government, seeking cooperation from the American Federation of Labor (AFL) during World War I. According to Irving Bernstein, local open-shop crusades like the one organized by the Industrial Association of San Francisco were "a local expression of the nation-wide open shop drive, primarily directed at the construction industry." Manufacturers, but also banks and insurance firms, were the chief organizers and financiers of the battle.[25]

The NAM's calculations for 1925 assured the crusaders that, of approximately 187,000 manufacturing establishments (minus the garment, news-paper, and commercial printing industries), roughly 97 percent were open or nonunion shop. (In the three others, the open or nonunion shop covered only 41 percent). After building, the remaining big trouble spots were transporta-tion and mining.[26] By the mid-1920s, therefore, the only reason the open-shop movement raged on was manufacturers' desire to clean up the building trades and other nonmanufacturing sectors.

Thus, the Associated Employers of Indianapolis (AEI), having achieved ex-traordinary success in establishing and defending the open shop in manufac-turing since around 1905, set about in the 1920s, in Bonnett's words, to "aid the contractors in the closed-shop branches of the building trades to put these on an open-shop basis whenever these contractors desire or become willing to make the change." Closely aligned with the Indianapolis branches of the NMTA and the NFA, and assisting in those national organizations' work across the country, the AEI had succeeded only temporarily in doing this back in 1909. Because of its work in "industrial hygiene of the highest order," as the NAM's James Emery put it, labor radicals regarded the city as the "scabbiest hellhole in the United States," even if the AEI failed miserably in ridding the city of building trades unions. In Cleveland, too, William Frew Long's "well-planned offensive" by the AIC against the building trades unions enjoyed only tempo-rary success, because of building contractors' divisions and lack of interest.[27]

Two interesting and distinctive cases were those of San Francisco and Chi-cago, whose temporarily successful campaigns inspired the one in Cleveland. (The AIC, founded in 1920, was initially called the "American Plan Associa-tion of Cleveland "in admiration of the "American Plan" issued by the Indus-trial Association of San Francisco, the nemesis of that city's powerful building trade unions.) In Chicago, a citadel of building trades union strength, a "Citi-zen's Committee" headed by manufacturing employers raised $5,000,000, and hired 12,000 strikebreakers and 600 private guards, to enforce a harsh ar-bitration award in 1921 (the "Landis award") on the militant unions. The same Chicago group, union officials believed at the time, figured prominently in the organization and financing of the NAM's nationwide open-shop drive. The Landis award included reductions of wages to levels—as in Sweden in 1934—"considerably below those which the [building] employers had been willing to grant." This proved to be a bad miscalculation, for contractors sys-tematically violated the wage reductions, and within six years fully repudiated what manufacturers had tried to impose. In San Francisco, it took a little longer, but only a decade, before total success in eliminating union control gave way to contractors' invitation to the building trade unions in 1931 to nominate representatives to their "Impartial Wage Board."[28]

It is telling that the most belligerent and effective of all building employers associations, the National Erectors' Association (NEA), represented national-level manufacturers' interests more than those of local contractors. Accord-ing to Sidney Fine, steel magnates early in the century were haunted by the ef-forts of the militant International Association of Bridge and Structural Iron

Workers (IABSIW) to unionize the production as well as use of structural steel by refusing to build with nonunion products. Thus, big contractors established the NEA in 1903 to stop the AFL, as the NEA's Walter Drew put it, from using the tough IABSIW "as an entering wedge for the closed shop in the steel industry." Dominant among the contractors was U.S. Steel's American Bridge Company, formed in 1900 with a merger, financed by J. P. Morgan, of 25 smaller companies. In fact, the principal NEA members were primarily fabricators rather than erectors of structural steel: the entire membership fabricated twice as much steel as they used. Not surprisingly, then, Drew claimed that the NEA's labor policy was "more largely and directly a matter concerned with the steel industry than with the building industry."[29]

Getting rid of unionism in the erection of structural steel was relatively easy, given the integration of fabrication and erection in leading companies and their ability to withhold steel from other more union-friendly users. In the pre–World War I era, the NEA was therefore able to keep structural steel erection in Pittsburgh, Hartford, Buffalo, and Milwaukee on an open-shop basis. In the interwar period up to 1930, the NEA made considerable progress imposing the open shop on structural steel erection in Philadelphia, Minneapolis, St. Paul, Milwaukee, San Francisco, Los Angeles, Seattle, and Dallas. But the closed shop remained strong in Chicago, Detroit, St. Louis, Cleveland, Pittsburgh, Baltimore, Kansas City, Boston, and Jersey City.[30]

Open-shop crusaders across the country saw the big general contractors as "the weak link in the open shop chain," to quote Walter Drew again. These big firms usually dealt willingly with unions in cities where the building trades were strong. Then, in order to preserve unions' favor in those places, they accepted unionism in other cities.[31] Observing the behavior of these "indifferent and uncertain" large contractors operating in many localities, "American Plan Conference" organizers declared it imperative for the movement to maintain momentum in local victories with a nationwide one across the country. In the words of the 1925 conference, "large contractors must operate over a wide field and cannot adopt the attitude of the Open Shop in the community in which he resides and the closed shop attitude in another. With uniform open shop conditions in all communities the larger contractors will more readily yield to the Open Shop sentiment."[32]

Employer Motives

Organized manufacturing employers outside construction battled the building trades unions for multiple reasons. Some were different from those of their Swedish counterparts, and some similar, though not identical. The most important probably relate to segmentalists' dual objectives of maintaining managerial control in the manufacturing sector and limiting the upward pull on wage differentials required to maintain efficiency wage advantages. On the whole, organizations like the NAM, the NMTA, and the NFA agreed with the Detroit employers' motives in 1907, cited earlier, who saw the building trades unions as a constant threat to the open shop, and therefore untrammeled managerial rights, in manufacturing. In 1925, NAM's Noel Sargent declared that building unions' efforts to establish the closed shop in Detroit "will, if successful, be used to create a closed shop nucleus to establish complete unionization in the home of the American automobile industry." (Until 1933, General Motors had no dealings with labor unions except for a few craft unions in the building trades.) In short, as LaFollette's Senate committee reported, "Strong and successful, the building-trades unions gave great impetus, both by their example and by their activities, to unionization in other industries."[33]

Manufacturers had another important motive for their attack on unionism in the building trades. High and increasing wages in construction sabotaged their own wage policies. According to discussions at the 1925 "American Plan Open Shop Conference" in Kansas City, "wages in the building crafts exert a tremendous influence upon the wages in other lines of endeavor," so building contractors "should not be permitted to grant indiscriminate wage increases without conferring with all other agencies concerned through the industrial association." For this, "a solid phalanx in all lines of business" was needed. The "Handbook" of the American Plan Conference in Detroit the following year proclaimed, "There should be no isolated, independent action on the part of any employer or group of employers in establishing a wage scale in complete disregard of the effect it will have upon the entire industrial and community life." That the highly seasonal building industry was the worst transgressor in this regard reads implicitly in the Handbook's declaration that

> [t]here is a natural and logical relationship that should be recognized between wages in permanent occupations and those of a seasonal character. There should be no competition that would result in increased labor turnover or a continuing ebb and flow between industries of the two kinds described. This harmonizing can be brought about by conferences between employers having seasonal work and those in permanent industries.[34]

Ongoing wage trends explain their preoccupation with the intersectoral problem. In 1919 and 1920, the postwar construction boom following the wartime decline gave building wages an almost 50 percent boost while manufacturing wage rates were dropping. Intense competition in industry brought sluggish wage growth in the 1920s, but wages in construction climbed steadily as residential construction soared and skilled craftsmen took advantage of their scarce supply. Between 1923 and 1929, for example, hourly wages in the building trades in 23 cities increased by 22 percent, while skilled and semi-skilled pay in manufacturing only rose about 8 percent.[35] Manufacturers' problem with high wages being paid by building trades contractors continued into the early years of the Depression—while in their own sectors low wages were the cause for alarm. In reference to the building trades, Noel Sargent, the NAM's Industrial Relations Department manager, complained in 1931 that "there exists unjust alignments of wages in certain trades as compared with wages of workers in other trades who must possess substantially the same degree of ability." Meanwhile, in San Francisco that year, employers in the building trades saw no need for wage reductions, and some even called for increases, as big segmentalists like U.S. Steel, International Harvester, and Ford were making their first big cuts. Four years later American Management Association president M. C. Rorty complained that recovery was seriously handicapped "by the rigid maintenance of . . . high levels of building wages."[36]

Even for leading segmentalists, the best of the welfare capitalists during the 1920s and early 1930s, wages being paid in construction confronted them with a disruptive standard of reference for what workers would consider "good wages." In other words, the higher the wages were in construction, the more a good employer probably had to spend for an efficiency effect. In 1921 Eastman Kodak created its own nonunion building division oriented to union wages and working conditions and provided a premium in the form of and steady employment for its building workers. Other welfare capitalists could not afford to be so generous. General Electric paid its in-house building craftsmen 20 percent less, and Procter and Gamble 35 percent less, than independent contractors. They made up for the differential, however, with more regular and often indoor work, lower transportation costs, and welfare benefits that regular building craftsmen never enjoyed.[37]

Probably all manufacturers had to orient themselves to building trade wages in the external labor market. For the big segmentalists, upward adjustments in their own wages for in-house work would disrupt internal wage differentials often carefully maintained to reduce turnover, preserve a sense of equity across occupations, and therefore overall morale, within the company. Therefore, changes in intersectoral differentials could easily disrupt the harmony and productive efficiency that the enlightened pay practices, practiced by segmentalist employers, were designed to promote. To the extent that the belligerent anti-union open-shop movement of the 1920s and early 1930s fought to control wages in construction, and therefore what the NAM called "unjust alignments of wages," they were also helping leading manufacturers deal with their own local labor markets on a segmentalist basis. Thus while in Sweden intersectoral control by manufacturers had been part and parcel of a strategy to impose solidarism on an encompassing, centralized basis, in the United States it was aimed at stabilizing a highly decentralized strategy of segmentalism.

Appealing to the Public:
Cutting the Costs of Cartelism

In the bitter political battle for public opinion, the open-shop movement focused not on the intersectoral wage problem, but on the more visible problem of building costs. Here they had a better chance of convincing the public that as consumers, taxpayers, and even churchgoers they shared interests in controlling unions. In 1907, the NMTA's *Open Shop* magazine attributed the "universal complaint of high prices in building" to the "heresy" and "pernicious teachings of unionism." In the 1920s they played the same tune louder and longer. The NAM's "Open Shop Department," established in October 1920 for "informational" and "education" purposes ("to convince the general public of the justice of the Open Shop") devoted a great deal of its publicity to the role of unions in raising building costs, though nonunion wages had been rising too, along with cost of building materials. A barrage of NAM pamphlets, bulletins, and press releases pounded away at the subject. The NEA's Drew was the author of an important one in 1922, "Building and the Public," which declared unions responsible for, among many other things, "a high overhead for the manufacturer and merchant" and for "the heavy burden of rent." Likewise, reasonable building costs headed the list of likely benefits to the community from the open shop in the 1926 "Handbook of the American Plan Open Shop."[38]

NAM press releases fired away at these issues to win public sympathy. Most focused on the high cost of residential building, reporting on NAM studies showing, for example, that the amount of building per capita was 45 percent greater in open shop towns or that rent increases had been three times as great in the past two years in closed-shop cities. Others aimed at buyers of America's affordable cars by trumpeting the successes of the country's union-free auto industry and warned of threats to that industry from building trade unions. Yet others aimed to show how religion and education paid forced tribute to the building trades unions in the form of expensive churches and schools. On the education issue, the NAM also targeted an elite audience, distributing an address by former Harvard University President Charles Eliot recounting his horror stories about delays and costs that he had personally seen on Harvard construction projects and his retirement mansion.[39]

No doubt, the publicity campaign against the building trades unions fell on sympathetic working class ears, too. After all, these unions dominated the crafts-based AFL, which during the 1920s and 1930s collaborated in an unholy alliance with employers to obstruct unionization of unskilled and semi-skilled workers in big manufacturing enterprises and to revise the National Labor Relations Act after 1935 to weaken the CIO.[40] Thus, deep division within the American labor movement over the AFL's obstruction of industrial unionism created at least a fragile basis for a potential cross-class alliance for intersectoral control late in the 1930s—once industrial unionism in manufacturing was taking root with the encouragement of the Wagner Act and the National Labor Relations Board it established.

Indeed, in 1938, the UMW's John L. Lewis and the new Congress of Industrial Organizations (CIO) made moves that might well have helped thaw relations with anti-union belligerents. Their newly formed Construction Workers' Organizing Committee (CWOC) offered attractive services to American segmentalists and promised a punch or two in the jaw to the AFL. These included providing (1) lower, more uniform, and more compressed pay scales in the building trades; (2) no crafts divisions and therefore no costly jurisdictional disputes; (3) no interference with new methods of production beneficial to manufacturers, including prefabrication; and (4) less racketeering and corruption.[41]

But wartime exigencies smothered any nascent cross-class friendship that manufacturing employers might have extended in support of the CIO and a negotiated system of intersectoral control. Of all people, CIO and garment union statesman Sidney Hillman, Roosevelt's labor representative on the National Defense Advisory Committee, found it expedient to kill the CWOC. He bypassed the fledgling union in brokering an agreement between the Building and Construction Trades Department of the AFL and government agencies desiring to get defense projects quickly under way with a minimum of intra-class jurisdictional warfare. To the CIO's indignation, one of the CWOC's favored contractors was passed over in 1941 even though its bid for a defense housing project in Detroit was substantially lower than the winner's. Even Harry Truman's Senate committee overseeing mobilization efforts pressured Hillman and the administration to rescind the contract, but failed. Now the war emergency brought forth an entirely different machinery of intersectoral control, as described earlier, a temporary system of state-imposed solidarism. Holding peak hourly rates in building and construction down was particularly high priority for the NWLB. Interestingly, the last solidaristic controls to be dismantled were those over the building and construction industry, in February 1947. Accumulated demand for civilian housing threatened skyrocketing wages, just as after World War I.[42]

No contrast with the Swedish case can better illustrate the fundamental difference between class politics in the two countries than manufacturers' relations with the building trades. The fact that the Swedish employers could look with such equanimity on the social democratic labor movement in the 1930s and onward can be attributed in large measure, especially early on, to the cross-class alliance against the building trades. Such an alliance was only possible because employers had helped institutionalize a kind of unionism that could live happily with virtually untrammeled employer prerogatives. In the United States, by contrast, manufacturing employers had been unable to force unions in manufacturing to accept managerial absolutism. They chose instead to disable and shut out those unions, eliminating them as potential allies against construction later. Thus, they were left to their own devices against the distributional and other disturbances emanating from the building trades. Class politics in America remained embittered; in Sweden they became a model to be widely admired and misunderstood.

Postwar Class Relations: Negotiated Segmentalism

During the interwar period, General Electric executive Gerard Swope (probably together with GE's Owen Young) broke ranks in a surprisingly big way with other large anti-union segmentalist employers. In 1926 Swope personally invited William Green, president of the AFL, to organize a union on a non-crafts industrial basis which he could, as he told reformer Alice Hamilton, "gladly" work with. Collective bargaining with a host of competing craft unions, all with their conflicting traditions and contested jurisdictions, remained unappealing. Governor Franklin Roosevelt, cross-class alliance maker for the garment industry, picked up on the employer statesman's initiative and tried to broker an arrangement with the New York State Federation of Labor. No doubt, the deal would have involved a hands-off clause for the union regarding managerial decision making. But Roosevelt's efforts came to nothing because of the rigid craft-based traditions and power configurations in the AFL. Some of its unions had already staked out turf at GE.[43]

Thirteen years later, shortly before World War II broke out, Allen Gates, Eastman Kodak's director of training, conceded the perfect feasibility, though not pressing desirability, of combining collective bargaining with enlightened company wage and benefit practices. What actually emerged after the war—a system of negotiated segmentalism—bore great resemblance to what he and Swope thought workable. Unions strengthened by the Wagner Act of 1935 and by wartime political deals ("maintenance of membership" or union security in exchange for collaboration in wage controls) were now brought into the system as joint participants in company-level policy making. But first the postwar employer backlash against wartime encroachments on managerial rights had to create a tolerable bargaining partner in organized labor.[44]

Wartime solidarism left only obscure traces. Uniform multi-plant and multi-employer job evaluation, as in California's aircraft industry, was one feature that survived here and there, with unions' blessings. In steel, uniform job evaluation and "pattern bargaining" probably served a subsidiary cartelist function in imposing standards on "little steel" to the benefit of the big companies. At the same time, high wages and good benefits relative to standards in local labor markets in which various steel plants were located continued to serve their efficiency wage function.[45] Wartime regulations also help explain the enormous importance of company welfare benefits in the postwar efficiency wage package. While holding the brakes on wage increases during the war, the NWLB gave vent to intense employer and union pressures for increases by ruling in 1943 that employer contributions to group insurance and pension plans, and other "fringe benefits" like paid holidays, vacations, and sick leave, would not be counted as wages. Tax laws were rewritten too, to give firms powerful incentives to shift remuneration into insurance benefits, at an estimated loss to the Treasury of $3 billion a year.[46]

Hence, during the war, worker coverage under company pensions increased dramatically. In manufacturing, roughly one quarter of all firms offered pensions on top of Social Security coverage by the end of the war. Only about 8 percent had done so in 1940. In all private sectors, the number of beneficiaries almost doubled. The share of firms providing medical and hospitalization insurance reached about two thirds in 1946, double the figure in 1940. Hospital coverage in Blue Cross and other group plans almost quadrupled. This rapid spread of benefits had not been intended, but the genie was out of the bottle. The best the NWLB could then do was try to impose fairly uniform standards, and therefore limits on their upward drift.[47] The Swedish Employers' Confederation experienced similar problems later in the 1940s, when company benefits took off under conditions of acute labor scarcity, flying out of reach of the organization's powers of solidaristic enforcement.

Not long after the war, union pressure and the Supreme Court, in the 1949 *Inland Steel* case, forced employers to include unions in collective bargaining over company fringe benefits. Organized labor would henceforth become intimately implicated in America's highly inegalitarian system of social protection. But the decision only forced employers to bring unions into decision making about things they were already eager to provide. Unions had once been generally hostile or at least highly ambivalent about things like group health insurance, preferring more wages instead. Employers were the original source of most benefits. An important case in point is paid vacations, which many employers introduced in the 1920s to improve productivity and reduce turnover. According to an astute study by Donna Allen, unions had begun incorporating already existing vacation plans in their contracts and taking full credit for their existence by the 1940s. Part of the reason was that the NWLB forced them to choose between benefits like these, in lieu of wage increases, or nothing at all.[48]

In the 1950s and 1960s, employers continued to roll out the benefits carpet as a path of low resistance compared to wage increases. Some of their resistance was probably feigned in order that unions and workers could come away with a feeling of victory for their militant efforts. This was the case for benefits at General Motors, where, according to President Charlie Wilson, the union leaders "won't go along" with the welfare benefits he favored "unless it's a 'demand' we resist and they 'win'." By the 1960s, according to Allen, on the whole "the employers were content to let the unions take credit for the fringe benefit movement." They remained, however, after as before the war, a major source and beneficiary of this "hard-headed business device." Now that unions could claim responsibility for a complex system of negotiated benefits, they no longer portrayed welfare capitalism as an evil. Despite the bilateral nature of benefits growth, the 1960s was in reality, Allen concludes, "Management's Decade." So advantageous were fringe benefits to employers, she says, "that had there been no unions at all, there would have been a fringe benefit movement."[49]

Thus, segmentalism reemerged ascendant in manufacturing after World War II, with bilateral and unilateral variants coexisting side by side. Major manufacturers like Kodak, Du Pont, and IBM managed to maintain their nonunion status while most major segmentalists reconciled themselves to collective bargaining on a company-by-company basis. Tensions endured, of course, between unionized companies and organized labor about the terms of segmentalism. In 1941, the United Electrical Workers forced General Electric to abandon its "community survey" method of wage setting for different plants in Lynn, Schenectady, and Erie. That method had fixed wages according to local market conditions and made sense from an efficiency wage standpoint. The union's militant push for company-wide leveling added to the many provocations that produced GE's newly belligerent stance toward unions. In the 1950s, the United Auto Workers and the United Steel Workers also pushed through, with some success, company-by-company pattern bargaining, for increasingly uniform conditions across plants and firms within the industry, while agitating for industry-wide centralization of bargaining. The big auto and steel makers were probably ambivalent, tacitly recognizing the cartelist benefits associated with piecemeal imposition of standards against smaller competitors while loudly resisting demands to equalize wages across their own corporations' far-flung operations.[50]

Despite any good feelings mixed in with the bad about pattern bargaining, unionized segmentalists completely rejected industry-wide multi-employer bargaining that unions like the UAW and the USW hoped to bring about during and immediately after World War II. They therefore joined forces with their nonunionized counterparts in a battle for the amendments to the National Labor Relations Act of 1935 that would outlaw multi-employer bargaining. The NAM, revitalized in the early 1940s under the leadership of welfare capitalist Frederick Crawford from Thompson Products of the aircraft industry, the best-paying employer in the Cleveland area, took charge of the battle. The NAM succeeded in 1947 with the passage of the Taft-Hartley Act, which was supposed to partially untie employers' hands in dealing with untrammeled union aggression, and took particular aim at cartelist unions in coal and construction. But they failed in including a prohibition against all multi-employer bargaining in the legislation.[51]

Some indecision and debate among major manufacturers about industry-wide multi-employer bargaining had resulted from the FDR commission's unanimous and entirely flattering 1938 reports on Sweden and Britain, signed by GE's Gerard Swope, U.S. Chamber of Commerce president Henry Harriman, and even Charles R. Hook, NAM president. By the end of the war, however, big manufacturers chafing at union encroachments on management were not about to grant them even more leverage. For example, George Romney, managing director of the Automotive Council for War Production, spoke for the entire industry in blasting the UAW's push for postwar industry-wide bargaining. In the ensuing years' debate, only a few manufacturing industries stood up for the practice. For example, positive experiences were reported from national or regional industry-wide bargaining in pulp and paper, flat glass, elevator manufacturing, and breweries, and especially in the San Francisco area, where the metal trades and some light manufacturing joined many other nonmanufacturing sectors in peaceful multi-employer bargaining.[52]

Centralization never had much of a chance among segmentalists in more important areas. Some of their hostility to industry-wide bargaining might be attributable to worries about the disruptiveness of industry-wide rather than company-level strikes on the rest of the economy. That, in any case, was an issue the NAM hammered away at, pointing out that in 1946, a year with an unprecedented number of labor disputes, almost half of all man-hour losses resulted from industry-wide strikes. The biggest of such disputes sometimes brought on government intervention and unwelcome outcomes. In coal they occasioned seizure of the mines in 1943 by the government. To make matters worse, the Department of the Interior agreed with John L. Lewis to impose employer payments into the new Welfare and Retirement Fund for the entire industry, centralizing union control over what segmentalists in other sectors thought should remain a strictly company affair. Nationwide shutdowns in coal mining during the war and in the fall and winter of 1949 led by the defiant United Mine Workers' leader gave the NAM and other organizations ample material for effective propaganda against "union monopoly" and the power of a single man to paralyze an entire industry and thus disrupt others. Even after its failure to outlaw multi-employer bargaining in 1947, angry NAM propaganda flowed, sometimes torrentially, against the UMW. It now joined the other currents of criticism against union monopoly and racketeering, especially against the building trade unions and the Teamsters. Lobbying pressure on Congress continued.[53]

Some reflection on the matter suggests that it would have been illogical for unionized segmentalists to see any advantage in centralization. After all, they linked their premium efficiency wages and benefits to prevailing standards in relevant labor markets. Those labor markets were local or regional, not national. As an executive of American Locomotive Corporation, a manufacturer with plants across New York State and Pennsylvania, put it to Congress, "Industry-wide bargaining gives no recognition to the widely varying economic and social factors applicable to the employers of the various union members, and of the localities in which they reside." Thus, GM's Charlie Wilson, who was more than happy to deal with the UAW on a company-by-company basis, also weighed in with those favoring legal prohibitions against multi-employer industry-wide bargaining in his testimony to Congress for the Taft-Hartley bill.[54]

Only 6 out of 48 major "interregional concerns" paid the same wage scales across the country in 1945, among them Ford and Standard Oil, according to economist Richard Lester. In 1950, according to the NAM's Earl Bunting, the majority of the larger corporations operating on a nation-wide basis adhered to some form of plant or local bargaining. But because union pressure was building for contracts that "wipe out local or geographical wage differentials," and "completely ignoring prevailing wage rates in the communities," he said, "it is becoming increasingly difficult for them to stick to this program."[55] Thus, well into the 1950s, leading elements in the NAM sought to outlaw multi-employer bargaining, especially on a national scale, probably hoping at the least to check any ambitions the unions might have in that direction.

The NAM's efforts along these lines helped perpetuate America's postwar climate of political hostility over labor issues. "Industry-wide bargaining, group bargaining, and pattern bargaining" came at the top of the list of topics suggested for investigation by a NAM "Study Group on Monopolistic Aspects of Unions" meeting in 1955, the very year when Swedish employers and unions were about to establish solidaristic wage bargaining on a multi-industry, not just industry-wide, basis. Of course, many of the American industries most active in multi-employer bargaining were not represented in NAM and lobbied to preserve its legality in the form of exemption from anti-trust restrictions. Thus, for all its efforts to close the loophole, the NAM was able to achieve no more against what it called "union monopoly" than the Landrum-Griffin Act of 1959. This act was directed specifically against labor racketeering practices, not multi-employer bargaining or bilateral cartelism itself, which to a certain extent provided the breeding ground for such corruption in the first place.[56] In the end, the attack on cartelists from the segmentalist camp resulted in a draw, while the politics of labor relations would remain fraught with tensions far exceeding those in Sweden.

Conclusion: From Labor Markets to Welfare States

The division of American employers between segmentalists and cartelists, artificially and temporarily obliterated by wartime labor scarcities and the solidarism they engendered, made for an enduring but always indecisive political warfare against unionism in the interwar and postwar periods. Despite the relative unimportance of socialist ideology in the American labor movement, class relations were on the whole far more hostile than in Sweden, where the labor movement never formally renounced its socialist origins. The service the Social Democratic Party and its trade union confederation offered manufacturers in intersectoral control over the building trades, something American employers tried to assert unilaterally, contributed immeasurably to the peaceful result.

American cartelists and many, if not most, segmentalists had one thing in common, though: vulnerability to cheap domestic product market competition. For example, according to historian Stanley Vittoz, because of high levels of investment in efficient capital-intensive manufacturing plant, major sectors of American industry were repeatedly rocked by "severe competitive dislocations and a superabundance of labor . . . during periods of stagnation and deflationary crises." Unchecked inflows of foreign workers in the years immediately after World War I added insult to injury, providing competitors using less enlightened labor practices with added opportunity to chisel on wages and prices. Thus, sentiment in leading business circles "seemingly edged toward acceptance of a permanent but 'flexible' policy of restriction," according to Vittoz. Major industrial trade journals reported an "increasingly widespread belief that unrestricted immigration was no longer either necessary or desirable." As Secretary of Commerce Herbert Hoover put it in 1926, there was a marked change in the attitude of employers, who "not so many years ago . . . considered it was in [their] interest to use the opportunities of unemployment and immigration to lower wages." He may have had in mind, among other things, positions taken by mid-1923 by the U.S. Chamber of Commerce and the

National Association of Manufacturers in calling for a policy flexibly moderating the labor influx. As President Warren G. Harding saw it, legislation was not the result of a struggle between capital and labor. Both capital and labor were winners, he thought.[57]

Segmentalists from the steel industry appear to have been important sources of encouragement. Elbert Gary, still head of U.S. Steel, adamantly denied journalists' declarations in 1923 that he was against restriction. Senator David A. Reed, the Pennsylvania Republican who sponsored the 1924 Immigration Act, descended from an old Pittsburgh steel dynasty. Apparently a cross-class alliance broker, he played a key role a decade earlier in the state's workmen's compensation legislation, which ultimately gathered the industry's blessings (see next chapter). His father had been Andrew Carnegie's attorney, helped found the U.S. Steel Corporation, and sat on its board of directors into the 1920s. Not surprisingly, then, as *Iron Age* reported, "the iron and steel industry and employing interests of the country generally have accepted . . . restrictive immigration legislation with comparatively little complaint."[58]

Vittoz concludes from this kind of evidence that immigration restriction in the 1920s should not be held up as a clear and shining example of labor political victory against a capitalist class always thirsty for a pool of cheaper labor. The cross-class, bipartisan nature of support for the Davis-Bacon Act, discussed in the previous chapter, and similar state legislation, recommends the same conclusion. Since 1927, Congress had extensively discussed "prevailing wage" bills to assist established building contractors, many engaged in cartelist labor market regulation, against underbidders bringing in "outside," "itinerant," or "bootleg" labor—often recent immigrants.[59]

Hence, for all the unresolvable strains across America's business sectors about the role of unions, electoral politicians were aware of a profound and growing commonality in their regulatory interests before and during the Great Depression, the decade of the "big bang" in America's welfare state development. Segmentalists and cartelists shared vulnerability to product market competitors willing to cut wages and otherwise operate on a substandard basis. In short, as the next chapters show, the cross-class alliance makers of the New Deal sought social and labor legislation to provide market security to struggling capitalists as well as social security to workers. In Sweden, because of solidarism, the story differs both in content and in timing. The next chapter begins the analysis with a focus on the New Deal, because it actually preceded the major social policy innovations of social democracy in Sweden by a decade and more.

Part III

Welfare States

9

THE NEW DEAL FOR
MARKET SECURITY

In 1939, only about four years after passage of the Social Security Act (SSA), Walter Fuller of the National Association of Manufacturers testified strongly in its defense. Speaking as chairman of the NAM's Economic Security Committee, he informed a Senate hearing that, while of course the organization would welcome a reduction in its unemployment insurance taxes, "we do not feel that a reduction should be made in such a way as to endanger the ultimate success of the program." The year before he had supported extension of old age insurance benefits to domestic and agricultural labor, along with widows and orphans of the insured. He also called for the earlier start of payments to help reduce the Social Security Act's anticipated enormous reserve fund.[1]

Fuller was not out of touch with the American business community. A survey conducted by *Fortune* magazine the same year he testified reported that "the impressive fact remains that whatever changes business might demand in such laws as the Wagner Act, Social Security, and the Wages and Hours Law, business seems to embrace the principles of this legislation—collective bargaining under federal supervision, federal provision for old age, and a federal floor to the wage and ceiling to the hours of the country's working week." Because sampling methods were still crude at the time, and in light of *Fortune's* outspoken editorial mission to reconcile businessmen to government activism, the results need to be taken with a grain of salt. In any event, they were not far from what was now coming out of the NAM. Of those surveyed, 76.8 percent favored keeping or adjusting wage and hour regulation; 72.2 percent thought the same about social insurance. A surprising 51.7 percent even accepted the new labor law protecting unions (the vast majority of those favoring modifications). An amazing 80 percent actually regarded union efforts to raise standards and regulate or stabilize the labor market as a good thing. The closed shop, violence, and racketeering probably made unions most unappealing, not their wage objectives. In conclusion, *Fortune* concluded, the results seemed to belie the theory that the business community "is ready with one accord to scuttle the whole New Deal and set up a regime of black reaction the moment it gets a chance."[2]

Within a few years, the normally ultra-reactionary NAM brought its official position into line. In its "Better America" program of November 1943, when much larger membership figures actually made it more broadly representative of American manufacturing than when it had spoken out against compulsory social insurance in 1935, the NAM declared flatly that "the need for Social Security is not questioned."[3] Similar things happened in the U.S. Chamber of Commerce, an organization roiled by internal controversy. In 1935, its previously reform-friendly leadership had been toppled by truculent opponents. The newly donned anti-FDR war mask concealed deep uncertainty and differences of opinion riddling the organization, however. In 1942, another insurgent leadership took control, having campaigned on a platform of "less Roosevelt-baiting" and more cooperation with government and labor. Around the same time, "much to the surprise of everybody," according to Marion Folsom of Eastman Kodak, a membership referendum came back with the necessary qualified majority for an official change of policy. Two thirds or more voted in favor of every important feature of the Social Security Act.[4]

Anticipated Alliances: Arranging the New Deal

Before passage of the Social Security Act, most business organizations in America rattled swords in noisy opposition to practically all aspects of the New Deal. Among them were the NAM, the NMTA, and state manufacturers' associations and chambers of commerce. But individually, rather than through organizations, a good number of prominent businessmen sent clear signals of support. A handful of them were personally involved in deliberations about legislative design. Among them was Kodak's Folsom. As he put it in retrospect, "during the early stages, organized business had very little to do with the development of this far-reaching system, leaving it up to a few individuals to present a business point of view and assist in putting it on a sound basis." Sanford Jacoby argues that their very scarcity made people like Folsom influential: "Precisely because so many employers opposed social security, the few who endorsed it wielded enormous influence."[5]

But they wielded this influence only because prodigious reformers like Franklin Roosevelt called on them to speak and chose to listen closely to what they had to say. But why listen? Edwin E. Witte, director of the Roosevelt administration's Committee on Economic Security (CES), the cabinet-level group charged with researching and drafting legislation, explained why. In his view, the administration could have shrugged off concerns about support from business for the SSA, or from labor for that matter, "and still force a measure through Congress." But the reformers wanted robust, deeply rooted legislation capable of weathering future challenges from any quarter. "The violent opposition of either group is likely to mean trouble hereafter," Witte wrote as deliberation proceeded.[6]

Senator Robert Wagner of New York, the legislative pilot of the New Deal, strategically aimed to avoid "trouble hereafter" from business, too. As it turns out, he was only partially successful with the labor relations legislation that bears his name. According to his biographer, Wagner was well aware, from earlier experiences with social and labor reform in the state of New York, that "passage of a measure [did not] mean that it was permanently secure." In other words, "Manufacturers, canners, and real-estate operators maintained powerful lobbies at Albany and could always find lawmakers who were willing to sponsor bills that would repeal, or amend into insignificance, the Factory Commission laws." Fear of a backlash uniting reactionary elements in business with ideologically motivated politicians made Roosevelt adamant about designing legislation with staying power. For example, he insisted that workers make payroll contributions to help finance old age insurance and so assert a "legal, moral, and political right" to their benefits. That way "no damn politician can ever scrap my social security program."[7]

So Roosevelt chose also to listen to voices from business about what might be necessary to create robust legislation. He ignored, however, the shrill voices of many organization leaders. Too often they were drawn to the job by a personal ideological mission against unreliable unions and politicians and played on members' anxieties and ideological predilections about the same. FDR's understanding of them was informed by New York state experiences he shared with Wagner. Important pieces of progressive legislation, he recalled, were "fought by chambers of commerce, manufacturers' associations and other business organizations." But the factory inspection law, for example, prepared by a legislative committee chaired by Wagner (with Frances Perkins, FDR's current secretary of labor, as its top aide), was ultimately supported by the great majority of manufacturers. Hence, Roosevelt confidently asserted, "in altogether too many cases the general views of business did not lend themselves to expression through its organizations."[8] There is good evidence that American reformers, on the whole, believed "the general views of business" about New Deal reforms were or would turn positive. It is for this reason they moved as resolutely as they did. These were pragmatic, business-financed politicians, not revolutionaries.

Strategic Anticipation of Support

Passage of a reform does not guarantee its survival, so what politicians anticipate about the future matters in their strategic timing and crafting of reforms. Though they may see in electoral and parliamentary majorities a chance to impose unwanted change, they know they cannot necessarily count on sustaining uncertain majorities against a united business community crouched and waiting to strike back at the next propitious moment. A delayed business reaction would put them between the rock of well-financed ideological and electoral challenges and the hard place of constituents ready to defend their new entitlements. To avoid this bind, reformers time and shape their reforms strategically, anchoring them in a foundation of elite as well as mass support.

Evidence and arguments in this and the following chapter strongly indicate that forward-looking political reformers like Roosevelt and Wagner responded selectively and strategically to signals from employers about the potential for durable cross-class alliances. They proceeded with a realistic degree of optimism based on learning experiences from earlier in the century. They had plenty of expert knowledge about businessmen and their markets and could see through the distracting smoke screen of ideology emanating from business organizations. Though concerned to win business support, they could ignore the bluster of business leaders and closely connected politicos who trafficked in anxieties about government's growing appetite for intervention in all economic affairs. Reformers were thus motivated to design legislation that would allay those fears, and so neutralize the ideologues in the end.

The reformers were not, to be sure, pressured into action by business interests. Actual pressure for reform came from other social groups mobilized on mass basis in elections and other modes of direct political participation.[9] What they sought in responding to those pressures was post facto cross-class alliances, and therefore durable, politically robust legislation.

Segmentalism and Cartelism in Shock

There was a clear regulatory logic to the social and labor legislation that the New Dealers anticipated would meet with American employers' ultimate approval.[10] During the 1930s, stagnant demand and industrial overcapacity gave rise to furious competition in national and local product markets. Surplus labor associated with high unemployment transformed "chiseling" or "cut-throat competition" from a chronic but manageable nuisance to a dire threat. Flying through the turbulence of the depression, vast numbers of businessmen felt as if the floor suddenly dropped out from under them. As different as they were on many dimensions, especially relations with unions, both segmentalists and cartelists suffered. The solutions, broadly speaking, were the same: establish a firmer floor on sinking competitive standards by imposing costs on "Poorpay, Skinflint, and Chisel," to use the NAM's colorful terminology.

From the ranks of big segmentalists, in particular, the most prominent foul weather friends of the welfare state came forth. Their voices gained disproportionate influence in the Roosevelt administration. Idiosyncratic personalities and experiences, more than objective interests, made them more active and progressive than others. Marion Folsom combined unusual technocratic skills for complex industrial planning with an abiding fascination with the big social welfare issues. Gerard Swope's years as a young man at Chicago's Hull House before his phenomenal career at General Electric may have made a difference, although his decision to go there in the first place already speaks of an unusual character. Though non-religious, his Jewish roots also set him apart. An-archic competitive conditions in oil suggest why Walter Teagle, from Standard Oil of New Jersey encouraged the New Dealers in their efforts. Why Teagle, and not someone else from oil, cannot really be known.

It is telling that "corporate liberals" never argued that they needed to sacrifice general business interests, and certainly not their companies' own, for a greater good. Quite the contrary, in fact. Probably what distinguished them, in the end, therefore, was open-minded study of unsentimental arguments for social insurance, lower assessment of the risks of government intervention, and less aversion to taking whatever risks they saw. In any case, objective interests or traumatizing experiences with government among segmentalists probably varied a great deal less than their personal idiosyncracies. Those variations filtered their perceptions of interests and moved them, or did not move them, into becoming activist corporate progressives. Some segmentalists, like Pierre du Pont, would thus join the ruin-prophesying conservatives. Others, like his cousin Alfred, would support the New Deal. But most segmentalists, if the truth be known, would remain uncertain at best and suspicious at worst. Mostly, they were nervous, watchful, and politically silent.

Segmentalists, according to theory elaborated earlier, voluntarily offered premium wages and benefits above what would have been necessary to clear their labor markets. They did so for efficiency effects that compensated for the extra costs. Under stable or expansionary macro-economic conditions, their strategy allowed them to dominate product markets in which competing producers still could turn a profit with lower wages and less generous benefits. Chiselers were a perpetual nuisance, but not much more than that. Under the shock of depressionary conditions, however, segmentalists experienced a distinct disadvantage. Their marginal competitors could hire and fire workers and raise and lower wages more freely. But the segmentalists were tied up in more long-term trust transactions with their workers. They had, to put it another way, expensive relationship-specific investments to protect.

As the New Dealers were well aware, segmentalists only very hesitantly and regretfully responded to competitive stress by slashing wages and welfare commitments. Big employers were so reluctant that they even waited until 1931 before starting to make deep cuts. Adding to their worries about the effects of widespread wage reductions on purchasing power, segmentalists also feared, rightly, the bitter reactions of workers whose efforts and loyalties had been courted with inflated promises of company-based security and protection. Thus, they teetered on the edge, looking into the frying pan of devastating price competition on one side and the fire of labor discontent and militant union organization drives on the other. Many employers had to jump into that fire, violating their "moral economy," the normatively constrained exchange relationships they had created (or at least espoused) before the SSA had a chance to save them. Those who were most able to preserve their benefits and therefore fulfill the promises of welfare capitalism were also more likely to emerge union-free out of the Depression and beyond.[11]

Social security legislation, the New Dealers understood, would reduce market pressures on segmentalists to cut wages and benefits at the risk of violating their company-level moral economy. Hence they designed their reforms to recover the segmentalists' advantage. Social insurance taxes could squeeze, from below, growing wage-related cost differentials back to an acceptable and appropriate size. For this reason, the New Dealers anticipated support after the fact, once it became clear that, for the segmentalists at least, only good and no harm was done.

The New Dealers also knew that the cartelists among employers were highly vulnerable to exogenous deflationary shocks to their negotiated system. Like segmentalists, they too set wages above market clearing levels, leaving their businesses vulnerable to low-wage, low-price competition. Their vulnerability was in direct proportion to unions' relative inability to accomplish two ends: (1) enforce standards upon freely entering product market competitors who, because of mass unemployment, enjoyed great flexibility to pay lower wages and cut prices in the face of slumping demand, or (2) persuade members to accept a downward revision of contract wages across the board. The New Dealers, especially Robert Wagner, emboldened by knowledge of cartelism's vulnerability, proceeded on two fronts: with labor relations legislation to strengthen unions and employers' associations against nonunion employers, and labor standards legislation designed to help employers where unions could not reach.

Wagner's National Labor Relations Act, not surprisingly, was opposed by practically all segmentalists, even those who looked at compulsory social insurance pragmatically and even optimistically. Their fear of union-sponsored encroachments on management through collective bargaining even exceeded their uncertainty about politicians and their legislative interventionism. Robert Wagner, for one, was bold enough to forge ahead, recognizing that there was enough support from sectors that were already engaged in negotiated cartelism, or would soon be (as in the case of trucking starting in 1937), to make for robust legislation.[12]

The failure of the anti-Wagner Act forces to include a prohibition of multi-employer bargaining in the Taft-Hartley Act of 1947 proved him right. Some evidence suggests, also, that the New Dealers anticipated that the National Labor Relations Act might prove its worth over time even to segmentalists. It could, Wagner hoped, empower unions to impose a floor on wage costs while preserving for management its ability to benefit from segmentalist largesse, and without undermining efficient management practices. As implausible as this may seem to those familiar with the intense controversy surrounding the legislation, the *Fortune* survey responses about unions' role in upholding wage standards, scattered evidence from the steel industry, and other experience in the postwar period suggest that the New Dealers in this regard were neither revolutionary nor delusionary. They were simply pragmatic reformers solicitous of employer interests and intelligently optimistic in anticipating their support.[13]

From the Progressive Experience
to Fair Labor Standards

"The large majority of employers want to be fair with their employees," Robert Wagner once remarked in an exchange with James Emery, general counsel of the NAM. During Senate hearings in 1934 concerning his bill to protect labor's right to organize and bargain, this legislative pilot of the New Deal added, however, "sometimes they are unable to be as fair as they would like to be, because of the keen competition with [employers] who are unfair to other workers, and these laws are always passed for the minority recalcitrants, not for the majority." Emery interjected, sarcastically, "Well, I suppose the Senator noticed the vast number of employers who flocked into this committee room last week, to support this bill."

SENATOR WAGNER: Well, that is the history of all acts.

MR. EMERY: Yes.

SENATOR WAGNER: The Workmen's Compensation Law [workplace accident insurance]. I do not know whether you were an active opponent of that in 1913, in New York State. That was a bill I introduced.

MR. EMERY: On the contrary, I was a strong proponent of it.

SENATOR WAGNER: Then you were not articulate, because there were no employers that came before the committee, favoring it.

MR. EMERY: I was very articulate. . . . I remember we began the agitation in the National Association of Manufacturers, for the substitution of workmen's compensation for employers' liability, in 1909.

SENATOR WAGNER: Well, if you will look at the record of 1913, every employer that was represented at a hearing opposed the act. There was only one, the enlightened Chamber of Commerce of Rochester, that, with some modifications, which modifications were made [sic], favored the act.[14]

Both Wagner and Emery were right on various details. At the national level, NAM had touted compulsory workers' accident insurance to shelter manufacturers from increasingly expensive litigation and unpredictable damages pried out of them by liability lawyers and their clients. But as a nonfederated national organization of individual manufacturers, it was not very active in state politics. Employers had not assiduously promoted the New York legislation, though they had done a little more in other states. Summing up, one of the country's most eager and busy proponents of legislation among manufacturers lamented the business community's great inertia and even occasional unfriendliness—as in Massachusetts—to compulsory workplace injury insurance.[15]

Most interesting is Wagner's point that legislators need not act as if employer opposition today inevitably means trouble tomorrow. As he recalled during the Senate hearing, New York employers "discovered . . . within a year or two that [workmen's compensation] was a great blessing, a great boon for industry." His perceptions were widely shared by reformers in the 1930s. In 1932, the welfare capitalist and corporate progressive Ernest Draper, of the Hills Brothers Company, recalled that "the heavens resounded with the wails of those who prophesied quick and complete disintegration of industry" before passage of workmen's compensation laws in 43 states between 1909 and 1920. Afterward, however, "American industry gave up wailing, and went to work seriously on the problem of prevention." The eminent progressive social reformer Isaac Rubinow, publishing in 1934, recalled that the laws enjoyed enthusiastic support from many employers, individual and organized, after passage: "Those who strenuously opposed it not so very long ago are a little bit ashamed when reminded of their opposition."[16]

This was not a wishful reconstruction of a forgotten reality. Wisconsin reformer John Commons had reported back in 1913 that the better employers in that state very quickly learned to appreciate the regulatory value of its workmen's compensation law. Before the law was introduced, "the competition of the worst employers [tended] to drag down the best employers to their level"; afterward, when employers were brought into the combined administration of safety laws and workmen's compensation, "the most progressive employers in the line of safety . . . [drew] up the law" and the Industrial Commission went out to enforce it and "bring the backward ones up to their level."[17]

Progressive-era experience with state-level wage and hour regulation was similar, providing an even more encouraging lesson to New Dealers now pushing for national fair labor standards law. Middle class reformers, and above all the National Consumers' League, took the initiative in promoting minimum wage and maximum hour regulations for women and children at the state level between 1912 and 1919. Apparently, according to Theda Skocpol, "business organizations and state Federations of Labor opposed minimum wage statutes in most places." In California, according to a report by three prominent reform intellectuals, the state minimum wage law met with "more or less opposition" from employers of women and minors at the time of passage. Among them were those in the fruit and vegetable canning industry, the largest employer of female workers of any industry in the state. One canner recalled that, at the time, "we all felt it would ruin us."[18]

Later, however, the same canner had nothing but praise, according to Felix Frankfurter, John Commons, and Mary Dewson, authors of the 1924 report. All were influential in their own ways in the New Deal. Dewson, for example, served on a citizens' advisory committee to the cabinet committee responsible for drafting the SSA. Their report also quoted the president of the Canners' League of California declaring, ten years into the operation of the law, that "I do not believe you could find a reputable canner or other large employer of women who would ask to have this law repealed." The report also presented enthusiastic testimony from employers in canning, laundries, retail, and manufacturing that "unfair competition" was prevented and industrial efficiency was enhanced. It cited a 1923 meeting of the San Francisco Retail Merchants' Association, where "resolutions galore" were passed praising the work of the Minimum Wage Commission. Most retailers were now opposing reductions the commission was contemplating. The managing director of the San Francisco Retail Merchants' Association observed how the merchants had acquired a distinct liking for the law's regulatory impact: "[T]he greatest boon to them is that it takes the question of wages very largely out of competition and saves them from the necessity of holding wages down to the level of their hardest and shrewdest competitor."[19]

Deeper research on California would possibly show that at least a few prominent employers signaled early approval. A 1930 study of the Oregon experience in the 1920s found that although "relatively few business men came out personally into the open in favor of the law," the Board of Governors of the Portland Chamber of Commerce actually endorsed it. Also, "the main representatives of more enlightened business interests, especially if they reflected even slightly a community standpoint, accorded cordial support to the measure." After the law was in force, many businessmen adopted new views, sometimes "strikingly" new ones. In 1923, shortly after the Supreme Court ruled down a District of Columbia measure, employers in Oregon "displayed no disposition to welcome the Supreme Court decision; in fact their openly declared sentiments were against the Court decree." The Manufacturers' and Merchants' Association of Oregon, among others, vowed to help fight legal challenges to the Oregon law.[20]

By the mid-1930s, therefore, the New Dealers could reasonably gamble on the proposition that minimum standards legislation would enjoy considerable post facto, if not always immediate, business support. Their recent memories of the Republican Party's Davis-Bacon Act of 1931, guaranteeing prevailing wage standards on federal building projects, could only have reinforced that view, favored as it was by building contractors. Now if manufacturers subjected federal standards to the same abuse that NAM had leveled at state minimum wage legislation—proclaiming the laws "fantastic and grotesque," and "pure socialism"—the New Dealers could calmly dismiss the opposition as the recreational barking of a toothless dog.[21]

But encouraging signals even came out of the supposedly reactionary NAM in the mid-1930s. In 1934 the highly intrusive state-sponsored corporatist regulation of "fair trade practices" under the National Recovery Administration (NRA) industry codes was confronting an ultimately successful challenge through the courts. Contrary to its reputation, the NAM was far from enthusiastic about sacrificing wage standards along with all the increasingly unpopular industry-by-industry regulation of cut-throat and predatory business practices. A NAM committee—backed by a membership survey—recommended to the NAM's December 1934 convention that it promote continuation of the labor provisions of the NRA's industry codes "pertaining to child labor, minimum wages, maximum hours, and collective bargaining, with clarifying definitions of collective bargaining and provisions for more elastic working hours added." These aspects of the committee's recommendation sparked no open debate; only the committee's recommendations against extending trade regulations did.[22]

When the Supreme Court finally ruled the NIRA unconstitutional in 1935, business and political interest in intrusive corporatist regulation of business decision making died away forever. That was not the case for wage and hour standards. For certain, Justice Brandeis, who joined the unanimous opinion, hoped they could be replaced by alternative and constitutionally more acceptable means. Prominent businessmen immediately intervened in that spirit. According to historian Steven Fraser, Robert Johnson, of Johnson & Johnson, a major manufacturer of textiles, especially hospital and surgical supplies, lobbied "tirelessly" among other politically active big businessmen in and outside the Commerce Department's Business Advisory Council (BAC) to line up supporters for wage and hour legislation. Among those he thought he could influence with his deluge of letters were, along with other big textile manufacturers, Walter Chrysler of Chrysler Motors, Myron Taylor of U.S. Steel, and the president of Otis Elevator. Johnson apparently promised politicians he could gather support from big retailers, including for example Donald Nelson of Sears Roebuck, and leading executives at Gimbel Brothers, Strawbridge & Clothier, and Roos Brothers. Nelson's boss, Sears Chairman Robert E. Wood, had supported the NRA because, according to Jacoby, "its wage codes intensified the economic pressures felt by low-wage retailers, especially smaller stores." Other major supporters from the retail sector were Edward A. Filene and Louis Kirstein of Filene's in Boston. As early as 1923, Filene had proselytized for minimum wages, partly to eliminate low-quality cut-throat competition in the retail sector, partly to increase efficiency and stability in both industry and retailing, and finally, to maintain the "consuming power" of working class customers.[23]

Though the textile industry was divided, pitting socially minded welfare capitalists in competition with the worst exploiters of child labor, its associations were key actors behind the Black-Connery wage and hour bill. Formulated under Labor Secretary Perkins under the expert guidance of Felix Frankfurter, it became the Fair Labor Standards Act (FLSA) in 1938. (Both had also been influential in shaping the NIRA, whose most broadly popular aspect had been wage and hour regulations.) William P. Connery of Massachusetts, chairman of the House Committee on Labor, put his name on the bill, for in Perkins's account, "his experience in Massachusetts, which had suffered from the exodus of textile and shoe industries to lower wage areas, had convinced him that national legislation was necessary to eliminate this destructive competition." Co-sponsor Hugo Black, Democratic senator from Alabama, had business support too, even from the southern textile industry. Most notable was fellow Alabaman Donald Comer of Avondale Mills, who had long favored federal child labor legislation, minimum wages, and maximum hours.[24]

In the end, the NAM officially opposed the relatively modest and far from encompassing FLSA in 1938, hell-bent as it was to stanch the flow of all reform. The reality, which could hardly have been overlooked by the New Dealers, was that the organization's official position masked a strong and steady undercurrent of approval among American manufacturers. The organization's official opposition was animated by the ideologically conditioned strategic concern to oppose on principle all government intervention to slow the passage of far more offensive legislation down the road. Even the AFL leadership initially opposed legislated wage and hour standards, probably seeing them as a substitute, and therefore an obstacle to unionization and collective bargaining. (For the same reason, a big textile employer like Comer saw them as icing on the cake.)[25]

Opposition and ambivalence on the part of organized capital and labor camouflaged the broad, though not entirely comprehensive, cross-class agreement in America about the need for emergency measures to prop up wages. The NAM's opposition does not indicate that the New Dealers acted in the bold defiance of capitalists. Organized labor's hesitancy does not indicate that workers' economic interests were irrelevant in their political calculations. Roosevelt and others knew that federal minimum wage and maximum hour legislation was rooted in a strong cross-class basis of support that would, if history was any indication, grow over time, and they acted resolutely on the basis of that knowledge.[26]

Unemployment Insurance as Restraint on Competition

Experience with Progressive-era wage and hour legislation at the state level no doubt fed the reformers' optimism about the federal standards finally passed in 1938. In the case of compulsory unemployment insurance (UI), a key element of the SSA, they had received even more recent reassurances about post facto business support. In 1928, after four years of pressure, the Amalgamated Clothing Workers union prevailed upon New York City men's clothing manufacturers to set up an unemployment benefit scheme for over 400 firms and 22,000 union members. "Once the manufacturers had accepted it," according to Daniel Nelson's important history of unemployment insurance, "they insisted that unemployment insurance was good business and not merely a system of charitable payments to unfortunate workmen." One prominent employer argued that unemployment insurance would serve the organized employers' and union's ambitions to "stabilize the industry"—code words, of course, for the joint cartelists' mission of imposing more uniform costs and standards to inhibit cut-throat competition.[27]

President Roosevelt and Senator Wagner were both, as New Yorkers, intimately familiar with the problems of the unions and employers alike in the needle trades, the state's most important manufacturing industry in employment terms. Wagner had been a key figure in the Factory Investigating Committee investigations of sweat-shop operations after 1911 and in passing the Factory Commission Laws, which helped elevate garment industry standards to those followed by "legitimate" manufacturers dragged down by low-wage and therefore low-price sweat-shop competition.[28] As governor, and out of enthusiasm for negotiated cartelism, Roosevelt appointed Herbert H. Lehman as chairman of the Board of Conciliation in 1929, to help the two sides resolve their differences and bolster each other's strength. Lehman, who would later replace FDR in the state house, had recently served from 1924 to 1926 on Governor Alfred E. Smith's Special Advisory Commission on the women's cloak and suit industry. Its mission was to protect "legitimate" or "inside" manufacturers against nonunionized, fly-by-night contractors. One of the advisory commission's successful recommendations was to set up an unemployment insurance fund like the one in men's clothing. In 1935, Governor Lehman, who in his own words "maintained very close relationships both with labor and with industry," signed the first state unemployment legislation since Wisconsin's, which had passed in 1932.[29]

Wisconsin's enactment of the first state unemployment insurance law provided a direct lesson for the New Dealers about the shifting rainy-day nature of business support. Organized employers in the Wisconsin Manufacturers' Association (WMA) had energetically and effectively opposed compulsory unemployment insurance through much of the 1920s. Once again, forces outside the business community were largely responsible for initiating the legislation—just as civic reformers had led the campaign for state-level wage and hour regulation and unions had initiated collectively bargained unemployment insurance in the needle trades. Reform experts, liberal members of the legislature, Governor Philip F. La Follette, and organized labor finally prevailed during the Depression. Organized farmers, who were often employers themselves (e.g., the Pure Milk Products Cooperative, representing five thousand dairy farmers) were persuaded wholesale, after being conveniently exempted from payment of the new contributions. The reformers argued that the scheme would support purchasing power for their agricultural products, which helps explain their broad endorsement of the legislation.[30]

Come the Depression, though, and things started to look different to manufacturers. Their hard resistance began to crumble about the edges. Four nonagricultural employers testified in favor during legislative hearings, still a surprisingly small number to historian Daniel Nelson, for, in his words, the plan "was calculated to win the approval of the progressive employers." But, to repeat a pattern becoming familiar by now to politicians, employers began to look at the Wisconsin legislation "in a different light" only after it was passed, according to Nelson. Partly they saw it as a better and cheaper alternative to more radical proposals being considered in national debates. But they also came to appreciate its "preventive" or regulatory virtues, the very thing that the reformers had incorporated to attract the progressive segmentalists.[31]

The Wisconsin plan, crafted in large part by Louis Brandeis's daughter Elizabeth and her husband Paul Raushenbush, called for individual employers to set up separate funds or "reserves" into which they paid a yearly fee until it accumulated a fixed balance. No further payments were required unless layoffs occurred and thus the reserves were drawn down. This arrangement would impose heavier costs on product market competitors with more labor-intensive operations and often more casual relations with workers. Thus, it would give big employers a reward for regularizing employment, which they were better at already, and punish those who treated workers as a highly variable and expendable factor. It would be hard to imagine that progressive employers failed to notice and relish the regulatory if not predatory potential of such welfare legislation. If so, it would not have been in their interest to mention it out loud.[32]

Thus, initial opponents George Kull, executive secretary of the WMA, and Frederick Clausen of the J. I. Case Company of Racine, which had installed its own company unemployment plan for its various factories in 1931, now served happily on the employers' advisory board of the Wisconsin Industrial Commission to help implement and administer the legislation. They also became active propagandists for Wisconsin-style legislation as the movement for reform spread in other states and to Washington. H. W. Story, an executive of agricultural machinery manufacturer Allis Chalmers, who along with Clausen and Kull once attacked the plan as visionary and impractical, appeared as its advocate at the Senate hearings on the SSA in 1935.[33]

Because Wisconsin experts, Edwin Witte most notably, figured so prominently in the drafting process in Washington, the Wisconsin experience was no doubt well known by others in the Roosevelt administration. But the example of workmen's compensation, state minimum wages, the New York garment industry plan, and the Wisconsin unemployment legislation were not the sole factors emboldening Depression-era politicians to proceed with compulsory unemployment insurance legislation, despite ideologically tinged business opposition. A handful of successful businesses—and some supremely successful ones—had signaled the practicability of legislation by setting up their own company plans. General Electric was a leader in this field. Three manufacturers in Fond du Lac, Wisconsin, formed a fund in 1930. Eastman Kodak established a joint plan with seven other companies in the Rochester, New York, area in 1931. Wrigley's in Chicago had a plan, which is possibly why Roosevelt asked William P. Wrigley to join GE's Swope and Kodak's Folsom on his advisory committee. About two dozen firms promised benefits between 1916 and 1934.[34]

Of course, the number of company experiments was not impressive, and some of them foundered. Two disappeared in the 1920s before the Depression, one was started and failed in 1929, and another four were discontinued between 1931 and 1932. But another fifteen companies (including the Rochester and Wisconsin firms) started up between 1930 and 1934 despite the Depression. The paucity and precariousness of the companies' "voluntary" plans would not, however, have invalidated the idea of legislation and compulsion. They would simply have impressed upon politicians seeking cross-class support the virtues of legislation that could force upon competitors the standards that progressive employers were struggling to adopt. By imposing costs on their competitors, it would probably put them in a better position to sustain their own plans. "Forcing other companies to share the burden," as Jacoby puts it, was probably a strong consideration behind Folsom's depression-induced shift of opinion in favor of government compulsion.[35]

General Electric was one of the few big firms to offer unemployment benefits. Gerard Swope, GE's chief executive and friend of FDR, made it explicit that unemployment legislation would have regulatory benefits for segmentalists, not just smaller employers in sectors like clothing. The famous "Swope Plan," which he zealously publicized in 1931, is widely regarded as a major source of inspiration behind the corporatist NRA. One of its main purposes was to give more reputable and progressive businessmen a chance to fashion and enforce uplifted standards of competition on underpricing rivals, who chiseled away at any and all standards of quality and decency. In the plan, and in the same spirit, Swope advocated compulsory industry-wide unemployment insurance along with pensions and disability benefits. The government, he thought, should allow and empower trade associations of interstate businesses to "place the same social burdens on companies competing in various parts of the United States." Segmentalists in their local labor markets would become cartelists in their national product markets. Swope revealed how much national and even international product market competition was weighing heavily on his mind in the plan's "addendum," where he called for tax abatement for those companies vulnerable to international competition when their foreign competitors were free from similar "provisions for the benefit of employees."[36]

In spring 1932, the employer statesman even met with AFL leaders William Green and Matthew Woll and urged the doubters to line up behind unemployment insurance. According to Irving Bernstein, Swope found that the labor leaders' opposition "was largely based upon prejudice and their denouncement of the British system." He was optimistic that they would soon change their views, as they did. Swope met personally in March 1934 with Roosevelt, who requested a detailed proposal for unemployment, pension, and disability benefits, which Swope delivered two weeks later. This, apparently, was an important source of encouragement for the president to move ahead with legislation, according to a biographer who interviewed Swope extensively. After consultation with Swope and Owen Young of GE, as well as John Raskob of GM, Roosevelt appointed his Committee on Economic Security (CES) of cabinet members headed by Labor Secretary and fellow New Yorker Frances Perkins, and directed by Edwin Witte from Wisconsin. Attached to the CES was the "citizens'" Advisory Council on Economic Security, composed of prominent businessmen, labor leaders, and social reformers. Swope, along with Walter Teagle of Standard Oil of New Jersey, Kodak's Marion Folsom, Morris Leeds of Leeds & Northrup (Philadelphia), and Sam Lewisohn of Miami Copper (New York City) represented the business progressives. Except for Lewisohn, they were active members of the Commerce Department's Business Advisory Council

(BAC), set up by FDR's Secretary of Commerce, Daniel Roper, and composed of several dozen mostly broad-minded executives.[37]

Behind the BAC stood the Special Conference Committee (SCC), the secretive group of prominent segmentalist executives, including Swope and Jersey Standard's Walter Teagle. The SCC had exercised considerable influence in the NRA's Industrial Advisory Board and was a forum where encouraging views were developed and transmitted into the BAC. Some of the BAC's reports, studied by the CES staff, may even have been ghost-written by the SCC, according to Colin Gordon. In its 1934 report, the SCC argued for a government solution: "[F]or the protection of employers in general and to equalize cost burdens among competitors, there probably will be need for funds built up and administered under the direction of public authorities."[38]

There is at least some striking evidence that other important manufacturers were gravitating toward the view that unemployment insurance was politically practical and could have great regulatory value. Among the most enthusiastic and politically vocal was Ernest Draper of Hills Brothers of the food processing industry. More important economically, but less busy in reform circles, was occasional BAC member Paul W. Litchfield, president of Goodyear Tire and Rubber. Overcapacity and ferocious competition in rubber made it particularly difficult for Goodyear to maintain and improve its welfare benefits. Litchfield therefore publicly promoted compulsory unemployment legislation. As much as he would have liked to provide unemployment benefits to his workers, he wrote, "the goal is simply not attainable for most of the concerns engaged in the rough-and-tumble competition of industry today, no matter how high their motives or how strong their treasuries." In other words, "There are always enough establishments in any industry which would be willing to cut prices by the amounts that a competitor was laying aside for unemployment benefits."[39]

Of inestimable significance for emboldening politicians and reformers willing to defy the business community's loud reactionaries was the direct participation of the Industrial Relations Counselors (IRC) in legislative groundwork for compulsory unemployment insurance. According to valuable and persuasive research by G. William Domhoff, the consultancy outfits' board of directors in the late 1920s and early 1930s included top executives of General Electric, International Harvester, U.S. Steel, and Standard Oil of New Jersey, all members of the SCC. Domhoff proves that the IRC remained heavily dependent financially on John D. Rockefeller, Jr., from 1926 and well into the 1930s. Service revenue, retainers from firms, and other sources covered less than half of its expenses in 1933, for example. That year, Rockefeller personally received a glowing report from Raymond Fosdick, his attorney and close advisor (and friend of FDR), about its activities in "shaping and administering legislation" in Wisconsin and Minnesota. Fosdick added that the IRC was also pursuing contracts to do the same in two other states, and Canada too. About these and other IRC activities, Fosdick told Rockefeller, "I cannot speak too highly." This he said in an appeal calculated to keep the Rockefeller money flowing.[40]

According to Edwin Witte, executive director of Roosevelt's CES, "almost the entire research staff of the Industrial Relations Counselors, Inc. was placed on the payroll of the Committee on Economic Security, so that the arrangement in effect amounted to employing the Industrial Relations Counselors, Inc. to make this study [on UI]." In other words, the country's leading management consultants, dependent on both corporate progressive largesse and profits—not altruistic do-gooders—were invited by the reformers to design legislation. Bryce Stewart, the IRC's director of research, had helped set up and administer the Amalgamated Clothing Workers' Union's jointly negotiated unemployment insurance funds before coming to the IRC. In charge of the CES study, he did the work for free, unlike the other IRC staff members, so he could remain in New York and continue directing IRC work as well.[41] By paying Stewart's salary, the IRC even helped finance the CES. That segmentalists sent encouraging signals to the New Dealers is only inaccurate as an understatement, when held up against the IRC's role.

As with the wage and hour legislation later, big retail merchandisers spoke with extraordinary unity and clarity in support of unemployment insurance. In part, their concern was the same as that of other segmentalists: to impose costs on chiseling competitors now that the shock of slumping demand and unemployment made it imperative. Big department stores also felt an urgent need to stabilize workers' purchasing power. In 1931, Lessing Rosenwald and Robert E. Wood of Sears Roebuck helped set up and lead a "Committee for the Nation" (along with James Rand of Remington Rand and Vincent Bendix of Bendix Corporation). Heavily backed by Rockefeller's and Teagle's Standard Oil of New Jersey, as well as other industrial firms, it was dedicated to propping up prices and purchasing power with macro-economic policy. Social Science Research Council (SSRC) founder Beardsley Ruml, recruited out of academia in 1934 to be Macy's treasurer, was also an early convert to Keynesian thinking. Like Walter Teagle, he was a close Rockefeller advisor (the SSRC depended heavily on Rockefeller money) and an influential figure among New Dealers. He was appointed director of the Federal Reserve Bank of New York by the chairman of the Federal Reserve, Marriner Eccles, who himself was inspired by proto-Keynesian "underconsumptionist" theory.[42]

Owners and executives of Filene & Sons of Boston were prominent enthusiasts of unemployment insurance, along with minimum wages, as ways of propping up worker income. So many other department store executives were persuaded that the National Retail Dry Goods Association, which included in its membership R. H. Macy & Co. and Sears Roebuck, and claimed to represent "a large section of the business life of the country," was by far the most vociferous sectoral business organization openly supporting the Social Security Act in 1935. The New York Retailers' Association came out openly in support of unemployment legislation while it was being debated in that state. In California and Ohio, state retailers' associations even played a direct role in drafting their laws.[43]

As the leadership and financing of the Committee for the Nation indicate, retailers were not alone in their desire to pump up aggregate demand. They had even been motivated enough to coordinate voluntary restraint against wage cuts until 1931, with President Hoover's encouragement. On the whole, however, they were perhaps only belated converts to the Keynesian interventionism of people like Ruml, according to historian Robert Collins. But Albert L. Deane of General Motors Assistance Corporation, which was set up to help people with modest incomes finance car purchases, was among the vanguard. In 1934, Deane published a proposal for a tax on overtime in manufacturing to finance unemployment benefits. It would even out worker demand and thereby help the auto industry stabilize its own production and employment levels.[44]

Ultimately, businessmen like these, communicating through the IRC, the BAC, retailers' associations, and informally through other channels, were probably decisive in motivating the Roosevelt administration and reassuring Congress that UI was practical and safe from a business backlash after passage. Domhoff's recent research on the role of the "Rockefeller network," especially the IRC, makes it hard to imagine that Rockefeller himself was unfriendly to the enterprise. For him to keep a low profile instead of personally speaking out in its favor made perfect sense. He would not have wanted to besmirch the enterprise by adding his controversial name to the list of endorsers. We know from Domhoff that maintaining anonymity in some of their reform endeavors was important to the Rockefellers. "It would be fatal to have the Director [J. Douglas Brown, of Princeton University's Industrial Relations Section] thought of as a Rockefeller man," John D. Rockefeller, III, wrote to his father in 1930, for example. This was in the context of discussions about increasing the family's endowment to the university's Industrial Relations Section up to $300,000 and possibly more. In exchange, he argued, the university should start paying Brown's salary out of its regular funds, which up to then came directly from Rockefeller.[45]

For reasons like these, the New Dealers knew that organizations like the NAM could be disregarded—for their "lack of objective approach and understanding by the leaders, as well as inept staff work," to invoke Marion Folsom's withering criticism. Folsom, a graduate of Harvard Business School, had been hired by George Eastman to head Kodak's statistical department, which collected and processed data for complex production planning. No soft-headed liberal ideologue, he later became Kodak's treasurer and, by administering the company's welfare programs, an insurance expert in his own right. "Objectivity" and top-flight executive expertise were therefore the province of people like him, Swope, Teagle, and the IRC staff, and Roosevelt knew it.[46] Brilliantly successful businessmen were making practical proposals with positive prospects for segmentalism's bottom lines. This was a comforting thing for insecure politicians depending on capitalists' money. They did not relish the prospect of unified business pressure to withdraw mass entitlements once the Great Depression's social and political emergency passed.

Social Security as Market Security

CES staff member J. Douglas Brown was one of those top quality staffers recruited by Witte from the network of Rockefeller-funded but nominally independent policy experts. According to his retrospective account, Perkins, Witte, and their cabinet committee at one point reached a moment of indecision, sometime in December 1934, about whether to include old age insurance (OAI) in the omnibus Social Security Act. Unemployment insurance was still top priority. At the moment of doubt, he recalled, "help came from an unexpected source, the industrial executives on the Committee's Advisory Council." They were, along with Swope and Folsom, Walter Teagle from Standard Oil of New Jersey, a person very close to John D. Rockefeller. Teagle, according to Domhoff, coordinated the work of IRC people responsible for OAI.[47]

While the industrial executives kept the ball rolling, IRC consultant Murray Latimer, one of the CES's key experts, did his best to make it bigger. The author of an influential survey and critique of company pensions published by the IRC, he insisted that OAI benefits be large enough for older workers to retire comfortably so younger ones could be absorbed into the active labor force. Latimer was no academic amateur: he had helped develop company pension plans at Standard Oil of New Jersey, at three other Rockefeller oil companies, and at American Rolling Mill. Latimer's concern was apparently a common one among welfare capitalists, Folsom among them. Because of low turnover, they were saddled with many older unproductive workers they greatly needed to retire and replace. It was a painful three-way choice between the high costs of keeping them around, retiring them with pensions, and the "loss of morale," as Brown put it, "which the discard of the old without compensation would involve."[48]

As the IRC's Brown explained in Senate testimony, the employer contribution "levels up the cost of old-age protection." Before the shock of deflation and mass unemployment, segmentalists had not felt much need for this. But now they could use some protection themselves. Even before the Depression hit, they had begun to worry, as the insurance industry and Latimer warned, that their pension promises were "actuarially unsound." That is to say, because they had failed for years to set aside the proper funds, their pensions were unaffordable. As drafted, Brown testified, OAI "protects the more liberal employer" who promised reitrement benefits "from the competition of the employer who otherwise fires the old person without a pension."[49] Had liberal employers prudently accumulated reserves, or had they been able to renege on pensions without repercussions, they would not have needed such government protection.

Also, it should be noted, the SSA disqualified from benefits anyone picking up more than a paltry $15 in earned income. Had it not, some workers over 65, retired by segmentalists, would have simply re-entered the labor market to work for low-standard employers, possibly even their competitors, to supplement their retirement benefits. Substandard employers might then have been able to retain or hire older relatively unproductive workers at an extremely low wage, depressing standards even further. Without the $15 per year limit, the government might have subsidized chiselers and negated the regulatory purpose of the new tax.[50]

Protection of high-standard employers from chiseling competitors certainly helps explains big retailers' exceptional enthusiasm for legislated OAI, for they were about the most likely of all employers to have installed company plans. Kodak's Folsom was also motivated, according to Jacoby, by the possibility of payroll taxes that "narrowed costs between Kodak and those employers who spent little or nothing on welfare benefits." Although executives from International Harvester do not figure in the record as vocal proponents of the legislation, once passed, it gave the company "a welcome opportunity to escape from the expensive pension plan and the same time put the company on an equal pension cost basis with the growing number of farm implement competitors," according to Harvester historian Robert Ozanne.[51]

As in the case of unemployment insurance, few busy corporate executives actually went out of their way to advocate compulsory old age insurance. In addition to the usual suspects, one worthy of mention is Alfred I. du Pont. Alfred served as vice president of production in the E. I. Du Pont corporation through many successful years. In 1915, however, he was ousted by cousins Pierre S. du Pont and Thomas Coleman. Had he prevailed, the corporation would possibly have joined the ranks of the corporate progressives and certainly not funded the ultra-reactionary American Liberty League. One of several reasons for the ouster, including personality, was serious differences over expansion strategies: as a champion of free and vigorous competition in the realm of innovation, Alfred rejected his rivals' monopolistic strategy, especially the swallowing up of competitors. While still the second largest shareholder in Du Pont, he devoted considerable energies to advocacy of pension legislation. Alfred was possibly the single most instrumental figure in the passage of Delaware's relatively advanced statewide pension plan in 1931. He became a consistent supporter of Franklin Roosevelt and a strong proponent of the SSA. It is possible Alfred saw legislated pensions as a way to stabilize competition without the baneful effects of monopoly. According to his biographer, he had greeted the NRA "as a major step toward bringing together labor and capital, as well as for setting standards for both production and wages." He died of a heart attack four years later while the Social Security Act was working its way through Congress.[52]

It would be wrong to conclude, solely on the basis of their small numbers, that energetic and vocal corporate progressives were such a rare species unable ever to propagate their views among the garden-variety employers and businessmen. In fact, the New Dealers had good reason to think that corporate liberal views would, for regulatory reasons, resonate widely. The purchasing power logic behind social insurance also gave it resonance.[53] Many of the noisy opponents among businessmen were only temporarily stupefied by ideology and inexperience; Folsom and his like were the ones with a clear and objective view that would surely spread.

In February 1935, the New Dealers got confirmation that the corporate progressives were the highly visible tip of a deep iceberg. These businessmen, it seemed, were not completely disconnected from cold capitalist reality. The size of the iceberg was uncertain, but it seemed to be growing, as indicated by an informal survey of editors at industry journals. Conducted for the Senate by the National Publishers' Association, it cited, for example, an editor of *National Petroleum News* declaring that most, if not all, of the bigger oil companies had pensions, while over 200,000 small oil producers, marketers, and retailers had "no protective features for their employees." The editor ventured that "if these last were forced to contribute to such protection as bigger companies are now doing, it might help to lessen some of their price cutting by bringing up their costs."[54]

The editor of *Iron Age* responded that in metal manufacturing and processing, "industry is in sympathy with the broad objectives leading to social security" and that it had "no objection to having these burdens transferred to Uncle Sam's shoulders, provided it is a practical load for him to carry." The editor of *Steel* ventured that iron, steel, and allied industries, though fearing hasty and ill-conceived legislation, in principle favored pensions and unemployment plans and "would strongly prefer . . . uniform plans." Uniformity, the suggestion was, would help bring the wage costs of smaller product market competitors closer to those of the larger ones and make it less imperative to lower their own labor standards in response to the Depression.[55]

"I am sure you will find the chemicals industry behind any program of sound legislation provided ample time is given for thorough investigation and study" was the cautious response from the editor of *Chemical and Metallurgical Engineering.* "Rapidly increasing numbers" of textile industrialists, perpetually worried about low-wage substandard competition, had lately been coming around to a favorable position on Social Security, the editor of *Textile World* responded to the inquiry. No doubt the thinking was similar to what was behind support for wage and hour standards. Other cautious but moderately encouraging results of inquiries were conveyed by journal editors and others associated with the California Metal and Mineral Producers' Association, the National Supply and Machinery Distributors' Association, the National Electrical Contractors' Association, the American Transit Association, the National Retail Dry Goods Association, and the New York Building Congress.[56]

Some of the most discouraging responses came from engineering. Chicago's Metal and Allied Products Association declared opposition. The NMTA did not answer the survey but sent a representative to testify firmly against the SSA. That organization, of course, was dominated by the nay-sayers of open-shopism. But even the American Gear and Manufacturers' Association called for Swope-style self-imposition of uniform Social Security arrangements within sectors. So there was no towering wall of hostile opposition even in engineering. L. C.

Morrow, editor of *Factory Management and Maintenance*, and speaking for the National Publishers' Association, summed up: "Industry, as a whole, is favorable toward the aims of social security and believes that some such legislation must be in effect some day."[57]

Generally, when opinions were not favorable, they were not unfavorable either. A good number of trade journal editors reported that official positions had not been taken or that a consensus had not yet developed one way or the other. Caution and ambivalence prevailed here, not the implacable opposition that leaders of the NAM (dominated by the NMTA) and the Chamber of Commerce (where New Deal haters had just staged a divisive coup) were trying with success to convey. As the editor of *Textile World* put it, the legislation was so complex that "it seems to be beyond the grasp of the average man in our industry." Only a few expressed very strong doubts, sometimes because the legislation might exacerbate rather than relieve competitive problems. Though the industry was generally friendly to the idea of legislation, according to the editor of *Paper Mill and Wood Pulp News*, some paper manufacturers exposed to ruinous international competition were nervous. Newsprint manufacturers, for example, were menaced by extremely low-price foreign competitors in Russia and Finland. (Swope had written the addendum to his plan to deal with such fears.) Fear of domestic rather than international competition made one sector particularly anxious. The editor of *Laundry Age* noted that the industry's customers were also its competitors; more laundering might be done at home if Social Security taxes drove prices higher. Domestic laundry already accounted for the loss of about half of the industry's 1929 volume, and with even higher costs the industry would come close to being all washed up itself.[58]

The bus industry's problem was a little less worrisome, even if buses would miss the riders who chose to walk instead of paying higher fares. More worrisome, according to the editor of *Bus Transportation*, was the provision exempting companies with fewer than four employees. It would "leave the door wide open for the small, shoestring company to operate at cut rates and to seriously hamper the larger companies who must comply with the law." Otherwise, he said, though extreme caution was necessary, "I believe the industry is not too strongly opposed to the general principles involved." John Edgerton, president of the NAM in 1931 when Swope first announced his plan, had anticipated fears like these. In reference to Swope's dividing line of 50 employees, he responded, "Any plan which does not embrace in its application and direct benefits all of the people who are employed in America, will not be a thoroughly sound and saving plan." A sound and therapeutic plan was a real possibility, Edgerton clearly meant to indicate.[59]

After passage of the SSA, few segmentalists left the business of providing private pension benefits. Most just revised their plans downward. Extremely few, it seems, favored completely opting out of the federal plan by providing their own equivalent. That had been the idea behind the controversial Clark amendment, which temporarily held up the legislation in the Senate in 1935 and provoked a veto threat from Roosevelt. An unspecified number of unnamed companies had apparently been prompted by Walter Forster of Towers, Perrin, Forster & Crosby, an insurance consulting and brokerage firm, to write letters to Congress requesting the opt-out provision. In all probability, not many major segmentalists wrote letters. Domhoff brings to light decisive evidence that big business executives across the country, including major segmentalists like U.S. Steel, AT&T, Du Pont, U.S. Rubber, Union Carbide, and Western Electric, became convinced even before passage of the SSA that their workers would receive the basic OAI benefits at a cheaper cost to their companies than their own plans. Thus, they could even economize by cutting back their company pensions and still stay ahead of the crowd.[60]

Folsom agreed. "I doubt if many companies with sound pension plans would find it to their advantage to be exempted from the Federal plan," he was quoted as saying in SSRC discussions, recommending that they simply supplement the government pensions with scaled-back company pensions. In 1936 he published an article in the *Harvard Business Review* revealing publicly what the major segmentalists knew and what we can fairly assume was a reason why he, Swope, and Teagle had intervened, as J. Douglas Brown reported, to keep the CES moving on old-age insurance at its moment of doubt. Here are Folsom's own words: "During the first few years"—fifteen or twenty he meant—"the combined cost [of Social Security taxes plus company supplements] will be somewhat lower because the benefits payable to those who retire in the next few years will be greater than could be purchased for the same payments to the insurance company." This was the same argument Folsom and Brown made to the American Management Association in 1935, shortly after passage of the SSA. As Brown put it then, "the favorable rates of the federal system should prove a boon" to companies with existing plans. Many segmentalists would have lost a huge bargain had the industrialists let the CES drop the ball.[61]

In various contexts, including a speech to the U.S. Chamber of Commerce the following year, and in his *Harvard Business Review* article, Folsom went public with two arguments against reviving the opt-out amendment. First of all, he warned companies that they would find no benefits and only costs in the form of constant federal regulation and monitoring of their private plans to make sure they qualified. If that failed to undermine support for the Clark amendment, he had an even better argument, one shared with noncapitalist reformers. This argument opposed giving capitalists a free market choice in the first place. In practice, only companies with a young workforce would find it advantageous to ask for exemption. That would be new entrants or existing nonsegmentalist competitors. Their "selection against the Federal plan" would make it more expensive for large segmentalists with low turnover, and therefore with older unproductive workers now ready to retire, to fund the system adequately. In other words, it would give back the advantage over competitors that the segmentalists had just gained. To put it bluntly, the Clark amendment was worthless—and even potentially costly—to America's big employers. After 1936, the idea died completely.[62]

As Folsom advocated and predicted, American segmentalists would not get out of the business of private welfare provision. They simply adjusted their company pension costs downward by the amount, more or less, that they now paid in Social Security taxes. For the first fifteen years or so, the combined cost of payroll taxes and their "supplemental plans" could actually be lower for the same level of benefits companies previously provided. Kodak modified its own plan "so that the cost to the company remained practically the same as before and the employee received the same benefits from the company contribution he previously received, part coming from the Government and part from the insurance company." (By saying "practically the same," Folsom left open the possibility that Kodak was actually saving money. Boasting that it was may have put his unusual efforts on OAI's behalf in an unflattering light.) Not surprisingly, the company pension movement actually grew through the rest of the 1930s, as Folsom also predicted. Even the insurance industry reaped benefits from expanding business, and lo and behold, soon came to love Social Security not as a threat but as a "gigantic advertisement" for the insurance idea.[63]

By preserving a company component, segmentalists like Kodak could maintain, even at a lower cost than before, their traditional efficiency wage differential in their respective local labor markets. Of course, the differential would now be compressed from below, but appropriately so in the context of high unemployment and sagging wages. Compression from above, in the form of cutbacks they preferred not to make, proved entirely unnecessary to cope with product market competition. Better yet, compulsory legislation squeezed costs upward for competitors who previously offered no pension benefits. Thus did progressive segmentalists support OAI, with their most prominent representatives vigorously defending its compulsory nature after passage. Seeing competitive advantages for themselves, big businessmen signaled to wary politicians and reformers that a broad-based business reaction to OAI was unlikely, prodded them along at a moment of doubt, and argued for preserving the integrity of the reformers' compulsory legislation after passage. The New Dealers were fully vindicated in their belief that they were crafting politically robust legislation anchored in a cross-class alliance of interests.

The Wagner Act: Trouble Hereafter?

The year 1935 also brought forth the National Labor Relations Act (NLRA). Unlike the SSA, it was legislation that mobilized a ferocious and virtually monolithic attack from the business community. Even progressive executives close to the Roosevelt administration opposed it, though some of that opposition may have been fairly mild. People like Swope remained silent, possibly so as not to entirely discredit themselves among fellow welfare capitalists more dedicated to maintaining their tame "employee representation plans" or company unions.[64] According to the law, unions were now to enjoy legal protection against employer belligerence. It also cleared company-sponsored unions or "representation plans" out of the labor movement's road to organizational strength.

New York Senator Robert Wagner, who invested prodigious energies in bringing the legislation to pass, regarded the unionism it would spawn as a means for "protecting the fair-minded employer from the cutthroat tactics of the exploiting few," and thus from excessive competitive turbulence. After all, "to encourage the establishment of uniform labor standards," along with supporting mass purchasing power, was among the central purposes of the Wagner Act. It was not about unionism or industrial democracy for its own sake without regard to its economic effects.[65]

As he indicated in his exchange with the NAM's Emery in the 1934 Senate hearing quoted earlier, Wagner expected those employers "who want to be fair to their employees" to come around later as they did for workmen's compensation. In introducing the 1935 bill, he identified protection of "the fair-minded employer from the cutthroat tactics of the exploiting few" as of equal importance to fixing wages at a level that would "prime the pump of business." Of course, as we now know, major employers in America never quite regarded the Wagner Act as "a great blessing, a great boon for industry" like compulsory on-the-job accident insurance. On the other hand, Wagner was not entirely delusional in his optimism. Within two years the NEA's Walter Drew, of all people, glimpsed a silver lining. "As long as we have this [Wagner] Act with us," the open-shop belligerent said, "it ought to be made to apply in as wide a scope as possible in order to stop chiseling."[66] His organization wrestled constantly against the chiseling problem, not just union inroads in structural steel. Regulatory virtue could now be made out of political necessity.

One might reasonably ask whether someone like Wagner would have invested such enormous energies in labor and other New Deal legislation had he anticipated nothing down the road but a relentless and massive business reaction that might lay waste to his entire investment. Because the organizationally weak AFL was a rather passive and uninvolved ally, he could hardly bank on a strong labor movement to neutralize a massive counterattack. The politically potent railroad unions actually testified against the Wagner Act on technical grounds, fearing it would disrupt relations they had established on the basis of the Railway Labor Act of 1926, passed on the basis of cross-class support. Instead, Wagner probably counted on the business community to be divided between opponents and proponents. Being from New York, he certainly knew that at least a major part of his politically relevant business world, the clothing industry, was already favorable to joint cartelism and, therefore, strong unions.[67]

Wagner also had good enough reason to think that other important sectors would welcome legislation that could strengthen unions' ability to police the terms of cartelism. Coal operators, large numbers of whom favored collective bargaining, contributed nothing directly to the Democratic National Committee (DNC) in 1936, but they did so at least indirectly with the automatic check-off of union dues to the United Mine Workers, which many operators supported as a way of strengthening the union. Out of these dues, in turn, the UMW contributed about $100,000, over half of all the union money given to the DNC, and lent it another $50,000. Perhaps Republican loyalties, extended to friends of collective bargaining from Hanna to Hoover, were still at work. John L. Lewis had backed the Republicans in 1932; Hoover had, after all, backed Lewis's legislative efforts to regulate the coal industry. In any case, according to Gordon, Wagner apparently planned, but failed, to bring in coal operators and garment manufacturers to testify in 1935 in favor of legislation. Only further research will tell why, curiously, such testimony did not materialize. Perhaps these employer groups feared the meddling of the proposed National Labor Relations Board, while finding unions' ability to organize already acceptably unfettered.[68]

Large numbers of building contractors, big and small, were often appreciative of collective bargaining's value in controlling their markets, so Wagner could be fairly sure that builders would not be motivated to mount a unified backlash. Numerous specialized and local contractors' associations certainly supported collective bargaining, and many probably favored a law that would boost their union counterparts' ability to impose union terms across the board. The director of the New York Building Congress, a cross-class confederation composed of over 600 municipal contractor associations and unions, testified that the Wagner bill was necessary to empower workers to standardize wages "for the benefit in the long run of the employers of that industry." Although the Associated General Contractors officially opposed the Wagner Act in Senate testimony, its position conceals the fact that there was deep internal division on labor relations. In the 1930s, labor issues had been mostly a "taboo subject within the association." That there was a strong undercurrent of interest in cartelist control even among big general contractors is certainly evident in its hearty support a few years earlier, in 1931, for the Davis-Bacon Act.[69]

Major textile manufacturers were among the employer groups New Dealers also had realistically in mind as a future support base. In July 1935, shortly before Roosevelt signed the Wagner Act, textile manufacturer Howell Cheney wrote to the president expressing fear for the industry's stability and health "unless further legislation lays a firm foundation for trade practices and labor agreements rather promptly." It was common knowledge that Roosevelt sympathized, for in radio addresses in May and July 1933, he used the textile industry as an example of the need for government help to prevent "the unfair 10 percent" from dragging the rest down. In one of these "fireside chats," he explained, "If all employers in each competitive group agree to pay their workers the same wages—reasonable wages—and require the same hours—reasonable hours—then higher wages and shorter hours will hurt no employer."[70] He meant, of course, that it would hurt no unfair employer.

The main electoral constituency for David Walsh, Massachusetts senator and Democratic chairman of the Committee on Education and Labor, was workers in the state's two leading but ailing industries, shoes and textiles. On several occasions, Walsh deliberately led witnesses in Senate hearings to express or affirm his argument for collective bargaining, which had a fairly good foothold in these two Massachusetts industries, "in the interest of the employer," he thought. As he explained, "a company recognizing collective bargaining will be driven out of business, if it must compete with a company that will not recognize collective bargaining, if one agrees to pay higher wages than the other." In short, "the employer who lives up to the spirit of the collective bargaining idea and who recognizes the union and meets the wages simply cannot survive unless all the industry is subjected to collective bargaining."[71]

Confirmation of Wagner's realism about employer support came during the 1937–1939 campaign of the Textile Worker's Organizing Committee (TWOC), led by the ACWU's Sidney Hillman. Hillman appealed to industrialists with the argument that "textile unionization means profits." Major producers, like the union-friendly Amoskeag Manufacturing in Manchester, New Hampshire, the largest mill in the country, hoped the fledgling union would bring an end to chiseling by low-wage competitors. The TWOC adopted the wage standards of the Chicopee Mills in Massachusetts and Georgia, a captive producer for Johnson & Johnson, for its campaign. Robert Johnson, an admirer of Hillman's, was the most enthusiastic of a number of textile industrialists about the TWOC's ultimately ill-fated efforts to enforce these elevated standards on chiselers. Even Donald Nelson of Sears offered to help out by boycotting a regular supplier (Hardwick Woolen Mills) if it failed to meet union standards. The TWOC's biggest victory came at American Woolen in Lawrence, Massachusetts. Easily the largest company in its sector, its president was rumored to harbor union sympathies. Collective bargaining at a number of other large mills was also achieved without strikes.[72]

New Dealers even saw beacons of support from a few prominent segmentalist firms battered by the especially brutal competition of the Depression economy. In a 1934 meeting of the National Industrial Conference Board, Cyrus Ching of U.S. Rubber expressed the view that unions "would be perfectly justified in saying, 'We will have to step in and do the job for you'" if manufacturers alone, or through the NRA code authorities, could not raise wages and impose a wage floor to stabilize the "competitive situation" and eliminate "substandard conditions which exist in that industry." U.S. Rubber was one firm to immediately accept national unions and attempt to work with them. The paper industry was also a hospitable site. According to Colin Gordon, big Northwestern paper producer Philip Weyerhauser "saw the potential of union-regulated wages as early as 1932" and hoped for their stabilization at higher, not lower, levels. George Mead of Mead Paper, it seems, may have endorsed the Wagner Act, and Crown Zellerbach accepted collective bargaining willingly.[73]

It may be relevant too that New Dealers, one can well presume, were familiar with Gerard Swope's invitation back in 1926 to the AFL's William Green to create an industrial union that would then organize the plants of all electrical manufacturers, pressure them to impose a floor under the standards of GE's product market competitors, and thus impose a hybrid mix of segmentalism and cartelism (see chapter 8). GE was, not surprisingly therefore, one of the first major firms to accept collective bargaining with national industrial unions. Swope was then invited by New York state's Democratic party to run for governor in 1936, with the promise of help from the American Labor Party and the CIO. At least one big retail firm, from the New Deal's most friendly sector, supported labor legislation to strengthen unions and collective bargaining for the same reason it assisted the garment and textile industry unions and supported unemployment insurance—to stabilize industry. As Edward Filene testified in the Senate, "Our labor unions have a better understanding of what is good for business today than our chambers of commerce have." The Twentieth Century Fund, his creation, "assisted the lobbying effort, arranging testimony and helping to defray some of the costs Wagner was incurring," according to Tom Ferguson.[74]

The legislation as passed did not command businessmen into industrywide collective bargaining over wages and working conditions. Perhaps opposition from some quarters before and after legislation followed from the fact that it could not prevent dangerously uneven union inroads into an industry. Thus, firms risked being forced by regional or other variations in union strength into accepting highly uncompetitive wage levels. But, without a doubt, most of the intense business opposition stemmed from the fact that most big employers worried about losing control of the workplace to unions, which in the American case were often still wedded to the idea of the closed shop and other restrictions on managerial prerogatives. Even M. C. Rorty, president of the American Management Association in 1935, begrudgingly saw a potentially useful role for unions—outside of the segmentalist's sphere of course—in stabilizing wages and therefore preventing "the evils of excessive wage reductions." But as Gordon puts it nicely, the big question for many employers was "whether or not the managerial threat of unionism outweighed the regulatory benefits."[75] The managerial risks were very high, and regulatory benefits equally uncertain. Furthermore, those benefits would start to decline once prosperity returned.

Possibly more support from businessmen would have been generated, or at least much less shrill opposition aroused, if Wagner's NLRA had contained iron-clad protection of "management's right to manage" and clear restriction of the collective bargaining agenda to distributional issues like wages and working hours. After all, many businessmen wanted these things regulated, by the defunct NRA code authorities or by other means. But given the character of negotiated cartelism in the needle trades, with which Wagner was intimately familiar, it is perhaps no mystery why such limitations never appeared. In garments, extraordinarily detailed negotiation over managerial and entrepreneurial prerogatives in multi-employer bargaining units was regarded by both sides of the class divide as essential for realizing their shared cartelist ambitions.[76]

Also, as historian Mark Barenberg argues, Wagner genuinely thought business could benefit from, and therefore accept, unions after the fact for their efficiency effects—because of the "trusting cooperation" that would evolve when independent unions, unlike company unions, eliminated traditional workplace hierarchies. Wagner was well initiated in the Brandeisian synthesis of Taylorism and unionism that had moved the Taylor Society to the left starting in the 1920s. "Getting together" is what Fred J. Miller, the president of the American Society of Mechanical Engineers had called for in 1920, criticizing what he called industry's "reactionaries and stiff-necked autocrats." Future Taylor Society President Morris Cooke agreed. In the same publication, which he edited in collaboration with Miller and AFL leader Samuel Gompers, Cooke argued that "[c]apital, labor, management and the public can unite in a common onslaught on the inefficiencies and wastes everywhere prevalent in American industry."[77] Wagner, however bold in his heroic legislative effort, was a pragmatic optimist, not an impractical dreamer.

The Wagner Act did experience a good deal of what Witte called "trouble hereafter," especially from a strange and reactionary cross-class alliance of the NAM and the crafts-based American Federation of Labor, which feared being outmaneuvered by the new Congress of Industrial Organizations. For engineering, which dominated the NAM, any partial and temporary regulatory advantage of standardized union wages was still probably not worth the risks entailed in sharing control over production and other managerial decisions. (Garment manufacturers and coal operators, not surprisingly, with their friendly cartelist and efficiency-promoting relations with unions, did not belong to the NAM.) The NAM agitation led to the Taft-Hartley law of 1947, which shifted the advantage partially back to anti-union employers and against the newer and more radical CIO. But the success of the backlash, just like the opposition from employers, was limited. It did not touch the regulatory potential of collective bargaining by removing unions' anti-trust exemptions and outlawing multi-employer bargaining. Even within the NAM, there was considerable internal division on the issue of industry-wide or multi-employer bargaining into the 1950s; in fact, it was possibly one of the most divisive issues within the association during the period.[78]

Thus, the partial robustness the Wagner Act, which helped unions in some sectors perform their essential role in joint cartelism, indicates that politicians' anticipation of substantial post facto support from employers was not simply wishful thinking or haughty defiance of capitalist interests. Unionism even proved of some worth to segmentalists. Events in the steel industry, where big segmentalists struggled mightily during the Depression on two fronts—against chiseling as well as against unionization—corroborate this conclusion.

On the chiseling front, as the *Wall Street Journal* reported in 1935, "the steel trade has decided to trust a combination of agreed wage standards and employer self-interest to prevent renewal of predatory competition" after the Supreme Court's rejection of the NRA. The next step, from the entirely predictable failure of voluntary agreements among fiercely competitive capitalists to acceptance of a strong union offering regulatory services, was apparently not a long one. On 28 February 1937, U.S. Steel's Myron Taylor signed an agreement with the mineworkers' leader John L. Lewis, who headed the CIO's Steel

Workers' Organizing Committee (SWOC). A strike proved unnecessary. Although controlling low-wage competition was not the immediate motive, big steel executives may have anticipated that Lewis would do them a service in organizing the rest of the steel industry and checking the depressionary drop in standards. Indeed, Thomas Lamont, who represented J. P. Morgan, Jr., in its relations with the company, and who regarded FDR as "a bulwark for sane policies," noted in a letter to the president the following year that SWOC could help protect U.S. Steel's leading, but ever-declining, position by preventing "the spectacle of 'the independents' jumping in and slashing wages roughshod."[79]

At this point, the company abandoned American industry's elite division in the intersectoral trench warfare against unions in construction, the National Erectors' Association (NEA). U.S. Steel's legendary stature as a fortress of antiunionism in America came to an abrupt end, both in the industrial relations and political sphere. The NEA had long been dominated by a U.S. Steel subsidiary in structural steel production and erection, American Bridge, which also signed with the SWOC in the weeks following the settlement between Taylor and Lewis. Now, Drew thought, we might get help from unions in imposing the regulatory control we once tried to maintain on a unilateral basis. Thus, by 1941, the steelworkers' union succeeded in organizing the rest of basic steel and helped impose unprecedented regulatory order to the industry.[80]

Wagner's gamble on belated employer recognition of the regulatory, macroeconomic, and efficiency value of unions showed strategic realism by a pragmatic politician, not a naive dreamer or defiant class warrior. If the cross-class alliance proved weaker in the case of the Wagner Act, in contrast to the SSA, it was because the legislation could never guarantee that unions would not go too far in the area of managerial control. It did not demand a sharing of management rights, but it did undermine employers' traditional defenses of them. Also, at least during the 1940s, it threatened to empower unions like the United Auto Workers in their ambition, which they eventually gave up, to impose multi-employer bargaining. Even though the big three manufacturers in the auto industry benefitted somewhat from the regulatory effects of unionization, they never welcomed the idea of industry-wide multi-employer bargaining. Negotiated segmentalism, that is, decentralized collective bargaining over good wages, and perhaps over benefits, was going quite far enough.[81]

Conclusion

Plenty of evidence indicates that mass popular and electoral pressures unleashed by the Depression were not the only forces that moved politicians in their New Deal reform efforts. In fact, the New Dealers also responded to strongly favorable signals from important parts of the business community about the need for regulation. On the basis of those signals, interpreted by sophisticated knowledge of employers' market problems, they realistically expected business support to congeal afterward. Those businessmen who were most enthusiastic were even invited to help deliberate over the legislative details, at least for the Social Security Act. Cooperation from prominent and supremely successful businessmen combined with learning experiences in cross-class alliance making earlier in the century stiffened the New Dealers' resolve against vocal and organized business opposition. Without knowledge of these things, their enthusiasm for reform would probably have been substantially weaker. They were not socialist radicals. They relied heavily on business money for their political survival.

Business interests in reform moved in a predictably progressive direction in response to the macro-economic shock of depression. American employers were foul weather friends of the welfare state, but they did not become mortal enemies with the return to prosperity. (They did, however, as the concluding chapter notes, mostly apply the brakes on its expansion.) Because of the Depression, both segmentalists and cartelists experienced alarming levels of low-wage and low-benefit competition in their respective product markets. The New Deal promised to "uplift" competition by imposing new costs and rigidities on chiselers. The social policy that resulted—and endured after the social emergency passed—was secured by a cross-class coalition anticipated by electoral politicians. A partial exception was the Wagner labor relations legislation, whose business support, as *Fortune* magazine reported, was significant but not as deep as Wagner and others probably hoped.

It was, in any case, far deeper than before passage. The Wagner Act, along with Roosevelt's tax policies, caused most of the anti-New Deal fright that seized many American businessmen in 1935. It was probably out of fear and anger about these things, more than hostility to social welfare legislation, that major business organizations attacked Roosevelt's Social Security bill before Congress. It was, as Jacoby puts it, "calculated strategy" to punish and weaken Roosevelt for other more threatening policies.[82] Just like conventional thinking, however, influential theory about the origins of the New Deal takes this opposition at face value. The following chapter looks critically at this theory in light of further evidence about employers and reformers.

10

WHOSE BUSINESS WERE THE
NEW DEALERS MINDING?

Probably no advisor close to Franklin Roosevelt wanted to keep things on good terms with big business in America more than Raymond Moley. The central figure in FDR's "Brains Trust" and coiner of the term New Deal, Moley barely mentions the Social Security Act in his first-hand account of the hostility between Roosevelt and much of the business community in 1935. Businessmen, he explained in 1939, were reacting with "paroxysms of fright" to Roosevelt's "soak the rich" talk accompanying his inheritance and corporate profits tax plans. Roosevelt and other Democratic Party leaders had gotten their own attack of jitters about Louisiana Senator Huey Long and the growing popularity of his Share Our Wealth movement. It looked like Long would even campaign outside Louisiana for promising Share Our Wealth candidates and possibly spoil FDR's chances in the next presidential election. Roosevelt told Moley he thought it necessary to "steal Long's thunder." Moley, alarmed by Roosevelt's cocky defiance, thought the taxes an overreaction.

Roosevelt, it seemed, now welcomed the business world's outrage as if "the proof of a measure's merit was the extent to which it offended the business community"—though all the while expressing amazement "that capitalists did not understand that he was their savior, the only bulwark between them and revolution." [1] He was deeply vexed by the intemperate carping and insults that vocal businessmen heaped on him, his wife, and his New Deal. Moley fully agreed with FDR that their grounds for complaint were mostly "purely imaginary" and "a question of psychology." (As historian Arthur Schlesinger, Jr., put it, FDR thought that many businessmen were "inclined to be ignorant and hysterical" and so "declined to pay the rich the compliment of fearing them.") Roosevelt even endorsed Wagner's labor relations bill, which corporate progressives hoped would fail. But on this, compared with the soak the rich rhetoric, Moley was more sympathetic. Roosevelt had changed his mind in favor of the act partly because he needed Wagner's help on other legislation. It was also a surrogate for the regulatory mechanisms of the NIRA, which Moley had helped bring to pass, after it met its demise at the hands of the Supreme Court. In the large, Moley wrote, the Wagner Act was a measure passed in the spirt of imposing collective control and uplift on competition. This was a goal with appeal to businessmen of all sorts, even if they feared what else the means to that end might bring.[2]

The "Institutionalists"

In a well-respected study of the New Deal, historian William Leuchtenberg notes that "[e]ven the most precedent-breaking New Deal projects reflected capitalist thinking and deferred to business sensibilities." Curiously, however, his discussion of businessmen focuses almost exclusively on the tensions that alarmed Raymond Moley. Likewise, Arthur Schlesinger's celebrated historical work also dwells only on antagonistic relations. In the context of Social Security legislation Schlesinger never mentions the supportive role of Swope, Folsom, Teagle, and the friends of big business in the Industrial Relations Counselors.[3]

We should hardly be surprised, therefore, that social scientists who theorize about private and public power in the making of social reform often construct their thinking around an impression of monolithic capitalist opposition left by mainstream historical narratives. Thus, a highly influential line of analysis about reformist politics in capitalist society, associated with sociologist Theda Skocpol and her collaborators, holds that the Roosevelt administration boldly defied widespread employer opposition to Social Security and even betrayed the few progressive businessmen willing to cooperate in exchange for some influence in its design.[4]

This "institutionalist" analysis, a distinctively and perhaps unrepresentatively "state-centered" one, makes the following highly intriguing argument. In a nutshell, the New Deal emerged when intense but inchoate and manipulable popular pressure from below was shaped, channeled, and extruded into policy form through the relatively rigid institutional machinery of government and electoral politics. This institutional machinery was tended by politicians and "policy intellectuals" ruled more by their vested interests in maintaining and developing those autonomous institutions than by outside economic or social interests, above all, capitalist ones. To the extent that ideas mattered in the process, their shape, reception, and influence were governed by institutions as well. Organized business was so monolithically hostile that, by implication, reformers acted in bold, conscious, and successful defiance of capitalist interests and ideology. Business support from a "handful of liberal-reformist businessmen" was evidently of no consequence because these individuals were actually disappointed by significant details of legislation that autonomous politicians and policy intellectuals ultimately passed.[5]

This coherent institutionalist position on the New Deal complements mainstream historical interpretations of the legislation as a liberal response to popular discontent with the failures of the business-dominated market and political system during the 1930s Depression. Like James MacGregor Burns's depiction of the New Deal's "Grand Coalition" of urban and often immigrant workers, Catholics, Jews, blacks, farmers, and the elderly poor with the scholarly and cultural intelligentsia, the institutionalists' analysis partially concedes the importance of social foundations. In doing so, their work also fits comfortably alongside the political science and political economy literature depicting the New Deal as resting on a capital-exclusive cross-class alliance of popular agrarian and urban working class support. Although generally shying away from "society-centered" explanations, it regards European welfare states, and Scandinavian ones in particular, as founded on the basis of strong working class organization. "Certainly," as Skocpol puts it—incorrectly, as we will see—"the political class struggle between workers and capital helps to explain why the United States has not developed a comprehensive full-employment welfare state along postwar Scandinavian lines."[6]

Interests and Institutions

The following critique shows that this comprehensive understanding of the New Deal completely unravels in the face of historical evidence. First, it brings to light additional evidence that monolithic business opposition was illusory. Second, the analysis shows that liberal corporate executives were not at all disappointed in any profound and unanimous ways by details of the legislation that institutionalists identify as contradictory to their wishes; in some ways, they were even pleased. Third, it shows that policy intellectuals were shrewd alliance brokers, eager to protect existing cross-class alliances rooted in segmentalist and joint cartelist interests and institutionalized in corporatist arrangements. They also wanted to promote new ones. They did not want to protect their vested interests and expand their power in autonomous state structures. Finally, the analysis shows that to the limited extent the institutionalist literature on the New Deal draws on class interests rather than institutional factors to explain outcomes, it incorrectly characterizes labor's success as capital's loss.[7]

Bold Defiance of Monolithic Opposition?

A critique of the state-institutionalist position on the New Deal must first look beneath the public record of apparently unequivocal official positions taken by business associations about New Deal legislation. The look reveals a complex tangle of internal controversy, self-censorship in the context of pack behavior, uncertainty, and finally a good deal of sheer ignorance among businessmen. Statements by relatively cautious and rational politicians suggest they probably had a fairly accurate picture of the complex reality and were thus emboldened to proceed rationally with the arranging of alliances that could protect their large investments in reform.

To the New Dealers, the fact that the U.S. Chamber of Commerce only recently reversed its previously favorable position in May 1935 probably weakened any deterrent effect its oppositional stance might have had. Without appearing far out of touch with the business community, Henry Harriman, the organization's former president, had for a number of years spoken with impunity in support of social insurance legislation. Suddenly, at its 1935 national conference, however, Harriman and prominent leaders of important committees and the permanent staff of the chamber found themselves unable to mobilize enough influence to block "derogatory" and "churlish" resolutions against the Roosevelt administration.[8]

The result of this meeting, "the most tempestuous in the chamber's annals," according to the *New York Times,* was "the appearance of a split in the organization," not anything like unanimity. Peter Van Horn, head of the National Federation of Textiles, charged that a "minority group with selfish political and business interests" was using the chamber as a "cat's-paw"—an unwitting tool, or dupe—against the Roosevelt administration, especially against its efforts to extend the NRA. *Business Week,* criticizing sensationalist press reports, claimed that the Chamber action "came from a single maneuver engineered by that body's way-right wingers." Harper Sibley, the new president, promised to adhere to the majority mandates but this close friend of FDR added most curiously that "[t]he difficulty, of course, in a large hall like that, is that people didn't really know what they were voting on."[9] As *Business Week* put it a few years later, "a small group of strong men had gradually obtained the upper hand," something that "often happens in all sorts of organizations." The rebels' claim to be representative of anything close to unanimity was quickly weakened by some local chamber withdrawals from the national organization. Only seven years later a new rebellion led to the election of insurgent Eric A. Johnston on a platform of "more cooperation with government and labor, less 'Roosevelt-baiting.'"[10]

Roosevelt's view about the deceptiveness or superficiality of opposition mobilized by ideologically motivated business organizers was certainly confirmed by the new Chamber president's assessment in 1935 that the delegates did not really know what they were voting for. Politicians got the same message from other people close to businessmen. As the editor of *Textile World* put it in a statement received by the Senate, textile manufacturers, who were now responding favorably toward persuasive efforts, "have not been able to formulate their own ideas as to just what lines [Social Security] legislation ought to follow; naturally, when it comes to details, they are completely lost." Big business friend Raymond Moley no doubt discussed with Roosevelt what he told readers of *Today* (which later merged with *Newsweek*) about the demagogic manipulability of businessmen, not just the lower classes. Business organizations, he wrote, were "misrepresenting American business."[11]

Open cracks in the apparent wall of opposition appeared in cities like Knoxville, Tennessee, Columbia, South Carolina, and Sheffield, Alabama. There, local chambers of commerce protested the national organization's shift against various aspects of the New Deal, including its public works. In Oklahoma City, Oklahoma, for example, the powerful chamber leader and civic promoter Stanley Draper had roundly praised FDR to conservative businessmen in his city's "Bone Head Club" in 1934 and continued to support the president's efforts for "relief, recovery, and reform" in the years thereafter. Some local units of the Chamber of Commerce resented manipulation and therefore refused to participate in a survey conducted by the national organization in November 1935. Heavily loaded with what the Decatur, Illinois, chamber called "trick questions," it was designed to elicit a massive negative response that could be used against Roosevelt. The survey of 1,500 local chambers found that they opposed, by a ratio of 35 to 1, (1) extension of federal jurisdiction into matters of state and local concern, (2) federal spending without relation to revenues, (3) government competition with private enterprise, and (4) unclear grants of authority to the executive branch. Only by a contorted stretch of the imagination could one conclude that this survey tapped into views about Social Security. Nevertheless, institutionalists rely on it for their conclusions about the depth and vastness of capitalist opposition. A better survey was conducted by the Chamber of Commerce around 1942. It showed overwhelming support for the specific details of the actual legislation.[12]

Beneath the surface, therefore, of opinions conveyed by national business organizations, large numbers of employers were probably uncertain and open to persuasion. The openly supportive ones, Marion Folsom estimated in recollections 35 years later, amounted to about 5 percent. John D. Rockefeller Jr. had his own reasons for hiding—while letting his money do some persuasive talking. If other open-minded businessman did not speak up, they were like most of their species, politically inactive. These were busy businessmen, after all. It also made perfect sense for them to avoid, especially in the Depression, unnecessarily alienating even a minority among their bankers, stockholders, board members, buyers, and suppliers who might have been resolutely hostile to Roosevelt and willing to take their business elsewhere. As social insurance reformer Isaac Rubinow put it, "Individual employers are found to be much more ready to express their acceptance of [unemployment insurance] proposals in private." When asked for open endorsements, however, "They prefer 'to have their name kept out of this.'" This might help explain why, for example, the segmentalist candy manufacturer William P. Wrigley was unavailable to join Perkins's and Witte's advisory committee and why, according to Folsom, Roosevelt had been lucky to get five other members.[13]

It is not surprising, then, that Roosevelt would so confidently proceed with legislation, given his belief that "in altogether too many cases the general views of business did not lend themselves to expression through its organizations." Individual expression of support from many progressively inclined businessmen, he probably believed, was suffocated by a wish to avoid the social if not economic censure that can be meted out in boardrooms and clubs across America. That is what corporate liberal Edward Filene witnessed. The "loneliness of the liberal business man" was the price paid for "approaching the problems of the business and industry in a scientific and liberal spirit." Sooner or later it "brings down upon his head the criticism of important groups of his fellow business men" and a "reputation for radicalism that hampers them for further influence in business circles."[14] Thus, the institutionalists' assessment about the belligerent thrust of vocal opinion among most politically and organizationally active businessmen may be correct. But it does not comprehend the full spectrum of politically consequential businessmen whom the New Dealers knew they were dealing with as they prepared their legislation—and, even more important, in the future.

Disappointed Corporate Progressives?

In addition to arguing that the business community as a whole locked arms in a broad phalanx against the SSA, the institutionalists try to bolster their case by showing that even the renegade employers on the CES's citizens' Advisory Committee failed to get their way in the design of the legislation. They see, for example, a discrepancy between the progressives' desires and the SSA in the imposition of the unemployment insurance tax entirely on employers. Indeed, the progressive capitalists had wanted to share the tax, speculating that employee contributions would cause workers to regard the plan as their own and not a gratuity, and thus form a constituency against squandering of funds by other workers.[15]

But the evidence seems to show that the lack of worker contributions was no more than a pebble in employers' shoes. As Daniel Nelson argues, the liberal employers' objections were "relatively innocuous." Reform intellectuals like Abraham Epstein and Isaac Rubinow, by contrast, experienced bitter disappointment about the corporate progressives' major victory on another matter, the goal of "prevention" or employment stabilization through "experience rating" and "employer reserves."[16] For the corporate liberals, the legislation's main virtue was prevention of unemployment through tax incentives on employers to reduce layoffs. Thus, those with highly unstable employment would pay more into unemployment funds. The liberal intellectuals preferred a different system that actually cross-subsidized rather than penalized firms and sectors (like garments) with highly unstable employment patterns.

The absence of worker contributions in no way contradicted the corporate progressives' prevention idea, which was closer to their hearts. Marion Folsom testified that worker contributions had nothing to do with the stabilization logic of the legislation, which involved manipulating the costs of doing business. Because of their overriding regulatory interests, he was, in fact, entirely agreeable to the idea of imposing the biggest burden on the employer, because "as he can do something about reducing unemployment . . . the employee can do very little." For the same reason, one big businessman active in state reform efforts actually spoke against worker contributions. Lincoln Filene, of the Boston retail firm William Filene's Sons Co., echoed Folsom in telling Congress that "it is the employer, not the employee, who can exercise control over conditions of employment." He objected to employee contributions because "the underlying principle is that unemployment is a business cost and should be so charged and hence paid by business, not by the employee."[17]

Institutionalists have generated even more confusion on the prevention issue than on the worker contribution issue by arguing that progressive capitalist advisors failed in their efforts to get the CES to accept a "nationally uniform" unemployment system, or "a kind of Ohio plan at the national level." In their view, because such a plan would impose a uniform system of taxes and benefits, it was favored by the liberal businessmen who did not want "balkanization of benefit standards or (worse) irregular taxes on business."[18] The "Ohio plan" they refer to, widely favored in liberal reform circles for the higher benefits it would allow, was a proposal calling for pooling uniform employer and employee contributions in large state-level unemployment insurance funds. With the Ohio plan, firms and sectors with stable employment levels would therefore subsidize unstable ones, and broad-based pooling would allow for more generous benefits to workers. In Wisconsin, by contrast, the prevention idea had won in 1931. Its plan required separate reserves for each individual employer and therefore meant highly irregular taxation. Employers would be charged for laying off workers because they paid taxes into their separate reserves only until a certain balance accumulated; no further payments were required unless layoffs occurred and the reserves were drawn down. As a result, employers with stable employment records would not subsidize others and their workers.

Contrary to the institutionalists, the record shows indisputably that practically every corporate executive close to the Roosevelt administration abhorred anything like the Ohio plan that pooled insurance funds at the national or any other level. Paul Litchfield from Akron, Ohio's Goodyear, was probably the lone exception. Instead, they favored the Wisconsin plan. This stance, after all, conforms entirely to their interests as segmentalists. The Wisconsin option, or any kind of differential taxation applying the insurance industry's principle of "experience rating," leveled the competitive playing field with low-standard employers. It actually gave their competitors an uphill battle.

Thus, in September 1934, Swope, Leeds, Teagle, and other business leaders on the Commerce Department's Business Advisory Commission (BAC) drew up a report advocating federal legislation to promote state systems with no pooling. Instead, they explicitly called for experimentation with stabilization incentives. Witte now had every reason to be optimistic about business defense of continued legislative efforts and resulting legislation. The following December Raymond Moley joined Folsom, Swope, Teagle, and Leeds in a letter to Labor Secretary Perkins, in which they explained their strong preference for a "federal subsidy" plan (or "grants-in-aid" plan). It called for the federal government to encourage states to set up unemployment insurance systems with large subsidies out of federal revenues. It would impose minimum standards on states for them to qualify for the subsidy but also allow for experimentation with prevention schemes.[19]

Because the progressives praised the subsidy plan for its inclusion of minimum standards, the institutionalists conclude they were for uniformity and the Ohio plan. In other words they confuse minimum standards with uniformity. The alternative arrangement, the Wagner-Lewis or "tax-offset" plan, actually provided less leverage for imposing minimum standards. It was to impose a federal payroll tax on most employers over a certain size (excluding those employing farm workers and domestic servants), who could then deduct, or "offset" against the tax, up to 90 percent of the amount that they contributed to UI schemes designed by states more or less in the form they pleased, if they pleased.

The main reason the corporate liberals favored the subsidy plan was not the minimum standards regulation but the flexibility it left open for experimentation with the kind of *industry-specific interstate arrangements,* complete with either company reserves or experience rating, that Swope had advocated in his famous plan. They made their complete happiness with the prospect of unevenness crystal clear in advocating that the "widest opportunity for experimentation and encouragement should be given to companies and industries, whether intrastate or interstate, to experiment with standards not less favorable than those approved by a governmental administrative body."[20] In a statement submitted to the Senate Finance Committee, Folsom summarized at length why the business members of CES advisory council, joined by William Green of the AFL, had favored the federal subsidy plan over the Wagner-Lewis tax-offset plan that Roosevelt had ultimately sent to Congress. Here he ranked "uniformity" low as far as businessmen, rather than workers, were concerned:

> We felt that under the [federal subsidy] system it would be possible to set up industrial plans covering more than one State, and that an entire industry could do a better job in stabilizing and reducing unemployment than individual companies in any industry could do in individual States. We thought there should be experimentation along industrial as well as State lines. It was also felt that the workers would be better protected because more minimum standards could be included in the Federal law under the grants-in-aid plan than under the proposed plan. There would still be considerable freedom to the States, but only above certain minimum standards.[21]

Again, he argued that firms and industries that through fortune or merit had stable employment should not be forced to subsidize others (in autos, construction, and needle trades for example) by contributing to a common pool.[22] "Balkanization" and irregular taxes were a good thing in other words, not as the institutionalists suppose, undesirable. Folsom's mention of minimum— but not uniform—standards suggests that it might have been a factor helping cement an alliance with the AFL president.

Ultimately the coalition of liberal businessmen and the country's top labor leader failed to persuade the CES to pursue the federal subsidy plan. The tax-offset plan, Supreme Court Justice Louis Brandeis's idea, was simply superior in its ability to satisfy a constitutional challenge on states' rights grounds, and not coincidentally to satisfy powerful agricultural employers in Southern states desiring to exclude blacks from federal minimum standards. And it was no big defeat for big industrial employers outside the South. In the end, according to Wilbur Cohen, Edwin Witte's protégé and aide, when a provision encouraging states to incorporate company reserves or merit rating was finally introduced into the tax-offset bill, "the employers were reasonably satisfied and dropped their support for the subsidy plan." Folsom, now so satisfied with the tax-offset plan, even authored a motion adopted by the council advising the CES that to secure federal and state legislation it may find it advisable to omit or amend some standards. In Senate testimony, he indicated nothing even close to great disappointment, much less opposition, appreciating that "there are also good reasons for adopting the proposed type of bill."[23]

In reference to the change, and as if speaking directly to the liberal segmentalists, Senator Robert Wagner emphasized in an opening statement that the plan's "chief merit" was the regulatory "stabilization of industry." An important feature serving that end was the "special encouragement" for states to incorporate preventive features: "If any State law enables an employer to reduce the amount of his State contribution because of his good business record, he may offset against his Federal tax not only the amount of his actual payment under the State law, but also the amount of the reduction that he has won." He then pointed out that Wisconsin had such a law and would so benefit.[24]

By dropping opposition to the tax-offset plan, the segmentalist employers acknowledged the close attention their interests had been given. Confirming their influence, Franklin Roosevelt—probably with Raymond Moley's help, according to Witte—added reference to the need for stabilization incentives in his special message to Congress on 17 January 1935, about the CES draft. In one important way, too, the corporate liberals actually emerged with an even better plan than the one sent to Congress by Roosevelt, as drafted by the CES. Folsom's testimony, which "greatly impressed the Senate Finance Committee," helped ultimately bring about the elimination of a partial pooling arrangement to be imposed on state systems that opted for company reserves.[25]

At that point, the only "trouble thereafter" being risked was from labor, reform intellectuals, and other liberals not from big business. As one extreme liberal—who happened also to be a small employer—testified, "I am convinced that the unemployment-insurance features embody a complete surrender to big business." According to reformer Paul Douglas, criticism of this nature about the "pronounced inequalities" in contributions and benefits associated with the bill caused the House of Representatives to omit the provision encouraging the reserves system. At that point, advocates of the Wisconsin plan, "who . . . occupied some powerful positions of vantage in the Washington scene," were among the "forces behind [the] return to the original draft" in the Senate. Douglas could only have meant the corporate progressives like Folsom. Their work then sailed intact through the joint conference committee of the two houses and into the final law.[26]

What the corporate liberals got in the end was not perfect. Their loss was not uniformity, but the possibility of national experimentation on a sectoral, interstate basis. Here, they bowed not to reformers acting against their interests in stabilization but to the reality of Supreme Court interventionism, which threatened to upset more centralized regulation. This interventionism was powered in part by Southern congressmen, doing the bidding of Southern plantation employers who opposed all compulsory federal standards and rules of inclusion that might weaken their powerful grip on the low-wage agricultural, and largely black, labor force. In this case, the outcome was the result of a minor but bridgeable division of interests between one group of influential employers and another, not employers versus reformers acting autonomously of business interests.[27]

In conclusion, the segmentalist corporation men suffered nothing like the defeat posited in the institutionalist analysis of UI. What they preferred above all was legislation that encouraged experimentation with company reserves or experience rating, exactly what Roosevelt had insisted on in a message to Congress back in June 1934 and repeatedly thereafter. Standards may well have been more important to the AFL's William Green, who had allied with the corporate liberals in the advisory council in support of the federal subsidy plan. Even the corporate liberals' minor defeat regarding contributions from workers, in combination with this success, may have been a blessing in disguise: according to the CES's Arthur Altmeyer, "if employee contributions had been included, the effect of experience rating on keeping benefits low would have been far less."[28] Thus, there were no disappointed liberal segmentalists—yet, that is. If they were disappointed about UI, it was later, and because they were ambushed by other employers in state-level cross-class alliance politics.

On the old age insurance portion of the SSA, institutionalists present no argument about the foiling of liberal employers' efforts. They could have found one, however, in the creation of the OAI system's large reserve fund. For various reasons, Folsom and others strongly opposed a fully funded system, preferring a "pay-as-you-go" system in which current payments into the system go to current beneficiaries. Their biggest concern was that big government spenders would find it impossible to keep their hands off the large fund. On this issue, Roosevelt was probably swayed by the fiscally conservative Treasury Secretary Henry Morgenthau, who wanted to use the surplus revenues to reduce the federal government's operating deficit. But the corporate progressives' position prevailed in a short time, bolstered by Keynesian, as well as conservative, logic. In 1939, they led a broad coalition of forces, including the private insurance industry and the NAM, pressuring successfully for a large move in the direction of pay-as-you-go financing. By delaying scheduled increases in Social Security taxes, and extending benefits to survivors and other categories, only a smaller contingency fund was to be built up.[29]

If the modification of the funding system in 1939 removed one cause for corporate liberals' disappointment, another change gave them cause for jubilation: exemption of company payments into private retirement or other welfare plans from the definition of wages to be taxed for Social Security. Even hidebound reactionaries like Lammot du Pont got something they wanted here. Once again, Folsom was instrumental in bringing about the change. By sheltering company expenditures from payroll taxes, the change reduced the costs of maintaining an efficiency premium relative to prevailing conditions in their respective labor markets—and therefore the cost disadvantage segmentalists experienced relative to chiselers in depressed product market competition. This reform made a good deal even better. In short, for segmentalists there was nothing disappointing about OAI. As Folsom conceived it, in Jacoby's words, OAI "would require government to subsidize the cost of private welfare capitalism." While imposing extra costs on their product market competitors who offered no company benefits, it gave them cheaper costs for their own, scaled back, supplementary plans.[30]

Bureaucracy on Top?

The institutionalist argument holds that New Deal reformers acted with virtually no regard for business interests or preferences and utmost regard for those of autonomous bureaucrats and policy experts. Thus, for example, it attributes the state-level autonomy provided for in the UI system largely to the protective efforts of reformers on behalf of "pre-existing state-level programs or administrative structures." The interests of white land-owning employers did not figure. Hence, CES director Edwin Witte, who was brought by Frances Perkins to Washington from Madison, sought "to protect the autonomy of the state of Wisconsin" and therefore its groundbreaking unemployment insurance law of 1931. Witte, it seems, hailed from Wisconsin's unusual "academic-political complex," a policy network connecting the University of Wisconsin in Madison and the state's unique administrative apparatus, the Wisconsin Industrial Commission, and the Legislative Reference Library. Witte was thus a quintessential example of a "third force" mediator—a policy expert with bureaucratic leverage and an agenda that looks well beyond private or class interests.[31]

It is indeed true that Witte viewed social insurance as "a matter for state action." He coordinated efforts with Wisconsin Senator Robert La Follette, Jr., whose amendment, passed in Senate committee with the help of Folsom's argumentation, removed all obligatory pooling and therefore left Wisconsin's system intact. Witte's own preference was partial pooling. So here, as the evidence will show, he was acting not upon his own, but upon the preferences of Wisconsin employers and others, like the CES business advisors, favoring a company reserves system.[32] In doing so, he simultaneously acted out of loyal commitment to Wisconsin's institutions and policies. This was no coincidence, for business interests and those institutions were far from distinct.

For the institutionalists, the relevant administrative structures and practices are those of the Wisconsin Industrial Commission (WIC), which Witte at one time directed. It was set up early in the century to administer workmen's compensation and factory safety regulation. It was then handed the job of implementing and overseeing the state unemployment insurance scheme in 1931. The institutionalists identify as the WIC's chief virtue its broad integration of administrative functions in diverse realms of labor and social policy. With comprehensive coordination came an unusual capacity to generate innovative policy. Moreover, it received the help of "America's most influential 'academic-administrative' complex, with a major research-oriented state university right in its capital city, Madison, and a strong Legislative Reference Bureau creating ties between legislators and academics." Arthur Altmeyer, Elizabeth Brandeis, Paul Raushenbush, and Edwin Witte, the "experts from Wisconsin who played the controlling roles in formulating the Social Security Act," came out of this network and therefore answered to their own "autonomous roots and orientations."[33]

John R. Commons, who trained the experts and helped set up the WIC, would probably not have much liked this characterization of Wisconsin policy making. He was a corporatist, not a builder of autonomous state institutions. The supreme doyen of business-friendly progressive reform experts in America at the time, Commons saw the WIC above all as the legal-administrative exoskeleton for policy making by private interests. It was inspired, he wrote, by Belgium's cross-class "Superior Council of Labor" and his experience with the National Civic Federation during the heyday of cross-class collaboration between industrialist-politician Marcus Hanna and mineworkers' leader John Mitchell.[34]

The essentials of the WIC were therefore not to be found in an expert staff recruited along civil service lines and engaged in policy discourse with independent liberal scholars. These types were either too inflexible or impractical compared to the industrial and labor leaders recruited onto the WIC "advisory boards," the heart and brains of the system.

> If one examines the three hundred pages of the labor law of the state he will find that the legislature enacted only one hundred pages and these advisory committees of employers and employees drafted two hundred pages. These were then issued as "orders" by the Industrial Commission. Two-thirds of the labor laws of the state are actually made by the men in the industries, who must obey the laws and who therefore frame them.

In other words, the corporatist WIC "combines to a certain degree, the activities of legislation, execution and judgment," surrendering all three to representatives of private interests.[35]

Administrative corporatism—legislation through collective bargaining—was the next best thing to Commons's "collective bargaining instead of legislation." And collective bargaining, as Commons preached ever since his NCF days early in the century, was all about managing competition. The WIC, as he pointed out, was partly modeled after the corporatist Wisconsin Railroad Commission, which was set up for industrial self-governance. But its regulatory function was different: "The railroad Commission regulates monopoly— the Industrial Commission regulates competition." In other words, "It endeavors to enforce 'reasonable' competition in so far as dealings with employers are concerned, by raising the level of labor competition." Thus, in Wisconsin, Commons noted, "it has been found that the employers on the [advisory] committees have been more exacting in their search for the highest practicable standards than the representatives of labor on the committees."[36]

Commons himself saw the Wisconsin unemployment law, which was drawn up by his students Elizabeth Brandeis and Paul Raushenbush, incorporating features of the negotiated multi-employer plan he helped set up for the Chicago clothing industry, as "an enabling act, setting up an administrative system of collective bargaining." In short, it "cannot be understood as a mere statute administered by a bureaucratic commission with appeals to the courts. It is as nearly a voluntary system of collective bargaining as the nature of our constitutional government will permit, and it can be understood only in so far as the concerted action of voluntary private associations is understood." The bureaucratic autonomy of the WIC and its experts, therefore, did not exist. The fact that the industry advisors, nominated by the Wisconsin Manufacturers' Association, served without compensation, not as full-time salaried civil servants, only strengthens this conclusion. They gave "an astonishing amount of time, at their own expense, which if paid for at commercial rates, would have required an expenditure far beyond the appropriation which the legislature allowed to the commission." They did not regard their work as "merely a public service, but mainly as a vital matter in the future conduct of manufacturing in the state."[37] Private financing of state activity complemented delegation of state powers to private interests. To see state autonomy here is to construct evidence from theory.

Commons was openly skeptical about the autonomous power of the academic side of the "academic-political complex." He dismissed journalists' typical stories about how "a university governs a state." To a conservative employer upset about the "socialistic" university, Commons pointed out "that the University had a great majority of its faculty in several colleges—engineering, law, commerce, the college of liberal arts, the economics department—mainly devoted to training students to serve the interests of business and employers." The visitor then "verified my statement and so advised me." In his autobiography, Commons states unabashedly that "private capitalists" doubled his own university salary in 1904 and otherwise augmented his income in following years, never hastening to clear up in advance any questions this might raise about his own autonomy. Instead, he added flippantly, "I guess I am an opportunist."[38]

Commons had taught CES director Edwin Witte well, for according to

Witte's biographer, he "conceived social insurance to be 'a form of labor legislation' and hence of regulation." As a University of Wisconsin economics professor, former chief of the state's Legislative Reference Library and secretary of the Industrial Commission, Witte had been and remained a central figure in the academic-corporatist network. He fully agreed with the Commons approach to merging interest group representation into law making and enforcement. After serving as the CES director and returning to Wisconsin, he wrote it into a 1937 Wisconsin labor relations act, which created a board where "both industry and labor shall have an opportunity to set their own houses in order without governmental intervention."[39] Clearly Witte was not the builder and defender of autonomous state institutions. Instead, he acted out of a pragmatic recognition of the need for cross-class regulatory alliances, institutionalized in corporatist administrative structures.

Not surprisingly, Wisconsin's Arthur Altmeyer, chairman of the Social Security Board in 1940, was a chief proponent of working corporatist advisory boards into the administration of the U.S. Employment Service and the Social Security Board. "It is only through representative advisory committees that *bureaucracies can be kept on tap instead of on top*," he said. So, after all, there was corporatism in America. And it was not only in Wisconsin. In the area of unemployment insurance, Wisconsin practices were replicated to varying degrees, and with varying success, in at least 26 other states. In 1965, according to the executive vice president of the Wisconsin Manufacturers' Association, 35 of the 37 most industrialized states of the union had advisory councils in which "the views of management and unions are well represented." In 26 of those, he said, the councils constructively "assist the legislature in developing revisions in the law." No better evidence can be found that corporatist institution building through regulatory cross-class alliance making—or "shared government" as Becker calls it in his study of state unemployment insurance administration—was in the minds of the New Deal's policy experts.[40]

In the case of federal old age insurance, institutionalists have little to say about an alliance of autonomous policy intellectuals and preexisting administrative structures, even though a few states had begun setting up their own separate arrangements. Here, administrative institution building actually drew on what institutionalists would regard as rather unlikely sources. In fact, experts from the sphere of corporate progressives—with little or no government loyalties—helped give birth to one of America's most successful government bureaucracies.

In setting up the administrative apparatus for OAI after passage of the Social Security Act, the New Dealers got free help from corporate progressives—just as Bryce Stewart from the IRC helped Wisconsin draft a plan in 1932 for administering its new unemployment system created by Commons's students. Experts in the Social Science Research Council (SSRC), an outfit, like the IRC, heavily dependent on Rockefeller money, were instrumental in developing the necessary infrastructure for OAI. In collaboration with the IRC, the

SSRC participated in preliminary studies consulted by Roosevelt advisors before establishing the CES in 1934. In 1935, the SSRC's Committee on Social Security began work right away on solving the organizational, personnel, and procedural problems to be faced by the as yet nonexistent Social Security Administration. With the intervention of corporate executives in the Commerce Department's BAC, the director of the Industrial Bureau of the Philadelphia Chamber of Commerce was hired to organize the massive bureaucracy. Then, for about a year or so, the SSRC remained the only available source of technical assistance.[41] If any conclusion can be drawn, it is this: because interests helped give rise to institutions, institution makers could not possibly have ignored interests.

State-Level Implementation: Disappointment after All?

Although progressive corporate executives were pleased by the unemployment insurance portion of the SSA—because it imposed no obligatory pooling and explicitly allowed states to follow in Wisconsin's footsteps—their hopes were sorely disappointed when most states failed to incorporate experience rating until well into the 1940s. Thus, when the institutionalists turn to analysis of state-level implementation, they find that employers were flattened by the combined forces of organized labor, professional reformers, and electoral politicians. Organized business, they find, opposed all legislation in the five states examined, especially when it provided for pooling. The only exception they note is the Boston Chamber of Commerce, missing the fact that organized retailers in New York, California, Ohio, and probably other states, were in favor. Retailers in Ohio and California helped draft their states' laws. Curiously, the institutionalist position in this state-level analysis is that the widespread success of statewide pooling systems demonstrates the weakness of the corporate progressives, having once wanted uniformity and pooling during the SSA debate.[42]

Cross-class alliances in state-level political processes need to be included in explanations of these outcomes. The evidence indicates that governors and state legislators responding to well-articulated union pressure for the "Ohio" or state-wide pooling option anticipated post facto alliances with politically influential industries in their states, especially seasonal and otherwise unstable industries like rubber, construction, mining, textiles, and clothing. These industries favored the cross-subsidization that corporate progressives, like most of those in the BAC, objected to. One who did not object—perhaps not coincidentally—was from Ohio. Paul Litchfield, president of Goodyear, spoke for the state's important rubber industry, which suffered heavy cyclical and seasonal unemployment that "good management" could exercise little control over. Thus, he for one pleaded for national legislation with pooling, arguing that the Wisconsin system "would bear with too great harshness" upon industries like his.[43]

Research indicates that unstable industries like rubber enjoyed greater leverage through state politics at the expense of experience rating, depending on their prevalence in each state's economy. Thus, in Ohio, rubber did better than in Washington, DC. From 1939 into the 1950s, one of the two employer representatives on the unemployment scheme's "advisory council" was "influential in the rubber industry, which is influential in the Ohio Chamber of Commerce, which is very influential in unemployment compensation matters." Institutional variations in sectoral leverage may also explain why pooling did better in the House of Representatives than in the Senate and White House.[44]

Labor was often able to ally with business interests to fight experience rating; in places like Wisconsin and New Hampshire, they accepted it. In Pennsylvania, for example, where coal mining was of course still a politically and economically important industry, politicians may well have been responding to a cohesive cross-class alliance for pooling. Company reserves and experience or merit rating were initially not permitted in the first state legislation passed pursuant to the SSA. Therefore, the "sick" mining industry was favored at the expense of more stable or growing sectors. Conflict between coal operators and other employer groups over reform of the system in following years continued, with the industry and its union often lining up together against a cross-class alliance of experience rating enthusiasts. Another interesting example is Rhode Island, where employers from the ailing textile industry and its important jewelry industry, whose output fluctuated seasonally, successfully joined forces with labor in sharp conflict with other employers on the issue. State-level cross-class alliance politics also affected post–New Deal outcomes in Utah, where steel, oil, retail merchandising, and auto dealers clashed with mining and seasonal industries like construction favoring the more liberal pooling system; in California, the "high cost" industries like motion pictures and retail trade lined up against "low cost" employers like California's economically weighty utilities.[45]

The New York case is worth dwelling on because its legislation in 1935 and beyond seemed to defy the corporate progressives so completely and directly favor labor unions. To the great disappointment of New York industrialists Swope and Folsom, their state's 1935 legislation explicitly rejected all prevention features. In effect, big segmentalists were forced to subsidize garment workers during slow periods and thereby reduce downward wage and price pressures bothersome to workers and employers alike. The law's relatively generous benefits would also help keep good workers available when production picked up again. The fact that Governor Lehman changed his initial opposition to the pooling system was probably due to the good relations he kept with the garment industry, not just the fact that the sector's labor force was the largest in the state's electorate. According to Becker's detailed analysis of corporatist input into UI in various states, the industry "had labor's viewpoint on many crucial issues," among them statewide pooling. For Swope at least, the arrangement was no huge betrayal. Despite Lehman's bias, Swope supported his re-election to the governorship in 1936–after having rejected an invitation from the Democratic Party to run himself. Later, in 1939 and 1940, Lehman vetoed experience-rating amendments passed by the state legislature. His successor, Democratic Governor Averell Harriman, did the same things three times later in the mid-1950s. Here was a cross-class alliance behind a policy well-tailored to the New York political economy.[46]

As evidence in support of labor's influence and therefore businessmen's continuing impotence in the process, the institutionalists cite the fact that the New York law "provided benefits to strikers that could help unions prolong strikes." That any sane capitalist would resist this almost goes without saying– but should not. Pursuant to the joint-cartelist strategy, garment makers dominating employers' associations often welcomed strikes. Work stoppages halted overproduction and imposed standards on chiselers. Fully endorsing strikes as negotiated cartelism's primary enforcement tool, the cartelists often refused to do work on contract for struck firms, assisted in the planning and financing of strikes, and explicitly exempted general organizing strikes from no-strike clauses in their contracts. They sometimes even colluded in the planning of general strikes to help drive workers into the union and force union terms on competitors (see chapter 7).[47] Because unions could not always afford strikes, subsidizing them with unemployment benefits was in these employers' interests too.

The garment industry probably made New York extreme in its insistence on pooling and unemployment benefits to strikers. Even that state eventually succumbed to the prevention idea, however. By 1943, 40 states—and by 1948 every state—had introduced the principle to some degree. New York moved slowly in that direction, possibly in step with the decline in relative importance of the clothing sector. Kodak's Folsom had to spend years on New York's advisory committee fighting the cross-class exploitation of the law's advantages by capital and labor in the needle trades. In 1965, he complained, despite improvements, that "we're still being drained by the seasonal industries."[48]

All in all, gradually, corporate progressives would get their satisfaction. Relentless pressure from stable industries recovered the advantage for the prevention idea. Division among employers explains some of the delay. For example, the National Association of Manufacturers strongly favored experience rating after 1939 only after some uncertainty. Also, the shift probably took place in cross-class alliance with labor interests less in need of intersectoral cross-subsidization. In New York, George Meany of the plumbers' union, for what reason it is not clear, took a more conciliatory posture on the experience rating question in the 1930s than other union leaders. Perhaps his move out of the state to take the national leadership of AFL leadership delayed the shift there.[49] Across the country, in varying degrees and speeds, a strong and durable constituency for experience rating prevailed. Only changeable and manipulable cross-class alliance making can explain the twists, turns, and delays along the way.

Other Theory: Structural Mechanisms, Sectoral Interests, and Instrumental Pressure

It bears repeating that key Roosevelt advisor Edwin Witte "conceived social insurance to be 'a form of labor legislation' and hence of regulation." He had listened well to John Commons's teaching. Institutionalist theory, pointing to people like Witte, makes serious errors in resolutely ignoring how he and other New Dealers were moved by employers' signaled and anticipated labor market interests in the design and passage of regulatory social legislation. Competing theories about major social policy reform in America also ignore these processes. Some lean too heavily on capitalism's even more indirect and impersonal "structural mechanisms" to explain outcomes. Others rely too much on the personal or instrumental intervention of individual capitalists on behalf of their sectoral interests. Analysis of employer interests in market governance, often shared across class lines, reveals their errors of interpretation and explanation as well. The critique helps justify the search for theory that neither ignores nor exaggerates capitalist influence.

Class Conflict and Business Confidence

One of the most important and influential theoretical treatments of major social policy reforms is that of Fred Block. His intriguing and well-crafted attempt to explain reform in capitalist society differs in a number of ways from the institutionalist analysis. For one thing, he attributes far greater importance to class struggle in bringing reforms into being. In the case of the New Deal, Block can justifiably support his case on the unprecedented ideological, organizational, and electoral mobilization of typically inert masses of the population. Economic depressions also play a more prominent role. While they trigger the mobilization of mass pressure for reform, he says, they also neutralize the obstructionary force of capitalists against it.[50]

In other words, economic crisis disables what Block calls a major "structural mechanism"—investment strikes and capital flight—operating more or less smoothly during normal economic times to stymie reform. In Block's own words, during depressions, "low levels of economic activity mean that the threat of declining business confidence loses its power, at the same time that popular demands for economic revival are strong." At such times, therefore, "the state managers can pay less attention to business opinion and can concentrate on responding to the popular pressure, while acting to expand their own power." After economic recovery, however, business confidence revives as a force in favor of capitalists' interests in a partial rolling back of reforms, which they achieve "through intense political struggle."[51]

A major flaw in Block's theory is its neglect of the fact that depressions can heighten employers' regulatory interests in reformist social or labor legislation. This is true whether or not economic crisis weakens their impersonal, structural resistance to reform, in itself a debatable matter. Politicians hoping desperately, for their own sake, for a recovery in business activity are probably all ears to signals from businessmen and their experts about what might work and what might make things worse. Block's mistake arises directly from his exclusive focus on class struggle and neglect of the fierce internecine struggle over dwindling profits and business survival within the diverse capitalist class. In this context, as history shows, cross-class alliances for regulation of ruinous competition are no less likely in principle than radical mobilization of a polarizing nature. Block's mistake also derives directly from his exclusive focus on the mobility of capital, while neglecting the mobility of low-priced goods across vast territory in integrated product markets. Here, consumers exercise their collective veto power against high-standard employers and union-friendly employers. Cross-class coalitions for compulsory reform neutralize that veto power.

Thus, politicians and reformers can seize the opportunity provided by depression to arrange cross-class alliances that in normal times are difficult to arrange. Depression divides capitalists among themselves over market control strategy that some favor and others oppose. Indeed, capitalists in some sectors may be the most eager reformers of all—especially big retailers, as the American case shows, for its effect on mass purchasing power. Within sectors, some employers may see more clearly than others through the smoke screen of anti-government ideology how reform may benefit them by imposing extra costs on their skinflint competitors. With the window of political opportunity opened by depression, reformers do not harness the working class to their state building projects because unanimous capitalists are collectively at bay. They harness capitalists and workers, or at least some of them, together.

Historical evidence indicates another problem with Block's theory. Overall, an "intense political struggle" did not ensue with economic recovery to roll back reforms in ways favorable to capitalists. Even the supposedly hidebound reactionaries dominating the NAM came around and played a progressive role in supporting the Social Security Act. Adjustments favored by capitalists did occur, but little in the way of rollbacks and seldom through a process resembling class struggle. At most, capitalists applied pressure to limit costly expansion of reforms. Only in the case of the campaign for the Taft-Hartley revisions of the Wagner Act does Block's prediction seem at all valid, and that may be what he had in mind. But the cross-class alliance argument explains the variation in ways that he does not. The revisions mostly involved aspects of the labor legislation that offered no clear regulatory advantage. Instead, they protected highly disruptive and systemically subversive practices (the closed shop, unionization of supervisory personnel, jurisdictional strikes, election of Communist officers, wildcat strikes, and racketeering).[52]

Sectoral and Instrumental
Determinism

On one matter, Block agrees with the institutionalists. By identifying "state managers" as the key instrumental agents in the reform process, Block shares their exclusive focus on the autonomous roles and interests of bureaucrats, politicians, and reform intellectuals in initiating reform and expanding their power. Both therefore neglect or attach no importance to prominent business-men's support of the New Deal. Other literature tends toward the other ex-treme, arguing that business support from certain quarters, or for certain rea-sons, mattered more than it did. Sometimes this literature suffers from a fatal inability to elaborate and substantiate why correlation (i.e., between business groups' support for legislation and the legislation that actually results) might also be causation.[53] Others avoid this "instrumentalist" determinism but inac-curately identify the nature and logic of business support.

Thomas Ferguson avoids instrumentalist determinism by focusing on the dynamics of vigorous competition among electoral politicians over support from various business sectors, not just votes. Thus, he plausibly suggests that the movement of money into the hands of electoral politicians, research foun-dations, and the media is a major causal force connecting business support with electoral and policy outcomes. Also, by focusing analysis on variations in interests across business groups and over time, he is able to incorporate the role of partisan politicians and cross-class alliances in a fairly well-elaborated theory.[54]

In some ways, Ferguson's argument resembles the cross-class alliance ex-planation offered here. However, it differs radically in one fundamental way, misspecifying the nature of business support for the New Deal's social and labor legislation and therefore the behavior and calculations of the New Deal-ers. The decisive business groups in his analysis were free-trading "interna-tionalists," especially the dynamic and highly competitive capital-intensive ones among them. The New Deal, he says, gave them measures favoring open international trade at the expense of enabling the New Dealers to pursue so-cial and labor legislation. This legislation cost them very little, for being capital intensive, they were less "labor sensitive"—that is, relatively indifferent to extra labor and payroll costs associated with progressive legislation. Thus Fer-guson depicts the New Deal as a logroll. Labor got welfare and labor law. In ex-change, the internationalists got freer trade, which more than compensated them for the limited price they paid to labor.[55]

Ferguson fails entirely to capture the regulatory logic of corporate liberal support for the New Deal. Corporate progressives backed Roosevelt and his so-cial legislation not as a necessary evil in order to obtain a greater virtue. They valued it for its own sake. Hence, he attaches no importance to crisis-induced business interests in regulation of domestic product market competition through the imposition of floors on labor and social costs. In the case of pen-sions, the liberal segmentalists were far from indifferent to labor costs. They cared so much about labor costs that they helped craft and pass legislation that would reduce their own burdens while raising their competitors'. The experience rating they expected and ultimately got in unemployment insurance promised to raise their competitors' costs in part so that they would not have to reduce their own burdens.

Employers in many sectors could see advantages quite independent of any political payoff in the form of trade policy. Huge capital-intensive segmentalists were primarily motivated by problems in domestic, not international competition. GE officials worried about low-wage, low-quality, low-price domestic competition in the unsteady mass market for electrical goods like light bulbs. Competitors could count on badly strapped consumers buying cheaper, though lower quality, bulbs. Standard Oil of New Jersey was pestered by a multitude of overproducing "independents," especially in east Texas, with their substandard labor practices. Kodak may have had problems with competing camera and photographic chemical manufacturers offering little to nothing in the way of pensions, unemployment benefits, or employment security—though perhaps not lower pay in the case of camera makers. Goodyear had problems dealing with low-wage producers of miscellaneous but important rubber items. Its sole and heel division had to move to Vermont because in Akron it had to keep its wages in line with those of the tire builders.[56]

Thus, firms like these shared interests with those in more labor-intensive sectors, where small firms engaged almost exclusively in domestic competition. Garment manufacturers and coal mining are notable cases. Their mostly supportive response to the New Deal can easily be accounted for. Ferguson fails to mention these industries entirely; nor does he mention the building industry, which was of course labor-intensive, practically exclusively engaged in local competition, and an enormous beneficiary of New Deal public works and other support. Not surprisingly, the Associated General Contractors supported much of the New Deal, especially public works and financial regulation.[57] Ferguson also overlooks the reason why big retailers were so enthusiastic about the New Deal—while having virtually nothing to do with international trade. They desired loyal, efficient, and therefore high-cost employees and worried about covering relatively fixed labor costs with stable demand. They faced intense domestic competition from low-wage smaller retailers, prepared to lay off and hire as demand permitted, and probably also less concerned about high and invariant real estate costs.

It is therefore probably true that, within sectors, the more capital-intensive firms were the most supportive of Social Security reforms. Major textile executives in the northeast were friends of various reforms, while those in the South were far less friendly. The Northerners operated, as Ferguson argues, on the basis of more advanced "best practice" technology and management in a highly labor-intensive industry, trying to compete with more ruthless low-wage, child-labor exploiting Southern competitors. Ferguson acknowledges that their support for the New Deal is a problem for his theory. He speculates, therefore, that were it not for their personal contacts with progressive businessmen from other sectors that fit his argument better (through the Taylor Society, whose managing director, H. S. Person, favored obligatory unemployment insurance), their support was "otherwise inexplicable." The argument presented here makes their support as easy to explain as Jersey Standard's, GE's, and Kodak's.[58] They simply wanted to "uplift" the competition.

Historian Colin Gordon's analysis fits the reality of business interests far better than Ferguson's. Gordon argues that reform was "driven more by the competitive anxieties of a wide range of business interests" and not the result of "the ideological and political power of a few corporate interests or the ascendance of certain types or groups of industries." Drawing on voluminous archival research, he concludes that "[f]ederal social security and labor law grew directly from the search for competitive order," a formulation broadly consistent with the economic logic of the cross-class alliance argument elaborated here. In other words, Social Security legislation "was largely an effort (made more urgent by the Depression) to 'even out' the competitive disparities resulting from two decades of private and state-level experimentation with work benefits."[59]

The problem with Gordon's analysis lies in his numerous instrumentalist claims that New Deal social policy was "business driven" and "a creature of business demands." Businessmen, Gordon says repeatedly in his analysis of the SSA, "demanded" that government "compel marginal competitors to respect standard labor costs and trade practices" and "pressed," "lobbied," or "pushed" for comprehensive federal law to "regulate competition by imposing higher labor costs on their rivals." In short, the Social Security Act "was largely the work of a motley coalition of business interests grasping for solutions to the ravages of economic competition and federated economic regulation."[60]

Gordon offers abundant archival evidence showing that a notable number of businessmen clearly signaled their and others' amenability to an arranged alliance and that some among them even participated in deliberations about legislation that might generate one. However, he presents none at all showing urgent lobbying, much less direct pressure—that is, that rewards were offered for legislation, or promises of trouble if nothing happened. Thus, he fails to show why pressure for reform, to the limited extent it might actually have arisen, overwhelmed business pressure against it, which was probably much more organized and intense.

Strangely, Gordon asserts without documentation that business opposition to the SSA "spread quickly after 1935 and by the late 1930s had found a voice among some of the earliest and strongest proponents." Such a turn of events would conform better to Block's theory than Gordon's own. This does not square with the facts about the NAM position, the *Fortune* survey, and the U.S. Chamber of Commerce referendum discussed earlier. As Marion Folsom recalled in 1965, it only "took several years to get the business community sold" on Social Security. This rapid shift helps explain why in 1939 Wilbur Cohen, Witte's protégé, could claim so confidently that "Republicans, as well as Democrats, accept the principle of social security and realize that there is no possibility of turning backward."[61] That the reforms should have proven so robust and durable jars with Gordon's instrumentalist claims about its origins—if business truly *had* turned against the reform.

Conclusion: "The History of All Social Policy Acts"?

The American story of post facto cross-class alliances for social reform might actually begin as early as the late nineteenth century. Among the most powerful defenders of local outdoor poor relief (cash benefits) at the time were small businesses, merchants, and manufacturers, according to historian Michael Katz. That is not to say that these same businessmen were prime movers in introducing cash benefits. The history of the progressive-era social legislation, as understood by Robert Wagner and Franklin Roosevelt, and then the New Deal, would lead us to think not.

Progressive reformer and cross-class alliance maker John Commons argued that employers do not normally open their minds in advance of legislated social reform "until they are faced by an alternative which seems worse to them than the one they 'willingly' accept."[62] But as a reform practitioner, Commons knew that what mattered more in the long run than scaring businessmen into welcoming moderate reforms was their conversion after the fact. In Wisconsin he witnessed first hand how, as in other states, many employers initially opposed workmen's accident insurance laws. "Not until the compensation laws came into effect did the employers, as a whole, become friendly to the safety laws," he wrote shortly after their passage. Commons's formula for ensuring this outcome was to incorporate business as well as labor influence into the administration and adaptation of regulatory social legislation. Isaac Rubinow, a contemporary and equally passionate reform intellectual and contemporary, shared Commons's faith, based also on experience early in the century with workmen's compensation. "The employing class," he said, would at first be "frankly antagonistic" to Depression-era reform. Later they would come around, as they did in the past, when they "learned to accept its value and sometimes—sometimes—[were] honest enough to admit it." Others were not so honest and "would rather shame-facedly deny both their opposition and their arguments" after the fact.[63]

This wisdom was passed along to New Deal reformers. They knew that the success and durability of reform depended on employers "getting sold," as Marion Folsom put it years later. Franklin Roosevelt clearly understood the dynamics of reform politics after legislation was passed and consciously designed his own strategies in that light. As New York governor, he once vetoed a bill passed by the state legislature allowing private insurance companies to enter the unemployment insurance business, hoping instead on passing compulsory legislation, which is what his successor Herbert Lehman did. "It is fairly obvious that if private corporations are permitted now to begin to write unemployment insurance, this will make it impossible to have the full and free consideration of other methods," he said, adding that "they will hereafter claim a kind of vested right in this business."[64]

These observations suggest that, despite flaws in existing institutionalist analysis of the New Deal, an institutionalism open to the notion that capitalists are a force to be reckoned with in capitalist society can yet offer some help in explaining the development of welfare states. It can do so with attention to the role of "policy feedback" anticipated and instrumentally manipulated by political entrepreneurs like Roosevelt or Wagner. In other words, reformist politicians, responding to their own agendas and popular pressures, anticipate the supportive, stabilizing effect that the institutionalization of post facto cross-class coalitions can have.[65] Even an institutionalist like Skocpol applies this kind of logic to European welfare states, which she posits were political elites' efforts at "anticipatory political incorporation of the industrial working class." The evidence strongly suggests her speculative insight badly needs extension to capitalists—both in the United States and, as the following chapters suggest, in broader comparative analysis.[66]

11

FROM SOLIDARISM TO
SOCIAL DEMOCRACY

Industrialist and employer leader Sigfrid Edström was visiting the Riksdag one day in spring 1934 to discuss with Per Albin Hansson, the Social Democratic prime minister, a matter affecting ASEA, Sweden's leading electrical engineering company. In his diary, he recalled the following:

> As I was leaving the room he called me back, asked me to sit down and continue our conversation. To my surprise the Prime Minister expressed the view that industry ought to have better representation in the Riksdag. In jest I answered: "Can you give me some votes so we get a Riksdagsman in?" P.A. smiled. We won't get far that way, he said, but one can imagine other solutions. I promised him I would think about the matter.[1]

Hansson's prodding, Edström recounted, soon came up for discussion in the "Directors' Club," through which the five leading engineering firms coordinated strategy for pursuing mutual economic and political interests. Discussion led ultimately to the founding in 1938 of the Institute for Industrial Research (*Industrins Utredningsinstitut*, or IUI), to sponsor research and shape public opinion about industry's interests. It was financed in part by SAF, the employers' confederation. That organization, together with the Directors' Club, the Swedish Engineering Employers' Association, and ASEA—Sweden's "General Electric"—was also chaired by Edström.[2]

Relations between Sweden's pre-eminent industrialist and its Social Democratic prime minister possibly approached the level of friendship and respect achieved between fellow employer statesman Gerard Swope of GE and President Franklin Roosevelt. In the following years until his death in 1946, Hansson enjoyed great confidence from other leading Swedish industrialists, too.

Some of them played poker with him regularly and hosted him at business gatherings. Employer lore has it that Hansson regretted the fracturing of his own party's opponents into three parties in parliamentary and electoral politics. He thought bourgeois unity would make for more sound reform carried out at a less hasty pace. Thus, he was disappointed when organized capital declined his offer to promote the current chiefs of the Swedish Trade Federation (*Sveriges Industriförbund*) and the Export Association (*Exportföreningen*) into regional governorships. His idea was that the organizations could then frictionlessly merge with SAF, the employers' confederation, under the unifying leadership of chairman Edström and its current executive director, Gustaf Söderlund. In the telling of these things, future SAF director Bertil Kugelberg understood Hansson's motive to have been "to achieve a strengthening and consolidation of industry's interests and influence." Recalling in his memoirs Hansson's "disarming charm" and "extraordinary ability to inspire confidence," Kugelberg wrote that "we had no reason to feel particularly worried about policies he advocated."[3]

As Edström put it, Hansson "tried with all his might to accommodate the balancing of forces in 'the People's Home.'" The People's Home (*Folkhemmet*) was Hansson's slogan for the kind of protective and nurturing society Swedish social democracy should create. By balancing of forces, Hansson probably wanted to gain leverage against excessive pressure from organized labor in the Social Democratic Party, and through it, on the government.[4] The prime minister's surprising observation to Edström in his Riksdag office was no doubt made in that spirit. It was uttered at the very time the Riksdag was intensively deliberating a highly controversial unemployment insurance bill.

The unions had long been pushing for a tax-financed system for insuring against the risks of unemployment. The employers' confederation opposed it, and the bourgeois parties were divided. As it turned out, the unemployment insurance legislation of 1934 was the only major innovation in social insurance passed by the Social Democrats in the 1930s. "Major" may be an exaggeration, however. Considering Hansson's overall guidance in the legislative process, and the need for parliamentary compromise recognized by Minister of Social Affairs Gustav Möller, it is not surprising that "outbreaks of rapture could hardly be discerned from the labor movement" upon passage of the law, according to historian Per Gunnar Edebalk. "A pathetic little rat" had been delivered, one union journal said—when an elephant had long been hoped for.[5]

American reformers like Abraham Epstein, who had a similar reaction to the Social Security Act's unemployment provisions, would not have seen in the Swedish version anything so substantial as a rat. By the end of 1935, it covered no more than about 77,000 workers in six separate funds for low-pay and mostly tiny sectors (clothing, saddles and luggage, stone quarries, retail, shoe and leather, and woodworking). Only their unions chose immediately to take advantage of the state subsidy and set up "authorized" funds or accept subsidies and therefore government regulation of their existing funds. Major growth in government-subsidized voluntary insurance did not occur until 1942 when the metalworkers' union accepted a newly enlarged subsidy for their fund. The unions in the building trades did not accept government subsidization and regulation until 1947. The paper workers' union finally formed an authorized fund in 1954 during a second growth spurt that finally brought most blue-collar workers into the system. Still, the system left out about half of the Swedish labor force, for white-collar unions had not yet acted. Municipal workers attached their fund in 1964, and most white-collar coverage started in 1969 and 1970. Coverage finally spread to the 80 percent range in the 1980s.[6]

Despite their unequivocal opposition beforehand, employers issued no cries of pain and woe after the law took effect. The confederation's 1935 yearly report calmly and dispassionately noted the law's passage without negative commentary. It even praised subsidiary measures to beef up the employment bureaus so they could play their role, described later, in the new system. Hansson's balance had been achieved, it appeared, by passing a very limited reform.

It was not until the 1940s and 1950s that Swedish social democracy took off with its truly major innovations and expansions in social insurance and labor market policy. The first of these, the People's Pension reform of 1946, will be analyzed in this chapter. Health, pension, and labor market reforms of the 1950s will be the subject of the following chapter. In contrast to unemployment insurance, these later reforms were much bigger. They also, not coincidentally, had employer support that was more solid, especially after passage. In three of four cases, support was certain even before passage.

The Logic and Timing of Employer Support

"Well designed and wisely considered social insurance is a great blessing for a people," declared Hjalmar von Sydow, Sweden's foremost employer leader and prominent Conservative politician, in the opening line of his address to a gathering of Swedish capitalists in December 1915. Roughly two years had passed since passage of a landmark pension law, which industrialists had welcomed. They also liked the work accident insurance law passed in 1916, the year after von Sydow's speech praising the draft bill. Recalling great concern that emigration to America stirred among industrial employers, and extended periods of labor scarcity, the executive director of the Employers' Confederation had raised the specter of even greater foreign demand for Swedish workers in the coming years. Only a month before, emigration of metalworkers, and poaching by foreign employers, had rankled engineering employers. Further loss might, however, be averted, von Sydow told them, by passing "fully modern and rational legislation."[7]

Four years earlier, with the labor market in better balance, von Sydow had been a bit less enthusiastic about social insurance. He ventured, however, that one ought not expect any "principled resistance" so long as it did not step out ahead of international trends. One had to worry after all about the damage its costs could do to Swedish export interests.[8] But now, when the prospect of labor scarcity loomed in 1915, work accident and sickness insurance looked like a valuable investment. Germany, after all, had demonstrated to Sweden "that well designed social insurance is the best means to inhibit emigration." It was also a way that other countries with labor-scarce war economies were getting hold of Swedes. The following year, the French government courted them with free health insurance and travel expenses.[9]

One thing speaking for legislation, von Sydow pointed out, was that many workers already enjoyed social benefits from their employers. Why this was a reason for government action he left unsaid, as if not requiring explanation. We know he was not thinking about government imposition of social costs on chiseling low-standard competitors, which is partly what had made social legislation logical to New Dealers minding American businessmen's interests in the 1930s. That made sense in the context of slumping prices and labor surplus, not labor scarcity. The scarcity problem meant that von Sydow was probably invoking a radically different argument. National legislation might level the playing field in the competition over scarce labor, both within Sweden and beyond. Recall that, for the same reason, major associations in SAF were currently trying to suppress welfare capitalism, if not eliminate company benefits altogether. We can fairly speculate therefore that the generosity of the 1916 law—in SAF's own words, "more advantageous to workers than corresponding laws in any other land"—was one reason for praising it. The high compensation levels could now be invoked to check private supplements that companies or industries might be tempted to offer, both to please their unions and attract workers.[10]

The scarcity motive offers a clue about the radically different timing for Swedish employer interests in welfare state expansion, surfacing as they did in the 1940s and 1950s. Labor scarcity remained central, especially the severe shortages during and after World War II. In the meantime, emigration had ceased to be much of a problem. (A legislative solution came in the 1920s not out of the Riksdag but as a gift from the U.S. Congress. Immigration restrictions responded in part to major American employers' dawning recognition of the need to limit waves of immigration and thereby check the disruptive wage and price chiseling it occasioned.) Sweden's unusually low birthrate was another factor in the progressive equation. Thus, the Social Democrats' family welfare legislation of the 1930s, famously associated with Alva and Gunnar Myrdal, united Right and Left. Both sides were concerned about Sweden's extraordinarily low birthrate. Its main purpose was to spread the cost of childbearing and child rearing. It left a greater mark on Swedish society, culture, and politics than the unemployment insurance law.[11]

Even more important in the end for the timing and shaping of welfare state development in Sweden was the labor scarcity that arose from employers' enormous success with solidaristic governance of the labor market. Success coincided with a long period of Social Democratic rule—in part because of that rule. Only in the context of that labor scarcity can the overall shape and timing of the Social Democrats' reforms be understood.

Solidarism, Scarcity, and Macro-economic Forces

The macro-economic shock of the Great Depression destabilized both segmentalism and negotiated cartelism, the dominant modes of labor market governance in America. In both systems, employers acted in a sense as price makers instead of price takers, setting wages above market clearing levels. In one case, they did it individually and unilaterally, and in the other, collectively and in negotiation with unions. Both systems left employers vulnerable to wage and price chiselers. These were product market competitors ready and able to take advantage of unexpected labor surplus by cutting wages for their current workers, replacing them with ones willing to accept less, or simply entering competition for the first time using workers ready to work for cheap. Democratic New Dealers stepped in, offering social and labor legislation that imposed extra costs on these chiselers and even reduced costs for high-standard employers.

By contrast, Social Democratic welfare state builders did not step in during the Depression with much in the way of social insurance and labor market legislation. The exception was unemployment insurance legislation far inferior to the New Deal's in eligibility and coverage. Social insurance, a form of labor legislation and therefore market regulation, as New Dealer Edwin Witte conceived it, coincided with a radically different macro-economic disturbance—the high demand and growth of the postwar world economy. Such macro-economic conditions did not put segmentalism and cartelism under duress in the United States. They did, however, subject Sweden's solidaristic system of labor market governance to serious strains.

In Swedish solidarism, employers were also price makers, just as in American segmentalism and cartelism. But solidarism meant holding wages below market clearing levels, not above. In the negotiated system, organized labor submitted to the pressure and economic logic of restraint, and took credit for compressing wages across firms and sectors. The labor scarcity that resulted from setting wages below market clearing levels for large numbers of employers created strong incentives to economize on the use of currently employed labor when demand picked up—instead of expanding production using existing technology and additional labor acquired easily in a loose external labor market. Solidarism probably accelerated the innovative introduction of labor-saving technologies and would therefore help explain Sweden's rapid growth and success in the international marketplace.[12] Of course, labor scarcity associated with wage restraint and compression also generated a powerful temptation to raise wages and benefits against the dictates of solidarism. Cheating was so rampant at times that extraordinary measures to stop it had to be taken. Social legislation was among such measures.

Systemic Crisis: Postwar Wage
and Benefit Drift

Organized employers already began experiencing frustration with the consequences of solidaristic disequilibrium as early as the mid 1930s when economic
recovery, driven in considerable measure by German rearmament, brought
extra-contractual wage increases ("wage drift") above negotiated levels. Wartime scarcities brought more of the same. Concern gradually turned into alarm
as wage drift associated with piece work and "disloyal recruitment" or "disloyal advertising" *(illojal värvning)* in competition over labor became rampant
in the spring of 1945.[13]

The years 1945 and 1946 were extreme but offer good examples of what
havoc solidaristic wage restraint in the face of strong growth would continue
to create in following years.[14] Low-pay sectors were particularly disturbed.
Some textile employers, frustrated with wage freezes and labor scarcities, and
enjoying good profits on average, wished to grant higher wages for fear of losing workers to higher-pay sectors like engineering. They were having to shut
down production for lack of labor. Engineering employers also stole workers
from each other. Hence, their national association tightened its rules against
poaching, and some regional units bound their members not to hire workers
until a full month had passed since their departure from a fellow engineering
employer.[15]

Growth in the face of continuing centralized wage restraint brought such
unquenchable demand for labor that by June 1946 only about 104 men sought
jobs through the government employment exchanges for every 100 nonagricultural blue-collar jobs the employers registered as vacant. The situation was
worse for employers seeking female workers: only 75 turned to the exchanges
for every 100 jobs registered. Engineering wished to increase its female labor
force by no less than 24 percent, no doubt at the expense of the still-profitable
textile industry. Textile employers could do little but sharpen their own restrictions against advertising for labor and poaching from each other, just as engineering employers did the year before.[16]

Unemployment among union members reached an all-time low of about
2 percent in 1946. SAF calculated that Swedish industry could easily have absorbed another 100,000 to 120,000 workers at current wage levels; labor mobility and turnover was "abnormally high." About 5 percent of all workers
changed jobs on a monthly basis. The labor confederation made common cause
with SAF in colorful but probably ineffective poster campaign exhorting workers not to be "job hoppers" *(hoppjerker).*[17] SAF now began actively pressing
for importation of labor, in particular from Italy. The confederation leadership
also contemplated setting up a Danish style "collegiality council" to monitor
"overpayment" in the overheated labor market. The Social Democratic government pitched in by admitting some foreign workers, and prolonging wartime
building controls, withholding building permits to check upward wage pressures emanating from construction. A special emergency meeting of important

industrialists, called by SAF chairman Edström, recommended the building controls. Collectively they resolved not to "let wage competition run loose."[18]

Internal discussions about wage drift, sometimes called "black market wages" *(svartabörslöner)*, naturally increased in volume. Small firms and unorganized employers were hardly better than common thieves in their "disloyal recruitment" of manpower.[19] Big firms got their share of the blame for providing "all manner of generous perquisites, vacation cottages, and benefit funds for workers." Two breweries were actually expelled from SAF for granting extra high pay raises without permission from SAF or the brewers' association. Their defense was that other companies had been enticing workers away with lavish company benefits. SAF began issuing circulars to members harshly criticizing the "unhealthy" but growing phenomenon of year-end bonuses. Such things were being used, SAF said, to "gain advantage in competition over labor." In its circulars, it reminded employers that collective agreements carry with them not just a commitment to workers but also, with respect to other employers, "an obligation not to exceed contractual wages."[20]

Upward drift in company benefits continued apace in the following years, when SAF began collecting statistics. A survey conducted in 1948 concluded that fringe benefits (for both manual and white-collar workers) constituted on average about 3.8 percent, and at most up to 5.7 percent of total labor costs. A lower figure would have applied to manual workers alone. A second survey in 1952 found that, now, fully 8 percent of manual labor-related costs (and about 12 percent for both manual and white-collar employees) consisted of housing, health, pension, and other nonwage labor costs. For workers across mining, forest products, and chemicals, the averages were roughly 18 percent or more, where housing benefits accounted for something between 3 and 9 percent of blue-collar wages. The figures would have been higher if they had included paid vacation time. As SAF's social policy expert Sven Hydén observed in 1953, "overfull employment" at the end of the 1940s brought forth an unusually rapid growth in social benefits, "which were used as a means of struggle over manpower."[21]

The Failure to Establish
Unilateral Control

The upward drift in labor costs not accounted for by hourly wages or incentive pay earnings triggered efforts by the SAF leadership to acquire new unilateral powers to regulate the labor market. These efforts began in 1948, when as SAF historian Hans De Geer notes, the acute shortage of labor and "keen wage competition between employers" persisted. One major precipitant was the upward drift of company pensions. Another was an action taken by the Textile Industry Association (TIF), which disobeyed instructions from SAF's contract council when it offered the textile union extra pay increases for shift-workers. SAF's executive director Fritiof Söderbäck expressed dismay that the shift premium had not even been a worker demand, "but rather had come about entirely on the initiative of the textile industry association." The textile association, in its defense, pointed to the shortage of labor and the difficulty of getting women to do late shifts. Looking closely at their statutes, SAF leaders discovered that they lacked authority to sanction TIF with fines. Their only recourse was the far too draconian one of expulsion.[22]

SAF's director Kugelberg was sure of one thing: there was hardly any prospect of getting the unions to a central bargaining table to help employers regulate their affairs in this matter equitably to avoid more embarrassing crises like the one with TIF. An alternative worth pursuing was to impose greater solidarism unilaterally. Consequently, the next year saw energetic and heatedly challenged efforts to revise SAF's statutes. Engineering employers, represented by VF, which exercised more centralized authority over its member firms than SAF did over its member associations, strongly supported Kugelberg. He wanted a majority of the SAF board to be similarly empowered to issue more binding directives and exact fines for violations from disloyal firms and sectoral associations.[23]

Resistance was strong. Employers in the forest products industries, most of all, seemed to fear giving more authority to SAF. It might empower VF, the largest association, to set unfavorable terms of labor market competition-namely, the same kinds of restrictions it currently subjected engineering employers to. For example, VF was the only SAF affiliate with a long-standing prohibition against advertising for labor, a solidaristic measure accompanied by an informal requirement that all member firms keep about 15 percent of their workforce in apprenticeship and other training. VF claimed it was unable to maintain the prohibition alone when firms in other sectors were free to direct advertisements at metalworkers. On this particular point, SAF board member Per Hägglund dug in his heels, fearing that should the job situation improve in northern Sweden after years of loss of labor to the south, paper employers like him would need advertisements to shift the tide.[24]

Gunnar Larsson, executive director of the Paper Industry Association, also opposed the augmentation of SAF's unilateral power. In his industry, like other traditionally rural-based sectors producing lumber, pulp, and iron, "social benefits" remained standard practice for tying workers to the firm and providing services, including housing and health, that were more accessible for sale in urban settings. Although the associations for these sectors tried their best to limit the practices, they preferred to do so at their own pace and discretion. When Kugelberg of SAF bemoaned the fact that existing statutes did not allow the confederation to intervene against "inappropriate" use of benefits, Larsson warned him that his Norwegian counterparts stood outside the Norwegian Employers' Confederation for the very reason that it regulated such things. "Caution should be exercised," he declared ominously, about rules changes that could "cause an entire association to leave."[25]

Trying to calm the opposition, Kugelberg reassured rural industries that regulating company housing subsidies and other such benefits was not on the agenda. Instead, the targets were to be work-week reductions, disloyal advertising for labor, year-end bonuses, and other "inappropriate forms of remuneration." If "certain big companies" bolted, he was ready to deal with the consequences. In the end he never had to, for the new rules, established in December 1948, allowed only a qualified majority of SAF's board the power to issue directives and prohibitions, backed by heavy "damages" *(skadestånd)* levied for violations. The rural-based industries, in other words, maintained veto power. Indeed, except on working-time issues, few new directives were ever issued. Even advertising across sectoral lines remained unregulated.[26]

By 1948, then, it was clear that solidaristic regulation of social benefits would have to be achieved, as in the past, on a negotiated, cross-class basis. Recent but only transitory success had been achieved using negotiated wage increases for buyouts of company housing benefits in 1943 and 1945. The changes, negotiated in various sectors with LO unions, altered the remuneration structure in favor of younger, childless, and therefore more mobile workers. They gravitated to urban lives and occupations just as employers in the forest products industries were facing, in their words, a "catastrophic labor shortage." As Fritiof Söderbäck, SAF's executive director, put it, liquidation meant "a correction of the injustice" suffered by younger workers relative to those living in company houses. The Metalworkers' Union had strongly opposed retiring housing benefits for steelworkers but relented in 1943 under employer association pressure. On the whole, this strategy lacked promise. Workers tended to prize their company's social benefits and thus their employers were strongly tempted to reinstate them. SAF and its associations lacked effective mechanisms preventing this micro-level collusion.[27]

In short, from 1945 onward, SAF experienced severe difficulties in controlling membership use of company benefits to cope with acute labor shortages. Wage restraint and compression in the face of strong demand for Swedish goods caused those shortages, and companies responded by cheating on restraint with social benefits. During this time, the Social Democrats began moving confidently and aggressively to promote compulsory social insurance with generous benefits and broad eligibility. SAF did not resist but rather openly signaled support. Legislation, the confederation recognized, would help relieve pressure building from below on member companies, whose managers were only too happy to deliver the noncontractual social benefits workers demanded.

Analysis of pension politics at the end of this chapter shows how the institutions of labor market regulation in general, and labor scarcity in particular, affected the timing and shaping of Swedish pension reform in the 1930s and 1940s. It was a highly consensual process of cross-class alliance making. Before turning to pensions, however, the chapter will step back in time to examine the politics of unemployment insurance in the 1930s. Although employers opposed reform, they accepted it with great equanimity. Why they did so can be understood only in the context of, among other things, the evolving cross-class alliance behind intersectoral control, especially over the building trades.

Unemployment Insurance

In 1934, especially during the nervous months before the Social Democratic government's welcome intervention in the building trades conflict, employers must have wondered what the self-professed socialists might try to spring on them in the form of social and labor legislation. A particular cause for worry was unemployment insurance, a major election promise. The unions had called eagerly for legislation for many years, and expected now to harvest the fruits of power. When a bill finally appeared, employers tried to suffocate it with a seamless blanket of criticism. Unlike in the United States, there were, it appears, no prominent individual capitalists or sectoral organizations—even retailers—promoting unemployment insurance. No firms like GE and Kodak, it seems, had experimented with their own schemes. In 1929 SAF coldly vetoed an exotic collectively bargained version of unemployment insurance for stone quarry workers. It was not unlike the kind recently appearing, with John Commons's help, in the American garment industry. Even the tiniest of experiments with negotiated cartelism was not to be tolerated.[28]

On unemployment insurance, the labor movement truly did seem to boldly defy fundamental capitalist interests as only Robert Wagner, joined by a large majority of the U.S. Congress, appears to have done in the United States with his labor law. But that was not, in reality, the conscious intent of either. Certainly Hansson wanted the party to tread as lightly as possible upon, if not gingerly around, employers' toes. As indicated by his conversation with Edström, he probably welcomed strong countervailing arguments against more impatient reformers in the unions, party, and government—probably Minister of Social Affairs Gustav Möller, for one.

With the help of the larger of two liberal parties (*Frisinnade Folkpartiet*), which was jittery about the loss of electoral support to the Left, the Social Democrats finally passed legislation in May 1934—a couple of months after the happy end to the building trades conflict. To take effect on January 1, 1935, the law provided for government subsidization of private insurance arrangements set up by individual unions—the so-called Ghent, or voluntary, system. In exchange for accepting government funds, the union-administered funds would have to submit to heavy regulation and oversight of their operation. The legislation was far from universalistic, of course. Because the system was a voluntary one, eligibility and benefits would vary widely across occupations. The law also even left the possibility open for the funds to reduce benefits on a needs basis.[29]

SAF leaders advanced three major arguments against the legislation. All of them proved illusory after passage. One widely held view was that unemployment insurance would bolster union militancy and therefore prop up wages at levels that would harm Swedish industry's competitiveness in international markets. VF's executive director, Georg Styrman, for example, feared that money from the union-controlled funds would somehow find its way into the hands of striking workers. In his statement officially representing SAF's position, SAF director Söderlund singled out only one group for illustration of the dangers: the building and construction trades, whose unjustifiably high wages might be supported by unemployment insurance.[30] Employers leveled a second criticism with equal, if not greater, urgency. They fretted about the effects of the Ghent system on labor mobility. Disregarding unions' strong incentives to husband members' contributions—the American corporate liberal's argument for worker contributions—employer critics reasoned that unions would be disinclined to deny benefits, as the law required, to members who spurned "reasonable" or "suitable" job opportunities in lines of work outside the union's ambit. Therefore, there was a risk that union fund managers would be inclined to regard only work that falls within the member's own occupation as suitable.

In the confederation's official statement, Söderlund noted how conditions peculiar to Sweden made the country's economic success highly dependent on the mobility of labor. It would be dangerous, therefore, if workers were to be insured "against the risk of being forced to take work in a new occupation with potentially lower pay." This would "reduce the mobility of manpower between different sectors and localities."[31] His statement resonated with arguments emanating from all of SAF's major affiliates. Styrman argued that the law would lock workers into jobs for which they were not well suited. The forest product industries, where labor needed to follow the product as it crossed sectoral lines from forestry and logging to sawmills or pulp and paper mills, prepared a joint position statement against the reform. Karl Wistrand from steel summed up, warning that the legislation would "counteract . . . the movement from one occupation to another, from one workplace to another, which is essential for a viable economy."[32]

A third argument echoed the view of former SAF leader von Sydow in the 1920s and now expressed by right-wing politicians concerned about union growth and power. They feared that the Ghent system would help drive workers into unions. VF's Styrman expected that union-dominated boards could not avoid the temptation to pressure a person wishing to join the unemployment insurance fund to join the union itself. Language in the law guaranteeing openness to nonunionists, he thought, was worth little.[33] The most notable thing about this objection was that only Styrman raised it. Curiously, no one else in SAF's recorded debate seems to have repeated the objection.

The Ghent System: Stronger Unions?

Minister of Social Affairs Gustav Möller, who was not as solicitous of employer interests as the prime minister, touted the Ghent system as a way to get workers into the unions. Right-wing politicians feared it for the same reason. That Styrman was alone among employer leaders in his criticism of this aspect of the proposed legislation, therefore, seems puzzling. But there is a ready explanation: Styrman was out of touch with the increasingly friendly climate developing at the highest levels between LO and SAF. SAF's view of LO, published for all to read in its 1930 yearly report, was that its leadership was increasingly dominated by "socially-minded, calm and deliberate attitudes."[34] VF and SAF chairman Edström, who had recruited Gustav Söderlund specifically for his ability to work smoothly with union leaders, found Styrman lacking in the same necessary graces and on more than one occasion discussed the idea of firing him from his VF post. In 1945 he even enlisted Söderlund's and the Directors' Club's help, but Styrman held on until his retirement in 1949. Why Edström failed is not certain, but probably Styrman had a strong enough constituency among VF's smaller members to make an ouster far too divisive.[35]

Tellingly, the secretary of the Directors' Club, recruited by Edström, had by 1935 become an advocate of the extreme corporatist principle of obligatory membership in encompassing private organizations regulated by the state. "I have come to the conclusion," Sven Erik Österberg wrote, "that such a solution to the issue, which in all probability is going to be forced by circumstances anyway, would be the most useful for society."[36] Edström and the other directors were possibly not so extreme in their views, but they probably sympathized. For them, unemployment insurance linked to membership in a union confederation trying to clean up its own house—in ways welcomed by SAF—was certainly a less heavy-handed government move in the same direction. This is of course why Communists and Syndicalists, common enemies of LO and SAF, were the most vehement critics of the Ghent system.[37]

Hence, we can conclude with some confidence that the SAF leadership as a whole probably looked with some favor, or at least benign ambivalence, at the prospect of the unemployment insurance system adding to the Social Democratic unions' membership. The real problems in the Ghent system lay elsewhere. In any event, while the proposed legislation gave with one hand, it took with another. Currently, the unions' independent funds often differentiated benefits according to length of membership. They did this, Edebalk says, for "membership consolidating purposes." By abolishing this practice, the law possibly discouraged a number of unions from seeking the subsidies.[38]

Thus, the exceedingly slow growth of the system in the three decades after 1935 proved all of employers' residual fears unfounded. By the 1950s, when the system was still underdeveloped, it was fully clear that any recruitment effects of the Ghent system would go with, rather than against, the grain of employer solidarism, aided as it was by strong centralized unions. In the 1940s, many companies began collecting membership dues for unions. Although the SAF board voted in 1953 to reaffirm the confederation's official disapproval, there was no support for an effective ban. Lennart Bratt, the prominent executive director of the General Employers' Group (chemicals, plastics, nonmetal manufacturing), argued that combating unions was "outdated" and that refusing to collect dues for them was "pure pettiness." In his view, "employers gain extraordinary benefits from strong organizations on the opposing side." It is well known, he said, "that the greatest difficulties in negotiations arise in cases where there is a large number of workers who are not organized."[39] Only labor scarcity can explain that phenomenon. Under conditions of scarcity, collective bargaining for administrative pricing of labor was superior to market processes.

Employers' practice of collecting union dues spread steadily throughout industry in the 1950s and 1960s, and sentiment grew for dropping SAF's negative policy. It had become dead-letter anyway. Because of repeated bouts of labor scarcity, in many cases employers happily collected dues for the unions in exchange for their efforts to soften rank-and-file resistance to the hiring of foreign workers. For this, personnel managers would even direct the immigrants to open-armed union officials. In 1966, VF formally agreed "to advise employers to recommend that foreign workers join Metall."[40] Four years later, by which time around 50 percent of all union members' dues were being collected for the unions by employers, VF agreed with Metall to require member firms to encourage unionization of their foreign workers. The practice spread across other sectors, helping LO gather up to 120 million extra crowns per year in hard-to-collect dues. In the end, large numbers of employers collected both union dues and unemployment insurance contributions and handed them over to the unions to divide between their organizations and the unemployment funds.[41] Whatever minor worries employers had in the beginning about the recruitment effects of the Ghent system—and there were not many effects—in the end, they proved entirely benign.

Unemployment Insurance: More Wage Militancy?

It is possible that recruitment effects worked both ways. In other words, Sweden's very high union membership levels in the 1950s and 1960s might help account for high levels of participation in the unemployment system. It became common practice for unions to make joining the unemployment system a condition of union membership. In the insurance funds' view at least, this brought participation levels among some groups to levels that could not otherwise be explained, considering Swedish workers' low rate of joblessness.[42] Low unemployment, in turn, was in large part attributable to solidaristic wage restraint in the face of macro-economic pressures pushing in the opposite direction. In the debate about unemployment insurance, SAF had mistakenly feared that this restraint would be undermined by the legislation. That proved also to be a misapprehension.

Thus, employer acceptance of unemployment insurance can in part be explained by the absence of its predicted effects on wage militancy and the way strong unions served the solidaristic project. LO performed its most valuable such service ever during the very interval between SAF's criticisms of the bill in 1933 and its passage in 1934: its extraordinary intervention against the militant building workers. Also, in the month when the insurance law went into effect, SAF's Söderlund noted with great pleasure LO's intention (carried out in 1941) to eliminate membership contract votes. These referenda had long stood in the way of wage moderation, especially in the building trades, and often dragged LO unions into costly collisions with SAF lockouts.[43]

One thing SAF had criticized in the government's original proposal was a rule ensuring unemployment support for workers idled because of conflicts in other firms or sectors. But the final language in the legislation imposed a more conservative eligibility rule. Idled workers would be denied benefits even if they were not direct participants in a strike or the object of a lockout—if their wages and working conditions could be affected by the outcome of the dispute. This meant a limited strike or lockout would disqualify from benefits all workers in the same large national contract unit and make them entirely dependent on their union for any support.[44] In effect, the amendment increased the leverage of lockouts against strikes. It also strengthened workers' incentive to join unions for lockout insurance.

Calming SAF's deepest fears about the direct effect of the law on union militancy was its intent to discriminate against high-wage sectors with seasonal employment patterns—in other words, their nemesis, the building sector. Edebalk argues, interestingly, that it was really the Liberal Party that tipped the scale in favor of the Ghent system, while the unions were divided. In addition to its cost and administrative advantages, the Liberals liked the Ghent system for the ease with which it incorporated discriminatory features against seasonal industries in its design.[45]

Discriminatory features helped dissuade unions in high-pay sheltered sectors like the building trades and printing from taking advantage of the subsidies. Among the disadvantages were lower rates of subsidization to high-pay sectors, which reduced the payoff for giving up full discretion over how existing funds were used. The law also imposed longer waiting periods for workers in seasonal trades and possible suspension of benefits during the winter off-seasons. It restricted eligibility to workers who had contributed to the fund for at least 52 weeks of the 24 months before unemployment, a condition seasonal workers would find hard to meet. State-subsidized funds could not be spent to support labor boycotts of firms, which made the system unattractive to the building trades unions, as well as the high-pay, sheltered printers' union. They were reluctant to abandon their closed-shop and managerial control tactics so hated by SAF and officially disapproved of by LO. In general, legal restrictions on the use of unemployment funds so discredited the law in the eyes of worker militants distributed throughout the labor confederation that even the leadership of the metalworkers' union would have faced too much grief had they joined the system right away. In short, radicals saw the system as a restraint on militancy, *not a supply line to the battlefront.*[46]

From the mid to late 1930s, and into the wartime 1940s, the administered pricing of labor through increasingly centralized industrial relations generated numerous symptoms of low-wage disequilibrium. This was prima facie evidence that employers' fears of the opposite disequilibrium had been overblown. SAF began to take special notice of how piece work earnings were slipping out ahead of negotiated wages in early 1935, shortly after the law's implementation, with concern intensifying in 1937.[47] Labor scarcity and wage drift made possible by plentiful company revenues were employers' chief headaches, not excessive wages and squeezed profits. By 1939, employers recognized that upward wage pressures were the result of job hopping and poaching for scarce skilled workers—the workings of the labor market—not union militancy. Hence, the most important group among them stepped up promotion of vocational training and tightened restrictions on advertising for workers.[48]

During the ensuing war years, consensual policies of centralized wage restraint and controlled adjustments for inflation created even greater scarcity. Social Democratic action continued to repress building and construction unions, who had in the past so effectively taken advantage of it. Discrimination against them succeeded in bringing their relative yearly earnings down so far that, when better statistics became available, they provoked considerable surprise in the SAF leadership.[49] In short, unemployment insurance did not and could not promote militancy. Whatever faults employers saw in the system as it evolved over the years, promotion of militancy was not one of them.

Labor Immobility?

Employers' fears about the effect of the Ghent system on labor mobility also proved entirely unwarranted. Instead, the Social Democratic labor movement would soon prove its merit as the best of allies in employers' efforts to keep labor mobile and adaptable to a dynamic industrial economy. Apparently, one motive unions had for speeding up the creation of new unemployment insurance funds where none had existed in the 1940s through the 1960s, was to facilitate movement between sectors. After all, they said, "members in unions with unemployment funds hesitated to move to unions lacking them." The belated growth and expansion of the unemployment insurance system, slow as it was, possibly facilitated mobility instead of impeding it.[50]

The Social Democrats even tried to accommodate employer wishes for mobility in the design of the legislation itself. According to historian Nils Unga, by agreeing that the insurance funds should direct unemployed workers to reserve jobs, and thus out of their traditional occupations, the Social Democrats ensured themselves a parliamentary majority with the Liberal Party. The law also required workers to show up daily at public labor exchanges to receive benefits for that day. If they refused "suitable" work (for their strength and skills, which in many cases were not sector-specific) at standard wages, benefits would stop flowing for four weeks. Edebalk points out that, in this particular regard, public funds were actually superior to the many independent union funds already in existence.[51] The law also explicitly provided for the use of unemployment funds for travel and moving expenses incurred by workers taking new jobs.

Companion legislation, passed simultaneously in 1934, beefed up the public labor exchanges' ability to direct workers into new jobs and out of dependency on unemployment benefits. It called for a major expansion of the public labor exchange system in ways that SAF had been advocating for a number of years. The number of exchange offices across the country's vast territory was to expand from 136 to 239. At the end of 1935, SAF was nothing but enthusiastic and called for even more to be done, despite the formation of 303 offices, even more than originally anticipated. "In many places there remains much to be done to arrive at a vigorous, vigilant, and effective referral system," SAF's yearly report said. The reason: "Strong seasonal changes, which characterize the Swedish labor market, along with the country's geographic dimensions, place great demands on the tasks of directing available manpower to those points where jobs open up at different times."[52]

Indeed, the 1930s legislation, which budgeted money for workers' moving expenses, and the expansion of the public labor exchange system that the union funds were to put unemployed workers in contact with, can justifiably be regarded as the first major precursors of Sweden's national-level, mobility-enhancing "active labor market policy" of the 1950s. That policy will be analyzed in the next chapter. More than any other piece of the "Swedish model," active labor market policy was designed in service of employer solidarism. Further stages in the policy's development in the 1940s and 1950s demonstrated the labor movement's profound commitment to the labor mobility so earnestly asserted by solidaristic employers—and dispelling all latent concerns about how the design of unemployment insurance might sectorally segment, and therefore structurally rigidify, the labor market.

SAF, it appears, never approved of unemployment insurance as much as other Social Democratic social legislation of the 1940s and 1950s and on frequent occasions called for adjustments and restraint in future revisions. Nevertheless, within two years after passage, it had so fully overcome its objections that it "showed sympathy" for the contributory system's full expansion, according to Edebalk.[53] SAF director Gustaf Söderlund found in 1937 that existing noncontributory means-tested cash assistance paid out of general government revenues was still so generous that workers were disinclined to join the relatively ungenerous unemployment insurance system. Over the years the Social Democrats fixed the problem, not by lowering social assistance levels but by increasing government subsidies and unemployment insurance benefits. The costs of this solution for employers were fairly small, considering the labor movement's contributions to wage restraint and labor mobility—and therefore low unemployment.

The People's Pension, 1935–1946

Referring in part to growing social spending, SAF's year-end report for 1934 voiced considerable nervousness about Social Democratic ambitions. In discussing the wording, Martin Waldenström, the prominent SAF board member from the huge Grängesberg mining company, complained that even the modestly formulated shot across the bow risked making the confederation sound like a pack of stiff-necked, hide-bound bosses (*förstockade arbetsgivare-patroner*). He objected to strengthening common misperceptions that SAF was simply an extension of the country's right-wing organizations. Director Söderlund acknowledged some sympathy but defended the report's statement.[54] Subsequent yearly reports for the decade and beyond, however, offered no reason for anyone to accuse employers of being hide-bound reactionaries. Staying blandly with the facts, the reports simply described the progress of Social Democratic legislation, betraying neither a hint of alarmism or satisfaction.

The flow of legislation was far from torrential. Nor was it, as the 1934 unemployment insurance legislation proved, designed in callous disregard for employers' interests. In fact, the relatively limited pension adjustments of 1935 and 1937 met with employer favor, not resistance, before and after passage. Bigger, and better yet from employers' standpoint, was the pension reform of 1946. At that time, labor scarcity had reached alarming levels. A truly groundbreaking piece of social legislation now appeared on the agenda, timed and designed in full consonance with the interests of employers in solidaristic management of the labor market.

Minor Reforms, 1935–1937

In 1935, the Social Democratic government modestly increased pension benefits provided by the existing compulsory system. It had been installed, with employers' blessings, in 1913. Workers' contributions into the system, and their benefits, were largely linked to their wage income. Benefits flowed out of a premium reserve fund that accumulated over time. In addition, there was a means-tested supplement for the elderly poor, but only those classified as disabled, financed from general revenues. This system, in the context of the depression, was failing miserably in keeping much of Sweden's elderly population off highly demeaning poor relief.

Despite Swedish social democracy's reputation for "universalism," the 1935 reform, to be implemented in 1937, mostly increased the supplementary means-tested benefits (i.e., only for those qualifying as poor), while eliminating the disability criterion. The basic, universalistic "People's Pension" was to continue providing roughly equal benefits for everyone, regardless of previous income. The system also moved away from premium reserve funding toward the pay-as-you-go principle. Like the 1939 Social Security revisions widely favored by American business leaders, shifting to the pay-as-you-go system, combined with modest increases in worker contributions, paid for the small increase in the basic public pension.[55]

In its official pronouncements, SAF supported every main feature of the Social Democrats' new law. The confederation welcomed in particular a provision that better accommodated an important residue of welfare capitalism that SAF, its solidarism still evolving, had not yet fully repudiated. This change now allowed workers to subtract their small company pension benefits of up to 300 crowns from the income figure used to test eligibility for the public supplement. In effect, the deductibility of company pensions meant a partial departure from means testing. Previously, the supplements had been reduced by company pensions. That practice had shifted government pension costs onto employers and undermined their segmentalist purpose—that is, to tie manpower to the firm and generate worker goodwill. Low-wage retirees had been able to receive similar amounts whether they stayed with their company or not. Now, with the Social Democrats' reform, employers could more rationally continue providing their "faithful servant pensions" (trotjänarpensioner) to long-term employees.[56]

The Social Democrats' 1937 revisions of the People's Pension was more controversial—though not with employers. Implemented in 1938, the changes improved on the earlier law by increasing the deduction of company pensions up to 400 crowns for workers in urban areas where costs for the elderly, especially housing, were greater. In response to concerns of the day about birthrates lower than practically anywhere else in Europe, the Social Democrats had argued that the increased benefits would help take the burden of the elderly off the backs of younger workers, freeing up more income to raise children. The same concern had also motivated some of the Social Democrats' innovative family policy initiatives in the 1930s, which provided an array of in-kind benefits and services to women and children.[57]

Political controversy centered primarily on the introduction of regional differences in the supplementary benefits. On this provision, SAF made common cause with the Social Democratic government, actually parting company with the parties to the right of them. In addition to their concerns about labor supply in Sweden, employers probably also hoped that reducing old people's dependency on their working progeny would somewhat reduce wage pressures from the latter. The divisive issue unified urban industrial Sweden against lower-cost rural areas that were strongly represented in the bourgeois parties. As the bill moved through the Riksdag, the provision was deleted. The Social Democrats, therefore, turned the measure into a parliamentary vote of no confidence, which it lost. During the ensuing election debate, in which the issue played a major role, the bourgeois parties beat a retreat, but lost votes anyway. Perhaps employer pressure figures in the change. In any event, the outcome was a victory for social democracy—in cross-class alliance with capitalist interests.[58]

The 1946 Reform

Swedish social democracy has earned a strong association with universalism as an underlying principle for social insurance. Universalism, broadly conceived, describes compulsory systems of tax-financed income transfers to individuals and households based on criteria other than need and applied to practically all citizens, regardless of occupation, race, or other dividing lines. It might come as a surprise that the first major advance along these lines had to wait until 1946, fourteen years after the Social Democratic Party's rise to power, and eleven years after the New Deal's major innovations. Even the New

Deal reforms were markedly more universalistic, though far from completely so. For example, they excluded agricultural labor, largely because of the power of Southern landowners fearful that New Deal benefits would loosen their paternalistic and coercive grip over their many black tenants and share-croppers.[59] But Swedish farm workers were also excluded from unemployment insurance, so it was hardly superior on that account. Also, the Swedish system effectively discriminated against many other groups, unlike America's UI. The Social Democrats' pension legislation of 1935 improved more on the means-tested elements than universalistic ones, while the Social Security Act of the same year was intended to reduce old people's dependence on means-tested assistance.

The Social Democrats' shift to full-fledged universalism in old-age security policy had to wait until 1946. The major pension reform of that year passed, once again, with a remarkable degree of cross-class agreement between capital and labor. Universalism, it seems, was highly consonant with evolving employer interests. This time, in contrast to 1937, all parties to the right of the Social Democratic government lined up behind organized capital in support of the legislation and rejecting alternatives that would have increased the means-tested elements in the older law. To take effect in 1948, it provided a large increase in the flat-rate People's Pension. In addition to the flat sum to be received by all, poorer retirees were to receive a small means-tested supplement in the form of housing and "wife" benefits (*bostads- och hustrutillägg*).

This was not a case of a mobilized Left pushing boldly and victoriously in a long campaign against reactionary interests. Notably, as Åke Elmér puts it, "one looks in vain for any suggestion about thorough reform of the People's Pension" in the Social Democrats' relatively radical Postwar Program of 1944. Minister of Social Affairs Möller initially promoted a cheaper, more means-tested system, which would concentrate resources on the most needy. Apparently, he was obeying the dictates of more fiscally conservative members of the government. By contrast, Conservative leader Gösta Bagge came out early and openly against means testing. According to the conservative *Sydsvenska Dagbladet*, the reform was in fact a "triumph for the right," although it did report that in his heart of hearts, Möller preferred universalism. In reality, it was an occasion of national unity, as the Liberal *Dagens Nyheter* put it.[60]

Unity extended deep into and across the leading labor market organizations. SAF and LO both favored the most universalistic of the three alternatives floated by the government commission. Perhaps national unity flowed upward from them. An editorial in the daily *Dagens Nyheter*, entitled "Between Brothers," speculated suspiciously that some sort of secret agreement had been reached on the matter because of the great similarity in SAF's and LO's views.[61] In any event, SAF made its reasoning loud and clear, possibly informing the Conservative Party's views. The acute labor scarcity of 1945 and 1946, examined before, was the problem.

In a formal statement on the government commission report's alternatives, SAF "totally rejected" the cheaper plan with beefed up means-tested benefits.

Its flaw was that it could drive older workers out of the labor market and thus worsen the scarcity problem. The reasoning was simple: they might choose to quit their jobs if their current income, and savings from it, were to disqualify them from receiving full government pensions at the qualifying age of 67. SAF's executive director Fritiof Söderbäck echoed concerns explicitly stated in the government's report, taking special care to "emphasize how important it is that people in their later years, who have the ability and will to offer their manpower to the disposition of the national economy, should not . . . suffer a substantial reduction in their people's pension. Population developments make it necessary that as large a portion of the older age groups as possible are engaged in productive labor." In short, means testing would "reduce incentives for pension recipients to improve their situation through work and savings."[62]

Did the confederation advocate the universalistic option only because it was the lesser-despite its greater cost-of two politically unavoidable evils? Did organized employers actually prefer a private solution to the pension problem? The answer is an emphatic no. A close look inside SAF discussion, before and after the pension reform, indicates that they regarded legislation as a welcome alternative to company pensions. The eclipse of welfare capitalism was not a dark day for Swedish capitalism. The hope was that by shouldering the retirement burdens of older blue-collar workers, the state would do service for solidarism. It would reduce worker pressure on companies to introduce or raise pension benefits and thus violate the spirit, if not the letter, of solidarism.

A crisis in the transport sector illustrates the problem well. While the legislation was brewing, the Motor Vehicle Transport Employers' Association (*Biltrafikens Arbetsgivareförbund*) resolutely attempted to block the spread of company pensions from unorganized and public operators into its own membership. Legislation, it thought, might relieve the pressure. In January 1946, therefore, the association warmly endorsed the approaching pension reform, hoping "that the government pensions would assume such dimensions and form that the worker pension issue can thereby be regarded as completely settled and that requests for further pension benefits from employers can be rejected." Compulsory government pensions, not welfare capitalism; the bigger, the better. Unfortunately for the association, the legislated pensions were not big enough to stop the company pension movement in its tracks, for it continued to roll on in 1947, rupturing the organization.[63]

The organized trucking operators were not alone in their views. Leading figures from more heavyweight associations regarded the law as a welcome argument to check the advance of company benefits. Not a voice was raised complaining about the law, nor in support for the idea that continuing increases in company pensions should be welcomed. The only differences arose because continuing labor shortages in 1947 would tempt companies to expand existing pensions or introduce new ones on top of the new public ones. Debate raged about the need to formulate directives for freezing existing company pensions at their current levels, or even imposing ceilings at levels already exceeded by some firms. This debate fed into the following year's controversy about strengthening SAF's authority to issue binding directives and therefore unilaterally regulate the labor market.

The conflict revealed interesting lines of division within as well as between sectors about imposing a ceiling on company pensions. In May 1947, SAF board member Gösta Lundeqvist, executive director at a large shipbuilder in VF, advised against imposing too much rigidity, declaring that "many workers were now leaving private sector companies and going over to state or municipal employers where better pensions beckoned." Lundeqvist wanted SAF directives to allow company pensions equivalent to what government jobs offered. But Nils W. Lundblad, an executive from a large sugar producer, rejected Lundeqvist's proposal as excessively permissive toward the use of company pensions as a magnet or "drawing card [dragplåster] to get manpower." His view was closer to the dominant view in VF. So much division and uncertainty prevailed about imposing a ceiling that chairman Sven Schwartz had to end the discussion by asking for a voluntary freeze on existing company pensions pending further study.[64]

Debate a few months later settled nothing. The most eager spokesmen for imposing a ceiling came from the large and powerful export-oriented engineering industry, where average company social benefits (according to the 1952 survey) were meager. VF's Arvid Nilsson, an executive from one of the many moderate-sized engineering firms unlikely to have large pension benefits, was one of them. He argued that with pension legislation in place, it now made sense to demand the shrinking of large companies' pensions down to 400 kronor (or 600 for married workers) and to enforce a ceiling at that level. (These were the amounts currently deductible for the 1937 means-tested supplements.) But Evert Wijkander, executive director of Bofors, and leader of the steel industry's association, disagreed. Many steel producers, Bofors among them, would have to reduce their company pensions, an ill-advised move from a psychological standpoint in dealing with workers. In principle, however, he had no problem with the idea of putting a solidaristic freeze on company pensions at existing levels.[65]

In the following year's controversy regarding SAF's authority to issue binding directives, the lines of division were the same. VF was the sectoral association most interested in increasing SAF's authority, and the largely rural steel industry, along with other rural-based employers in the forest products industries, were VF's main opponents. They were still more dependent on social benefits for attracting and keeping workers and less inclined to give VF leverage through SAF to dictate their use on the engineering industry's terms. Nevertheless, there was considerable consensus that their growth should be restrained. SAF's official response to the bill had already summarized this consensus in 1946. The legislative reform, it said hopefully, would remove all cause for "building up workers' People's Pensions with pensions from employers, as is currently happening."[66] No tears would be shed for the demise of welfare capitalism, the private market's solution to the retirement problem.

Conclusion

Comparison of employer attitudes in Sweden and the United States regarding social and labor policy reforms of the 1930s reveals an intriguing difference. Among Swedish employers there was virtually no interest in social insurance and labor market measures that would prop up workers' wages to regulate product market competition and boost aggregate purchasing power. These were ideas that resonated broadly among American capitalists. By contrast, employer leader J. Sigfrid Edström had nothing good to say about Americans' efficiency wage and purchasing power theories and about the regulatory protections against chiseling in Roosevelt's National Industrial Recovery Act, inspired in good part by the "Swope Plan." The difference had nothing to do with variations in their progressiveness or the companies they represented. In fact, both Edström and Gerard Swope led their countries' respective "General Electrics," and both stood out as about the most constructive and statesmanlike of all industrialists in relations with their societies' progressive forces.[67]

The progress of Swedish pension reform from the Depression-era 1930s and into the labor-scarce 1940s shows how the evolution of the social democratic welfare state hewed closely to evolving employer interests. The growing clarity of employer hopes in the 1940s about what legislation could do to assist with their confederation's solidaristic agenda goes a long way in explaining the shaping as well as timing of the new pension legislation. For example, labor scarcity generated by solidaristic wage restraint in the face of powerful growth pressures made means testing inappropriate, as employers saw it, for by driving elderly workers out of the labor force, it would only make scarcity worse. Their views seem to have tipped the fiscally conservative Social Democratic government in the direction of the more expensive universalistic option.

Solidaristic motivations for employer support of the Social Democratic welfare state help explain major differences in the timing and shaping of pension legislation between the United States and Sweden. Progessive segmentalists in America desired pension legislation in the context of depression and high unemployment. Sweden's own "corporate liberals" desired it in a period of growth and labor scarcity. Legislative design followed logically. American segmentalists and their IRC experts working with the Roosevelt administration were extremely eager to make OAI financing cheap enough and benefits large enough to get rid of older workers and replace them with cheaper, more productive, and unemployed young ones. In other words, it was specifically designed to clear old people out of the labor market. Thus, the Social Security Act required workers to retire at 65 in order to begin receiving public pension benefits. Swedish solidarists, by contrast, were anxious to keep elderly workers in the labor force and not drive them out with legislation. The People's Pension reform of 1946 in Sweden was designed so that workers did not have to retire at 67 and could earn all they pleased without losing benefits. Strikingly different features in the reforms matched radical differences in the strong interests of capitalists. This was no coincidence. In postwar America, when surplus labor was no longer disruptive, retirees gained the right to earn much more before losing Social Security benefits ($17,000 in the 1990s). In 2000, because of labor scarcity, the ceiling was eliminated entirely. The measure received broad-based, bipartisan support; employers welcomed it enthusiastically.[68]

In short, progressive social legislation introduced in America during the 1930s was designed in part to engender support among capitalists because of its regulatory effects on depressed and unruly product market competition. By contrast, the development of the core elements of the social democratic welfare state in Sweden emerged only after the Depression and harmonized well with the evolving interests of employers in rule-bound competition among themselves over a labor force in short supply. In building the modern Swedish welfare state, a powerful and innovative social democratic labor movement catered to, rather than defied, the market governance interests of capitalists, just like the American New Dealers did before them.

12

EXPANDING THE SOLIDARISTIC
WELFARE STATE

Compared to every other step in Sweden's welfare state development, demands for full retirement security in the 1950s stirred
an unusually polarized debate. The social democratic labor movement insisted on legislation guaranteeing that, upon retirement, workers should no
longer have to suffer deep cuts in income down to the level provided for by the
People's Pension. After eight years of controversy, the Social Democrats' comprehensive pension bill finally passed in the Riksdag by only a single vote. But
conflict threatened to continue after passage in 1959. The Conservative Party
leadership promised to "rip up" the reform if ensuing election results offered a
chance to form a coalition. The narrowness of the Social Democrat's legislative victory inspired them with hope.

Behind the political scene, things looked strangely different. Arne Geijer,
the nation's top labor leader, confided all along to Bertil Kugelberg, his employer counterpart, that he preferred a collectively bargained solution instead
of legislation. Geijer knew that was SAF's preference too. But the Social Democratic Party had irrevocably hijacked the issue, and carried on with legislation. Be that as it may, Geijer reassured Kugelberg, the labor confederation had
exactly the same interest as Sweden's capitalists regarding how to administer
the new pension funds, the issue that aroused employers' anxiety the most. He
kept Kugelberg up to date on his successful efforts to secure those interests. A
rude surprise, therefore, lay in wait for the Conservative Party: SAF and leading business figures soon insisted that the party drop all talk of trashing the
legislation. Had they only known that employers would regard it as "not that
bad," rued future Conservative leader Gunnar Heckscher, his party would not
have opposed the legislation so aggressively.[1]

Swedish Social Democrats laid three major milestones in the development
of the welfare state during the 1950s: first, a comprehensive health insurance

reform with guaranteed sick pay linked to earnings; second, a costly expansion of an administratively innovative "active labor market policy" for retraining and relocating workers; and third, the new pension system guaranteeing for all workers a standard of living in old age commensurate with their situation before retirement. Just as in the pension debate, the politics behind the other two reforms fly in the face of conventional notions about class power and conflict. The labor confederation lined up behind SAF on the controversial sick pay issue, a central feature of the comprehensive health insurance reform. Together, they prevailed over the initial designs of the Social Democratic minister of Social Affairs. Gustav Möller's less generous plan intentionally reserved an important role for employers in provision of supplementary benefits. But that was a role they simply no longer wanted to play. The logic behind active labor market policy, promoted by the union confederation, was something the Social Democratic leadership initially dismissed with contempt. SAF never challenged it and had enthusiastically supported previous policy, administrative, and budgetary steps in its direction. Once major expansion had occurred, the employers' confederation regarded Conservative Party attempts to undermine the labor market policy as "entirely against our interests."[2]

There is widespread acceptance of the view that Sweden's world prominence as a welfare state can be accounted for by a "historic compromise" that, as one typical account puts it, "resulted in an exchange of industrial peace and wage restraint for a comprehensive set of welfare state programs." Thus, employers in Sweden, "are willing," though reluctant, "to shoulder a much greater share of the pension burden than in the United States." Behind this analysis is the notion that the labor movement's unusual extortionary power put it in position to force such a compromise. Analysis of the historical evidence shows that there is as little truth to this account as there is to the argument, criticized earlier, that unions exchanged wage restraint for solidaristic wage policy.[3] Examination of the three major welfare reforms of the 1950s—the same decade when solidaristic wage policy became a cross-class project—is followed by a critique of literature that explicitly or implicitly invokes a "balance of class power" favorable to labor, rather than a remarkable alignment of class interests, to explain Sweden's unusual developments.

Compulsory Health Insurance

Class conflict does not pervade the history of health and sickness insurance legislation in Sweden. SAF eagerly supported the 1931 law, a limited reform of the existing voluntary system, which passed before the Social Democrats came to power. Like the 1934 unemployment legislation, it subsidized and standardized the practices of voluntary private insurance funds. Employer approval had prominent solidaristic overtones. Gustaf Söderlund noted appreciatively how the legislation, by making generous protection broadly available, would reduce widely varying employer health care expenses. He also noted its cross-class appeal: it was "in employers' and workers' common interest."[4]

Söderlund's hopes were not fulfilled, however. In ensuing years labor-hungry employers simply began contributing workers' share of premiums into the system and provided unilateral (noncontractual) company benefits, and sometimes sectorally negotiated benefits, often in the form of sick pay. Meanwhile, many workers, especially but not exclusively in low-pay sectors, missed out on both government subsidies and private benefits. Thus, it was not until 1955 that implementation of a compulsory and universalistic system would fulfill employers' goal, pursued since early in the century, of taking decisions about health care and sick pay out of their hands. It would also serve the broad interests of the working class in widespread and equal access to medical care and income security, despite absence from work due to sickness and injuries.

Möller's Detour

The first Social Democratic move to introduce compulsory and therefore all-inclusive health care insurance and sick pay began auspiciously for employers with the presentation of a government commission report in 1944. Because Fritiof Söderbäck, SAF's current executive director, had been enlisted as a key expert by the government commission, it is not surprising that the confederation solidly supported the proposal. But then things went seriously awry. Gustav Möller, the headstrong minister of social affairs, mobilized support from within the Social Democratic Party for an alternative plan. The bone of contention within the party and between the party and employers was sick pay. Through his divisive maneuvering, Möller succeeded in replacing the commission's earnings-related sick pay scheme with a controversial flat-rate substitute. His legislation passed in 1946. In this, Möller was apparently inspired by Britain's William Beveridge, seeking a highly egalitarian safety net and administrative simplicity.

Further research will be needed to establish whether SAF's rejection played a part in ensuring that Möller's legislation, though passed, was never implemented. After five years of delay, against Möller's will and after his resignation, it was finally scrapped in 1951.[5] As SAF understood it, one reason the government delayed Möller's reform was the fiscal conservatism of other party leaders. Another was severe labor and other shortages. Sudden increased demand for health services unleashed by the reform would be impossible to meet because the labor and materials needed for hospital construction and patient care were simply not available. These misgivings matched some of the employer confederation's own—especially the problems that factor shortages and, therefore, pay inflation from hospital construction would cause for solidaristic control of the private sector labor market.[6]

But the resource problem was, ultimately, only a passing concern. What mattered more was SAF's problems with the sick-pay provision in Möller's legislation. One of its objections alluded to recruitment problems in a labor-scarce economy. Though low, the uniform benefit level, complemented with spouse and child supplements, was substantially higher than actual income for a significant number of families in agricultural employment.[7] Thus, industry's ability to dislodge scarce labor from rural life would be compromised, if perhaps only marginally.

Dominating SAF's critique of the Möller legislation was the fact that his 1946 law had dropped plans for "coordination" (*samordning*) of the existing work accident insurance legislation with the new system. SAF had looked eagerly forward to coordination—in fact, von Sydow had advocated it from the very beginning, in 1915, when workplace accident insurance was legislated. He had hoped that compulsory national health insurance would soon be introduced to pick up costs for the first 60 days after workplace injuries.[8] The idea behind coordination was that the regular insurance scheme, which was only partially funded by employer contributions, would provide sick pay and medical care for the numerous short-term cases lasting no more than two months or so. Employers would then pick up the entire tab only for the relatively few injuries keeping workers at home beyond that time. Employer-funded workmen's accident compensation that lacked such coordination with regular health insurance gave workers a strong incentive to submit fraudulent claims for off-the-job injuries to obtain any compensation at all. When that happened, employers were forced unjustly either to pay or engage in expensive and tiresome disputes. In sum, coordination would save employers money.

Whether or not SAF's objections were decisive in persuading the Social Democrats to delay and then trash Möller's legislation is impossible to say on the basis of SAF documents and existing historical research, which ignores SAF entirely. Möller resigned in 1951, apparently in frustration over stinging defeats on various pieces of social legislation at the hands of more fiscally conservative cabinet and party leaders. They regarded him as "economically irresponsible."[9] His resignation unblocked the way for new legislation, passed in 1953, better suiting Prime Minister Tage Erlander and his new finance minister from the leadership of LO, Gunnar Sträng.[10]

Starting in 1955, all citizens were finally to receive free hospitalization, generous health benefits, and up to two years' sick pay, financed by a combination of taxes on employer payrolls, workers' wages, and general revenue from national and local governments. Instead of Möller's uniform sick pay favoring low-income groups, it offered roughly two thirds of normal income for illnesses lasting a month and somewhat less for shorter illnesses because of a three-day waiting period (*karenstid*).[11] Coordination with the accident compensation system meant that the general scheme would take care of workers for the first 93 days after work-related accident cases—better even than von Sydow's 60. It also meant now that for the first time an absolute and uniform waiting period of three days would apply for all compensation, a feature missing in the accident scheme.

Thus, what Social Democratic leaders Erlander and Sträng preferred also answered SAF's main criticisms. This is not surprising, for they had enlisted Sven Hydén, SAF's chief expert on social policy matters, to help formulate the revision— just as Fritiof Söderbäck had been enlisted in the 1940s to help with the proposal that Möller buried. As for the finer details, improvements in the substitute legislation were possible in the eyes of practically everyone in SAF, though agreement was far from complete about which details exactly were objectionable. From the engineering employers' standpoint, the worst thing was elimination of experience rating in workplace accident insurance— that is, reduction of employer fees for firms with low accident levels. Because of average injury levels, the paper pulp industry neither gained nor lost. Textile employers agreed with VF, for they also had, on average, low accident rates. They were also more generally gloomy about the legislation and its new taxes, squeezed as they were on the one side by bruising price competition from abroad and on the other by high (engineering) wages in tight labor markets.[12]

The negatives, according to Hydén, did not outweigh the positives, however. He had entered only one formal reservation in the commission report about a relatively minor matter affecting employer costs—compensation for accidents on the way to and from work. Now the costs of accidents occurring in transit would be picked up by the employer-financed workmen's compensation system, though only after the regular system covered the first 93 days. Benefits received by injured workers during this first period would, "happily enough" according to one pleasantly surprised employer group, actually be lower than before.[13]

Hence, there was widespread employer enthusiasm for coordination of the workmen's accident insurance and the new health insurance scheme. Commentary by sectoral organizations in SAF was exclusively positive. VF, the engineering employers' association, "welcomed with satisfaction, above all, the proposal concerning coordination." Only the private insurance industry, which had a stake in the existing accident insurance arrangement, objected. A steel and iron ore industrialist dismissed its opposition as arising from the "instinct for self-preservation."[14]

Hydén acknowledged that the costs of eliminating experience rating from the accident scheme would, relative to past practice, hit different employer groups "very unfairly." But, he said, merit-based differentiation would still obtain for the period after three months. For the rest of the time, he pointed out, "if one accepts coordination, it would be impossible to accomplish any system other than one with uniform fees."[15] With this, Hydén justified a defect in the legislation that divided employers by explaining its necessary technical connection with a feature for which there was only widespread praise. After deliberating on the matter at some length, SAF leaders decided on a mild and "tactful" request for efforts in the future to find a way to differentiate payroll taxes or introduce other monetary incentives for low accident rates.[16] To hold out minor improvements like these would make SAF look, incorrectly, like it was stuck in a "reactionary mentality" (baksträvarmentalitet).[17]

The Cross-Class Alliance
against Welfare Capitalism

Hydén's view, shared by Tore Browaldh, SAF's vice-director,was that, given the Social Democrats' strong urge to act after the long delay, disagreement on complex and minor details would play into the hands of less cautious reformers in the Social Democratic camp happy to write off SAF and incorporate worse flaws than those remaining. The current proposal, in fact was "not unacceptable" at all.[18] Hydén's point poses the following question, of course: did SAF really favor some private solution, but strategically support this reform only because it feared legislation was inevitable and worse legislation if it failed to compromise? Were its interests in legislation only strategic?

All evidence indicates that the support for legislation was genuine. A remarkable thing about employers' internal debate before and after passage of the expensive health care reform was that not a single voice of opposition was recorded in defense of private employment-based benefits. None objected in spirit or principle to the socialization of health care and sick pay. The consensus was as great as it had been on private company pensions in 1946. A history of the paper pulp industry association, published only two years after the reform became law, concluded flatly and simply—too simplistically, in fact—that "an administratively burdensome task had been transferred to a social agency."[19]

By the mid-1950s, practically all employers throughout SAF had been providing at least one and usually more of the following benefits: sick pay, free or subsidized physician's services and hospitalization, and contributions toward workers' membership payments into private (state subsidized and regulated) health insurance funds.[20] Often they were provided on a company basis, though due to SAF's intervention not secured in collective agreements negotiated at company level. Sometimes they were collectively bargained on a uniform multi-employer basis to keep a lid on company practices. The reform meant that Swedish employers would busily and happily set about retiring all of these benefits. High-level strategy sessions emphasized flatly the need, in the words of Erik Brodén, vice executive director, to seize the opportunity and "clear out health benefits." This would be, as Hydén energetically exhorted, "to the employer's advantage."[21]

Consensus extended across class lines from SAF to LO, fully bypassing Möller. His plan had called for a simple, flat, and relatively low sick pay benefit. Employers and workers, he explicitly recommended, should work out voluntary supplements on top of the flat rate to achieve adequate income security in case of illness. Higher pay workers would insist on it, and individual employers would be only too happy to oblige them in times of scarcity. But, collectively, employers wanted out of the business. Also, they dearly wanted relief from full financial responsibility for the first three months after a workplace accident, by which time, of course, most injured workers would be rehabilitated. Möller's scheme made that impossible. Its relatively small benefits for higher paid workers would keep employers in the business of providing supplementary accident benefits during the first three months. Coordination on the basis of legislated accident as well as sick pay linked to wage earnings, though more costly for the government, was a better deal for employers.

The labor confederation ultimately lined up in solidarity with SAF's position. Even early on, in 1945 and 1946, LO treasurer and Riksdag member Axel Strand had spoken out loud and clear against Möller's version, joining other critics in the party who agreed with SAF. According to Torsten Svensson's research, views in LO were, in contrast to Strand's certainty, still divided and ambivalent in the mid-1940s. By 1953, however, they were solidly behind income-related sick pay, which made for easier coordination with income-related work injury insurance. For the unions, including the important metalworkers' union, Möller's basic sick pay benefits were just too small, and they held slim hopes that a system of voluntary supplements would ever be adequate and equitable. Gunnar Sträng, the new minister of social affairs, steered the legislation to be enacted in the new direction. He had, Edebalk points out, a trade union background, unlike Möller.[22]

Gustav Möller is sometimes credited with being the central figure, "the legendary architect" in the designing of the Swedish welfare state. Ironically, though he is identified with a certain kind of universalism, his health insurance plan explicitly called for preserving an important role for private, employer-provided benefits. In this instance, his designs were overruled with legislation backed by a remarkable cross-class alliance of employer and union preferences. This legislation, in one sense, was actually more universalistic in its overall implications. The detour he led the Social Democratic Party down, against employers' objections, turned out to be a dead end, and the frustrations he experienced in the process contributed to his retirement from politics. If the evolving Social Democratic welfare state was a solidaristic one founded on a cross-class alliance with organized capital, it came at the expense of Möller's distinctive influence.[23]

Active Labor Market Policy

In perhaps no other policy area have Swedish Social Democrats gained such international renown and praise as in their massive interventions to influence the supply and movement of labor. Expenditures associated with the country's "active labor market policy" took off after the mid-1950s with innovative programs for retraining and geographic relocation of workers made redundant by rapid technological and market change. By the 1970s, large amounts of money were devoted to the policy, reaching about 2 percent of GNP and 6 percent of total government budgets.[24] Retraining and relocation were also complemented by things like temporary job creation to keep people off "passive" measures—that is, unemployment insurance—and therefore in healthy circulation through the labor market. However, the active "supply-oriented programs" like retraining and relocation grew more rapidly, reaching nearly 40 percent of total spending by labor market authorities in 1982 from only a few percent before 1960.[25]

Active labor market policy is conventionally attributed to the ideas, interests, and power of the strong Swedish labor movement. Indeed, that is one source of the stepped up activity in the 1950s. In the words of Gösta Rehn, who was, along with his fellow LO economist Rudolf Meidner, a driving intellectual force behind the expansion of active measures, labor market policy should not simply compensate for the crushing individual burdens of unemployment. Instead, it should enhance workers' freedom by increasing their ability to change jobs. By promoting mobility, active labor market policy would facilitate dynamic economic change and, therefore, growth. The "safety of wings," as opposed to "safety of the snail shell," was Rehn's felicitous description of the policy's goals—to reconcile and combine liberty, through labor market mobility, with equality and security.[26] Thus, active labor market policy and solidaristic wage policy, accompanied by stringent macro-economic policy, were the three main pillars of what came to be known as the Rehn-Meidner model, first presented in a report to the 1951 LO congress.[27]

The Employer View

What was the view of organized capital about the Rehn-Meidner model? As regards solidaristic wage policy, the answer is already clear: they agreed with all its essentials (see chapter 6), but were strategically coy about admitting it openly. As regards active labor market policy, one would expect them to have responded positively, considering the deep concerns they expressed about promoting labor mobility in the debate over unemployment insurance. Indeed, because active labor market policy was designed to reduce dependence on unemployment insurance, and promote geographic and occupational mobility, that is exactly what happened. In essays and other publications of the 1960s, SAF's executive director Curt-Steffan Giesecke, Kugelberg's successor, claimed that "[t]here has long been a high degree of unity regarding labor market policy in our land," mentioning in particular agreement about the need for interoccupational mobility and strategic training of youths in skills needed by a rapidly changing industry. The reason for agreement lay in the fact that "during the whole post-war period there has been an extreme shortage of trained manpower." In short, he argued, it was "extremely important from industry's standpoint" to spend more rather than less on policies like adult vocational training to promote occupational mobility.[28]

No wonder then that the corporatist administration of labor market policies—that is, by the Labor Market Board (*Arbetsmarknadsstyrelsen*, or AMS, consisting of three SAF representatives along with representatives of LO and the white-collar union confederation, TCO)—operated so frictionlessly during the 1960s and even into the 1980s. Curiously, in a vivid description of his and Rudolf Meidner's efforts to promote active labor market policy from about

1948 through the 1960s, Gösta Rehn never mentions employers except perhaps in a veiled confession of their role in the cross-class alliance. Modestly dismissing the idea that he and other LO economists invented the idea of mobility measures, he said that demands for them come "from outside" the unions. By this, he probably meant employers. According to his writings in the 1950s, the main objective with permanently stepped up measures was "to stimulate the adaptation of manpower to industry's needs."[29]

Rehn could not have meant that the demands came from the current party and government leaders. In fact, they stood in the way of rapid expansion of active measures in the time between Rehn's and Meidner's analyses in 1948 and legislative action about ten years later. Per-Edvin Sköld, Social Democratic finance minister, personally informed Rehn that his and Meidner's 1951 report was "the dumbest thing I've read" (*det dummaste jag har läst*). On various occasions Sköld reacted with "wrath" and "indignation" to Rehn's and Meidner's criticisms of the government's economic and employment policy, which derived from their thinking in the LO report.[30]

The conflict concerned what the "gang of querulants" (*kverulantgänget*)—the young LO and party upstarts—said about the government's reliance on traditional and very clumsy expansionary Keynesian fiscal and monetary policies to counteract cyclical increases in unemployment. They regarded as naive the government's expectations that the unions could and would restrain wages to stop inflation when excessive government measures sometimes pushed unemployment below 1 percent.[31] Predictably, as in 1948, 1951, and 1955, the result of macro-economic policy was an explosion of wages and prices triggered both by wage militancy and by wage drift, that is, atomistic market forces. In fact, wage drift in one place probably fueled militancy in another. At those times, individual employers trampled all over each other in violation of centrally negotiated guidelines for restrained wage increases. That employers would willingly give away more than the unions had settled for, or even demanded, was a source of embarrassment for union officials. They would then have to rush in and redeem themselves with militant demands to restore equitable pay relations disturbed by uncontrolled wage drift.[32]

Thus, Rehn and Meidner prescribed more restrictive and careful fiscal policy, the third major pillar of their model, after solidaristic wages and active labor market measures. Restrictive policy would activate employers, individually now as well as collectively, as the restraining force on wage drift after unions accepted moderate wage increases. Unions would thereby not have to shoulder the demeaning and thankless task of restraining wages. For this they were both ideologically ill suited and organizationally ill equipped. Active labor market policy, not macro-economic policy, would then take over to dry up remaining pools of unemployment. It would do so by retraining and relocating workers and delivering them into the hands of dynamic employers still facing inflationary labor supply bottlenecks, despite stringent fiscal policy.[33]

Gradually, the entire top leadership of the Social Democratic Party had bought into all three elements of the model, at least in principle if not always macro-economic practice. Prime Minister Tage Erlander admitted to the LO congress of 1961 that he had not understood the LO economists ten years earlier. Now he was putting their ideas to work. Even Per-Edvin Sköld finally came around, though the real breakthrough had to wait until his replacement, Gunnar Sträng, who was "totally sold on the idea," used a short cyclical downswing beginning in 1957 to initiate a large-scale increase in active, mobility-enhancing measures.[34]

Though the timing of the first major increase in labor market spending might suggest that the Social Democrats saw the policy largely as a remedy for cyclical unemployment, the Rehn-Meidner model itself, and the ensuing long-term expansion of active labor market policy, was neither anti- nor pro-cyclical in principle. It was structural, designed to remedy the sluggish adjustment of supply displayed by labor markets at all times. Meidner pointed out that it "ought to be pursued intensively even during good years" for stabilizing a full employment economy and promoting growth. "Adjustment measures taken during booms," he said, "strengthen the economy's defenses during international slumps."[35] This harmonized completely with employers' desire to step up efforts to deal with scarcities, not unemployment.

Origins and Precursors

In 1951, during the Korean War boom, the Social Democratic government made moves to cut the budget of the labor market authorities, whose active labor market measures were as yet still very limited. Against the Social Democrats, SAF rose in the bureaucracy's defense. The employers' organization objected in particular to the government's plan to hand over to clueless schoolteachers the important job of counseling working class youths about their important vocational decisions. More important, they also fought to defend the jobs of special occupational counselors across the country whose task was to expand the female labor force. "It is of greatest importance, " SAF wrote, "that the potential manpower reserve consisting of non-gainfully employed women, is supplied to production." The confederation also objected to taking the government out of the business of locating and placing nannies (hemvård-arinnor). It wanted the agency to ration the scarce supply of nannies and give priority to families with mothers prepared to join the industrial workforce.[36]

In this, we see with all clarity the source of demands coming from outside the labor movement that Rehn alluded to. Other evidence from the 1940s and even earlier corroborate the idea that SAF shared with LO great responsibility for putting active labor market policy on the agenda. The cross-class alliance actually began congealing and solidifying as early as 1935 when SAF heartily welcomed the growth in number and budgets of local labor exchanges provided for in the legislative package including unemployment insurance (see chapter 11). Shortly thereafter, SAF director Gustaf Söderlund joined a government commission mandated to suggest means for dealing with the effects of technological rationalization. It recommended in 1939 a broad spectrum of active mobilization measures, including beefing up vocational training. It proposed government assistance with workers' moving and travel expenses and help for home-owning workers in selling their property without a prohibitive loss of equity. This last measure would help dissolve some of the immobilizing bonds of segmentalist practices in the forest product sector, where employers had often helped workers finance the building of homes.[37]

A major matter in the 1939 report was the question of national-level centralization of authority and funding for mobilization measures needed during periods of labor scarcity. The need, as Söderlund probably helped clarify, was for greater "inter-regional mobility" to supply expansionary industries with workers from industries in decline. The problem was that local authorities' desire to spend money on labor mobilization rose with unemployment but sagged in times of growing labor scarcity—as was already happening in the late 1930s.[38] Employers were far more interested in the reverse timing and could assert those interests more effectively over a centralized, national labor market bureaucracy.

War in Europe gave rise to widespread expectations that Sweden's economy would be disrupted by severe labor shortages and imbalances. Thus, the employers' confederation welcomed the major features of a compulsory service law (*tjänstepliktslagen*), which gave a central government commission the power to draft workers for essential industries. It also strengthened the power of the labor exchanges to direct the flow of scarce labor and subsidize workers' travel costs.[39] SAF happily took on joint administrative custody, along with LO, of the new wartime National Labor Market Commission (*Statens Arbetsmarknadskommission*, or SAK). This corporatist agency sought to tap isolated surpluses and thus break open bottlenecks in service of wartime solidarism. SAK's most important tasks included training and retraining of semi-skilled operatives for the engineering industry. It directed workers from the stalled construction, sawmill, and paper pulp industries into timber production where labor was scarce. Its most illiberal measures forced 19-year-old boys into logging in 1942 and required building contractors to use the labor exchange system to check the flow of labor into housing construction. Also, to bring SAF's perennial bête noire under control, it limited the flow of building materials into the industry. Most important, it rationed building permits, a practice that would continue after the war. SAF director Söderlund had a direct hand in its development.[40]

Thus, there were many precedents, supported and probably actively promoted by employers, for the mobility-enhancing and steering policies associated with LO economists Rehn and Meidner. Even the term "active labor market policy," now so strongly associated with them, seems to have been coined before they entered the picture. According to Rothstein, Gustav Möller used the term "active" to describe wartime mobilization measures already being contemplated on a cross-class basis in the late 1930s. Immediately after the war, a government commission predicted continued labor shortages, due in part to Sweden's low population growth. Bertil Kugelberg sat on the commission and endorsed the report, dissenting on only one administrative matter. Prepared at least two years before Rehn and Meidner took the baton, it called for "activization of labor market policy" and pursuing "a more active labor market policy."[41]

The report also recommended that continued wartime measures now be permanently coordinated under the centralized roof of the national Labor Market Board (*Arbetsmarknadsstyrelsen*, or AMS). It was to concentrate on supply-side labor mobilization measures. It advocated one active demand-side measure, advising industries about the best place to locate production given available manpower. The only passive measure it promoted was transitional government subsidies or orders for firms whose workers eventually need to be moved.[42] Matts Bergom Larsson, who later served as executive director of the engineering employers' association from 1951 to 1973, submitted SAF's official approval of the new agency. Larsson, representing SAF, also took a seat on the corporatist board.[43] In that capacity, he would come to play an important role in the innovation and administration of labor market policies over the years, particularly in the realm of vocational education and mobilization of women into gainful employment. In all probability, he also saw to it that, by rationing labor, the authority favored the dynamic engineering industry over sectors like textiles, though they too had their chronic labor supply problems.

SAF supported the administration of labor market policy on a joint or corporatist basis with LO from the very beginning. It vigorously advocated handing over authority to itself and LO for implementing the compulsory service law and then administering the wartime SAK.[44] Now, in the 1940s, SAF also supported the extraordinary departure from standard civil service rules for recruiting and hiring personnel for the large new bureaucracy. Most of the personnel would be hired straight from the unions, upon recommendation from its officials. In principle, people from the employer camp were also welcomed, but the government salaries could not compete. There was apparently little concern from employers, including engineering's Larsson, regarding low qualifications, patronage, and corruption. In internal deliberations about personnel, SAF never demanded recruitment according to formal qualifications and officially indicated approval of this decidedly unorthodox administrative arrangement. It seems SAF appreciated the recruitment of people with flexibility and first-hand practical knowledge to serve the rapidly changing labor needs of a dynamic manufacturing economy. Hence, when in 1951 the Social Democratic government, trying to save money, proposed shifting vocational counseling functions over to schoolteachers, Larsson, speaking for SAF, objected strongly.[45]

Administered Pricing, Administrative Rationing

In 1956, shipbuilder and VF leader Nils Holmström explained the country's rampant wage drift, which accounted for roughly half of all wage increases in the next two decades, the way any economist would: the result of "a lack of balance between demand and supply in the labor market." That is why employers wanted to, and did, pay more than they were supposed to. The relatively moderate increases negotiated the two previous years and the subsequent heavy demand for Swedish goods, labor shortages, and high inflation had produced what another employer leader called "overfull employment." So untenable was the situation, according to Holmström, still speaking like an economist, that there were only two logical choices available. One was to let Swedish workers' already high wages rise at the expense of competitive problems in international markets and higher unemployment. This would not increase the supply of labor, however, as cement magnate Ernst Wehtje pointed out. The other was to continue holding wages down and "ration labor."[46]

Sweden's Social Democratic labor movement chose rationing, not wage increases. Active labor market policy, as conceived by Rehn and Meidner, and administered by AMS, was in some regard a rationing system. It was intended to allocate scarce labor across the Swedish economy. The supply and allocation of labor had to be administered to reduce inflationary pressures associated with wage restraint under very high levels of employment. Labor was to be moved and trained to open supply bottlenecks that would otherwise set off a chain reaction of inflationary wage increases. Administrative pricing of labor gave rise to administrative rationing.

In 1956, SAF economist Karl-Olof Faxén pontificated that an employers' organization would have difficulty supporting the planned and centrally administered rationing of labor in a labor-scarce economy. Favoring certain firms and sectors over others in the procurement of workers was simply too divisive.[47] Within a few years, however, it was clear that the employers' confederation could more than happily live with an innovative administrative alternative to market allocation that the Social Democratic government was offering. SAF, after all, had actively set up the centralized system for administered pricing that made rationing logical. The rationing authorities even showed systematic favoritism, promoting a developmental strategy behind which there was fundamental cross-class agreement: expansion of export-oriented industry, especially engineering. On the AMS board sat Matts Bergom Larsson, executive director of VF, the engineering association. This most powerful of SAF's sectoral associations prohibited its members from recruiting labor through advertising and strongly recommended they turn instead to the system of labor exchanges under the AMS.[48]

In sum, the alliance of forces behind solidaristic wage policy made common cause behind the active labor market policy needed to manage the disequilibrium caused by that same wage policy. In a book of essays he published in 1968, SAF director Giesecke noted the great and lasting cross-class unity in Sweden that marked labor market policy. "When speaking of state collaboration with industry," he said, "it is worth emphasizing that few areas are more crucial for government efforts than this particular one." Lars-Gunnar Albåge, one of SAF's chief negotiators, argued the same year that labor market policy ought to be seen as "employers' ally."[49]

Once the alliance between SAF and LO put active labor market policy into full-fledged practice—against the temporary resistance of Social Democratic politicians—SAF continued to support the Social Democratic policy against attack from right-wing politicians. Late into the 1960s SAF's labor market policy expert Gunnar Lindström blasted the Conservative Party's attempts to discredit Social Democratic labor market policy. They "militate totally against our interests" (*helt strider mot våra intressen*), he said.[50] This was not the first time that organized capital in Sweden found the Conservative Party a bit too reactionary. The same thing happened on the issue of a major pension reform, shortly after its passage in 1959.

The 1959 Pension Reform

The Social Democratic government's last great social insurance reform in the building of the Swedish welfare state passed the Riskdag by a single vote in 1959. Called the "General Supplementary Pension" (*Allmänna Tillägspensionen*, or ATP), it finally guaranteed all wage and salary earners a retirement income commensurate with the standard of living they grew accustomed to while gainfully employed (approximately 65 percent of former wage or salary earnings, inclusive of People's Pensions). But because of the reform's narrow margin of victory, the Conservative Party vowed not to give up the fight. The following winter, party leader Jarl Hjalmarsson vowed, if given the chance at power after new elections, to "rip up ATP."[51]

A strange and surprising thing then happened, as recorded in SAF Director Bertil Kugelberg's notes and other documents. Instead of an appreciative rally of business support, Hjalmarsson's promise stirred "great unrest." Numerous written protests "streamed in" to the Conservative Party. Many companies refused to send their usual contributions to the party's campaign chests, or in some cases postponed their decisions. Stora Kopparberg, one of Sweden's largest corporations, and an important part of the vast Wallenberg empire, was one of them. The following year companies showed a continuing "strong disinclination" to make large contributions.[52]

Gustaf Söderlund, SAF's executive director during much of the formative 1930s and 1940s, and now executive director of Skandinaviska Banken, entered personal reservations about his party's position.[53] Tore Browaldh, Handelsbanken's executive director, who had been vice director at SAF from 1951 to 1954, rued aloud to other bankers, industrialists, and politicians that "we have nagged so much about ATP." (In his final year at SAF Browaldh had delightedly accepted Rudolf Meidner's invitation to serve as an "opponent" at the LO economist's doctoral dissertation defense.) Years later, Browaldh wrote in his memoirs that "I never could understand the ferocious outcry against ATP from the Conservatives."[54]

Party and employer leaders met to sort out the "widespread dissatisfaction" and "distaste" in business circles about the party's intentions to turn back the clock on pension reform. Conservative leaders were naturally bewildered, having once received backing from the employers' confederation and extra financial support in an ATP referendum campaign. Now, indignant Conservatives watched in spring 1960 as SAF employers dropped the fight for a private, collectively bargained option allowed in the law for white-collar workers. According to future Conservative leader Gunnar Heckscher, had the party known earlier that industry would suddenly regard the ATP reform as "not that bad" (*inte så farlig*), then it "would not have been such a hard opponent."[55]

What makes these postreform events so strange is that the 1959 pension reform, even more than the unemployment insurance law of 1934, seems to have come about through a political victory of labor over capital and Left over Right. All important accounts of the ATP reform portray it that way, with apparently good reason. They focus, for example, on a highly unusual national referendum in October 1957, in which Left and Right, financed respectively by LO and SAF, mobilized unprecedented resources for and against compulsory earnings-related old-age insurance. In April 1958, the three bourgeois parties linked arms as a majority in parliamentary defeat of Social Democratic legislation, which had achieved plurality but not majority support in the referendum. The Social Democrats therefore called an election in June, which again gave them favorable but inconclusive results. The final legislation squeaked by in May 1959 with a mere one-vote majority in the lower chamber—only with the help of Communist votes and a defection by a working-class unionist in the Liberal Party.[56] Thus, according to the current consensus, ATP was a brilliant move on the part of Social Democrats risking capitalist wrath in order to gain an important new constituency. In fact, it helped Social Democrats mobilize roughly 200,000 apathetic voters in the 1958 election, among them significant numbers of white-collar workers. It therefore allowed them to abandon their traditional alliance with the Agrarian Party, whose rural electorate was dwindling, and shift its attention to a new and growing support base.[57]

During the referendum campaign and beyond, parties to the right of the Social Democrats warned that centralized government control of pension fund capital was a step on the way to socialism. Some on the Left accused employers—unjustly, in fact—of wishing to deny workers income maintenance and therefore material security in their old age.[58] Union officials were so caught up in the political campaign for an all-encompassing earnings-related pension that in fall 1957 construction employers would experience the smoothest wage negotiations since World War I's building bust.[59] Intense distributional struggle in the labor market was displaced to the political sphere, it seems, where the organizational and electoral resources of the labor movement, backed by the labor confederation mobilized as a huge vote-getting machine, was to rule the day. All of this was as class politics is supposed to be.

But a friendly calm quickly settled over Swedish politics and class relations after three years of polarization, stalemate, and the Social Democrats' narrow and apparently fragile victory. Instead of rancor and distrust, extraordinary cross-class harmony marked the ensuing decade. In summer 1960, a witty and surprisingly well-informed political cartoon by "Bertila" in *Aftonbladet*, a major daily, depicted ATP as a hefty and hardy toddler proudly on display by Papa Tage Erlander, the prime minister. Uncle Bertil (Kugelberg), the mirthfully entertained uncle, gets a severe scolding from "Aunt Hjalla" (Hjalmarsson), who berates him for abandoning his convictions and falling sway to the repulsive nephew's charms.[60]

As the cartoonist had somehow learned, Kugelberg led employer efforts to sort out problems between the party and industry and to urge the Conservative Party to accept the pension legislation. Like Söderlund before him, he had been recruited by employer statesman J. Sigfrid Edström for being a team player (*en samarbetets man*) in relations with labor. The well-tempered Kugelberg was even approached as a possible replacement for party leader Hjalmarsson in March 1961, but declined the honor. It was then offered to the relatively centrist Heckscher, who was "on the same wavelength as younger industrialists," according to the even more centrist Conservative Browaldh. Years later, Heckscher would write a blandly positive book on the welfare state.[61]

The Tectonics of Solidarism: Reform Blockage and Breakthrough

The ATP reform was a seismic event of great consequence in the history of the Swedish welfare state. The raucous politics of polarization before and eerie calm afterward can only be understood in light of a distinct flaw in the industrial relations system. In a nutshell the argument is this: SAF's unilateral solidarism applied the brake with great force on growth of individual company pensions for blue-collar workers through the 1940s and well into the early 1950s. Suppression of this growth, combined with obstacles and delays (described later) in arranging service pensions through multi-employer collective bargaining, brought on the political earthquake. But instead of shaking the cross-class solidaristic consensus at its foundations, the political earthquake simply adjusted, as it were, a misalignment of labor market conditions in a way that would help maintain the consensus in the years to come. The Social Democrats benefitted politically by preserving good relations with capital, not just in acquiring white-collar support.

A majority of SAF's member firms did not provide company pensions in the early 1950s. Virtually all larger ones did, however, and because of them, a majority of workers employed by SAF members had at least some prospect of receiving benefits on top of the People's Pension. But they rarely amounted to more than a meager 400 to 600 crowns a year, and then only for long years of service.[62] Major engineering employers had endeavored since the 1938 to hold down their vestiges of "loyal servant pensions" (*trotjänarpensioner*) at identical levels and promote the same for the rest of the sector, to restrict the use of pension increases as a device to attract labor. For example, in 1944, the six leading firms (of the so-called Directors' Club) closed ranks to limit their gratuity pensions to the rather paltry sum of 400 to 500 crowns—in line with SAF recommendations in 1940. This policy preserved but encapsulated the small, alien vestiges of segmentalism inside the larger solidaristic system. The People's Pension reform of 1946, which employers had supported, helped justify keeping the figure frozen at that low level by allowing no more than that amount to be deducted from income used to establish eligibility for means-tested supplements. By 1951, at least one major employer recognized that this provision in the law imposed an undesirable "stalemate" (*dödläge*) in company pensions.[63]

The effective freeze on company pensions and slow expansion of the flat-rate People's Pension meant that blue-collar retiree income in the latter part of the 1940s and early 1950s lagged far behind growth in income from gainful employment. Meanwhile, private income-related pensions for white-collar workers, both company-based and collectively bargained, grew apace, adding insult to injury to blue-collar workers organized in LO and voting loyally for the Social Democratic party. But while solidarism, combined with existing pension law, arrested the growth of company pensions, it did not in principle foreclose a collectively bargained superannuation system. A negotiated system could have imposed all the uniformity solidarism required.

In practice, however, SAF's unilateral efforts on behalf of solidarism also blocked a negotiated, multi-employer correction of the distributional misalignment. In private conversation with SAF's Kugelberg, LO's Arne Geijer voiced regret in 1957 that big steel employers had not gone for the decidedly unsolidaristic suggestion he had once made, as head of Metall sometime before 1956, to raise their company pensions to 1500 crowns. Had they done so, Geijer rued privately, "we would never have gotten into the trying situation we now find ourselves in." By this, he meant the intensely politicized and polarized debate surrounding the referendum.[64] These increases would, he implied, have induced other workers across industry to start demanding similar increases and thus propel the issue onto the centralized and solidaristic collective bargaining agenda—before it became politicized. Once he got roped into the political debate, Geijer put the blame on employers. "The employer in this land," he said, is responsible for "turning social issues into legislative issues."[65]

In the absence of strong "benefits rivalry" that stronger benefits drift would have unleashed, demands from workers remained spotty and weak. LO leader Axel Strand tried, for a while it seems, to persuade union leaders in various sectors to take interest in the cause of negotiated multi-employer pensions. Metall's Geijer responded appropriately, while most of the rest preferred to concentrate on wages instead. As Hydén put it in 1953, "Workers, as is well known, aim to get the largest possible cash wages, so pensions have not been a burning problem." Had workers pressured harder, employers would not have put up principled resistance. As Kugelberg put it to Liberal Party leader Ohlin in 1957, SAF had informed LO that "it was a matter of indifference whether a certain increase in productivity was taken out in the form of increased wages or in the form of pension premiums," adding "it was a position we had taken a long time ago, and we still stand by it."[66]

Thus, none of the issues that blocked the road to a collectively bargained pension system was ideological or clearly win-lose in nature for capital or labor. Instead, interest diversity and tactical confusion within employer and union camps were responsible. Out of both sides emanated mixed and confused signals. Up to 1951, according to SAF's social policy expert Hydén, on the occasions when unions did bring up the idea of pension improvements, employers put them off "with reference to anticipated general old-age insurance"—in other words, legislation.[67] Employers' initial reactions to the 1951 Åkesson Commission report, which called for compulsory legislation, had after all been generally favorable and certainly far from hostile. Indeed, Erik Brodén, SAF's representative in the commission, explicitly endorsed a statutory solution. He had also been an enthusiast for the earlier health insurance and sick pay legislation.[68]

Though SAF initially raised no strong objections to the idea of legislation, they began upon reflection to suffer an acute case of jitters about some implications of the Åkesson 1951 report. The question of funding, especially, gave them pause. But they could not summon the necessary unity to throw their weight behind a collectively bargained alternative. Only strong worker pressure for immediate results could have forced them to overcome their heterogeneity and unite behind a viable initiative. But the only impulse came, as mentioned, from Geijer at Metall. In 1953, he signaled to Matts Larsson of VF that it might be good to head off more expensive legislation with an LO-SAF agreement. Because legislation under debate called for the accumulation of pension money in large funds, money otherwise available for wage increases would be siphoned off. A peak agreement, presumably on a pay-as-you-go system, would leave more room for wage increases.[69]

In 1954, SAF finally issued a set of principles, though hardly a proposal, for a bargained scheme. Despite the low-risk nature of the vague scheme envisaged (no protection of pension benefits against inflation), its sectoral associations remained so split on details and strategy that SAF could only present it to LO "for discussion," not negotiation. A classic case, this was, of too little, too late. Both sides' lack of resolve now allowed politicians to proceed with legislative efforts, even as Geijer engaged in continuing discussions with VF about a collectively bargained solution.[70]

In short, because LO as a whole failed to push aggressively for a bargained solution, SAF failed to summon unity behind a good proposal. And because of SAF's ambivalent, irresolute, and ineffectual behavior in the face of looming legislative action, both sides allowed Social Democratic politicians to proceed, for potential electoral payoff, with their legislative ambitions. Politicization and polarization became irreversible when the Liberal and Conservative parties, in a tactical move they would later regret, badgered the reluctant Social Democratic government into scheduling a general referendum in October 1957.

The referendum's three-part formulation gave the Social Democratic leadership—and compulsory legislation—a plurality and therefore symbolic, if not

conclusive, victory over the collectively bargained or individualistic private solutions. Geijer, having taken over leadership of LO in 1956, vehemently argued
against holding the referendum, still expressing regret to Kugelberg that big
companies had honored their unilateral solidaristic commitments by not going
ahead and individually raising their pensions. The day after the referendum
Geijer told Kugelberg "It's terrible what a mess politicians can make" (det är
förfärligt vad politikerna kan ställa till). The following month, Geijer still hoped
for some way for LO and SAF to get the politicians out of the picture at least in
crafting the details of the legislation. SAF, in deference to the Conservatives
and Liberals, who had harbored false hopes that the referendum and elections
would go their way, chose not to meet officially with Geijer.[71] In public, therefore, Geijer had to present a different face. Swept up in the dynamics of polarizing electoral politics, he was now a class warrior. But behind the scenes, he
could still play a role in keeping the legislative result within the bounds of the
solidaristic cross-class consensus.

ATP as Solidaristic Reform:
The Uniformity Issue

In one important regard, employers recognized that legislation was superior for
achieving uniformity across the labor market, a central solidaristic concern.
To that extent, there was little Geijer had to do to make sure that employers
would be satisfied. SAF board member Nils Danielsen, a leading figure in the
steel industry, wanted a centralized and uniform solution one way or another,
even if had to be legislated, to "prevent the abuse of the benefit by exploiting it
in competition over labor."[72] In 1955, Sven Hydén predicted that "a good many
of the association's members" would probably find a legislative solution satis-
factory in view of the fact "that it will even include the unorganized firms"—
no doubt to eliminate undesirable competition over labor.[73] The problem at the
time of acute labor scarcity and wage drift was, to be sure, not chiseling by the
unorganized employer. (For example big Swedish shipbuilders had begun subcontracting out production to small, unorganized firms in the 1950s who routinely offered higher wages than the big shipbuilders were allowed to pay.[74])
The same logic explains why Kugelberg harbored doubts, recorded in his memoirs, about the merits of allowing variations in pension levels in the collective
bargaining approach that SAF officially, but irresolutely, favored. Only one association openly advocated unsolidaristic differentiation as a recruitment device—electrical contractors in the trade-sheltered building industry, where
extra costs could easily be shifted onto others.[75]

Once publicly tied down to legislation as the road to adequate pensions,
Geijer's arguments rang with solidaristic themes. He argued that because
much of the labor force—and the Social Democratic party's constituency—
was organized outside SAF's ambit, a negotiated solution would not cover
them. In one-on-one discussions with Kugelberg, he argued that legislation
was in SAF's own interests, echoing sentiments uttered in SAF's own debates,

including those of Kugelberg. "If anything," Geijer apparently told him, "it should be an advantage that the pension issue is automatically solved uniformly across the board." That a mandatory and therefore uniform pension system could really be so downright unappealing to SAF was not, he told Kugelberg, particularly credible—a point Kugelberg confirmed in his memoirs. In any event, as he told the employer leader in late 1957, compulsory and uniform legislation had become virtually nonnegotiable. He reassured the employer leader, however, saying "on the other hand, concerning the details of the mandate, practically everything is up for discussion."[76] In short: the only nonnegotiable component was something that served both SAF's solidarism and the Social Democratic Party's larger constituency.

By now SAF too was blocked by its loyalties to the bourgeois parties' calculated electoral strategy against legislation to admit there was any silver lining in the legislative approach or openly express confidence that negotiations on legislative details could lead to a happy conclusion. Both Kugelberg and Geijer now had to assume a confrontational posture that neither wanted, since politicians had hijacked the issue and made a terrible mess of things.[77] So it was the labor movement alone that advanced the solidaristic argument for uniform legislation. For example, when Bertil Ohlin of the Liberal Party proposed an opt-out provision (*dispositivitet*) for individuals or bargaining units, top SAF leaders Kugelberg, Sven Schwartz, Curt-Steffan Giesecke, and Ernst Wehtje reasoned privately among themselves that this would be a "rather unpleasant" thing. "To conduct negotiations under those circumstances would be very difficult," they concluded among themselves.[78] Publicly, Torsten Nilsson, minister of Social Affairs, expressed one concern that had probably been on their minds. Unorganized sectors of the labor market "could give employees a not insubstantially higher wage in exchange for waiving their pension rights." This would be especially tempting to younger workers, objected Per-Edvin Sköld and Gunnar Sträng, former and current finance ministers. Their high wage increases would then complicate restraint by other workers whose employers had to pay into pensions. Such an arrangement, recalled Minister Erlander, from an astute solidaristic perspective, would have been "an extremely bothersome thing with regard to organizations in the labor market."[79]

In other words, organized wage solidarity across firms competing intensely over low-skill, entry-level labor would be disturbed by an opt-out possibility. That was the same worry raised in SAF's own discussions, especially by the textile and garment employers, with regard to a pension system constructed through collective bargaining—which, by its very nature, allowed for opting out. The leadership of the Textile Employers' Association warned that the association could suffer severe damage from the resignation of a significant number of members wishing to avoid the cost of pensions. The bolters would then be able to use extra wage increases "to continue competing for manpower."[80] Ultimately, the Social Democrats included an opt-out provision in the law, but available only on a negotiated, collective basis with centralized unions, and probably to appeal to the bourgeois parties and the growing white-collar unions, not employers. After the law was passed, employers did not push strongly for use of the option, which was never exercised. No doubt they feared the effects of differentiation on solidaristic management of the labor market. Also, the white-collar unions discovered that legislation actually offered a better deal than their existing schemes, leaving more money behind for salary increases.

ATP as Solidaristic Reform: The Mobility Issue

Employers probably also recognized that uniform legislation was superior to collectively bargained pensions for promoting healthy labor mobility, another key solidaristic concern. Here we find another explanation for their remarkably supportive reaction after passage of ATP and reason to think that Geijer and other Social Democratic reformers could proceed without fear of disturbing the cross-class solidaristic consensus that stabilized their domination of Sweden's political system.

As we know from the debate about unemployment insurance in 1934, employers in Sweden strove to foster and preserve a high degree of healthy labor mobility in the labor scarce economy for both seasonal and structural reasons. The Åkesson Commission's mandate insisted flatly that the system "should be devoted to fostering mobility in the labor market."[81] According to Prime Minister Tage Erlander's memoirs, LO's Per Holmberg criticized the collectively bargained route for generating "inadequate mobility in the labor market." Holmberg probably meant that benefits might be uneven and hard to transfer from job to job—and thus create a lock-in effect.[82]

Indeed, SAF fully affirmed the principle of vesting or portability of pension benefits (*oantastbarhet*) advocated in the Åkesson Commission's 1951 report. Heretofore many manual workers risked losing their faithful servant pensions if they changed jobs or their employers shut down. Thus, nonvested pensions reinforced what might be called structural immobility. Capital and labor alike agreed on the need to gently uproot and redirect manpower from some sectors, for example, the forest products industry where mechanization was proceeding rapidly, to regions with sectors like engineering seeking to enlarge their labor force. More structural mobility would reduce the pathologies of what might be called frictional mobility (job hopping within sectors). Without greater structural mobility, the dynamic, expansionary sectors faced stronger temptation to use higher wages to poach workers in local labor markets and thus increase frictional mobility.

As early as 1944, employer views on the value of portable pensions had begun shifting radically. Fritiof Söderbäck, SAF's executive director, declared in discussions with LO leaders that vesting was "something I regard as one of the most important features one must demand of a rational pension system." SAF chairman Söderlund agreed, calling for a centralized system negotiated with the unions, for whom vesting was also nonnegotiable. By 1953, according to Hydén, employers were fully converted to the idea "that long-term employment in industry in and of itself ought to bring with it greater old-age security . . . regardless of whether the worker had worked for one or for several employers."[83] According to SAF's and its chemical group's board member Sven Hammarskiöld (director of Sweden's largest sugar producer), vesting would relieve employers of their "psychological" inhibition against shedding workers who might, with some looking and perhaps help, find more suitable employment. Thus, all SAF sectoral associations signed on to the principle.[84] Though the mobility promoting effects of vesting could fairly easily have been achieved through peak-level LO-SAF negotiations, legislation at least would do a better job across the entire labor market and thus more completely serve the needs of organized employers.

Within Capitalism's Bounds: The Capital Control and Supply Issue

Though initially favorable to the idea of legislation recommended in the 1951 Åkesson Commission report, in part because it promised uniformity and vesting, SAF quickly pulled back when worries spread among the country's capitalists about another matter—the large central funds that were to be created. Statements from the more radical elements in the Social Democratic Party about what the money could be used for no doubt fed the anxiety. As SAF's social policy expert Sven Hydén put it, "What employers fear first and foremost is the power that will fall into the state's hands."[85]

Industrial employers fretted in particular about losing access to capital at a time when the central bank's restrictive credit policy, accompanying and because of its low-interest rate policy, was rationing credit among competing users, some of them with considerable political clout.[86] While collective bargaining might have had some bothersome deficiencies in the area of uniformity and mobility, legislation posed profound risks from the standpoint of control over capital. A collectively bargained solution promised more secure control. Employers in general probably agreed with banker Jacob Wallenberg and publisher Tor Bonnier that if it were possible to get a legislated pension system without any funds at all, a compromise with the government and continued Social Democratic rule were well "worth thinking about." Encouraging signals from Arne Geijer, who was favorable to collective bargaining and against funding, probably encouraged SAF leaders to hold out against legislation. The SAF board understood that Geijer himself had not been pleased with the idea of building up funds, for it would tap away additional income otherwise available for higher wages.[87]

Ultimately, however, SAF joined a consensus that emerged across the board—assisted in no small way by the Liberal economist and politician Bertil Ohlin—that an accumulation of funds was necessary. Personal retirement savings, he calculated, would decline as a result of pension legislation, and the resulting shortfall in capital available for investment would have to come out of compulsory savings. The burning question, of course, was about who could get their hands on these funds. The question did not burn bridges between LO and SAF, however. In fact, LO Chairman Geijer attempted to resolve the issue in a way that appeased employers, allowing them to accept the legislation and reap its solidaristic benefits.

In their private conversations, Geijer repeatedly reassured Kugelberg that as far as pension funds were concerned, LO, like SAF, did not want a fund system controlled by the government, "regardless of its political color." It was imperative, Geijer insisted, "that industry is given disposition of the resources," and therefore he favored rules that gave companies a right to borrow from them "along the lines SAF is contemplating."[88] To be sure, not all business figures were completely satisfied. Banker Ernfrid Browaldh (Tore's more right-wing father) dismissed as "pure utopia" any notion that the funds would be used only to benefit industry. Liberal leader Ohlin, likewise, had the impression that the labor leader "was bluffing to a great extent" on the frequent occasions he insisted that industry would have privileged access.[89] For Kugelberg, however, the labor confederation's chairman was a man of his word. Kugelberg's memoirs exude trust and admiration not just for Geijer but other Swedish labor leaders as well.[90]

In the end, Geijer made sure that an automatic right for firms to borrow from their payments into the fund was written into the law. He kept a watchful eye on the work of a government commission set up in April 1957, including union and business representatives, and headed by central bank chief Erik Åsbrink, to draw up rules for administering the funds. When, at one point, the group reached an impasse on the fund issue, Geijer informed Kugelberg that he had instructed Rudolf Meidner, the LO economist on the commission, "that the way we fix that detail is not something that can block agreement."[91]

As the Åsbrink Commission was continuing its work under Geijer's watchful eye, Geijer repeated to Kugelberg that it was "most essential" that the funds not get in politicians' hands. In that regard, he added, "LO has exactly the same interest as the employers" (*precis samma intresse som arbetsgivarna*). Thereupon, Geijer exclaimed, according to Kugelberg's notes on the conversation, "You should have been there and heard what we told the government!" In the same conversation, Geijer expressed to Kugelberg his surprise and consternation that the commission had agreed on seating three government representatives, instead of only one, on each of the three boards to oversee the three separate funds. He had apparently instructed Meidner to insist that only one politician share representation with a crushing majority of three employer and three union representatives.[92] It was the leftward sliding banker and former SAF executive Tore Browaldh who had accepted the setup for the sake of unanimity. On this matter, Geijer chided Kugelberg for SAF's "great oversight" in failing to intervene.[93]

Wasting little time, the Åsbrink Commission produced a unanimous report in January 1958. It drew up the designs for administering the system legislated the following year, on 14 May 1959.[94] During the intervening election, SAF maintained a curiously low profile, despite the centrality of the pension issue in the campaign. Only the Åsbrink Commission's work can explain why. As Kugelberg understood it, the fact that the Social Democrats did not go even further than they did to assuage employer fears was the fear of losing Communist votes in other legislative matters. Collaboration between SAF and LO even continued in January 1960, when the law first took force, to negotiate rules for the three ATP fund boards to ensure that industry could dispose of adequate capital from them. Torsten Nilsson, minister of social affairs, reassured Kugelberg during a lunch at the ministry that the government stood behind these efforts and that if existing rules were not good enough, they would be improved.[95]

In light of the trustful communication and cooperation between the LO and SAF leaders, it is no surprise that Kugelberg would lead the chorus of critics inside the Conservative Party after it promised to tear up the new pension system. In January 1961, when high-level discussions continued about the Conservative Party's controversial threat to repeal the legislation, Bertil Kugelberg reported to an assembly of fourteen top party, banking, industry, and employer figures that

[a]ll the gentlemen here are well aware that SAF has taken up the question of future capital supply to industry with LO, KF [the Cooperative Association] and TCO [the white-collar union confederation]. We have received extraordinarily clear messages from all three indicating that the ATP funds ought to benefit industry and not be sluiced over to the state. I myself believe that they are fully sincere when they say that. I myself am convinced of the reality that the Social Democratic and union representatives on the fund boards will do their best to ensure that the money benefits private enterprise.

He concluded saying, "And therefore I am disturbed by the idea that the Conservatives should simultaneously adopt proposals in the Riksdag that could infect things politically."[96]

Ultimately, the rules governing the ATP system largely satisfied Swedish industry's demand for privileged access to capital from the funds and for restrictions that prevented their abuse as an instrument of socialist control. Banker Tore Browaldh and Conservative leader Heckscher both agreed that private savings levels appeared unaffected any time after the reform.[97] Three funds were created instead of one probably to dispel the fears of the industrialists and bankers. Roughly a third of their lending went to the private sector, excluding housing, while between 35 and 50 percent went toward financing public and private sector housing into the 1970s. Corporations were more or less automatically allowed to borrow up to 50 percent of the fees they paid the preceding year if a bank assumed the risks of these "retroverse loans." The funds could also lend directly against a promissory note to banks and other financial intermediaries, who would then pass the money on to industry. Finally, they could purchase bonds issued by corporations. Because purchase of equity and direct lending to firms was disallowed, the funds were denied the opportunity to exercise discretionary influence over the corporate sector.[98]

In conclusion, the final result was legislation that conformed squarely with capitalists' demand for continued domination of industrial finance and investment while at the same time serving employers' solidaristic labor market interests.[99] The polarized political debate had resulted not from fundamental distributional or ideological conflicts between organized labor and organized capital. By taking over, in Kugelberg's view, politicians led things down a "dead-end street," generating the kind of mass electoral politics that locked the parties into uncompromising positions. In short, "no one wished to lose face," he observed in the thick of it all.[100] The nation's most powerful banker, Marcus Wallenberg, Jr., agreed, saying that bourgeois politicians had "tied themselves down somewhat too hard" to an uncompromising position. Geijer, the top labor leader, agreed, saying that politicians had caused everything to "run aground."[101]

Åke Elmstedt, a leading SAF official, came to a similar conclusion in his retrospective account. Once the issue became politicized, it had been too tricky, Elmstedt argues, for SAF to "go behind the backs of the parties" in efforts to work out a compromise with the labor movement.[102] In fact, as mentioned before, the Conservatives and Liberals had blocked SAF from doing just that in 1957. LO too had been paralyzed by the issue's politicization, pulling an initially reluctant Geijer into the process, and tying him down to the party's legislative strategy. The events and heated rhetoric of the time therefore easily blind us to the cross-class interests that the labor movement responded to in the actual legislation crafted. They also blind us to the fact that the labor movement continued to honor capitalist control over industry—in the realm of investment as well as, in the past, of management. The highly conflictual process was one whose appearances did not square accurately with the reality of the result—cross-class consensus.[103]

To understand the entire dramatic arc of the 1959 pension reform, therefore, one must grasp how employer solidarism contributed to the blockage of change and seismic buildup of tensions; how the Social Democratic reformers contributed to the sudden relaxation of class tensions both by serving solidarism and preserving capitalist control; and why, because of employers' favorable response, Sweden's most right-wing party adjusted its position leftward. Gøsta Esping-Andersen is mistaken in arguing that the reform battle reinstated "with utmost clarity the essential ideological differences between the two political blocs" after a period marked by the blurring of ideologies.[104] Electorally, the Social Democratic Party came out ahead, having engineered a realignment of white-collar support in its favor. But there was more to their success than that. By reaffirming the labor movement's commitment to employers' interests, capitalist satisfaction, not just white-collar support, probably helped the party maintain its continued domination in Swedish politics.

Other Theories about the
Swedish Welfare State

At each step of the way, from the 1930s through the 1950s, employers either welcomed each major new piece of the Swedish welfare state or rather quickly dropped their opposition after its passage. In the latter instances, they came to understand that its components either contributed to or proved entirely benign to their collective interests in solidaristic governance of the labor market. Equally important, none of the legislation came to be seen as the nose of the socialist camel under the capitalists' tent. By and large, Social Democratic reformers acted cautiously, aligning reforms with employers' interests and keeping within the bounds of the Swedish variety of capitalism. In Sweden, as in the United States, employers quietly endorsed the main components of the welfare state, not out of resignation but out of self-interest. In Sweden, the historical facts suggest, the enduring political success of the Social Democratic labor movement and the durability of its famous social and labor market policy reforms would not have been possible had they been imposed against the interests of capital. Most theoretical treatments of the Swedish social and labor market policy implicitly or explicitly suggest otherwise.

Institutions and the Balance
of Class Power

Unlike the literature on the American welfare state, most of what has been said about Swedish labor and social policy attributes its development to the exceptional power of its labor movement. In Sweden, "more than in any other European nation," according to Esping-Andersen, the "working class has been capable of initiating and imposing its policy preferences." Thus, the power of the Swedish working class "is the key to the evolution of Sweden's postwar political economy." Even SAF's favorite of all Social Democratic initiatives, active labor market policy, he argues, "was only possible due to the extraordinary labor market powers of the union movement."[105]

Bo Rothstein, whose influential and more historically rich analyses of Swedish social policy fit more generally in the institutionalist camp, also incorporates the balance of power logic and its characteristic equivalency premise about employer interests against the welfare state. Writing about employers' participation in corporatist or shared administration of welfare and labor market policies, Rothstein argues, for example, that there is "no reason why a major capitalist organization should occupy itself with administrating the implementation of any Social Democratic welfare policy" other than a labor movement so strong that, one way or the other, it is going to enforce its policies. "Confronted with such an opponent," he says, "business has had to choose between Scylla and Charybdis, to take part in the administration of Social Democratic policies and thereby legitimate them in order to gain a minor influence in the stage of implementation, or to refuse to participate, thereby risking a more severe implementation of the policies in question, maybe to the point of threatening fundamental capitalist interests."[106]

At another point on the spectrum is Hugh Heclo's institutionalism, which rejects the class power argument and the equivalency premise along with it. Interestingly, Heclo's comparative analysis of Sweden and Great Britain strongly inspired Skocpol's subsequent analysis of the New Deal. His historical analysis of unemployment and pension reform in the two countries suggested that private interests explain little about the shape and timing of social policy. Though not entirely irrelevant, he found their interests too unpredictable and manipulable to matter greatly. In other words, "neither capital nor labor, employers nor employees have consistently been on one side or the other of the question of an expansionary social policy."[107] Heclo attempts to explain this unpredictability by turning to the autonomous role of state actors in persuading irresolute economic actors that they should like the legislation public officials autonomously promote.

On Britain's groundbreaking unemployment insurance law of 1911, for example, Heclo writes that "[a]s for the interest groups, it was a question of the government department lobbying to persuade them rather than vice versa." While the attitudes of the unions was admittedly "most crucial," it was not the moving force, for government officials had to undertake "a vigorous campaign . . . to obtain union agreement."[108] In Sweden, he correctly notes, employers accepted all major aspects of the 1935 pension reform, and in 1946 the Conservative Party, which they were closely aligned with, even favored a pension plan that was more expensive than the alternative initially favored by leading Social Democrats. Heclo leaves the economic reasoning for these seemingly counterintuitive positions entirely unexamined, implicitly declaring private sectors' interests too labile, amorphous, and manipulable to be a reliable source of explanation. Instead, the dynamics of policy legacies were more important: "the momentum from past policy" decisively shaped new policies sought and achieved by public officials.[109] In short, private interests were simply overwhelmed by state officials and policy experts with their autonomous problems, ideals, ambitions, and powers.

By and large, Heclo's state-centric institutionalism, though drawing on research in Sweden, has had more influence on analysis of the United States.[110] His analysis of Sweden, by fully downplaying the role of economic interests, could never have fulfilled a widely recognized need for illuminating class analysis. The biggest influence along those lines has been the balance of power analysis associated most of all with Gøsta Esping-Andersen and Walter Korpi. Often in collaboration with Esping-Andersen, Korpi's seminal work attributes the success of the Swedish labor movement to its superior resources in the labor market and electoral politics. The dramatic decline of industrial conflict in and after the 1930s, he contends, resulted "not from better consensus [samförstånd] between the two sides," but from a change of strategy allowed by a shift in the power balance between classes.[111] In other words, the labor movement displaced its efforts in distributional conflict to the political sphere. With its superior position in the Riksdag—guaranteed in part by the power resources of unions acting as an electoral machine—it could prevail over capital on redistributive social and labor policy without the disruption of strikes. But the fact that the dramatic decline in strikes occurred in the early 1930s, well before major welfare developments occurred in the 1940s and 1950s, weakens the historical plausibility of Korpi's analysis.[112]

In a subsidiary and essentially contradictory elaboration, Korpi attributes Sweden's "historic compromise" of the 1930s to a cross-class alliance including a part of capital, not simply a shift in the power balance in labor's favor at capital's expense. Here, however, he attributes labor's success to an alliance with domestic business sectors benefitting from Keynesian expansionary policy. SAF, he argues, was dominated by "home market industries." Thus director Gustaf Söderlund represented the doves of industry against the hawks of the export sector who "were against [the] compromise with Social Democrats and LO" in the 1930s.[113]

For this argument, Korpi draws, like many others, on a work by historian Sven-Anders Söderpalm, who asserted without evidence that the big export-oriented engineering employers' political activity, coordinated by the "Directors' Club," was motivated by their need to counteract the home-market–friendly policies of the Social Democrats.[114] This notion that export-oriented capitalists were overshadowed in SAF and an opponent of compromise is mistaken, to say the least. SAF and VF Chairman J. Sigfrid Edström ran ASEA, the country's leading export-oriented electrical engineering company. He had been recruited to that job by the powerful banker, Marcus Wallenberg, Sr., whose vast industrial interests were almost entirely export-oriented. Within a decade or so, ASEA would become Sweden's largest industrial enterprise. Edström actively promoted the cross-class consensus building of the 1930s and was warmly appreciated by labor leaders like LO Chairman August Lindberg. He personally oversaw the recruitment of executive directors Söderlund (and later Kugelberg), looking for personal qualities suited to cross-class consensus building. He participated eagerly, as chairman, in the Saltsjöbaden negotiations.[115]

Edström and the "Big Five" in his Directors' Club did indeed continue to support the bourgeois opposition, but largely and successfully to counterbalance the radical elements in the Social Democratic Party and their ambitions in the realm of planning and socialization of ownership. This is exactly as Social Democratic Prime Minister Hansson hoped. By 1941, the Social Democratic leadership had so proved its merit that Edström decided to cut off financial life support to numerous small Conservative newspapers. In exasperation at the unprofitable newspapers' unending requests for handouts, Edström justified the move saying, only half-facetiously, that "for that matter, the Soshies are becoming Conservatives themselves" (*förresten håller ju sossarna på att bli högermän själva*).[116]

Esping-Anderson's more recent comparative work also emphasizes a "class-coalitional approach" and thus avoids problems of comparative explanation relying all too simplistically on the "relative power of labor."[117] But, in this analysis, unlike Korpi's version, employers remain an exclusively hostile and therefore relatively weak force. As the argument goes, a working class with formidable organizational and electoral resources was assisted by alliances with agrarians (e.g., the 1933 crisis agreement) and with white-collar segments of the population (the 1959 pension reform) against capitalist organization and interests. Thus, for example, the Swedish Social Democrats succeeded better than their well-organized Austrian counterparts in the 1930s because of the latter's political "ghettoization" and because Austria's rural classes in the 1930s were already "captured by a conservative coalition."[118] All along, capital is excluded, not favored; never a word is wasted on their complex and variable interests.

Esping-Andersen's and Korpi's arguments mesh well with that of Francis Castles, who attributes the relative success of Scandinavian (and Dutch) labor movements to partisan division, and therefore weakness, of the Right.[119] There is no doubt some truth that Social Democrats in Sweden benefitted somehow from the Right's division and weakness, especially electorally. On the other hand, their overall success is quite possibly attributable to their considerable restraint in divisive parliamentary exploits—so as not to inflame capitalist opposition. Recall Per Albin Hansson, prime minister during the 1930s, who gained enormous confidence from leading Swedish industrialists by making clear his view that their interests were badly served by the bourgeois parties— and that he favored a "strengthening and consolidation of industry's interests and influence." Divide and rule was not Hansson's preferred strategy. Hesitation to exploit all its possibilities may explain something about cross-class consensus and the absence of capitalist backlash—and therefore stable Social Democratic rule.[120]

Much can be said for Bo Rothstein's more historically sophisticated analyses mentioned earlier. Usually he avoids direct reference to "labor power" in explaining the particulars of the Swedish welfare state. Nevertheless, while incorporating a broad mix of institutional, coalitional, and leadership factors, Rothstein joins the class power theorists in misconceiving or ignoring the interests of capitalists that reformers had to reckon with in order to reproduce the politics of *samförstånd* over time. He therefore misses many essentials about the timing, design, and political durability of Social Democratic reforms. Because of their unusually rich historical detail, as well as provocative and engaging formulation, Rothstein's analyses deserve focused attention.

In identifying correctly the importance of early-twentieth-century corporatist relations in local labor exchanges for later developments in labor market policy under Social Democratic rule, Rothstein concludes, incorrectly, that SAF only rather begrudgingly accepted the "neutral" exchanges installed by bourgeois liberal reformers instead of employer-controlled institutions. They were a fait accompli; the unions were too strong to eliminate from the picture, Rothstein suggests. But, in fact, what made the early corporatist experiment successful was not employer resignation. Instead, it was their recognition of its great value in the context of labor scarcity. The year 1907, which Rothstein identifies as the time SAF accepted the corporatist exchanges, came at the conclusion of a peak period of emigration to America. Market-driven wage drift and frequent poaching of workers by engineering employers raged because of remarkable wage restraint by the metalworkers' union after their groundbreaking central agreement in 1905. Thus, engineering employers encouraged members to turn to the exchanges—to which workers also turned because of their neutrality—to recruit scarce labor. That was more in their interest than stealing workers from each other, even as American employers were stealing from them.[121]

Rothstein agrees with Esping-Andersen and others about the importance of the farmer-labor alliance of the 1930s, a "formative moment" in the Swedish system. He highlights the capital-exclusive nature of the alliance by emphasizing terms of the arrangement that supposedly strengthened labor's "monopoly over the supply of manpower" against employers. Here, however, he provocatively argues against the conventional cow-trade or log-roll depiction of the 1933 crisis agreement in which workers got jobs at good wages and for that reason gave up their resistance to further agricultural protections and higher food prices. Instead, he argues, the program sealed a "genuine class alliance" in which labor and agriculture joined forces to obtain something they both wanted—state assistance in organizing both agrarian and industrial working classes.[122]

Problems abound. Rothstein neglects to specify what exactly the Social Democratic government actually offered and supplied to help farmers organize in 1933 beyond what they had already gotten in 1932 from Conservatives and Liberals—against Social Democratic opposition. (That was a complicated tax system that, in effect, forced unorganized dairy competitors either to join dairy associations and abide by their pricing agreements, or to pay a prohibitively high "fee," part of which the association would receive.) Once in power a few months later, the first thing the Social Democratic government did was to reduce the fee and partially undermine the arrangement.[123] Yet another difficulty is that in 1934 the Agrarian Party maneuvered with other parties to bring down the Social Democratic government on labor law issues. It also voted against the Ghent unemployment insurance system, which Rothstein himself emphasizes was designed to support all-inclusive class organization. If Rothstein is right that the Agrarian Party was so dependent on the Social Democrats and that the two parties had the "same fundamental view about interest organizations' relationship to the state," Gustav Möller should have had the farmers' votes for unemployment insurance in his pocket. Not having that luxury, he was forced to make major compromises with the Liberal Party instead.[124]

Rothstein vastly overestimates the union-strengthening features of the crisis agreement. In his view, the old rules regulating reserve jobs it replaced had threatened "to an essential degree the very foundations of labor organization." This cannot be true. The strike-breaking provision in the law, which could require workers wanting relief jobs to replace strikers, was used only three times between 1926 and 1932 under non-Social Democratic governments. If the truth be told, the old rules probably only helped LO as well as SAF, though only marginally, by discriminating against Communists and Syndicalists. In practice as well as principle, it could be used only against unions using strike tactics that violated the labor law, which LO's own regulations, and practically all its actions, abided by. Thus, although the rules change probably had considerable symbolic importance for maintaining internal party unity, it was of absolutely no significance for securing the unions' survival or increasing their strike potential.[125]

Rothstein contends that the old wage rules for reserve jobs, revised in the crisis agreement, mortally threatened unions by playing unemployed workers off against union members. In other words, the unemployed "underbid" other workers by taking reserve jobs at wages below union standards. But this was not a big problem. It was faced almost exclusively by workers in the public sector, where unskilled relief work was performed. Not surprisingly, it was mostly the municipal workers' union that drove the labor confederation's policy in this realm.[126] Underbidding was virtually nonexistent in other sectors. Instead, *overbidding*, or poaching by one employer at another's expense was the usual problem, even in sectors like garments and even, astonishingly, in the 1930s.

In light of these facts, it is no mystery that internal discussions in SAF records offer no grounds to think that employers mourned the loss of a weapon to diminish or weaken labor organizations as a consequence of the crisis agreement between the Social Democrats and the Agrarian Party. This lack of concern dovetails well with the observation that only one rather exceptional employer leader worried about the effect of the following year's unemployment insurance law on unions' organizational strength. Hence, the conventional cow-trade view of the deal between labor and agriculture, which Rothstein criticizes, remains valid. It should, however, be modified by inclusion of capital as one of its cross-class foundations, predicated as it was on settling the 1933–1934 building trades conflict. The deep reductions in wages accomplished in the settlement delighted employer leaders like Edström as much or more than farmers, and they even suited other unions in LO.

Rothstein's analysis of Sweden's distinctive unemployment insurance system also contains problematic elements directly connected to a misconceptualization of class interests and excessive reliance on state institutions for explanation. He argues that Sweden's remarkably high organization levels, at least in the postwar years, "can to a large extent be explained by historical variation in national *political institutions*" (his italics). Thus, he gives credit to the Ghent system for labor's unusual ability "to organize and take collective action against capitalists" because "the main power resource unions possess" in conflict against capital is "their control over the supply of labor power."[127]

In all probability, the Ghent system does explain some of Sweden's unusual levels of union membership growth, but if so, only after 1950, as Rothstein recognizes, when its benefits had been greatly improved with subsidies from general revenues. If their wage and welfare accomplishments followed causally, they did not come at the expense of capital. Before the 1950s, Swedish unions had already reached extraordinarily high levels other countries have never reached. Thus, it remains highly contestable that differences across countries can "to a great extent" be explained by political institutions. A big part of the full historical explanation would have to be employer policies. As SAF's von Sydow pointed out, the confederation could have delivered a permanently crippling blow to the Social Democratic unions after their terrible defeat in the mass strike of 1909. Instead, the confederation wanted to bring the reformist unions back to the centralized bargaining table, in full knowledge that this would help them recuperate. Also, employers adopted a policy of indiscriminately locking out the unorganized along with organized workers, who then, according to unemployment relief policy of the 1920s through the 1930s, could not receive government jobs or cash support. Consequently, many Swedish workers probably joined unions for lockout insurance, paying their dues as premiums. Employer rather than state institutions, at least through the 1940s, therefore, probably explain more variation across countries than anything else. Thus, it is also a mistake to automatically equate, as Rothstein does, "degree of unionization with working class strength."[128] Very strong employers helped create very strong unions.

Collection of union dues by employers quite probably accounts for a good deal of the growth and stability in union membership in later years. This widespread practice also casts another large shadow of doubt on Rothstein's equation of union membership with union power against capital, which logically requires that employers could not be interested in promoting unionization. As one prominent Swedish employer official put it—defending the practice to confederation officials—"In reality, employers benefit extraordinarily from strong organizations on the other side," adding that "the greatest difficulties in negotiations arise in cases where there is a large number of workers who are not organized."[129] Comparative analysis of employer behavior in certain sectors in the United States closes the case. In coal mining, clothing, and construction, employer organizations welcomed well-organized unions capable of enforcing standards on cut-throat competitors. Employers often agreed to help unions collect members' dues, which then stocked the funds for strikes that employers welcomed against their competitors. In garments, when those funds were not sufficient, employers sometimes even helped finance strikes (see chapter 7).

Finally, in his analysis of active labor market policy, Rothstein misses an essential point by ignoring employers' manifest interests in the policy measures. He identifies a peculiar administrative feature—what he calls a "social democratic cadre organization within the Swedish state apparatus"—as a necessary condition for the labor market policy's success. Creating a highly dedicated and appropriately flexible bureaucracy of this nature meant inculcating in it a quasi-ideological commitment to the policy being carried out. All this, Rothstein argues, was possible only because the relevant legislation allowed, extraordinarily, for the hiring of union people to staff much of its bureaucracy from the street level up. Traditional strict civil service rules for hiring and recruitment would not have allowed this.[130]

The connection between active labor market policy's administration and its apparent success is intriguing and indeed plausible. What is missing is a factor that was equally necessary, if not more important. As Rothstein himself points out, the administrative practices he describes were calmly accepted by the employers' confederation. He misses the fact that the most important sectoral association strongly preferred that its members use the system while discouraging them from recruiting labor on their own through advertising. Had the engineering association strongly disagreed with the system, it would hardly have so energetically defended the labor board's monopoly. Active labor market policy would not have worked so smoothly. The reason employers did not put up a fight can be explained only by their fundamental agreement with the mission being pursued. In short, they agreed profoundly with the technocratic logic behind active labor market policy—the rationing of labor whose scarcity resulted directly from a system of administered pricing they themselves helped establish. This technocratic logic overlapped almost perfectly with the reform mission being pursued by Swedish Social Democracy—full employment and solidaristic wage policy. There was profound cross-class agreement behind employer support and cooperation, not fatalistic resignation to the power of labor.

Conclusion: Interest Analysis
Prior to Power Analysis

The full story of the building of welfare states needs to incorporate analysis of employer interests in governing markets, and the concerns of politicians to accommodate them. Those interests, as research indicates, were not infrequently progressive. Inferences about labor's power against capital drawn solely from the progressiveness of political outcomes lack compelling empirical as well as logical foundation. Interest analysis is prior to power analysis, something astute and cautious politicians who want to hold on to their precarious power know quite well. Left-wing welfare state builders in Sweden took into account, sometimes begrudgingly and sometimes wholeheartedly, what employers deemed necessary in their market interests. Like their liberal American counterparts in the 1930s, Social Democratic politicians anchored their reforms in a cross-class foundation of support. The historical puzzle of why the Swedish Social Democrats' greatest accomplishments occurred in the 1940s and 1950s, not in the 1930s as in America, can be explained only by the peculiar logic of solidarism. Reforms timed and designed to serve interests deriving from solidarism spared them open and intense conflict that easily could have undermined their extraordinary electoral and parliamentary control.

Part IV

*Conclusion: The 1950s
to the 1990s*

13

LEGACIES AND TRANSFORMATIONS

Side by side, jointly regulated segmentalism and cartelism in the United States worked reasonably well for capital and labor as a complex regime of labor market governance in the 1950s and 1960s. A more uniform and consensual regime of solidarism functioned even better in Sweden. In both countries, there were tensions, of course, usually manifested in benign, routinized conflicts over the details of regulation. There were also deeper systemic stresses. In the United States, the rate of private sector unionization started its long slide downward in the mid-1950s. Still a dark lining in a silver cloud, the membership decline coincided, however, with remarkable signs of vitality. Take, for example, the American steel industry. Once the vanguard of belligerent anti-unionism, and then of negotiated segmentalism, steel employers continued to lead the forward march with their entry into industry-wide multi-employer bargaining in 1956. With this, they achieved a workable hybridization of segmentalism in their separate labor markets with cartelism across a shared national product market. Negotiated cartelism also seemed to advance and thrive in more predictable places. Nationwide centralized bargaining in coal solidified in 1950 and dominated the industry through the 1960s. In 1964, a confederation of 28 trucking employer associations signed the first of a series of nationwide market-controlling Master Freight Agreements with the International Brotherhood of Teamsters.[1]

Today, in retrospect, the stresses appear more fatal than they did at the time to optimistic industrial relations experts. Many if not most big American employers nursed an abiding aversion to unions. Because of the constant threat they posed to managerial authority, employers pragmatically accommodated unions, but only on segmentalist terms. They were reminded by the scattering of successful union-free giants like Kodak, Du Pont, Procter and Gamble, and IBM that unilateral segmentalism might yet prevail. Southern states, meanwhile, extended employers an open invitation to set up production in cheaper labor markets without unions' constant nibbling away at managerial sovereignty. Over time, ever increasing numbers of big employers accepted that invitation.[2]

In the 1950s and 1960s, Swedish employers showed far more favor than American ones to unions and collective bargaining, despite the unions' socialist rhetoric and pervasive influence in industrial relations and politics. For one thing, they had more thoroughly disabused the Swedish labor movement of its early ambitions to share management powers. Unions stuck to a highly negotiable distributionist agenda, avoiding trench and guerilla warfare on the harsh terrain of managerial control. Employers built and enforced their solidaristic system with the help of a strong labor movement in both labor markets and politics, and could not have succeeded otherwise. Thus, by 1970 individual employers happily collected dues for half of all union members, because of unions' absolute respect for management control, and partly in gratitude for their efforts to soften worker resistance to the hiring of foreign workers in tight labor markets. Soon thereafter, most sectoral associations required member firms to encourage unionization of foreign workers in exchange for the labor movement's cooperation in immigration policy.[3]

Ironically, residual or inherent tensions in the Swedish system originated more from collusive rather than hostile relations between big companies and their workforces. At that level, both sides agreeably sought to raise wages above restrained, centrally negotiated levels. This meant defying central employer authority by exceeding, not undercutting, negotiated increases, which consistently remained below productivity growth rates. The result was upward "wage drift," a clear symptom of solidarism's micro-economic disequilibrium (that is, excess demand for labor). Drift accounted for between 40 and 50 percent of blue-collar earnings increases from the late 1950s through the 1970s.[4]

Solidaristic setting of pay below market clearing for major employers led to the very curious phenomenon—from an American standpoint—of big Swedish shipbuilders subcontracting out production tasks to small, unorganized firms because they routinely offered higher, not lower, wages than the big shipbuilders were allowed to pay. This practice enabled the large companies to expand employment and output at other sectors' expense in order to meet strong demand for Swedish ships. Both SAF and LO objected. Labor leaders even quietly reported excess wage payments to the employer confederation, requesting "more decisive action" against its members' generosity. Employers' solidaristic action sometimes took the form of fines for excessive wage increases—200,000 and 100,000 crowns for Volvo and SAAB in 1978, for two sensational examples.[5]

The American and Swedish welfare states continued to evolve through these decades in ways that suited, or at least did not negatively impinge on, employers' labor market regimes. Of course, there were tensions too, but nothing alarming. By 1953, according to Marion Folsom, former Kodak executive and now secretary of the Department of Health, Education, and Welfare in the Eisenhower cabinet, "You didn't find any business people against social security." In 1965, according to an official in the National Association of Manufacturers, "I suppose there are people in management . . . who now feel this country could get along without government-operated unemployment compensation, but I haven't met any lately who hold this viewpoint." This secure support had a lot to do with the fact that the American welfare state kept to the bounds of what Folsom called for in the 1930s and later—a minimum or basic welfare state on which to build a growing system of private, employment-based benefits.[6]

Minimalism is also what Charlie Wilson of GM advocated in 1950, following Folsom. The system's ultimate objective should be, he said, to cover all those gainfully employed but only "on a minimum basis." Private company pensions should supplement Social Security "in high production industries where wages are high and employees are accustomed to a higher standard of living." As partners in negotiated segmentalism, or what one account calls "unionized welfare capitalism," unions enthusiastically obliged, and from that decade onward helped to build up America's noncomprehensive, inegalitarian "private welfare state." Top labor officials believed that their success in negotiating benefits for their members took the steam out of pressure for welfare state expansion. In effect, they helped form a cross-class alliance for welfare state minimalism, but took little pride in the fact.[7]

Despite their views on minimalism, both Folsom and Wilson strongly supported large increases in Social Security taxes and benefits in 1950. So did the Social Security Advisory Council, composed largely of businessmen. Social Security (i.e., old age insurance), they thought, had become too minimal. This was probably affecting segmentalists adversely. It seems that means-tested old age assistance (OAA), administered by the states with joint federal funding, was taking over the job (unevenly across states and races, of course) of keeping many old people out of poverty. In places, OAA actually exceeded stagnant OAI benefits. Thus, OAA benefits would have been rising dangerously close in value to the retirement income of pensioners relying on a combination of OAI and employer-provided pensions. Because segmentalists' supplementary pensions would disqualify their retirees from means-tested OAA, they were paying twice—first for their own workers' retirement and, then, through general taxation for OAA, for the equally advantageous retirement of other employers' workers. Some of those other employers would have been competitors. Increasing Social Security taxes and improving benefits would right the competitive and distributional balance favored by segmentalists. Thus follows their strong support and Wilson's hope that OAA be eclipsed. The marginalization of OAA would also make it easier to administer uniform company pensions across states.[8]

Segmentalist "corporate liberals" in the Committee for Economic Development, founded by Folsom in 1942, also supported the extension of unemployment benefits during recessions, something that did not happen until the early 1970s. In their Keynesian progressivism, at least in this regard, they were well ahead of politicians. Further research may well show that some segmentalists, acting in enlightened self-interest, signaled friendliness to Medicare legislation in 1965 and quietly approved of union initiatives in that direction. They, as well as unions, might have seen the potential for shifting retirees' health costs (that cut into current workers' take-home wages) away from negotiated plans and onto broader revenue shoulders (employers with higher proportions of younger workers or not providing retiree benefits). In any event, as Folsom noted, "organized business" (e.g., the NAM) continued with its typical "lack of objective approach and understanding, as well as inept staff work" that it once showed toward the Social Security Act. In the year Medicare passed, Folsom accurately predicted that when businessmen thought it through they would come around. Thus, in the 1990s, corporations argued vehemently against cuts in Medicare that threatened to shift retiree health costs back onto their shoulders. Is it possible, too, that more informed and less ideologically aroused businessmen also signaled friendliness to the major expansion of Social Security's retirement benefits in the late 1960s and early 1970s? After all, partial release from the prospective costs of their promise to take care of retirees was an important reason they signaled support for the old age insurance in the first place in the 1930s. Indeed, in the 1960s employers would have regarded all the baby boomers now of working age, or soon entering, as a rich lode of cheaper substitute labor.[9]

In Sweden, the welfare state grew dramatically from the 1960s on, and even somewhat into the 1980s, rapidly bypassing America's slowly growing minimalist welfare state. Theory suggests that unlike segmentalism, solidarism tended to reinforce welfare state growth during periods of economic expansion. The ideological legacy of employer congeniality to the welfare state surely hobbled conservative parties' political ability to counter popular pressures for welfare expansion. The most notable growth was in public service sector employment from about 17 percent of the adult population in the early 1970s to 26 percent in the early 1980s, especially in female labor-intensive municipal government services. This phenomenon is what turned Sweden into a distinct and preeminent "social democratic welfare regime," according to Esping-Andersen's useful and influential categorization. Continental European or "conservative" regimes, though also spending far larger amounts than the limited "liberal regime" in America, concentrated far more on cash transfers, keeping direct provision of services at levels similar to America's. Government jobs in Sweden even continued to multiply until 1990, while public sector employment in the United States remained stagnant at 10 to 11 percent of the adult population from the 1970s to the 1990s. In Germany and the Netherlands, it also stagnated at similarly low levels.[10]

Solidarism's labor scarcity, manifested in wage drift, was both a cause and partly a consequence of the "service-intensive" welfare state. For example, public child care began to take off in the mid-1960s during solidarism's most consensual golden years. Capacity, measured as child care places as a percentage of children up to 6 years old, reached about 10 percent in 1970 and only started to level off at a little less than 50 percent in 1990. Research shows unmistakably that employers keenly favored this development to dislodge mothers from their homes and mobilize them for industrial work. Institutional child care was less labor-intensive, after all, than home care, promising at least a modest net gain in the female labor supply. Engineering employers were especially pleased, desiring to bring large numbers of women into mass production. (In the early 1950s, they hoped also that the household appliances they manufactured would "rationalize housework" to facilitate female participation in the labor market. Other employers, they thought, should lend their workers the money to buy household appliances. Some employers had already installed laundry facilities for employees' domestic needs.) Engineering's female blue-collar labor force began increasing steadily since 1949 from 2.5 percent to about 12 percent through the 1970s. It continued to increase to 17 percent in the 1980s, by which time the sector employed almost one quarter of all women in manufacturing. Industry as a whole continued to make demands for public day care and get action into the late 1980s.[11] Growth in government employment of women to provide free public care for the elderly and infirm also grew considerably during the 1970s and 1980s. Further research may well show that manufacturing employers also favored the socialization of these services to free up female labor for industry.[12]

All in all, we can reasonably suspect that there was a cross-class alliance of forces behind the growth of this extraordinary service-intensive welfare state, at least into the 1970s. The power resources and coalitional possibilities of labor (with women's groups, for example) against opposing interests of capital had little to do with it. Whether employers should have preferred importing foreign workers rather than commodifying household labor is not clear; in any case, the labor movement cooperated with both. Employers even aligned with labor against physicians in supporting the "Seven Crowns Reform" of 1969, which turned most Swedish doctors into full-time employees of the state. This is not to say that employers actually pushed for the 1970s expansion of employment in all health service occupations. But expand it had to, just as in America and the rest of the world. The fact that expansion took place almost exclusively in the public sector can, however, be explained by the fact that, historically, employers were in the coalition of forces that put health services there in the first place (see chapter 12).[13]

Some public policies that made Sweden distinctive are also widely credited for its high female labor force participation—and thus its high labor force participation overall in international comparisons. These include the tax reform of 1971, which introduced separate taxation of marital couples. Long before, in 1951, SAF and LO had called in unison for this reform to reduce women's high marginal taxes and therefore their large disincentive to seek gainful employment. A scheme of parental insurance, introduced in 1974, and expanded later, worked hand in hand with the tax law of 1971 and expanding day care to spur women's massive labor market participation. Thus was the household sector progressively "monetized." Day care encouraged both parents to work (or study) as both had to do so to qualify for slots; the leave system encouraged women to establish a work history before having children because benefits were linked to previous earnings.[14]

Other policies rewarded labor market participation, and so responded to employers' desire to increase the labor supply—the old concern that explained their 1940s opposition to means testing in the public pension system (see chapter 11). The unemployment insurance authorities, for example, closely monitored workers' job searches and pushed workers to take available jobs. So much of Sweden's social legislation required some labor market participation as a condition for receiving benefits that, in some economists' views, "the term *workfare state* is arguably a more appropriate appellation for Sweden than *welfare state.*"[15]

Major improvements over time in unemployment benefits were not so worrisome in a context of very low unemployment and systemic incentives to stay in or return to gainful employment. The welfare state's early legacy of consonance with employer interests probably helps explain the fact that even into the early 1980s, top SAF representatives on corporatist government boards consistently joined their labor movement counterparts in requests for welfare program budgets exceeding what Social Democratic finance ministers were willing to consider. Some of them had first occupied these positions in the period of welfare state consensus in the 1960s and 1970s, important developmental years for their own thinking as well as the welfare state's.[16]

Turnaround: The 1970s to the 2000s

During the 1970s and 1980s, both countries started to chart a deviant course. Dramatic welfare changes accompanied the crumbling of labor market regimes. One might suspect that the overall coincidence of trends was no accident, although some concurrent changes may be distantly related, if at all. In the United States, centralized negotiated cartelism in coal mining fell victim to decay. By 1980, nonunion mines with lower wages and benefit costs produced about half of the nation's coal. In 1989, they produced two thirds. Joint cartelism fell apart in the clothing industry, ravaged by foreign and renewed domestic sweatshop competition. Nonunion construction made major inroads into that traditionally cartelist sector. In trucking, the centralized relations of 1964 onward collapsed in the early 1980s. Real hourly earnings there declined drastically by 1990 back to their 1962 levels.[17]

By 1986, centralized multi-employer bargaining in the American steel industry was also finished. In meatpacking, "pattern bargaining" had brought increasingly uniform conditions across different companies and plants in the 1960s, but disruptions in the practice brought predictable distributional consequences in the 1980s. Diversity in industrial relations outcomes across operations within and across firms in the automobile sector, especially between assemblers and parts suppliers, increased dramatically.[18] Unilateral segmentalism emerged ascendant across manufacturing, as foreign manufacturers moved in to set up operations in the South and elsewhere. Domestic corporations also shifted production to nonunionized areas, fought off unionization efforts in new facilities generally, and even pulled off successful union decertifying elections. Their purpose was to get lower labor costs and assert greater managerial control. As segmentalists, however, they did not intend to abandon above-market wages and benefits.

To some extent, unions brought on the backlash by using their labor market and political power in aggressive violation of the principles of workable negotiated segmentalism, which reserved control over managerial and investment decision making almost exclusively for management. Unions took risky advantage of their political influence in the 1960s, especially over presidential appointments to the highly politicized National Labor Relations Board (NLRB). Employers were alarmed by a handful of decisions handed down by the Kennedy-Johnson–era NLRB, which had begun forcing them to negotiate about management decisions. According to an important account, they feared for American industry's competitiveness if labor law empowered unions to prevent the discontinuance of unprofitable products; inhibit automation, mergers, and consolidations; and check geographic relocation whenever a union forced through too costly a deal.[19]

Fears that the NLRB was closing the geographical escape route from unionism were magnified by unions' increasingly systematic violation of an important segmentalist principle: that wages and benefits should be high relative to varying local labor markets, but not uniform across product markets. In the 1960s, multi-union efforts to centralize control by coordinating bargaining strategy within and among large companies in a sector ferociously antagonized segmentalists like GE and Westinghouse. They did not regard taking wages out of competition as adequate compensation for the loss of managerial flexibility. Union efforts along these lines probably accelerated bigger employers' proclivity to move or set up new lower-pay operations in the South, where it was possible to do so on a nonunion basis.[20]

By and large, though, it was not transgressive labor militancy but intensified international product market competition that bears most responsibility for undermining the American labor market regime, which had evolved, after all, in the absence of significant international competition. Imported clothing, of course, was directly responsible for the devastation of unionism and cartelist collective bargaining in the garment industry. International competition in steel's increasingly heterogeneous product market wiped out any advantages associated with uniformity for reinforcing stable oligopoly pricing. Thus followed the collapse of nationwide multi-employer bargaining in that sector in 1986. In the automobile sector, foreign competition transformed the UAW's pattern bargaining strategy from something relatively innocuous and even partially beneficial into a dangerous brake on flexible strategies to face the international challenges of the 1970s and 1980s.[21]

Market pressures from abroad also bear indirect, though some ultimate, responsibility for the destruction of negotiated cartelism in trucking and coal mining. Manufacturers seeking lower transportation costs to meet foreign competition agitated successfully for trucking deregulation. With freer entry and competition, nonunion firms sprang to life with devastating effect on the National Master Freight Agreement in the early 1980s. Users of coal seeking shelter from high oil prices may well have played a role in the decline of unionization and cartelist collective bargaining in coal mining. Industrialists' increased demand for alternative fuel sources fuel sped the entry of nonunion surface mining in the West in the 1970s. Oil companies, now flush with profits to invest, thanks to the international oil embargo, lavishly financed the expansion of capital intensive surface-mining operations.[22]

International forces had their way with construction too, even though, like trucking, it was fully sheltered from international competition. The political ramifications were enormous. Leading manufacturers, squeezed from one side by price competition from abroad and cost pressures emanating from construction on the other side, were key agents responsible for the decline of collective bargaining relations. Out of this process emerged the Business Roundtable, an organization consisting of CEOs from the nation's leading corporations. The Roundtable was to become, according to one assessment, "the peak organization of big business political power in the United States." In short, much of the new organizational and political mobilization against labor in the 1970s—exactly as in the two open-shop movements earlier in the twentieth century—arose in part from intersectoral strains between manufacturing and construction.[23]

Formed in 1972, the Business Roundtable merged two already existing elite groups—the Labor Law Study Group (LLSG), formed in 1965 in reaction to the decisions of the Kennedy-Johnson–era NLRB, and the Construction Users' Anti-Inflation Roundtable (CUAR). The CUAR materialized in 1969 for a multi-front assault on the rapidly rising costs of construction. The CUAR, and later the roundtable, was headed by Roger Blough, former chairman of U.S. Steel. Throughout the 1960s, wages in construction had shot wildly ahead of those in steel and other manufacturing (from about 125 percent to 150 percent of wages in engineering between 1960 and 1972). This trend forced building costs up during a boom in industrial plant construction and whipped up the wage expectations of industrial workers. Like other major manufacturers, the big steel firm was now feeling the bite of serious foreign competition for the first time in the industry's history and, therefore, hurriedly tried to catch up from far behind in the technology race. In 1969, Japan became the world's largest exporter of steel. Imports as a percentage of total U.S. consumption of steel quadrupled between 1960 and 1971.[24]

According to congressional testimony by top unionists, the Roundtable was a "guerilla army in three piece suits" leading a revival of the burgeoning open-shop movement. Two of the movement's biggest political successes in the backlash against construction unions were NLRB rulings in the early 1970s giving contractors greater freedom to build on a nonunion basis. The open shop push took a large toll: Between 1971 and 1988, union membership in construction dropped from about 42 percent to 22 percent, and union pay stagnated. But the Roundtable also agitated among manufacturers for concerted efforts to pressure normally weak-willed and disorganized contractors into aggressive discipline of unions where they could not be completely dislodged. Hence, the somewhat anomalous growth of multi-trade collective bargaining at local levels and coordinated multi-employer lockouts. With these new tools, the broader employer community helped reduce strikes and whipsawing and eliminate what they regarded as inefficient work rules and pay structures.[25]

Intensified international competition, which spurred a bipartisan deregulation movement and therefore intensified domestic competition, interacted with more impatient capital markets to account for other major changes in the American labor market. The 1980s and 1990s were decades when former "welfare capitalists," both unionized and nonunion, engaged in permanent layoffs of unprecedented size even when profits looked good. Previously, segmentalists avoided such layoffs except in truly hard times. Major segmentalists also turned increasingly, though not massively, to the recruitment of temporary or contingent workers for their peripheral and easily shed workforces on a lower-pay, no-benefit basis.[26]

Though far from disappearing, segmentalism receded in its coverage with the decline of blue-collar manufacturing employment. In the late 1970s, private sector pension coverage started declining. Segmentalism also hardened as it shrank. In the 1980s, many employers started terminating their traditional "defined benefit" pension plans, which guaranteed secure benefits throughout one's retirement. Optional "defined contribution" plans took their place. Now employers matched employees' voluntary contributions into private market accounts of uncertain value at retirement. Some companies terminated their traditional plans to get at accumulated assets, especially during mergers and "leveraged buyouts." Hundreds of major companies in the 1990s like Kodak and IBM retained their plans but converted them to "cash balance" schemes, which reduced retirement obligations, especially to older workers, and liberated fund assets for corporate use. Between 1983 and 1993, underfinancing of future company pension obligations rose from about $10 billion to $70 billion before action by the government's Pension Benefit Guaranty Corporation enforced more responsible behavior.[27]

A marked fall in private-sector workers' health insurance coverage commenced in the mid-1970s. Segmentalists contributed to this decline by making health coverage optional, letting workers choose between paying a growing share of rising group insurance premiums and passing up health insurance for more take-home pay. For those declining numbers of low and moderate income workers who continued to get health coverage, its quality on a number of dimensions declined too, with risks and costs being shifted off employers' shoulders. By 1999, employers with health plans had moved about 90 percent of their workers out of traditional schemes into HMOs and other forms of managed care with less patient choice and guaranteed service, or forced them to pick up more of their health costs in traditional plans through higher co-payments, deductibles, and out-of-pocket maximums. The percentage of employers offering retiree medical coverage to fill gaps in Medicare declined from 40 percent in 1994 to less than 25 percent in 2000. (Because of these cuts, increasing health costs ate up many retirees' declining pensions. Thus, not surprisingly, the mid-1990s saw a reversal of the decades-long decline in the retirement age.) Because of the wage-benefit tradeoff, unions sometimes participated and sometimes resisted these adjustments to segmentalism. The managed care revolution for checking the rise in health costs was, at least initially, a cross-class project.[28]

Whereas international forces probably did the most damage to the American labor market regime, the same probably cannot be said for Sweden. Solidarism, after all, grew in the hothouse of intense exposure to international trade. Unprecedented labor and political militancy for ends of a system-transgressive nature were more important. Beginning around 1969, the labor confederation shifted into confrontational gear, willfully choosing to take full advantage of its considerable short-term situational power to violate the consensual terms of Sweden's solidaristic labor market regime. The employer backlash of the 1980s undid the damage rather quickly, producing a decentralization of collective bargaining and wage setting down to the sectoral and firm level. Employers repudiated centralized wage policy, now that the unions could no longer be relied on to co-administer it on consensual terms, and embarked on a policy of greater autonomy for firms and industries in setting wages. With the breakdown of solidarism came a strikingly inegalitarian turnaround in the movement of wages starting in the early 1980s.[29]

One of the principles of consensual solidarism that unions routinely violated in the 1970s, starting in 1969, was substantive: compression across firms and industries only, or equal pay for equal or similar work. Through the 1970s, the unions began demanding much more—a compression of pay across skills and occupations within firms. Engineering employers organized in VF were the most outraged by this "repugnant" (*motbjudande*) wage policy. Pressure from the metalworkers' union (Metall) enforced the policy with threats of strikes. The employers' confederation was unable to summon the necessary unity to counterattack with sympathy lockouts. Reacting against the engineering sector's characteristically high degree of wage inequality within firms, Metall's low-pay members were activated by the spirit of egalitarianism implicit in traditional wage solidarism, which, being more conservative, had also been more consensual. The radical new leftism of the student movement of the late 1960s and the 1970s poured oil on the fire. Metalworkers were also motivated by the ongoing compression of wages in the public sector. There, different economic and political constraints, and the rapidly growing sector's need for labor, allowed its low-skilled workers to make greater progress than in the private sector. Thus, labor market forces pushed in the same direction as the new egalitarian agenda. By 1974, because of the unions' radicalized egalitarian wage policy, VF's executive director personally concluded that "it is necessary to decentralize wage negotiations." Views on the wisdom of decentralization, however, still varied and wavered in the engineering association.[30]

SAF as a whole was far from eager to resort to massive lockouts against the unions' radicalized wage egalitarianism. One reason was that unions in sectors other than engineering often chose not to take advantage of the new wage leveling clauses in the post-1969 LO-SAF agreements in the sector-level implementation process. Where they did so choose, firms were often better able, because of their predominantly domestic markets (as in the retail sector), to pass on the costs to consumers. When engineering firms reacted to wage leveling that had been forced on them from above by topping off their skilled workers' wages—to restore company differentials—this registered as wage drift. Then automatic wage drift clauses (*förtjänstutvecklingsgarantier*) negotiated at the LO-SAF level gave workers and firms elsewhere compensation to maintain wage parity and, thus, recruitment competitiveness in tight labor markets. This wage-wage spiral was a managerial nuisance and, of course, highly inflationary.[31]

All of this was happening when international competition made inflation and limits on flexible managerial manipulation of wage differentials increasingly costly. Thus, international forces probably share some blame for what happened. For example, international monetary institutions and financial markets made the repeated devaluations of the 1970s to restore export industry's competitiveness and profits an increasingly self-destructive policy. Differential sensitivity to international competition helps explain why other SAF associations were less resistant to the new egalitarian wage policy, a source of much indignation voiced in and by VF in 1974. In 1975, therefore, VF leaders began seriously examining the possibility, recommended strongly by many in the ranks as early as 1972, of more decentralized, sectoral level bargaining and lockouts. In 1977, VF's board came out strongly for decentralization as the remedy for the labor movement's new "wage policy insanity" (*lönepolitiskt vansinne*)—if not in the next wage round, then sooner or later. The confederation, they concluded, had become so heterogeneous that "it is currently impossible to reach solutions that suit export industry" while simultaneously satisfying home market and service industries. Virtually every other sectoral association, however, still preferred to stick with centralization and bombarded VF with arguments against its struggle for independence.[32]

By 1980, VF finally gave up on peak-level centralization, disappointed by the behavior of other sectors and the bourgeois coalition government during SAF's first major lockout in years. VF even threatened to leave SAF if the confederation disallowed independent action. It used the same threat later in 1989 to force SAF to dismantle its machinery for multi-industry bargaining on behalf of the other sectoral associations. SAF, in the end, chose immediate disablement over dismemberment. In 1983, VF cut a deal with the new leadership of Metall, now more responsive to high-pay members who had been held back by radicalized solidarism. It even offered to give Metall more than LO was demanding on its behalf in exchange for a decompression of wages within firms and elimination of wage drift clauses. The new more decentralized order wrought by engineering represented a realignment of cross-class relations against home market sectors, including the public sector. Most important, it tended to redistribute income away from the public sector and its workers and redirect it toward private manufacturing employers and their own workers. It was not simply an overpowering of labor by capital. Indeed, Metall now joined VF in renouncing solidaristic wage policy.[33]

Thus, just as engineering played a key role in setting up and supporting the centralized solidaristic system, its actions were the first in a series of events leading to other major decentralizing and inegalitarian trends in the country's bargaining and pay-setting system. By the end of the 1990s, employers displayed, for the first time in the century, a principled openness to company-level provision and differentiation of social benefits—in other words, a door open in the direction of American-style segmentalism within the institutional shell of multi-employer bargaining. Major reforms of 1996 and 2000 in LO and SAF's centrally bargained supplementary pensions (introduced in 1972) dropped the pay-as-you-go defined benefits features, replacing them with funding through defined contributions. Workers would now have to choose market funds in which to invest money going into their individual accounts. Increases in 2000 came at the expense of requiring local, company-level agreements to implement the plan, thus opening the possibility for some employers (with a younger labor force, for example) to avoid payments altogether. From then on, company-level agreements with local unions would be able to implement terms differing from the central agreement. This was a quiet but giant step by SAF into a new century—out of its past century of solidarism.[34]

The radicalization of the Swedish labor movement in the 1970s blocked the return to consensual solidarism by violating its most important foundational terms: the virtually untrammeled managerial absolutism that employers had so effectively established since early in the century, and even the principle of private ownership and control of capital. Social Democrats passed more than a dozen labor laws in the 1970s, chipping away at the famous (or from the radical's standpoint, notorious) Paragraph 32 of the SAF's constitution, which required member firms to treat their managerial rights as inalienable and therefore nonnegotiable. Now the law forced them to accept everything from union representation on company boards to codetermination over hiring, firing, and production decisions.[35]

Most abhorrent of all, from employers' standpoint, was the "Wage-Earner Funds" proposal, formulated initially by LO economist Rudolf Meidner, among others, and passed at the 1975 LO congress. It was designed in principle to shift ownership and control of the private sector to workers and their representatives. Few analyses of this remarkable plan recognize that this long-term goal, appealing to the radicalized labor movement, had a vital short-term solidaristic purpose that decisively propelled it onto the national political agenda. In short, the idea was to tax away and therefore sterilize "excess profits" left behind by solidaristic wage restraint in firms that could, and therefore often did, pay more (via wage drift). The diverted profits were then supposed to be kept in circulation for productive investment. Because the labor movement would control the flow of funds, workers' continued solidaristic restraint would be justified. Sterilization would thus reduce the wildcat militancy and high wage drift of the early 1970s that destabilized the centralized bargaining system, undermined solidaristic wage policy, and thereby threatened the labor confederation's position in the Swedish political economy. Of course, employers may have sympathized with the plan's solidaristic ends but could never have abided its socialistic means and consequences.[36]

Thus, with its radicalized egalitarian wage policy, followed by legislative challenges to managerial control and capitalist ownership, LO fatally undermined Sweden's renowned politics of progressive consensus. The Social Democratic government passed a version of wage-earner funds in 1983, albeit a heavily watered-down one. They did this largely to give LO something for continued wage restraint in the face of a huge 16 percent devaluation of the crown (after a 10 percent devaluation the previous year), which rechanneled a large share of the national income stream back to export capital. The funds were abolished in 1992 by a Conservative-led government, whose electoral base was no doubt strengthened by the unprecedented political mobilization of capital in the 1980s against labor's recent radicalism.[37]

Some might argue that the relatively radical labor legislation of the 1970s and then the extraordinarily confrontational wage-earner funds campaign explain the breakdown of the Swedish model of centralized bargaining in the 1980s. The argument is that employers sought decentralization in order to shatter the labor confederation's unity, and thus its ability to mobilize the electorate and, with its unified voice, control the Social Democratic Party in government. The near simultaneity of wage-earner fund legislation and the breakdown of centralization suggests as much. But so far, the evidence is sparse to nonexistent that engineering employers had any more justification than the unions' radicalized egalitarian wage policy when they first resolved to decentralize in the 1970s. By the 1980s, for sure, the political weakening of the radicalized labor movement looked like icing on the cake and good reason not to seek recentralization. Political embitterment across the camps made the requisite communication impossible. Thus, the squandering of trust once so carefully cultivated by employer and labor leaders alike—from Gustaf Söderlund and August Lindberg in the 1930s to Bertil Kugelberg and Arne Geijer in the 1950s and 1960s—drastically reduced the possibility for a return to more moderate and mutually satisfying terms of centralized governance.[38]

Why the Swedish labor movement departed from its earlier tradition of caution and coalition is a difficult question to answer. There were probably many causes, assisted in no small way by generational turnover in the ranks and leadership. An important reason, at least in the beginning, was that even the three political parties to the right of the Social Democrats, especially the Liberal and Center parties, contemplated action on the economic democracy agenda in 1969 and the early 1970s. As top SAF officials understood the situation, the bourgeois parties were "driving the Social Democrats from the rear" (*De borgerliga partierna driver socialdemokraterna framför sig*). In the employer view, the slow-moving LO was anxious about being "left behind" (*LO befarar att bli efter i utvecklingen*). To avoid the political embarrassment of being outflanked on the left by centrist parties, a leading employer official predicted correctly, LO leaders would probably be forced to seize the reins. Leaders of both confederations hoped—in vain, it turned out—to win time by depoliticizing the matter with negotiated experiments and so keep it out of the politicians' hands.[39]

An increasingly pervasive mythology about the relative strength of labor and capital's weakness in the country's politics of egalitarian compromises also helps explain the abandonment of the cross-class strategy. Repeated in practically all academic analyses and labor movement rhetoric—for example, about the highly politicized pension reform of 1959—the mythology was probably reinforced by labor's historical monopoly on reformist initiative taking. Also, strategic silence on the part of employers about what they gained from moderate reforms probably gave the mythology time to sink roots and spread foliage to obscure the more realistic view. By holding back on vocal support, employer leaders implicitly blamed labor's power for reforms that inevitably rubbed some employer group or the other the wrong way. Employer silence had simultaneously strengthened a trustworthy labor confederation's leadership vis-à-vis the rank and file. Thus, the labor movement was able to take credit, boasting that with each piece of progress its strength against capital, rather than cross-class agreement, made the difference. By the 1970s, mythology eclipsed reality in the minds of a new generation of labor leaders, and they threw caution to the wind. In doing so, they gambled against the possibility of an employer backlash and the loss of centralized influence, not fully aware of the odds against them.

Welfare in Decline

Predictably, American industry's increasing exposure to rocky international competition in and after the 1970s unified business as a whole behind state and federal politicians' austerity measures to reduce deficits and put the brake on tax increases and regulatory burdens. Big employers now linked arms with small, though not always in the same organizations or with the same particular objectives. Equally important, none spoke out against cutbacks. The steep decline in the real value of the minimum wage after the rapid inflation of the early 1970s was left unremedied through the rest of the decade, and by the end of the 1980s, it had sunk down to where it was in the 1940s. Despite later nominal increases in 1996 and 1997 it remained more than one dollar below what was needed on a full-time basis to bring a family of three to the official poverty level. Tellingly, the refundable Earned Income Tax Credit (EITC), whose passage and increases in 1975, 1987, 1990, and 1993 made up for some of the injury to the working poor, was an employer-friendly measure, subsidizing low-wage employment and shifting part of the labor supply curve to employers' advantage. According to one account, business interests and conservative politicians joined liberals in singing its praises.[40]

The value of unemployment benefits shrank by 12 percent in real terms between 1971 and 1994, and because of increasingly stringent eligibility rules imposed by states, the percentage of the unemployed receiving compensation fell from 81 percent in 1975 to a low of 26 percent in 1987, though rising again to a still modest 36 percent by 1995. Changes in Social Security backed by President Ronald Reagan partially undid improvements of the early 1970s, gradually reducing projected benefits as a percentage of preretirement earnings from about 64 percent to 51 percent between 1985 and 2030 for low earners. The real value of maximum Aid to Families with Dependent Children (AFDC) benefits fell in every state from 1970 to 1995, and in 1996 the federal entitlement program, a piece of the original Social Security Act, was scrapped entirely. It was replaced with block grants to the states with few major strings attached except work requirements and severe time limits on eligibility.[41]

How much American employers and the changes in their labor markets that they engineered had to do with all this, relative to the more easily identified political agents of the retrenchment process, must remain a matter of speculation. But we can be fairly sure of two things. First, protection against intense low-standard domestic competition once provided the regulatory logic of the cross-class alliance behind the limited welfare state. Therefore, low-cost international competition could not have motivated employers to rise in its defense. International competition, after all, spoke for reducing domestic costs, not building floors under them. Second, we can be sure that the extensive private provision of welfare benefits stunted the development of effective ideological and institutional defenses of the public welfare state throughout the American political system.

Organized labor could not even muster much effort to revive itself through expansion into the expanding service sectors of the economy, where workers were badly protected by both private and public welfare. The shrinking unionized labor force in the private sector remained relatively well looked after and largely indifferent to the losers. Indeed, their interests were actually somewhat divergent, given that low taxes left all the more behind for protecting their real take-home wages and shoring up private benefits. Thus despite all talk of the need for balanced budgets, limits on "tax expenditures"—or deductions from companies' taxable income for their health and pension expenses, and the exemption from taxation of individual benefits received—remained beyond the pale of serious political debate. Silence on the issue of tax breaks for private welfare gives eloquent testimony to the power of the continuing cross-class alliance for the minimal welfare state and extensive employment-based benefits. A powerful agent of this alliance in interest group lobbying was the Employee Benefits Research Institute (EBRI), formed in 1978 and sponsored by unions as well as employers, banks, insurance companies, and the country's army of benefits consultants. If anything, the call from Democrats from left to center was for more generous tax breaks for segmentalists' "good corporate citizenship" in the 1990s.[42]

An anomalous episode during the late-twentieth-century politics of the American welfare state care is instructive about the continued importance of cross-class alliances. For a time during the late 1980s and early 1990s, a gaping crack opened in the business world's generally united front against expanding the welfare state. By March 1993, Anheuser-Busch, Bethlehem Steel, Chrysler, Dayton Hudson, Del Monte, Ford, Georgia-Pacific, H. J. Heinz, Home Depot, Hormel & Co., Hunt-Wesson, Inland Steel, International Paper, James River, Lockheed, LTV Steel, Northern Telecom, Pacific Gas and Electric, Quaker Oats, Safeway Stores, Scott Paper, Southern California Edison, Time Warner, U.S. Bancorp, Westinghouse, Wheeling-Pittsburgh Steel, and Xerox joined forces with other major corporations, labor unions, and industrial associations to promote or endorse an outrageously un-American idea: corporatist or tripartite regulation of compulsory employment-based health insurance. This National Leadership Coalition for Health Care Reform (NLCHCR) had the agreement of over half of the benefits managers in a 1992 to 1993 sample of leading corporations at least in its advocacy of an "employer mandate" or legislation compelling employers to offer and help pay for their employees' health insurance. Even the National Association of Manufacturers and the U.S. Chamber of Commerce were on the bandwagon for universal coverage in the early 1990s.[43]

Top labor leaders had envisioned just such an alliance with big business to justify abandoning their traditional demands for a Canadian-style single-payer system instead of an employer-based multi-payer system. They saw clearly how many big employers, segmentalists all (especially in autos and steel) signaled strong interest in legislation that would suppress health inflation across the board and shift mushrooming health costs (especially for retirees) off their backs, while expanding coverage to over 40 million uninsured. Segmentalists, valuing stable worker relations, wanted above all to restrain or reduce overall labor costs to cope with intensified foreign competition (partly due to the rise in the dollar between 1988 and 1990) and recession (in 1990 and 1991) at the least expense to their workers' paychecks and benefits. Labor strife concentrated during the period, after all, largely on employers' aggressive efforts to economize on this part of private welfare. Thus, because of support from big employers, and despite the absence of a strong electoral mandate, President Bill Clinton enjoyed in most observers' eyes a clear shot at completion of the New Deal with the passage of a "Health Security Act." Ultimately Clinton's health plan—and all other comprehensive designs—died at the hands of small insurers, low-pay employers (small and large), in alliance with the Christian Coalition, the rabidly conservative wing of the Republican party, and a number of conservative Democrats in Congress.[44]

If the truth be told, however, segmentalists' loss of interest knocked the wind out of the Clinton Plan and all other designs by 1994, even though they had initially breathed life into it in 1992. Shortly after 1992, big employers' own private efforts to bring their own health costs under control began paying off handsomely. An alliance with large insurers scrambling to offer HMOs and other forms of managed care coverage at declining employer premiums did the trick. Employers' health cost inflation came to a standstill in the middle of the decade, even as their competitive position improved (the dollar fell) and growth picked up steam. By early 1994, the news media began reporting what business leaders already knew about—the stunning success (if only a short-term one, as it later turned out) of their private cost-control efforts. Reasons for remaining in an instrumental cross-class coalition for reform vanished. The fate of health reform followed that of the cross-class alliance, and a causal connection cannot be easily dismissed.[45]

Like their American counterparts, Swedish employers welcomed a broad array of welfare rollbacks and economizing measures in the 1990s. These were sponsored by the Social Democratic Party and its competitors alike, often in collaborative efforts. Aside from general pressures for austerity to lighten payroll costs, the reforms were greatly accelerated by the most severe economic crisis since the 1930s—a period of negative growth between 1991 and 1993 that produced the highest unemployment since the Great Depression. The bust followed several years of a dizzying speculative bubble in finance and real estate prices. Major macro-economic policy error in the context of a financial system liberalized by the Social Democrats in the late 1980s, in response to powerful international pressures, must bear responsibility for the disaster, though the welfare state had to pay some of the price. Benefit cuts limited the size of tax increases needed to pay for the social costs of mass unemployment. Later, unrestored, they helped bring taxes and social insurance contributions down as a percentage of GDP between 1990 and 1997.[46]

To deal with very high and costly absenteeism, a conservative coalition in power from 1991 to 1994 added "waiting days" (*karensdagar*) before eligibility for sick pay and shifted responsibility for the first fourteen days of sick pay to employers. This created an incentive for them (and, indirectly, unions) to reduce fraudulent or overly self-indulgent absenteeism at the public's expense. It also cut the "replacement rate" (percentage of previous earnings) for sick pay, parental leave, and unemployment insurance from 90 to 80. After returning to power, Social Democrats reduced these benefits further to 75 percent in 1996. They did restore the unemployment benefits back to the conservative coalition's more generous 80 percent after loud union protest. In exchange, the unions agreed in principle to eventual introduction of time limits on benefits sometime around 2002. Social Democrats also cut the universal child allowance from 750 to 640 crowns in 1996.[47]

Finally, a major reform hammered out among the five main political parties between 1991 and 1994 completely revamped the old-age insurance system to deal with long-term solvency problems associated with an aging population. The Social Democratic government began the 20-year implementation process in 1999. Benefits were no longer to be fully secure, for the reform converted to a defined contribution, rather than defined benefit basis. Hence, overall benefits were to depend on underlying economic growth. Many were to get less than the old system promised. Workers had to pay part of the pension contributions, where once employers paid all, the idea being to increase their cost awareness by itemizing the payroll deductions on paychecks. Finally, the system was partially "privatized," combining an element of insecurity along with possibility of higher earnings distributed unevenly as luck and the market would have it. Whereas 16 percent of income was to be taxed for pay-as-you-go coverage of current retiree benefits, 2.5 percent would now go into a funding system with separate accounts invested in market funds chosen by individual taxpayers.[48]

The cross-class foundation of these cuts and restructuring was apparent, at least on a superficial level, in a broadly consensual recognition of the need for austerity. The specific details of particular reforms do not, however, derive directly, with any immediate and transparent logic, from the needs or character of the changing labor market regime. It is more likely that they are direct responses to pressures for fiscal austerity that Sweden shares with all other advanced industrial democracies. Nevertheless, it is telling that one of the most dramatic changes of the 1990s in the Swedish welfare state was the cutback in public sector employment levels from their peak in 1989 at 26.1 percent to 21.9 percent in 1997, its lowest level since 1977. Sweden, in other words, severely cut back on the very dimension of welfare variation that distinguished it as the preeminent social democratic regime.[49]

Cutting back on the total public sector wage bill, by reducing overall government employment, conformed strongly with the interests of the recast labor market alliance of the 1980s, which unified private, export-oriented employers and unions serving their workers, especially Metall. Their repudiation of centralization and solidarism was directed in large part against the growing public sector and its expensive demands for interoccupational and intersectoral equality. The new cross-class alliance, it seems, helped neutralize public sector workers' and their clients' defenses in the new politics of welfare state dismantlement. Cross-class alliances, in other words, probably figure significantly in both the formative politics of the welfare state, the main subject of this book, and in its political setbacks.[50]

An Agenda

Writing in the early 1940s, and surveying the recent wreckage of economies and societies across the globe, economic and social historian Karl Polanyi looked into regulatory politics of the past for clues about what might bring forth a better sociopolitical order in the future. In a better world, he thought, markets would be harnessed to society so that they would never again throw economies into calamitous depression and classes and nations into war. In his masterful book, *The Great Transformation*, Polanyi noted that even if the ultimate causes of social and political change were usually international economic forces, classes or sectional interests would be the "natural vehicles" of reform. In this politics of class, he noted, one must realize that the monetary or economic nature of sectional demands are often fueled by, and in fact hard to distinguish from, normative motivations to regulate "standing or rank." In other words, economic conflict was also a struggle for fair shares fought with appeals to socially defined norms of equity and dignity—the "cement of society" as Jon Elster puts it.[51]

Paralyzing class conflict associated with inability to compromise on these terms could be a grave peril to society, as recent experience with depression, fascism, communism, and war showed. Experience also showed, however, that through self-interested action, classes could also bring about desirable change if they could only build bridges across interests. In other words, they need "to win support far outside their own membership, which again will depend upon their fulfillment of tasks set by interests wider than their own." Such cross-class bridge building, Polanyi noted, looking at the history of things like collective bargaining and social legislation, was "an everyday occurrence." It was not, to be sure, an unrealistic hope. Reform based on cross-class compromise and agreement could reconcile efficiency and society, allowing classes to work together for socially and environmentally healthy growth, political stability, and a widely shared, nonutopian kind of freedom. Even his egalitarianism was quite a pragmatic one. "Wage differentials," he wrote, for example, "must (and should) continue to play an essential part" in a planned and justly regulated economy that controls, motivates, dignifies, and liberates in a grand but realistic balance.[52]

As presented here, the history of labor markets and welfare states in the United States and Sweden into the 1970s accords with much of Polanyi's analysis and vision. Though he did not specifically investigate when and why capitalist interests would show progressive potential, his implication to that effect shines clearly through. His conclusions also square well with the evidence in this book that noncapitalist interests like unions and political parties dependent on broad-based working class support are most likely to play the active, instigating role in broadly beneficial social legislation. Active defense of broad social interests through early collectivist regulation, he said, "fell primarily to one section of the population in preference to another."[53] But in the case of the New Deal and Swedish welfare state, it appears, reformers usually kept a cautious eye on powerful capitalists, pragmatically adapting their goals in order also to appeal to capitalists' market interests.

The fact that labor leaders and progressive politicians usually play the instigating role calls for deeper analysis of the profound importance of strategic agency and choice, partisan politics, and ideology in the comparative analysis of welfare state variations. These issues are all more or less studiously neglected here, and some will think woefully so. For example, the ideology of conservative parties in power, their electoral strategies, and the institutions that condition them probably cause some societies to pass up chances for reform that progressive political agents in other societies choose to take good advantage of. Hence, institutional and ideological conditioning or strategic neglect of opportunities probably explains some countries' conservative choices better than capitalist opposition. Furthermore, the role of working class mobilization probably also deserves more attention. It can motivate elites of all stripes to undertake reforms that pass and endure not because mass unrest overwhelms capitalist resistance, but because it jolts pragmatic reformers into a more energetic search for solutions that resonate with the regulatory, anti-market interests of capitalists.

The complete agenda to be recommended for future comparative and historical research, Polanyiesque in its broad scope, would fully integrate historical analysis of varying and changing capitalist market interests with international forces; ideological processes; popular movements; all sorts of social, economic, and political institutions; and, finally, the strategic choices of the elites who dominate them. If political knowledge so generated somehow improved the chances for more equality and security across capitalist societies, or just halted current trends in the other direction, that would be a good thing.[54]

NOTES

1. A Historical Puzzle

1. Sweden's infant mortality is lowest in the world, and the country ranks among the top two or three in terms of life expectancy. The United States ranks in the vicinity of Portugal on both counts. *Statistical Abstract of the United States 1998* (Washington DC: U.S. Department of Commerce, 1998), 830–31; *1997 Demographic Yearbook* (New York: United Nations, 1999), 347–54 and 480–500. On the possible link between material equality and overall health, see Richard Wilkinson, *Unhealthy Societies: The Afflictions of Inequality* (New York: Routledge, 1996); Ichiro Kawachi and Bruce P. Kennedy, *The Health of Nations: Why Justice is Good for Our Health* (New York: New Press, 2001).

2. On centralization and wage equalization, see Richard B. Freeman, "Labour Market Institutions and Economic Performance," *Economic Policy* 6 (April 1988); Bob Rowthorn, "Corporatism and Labour Market Performance," in Jukka Pekkarinen, Matti Pohjola, and Bob Rowthorn eds., *Social Corporatism: A Superior Economic System?* (Oxford: Clarendon, 1992); Torben Iversen, *Contested Economic Institutions: The Politics of Macroeconomics and Wage Bargaining in Advanced Industrial Democracies* (New York: Cambridge University Press, 1998), esp. 36–37 and 72–77; and Michael Wallerstein, "Wage-Setting Institutions and Pay Inequality in Advanced Industrial Societies," *American Journal of Political Science* 43 (July 1999).

3. For differing versions and discussions of the strengths and weaknesses of the power resources argument, see Alexander Hicks and Joya Misra, "Political Resources and the Growth of Welfare in Affluent Capitalist Democracies, 1960–1982," and Evelyne Huber, Charles Ragin, and John Stephens, "Social Democracy, Christian Democracy, Constitutional Structure, and the Welfare State," both in *American Journal of Sociology* 99:3 (November 1993).

4. David Rueda and Jonas Pontusson directly link labor power in the labor market (union density) with equalization in "Wage Inequality and Varieties of Capitalism," *World Politics* 52:3 (April 2000). On the relationship between labor's electoral power resources and "corporatist" or centralized bargaining, which in turn is associated with wage compression (note 1), see John Stephens, *The Transition from Capitalism to Socialism* (London: Macmillan, 1979), 122–3; Alexander Hicks and Duane Swank, "Politics, Institutions, and Welfare Spending in Industrialized Democracies," *American Political Science Review* 86 (1992), 658–74, and Hicks, *Social*

Democracy and Welfare Capitalism: A Century of Income Security Politics (Ithaca: Cornell University Press, 1999), 138 and 148–50.

5. John Stephens and Harold Wilensky first brought the importance of Christian Democracy to comparativists' attention in Stephens, *The Transition from Capitalism to Socialism*, 99–101, and Wilensky, "Leftism, Catholicism, and Democratic Corporatism," in Peter Flora and Arnold Heidenheimer, eds., *The Development of Welfare States in Europe and America* (London: Transaction, 1981). See also Göran Therborn, "Pillarization and Popular Movements: Two Variants of Welfare State Capitalism," in Francis G. Castles, ed., *The Comparative Analysis of Public Policy* (New York: Oxford, 1989), and Kees van Kersbergen, *Social Capitalism: A Study of Christian Democracy and the Welfare State* (London: Routledge, 1995). Torben Iversen and Anne Wren identify Christian Democracy as a force for equalization of wages in "Equality, Employment, and Budgetary Restraint: The Trilemma of the Service Economy," *World Politics* 50 (July 1998).

6. James Bryce, *The American Commonwealth* (New York: Macmillan, 1893), 1:302.

7. Robert Salisbury, "Why No Corporatism in America?" in Philippe C. Schmitter and Gerhard Lehmbruch, eds., *Trends toward Corporatist Intermediation* (London: Sage, 1979), 218–19; Huber, Ragin, and Stephens, "Social Democracy, Christian Democracy, Constitutional Structure, and the Welfare State." In John Stephens's earlier work, at least, the anticapitalist nature of labor's power was explicit, and Christian Democratic success in developing the welfare state followed from "antiCapitalist aspects of Catholic ideology." *The Transition from Capitalism to Socialism*, 99–101.

8. Hicks and Misra summarize others' arguments in this way in "Political Resources and the Growth of Welfare," 677.

9. There are disputes about which kinds of capitalists gave to the Democrats and why, but no disagreement that the money was substantial. Louise Overacker, "Campaign Funds in the Presidential Election of 1936," *American Political Science Review* 31:3 (June 1937), 473–98; Michael J. Webber, "Business, The Democratic Party, and the New Deal: An Empirical Critique of Thomas Ferguson's 'Investment Theory of Politics'," *Sociological Perspectives* 34:4 (1991), 486–7; Michael J. Webber and G. William Domhoff, "Myth and Reality in Business Support for Democrats and Republicans in the 1936 Presidential Election," *American Political Science Review* 90:4 (December 1996), 824–33.

10. Marquis Childs, *Sweden: The Middle Way* (New Haven: Yale University Press, 1936), 161 (quote). See also Childs, *This is Democracy: Collective Bargaining in Scandinavia* (New Haven, Yale University Press, 1938). On the modesty of the decade's reforms, see Kurt Samuelsson, *Från stormakt till välfärdsstat–Svensk samhällsutveckling under 300 år* (Stockholm: Rabén & Sjögren, 1968), 271. Sweden also came into public view after a special commission appointed by President Roosevelt visited to study its centralized wage bargaining system and in 1938 published a flattering picture. Even business leaders Gerard Swope, of General Electric, and Charles R. Hook, director of the National Association of Manufacturers, signed the report, though they possibly prevented it from recommending centralization for the United States. U.S. Department of Labor, *Report of the President's Commission on Industrial Relations in Sweden* (1938); "President's Study of Swedish Labor Finds Peace is Key," *New York Times*, 25 September 1938, 1.

11. Edwin Amenta, *Bold Relief: Institutional Politics and the Origins of Modern American Social Policy* (Princeton: Princeton University Press, 1998), 5. It seems, though, that had Amenta counted "general" not just central government spend-

ing from his data source, Sweden would have surpassed the United States somewhat in terms of social spending as a percentage of GDP (about 8.5 percent for Sweden, 6.3 percent for the United States) and about matched it in percentage of government spending (27.6 percent in Sweden, 29.4 percent in the United States). The source for his and my calculations is Peter Flora et al., *State, Economy, and Society in Western Europe 1815–1975* (Chicago: St. James, 1983).

12. Peter Flora and Jens Alber, "Modernization, Democratization, and the Development of Welfare States in Western Europe," in Peter Flora and Arnold J. Heidenheimer, eds., *The Development of Welfare States in Europe and America* (New Brunswick, NJ: Transaction, 1981), 55.

13. The family welfare legislation united Right and Left in Sweden because of concerns about Sweden's extraordinarily low birth rate. Its main purpose was to spread the costs of childbearing and child rearing. Lisbet Rausing, "The Population Question: The Debate of Family Welfare Reforms in Sweden, 1930–38," *European Journal of Political Economy* 2:4 (1986), 536, 540, 544–47.

14. Therborn, "Pillarization and Popular Movements," 220.

15. Göran Therborn, "A Unique Chapter in the History of Social Democracy: The Social Democrats in Sweden," Klas Misgeld, Karl Molin, and Klas Åmark, *Creating Social Democracy: A Century of the Social Democratic Labor Party in Sweden* (University Park, PA: Pennsylvania State University Press, 1992), 24; Norman Ginsburg, "Sweden: The Social-Democratic Case," in Allan Cochrane and John Clarke, eds., *Comparing Welfare States: Britain in International Context* (London: Sage, 1993), 174.

16. *Politics Against Markets: The Social Democratic Road to Power* (Princeton: Princeton University Press, 1985), 157.

17. Ginsburg, "Sweden," 183; Esping-Andersen, *The Three Worlds of Welfare Capitalism* (Princeton: Princeton University Press, 1990), 50.

18. Esping-Andersen and Roger Friedland, "Class Coalitions in the Making of West European Economies," in *Political Power and Social Theory* 3 (1982), 47.

19. Sven Hydén, "Arbetsgivarna och socialpolitiken," *Sociala meddelanden* 5 (1953), 271; Lars Svensson, *Closing the Gender Gap: Determinants of Change in the Female-to-Male Blue Collar Wage Ratio in Swedish Manufacturing 1913–1990* (Lund: Ekonomisk-historiska föreningen, 1995), 118–19; Mary Ruggie, *The State and Working Women: A Comparative Study of Britain and Sweden* (Princeton: Princeton University Press, 1984), 16 and 261–85.

20. Esping-Andersen, *The Three Worlds of Welfare Capitalism*, 21–2.

21. Jonas Pontusson, "From Comparative Public Policy to Political Economy: Putting Political Institutions in Their Place and Taking Interests Seriously," *Comparative Political Studies* 28:1 (April 1995), 136.

22. Skocpol, *States and Social Revolutions: A Comparative Analysis of France, Russia, and China* (Cambridge: Cambridge University Press, 1979), especially 115.

23. Kathleen Thelen, *How Institutions Evolve: The Political Economy of Skills in Comparative-Historical Perspective*, manuscript, Northwestern University, 2001, and Thelen and Ikuo Kume, "The Rise of Nonmarket Training Regimes: Germany and Japan Compared," *Journal of Japanese Studies* 25:1 (1999), 33–64. This work, unlike most institutionalist analysis, analyzes employers' economic rationale for variable support and opposition in different national contexts. Cathie Jo Martin's institutionalism, like Thelen's, also explicitly allows for capitalist interests in social reform, though she does not go far into the economic reasoning for variations. *Stuck in Neutral: Business and the Politics of Human Capital Formation* (Princeton: Princeton University Press, 2000). See also Duane Swank and Cathie Jo Martin, "Em-

ployers and the Welfare State: The Political Economic Organization of Employers and Social Policy in Contemporary Capitalist Democracies," *Comparative Political Studies* 34:8 (October 2000), 889–923.

24. Ellen Immergut, *The Political Construction of Interests: National Health Insurance Politics in Switzerland, France, and Sweden* (New York: Cambridge University Press, 1992), 236. To be fair, Immergut is persuasive in showing the importance of institutional frictions and cannot be faulted merely for failing to examine all possible pivotal factors. See also Sven Steinmo and Jon Watts, "It's the Institutions, Stupid! Why Comprehensive National Health Insurance Always Fails in America," *Journal of Health Politics, Policy, and Law* 20:2 (Summer 1995). They imply that there is an open and shut case for political institutions as the cause of health reform failure in America, as opposed to other countries, and nothing distinctive and pivotal about American capitalists' interests and roles.

25. Fred Block, "The Ruling Class Does Not Rule: Notes on the Marxist Theory of the State," *Socialist Revolution* 33 (May–June 1977). See also the discussion on Block here, in chapter 10.

26. Esping-Andersen, *Three Worlds*, 105–38.

27. Esping-Andersen and Friedland, "Class Coalitions," 17–19.

28. Skocpol, *Social Policy in the United States: Future Possibilities in Historical Perspective* (Princeton: Princeton University Press, 1995), 18 and 237–38; Margaret Weir and Theda Skocpol, "State Structures and the Possibilities for 'Keynesian' Responses to the Great Depression in Sweden, Britain, and the United States," in Peter B. Evans, Dietrich Rueschemeyer, and Theda Skocpol, eds., *Bringing the State Back In* (Cambridge: Cambridge University Press, 1985), 147. For a forceful statement of the class power argument about differences between the United States and Sweden with regard to health insurance, complete with an explicit equivalency premise, see Vicente Navarro, *The Politics of Health Policy: The U.S. Reforms 1980–1994* (Oxford: Blackwell, 1994), especially 176–84.

29. Rueda and Pontusson, "Wage Inequality and Varieties of Capitalism." These authors make the extreme assumption that union density is an entirely unproblematic measure of labor power. In fact, union membership may increase with employer trust and recognition of unions' contributions toward their regulatory and other interests. See discussions of employer support for both unionization and different kinds of wage compression in the United States and Sweden in chapters 6, 7, and 8.

30. Esping-Andersen, *Three Worlds*, 138.

31. Employers thus have regulatory interests in "distributive" (e.g., welfare) as well as other strictly "regulatory" policies. The regulatory aspect of distributive policies makes Theodore Lowi's influential categorization somewhat problematic. See his "American Business, Public Policy, Case-Studies, and Political Theory," *World Politics* 16:4 (July 1964), 677–715. On the gap between capitalists' interests, ideology, and action, and the role of non-capitalists in advancing capitalists' interests, see David Vogel, "Why Businessmen Distrust Their State: Political Consciousness of American Corporate Executives," *British Journal of Political Science* 8:1 (January 1978), especially 65–74.

32. J. Joseph Huthmacher, *Senator Robert F. Wagner and the Rise of Urban Liberalism* (New York: Atheneum, 1968), 9; Theron F. Schlabach, *Edwin E. Witte: Cautious Reformer* (Madison: State Historical Society of Wisconsin, 1969), 123; Edwin E. Witte, "The Government and Unemployment," *American Labor Legislation Review* 25:1 (March 1935), 8.

33. Evelyne Huber and John D. Stephens typically use these correlations to

support their theory about the role of the "political power balance" between capital and labor in welfare state development. See their *Development and Crisis of the Welfare State: Parties and Policies in Global Markets* (Chicago: University of Chicago Press, 2001).

34. Earlier research on the interplay tends only to examine the reverse effects of welfare states on labor market behavior. Kåre Hagen, "The Interaction of Welfare States and Labor Markets: The Institutional Level," in Jon Eivind Kolberg, ed., *The Study of Welfare State Regimes* (Armonk, NY: Sharpe, 1992), 124–68.

2. Solidarity, Segmentation, and Market Control

1. Drucker, *Adventures of a Bystander* (New York: Harper and Row, 1978), 275.

2. GM's Alfred P. Sloan Jr. claimed credit for authoring the idea, as early as 1946. *My Years With General Motors* (New York: Doubleday, 1990), 405.

3. Drucker, *Adventures*, 274.

4. "The G.A.W. Man," *Time* 20, 1955 (June) 20. According to this story, Reuther accused Ford of colluding with GM when it revealed a stock-sharing plan of the same nature that GM had also proposed to parry the UAW's "Guaranteed Annual Wage" demand. If Reuther's accusation is true, it would suggest that the two companies collusively aimed at the outcome Wilson wanted. See also Jill Quadagno, *The Transformation of Old Age Security: Class and Politics in the American Welfare State* (Chicago: University of Chicago Press, 1988), 163–67.

5. Nelson Lichtenstein, *The Most Dangerous Man in Detroit: Walter Reuther and the Fate of American Labor* (New York: Basic, 1995), 285, 286; Drucker, *Adventures*, 274–78. While historian Lichtenstein gives Reuther credit for demanding the scheme's "actuarially stringent standards," it was Wilson, according to Drucker, who was behind them.

6. Wilson on Reuther: "He, not I, should be the next chief executive of GM, and he'd love it. In fact, if Walter had been born a few years earlier and gone to work before 1927 when the near-collapse of the Ford Motor Company destroyed opportunities for machinists to move into management, he'd be president of GM today." Some of this friendliness may have to do with the fact that as a young man Wilson had been a Debsian socialist and local leader of a patternmakers' union. Drucker, *Adventures*, 275; Lichtenstein, *The Most Dangerous Man in Detroit*, 283.

7. Nelson Lichtenstein, *The Most Dangerous Man in Detroit*, 286–87, 294, 297. Initially, there was some reason for optimism: Congress increased Social Security payments after the UAW's first pension breakthrough in 1949 and several states increased unemployment benefits in 1955 after the SUB agreement. Lichtenstein, *The Most Dangerous Man in Detroit*, 297; Quadagno, *Transformation of Old Age Security*, 166.

8. Quadagno, *Transformation of Old Age Security*, 171. See also Michael K. Brown, "Bargaining for Social Rights: Unions and the Reemergence of Welfare Capitalism," *Political Science Quarterly* 112:4 (Winter, 1997–1998).

9. "Interview with Marion Folsom," Social Security Project, Columbia University Oral History Collection (typescript, 1965), 165.

10. C. E. Wilson, "Pensions in Our Society" (talk before the Chicago Executives Club, 6 January 1950) in Neil W. Chamberlain, ed., *Sourcebook on Labor* (New York: McGraw-Hill, 1958), 999–1002.

11. Lichtenstein, *The Most Dangerous Man in Detroit*, 332–33, 337–38; Victor G. Reuther, *The Brothers Reuther* (Boston: Houghton Mifflin, 1976), 353–54; Charles Kassman, *Arne Geijer och hans tid, 1910–1956* (Stockholm: Tiden, 1989), 271–73.

12. Bertil Kugelberg, SAF's executive director, regarded Geijer with the same enormous esteem that Wilson had for Reuther. Conversations between the laconic Geijer and the more gregarious Kugelberg, according to the latter's memoirs, were often marked by a "playful tone" and "friendly jocularity." In 1962 the two traveled together for five weeks in the United States and Canada, after an invitation from JFK's secretary of labor Arthur Goldberg, jointly instructing American business, labor, and political leaders (including a Senate committee) about the Swedish model. Together they visited the United States again in June 1963. Geijer and his wife were regular guests at Kugelberg's summer cottage. Bertil Kugelberg, *Från en central utsiktspunkt* (Stockholm: Norstedts, 1986), 35, 72, 185, 243, 279, 292; Kassman, *Arne Geijer och hans tid*, 256–57.

13. Hans Söderlund, "Grundvalarna för SAF:s lönepolitik," Lönekommittén P.M. 6, 14 April 1955 [SAF/AO], 40–41.

14. On employers' earlier more outspoken attitudes before the 1941 rules change, see Sten Höglund, *Storföretagen, Svenska Arbetsgivareföreningen och beslutsordningen i arbetarnas fackliga organisationer—Arbetsgivaresynpunkter på LO:s och fackförbundens sätt att fatta beslut om förlikningsbud, perioden 1925–1941* (Department of Sociology, University of Umeå: Research Report No. 45, 1978).

15. Gustaf Söderlund in SAF, Minutes, Styrelse, 25 January 1935.

16. Axel Hadenius, *Facklig organisationsutveckling—En studie av Landsorganisationen i Sverige* (Stockholm: Rabén & Sjögren, 1976), 58.

17. Samuel Gompers, "The Eight-Hour Workday," *American Federationist* (May 1897).

18. See Oliver E. Williamson, "Wage Rates as a Barrier to Entry: The Pennington Case in Perspective," *Quarterly Journal of Economics* 82 (1968), 85–115; Ralph Flanders, "The Tradition of Voluntarism," *British Journal of Industrial Relations* 12 (November 1974), 352–70; Michael T. Maloney, Robert E. McCormick, and Ralph D. Tollison, "Achieving Cartel Profits through Unionization," *Southern Economic Journal* 46:2 (1979), 628–34.

19. For an excellent and enlightening analysis, see John Bowman, *Capitalist Collective Action: Competition, Cooperation and Conflict in the Coal Industry* (Cambridge: Cambridge University Press, 1989), 54–61, who shows how unions and why unions can be effective "external organizational mechanisms" for controlling competition.

20. Lloyd Reynolds, "Cutthroat Competition," *American Economic Review* 30 (December 1940); F. C. Pierson, "Prospects for Industry-Wide Bargaining," *Industrial and Labor Relations Review* 3 (April 1950), 341–61; Pierson, "Cooperation among Managements in Collective Bargaining," *Labor Law Journal* 11 (July 1960), 621–8; Pierson, "Recent Employer Alliances in Perspective," *Industrial Relations* 1 (October 1961), 39–57. Other motives, including a more secure monopoly of managerial control, are discussed in Keith Sisson, *The Management of Collective Bargaining: An International Comparison* (London: Basil Blackwell), 5–6, 12–13.

21. Sisson, *The Management of Collective Bargaining*, 13. Hugh Clegg, *Trade Unionism Under Collective Bargaining* (London: Social Science Research Council, 1976), emphasizes employer recognition and institutionalized collective bargaining between organized employers and workers as the main source of variations in union size and strength.

22. Bowman, *Capitalist Collective Action*, 107.

23. "The wages of labour are the encouragement of industry, which, like every other human quality, improves in proportion to the encouragement it receives." *An Inquiry into the Nature and Causes of the Wealth of Nations* (New York: Modern Li-

brary, 1937 [1776]), 81. Or as the workplace jokes go, "they pretend to pay us, we pretend to work," and "Pay peanuts and you get monkeys." Two seminal works are Joseph Stiglitz, "The Efficiency Wage Hypothesis, Surplus Labor, and the Distribution of Income in LDCs," *Oxford Economic Papers* 28 (1976), 185–207, and Robert Solow, "Another Possible Source of Wage Stickiness," *Journal of Macroeconomics* 1 (1979), 79–82. Useful introductions are Andrew Weiss, *Efficiency Wages: Models of Unemployment, Layoffs, and Wage Dispersion* (Princeton: Princeton University Press, 1990), and George Akerlof and Janet Yellen, "Introduction," in Akerlof and Yellen, eds., *Efficiency Wage Models of the Labor Market* (Cambridge: Cambridge University Press, 1986), 1–21.

24. Weiss, *Efficiency Wages*, 102.

25. Harvey Leibenstein, "The Theory of Underemployment in Densely Populated Backward Areas," in *Economic Backwardness and Economic Growth* (New York: Wiley, 1957), chapter 6; Stiglitz, "The Efficiency Wage Hypothesis," *Oxford Economic Papers* 28: (1976), 185–207; C. J. Bliss and N. H. Stern, "Productivity, Wages and Nutrition," *Journal of Development Economics* 5 (1978), 331–98; and P. Dasgupta and D. Ray, "Inequality as a Determinant of Malnutrition and Unemployment: Theory," *Economic Journal* 97 (1986), 1011–34.

26. The assumption here is that workers' ability and their "reservation wages" are positively correlated. See, for example, Andrew Weiss, "Job Queues and Layoffs in Labor Markets with Flexible Wages," *Journal of Political Economy* 88 (1980), 526–38; James Malcomson, "Unemployment and the Efficiency Wage Hypothesis," *Economic Journal* 91 (1981), 848–66.

27. D. Hammermesh and R. S. Goldfarb, "Manager Programs in a Local Labor Market: A Theoretical Note," *American Economic Review* 60:4 (1970), 706–09; Steven Salop, "Systematic Job Search and Unemployment," *Review of Economic Studies* 40(2):2 (1973), 191–201, "Wage Differentials in a Dynamic Theory of the Firm," *Journal of Economic Theory* 6:4 (1973), 321–44; Salop, "A Model of the Natural Rate of Unemployment," *American Economic Review* 69 (1979), 117–25; and Joseph Stiglitz, "Alternative Theories of Wage Determination and Unemployment in LDC's: The Labor Turnover Model," *Quarterly Journal of Economics* 88:2 (1974), 194–227.

28. See, for example, Guillermo Calvo, "Quasi-Walrasian Theories of Unemployment," *American Economic Review Proceedings* 69 (1979), 102–07; B. Curtis Eaton and William White, "Agent Compensation and the Limits of Bonding," *Economic Inquiry* 20 (1982), 330–43; James Foster and Henry Wan, "Involuntary Unemployment as Principal-Agent Equilibrium," *American Economic Review* 74 (1984), 476–84; Hajime Miyazaki, "Work Norms and Involuntary Unemployment," *Quarterly Journal of Economics* 99 (1984), 297–311; Carl Shapiro and Joseph Stiglitz, "Equilibrium Unemployment as a Worker-Discipline Device," *American Economic Review* 74 (1984), 433–44. An older argument, foreshadowing the efficiency wage literature, suggested that worker good will toward employers does not necessarily make them "more industrious or more painstaking," but rather renders workers "more responsive to demands made upon them by the management, and thus it enables alert and aggressive executives to obtain better results from their men." Sumner Slichter, "The Current Labor Policies of American Industries," *Quarterly Journal of Economics* 43:3 (May 1929), 425.

29. George Akerlof, "Labor Contracts as Partial Gift Exchange," *Quarterly Journal of Economics* 97 (1982), 543–69, and "Gift Exchange and Efficiency Wage Theory: Four Views," *American Economic Review Proceedings* 74 (1984), 79–83. See also Samuel Bowles, "The Production Process in a Competitive Economy: Walrasian, Neo-Hobbesian and Marxian Models," *American Economic Review* 75 (1985), 16–36.

30. Alan Krueger and Lawrence Summers, "Efficiency Wages and the Inter-Industry Wage Structure," *Econometrica* 56:2 (March 1988), 278; Lawrence F. Katz, "Some Recent Developments in Labor Economics and Their Implications for Macro-economics," *Journal of Money, Credit, and Banking* 20:3 (August 1988, Part 2), 515.

31. Weiss, *Efficiency Wages*, 1.

32. On involuntary unemployment as an element of the natural rate of unemployment, and caused by efficiency wages, see Steven C. Salop, "A Model of the Natural Rate of Unemployment," *American Economic Review* 69 (March 1979), 117–25; Carl Shapiro and Joseph E. Stiglitz, "Equilibrium Unemployment as a Worker Discipline Device," *American Economic Review* 74 (June 1984), 433–44. For the neo-classical view, which includes only voluntary unemployment in the natural rate, see Milton Friedman, "The Role of Monetary Policy," *American Economic Review* 58 (March 1968), 1–17.

33. Akerlof and Yellen, "Introduction," 3; Krueger and Summers, "Efficiency Wages and the Inter-Industry Wage Structure," 259–93.

34. Guillermo Calvo and Stanislaw Wellisz, "Hierarchy, Ability, and Income Distribution," *Journal of Political Economy* 87 (1979), 991–1010; Janet Yellen, "Efficiency Wage Models of Unemployment," 200–01; James Malcomson, "Work Incentives, Hierarchy and Internal Labor Markets," *Journal of Political Economy* 92 (1984), 486–507; Jeremy Bulow and Lawrence Summers, "A Theory of Dual Labor Markets with Application to Industrial Policy, Discrimination, and Keynesian Unemployment," *Journal of Labor Economics* 4:3, part 1 (1986), 376–414; Krueger and Summers, "Efficiency Wages and the Inter-Industry Wage Structure;" George Akerlof and L. F. Katz, "Workers' Trust Funds and the Logic of Wage Profiles," *Quarterly Journal of Eonomics* (August 1989), 525–37; and Erica Groshen, "Five Reasons Why Wages Vary Among Employers," *Industrial Relations* 30:3 (Fall 1991), esp. 369–73. A seminal book on labor market segmentation is Peter B. Doeringer and Michael J. Piore, *Internal Labor Markets and Manpower Analysis* (Lexington, Mass.: D.C. Heath and Company, 1971).

35. For Alan Krueger and Lawrence Summers, the rent sharing explanation of pay differentiation is intimately related to and therefore to be regarded as "a species of efficiency wage theory rather than as alternative explanation." "Efficiency Wages and the Inter-Industry Wage Structure," 280. See also Weiss, *Efficiency Wages*, 100; Karl Ove Moene and Michael Wallerstein, "Bargaining Structure and Economic Performance," in Robert J. Flanagan, K. O. Moene, and M. Wallerstein, *Trade Union Behavior, Pay Bargaining and Economic Performance* (Oxford: Clarendon, 1993), 105–09.

36. It is possible that benefits have an effect on gratitude and therefore reciprocity like the most effective of gifts—"luxuries" that we would not readily choose to buy ourselves, if given their dollar value in cash.

37. In labor economics, the "implicit contract" literature emerged to explain equilibrium unemployment and therefore usually refers to wage rigidity, not employment security, in firms. An early statement on the probable efficiency benefits of both wage stability and employment security is Sumner Slichter, "The Secret of High Wages," *The New Republic*, 28 March 1928, 185.

38. See Michael Hoel, "Efficiency Wages and Local Versus Central Wage Bargaining," *Economics Letters* 30:2 (August 1989), 175—79; Hoel, "Union Wage Policy: The Importance of Labour Mobility and the Degree of Centralization," *Economica* 58:230 (May 1991), 139–53; and Asbjørn Rødseth, "Efficiency Wages and Local Versus Central Bargaining," *Oxford Economic Papers* 45:3 (1993), 470–81. In the efficiency wage model, the cooperative reduction of wages means movement

away from the competitive equilibrium down employers' demand curve. In the monopsony model, the movement is down the labor supply curve. If the employers' cartel collapses, in the monopsony model employment also rises, for the effect of higher wages is to increase the supply of labor. In the efficiency wage model, however, employment falls because wage increases discourage firms from hiring.

39. Karl Ove Moene and Michael Wallerstein, "Bargaining Structure and Economic Performance," in Flanagan, Moene, and Wallerstein, *Trade Union Behavior,* esp. 90–93.

40. On the monitoring and compliance problem, see Hoel, "Efficiency Wages," 175, and Rødseth, "Efficiency Wages," 477.

41. For obvious reasons, "centralism" would be inadequate and "monopsonism" would be inaccurate (see note 38).

42. Some of these phenomena associated with employer solidarism in Sweden are discussed in Eskil Wadensjö, "Arbetsmarknadspolitiken och arbetsgivarorganisationerna," in *90-talets Arbetsmarknad* (Stockholm: Almänna Förlaget, 1988), 101–17.

43. Bob Rowthorn finds exactly this strange result. Highly intrusive solidaristic wage regulation in Sweden helped create an interfirm wage structure that "effectively mimicked the Walrasian ideal of perfect competition," much unlike what is found in decentralized systems. "Corporatism and Labour Market Performance," in Jukka Pekkarinen, Matti Pohjola, and Bob Rowthorn, eds., *Social Corporatism: A Superior Economic System?* (Oxford: Clarendon, 1992), 114–15.

44. For a related argument about the importance of fairness norms for the centralization of union authority, see Peter Swenson, *Fair Shares: Unions, Pay, and Politics in Sweden and West Germany* (Ithaca: Cornell University Press, 1989), 19–24.

45. Karl-Ove Moene and Michael Wallerstein would add an additional reason for unusually rapid innovation and replacement of old with new vintage capital under solidarism: the restraint of wages where they would otherwise be higher in more decentralized, inegalitarian labor markets subsidizes investment and speeds up the Schumpeterian process of creative destruction. "Pay Inequality," *Journal of Labor Economics* 15 (July 1997), 403–30.

46. Edward P. Lazear, "Salaries and Piece Rates," *Journal of Business* 59:3 (1986), 405–31; Janet Yellen, "Efficiency Wage Models," 201.

47. Workers also risk a great deal when they invest their own resources in training and education. The more specific the skills, the greater the risk in their becoming obsolete. The more general the skills, the greater the potential waste in acquiring skills that prove superfluous.

48. See Kathleen Thelen's original and enlightening comparative-historical analysis of employer interests, often overlapping with labor's, in different training regimes. *How Institutions Evolve: The Political Economic of Skills in Comparative-Historical Perspective,* manuscript, Northwestern University, 2001.

49. Excess profits, and the wildcat militancy and wage drift they probably contributed to, have often been a source of tension in Swedish industrial relations. On the three-way tradeoff or "trilemma" for unions between wage equality, employment, and the squeezing of profits in Sweden, and its political implications, see Swenson, *Fair Shares,* 111–20.

50. However, while the unintended side benefit may stabilize the arrangement, it probably will not be among employers' and unions' motives for setting it up.

51. Carl Mosk, *Competition and Cooperation in Japanese Labour Markets* (New York: St. Martin's, 1995), 3–6 and 158–63. See also Shigeru Wakita, "A Model for Patterns of Industrial Relations," in Isao Ohashi and Toshiaki Tachibanaki, eds.,

Internal Labour Markets, Incentives, and Employment (New York: St. Martin's, 1998), 126–40; Ronald Dore, *Stock Market Capitalism–Welfare Capitalism: Japan and Germany versus the Anglo-Saxons* (Oxford: Oxford University Press, 2000), 23–48.

52. John Maynard Keynes, *The General Theory of Employment, Interest, and Money* (London: Macmillan, 1936), chapter 2.

53. See Arthur Okun, "Upward Mobility in a High-Pressure Economy," *Brookings Papers on Economic Activity* 1 (1973), especially 237–41; and Andrew K. Rose, "Okun's Ladder Reexamined," *Economics Letters* 32:4 (1990), 383–87.

54. See George Akerlof and Janet Yellen, "Introduction," in Akerlof and Yellen, eds., *Efficiency Wage Models of the Labor Market*, 11–14; Akerlof and Yellen, "A Near-Rational Model of the Business Cycle, With Wage and Price Inertia," *Quarterly Journal of Economics* 100:Supplement (1985), 823–38; and "The Fair Wage-Effort Hypothesis and Unemployment," *Quarterly Journal of Economics* 105:2 (May 1990), especially 281.

55. Truman F. Bewley, *Why Wages Don't Fall During a Recession* (Cambridge: Harvard University Press, 1999), 17, 398–443. Bewley refers to Akerlof, "Labor Contracts as Partial Gift Exchange" and Solow, "Another Possible Source of Wage Stickiness." He also concedes that the shirking argument, or motivation by fear of job loss, may have been valid in an earlier day and age when authoritarian management was more the norm.

56. Arthur Okun, "The Invisible Handshake and the Inflationary Process," *Challenge* (January–February 1980), esp. 6; Akerlof, "Labor Contracts as a Partial Gift Exchange"; Akerlof and Yellen, "The Fair Wage-Effort Hypothesis and Unemployment"; Ernst Fehr and Simon Gächter, "Reciprocity and Economics: The Economic Implications of *Homo Reciprocans*," *European Economic Review* 42:3–5 (May 1998), 845–59; and Ernst Fehr and Armin Falk, "Wage Rigidity in a Competitive Incomplete Contract Market," *Journal of Political Economy* 107:1 (February 1999), 106–34.

57. Recent literature in comparative political economy tends to ignore or at least underplay the importance of relational contracting at the workplace in "liberal market economies" like the United States. See, for example, the depiction of the American economy as opposed to the more institution-rich "coordinated market economies" of Europe in Peter A. Hall and David Soskice, "An Introduction to Varieties of Capitalism," in Hall and Soskice, eds., *Varieties of Capitalism: The Institutional Foundations of Comparative Advantage* (Oxford: Oxford University Press, 2001), especially 6–33. In fact, long-term commitments in industrial relations are a constitutive feature of segmentalism, and are imposed and maintained not so much by institutions external to the firm but by microeconomic rationality.

3. Managerial Control

1. Howell John Harris, *The Right to Manage: Industrial Relations Policies of American Business in the 1940s* (Madison: University of Wisconsin Press, 1982), 4.

2. Harris, *The Right to Manage*, 170.

3. Ronald W. Schatz, *The Electrical Workers: A History of Labor at General Electric and Westinghouse 1923–1960* (Urbana: University of Illinois Press, 1983), 110.

4. Harry Katz, *Shifting Gears: Changing Labor Relations in the U.S. Automobile Industry* (Cambridge: MIT, 1985), 38–42.

5. Sanford Jacoby, *Modern Manors: Welfare Capitalism Since the New Deal* (Princeton: Princeton University Press, 1997).

6. Harris, *The Right to Manage*, 129–35, 139–58. Unlike Wilson, Boulware wanted to take credit back from the United Electrical, Radio and Machine Workers'

Union (UE) for its segmentalist policies. Since the 1930s, the UE "took all the credit, demanded more, and [in 1946] through a long strike forced the company to go far beyond what it deemed to be right and proper." Boulware therefore would present unions at the bargaining table with a "tempting dish" on a take it or leave it basis in order to curry favor with workers. The hope was to weaken the militant union, which unlike Reuther's UAW, was under Communist influence. Herbert Northrup, *Boulwarism: The Labor Relations Policies of the General Electric Company* (Ann Arbor: Bureau of Industrial Relations, University of Michigan, 1964), 21 and 29–30.

7. Sloan, *My Years with General Motors* (New York: Doubleday, 1990 [1963]), 406.

8. George Barnett, "National and District Systems of Collective Bargaining in the United States," *Quarterly Journal of Economics* 26:3 (May 1912), 427–28; Thomas A. Klug, *The Roots of the Open Shop: Employers, Trade Unions, and Craft Labor Markets in Detroit, 1959–1907*, dissertation, Wayne State University, 1993, 506.

9. Barnett, "National and District Systems of Collective Bargaining," 425–26.

10. Marguerite Green, *The National Civic Federation and the American Labor Movement* (Washington DC: Catholic University of America Press, 1956), especially 37–90.

11. Horizontal integration absorbed product market competitors; vertical integration gave control over key inputs to be denied competitors and entrants. Economies of scale and speed were not the only advantages gained, nor were they the main motivations for consolidation, it appears. Naomi R. Lamoreaux, *The Greater Merger Movement in American Business, 1895–1904* (Cambridge: Cambridge University Press, 1985), especially 87–117, 152–58, and 187–94. Cf. Alfred D. Chandler, "The Beginnings of 'Big Business' in American Industry," *Business History Review* 33 (Spring 1959), 1–31, and *The Visible Hand: The Managerial Revolution in American Business* (Cambridge: Harvard University Press, 1977).

12. David Brody, *Steelworkers in America: The Non-Union Era* (New York: Harper and Row, 1960), 51–55.

13. John A. Garraty, "The United States Steel Corporation Versus Labor: The Early Years," *Labor History* 1:1 (Winter 1960), 9, 23; Ron Chernow, *The House of Morgan: An American Banking Dynasty and the Rise of Modern Finance* (New York: Touchstone, 1990), 82. Morgan's "right-hand man," George W. Perkins, was an enthusiastic supporter of the National Civic Federation, an association representing both labor and capital and dedicated at the time to promoting joint cartelist relations. Perkins contributed a third of the $8,000 salary the NCF paid to John Mitchell of the United Mine Workers, who headed its collective bargaining or "trade agreements" department. On joint cartelism in coal mining, see chapter 7.

14. Many of the steel men had apparently insisted on an open-shop policy before joining U.S. Steel. Marguerite Green, *The National Civic Federation*, 25.

15. Thomas K. McCraw and Forest Reinhardt, "Losing to Win: U.S. Steel's Pricing, Investment Decisions, and Market Share, 1901–1938," *Journal of Economic History* 49:3 (September 1989).

16. Klug, *The Roots of the Open Shop*, 483; Russell S. Bauder, "National Collective Bargaining in the Foundry Industry," *American Economic Review* 24:3 (September 1934), 468.

17. Samuel Gompers, *Labor and the Employer* (New York: Dutton, 1920), 43.

18. Klug, *The Roots of the Open Shop*, 557.

19. H. W. Hoyt, "Manufacturers' Associations, Labor Organizations, and Arbitration," *The Engineering Magazine* 19:2 (May 1900), 174.

20. Klug, *The Roots of the Open Shop*, 613.

21. "National Founders' Association: Sixth Annual Convention," *Iron Age*, November 27, 1902, 31.

22. On scarcity and machines, see Haydu, "Employers, Unions, and American Exceptionalism: Pre-World War I Open Shops in the Machinery Trades in Comparative Perspective," *International Review of Social History* 33:1 (1988), 36; Klug, *The Roots of the Open Shop*, 593, 693; Bauder, "National Collective Bargaining in the Foundry Industry," 465, 469, 475; and William Lazonick, *Competitive Advantage on the Shop Floor* (Cambridge: Harvard University Press, 1990), 217–18. Employers also tried collectively to deal with scarcity problems with pressure on unions to relax restrictions on employment of apprentices. See, for example, "Features of the Founders' Convention," *Iron Age*, 27 November 1902, 38.

23. Frank maintained the union's demand that wages in cities should be higher "is only used for 'jacking up purposes.'" The convention ignored him, adopting a statement of principles calling for rates "to be governed by local or shop conditions." "The National Founders' Eighth Annual Convention: The New York Agreement Abrogated and Arbitration Principles Adopted," *Iron Age*, 24 November 1904, 20, 22.

24. "The National Founders' Eighth Annual Convention: The New York Agreement Abrogated and Arbitration Principles Adopted," *Iron Age*, 24 November 1904, 21; "National Founders Association: Sixth Annual Convention," and "Features of the Founders' Convention," *Iron Age*, 27 November 1902, 28, 31, and 38. See also William F. Willoughby, "Employers' Associations for Dealing With Labor in the United States," *Quarterly Journal of Economics* 20:1 (November 1904), 131–32.

25. "Arbitration in the Machinery Trade," *Iron Age*, 22 November 1900; "Hearings Before the Industrial Commission," *Iron Age*, 14 June 1900, 29.

26. "The Machinists' Demands," *Iron Age*, 16 May 1901, 49–50; Montgomery, *Workers' Control in America: Studies in the History of Work, Technology, and Labor Struggles* (Cambridge: Cambridge University Press, 1979), 54–55.

27. Montgomery, *Workers' Control* 55; Jeffrey Haydu, *Between Craft and Class: Skilled Workers, Factory Politics in the United States and Britain* (Berkeley: University of California Press, 1988), 83, and Haydu, "Employers, Unions, and American Exceptionalism," 32–33.

28. Montgomery, *Workers' Control*, 55. The year after the Murray Hill failure, the union officially outlawed working on piece rates. Bruno Ramirez, *When Workers Fight: The Politics of Industrial Relations in the Progressive Era, 1898–1916* (Westport, CT: Greenwood, 1978), 90.

29. "The Settlement of the Machinists' Strike," *Engineering Magazine* 19:4 (July 1900), 522; "Hearings Before the Industrial Commission," *Iron Age*, 14 June 1900, 28; Haydu, *Between Craft and Class*, 80; Klug, *The Roots of the Open Shop*, 592–93, 652 (note 41).

30. "Hearings Before the Industrial Commission," *Iron Age*, 14 June 1900, 29.

31. Introductions on this are Robert W. Dunn, *The Americanization of Labor: The Employers' Offensive Against the Trade Unions* (New York: International Publishers, 1927), especially 81–102 and Irving Bernstein, *The Lean Years: A History of the American Worker 1920–1933* (Boston: Houghton Mifflin, 1960), 144–57. The best single source on employers' organized, national-level activities is the report of the Senate Committee on Education and Labor, *Violation of Free Speech and Rights of Labor—Labor Policies of Employers' Associations, Part I: The National Metal Trades Association*, 76th Cong., 1st sess., 1939.

32. Important and useful discussions of welfare capitalism in America can be found in David Brody, "The Rise and Decline of Welfare Capitalism," in John Braeman et al., eds., *Change and Continuity in Twentieth Century America: The 1920's* (Columbus: Ohio State University Press, 1968), 147–78 [(revised and reprinted in

Brody, *Workers in Industrial America: Essays on the Twentieth Century Struggle* (New York: Oxford University Press, 1980), 48–81]; Stuart D. Brandes, *American Welfare Capitalism, 1880–1940* (Chicago: University of Chicago Press, 1970); Daniel Nelson, *Managers and Workers: Origins of the New Factory System in the United States, 1880–1920* (Madison: University of Wisconsin Press, 1975), 101–21; Ramirez, *When Workers Fight,* 147–59; Lizabeth Cohen, *Making a New Deal: Industrial Workers in Chicago 1919–1939* (Cambridge: Cambridge University Press, 1990), especially 159–211 and 238–46; Frank R. Dobbin, "The Origins of Private Social Insurance: Public Policy and Fringe Benefits in America, 1920–1950," *American Journal of Sociology* 97:5 (March 1992), 1416–50; and Sanford Jacoby, *Modern Manors.*

33. Jacoby, *Employing Bureaucracy: Managers, Unions, and the Transformation of Work in American Industry, 1900–1945* (New York: Columbia University Press, 1985), 198–99.

34. *Employing Bureaucracy,* 167–80.

35. Sumner Slichter, "The Current Labor Policies of American Industries," *Quarterly Journal of Economics* 43:3 (May 1929), 393–435; Paul Starr, *The Social Transformation of American Medicine: The Rise of a Sovereign Profession and the Making of a Vast Industry* (New York: Basic, 1982), 294.

36. Murray Webb Latimer, *Industrial Pension Systems in the United States and Canada* (New York: Industrial Relations Counselors, 1932), 42; Jacoby, *Employing Bureaucracy,* 199. See also Jacoby, *Modern Manors,* 26–34.

37. Ramirez, *When Workers Fight,* 151–52; John H. Patterson, "Altruism and Sympathy as Factors in Works Administration," *Engineering Magazine* 20 (January 1902), 579–80; Jacoby, *Modern Manors,* 62; Slichter, "Current Labor Policies," 398.

38. Green, *The National Civic Federation,* 274.

39. Howell Harris, "Open Shop, Part 4" at *H-Business* (www.eh.net/ehnet/ Archives, 16 December 1996), 1. Montgomery claims that the NAM and NMTA "engaged as heartily in it as did the NCF." *Workers' Control,* 61. However, Clarence Bonnett, in *Employers' Associations: A Study of Typical Associations* (New York: Macmillan, 1922), and Albion Guilford Taylor, *Labor Policies of the National Association of Manufacturers* (Urbana: University of Illinois, 1927), leave discussion of welfare work out of their extensive discussions.

40. NAM, Employment Relations Committee, letter No. 3, "Housing Assistance," 31 July 1926 (NAM/600/Industrial Relations Department, Employment Relations 1920–1933); Noel Sargent (Manager, NAM's Industrial Relations Department), "Company Plans to Reduce and Alleviate Unemployment," 9 October 1930 (NAM/I[149]/Industrial Relations Department, Public Social Insurance, 1928–1933); Edward S. Cowdrick [quote on pensions], Counselor in Personnel Administration; H. W. Forster, of Brown, Crosby & Co.; and S. W. Ashe, General Electric, "Plant Pension Plans and Mutual Benefit Associations: Addresses Delivered at the 1928 Annual Meeting of the National Association of Manufacturers," (New York: NAM, 1928).

41. National Industrial Conference Board, *Industrial Pensions in the United States* (New York: NICB, 1925), 31–40; G. William Domhoff, *State Autonomy or Class Dominance? Case Studies on Policy Making in America* (New York: Aldine de Gruyter, 1996), 32–33.

42. Robert Ozanne, *A Century of Labor-Management Relations at McCormick and International Harvester* (Madison: University of Wisconsin Press, 1967), 156–61.

43. On the AMA, see Jacoby, *Employing Bureaucracy,* 180–82 and 185. On the IRC, see Bernstein, *The Lean Years,* 168; G. William Domhoff, *The Power Elite and the State: How Policy is Made in America* (New York: Aldine de Gruyter, 1990), 57; *State*

Autonomy or Class Dominance?, 128–30; and Latimer, *Industrial Pension Systems*, 894–902. Latimer was not able to confirm that pensions reduced turnover, industrial militancy, and union formation. Their clear benefit was that companies could cheaply get rid of older employees whose wages outstripped their productivity (and persuade lower level supervisors to discharge them) without deleterious effects on morale, particularly among still productive workers approaching retirement age.

44. For a contemporary and rudimentary statement of the theory see Sumner Slichter, "The Secret of High Wages," *The New Republic*, 28 March, 1928, 185.

45. M. C. Rorty, "Is Collective Bargaining Compatible with a Free Price and Wage System?" *The Management Review* 24:2 (February 1935), 38–39.

46. Henry Ford, *My Life and Work* (Garden City, NY: Doubleday, Page & Co., 1923), 147. See also John R. Lee, "The So-Called Profit Sharing System in the Ford Plant," *Annals of the American Academy of Political and Social Science* 65 (May 1916), 307; Allan Nevins, *Ford: The Times, the Man, the Company* (New York: Scribner's, 1954), 512–57, especially 539; Keith Sward, *The Legend of Henry Ford* (New York: Rinehart, 1948), 47–63; and Stephen Meyer, *The Five Dollar Day: Labor Management and Social Control in the Ford Motor Company 1890–1921* (Albany: SUNY Press, 1976).

47. Daniel M. G. Raff, "Ford Welfare Capitalism in Its Economic Context," in Sanford Jacoby ed., *Masters to Managers: Historical and Comparative Perspectives on American Employers* (New York: Columbia University Press, 1991), 93, 95. See also Raff and Lawrence H. Summers, "Did Henry Ford Pay Efficiency Wages?" *Journal of Labor Economics* 5:4, part 2 (1987), s72–s75; Nevins, *Ford*, 537, 550.

48. John A. Garraty, "The United States Steel Corporation Versus Labor," 10 (quote), 20, 23–26; National Industrial Conference Board, *Wages in the United States 1914–1930* (New York: NICB, 1931), 48.

49. Ozanne, *A Century of Labor-Management Relations*, 109–10, 138–39, 141, 148, 177; Robert Ozanne, *Wages in Practice and Theory: McCormick and International Harvester 1860–1960* (Madison: University of Wisconsin Press, 1968), 7–8.

50. Clarence J. Hicks, *My Life in Industrial Relations: Fifty Years in the Growth of a Profession* (New York: Harper & Brothers, 1941), 41–52, 55–56; Stuart Chase, *A Generation of Industrial Peace: Thirty Years of Labor Relations at Standard Oil Company* (New Jersey: Standard Oil Company, 1947), 20.

51. Schatz, *The Electrical Workers*, 19, 24, 67, and 170.

52. Construction workers employed by the firm, by comparison, were paid lower than union rates, but their employment and therefore earnings were more regular, and at the end of the year, competitive. Herbert Feis, *Labor Relations: A Study Made in the Procter and Gamble Company* (New York: Adelphi, 1928), 44–6, 125–28.

53. Gerald Zahavi, *Workers, Managers, and Welfare Capitalism: The Shoeworkers and Tanners of Endicott Johnson, 1890–1950* (Urbana: University of Illinois Press, 1988), 37–38, 53, 104–5, 137.

54. Jacoby, *Modern Manors*, 63, 74.

55. Walter H. Uphoff, *Kohler on Strike: Thirty Years of Conflict* (Boston: Beacon, 1966), 6–18.

56. Charles Brown, James Hamilton, and James Medoff, *Employers Large and Small* (Cambridge: Harvard University Press, 1990), 50.

57. Taylor, "Shop Management," 25 and "Testimony before the Special House Committee," 37, in *Scientific Management* (New York: Harper & Row, 1911).

58. Harris, "Open Shop, Part 4," 4; "Employers' Collective Action in the Open-Shop Era: The Metal Manufacturers' Association of Philadelphia, c. 1903–1933,"

in Steven Tolliday and Jonathan Zeitlin, eds., *The Power to Manage? Employers and Industrial Relations in Comparative-Historical Perspective* (London: Routledge, 1991), 136. Recent research from the 1980s finds a strong association between firm size and wages, even controlling for worker quality, working conditions, and union avoidance efforts. Brown et al., *Employers Large and Small*, 42. On the NMTA surveys, see N. Arnold Tolles and Robert L. Raimon, *Sources of Wage Information: Employer Associations* (Ithaca: Cornell University, 1952), 124–27.

59. Address of James W. Van Cleave before the 5th Annual Convention of the Iowa State Manufacturers' Association, 7 June 1907 (NAM/Acc 1521/Reel 4).

60. Bonnett, *Employers' Associations*, 350–51.

61. Sidney Fine, *"Without Blare of Trumpets": Walter Drew, the National Erectors' Association, and the Open Shop Movement, 1903–57* (Ann Arbor: University of Michigan Press, 1995), 42, 55.

62. Bonnett, *Employers' Associations*, 139, 145.

63. Magnus W. Alexander, "Employers' Associations in the United States," *International Labour Review* 25:5 (May 1932), 612; Bonnett, *Employers' Associations*, 73, 102–3, 114; Klug, *Roots of the Open Shop*, 973; "The National Founders' Association: Important Questions Considered by the Ninth Annual Convention," *Iron Age*, 23 November 1905, 1384.

64. "Part of Address by Noel Sargent at Meeting of Pennsylvannia Trade Secretaries Association" (NAM/520/Industrial Relations Department; Open Shop/1921–1930).

65. NAM, *Open Shop Bulletin No. 5*, 3 June 1921, 8.

66. Bonnett, *Employers' Associations*, 503; "Newspaper article written by William Frew Long of the Associated Industries of Cleveland for the *New York Commercial* of December 11, 1925," in Senate Committee on Education and Labor, *Violation of Free Speech and Rights of Labor—Labor Policies of Employers' Associations, Part II: The Associated Industries of Cleveland* 76th Cong., 1st sess., 1939, 226.

67. "Wagner Bill Clinic/Held at Annual Meeting/National Association of Manufacturers," no date, probably 1936 (NAM/I/211/USGovernment—Labor—Wagner Act).

68. "Wagner Bill Clinic," 16–17. As Wagner himself told NAM's general counsel James Emery, it was the "minority recalcitrants" of unfair employers who brought this law upon them. Senate Committee on Education and Labor, *To Create a National Labor Board: Hearings on S. 2926: Hearings before the Committee on Education and Labor*, 73d Cong., 2d sess., 1934, 374–75.

69. For more on the logic of this mix, see chapter 2. Swope's initiative, which Franklin Roosevelt, as governor of New York, took up in an effort to persuade the State Federation of Labor, came to nothing because of the rigid crafts-based culture and power configurations of the AFL. Swope was apparently impressed by the joint cartelism of Sidney Hillman's Amalgamated Clothing Workers' Union (see chapter 7). David Loth, *Swope of General Electric: The Story of Gerard Swope and General Electric in American Business* (New York: Simon and Schuster, 1958), 167–72; Alice Hamilton, *Exploring the Dangerous Trades* (Boston: Little Brown, 1943), 291; Frances Perkins, *The Roosevelt I Knew* (New York: Viking, 1946), 309; and Josephine Young Chase and Everett Needham Chase, *Owen D. Young and American Enterprise* (Boston: David R. Godine, 1982), 379, 847.

70. NAM, *Thirty-ninth Annual Convention*, Waldorf-Astoria, New York, December 5–6, 1934, 149–206, imprints collection, Hagley Library. See also "Text of New Parts of Recovery Platform Adopted by Manufacturers' Association," *New York Times*, 7 December 1934.

71. Fine, *Without Blare of Trumpets*, 55.

72. Address of James W. Van Cleave, 7 June 1907.

73. Senate Committee on Education and Labor, *Violation of Free Speech and Rights of Labor, Part I*, 1939, 20–21 and 39–40.

74. Senate Committee on Education and Labor, *Violation of Free Speech and Rights of Labor, Part I*, 40.

75. E. F. Du Brul, "Piece Work," *Bulletin of the National Metal Trades Association* 3:1 (January 1904), 39.

76. Senate Committee on Education and Labor, *Violation of Free Speech and Rights of Labor, Part I*, 127; Bonnett, *Employers' Associations*, 115.

77. Bonnett, *Employers' Associations*, 74.

78. Bonnett, *Employers' Associations*, 109; Senate Committee on Education and Labor, *Violation of Free Speech and Rights of Labor, Part I*, 43.

79. Senate Committee on Education and Labor, *Violation of Free Speech and Rights of Labor, Part II*, 34, 88, and 132–33.

80. Bonnett, *Employers' Associations in the United States*, 510, 523.

81. Senate Committee on Education and Labor, *Violation of Free Speech and Rights of Labor, Part I*, 30.

82. Bonnett, *Employers' Associations in the United States*, 141; Fine, *Without Blare of Trumpets*, 236.

83. Herbert Hoover, *The Memoirs of Herbert Hoover: The Great Depression, 1929–41* (New York: Macmillan, 1952), 312; "Prosperity Pledgers," *Time*, 2 December 1929, 35–36; Brody, "The Rise and Decline of Welfare Capitalism," 73; Bernstein, *The Lean Years*, 180; Henry Ford, *My Life and Work* 116–30; and Ford, *Today and Tomorrow* (Garden City, NY: Doubleday, Page, 1926), 150–61.

84. Anthony Patrick O'Brien, "A Behavioral Explanation for Nominal Wage Rigidity during the Great Depression," *Quarterly Journal of Economics* 104:4 (1989), 719–21; Ozanne, *Wages in Practice and Theory*, 52.

85. Brody, "The Rise and Decline of Welfare Capitalism," 67; Ozanne, *A Century of Labor-Management Relations*, 159.

86. A. E. Outerbridge, Jr., "Labor-Saving Machinery the Secret of Cheap Production," *Engineering Magazine* 12:4 (January 1897), 653.

87. O. F. Carpenter, "Management's Opportunities with Labor Relations Today," *Factory and Industrial Management* 75 (January 1928), 80–81; L. W. Moffett, "Agitation for Wage Reduction Finds Administration Opposed," *Iron Age*, 23 April 1931, 1382-c.

88. Hoover, *The Memoirs of Herbert Hoover: The Cabinet and the Presidency 1920–1933* (New York: Macmillan, 1952), 108; National Industrial Conference Board, *Wages in the United States, 1914–1926* (New York: NICB, 1927), 3–4; O'Brien, "A Behavioral Explanation for Nominal Wage Rigidity," 719–22.

89. Slichter, "Current Labor Policies," 401, 431–32.

90. Ozanne, *Wages in Practice and Theory*, 52.

91. O'Brien gives great weight to the purchasing power motive but invokes Lawrence Summers's version of efficiency wage theory to help explain the absence of "free riding." "A Behavioral Explanation for Nominal Wage Rigidity," 730. See Summers, "Relative Wages, Efficiency Wages, and Keynesian Unemployment," *American Economic Review* 78 (May 1988), 383–88. In hundreds of interviews with employers, Truman Bewley found the micro-economic motivations of avoiding morale and recruitment problems pervasive ones behind their refusal to cut wages during the early 1990s recession. Purchasing power, not surprisingly, was not men-

tioned. *Why Wages Don't Fall during a Recession* (Cambridge: Harvard University Press, 1999).

92. Brody, "The Rise and Decline of Welfare Capitalism," 73; Rorty, "Is Collective Bargaining Compatible with a Free Price and Wage System?" 36.

93. Brandes, *American Welfare Capitalism*, 142; Brody, "The Rise and Decline of Welfare Capitalism," 78. See also Cohen, *Making a New Deal*, 238–46.

94. Dobbin, "The Origins of Private Social Insurance," 1423–31; Latimer, *Industrial Pension Systems*, 843.

95. Jacoby, *Modern Manors*, 33, 63, 74; Latimer, *Industrial Pension Systems*, 843. At Hershey's, apparently, old-fashioned paternalist and company town welfarism, along with sickness, accident, retirement, and death benefits, were not accompanied by particularly sweet wages and working hours during the Depression. This fact probably made the company vulnerable to labor unrest. Disarmed by hurt and dismay at workers' ingratitude, more than by anything else, Milton Hershey gave in to collective bargaining. Joel Glenn Brenner, *The Emperors of Chocolate: Inside the Secret World of Hershey and Mars* (New York: Random House, 1999), 116–17, 131–42.

96. Zahavi, *Workers, Managers, and Welfare Capitalism*, 37–38, 53, 104–5, and 137.

97. Uphoff, *Kohler on Strike*, 6–18.

98. Jacoby, *Modern Manors*, 32–33.

4. Employers Unite

1. J.S. Edström, "Anteckningar från ett sammanträde på Operakällarens entrésolvåning," 22 April 1932 (Edström 34[A14d]).

2. Edström to C. J. Malmros, 25 April 1932 (Edström 34 [A14d]). On Carl Kempe and MoDo, see Ragnar Björin, "Egnahemverksamheten vid Mo och Domsjö Aktiebolag," 169–80; Gunnar Sundblad, "Carl Kempe och skogsindustriens branschorganisationer," 845–5, in Bengt Lyberg, Sixten Ulfsparre and Bo Gyllensvärd, eds., *Festskrift tillägnad Carl Kempe 80 år, 1884–1964* (Uppsala: 1964); Karl Molin, "Patriarken möter byråkratin—En aspekt på svensk samhällsomvandling 1870–1914," in Thorsten Nybom and Rolf Torstendahl, eds., *Byråkratisering och maktfördelning* (Lund, 1989), 218–19; 238; and Gunnar Nordström, *Mo och Domsjö och arbetareorganisationerna intill 1940—Frans Kempes personalpolitiska program och Domsjö Arbetareföreningen* (Uppsala: Uppsala Universitet, 1993).

3. Edström, untitled memo, on ASEA stationery, no date (Edström 27 [A3g/styrelse m.m.]). The memo was probably written after Edström's visit to the United States sometime in April 1931. His handwritten note on the memo called for distributing "as many copies as possible." SAF's chief Hjalmar von Sydow seemed, for one, to have worried about the effect of wage reductions on purchasing power. SAF, Minutes, Styrelse, 1 April 1931. For more evidence of Ford's unpopularity among leading Swedish employers, see Georg Styrman to Edström, 18 January 1927 (Edström 25 [A3e/styrelsen]).

4. Söderlund to Edström, 30 April 1932 (Edström 34 [A14d]).

5. SAF, Minutes, Arbetsutskott, 31 October 1949.

6. Per-Anders Edin and Johnny Zetterberg, "Interindustry Wage Differentials: Evidence from Sweden and a Comparison with the United States," *American Economic Review* 82:5 (December 1992), 1342.

7. See also Peter Swenson, "Bringing Capital Back In, or Social Democracy Reconsidered: Employer Power, Cross-Class Alliances, and Centralization of Indus-

trial Relations in Denmark and Sweden," *World Politics* 43:4 (July 1991), 537–40. Employers' reaction to the wheelbarrow incident of 1928 is a good measure of the level of violence in Swedish industrial relations. Metalworkers in a Stockholm factory loaded a young piece rate buster who refused to join the union into a wheelbarrow and dispatched him down some iron-covered steps. SAF called special attention to the "scandalous" event in its yearly report. VF's executive director devoted more than a page to it—the only mention of worker violence—in his history of the association published in 1936. SAF, *Styrelse- och revisionsberättelser för år 1928*, 36–37; Georg Styrman, *Verkstadsföreningen* (Stockholm: P.A. Norstedt, 1936), 228–29.

8. See, for example, VF, Minutes, Extra allmänt möte, 21 February 1920.

9. "Arbetsgivarna och arbetsaftalslagstiftningen—Industrin uttalar sig mot regeringsförslaget," *Göteborgs handels- och sjöfartstidningen* 6 March 1911, 3. In 1926, Edström expressed similar fears about legislation, noting how in Norway in 1923 it inhibited use of the lockout. "Arbetsfredens fullgörande," 15 February 1926 (Edström 25 [A3e/Styrelsen]).

10. In 1920, exceptions were made but only on an individual, case-by-case basis, on behalf of older workers who had stood loyally behind their employers in past conflicts. Karl-Gustaf Hildebrand, Örjan Armfelt-Hansell and Arne Törnqvist, *Sågverksförbundet 1907–1957* (Stockholm: Almqvist & Wiksell, 1962), 240; von Sydow to Axel Palmgren, 17 December 1927 (Palmgren papers, Vol. 7); SAF, "P.M. rörande oorganiserade arbetares förhållande under arbetskonflikt," December 1934 (SAF, A555/20b); SAF, Minutes, Styrelse, 22 January 1920; VF, Minutes, Extra allmänt möte, 21 February 1920.

11. For example, engineering lockouts in 1903 and 1905 gave union organization a boost. Bo Stråth, *Varvsarbetare i två varvsstäder—En historisk studie av verkstadsklubbarna vid varven i Göteborg och Malmö* (Göteborg: Svenska Varv AB, 1982), 61–63.

12. Klas Åmark, *Facklig makt och fackligt medlemskap—De svenska fackförbundens medlemsutveckling 1890–1940* (Lund: Arkiv, 1986), 122; Anders Kjellberg, *Facklig organisering i tolv länder* (Lund: Arkiv, 1983), 269–319. Unions did not do as well in Denmark and Norway, where employers also locked out workers in large numbers. Evidence from those countries on (1) the guarantee of union support to all locked out workers, (2) lockout policy regarding unorganized workers, and (3) exclusion of locked out workers from public relief measures would be required to substantiate or refute this argument. Finnish employers did not lock out nonunion members. Von Sydow to Palmgren, 17 December 1927 (Palmgren papers).

13. "De svenska arbetsgivarnas organisationsformer," draft of an article for *Chalmerska jubileumsskriften*, no date (probably 1929), (Edström 34 [A14d]).

14. Angus Maddison, *The World Economy in the 20th Century* (Paris: OECD, 1989), 89; Gösta Ahlberg, *Stockholms befolkningsutveckling efter 1850* (Stockholm: Almqvist & Wiksell, 1958), 107; Dorothy Swaine Thomas, *Social and Economic Aspects of Swedish Population Movements, 1750–1933* (New York: Macmillan, 1941), especially Appendix D, Table 92.

15. Maddison, *The World Economy*, 89.

16. *Emigrationsutredningen—Betänkande* (Stockholm: Norstedt, 1913), 9–10 (motion from Ernst Beckman).

17. Hjalmar von Sydow, *Om arbetarstatistik och arbetsförmedling inom arbetsgifvarorganisationer* (Stockholm: SAF, 1907), 14.

18. This discussion is based on John Lindgren, *Svenska Metallindustriarbetareförbundets historia, Band I 1880–1905* (Stockholm: Tiden, 1938), 618–23 , and 633; Carl Hallendorff, *Svenska Arbetsgifvareföreningen 1902–1927* (Stockholm: 1927), 67–73; and Hans De Geer, *The Rise and Fall of the Swedish Model: The Swedish Em-*

ployers' Confederation and Industrial Relations over Ten Decades (Chichester, UK: Carden, 1992), 31–34.

19. Three pairs of rates were to apply in different parts of the country according to prevailing wage and living costs, with the greater Stockholm area taking the highest.

20. Sweden's first national level agreements, for the tobacco and printing industries, were negotiated in 1902, 1903, and 1904. These, however, regulated only general working conditions and procedural matters, not wages. Lennart Lohse, *Arbetsgivarnas inställning till föreningsrätt arbetareskydd och arbetstid i statsvetenskaplig belysning* (Stockholm: SAF, 1963), 63.

21. Thomas, *Social and Economic Aspects of Swedish Population Movements*, 419, 428–33; Aubrey Clayton to Edström, 12 February 1907 (Edström 21 [A3a/överstyrelsen]).

22. Edström and Carl O. Holmberg to VF's överstyrelse, 1 December 1907 (Edström 23 [A3c/Öfverstyrelse]); VF, Minutes, Styrelse för Norra kretsen, 7 November 1907 (Edström 21 [A3a/Norra kretsen]); VF, Överstyrelse 15 February 1908 and 18 May 1911; and VF, Cirkulär N:r 29 (26 September 1908). On the public labor exchanges, see Bo Rothstein, "Från 'Det svenska systemet' till 'Den svenska modellen' eller Fanns det en arbetsmarknadspolitik före AMS?" *Arkiv for studier i arbetarrörelsens historia* 23–24 (1982), 4–11.

23. Hallendorff, *Svenska Arbetsgifvareföreningen*, 78–80.

24. Lohse, *Arbetsgivarnas inställning till föreningsrätt*, 70–71; Bernt Schiller, *Storstrejken 1909—Förhistoria och orsaker* (Göteborg: Elanders, 1967), 39.

25. Ragnar Casparsson, *LO under fem årtionden, 1924–1947* (Stockholm: Tiden, 1948), 1:269–70, 258–65.

26. Casparsson, *LO under fem årtionden*, 1:274.

27. De Geer, *The Rise and Fall of the Swedish Model*, 36. An earlier SAF historian argued that "prominent elements in [LO] were rather well aware that the whipsaw tactics in the long run were injurious for workers themselves and deleterious for those aims that their leaders had to protect and advance." Hallendorff, *Svenska Arbetsgifvareföreningen*, 55 and 114.

28. Schiller, *Storstrejken*, 74–6; Bernt Schiller, *LO, paragraf 32 och företagsdemokratin* (Stockholm: LO/Prisma, 1974), 28.

29. Peter Billing, Lars Olsson, and Mikael Stigendal, "Malmö—Our Town": Local Politics in Social Democracy," in Klaus Misgeld, Karl Molin, and Klas Åmark, *Creating Social Democracy: A Century of the Social Democratic Labor Party in Sweden* (University Park, PA: Pennsylvania State University Press, 1992), 282; Schiller, *Storkstrejken*, 35 and 63–68. See also Klas Åmark, *Maktkamp i byggbransch—Avtalsrörelser och konflikter i byggbranschen 1914–1920* (Lund: Arkiv, 1989), 25.

30. Krister Gierow, *Sveriges Pappersbruksförbund 1907–1957* (Lund: Berlingska Boktryckeriet, 1957), 29–30.

31. The unions were once hostile to the old paternalistic benefits because they were sometimes withdrawn in punitive fashion against union activists. John Lindgren, Herbert Tingsten, and Jörgen Westerståhl, *Svenska metallindustriarbetareförbundets historia, Band II 1906–1925*, 2:126–8. The December Compromise prohibited such action.

32. Lindgren et al., *Svenska metallindustriarbetareförbundets historia* 2:113–36; Sven Olsson, *Järnbruksförbundet 1906–1956* (Stockholm: Esselte, 1958), 43–54.

33. Olsson, *Järnbruksförbundet*, 44.

34. M. Carlson, JBF, to Sveriges Verkstadsföreningen, 5 October 1908; Protokoll vid sammanträde med delegerade för Sveriges Verkstadsföreningen och Järnbruks-

förbundet, 27 November 1908 (Edström 24 [A3d/Samarbete]). See also Styrman, *Verkstadsföreningen*, 135–37; Olsson, *Järnbruksförbundet*, 54–5. Earlier, in June of that year, VF had invoked the absence of such a clause to explain why it could not back the building industry lockout with a sympathy lockout. VF, Överstyrelseprotokoll, 27 June 1908. Personal differences between VF and SAF leaders had obstructed VF's affiliation with SAF, now partially superfluous. On the importance of LO's overarching financial support as a motive for employers' centralization, see James Fulcher, *Labour Movements, Employers, and the State: Conflict and Co-operation in Britain and Sweden* (Oxford: Clarendon, 1991), 92.

35. Hildebrand et al., *Sågverksförbundet*, 233–37; Schiller, *Storstrejken*, 204.

36. Paper pulp producers and ready-to-wear clothing firms, for example, desired centralized pay agreements in part to bring about a downward leveling of wages across the board. To the extent they wanted to level the competitive playing field in their product markets, centralization was to lower standards in the high pay firms, not bring the lower-paying firms up to higher standards as in American negotiated cartelism (see chapter 7). Schiller, *Storstrejken*, 186–206, especially at 183 and 189.

37. Also, SAF wanted to impose a commitment to the open shop, employers' right to sympathy actions, and finally, a procedural agreement, with centralized conciliation, akin to the Danish employers' prized "September Agreement" of 1899 and the VF arrangement set up in 1905. Schiller, *Storstrejken*, 106–7.

38. Hjalmar von Sydow, *Om den svenska arbetsgivareorganisationen, dess verksamhet och betydelse* (Stockholm: SAF, 1932), 19.

39. Hjalmar von Sydow, *Riktlinier för Svenska Arbetsgivareföreningens verksamhet under gångna och kommande år,* (Stockholm: SAF, 1913), 36–37.

40. Nils Bergsten, *Sveriges Textilindustriförbund 1907–1950* (Stockholm: 1957), 224.

41. "Utdrag ur protokoll, hållet vid sammanträde med Styrelsen för Göteborgskretsen af Sveriges Textilindustriförbund den 18 April 1913," Appendix 16 to TIF, Minutes, Överstyrelsen, 26 April 1913.

42. Bergsten, *Sveriges Textilindustriförbund*, 228–30. Seniority differentials, presumably, were to be grandfathered too, so that as new employees were taken on, and the overall standards raised, they would gradually disappear.

43. Normal wages were partially differentiated according to regional zones and graduated downward for workers between 16 and 20 years of age. Workers already receiving wages above the standard were to keep those rates, but they were not to be increased. Their differentials, it appears, were to be closed over time as negotiated standards were raised to their levels. TIF, "Kollektivt aftal angående arbets- och löneförhållanden för textilarbetare jämte för samtlige fabriker gemensamma ordningsföreskrifter," 1914, 6.

44. So far, engineering, steel, sawmills, textiles, and glass were the major manufacturing sectors with national agreements.

45. Gösta Walldén, *Med Sveriges Träindustriförbund under 50 år* (Stockholm: Relieftryck, 1955), 148–49; Klas Åmark, *Faklig makt och fackligt medlemskap—De svenska fackförbundens medlemsutveckling 1890–1940* (Lund: Arkiv, 1986), 132.

46. Gierow, *Sveriges Pappersbruksförbund*, 29–30.

47. Åmark, *Maktkamp i byggbransch*, 277 and note 9, 362.

48. The cement embargo was largely successful, but bricks found their way into production, from among other places, Holland and Germany. For an in-depth analysis of the 1920 conflict, see Åmark, *Maktkamp i byggbransch*, 243–301. See also Thor Brunius, *Svenska Byggnadsindustriförbundet 25 år* (Stockholm: Victor Petterson, 1944), 20–108.

49. Tom Söderberg, "Pappersmasseförbundets första halvsekel," in *Pappers-masseförbundet 1907–1957* (Stockholm: Almqvist & Wiksell, 1957), 66–71.

50. E. W. Paues, "Avskrift," Appendix 2 to Sveriges Konfektionsindustriför-bund, Minutes, 11 December 1925.

51. Hallendorff, *Svenska Arbetsgifvareföreningen*, 6, 55; Hjalmar von Sydow, *Riktlinier för Svenska Arbetsgivareföreningens verksamhet*, 6–7.

52. Gierow, *Sveriges Pappersbruksförbund*, 90.

53. *Styrelse- och revisionsberättelser för år 1921* (Stockholm: SAF, 1921); Hallen-dorff, *Svenska Arbetsgifvareföreningen*, 156; Karl-Olof Faxén, "Några kommentarer till SAFs lönepolitiska uttalanden under 1920-talet," in Eskil Wadensjö et al., eds., *Ving-arnas trygghet—Arbetsmarknad, ekonomi och politik* (Lund: Dialogos, 1989), 69–75.

54. Thommy Svensson, *Från ackord till månadslön*, 118; "Edströmiana. Utdrag av tal vid direktör J.S. Edströms middag å Riche," 7 March 1939 (Kugelberg P6, Ed-ström, J. S.); Lars Magnusson, *Arbetet vid en svensk verkstad: Munktells 1900–1920* (Lund: Arkiv, 1987), 229.

55. Sven Anders Söderpalm, *Storföretagarna och det demokratiska genombrottet—Ett perspektiv på första världskrigets svenska historia* (Lund: Gleerups, 1969), espe-cially 194–96.

56. Styrman, *Verkstadsföreningen*, 181–85; P. S. Graham, G. A. Styrman et al., "Arbetskraftsbetänkande n:r 1: Ang. konkurrens om arbetskraft," appendix to VF, Ordinarie allmänt möte, 12 May 1920. See also, VF, Minutes, Överstyrelse, 11 No-vember 1919; 17 December 1919; Cirkulär n:r 38–1920, "Betr. annonsering efter arbetskraft," 26 March 1920; Cirkulär n:r 59–1920 "Ang. allmänna mötets behand-ling av arbetarerekryteringsfrågan," 17 May 1920; SAF, Minutes, Ombudsman-nakonferens, 20 February 1939.

57. Styrman, *Verkstadsföreningen*, 180–81; Appendix to VF, Minutes, Över-styrelse, 19 December 1921.

58. VF, Minutes, Överstyrelse, 8 December 1921; VF, Minutes, Extra allmänt möte, 29 December 1921.

59. VF, Minutes, Extra allmänt möte, 29 December 1921. Edström's resignation gesture was not reported in the minutes, but by executive director Georg Styrman in *Verkstadsföreningen 1896–1945*, 204–05. See also Ulf Olsson, *Lönepolitik och löne-struktur—Göteborgs verkstadsarbetare 1920–1949* (Göteborg: Ekonomiska-Historiska Institutionen vid Göteborgs Universitet, 1970), 27.

60. VF Cirkulär n:r 35–1921, 21 December 1921; VF, Direktiv N:r 1–1922, 5 January 1922.

61. VF [Kommitté tillsatt av överstyrelsen], "Verkstadsindustrin och den indus-triella demokratin," Appendix to VF, Överstyrelse, 17 June 1920; Stenografiska an-teckningar vid allmänt möte med medlemmar av Sveriges Verkstadsföreningen (Appendix to VF, Minutes, Allmänt möte, 30 June 1919).

62. Styrman, *Verkstadsföreningen*, 205; VF Cirkulär nr. 2, 1929 (Edström 26 [A3f/Allmänt]).

63. VF, Minutes, Överstyrelse, 20 February 1923 and 1 March 1923; Extra all-mänt möte, 8 March 1923; SAF, Minutes, Ombudsmannakonferens, 11 September, 13–14 November, and 20 December 1923; Styrman, *Verkstadsföreningen*, 216–7.

64. G. A. Styrman (VF) to AB Pumpseparator, 3 November 1925; E. A. Forsberg (AB Separator) to VF, 3 December 1925; VF, Memo, 18 January 1926; J. S. Edström to Styrman, 26 January 1926; VF (Edström) to AB Pumpseparator, 16 February 1926 (VF F515/1925–26).

65. VF, Minutes, Överstyrelse, 21 September 1978.

66. SAF, Minutes, Ombudsmannakonferens, 20 September 1921. Division over

minimum versus normal wages continued in the following years. SAF, Minutes, Ombudsmannakonferens, 19 May, 1924 and Styrelse, 16 January 1925.

67. Appendix E to SAF, Minutes, Styrelse, 16 November 1918.

68. VF, Minutes, Öfverstyrelse, 12 September and 8 December 1921; VF, Minutes, Extra kretsmöte med medlemmarna av Sveriges Verkstadsföreningens Norra krets, 30 November 1921. High and rising wages in meat processing (*charkuteribranschen*) transmitted upward wage pressure on engineering through food costs.

69. "Till Styrelsen för Svenska Arbetsgivareföreningen," Appendix A to SAF, Minutes, Styrelse, 11 November 1921.

70. SAF, Minutes, Styrelse, 11 November 1921.

71. SAF, Minutes, Styrelse, 20 December 1922, including Appendix A, N. E. Malmgren, Byggnadsämnesförbundet to Svenska Arbetsgivareföreningen, 16 December 1922.

72. SAF, Minutes, Ombudsmannakonferens, 20 December 1928.

73. SAF, *Styrelse- och revisionsberättelse för år 1925*, 36–39; Minutes, Styrelse, 10 September, 16 October, and 24 October 1925.

74. SAF, Minutes, Styrelse, 16 October and 21 December 1925; *Styrelse- och revisionsberättelse för år 1925*, 38.

75. The fourth, a nonmining operation, AB Express-Dynamit, remained in Allmänna Gruppen, which housed a diverse group of firms, especially in chemicals.

76. SAF, Minutes, Styrelse, 24 October, 12 November, and 21 December 1925.

77. It was also granted permission to negotiate with the militant Syndicalist union, which enjoyed majority support in the northern mines, on the peculiar condition that it receive the go-ahead from the Social Democratic union of miners (*Gruvindustriarbetareförbundet*) in LO, which was inclined to collaborate with the Syndicalists. SAF, Minutes, Styrelse, 24 October and 21 December 1925. On the LKAB strike, see Peter Swenson, *Fair Shares: Unions, Pay, and Politics in Sweden and West Germany* (Ithaca: Cornell University Press), 1989: 85–89.

78. Iwan Schyman, *Christian Storjohann—Mannen som byggde Billerud* (Stockholm: Bok och Bild, 1968), 110; SAF, Minutes, Styrelse, 12 November and 21 December 1925.

79. SAF, Minutes, Styrelse, 1 July 1932. Versteegh was apparently an unregenerate industrial tyrant; his pulp operations in Ådalen were consequently the site of strong Communist presence and the notorious deaths of workers at the hand of the Swedish military in 1931. He had directly benefitted when SAF footed the bill for the strike-breakers working for shipping companies loading Versteegh's pulp products in Ådalen, even though he was not in SAF. Casparsson, *LO under fem årtionden*, 2:214.

80. This division, von Sydow believed, gave him the ability to play off various units against each other. Von Sydow to Palmgren, 20 April 1927 (Palmgren papers).

81. Also, rates of capital intensity and vulnerability to loss of dedicated customers varied, making companies and sectors differently disposed to lockouts and lockout compensation from SAF. SAF, Minutes, Styrelse, 7 April 1930; Carl Wahren, memorandum to SAF's board from the Holmen board, 27 March 1930, (Edström 34 [A14d]); Storjohann to Edström, 18 September 1931, (Edström 34 [A14d]); SAF, Minutes, Styrelse, 6 May, 1932 and *Styrelse- och revisionsberättelser för år 1932*, 3.

82. VF, Minutes, Överstyrelse, 27 April 1931.

83. SAF, Minutes, Styrelse, 4 August 1931. Storjohann feared loss of business to other pulp producers in Sweden and abroad if he joined the lockout, and that Communists, who were making headway in much of the industry, would gain control of

the union at Billerud. They had done so temporarily in 1928 because of the poisoned atmosphere created by the badly executed lockout. SAF, Minutes, Styrelse, 4 August 1931.

84. SAF, Minutes, Styrelse, 4 August 1931; *Styrelse- och revisionsberättelser för år 1928*, 29, 32.

85. SAF, Minutes, Styrelse, 4 August 1931; *Styrelse- och revisionsberättelser för år 1928*, 32.

86. SAF, Minutes, Styrelse, 4 August 1931, and 9 March, 30 March, and 30 April 1928.

87. SAF, Minutes, Styrelse, 4 August, 1931; Edström to Storjohann, 23 September 1931. See also Storjohann to Edström, 18 September 1931 (Edström 34 [A14d]).

88. SAF, Minutes, Styrelse, 4 August 1931 and 1 July 1932; Gierow, *Sveriges Pappersbruksförbund*, 138–41.

89. VF, Minutes, Överstyrelse, 17 August 1931.

90. SAF, Minutes, Styrelse, 29 September 1931, and 28 September 1932.

91. SAF, Minutes, Styrelse, 9 March 1928. The following month LO forced its mineworkers' union in April 1928 to quit a "Swedish-Russian Unity Committee," an arrangement through which the Soviet Union channeled money to the union from its Russian counterpart. The Soviet Union had picked up 45 percent of the bill for an eight-month conflict, costing the industry 800,000 worker days. Casparsson, *LO under fem årtionden*, 2:89–108 and Ragnar Casparsson, *LO—Bakgrund, utveckling, verksamhet* (Stockholm: Prisma, 1966), 237–40. SAF was particularly pleased by Metall's vigorous actions against Communists. SAF, *Styrelse- och revisionsberättelser för år 1928*, 70–73.

92. SAF, Minutes, Styrelse, 9 March 1928.

93. Von Sydow to K. A. Lagergren, 6 October 1928, cited in Jörgen Westerståhl, *Svensk Fackföreningsrörelse—Organisationsproblem Verksamhetsformer Förhållande till staten* (Stockholm: Tiden, 1946), 154; SAF, Minutes, Styrelse, 9 March and 30 April 1928; SAF, *Styrelse- och revisionsberättelser för år 1928*, 33.

94. There was still pessimism. Paper industrialist Malmros thought LO might start offering lockout support to the pulp workers if SAF went to attack with a sympathy lockout of the paper industry. SAF, Minutes, Styrelse, 1 July 1932. On Storjohann and Söderlund, see Edström to Hugo Hammar, 20 June 1930 (Edström 34 [A14d]). Storjohann had good reason for remaining pessimistic: Edström had opposed having VF help PMF in 1928. Hugo Hammar to Edström, 24 February 1928 and Edström to Hammar, 2 March 1928 (Edström 34 [A14d]).

95. Tom Olsson, *Pappersmassestrejken 1932—En studie av facklig ledning och opposition* (Lund: Arkiv, 1980), 342. Olsson finds the report discussed in PMF, Minutes, Styrelse, 15 July 1932. Unfortunately, these minutes appear to have been lost from the current paper industry association's archives. The memo and JBF's response are cited in Sven Olsson, *Järnbruksförbundet*, 197.

96. SAF, Minutes, Styrelse, 3 August and 9 September 1932.

97. SAF, Minutes, Ombudsmannakonferens, 3 May 1932; Olsson, *Pappersmassestrejken*, 285–88, 323, and 451, note 37.

98. SAF, Minutes, Styrelse, 1 April, 6 May, 1 July, and 3 August 1932; *Styrelse- och revisionsberättelser för år 1932*, 35. See also Tom Söderberg, "Pappersmasseförbundets första halvsekel," 91; Olsson, *Pappersmassestrejken*, 310–11, 320, 324–25, 341–42, 363; and Casparsson, *LO under fem årtionden*, 2:287, 290–92, and 297.

99. Members of SPIAF's board believed that LO had withheld support so as not to provoke a mass lockout. Olsson, *Pappersmassestrejken*, 291.

100. SAF, Minutes, Styrelse, 9 September 1932. On the contract votes and other events, SAF, Minutes, Styrelse, 4 March, 1 April, 3 August 1932, and 9 September 1932; *Styrelse- och revisionsberättelser för år 1932*, 36.

5. Cross-Class Alliance

1. Söderlund to Edström, 6 February, 1934 (Edström 34 [A14d]); Larson to Palmgren, 15 February 1934; Larson to Palmgren, 13 February 1936 (Palmgren papers). The self-assessment is from Axel Brunius, "De svenska arbetsgivarnas organisationsformer," draft of article for *Chalmerska jubleumsskriften* (circa 1929), (Edström 34 [A14d]).

2. The therapeutic imagery of "draining," "bleeding," and "lancing" recur in SAF, Minutes, Ombudsmannakonferens, 30 August 1932; VF, Minutes, Överstyrelse, 8 September 1932; Ivar O. Larson to Axel Palmgren, 4 November 1932 (Palmgren papers).

3. SAF, Minutes, Styrelse, 24 November and 15 December 1933; 28 February and 31 May 1934; Appendix B to Minutes, 29 January 1934; and Ombudsmannakonferens, 27 February 1935; Statistiska Centralbyrån, *Statistisk årsbok för Sverige* (Stockholm: SCB, various years).

4. On Edström and forest products, see SAF, Minutes, Styrelse, 9 March 1928. While VF had successfully forced through 60 percent wage reductions during the post-WWI depression in engineering (other export sectors accomplished reductions between 62 percent and 86 percent), the building industry had only brought down its wages by about 40 percent between 1920 and 1922. For these and other comparisons, see N. P. Mathiasson, "Inledningsanförande vid Hälsingborgs Fackliga Centralorganisations diskussionsmöte, Folkets Hus, 28 April 1929" (Edström 34 [A14d]); Carl Hallendorff, *Svenska Arbetsgifvareföreningen 1902–1927* (Stockholm: 1927), 156. On the building boom of 1930, see SAF, Minutes, Styrelse, 7 April 1930.

5. Bertil Ohlin, "Lönenivåns söndersplittring," *Verkstäderna* 22:7 (1926), 246–50; Georg Styrman, *Sveriges Verkstadsföreningen 1896–1945* (Stockholm: P.A. Norstedt, 1946), 228.

6. See H. E. Pulver, *Construction Estimates and Costs* (New York: McGraw-Hill, 1947), 137, and Ralph P. Stoddard, *Brick Structures: How to Build Them* (New York: McGraw-Hill, 1946), 47–50; SAF, Minutes, Styrelse, 28 April 1933.

7. On the 1920s, see SAF, Minutes, Styrelse, 20 November 1920, 11 November 1921 (including Appendix A); 23 September 1922; 28 July 1923, 10 March 1924, 15 May 1925, and 16 October 1925; *Styrelse- och revisionsberättelser för år 1924*, 27–29, 35–36, and 41. See also VF, Minutes, Överstyrelse 12 May 1920 and 8 December 1921; Arbetsutskott, 17 June 1920; Styrelse för Norra Kretsen, 30 November 1921. In 1918, the large national telegraph, railroad, and waterworks, together with large municipal projects, led the way in introducing the 52-hour week, dragging the rest of SAF in its wake. Hallendorff, *Svenska Arbetsgivareföreningen*, 141.

8. Edström to von Sydow, 6 March 1918 (Appendix D to SAF, Minutes, Styrelse, 11 March 1918); VF, Minutes, Överstyrelse, 13 June 1930; Sven Olsson, *Järnbruksförbundet 1906–1956* (Stockholm: Esselte, 1958), 211; SAF, Minutes, Styrelse, 20 November 1920.

9. SAF, Minutes, Styrelse, 4 August 1931; Styrman, *Verkstadsförening*, 227–28; K. A. Bratt, *J. Sigfrid Edström—En levnadsteckning* (Stockholm: Norstedt, 1953), 2:151; SAF, Minutes, Styrelse, 1 April and 4 August 1931.

10. On in-house building, see *Socialt inom Asea* (Västerås: Västmanlands Allehandas Boktryckeri, 1950), 3–9; Styrman to Edström, 20 June 1929; Edström to

Styrman, 21 June 1929; Fritjof Ekman (Metall) to Sveriges Verkstadsförening, 14 June 1929 (Edström 26[A3f/Allmänt]); SAF, Minutes, Styrelse 5, November 1927, and Ombudsmannakonferens, 17 September 1929.

11. On Metall, see Fritjof Ekman (Metall) to Verkstadsföreningen, 23 September 1927; Georg Styrman to Svenska Metallindustriarbetareförbundet, 20 October 1927; Ekman to VF, 14 June 1929 (Edström 26 [A3f/Allmänt]); VF, Minutes, Överstyrelse, 13 June 1930; VF, Cirkulär Nr. 10–1933, 25 September 1933; Styrman, *Verkstadsföreningen,* 243; SAF, Minutes, Ombudsmannakonferens, 17 September 1929; Olsson, *Järnbruksförbundet,* 211. On the labor court's reasoning, see, for example, "Arbetsdomstolens dom i mål mellan Svenska Metallindustriarbetareförbundet, kärande, samt Sveriges Verkstadsföreningen och Eriksbergs Mekaniska Verkstad AB, Göteborg," 13 February 1933. On building workers' tactics against in-house work, see SAF, Minutes, Ombudsmannakonferens 14 March 1930; Olsson, *Järnbruksförbundet,* 211.

12. SAF, Minutes, Ombudsmannakonferens, 12 April 1924; Minutes, Styrelse, 16 January 1925. On the spread of wage increases from plumbing and electrical installation work to engineering, see SAF, Minutes, Styrelse, 17 December 1930.

13. Anders Vigen, *De Nordiske Arbejdsgiverforeningers Samarbejde gennem 20 Aar* (Copenhagen: Langkjaer, 1927), 33–34; Hallendorff, *Svenska Arbetsgifvareföreningen,* 97; SAF, Minutes, Styrelse, 16 November 1918, Appendix E.

14. SAF, Minutes, 3 May 1920; 19 June 1920 (including Appendix C); 16 September 1920 (and Appendix C) and 26 November 1920 (and Appendix B); Klas Åmark, *Maktkamp i byggbransch—Avtalsrörelser och konflikter i byggbranschen 1914–1920* (Lund: Arkiv, 1989), 270; "Till Styrelsen för Svenska Arbetsgivareföreningen," 24 August 1920, Appendix C to SAF, Minutes, Styrelse, 31 August 1920. Grängesberg's action would be remembered later in the angry debate over its behavior in 1925 (see chapter 4).

15. On the 1924 agreements, see SAF, *Styrelse- och revisionsberättelser för år 1924,* 27–32, 41; SAF, Minutes, Styrelse, 23 April 1924. On organizational problems in the building trades, see SAF, Minutes, Styrelse, 19 June 1922, including Appendices C and D; 15 and 30 June 1923; 11 March, 15 May, and 21 December 1925.

16. On 1925, see SAF, *Styrelse- och revisionsberättelser för år 1925,* 21–22; Minutes, Styrelse, 16 October 1925; Edström to Styrman, 20 August 1933 (Edström 28[A3h/Styrelse m.m.]). On problems with electrical installation in engineering, and at ASEA in particular, see "Betr. hissmontörers och kraftverksmontörers förhållande till VF, resp. verkstadsavtalet," 8 September 1933 (Edström 29[A3h/Styrelse m.m.]); SAF, Minutes, 16 January 1925 and 17 December 1930; Hallendorff, *Svenska Arbetsgivareföreningen,* 158–161; Styrman, *Verkstadsföreningen,* 220; VF, Minutes, Överstyrelse, 19 December 1929 and 24 February 1930; "P.M. beträffande hissmontörers ställning," 20 September 1933 (Edström 29 [A3h/Styrelse m.m.]); Edström to Georg Styrman, 5 December 1933 (Edström 28 [A3h/Allmänt]); Jan Glete, *Asea under hundra år 1883–1983—En studie i ett storföretags organisatoriska, tekniska och ekonomiska utveckling* (Västerås: Asea, 1984), 126.

17. Hartmut Apitzsch, "Byggnadsbranschen: Produktionsförhållanden och organisationsstruktur," *Arkiv för studier i arbetarrörelsens historia* 2 (1972), 33; SAF, *Styrelse- och revisionsberättelser för år 1924,* 29, 41; SAF, Minutes, Styrelse, 16 October 1925.

18. On defeatism, see SAF, Minutes, 8 July 1930; VF, Minutes, Överstyrelse, 16 December 1933. On solutions, see SAF, Minutes, Styrelse, 23 April 1924; 3 February and 11 March 1925; 21 September and 30 April 1928. Nominated by SAF's Board of Directors in February 1925, Edström was elected vice chairman of SAF's

supreme decision making body, the Congress of Delegates (*fullmäktige*). SAF, Minutes, Styrelse, 3 February 1925.

19. On the apprenticeship scheme, which bore lackluster results because militant masons boycotted employers training too many apprentices, see SAF, Minutes, Styrelse, 10 September 1925, 17 December 1926, 11 January 1928, and 23 January 1929. On the recruitment initiatives, see Edström to Gustaf Söderlund, 3 October 1933 (Edström 34 [A14d]); SAF, Minutes, Styrelse, 15 December 1933 and 28 February 1934, including Appendix C.

20. On SAF's ties with banks and therefore export industry, see von Sydow to Christian Storjohann, 13 May 1929; Edström to Wiking Johnsson, 22 May 1929; Johnsson to Edström, 23 May 1929, and Edström to Johnsson, 25 May 1929 (Edström 34[A14d]).

21. On the Labor Court, see Edström to von Sydow, 2 November 1928 (Edström 34 [A14d]). On the construction issues, see VF, Minutes, Överstyrelse, 24 February 1930, and Edström to Styrman, 5 December 1933 (Edström 28 [A3h/Allmänt]). On the high wages and purchasing power argument, see von Sydow's statement in SAF, Minutes, Styrelse, 1 April 1931. The same month, Edström visited the United States. A memo probably from that same year, on ASEA stationery and with Edström's handwritten corrections, criticized the theory. Edström's note on the untitled memo called for distributing "as many copies as can be gotten" (Edström 27 [A3g/styrelse m.m.]).

22. On early relations with banks, see SAF, Minutes, Styrelse, 21 January 1922, 8 April 1922, 30 June 1923, and 29 September 1931; Hallendorff, *Svenska Arbetsgivareförening*, 99, 120, and 160. On Edström's behind-the-scenes efforts to replace von Sydow, see "P.M. från sammanträde i Stockholm den 6 maj 1929;" "P.M. från sammanträde i Stockholm den 8 juli 1930;" Edström to Hugo Hammar, 20 June 1930; Hammar to Edström, 21 June 1930; Edström to Marcus Wallenberg, 20 June 1930; and Edström to Hammar, 11 July 1930 (Edström 34 [A14d]). The official efforts to find a replacement, including setting up a committee, began in August 1930, immediately after the end of the secret search. Edström to members of SAF's board, 2 August 1930 (Edström 34 [A14d]). On Larson and von Sydow, see Ivar O. Larson to Axel Palmgren, 10 August 1931 (Palmgren papers); Axel Brunius, "Ivar Larson och uppgiften," *Industria* 11 (1947), 13.

23. Evidence that Edström relied on bank connections to influence individual employers is in VF, Minutes, Överstyrelse, 12 May 1920; Edström to Gustaf Ekman (Göteborgsbanken), 18 October 1930 (Edström 34 [A14d]); SAF, Minutes, Styrelse, 6 May 1932; and Edström to Styrman, 29 January 1943 (Edström 30[A3j/Korrespondens]). Wallenberg, possibly prompted by Edström, wrote to Storjohann in 1932, blasting his withdrawal from SAF as "grave disloyalty." Schyrman, *Christian Storjohann*, 104. On ASEA and Wallenberg, see Jan Glete, *Storföretag i starkström— Ett svenskt industriföretags omvärldsrelationer* (Västerås: ASEA, 1984), 60–61.

24. Thor Brunius, *Svenska Byggnadsindustriförbundet 25 år*, (Stockholm: Viktor Petterson, 1944), 151; Kupferberg, "Byggnadsstrejken 1933–34," *Arkiv för studier i arbetarrörelsens historia* 2 (1972), 44 and 51–52; SAF, Minutes, 27 June and 20 October 1933; VF, Minutes, Överstyrelse 16 December 1933.

25. SAF, Minutes, Styrelse, 15 December 1933.

26. SAF, Minutes, Styrelse, 27 November and 15 December 1933; VF, Minutes, Överstyrelse, 16 December 1933. Söderlund did not expect construction employers to hold out until spring 1934.

27. SAF, Minutes, Styrelse, 15 December 1933.

28. On worker attitudes, see SAF, Minutes, 24 September 1930; Karlbom and

Pettersson, *Svenska Grov- och Fabriksarbetarförbundets historia* (Stockholm: 1944), 265; A. Helldén, *Svenska Byggnadsträarbetareförbundet 1924–1928* (Stockholm: 1954), 38–39. On attitudes about the conflict, see SAF, Minutes, Styrelse, 27 June 1933; Apitzsch, "Socialdemokrater och kommunister i byggnadsstrejken,"*Arkiv för studier i arbetarrörelsens historia* 2 (1972), 61–71; Apitzsch, "Byggbranschen," 34–35; and Kupferberg, "Byggnadsstrejken," 45–46.

29. On Skromberga, see Bill Sund, *Nattens vita slavar—Makt, politik och teknologi inom den svenska bagerinäringen 1896–1955* (Stockholm: Almqvist & Wiksell, 1987), 88–90. On the LO debate in the 1920s and 1930s about wage differentials and LO's centralized role, see especially Jörgen Ullenhag, *Den solidariska lönepolitiken i Sverige: Debatt och verklighet* (Stockholm: Läromedelsförlagen, 1971), 26–35; Axel Hadenius, *Facklig organisationsutveckling—En studie av Landsorganisationen i Sverige* (Stockholm: Rabén & Sjögren, 1976), 35–42. On Stockholm, see SAF, Minutes, Styrelse, 20 November 1920; 7 April, and 24 September 1930.

30. SAF, Minutes, Styrelse, 24 November 1933. On LO's press releases and Möller see Kupferberg, "Byggnadsstrejken," 45, and Apitzsch, "Socialdemokrater och kommunister," 63.

31. Quote from Edström's diary in Bratt, *J. Sigfrid Edström,* 2:64–65.

32. Apitzsch, "Socialdemokrater och kommunister," 71; Kupferberg, "Byggnadsstrejken," 53–57; SAF, Minutes, Styrelse, 28 February 1934; Bratt, *J. Sigfrid Edström,* 2:65.

33. See especially Söderlund's comments in SAF, Minutes, Styrelse, 27 June 1933.

34. Appendix B to SAF, Minutes, Styrelse 29 January 1934; SAF, Minutes, 28 February 1934; Söderlund to Edström, 6 February 1934 (Edström 34[C]).

35. Olle Nyman, *Svensk parlamentarism 1932–1936—Från minoritetsparlamentarism till majoritetskoalition* (Uppsala: Almqvist & Wicksell, 1947), especially 108–12, 136–37, 158, 528–32; Kupferberg, "Byggnadsstrejken," 44, 45, and 54. It is unclear from existing work whether the farmers spelled out substantive terms that had to be satisfied.

36. Stig Hadenius, Björn Molin, and Hans Wieslander, *Sverige efter 1900* (Stockholm: Aldus/Bonniers, 1974), 125–27; Gustaf Söderlund, "Yttrande över en . . . promemoria angående beredskapsarbeten till motverkande av arbetslöshet," 11 February 1933 (SAF A711141/1d).

37. F. Holmén (Svenska Byggnadsindustriförbundet) to SAF, 2 February 1933 (SAF A711141/1d/1933).

38. G. Hultman (Pappersmasseförbundet) to SAF, 4 February 1933, and Torsten Andersson (Sågverksförbundet) to SAF, 4 February 1933 (SAF/A711141/1d/1933).

39. On Stockholm, see Georg Styrman (Verkstadsföreningen) to SAF, 8 February 1933 (SAF A711141/1d/1933), 2. On wages for reserve jobs, see "Reservarbetenas konkurrens om arbetskraften," *Industria* 22 (1933), 569; "De höga reservarbetslönerna—Besvär av Svenska Arbetsgivareföreningen," *Industria* 25 (1933), 646–7; Eli Heckscher et al., *Bidrag till Sveriges ekonomiska och sociala historia under och efter världskriget, Del I* (Stockholm: Norstedt, 1926), 322–24. According to Heckscher's analysis, reserve jobs brought unskilled laborers without dependents on average 4 percent greater earnings than their counterparts in the regular labor market. Those without dependents, because they were less able to take advantage of in-kind housing and travel benefits, earned on average only 2 percent less.

40. E. W. Paues (Textilindustriförbund) to SAF, 6 February 1933 (SAF A711141/1d/1933); Andersson to SAF, 4 February 1933; G. Hultman to SAF, 4 February 1933; G. Styrman to SAF, 8 February 1933.

41. Gustaf Söderlund, "Yttrande över en . . . promemoria angående bered-skapsarbeten till motverkande av arbetslöshet," 11 February 1933 (SAF-A711141/ 1d/1933), 9–14, 18–20; SAF, Minutes, Styrelse, 24 November 1933.

42. SAF, Minutes, Styrelse, 24 November and 15 December 1933; 28 February and 31 May 1934; Appendix B to Minutes, Styrelse, 29 January 1934; and Minutes, Ombudsmannakonferens, 27 February 1935.

43. SAF, Minutes, Styrelse, 27 January 1933; Nils Unga, *Socialdemokratin och arbetslöshetsfrågan 1912—1934* (Stockholm: Arkiv, 1976), 168.

44. Edström, *P.M. angående utredning om vissa social-industriella problem m.m.*, 18 December 1936 (Edström 36 [I/A2. Sveriges Industriförbund]); Rolf G.H. Henriksson, *Som Edström ville—hur IUI blev till* (Stockholm: Industrins Utrednings-institut, 1990), 31–34; 201–04. Employers were also to take account of workers' seniority and family circumstances when choosing between workers of equal skill for layoffs. This was probably already established and prudent practice for most employers.

45. Klas Åmark, "Diskussion," in Sten Edlund et al., eds., *Saltsjöbadsavtalet 50 år—Forskare och parter begrundar en epok 1938–1988* (Stockholm: Arbetslivscen-trum, 1989), 112. On events in 1937, see Åmark, *Facklig makt och fackligt medlem-skap—De svenska fackförbundens medlemsutveckling 1890–1940* (Lund: Arkiv, 1986), 153; A. Helldén, *Svenska Byggnadsträarbetareförbundet*, 29–53.

46. Sten Edlund, "Saltsjöbadsavtalet i närbild," in Edlund et al., eds., *Saltsjö-badsavtalet*, 65; Ragnar Casparsson, *Saltsjöbadsavtalet i historisk belysning* (Tiden: Stockholm, 1966), 132; Sten Höglund, "En fallstudie i organisationsförändring— Vad drev fram 1941 års stadgeförändring i den svenska Landsorganisationen?" *Research Reports from the Department of Sociology* (Umeå: University of Umeå, 1979), 36 and 54–55; Sven Anders Söderpalm, *Arbetsgivarna och Saltsjöbadspolitiken—En historisk studie i samarbetet på svensk arbetsmarknad* (Stockholm: SAF, 1980), 32. See also the discussion and extensive list of such actions in one building sector in K. A. Winroth, Elektriska Arbetsgivareföreningen, till Styrelsen för SAF, 22 February 1933, Appendix C to SAF, Minutes, Styrelse, 31 March 1933.

47. For the text of the agreement, see Casparsson, *Saltsjöbadsavtalet*, 263–66. On the building trades' unions opposition and later refusal to sign, see Anders Jo-hansson, *Tillväxt och klasssamarbete—En studie av den svenska modellens uppkomst* (Stockholm: Tiden, 1989), 140, 145; Knut Johansson (chairman of Byggnadsar-betareförbundet 1952–1975), "Kommentar," in Edlund et al. (eds.), *Saltsjöbadsav-talet*, 100; "Byggnads godtar inte huvudavtal," *Arbetsgivaren* 23 April 1965, 7.

48. On Norway, see Edström, "Arbetsfredens fullgörande," February 1926 (Ed-ström 25 [A3e/styrelsen]).

49. On Åmark's conjecture, see "Diskussion," in Edlund et al. (eds.), *Saltsjö-badsavtalet*, 112, and Åmark, *Facklig makt och fackligt medlemskap—-De svenska fack-förbundens medlemsutveckling 1890–1940* (Lund: Arkiv, 1986), 148 and note 23, 189. Axel Hadenius asserts incorrectly in *Facklig organisationsutveckling* (1976), 54, that strikebreaking was explicitly forbidden in the Basic Agreement. Ingemar Flink speculates that with the Basic Agreement strikebreaking became fairly superflu-ous and that SAF might have made an informal promise to "hold back" on strike-breaking. Ingemar Flink, *Strejkbryteriet och arbetets frihet—En studie av svensk ar-betsmarknad fram till 1938* (Uppsala: Almqvist & Wiksell, 1978), 117 and 147. Åmark cites Jarl Torbacke, who found that newspaper publishers, organized inde-pendently of SAF, started constructing a strikebreaking apparatus in 1933 in preparation for efforts to impose wage reductions and their own separate "Basic Agreement." The disappearance of this activity seems to have followed the news-

papers' resounding success. Torbacke, "Före första 'fredsavtalet' 1937—Tidnings-utgivarpolitik i konfliktsituation," *Historisk tidskrift* 2 (1975). On Ådalen and strike-breaking, see Casparsson, *Saltsjöbadsavtalet*, 224; "Text of Report by Roosevelt's Commission on Labor Relations in Sweden," *New York Times* 25 September 1938, 40.

50. SAF, Minutes, Styrelse, 25 November 1932; 24 and 27 November 1933; Edström to Söderlund, 3 October, 1933 (Edström 34 C).

51. Three other organizations, *Föreningen för Arbetarskydd, Föreningen Norden, Föreningen Teknisk Samhällshjälp* were also budgeted a combined total of 7,700 crowns in 1944. On appropriations in that decade, see, for example, Appendix III, SAF, Minutes, Styrelse, 1944, 353; Appendix 1 to SAF, Minutes, Styrelse, 16 December 1948; Appendix 1 to SAF, Minutes, Styrelse, 15 February 1951. A large conflict in the agricultural sector against the construction unions in 1942 was the context of the rescue operation for *Arbetets Frihet.* SAF, Minutes, Styrelse, 29 October and 26 November 1942; Fritiof Söderbäck, SAF, to Sveriges Träindustriförbund, 20 January 1943 (in volume marked "1944 Svenska Arbetsgivareföreningen," at Träindustriförbundet's archive, Stockholm). On Boyton and Ådalen, see Flink, *Strejkbryteriet,* 81–85 and 89.

52. Flink, *Strejkbryteriet,* 110, 131–32, and 165–66.

53. On removing strikebreakers, see Flink, *Strejkbryteriet,* 130, 133, and 143. On LO's insufficient capacity and support, see SAF, Minutes, Ombudsmannakonferens, 11 April 1933; Ivar O. Larson, Karl Wistrand, and Thure Widefeldt, "P.M. angående åtgärder mot den syndikalistiska arbetarrörelsen," Appendix A to SAF, Minutes, Ombudsmannakonferens, 6 December 1933. On LO's problems with Syndicalists, see Valter Åman, *Svensk syndikalism* (Stockholm: LO, 1938).

54. Employer-organized strikebreaking in the public sector probably declined dramatically after Saltsjöbaden. Before, politicians across the board had been eager to legislate a stop to "socially dangerous conflicts" (*samhällsfarliga konflikter*) paralyzing essential public and private transportation, utilities, and other services. SAF helped prepare for these occasions by funding TSH, *Föreningen Teknisk Samhällshjälp.* With the Basic Agreement's conciliation provisions regarding such conflicts, LO committed itself to assert control in this area. Thus, Edström's ASEA, for one, announced it would drop its independent support of TSH in 1939, in reference to the 1938 agreement. See Casparsson, *Saltsjöbadsavtalet,* 134–37; Jörgen Westerståhl, *Svensk Fackföreningsrörelse—Organisationsproblem Verksamhetsformer Förhållande till staten* (Stockholm: Tiden, 1946), 362; Flink, *Strejkbryteriet,* 69–81, 124, and 145. Nevertheless, SAF would continue to give TSH small contributions through 1944, when it provided only 700 crowns. SAF, Minutes, Styrelse, 1944, Appendix III ("Diverse anslag"), 353.

55. Though he is correct in thinking SAF was friendly to the idea of a strong LO, Åmark mistakenly speculates that it might have promised in the 1930s to help take over collection of union membership fees. This practice, by individual employers, did not begin until much later, against official SAF disapproval. Åmark, "Diskussion," 113. For a discussion on employer collection of union fees, see chapter 11.

56. Sten Höglund, "Storföretagen, Svenska Arbetsgivareföreningen och beslutsordningen i arbetarnas fackliga organisationer—Arbetsgivaresynpunkter på LO:s och fackförbundens sätt att fatta beslut om förlikningsbud perioden 1925–1941," *Research Reports from the Department of Sociology* No. 45 (Umeå: University of Umeå, 1978), 27 and 51. The sawmill workers' constitution, though requiring referenda, stipulated that a 3/5 majority was necessary to approve a strike, and thus reject a contract.

57. Casparsson, *Saltsjöbadsavtalet,* 243–44; Höglund, "En fallstudie i organisa-

tionsförändring," 44 and 73, note 76. Söderlund's statement is in SAF, Minutes, Styrelse, 25 January 1935.

58. "Anteckningar från sammanträde på Operakällarens entrésolvåning;" Höglund, "Storföretagen," 20–24 and 44–57. For employers' standard arguments, see Karl Hildebrand, "Brister i förhandlingsordning och omröstning," in Hildebrand and Axel Brunius, *Fackföreningsrörelsen och samhället* (Stockholm: Hugo Geber, 1934), 52–59.

59. Casparsson, *LO—-Bakgrund, utveckling, verksamhet* (Stockholm: Tiden, 1966), 244. The yeas and abstainers about equaled the rejectors. Höglund, "Storföretagen,"13; Hadenius, *Facklig organisationsutveckling*, 125–26.

60. *Betänkande om folkförsörjning och arbetsfred* (SOU 1935:65), especially 108–09; Hadenius, *Facklig organisationsutveckling*, 49.

61. On the details and causes of the 1941 changes, see Ullenhag, *Den solidariska lönepolitiken*, 40–45; Hadenius, *Fackliga organisationsutveckling*, 45–68; Höglund, "En fallstudie i organisationsförändring," 28–56; Sten Höglund, "Centralisering och reduktion av medlemsinflytandet i en stor facklig organisation,"*Research Reports from the Department of Sociology* (Umeå: University of Umeå, 1979), 4–13. Hadenius and Höglund disagree with Ullenhag, saying that solidaristic wage policy was unimportant as a basis for the organizational reform. Indeed, the 1941 LO report argued that social policy, not wage policy, was the only feasible way of squeezing inequalities from below. It only gingerly and obliquely addressed the problem of high wages with its factual analysis of wage differentials between traded good sectors and home-market sectors. See Landsorganisationens Femtonmannakommité, *Fackföreningsrörelsen och näringslivet* (Stockholm: LO, 1941), 200–08, 215–66, and 273. Whether by intention or not, in strengthening LO vis-à-vis its high-pay unions, the reforms served solidaristic purposes. It is telling that high-pay unions were highly critical, while SAF was favorable. SAF, Minutes, Styrelse, 25 September 1941. Albin Lind's 1938 article "Solidarisk lönepolitik," is reprinted in Erik Zander, ed., *Fackliga klassiker—En antologi king facklig demokrati, ideologi och lönepolitik* (Stockholm: Rabén & Sjögren/LO, 1981); quotation from 98.

62. On the leadership search, see "P.M. från sammanträde i Stockholm," 6 May 1929; Edström to Wallenberg/Enskilda Banken, 20 June 1930; Edström to General G. R. J. Åkerman, 20 June 1930; Hugo Hammar to Edström, 21 June 1930; Edström to Ragnar Blomquist, 9 July 1930; Edström to Åkerman, 10 July 1930; Edström to Hammar, 11 July 1930; Åkerman to Edström, 13 July 1930; Edström to Blomquist, 28 July 1930; Edström to Åkerman, 26 August, 1930 (Edström 34 [A14d]). On Edström versus Larson, see SAF, Minutes, Styrelse, 28 April 1933. On Söderlund's mission to forge consensus, see Söderlund to Edström, 1 March 1931 (Edström 34 [A14d]).

63. SAF, Minutes, Styrelse, 28 February and 31 May 1934.

64. SAF, Minutes, Styrelse, 26 May, 20 October, and 24 November 1933; Söderlund to Edström, 17 October and 21 October 1933 (Edström 34 [A14d]).

65. Brunius, *Svenska Byggnadsindustriförbundet*, 77–79.

66. Söderlund to Edström, 23 March 1937 (Edström 35 [A14e]).

67. W. de Shàrengrad to Edström, 11 December 1939, and attached "P.M. angående avtalsförhandlingarnas centralisering" (Edström 35 [A14e]); SAF, Minutes, Styrelse, 26 September 1939.

68. SAF, Minutes, Styrelse, 12 September (Söderbäck quote) and 31 October 1940; 25 September 1941; and 24 September 1942. On Lindberg see Johansson, *Tillväxt och klassamarbete*, 213–18. On textiles and garments, see Otto Thurdin's statement in SAF, Minutes, Ombudsmannakonferens, 16 September 1947.

6. Egalitarian Employers

1. Hans De Geer, "Mellan effektivitet och rättvisa: Arbetsgivarna och lönen," in *Lönebildning i förändring* (Stockholm: SAF, 1992), 13, 20. See also De Geer, "En förnyad reflexion om den svenska modellen och arbetslivets förändringar," in Per Thullberg and Kjell Östberg eds., *Den svenska modellen* (Lund: Studentlitteratur, 1994), 108. Hugh Heclo and Henrik Madsen say the "policy of wage solidarity in return for centralized wage bargaining" was a "premeditated bargain." *Policy and Politics in Sweden: Principled Pragmatism* (Philadelphia: Temple University Press, 1987), 116. Drawing on Axel Hadenius's account (see note 4), I made the same mistake in Peter Swenson, *Fair Shares: Unions, Pay, and Politics in Sweden and West Germany* (Ithaca: Cornell University Press, 1989), especially 57.

2. Albin Lind's 1938 article "Solidarisk lönepolitik," is reprinted in Erik Zander, ed., *Fackliga klassiker—En antologi kring facklig demokrati, ideologi och lönepolitik* (Stockholm: Rabén & Sjögren/LO, 1981). Before then, "socialistic wage policy" seemed more common. In 1936 the metalworkers' union called for a "*socialistisk (solidaritetsbetonad) lönepolitik.*" Jörgen Ullenhag, *Den solidariska lönepolitiken i Sverige—Debatt och verklighet* (Stockholm: Läromedelsförlagen, 1971), 26, 34. See also Rudolf Meidner, *Samordning och solidarisk lönepolitik* (Stockholm: Prisma/LO, 1974), 7–25 and De Geer, "Mellan effektivitet och rättvisa," 15. For a recent analysis focusing exclusively on the worker interests behind solidarism, see Klas Fregert, "Relative Wage Struggles during the Interwar Period, General Equilibrium and the Rise of the Swedish Model," *Scandinavian Economic History Review* 42:2 (1994), 173–86. On the changed meaning of solidaristic wage policy in the 1970s, see chapter 13.

3. Details of the central agreements are in Meidner, *Samordning och solidarisk lönepolitik*, 26–44. On the results, see Ingvar Ohlsson, "Den solidariska lönepolitikens resultat," in *Lönepolitik och solidaritet. Debattinlägg vid Meidnerseminariet* (Stockholm: LO, 1980), 239.

4. This combines, in broad strokes, the core of the labor-centric analyses, which differ on the relative importance of particular details. See Ullenhag, *Den solidariska lönepolitiken*; Meidner, *Samordning och solidarisk lönepolitik*; Axel Hadenius, *Facklig organisationsutveckling: En studie av Landsorganisationen i Sverige* (Stockholm: Rabén & Sjögren, 1976); and Hans De Geer, *SAF i förhandlingar: Svenska Arbetsgivareföreningen och dess förhandlingsrelationer till LO och tjänstemannaorganisationerna 1930–1970* (Stockholm: SAF, 1986), 134–37, 143–46, 182–96. The "Rehn-Meidner model" was published as LO, *Fackföreningsrörelsen och den fulla sysselsssättningen—Betänkande och förslag från Landsorganisationens organisationskommitté* (Stockholm: LO, 1951).

5. SAF, Minutes, Arbetsutskott, 14 October 1952.

6. "Memorialanteckningar från sammanträde med Svenska Arbetsgivareföreningens lönekommitté," 10 December 1953 (SAF AO/Lönekommittén), 5.

7. Hans Söderlund, "Grundvalarna för SAF:s lönepolitik. Underlag för diskussion vid sammanträde med SAF:s lönekommitté," 14 April 1955, (SAF AO/Lönekommittén), 19–21, 40. See also Söderlund, "Synpunkter på bärkraftsprincipen," 22 November 1954 (SAF AO/Lönekommittén).

8. "Diskussion av lönekommitténs promemoria nr 6 angående grundvalarna för SAF:s lönepolitik," Appendix to SAF, "Memorialanteckningar från sammanträde med Svenska Arbetsgivareföreningens lönekommitté," 20–21 April 1955 (SAF AO/Lönekommittén).

9. Söderlund, "Grundvalarna för SAF:s lönepolitik," 41. On his father, see chapter 5.

10. "Diskussion av lönekommitténs promemoria nr 6." Kugelberg's talk was published as "Lönepolitik i ett progressivt samhälle," *Nationalekonomiska Föreningens förhandlingar* 5 (1955). For Schwartz's ideas on system-wide job evaluation, see his article "Följsamhet i löneutvecklingen," *Arbetsgivaren*, 28 June 1963, 4.

11. Faxén, "Grundvalarna för en arbetsgivareorganisations lönepolitik," 25 July 1956 (SAF AO/Lönekommittén), 20–25, 34.

12. Faxén, "Wage Policy and Attitudes of Industrial Relations Parties in Sweden," *Labour and Society* 2:1 (January 1977), 63–65. See also "Arbetsgivarorganisationer, lönepolitik och inflation," in *Erfarenheter av blandekonomin—Uppsatser och diskussioner vid Dahmén-symposiet om den svenska blandekonomin* (Stockholm: Skandinaviska Enskilda Banken, 1976), especially 119–20. In a historical analysis of SAF's earlier solidarism in the 1920s, Faxén wrote that uniformity in wage levels was an "independent objective," deriving not from union pressure but from SAF's character as a "buyers' cartel." "Några kommentarer till SAFs lönepolitiska uttalanden under 1920-talet,"in Eskil Wadensjö et al., eds., *Vingarnas trygghet. Arbetsmarknad, ekonomi och politik* (Lund: Dialogos, 1989), 72–73.

13. Axel Brunius, "Ivar O. Larson och uppgiften," *Industria* 11 (1947), 12.

14. The eavesdropper overhead Erlander's conversation with Erik Åsbrink, on board an airplane. Lennart [no last name], "Erlander och politiken. Minnesanteckningar för Direktör Kugelberg," 1 October 1955 (included with Kugelberg's own "Minnesanteckningar"). On Sköld's view, as reported to Kugelberg, see Kugelberg, "Minnesanteckningar från diskussion på Hotell Tunneln i Malmö," 8 November 1954.

15. Meidner, *Samordning och solidarisk lonepolitik*, 26–35; Hadenius, *Facklig organisationsutveckling*, 68–91.

16. See Hadenius, *Facklig organisationsutveckling*, 86, 90. Meidner's narrative is strangely silent about employer interests and the power issue. *Samordning och solidarisk lonepolitik*, 7–25.

17. SAF, Minutes, Ombudsmannakonferens, 13 December 1954.

18. SAF, Minutes, Styrelse, 20 September 1951 and 17 January 1952. Neither Hadenius nor De Geer mentions stiff resistance in their accounts of these events. Hadenius, *Facklig organisationsutveckling*, 82; De Geer, *SAF i förhandlingar*, 119–20.

19. On the volume of wage drift, see Meidner, *Samordning och solidarisk lönepolitik*, 46. Holmström quote in SAF, Minutes, Styrelse, 21–22 October 1954. Wehtje in SAF, Minutes, Styrelse, 18 November 1954 and Kugelberg, "Minnesanteckningar från diskussion på Hotell Tunneln i Malmö," 8 November 1954.

20. Hallström in SAF, Minutes, Ombudsmannakonferens, 13–14 September 1954. Bahrke's and Bager's remarks in Bertil Kugelberg, "Minnesanteckningar från diskussion på Hotell Tunneln i Malmö," 8 November 1954.

21. Bergh in SAF, Minutes, Styrelse, 16 September 1954 and 21–22 October 1954. Elmstedt in SAF, Minutes, Ombudsmannakonferens, 13 December 1954. On the textile industry, squeezed between the international product market and the domestic labor market, see Kurt Samuelsson, *Från stormakt till välfärdsstat—Svensk samhällsutveckling under 300 år* (Stockholm: Rabén & Sjögren, 1968), 288.

22. Björnemann, Wahlstedt, and Andersson in Bertil Kugelberg, "Minnesanteckningar från diskussion på Hotell Tunneln i Malmö," 8 November 1954. Bahrke and Björnemann in SAF, Minutes, Styrelse, 21–22 October 1954.

23. SAF, Minutes, Styrelse, 22 April 1955 and 20 October 1955.

24. Hadenius, *Facklig organisationsutveckling*, 85–86, note 61.

25. Åberg in SAF, Minutes, Förbundsdirektörskonferens, 12–13 November 1956. Kugelberg in SAF, Minutes, Styrelse, 16 December 1954.

26. On the drift of workers from engineering to construction see SAF, Minutes, Styrelse, 23 May 1950, 15 November 1951, and 15 September 1955. On the building boom, see SAF, Minutes, Styrelse, 16 September 1954, and Styrelse- och revisionsberättelser 1949, 51–52.

27. On the free Saturdays and steel, see SAF, Minutes, Styrelse, 22–23 April 1954. In 1952, SAF rejected VF's request for a waiver from SAF's directive against free summer Saturdays. In 1954, individual engineering firms in VF clamored for dispensation from SAF to allow the five-day week. They expected morale and productivity benefits, but mostly wanted to solve their recruitment problems. Seventy or so mostly unorganized small engineering firms had already instituted five-day summer weeks and, thus "had no difficulties getting workers." SAF, Minutes, Styrelse, 20 November 1952; 7 May, 16 September, and 21–22 October 1954.

28. Kugelberg, "Minnesanteckningar från samtal med Professor Bertil Ohlin," 6 May 1954; "Minnesanteckningar från samtal med Direktör Jarl Hjalmarsson," 6 May 1954. On the strategic discussions, see SAF, Minutes, Styrelse, 22–23 April and 7 May 1954. See also Kugelberg, "Minnesanteckningar från samtal med Ingenjör Sven Dahlberg," 4 May 1954.

29. Osvald in SAF, Minutes, Förbundsdirektörskonferens, 7 December 1965. Per Holmberg, "Aspekter på låglönefrågan, *Tiden* 1 (1965), 5; "Löneklyftorna i forskarljus," *Fackföreningsrörelsen* 1 (1965), 310; and "Perspektivet," *Fackföreningsrörelsen* (1965), 156. See also Joachim Israel, "Aspekter på låglönefrågan," *Tiden* 2 (1965), 69.

30. Minutes, Förbundsdirektörskonferens, 7 December 1965.

31. Giesecke in SAF, Minutes, Förbundsdirektörskonferens, 13 September 1965. See related thoughts in Bertil Kugelberg, "Låglöneproblemet är främst ett höglöneproblem," *Arbetsgivaren*, 8 October 1965. On the 1966 agreeement, see Meidner, *Samordning och solidarisk lönepolitik*, 36.

32. On the better firms' domination, see Faxén, "Grundvalarna för en arbetsgivareorganisations lönepolitik," 32.

33. SAF, Minutes, Styrelse, 29 December 1937; "Angående gratifikationer," SAF-cirkulär E/1946; Kugelberg to Patrik Rydbeck, 16 November 1946, Appendix A to Protokoll, SAF-styrelse, 22 November 1946. VF also fought the battle at the sectoral level. Ulf Olsson, *Lönepolitik och lönestruktur—Göteborgs verkstadsarbetare 1920–1949* (Göteborg: Ekonomiska-Historiska Institutionen vid Göteborgs Universitet, 1970), 28–29.

34. See SAF's circular, "Angående gratifikationer," SAF-cirkulär E/1946. On the study, see Charles A. Myers, *Industrial Relations in Sweden: Some Comparisons with American Experience* (Cambridge, MA: The Technology Press, 1951). On the textile industry, see Nils Bergsten, *Sveriges Textilindustriförbund 1907–1950* (Stockholm: TIF, 1957), 390–400, 89. For the 1947 circular, see SAF, "Angående överbetalning av arbetskraft," SAF-cirkulär B/1947.

35. Direktörsklubben, Minutes, No. 91, 4 October 1945.

36. SAF, Minutes, Styrelse, 18 October 1951; Schwartz in "Memorialanteckningar från sammanträde med Svenska Arbetsgivareföreningens lönekommitté,"10 December 1953, 9. SAF's future executive director Steffan Giesecke gave his view in "Vinstandelssystemet," 10 December 1953 (SAF AO/Lönekommittén), 8.

37. On "excess labor mobility," see Curt-Steffan Giesecke, "Organisation av och arbetsuppgifter för arbetsgivareföreningens lönekommitté," 16 March 1953, (SAF AO/Lönekommittén), 1. The seniority debate is in SAF, Minutes, Ombudsmannakonferens, 21 October 1947.

38. American segmentalists would have had no beef with this and the other

things Rehn apparently suggested, according to employer discussions: individualized increments based on skill and low absenteeism. SAF, Minutes, Ombudsmannakonferens, 16 October 1950. See also SAF, Minutes, Ombudsmannakonferens 11 December 1950.

39. SAF, Minutes, Ombudsmannakonferens, 15 March 1954.

40. SAF, Minutes, Ombudsmannakonferens, 15 March 1954; Minutes, Styrelse, 18 March 1954. On VF, see Faxén, "Grundvalarna för en arbetsgivareorganisations lönepolitik," 26. On Volvo etc., see Olsson, *Lönepolitik och lönestruktur,* 27–29.

41. Every advanced country except Switzerland lost ground relative to the United States between 1938 and 1950, though Switzerland lost ground, unlike Sweden, between 1929 and 1938. On comparative usage, see Hjalmar von Sydow, *Om den Svenska Arbetsgivareorganisationen, dess verksamhet och betydelse* (Stockholm: SAF, 1932), 15, and Sveriges Industriförbund, "Yttrande angående arbetslöshetsförsäkring", 17 February 1933 (SAF A711141/1d/1933), 7. On comparative productivity, see Angus Maddison, *The World Economy in the 20th Century* (Paris, OECD, 1989), 89; *Monitoring the World Economy 1820–1992* (Paris, OECD, 1995), 47. Maths Isacson discusses productivity growth in *Verkstadsindustrins arbetsmiljö: Hedemora Verkstäder under 1900-talet* (Lund, Arkiv, 1990), 43.

42. Kugelberg and Schwartz in SAF, Minutes, Styrelse, 26–27 April 1962 and 13 December 1962. For data on usage in the 1950s and 1960s, see International Labour Office, *Payment By Results* (Geneva: ILO, 1951), 81–88; OECD, *Forms of Wage and Salary Payment for High Productivity* (Paris: OECD, 1970), 42–43. Specific information on engineering and construction is from Georg Styrman, *Verkstadsföreningen 1896–1945* (Stockholm: Norstedt, 1946), 310; SAF, Minutes, Förbundsdirektörskonferenser 1961 (Appendix 3, "Timförtjänster 2:a kvartalet 1961"); "Payment by Results in the Building Industry," *International Labour Review* 63:1 (January-June, 1951); John T. Dunlop, *Industrial Relations Systems* (Boston: Harvard Business School, 1993), 221; and "Tidlön eller ackord? Löneformer inom byggfacket i olika länder," *Arbetsgivaren,* 17 December 1955, 6. On shipbuilding, see Tommy Svensson, *Från ackord till månadslön: En studie av lönepolitiken, fackföreningarna och rationaliseringarna inom svensk varvsindustri under 1900-talet* (Göteborg: Svenska Varv AB, 183), 385.

43. According to labor economist Edward Lazear, piece rates are a rational response to the heterogeneity of workers sifted from a shallow reserve pool and the unevenness of their efforts resulting from a minimal fear of being fired. "Salaries and Piece Rates," *Journal of Business* 59:3 (1986), 405–31. On piece work in the building trades, see "Memorialanteckningar från sammanträde med Svenska Arbetsgivareföreningens lönekommitté," 10 December 1953, 7. On the paper representative's view, see comment by Lars-Olof Ekeberg in "Minnesanteckningar från direktörskonferens på Yxteholm," 17 April 1957. Geijer's conversation with Reuther is in Frederic Fleisher, *The New Sweden: The Challenge of a Disciplined Democracy* (New York: David McKay, 1967), 93–94.

44. On the decline of output restriction, see SAF, Minutes, Styrelse, 25 April 1957. On Taylor, see Frederick Winslow Taylor, "Shop Management," 30–34; "The Principles of Scientific Management,"15–24; and "Testimony before the Special House Committee," 38, in *Scientific Management* (New York: Harper & Row, 1911). For more on the relationship between full employment and workers' "breaking through the ceiling" (*takgenombrytning*), see Gösta Rehn [1956], "Försök till statistisk belysning av löneglidningens orsaker," in *Full sysselsättning utan inflation: Skrifter i urval* (Stockholm: Tiden, 1988), 298.

45. Previous research has tended to emphasize top-down consensus building among high level union and employer officials regarding technological innovation. See, for example, Anders L. Johansson, *Tillväxt och klassamarbete—En studie av den svenska modellens uppkomst* (Stockholm: Tiden, 1989).

46. On local autonomy, see VF, Minutes, Överstyrelse, 26 April 1931. On the training of engineers and foremen, see Hans De Geer, *Rationaliseringsrörelsen i Sverige—Effektivitetsidéer och socialt ansvar under mellankrigstiden* (Stockholm: Studieförbundet Näringslivet och Samhälle, 1978), 147–57; SAF, Minutes, Styrelse, 22 March 1945.

47. Eric Giertz, "Utveckling och förändring av arbetsorganisation inom tillverkningsindustrin," in *Lönebildning i företagsperspektiv* (Stockholm: SAF, 1992), 129.

48. Kellgren in SAF, Minutes, Förbundsdirektörskonferens, 15 April 1957. Geijer in Kugelberg, "Minnesanteckningar från besök i Finspång," 2 January 1957. On the sawmill industry, see Lars-Olof Ekeberg, PMF, "Minnesanteckningar från direktörskonferens på Yxteholm," 17 April 1957. On flour milling, see H. W. Söderman and Per H. Osvald (Sveriges Kvarnyrkesförbund) to SAF, 30 August 1965; Östen Ericson (Svenska Livsmedelsarbetareförbundet) to Sveriges Kvarnyrkesförbund, 16 June 1965; Curt-Steffan Giesecke to Sveriges Kvarnyrkesförbund, 2 September 1965 (SAF AO:26).

49. The connection between scarcity, piece work, and wage drift is discussed by Kugelberg, Faxén, and Wahlquist, for example, in SAF, Minutes, Styrelse, 26–27 April and 13 December 1962. See also SAF chairman Sven Schwartz's analysis in "Löneglidning och arbetsmarknadsläge," *Arbetsgivaren*, 14 August, 1964. On overall wage drift levels in 1964, see SAF, Minutes, Styrelse, 17 November 1964.

50. On building, see SAF, Minutes, Styrelse, 26–27 April 1962, 19 April 1963, and 17 November 1964; Percy Bratt, "Rationalisering på byggnadsområdet," *Arbetsgivaren*, 29 January 1965, 3; "Rationellt byggande kräver stora serier," *Arbetsgivaren*, 8 October 1965, 6; SAF, *Rapport från kommittén för byggnadsindustrins lönesystem* (1965) (SAF AO:24); Sture Eskilsson, *Löneutveckling under kontroll* (Stockholm: SAF, 1966), 35; Nils Lagerström, "Löneskillnaden mellan byggfacket och annan industri beror främst på utvecklingen av ackordsförtjänsterna," *Arbetsgivaren*, 18 October, 1968, 4.

51. Gustav Nydahl, "Lönesystemet inom byggnadsindustrin anpassas till den nya byggtekniken," *Arbetsgivaren*, 22 April 1966, 4; Sven Kjellgren, "Nytt ackordssystem växer fram," *Arbetsgivaren*, 14 June 1968, 5.

52. See SAF, Minutes, Styrelse, 19 February 1957; "Minnesanteckningar från direktörskonferens på Yxtaholm," 17 April 1957; SAF, Minutes, Styrelse, 25 April 1957, 17 October 1957, and 14 November 1957.

7. Cartelism and Market Control

1. Ivan L. Willis, "Are the British and Swedish Systems of Collective Bargaining Applicable in the United States?" in Almon E. Roth, Ivan L. Willis, and A. B. Gates, *Employer Associations in Collective Bargaining* (New York: American Management Association, 1939), 20; Homer Sayre, "The Price of Industry-Wide Bargaining," August 1939 (NAM 512/Industrial Relations Department, Industry-Wide Collective Bargaining). Willis and Sayre would also have found an employer confederation's power to order a firm to lockout its workers intolerable.

2. See U.S. Department of Labor, *Report of the Commission on Industrial Relations in Sweden* (Washington: Department of Labor, 1938); "President's Study of

Swedish Labor Finds Peace Is Key," *New York Times*, 25 September 1938, 1; Edwin E. Witte, "Economic Aspects of Industry-Wide Collective Bargaining," in Colston E. Warne, ed., *Industry-Wide Collective Bargaining* (Boston: D.C. Heath, 1950), 55.

3. Edström to Fritiof Söderbäck, 11 June 1941 (Edström 35[A14e]). Apparently SAF leaders did not find preposterous the notion, suggested by Albin Johansson, a leading figure in Sweden's Cooperative movement, that LO might join in with business organizations to discuss propaganda promoting economic freedom or free enterprise (*näringslivets frihet*). Söderlund to Edström, 1 June 1942 (SAF P6/Edström, J.S.).

4. Herbert Croly, *Marcus Alonzo Hanna: His Life and Work* (New York: Macmillan, 1912), 90–95; Matthew Josephson, *The Politicos, 1865–1896* (New York: Harcourt, Brace, 1938), 637–61, 695–97.

5. Kenneth M. McCaffree, "A Theory of the Origin and Development of Employer Associations," *Proceedings of the Fifteenth Annual Meeting of the Industrial Relations Research Association* (December 1962), 65–68. Swedish employers even occasionally referred to their organization as a "cartel." For reasons to characterize their goal as solidarism rather than monopsony, see chapter 2. For a discussion of "joint union-employer monopoly," see Leo Wolman, *Industry-Wide Bargaining* (New York: Foundation for Economic Education, 1948), 41–45. See also Edward S. Mason, "Labor Monopoly and All That," and James R. Schlesinger, "Market Structure, Union Power, and Inflation," both in Walter Galenson and Seymour Martin Lipset, eds., *Labor and Trade Unionism: An Interdisciplinary Reader* (New York: Wiley, 1960), 119–49 and 155–69.

6. There were another 46 or so unions with more than 10,000 members, and 98 with more than 1,000 members. All figures here leave out railroads and the public sector. If unions in the railroad sector are included, where bargaining took place in effect on a multi-employer basis, the total percentage of union members in sectors where bargaining is usually or frequently with employers' associations reaches 79 percent. The categorization of sectors, and characterization of the railroads, comes from Helen S. Hoeber, "Collective Bargaining with Employers' Associations," *Monthly Labor Review* 49:2 (August 1939), 304 and 310. Union membership figures are from Leo Wolman, *Ebb and Flow in Trade Unionism* (New York: National Bureau of Economic Research, 1936), Appendix, Table I.

7. These terms are from Clarence Bonnett, *Employers' Associations in the United States* (New York: Macmillan, 1922). Bonnett associates employers' "appeasatory" behavior toward unions with cartelist "collusion" in his *History of Employers' Associations in the United States* (New York: Vantage, 1956), 481–93.

8. These ideas are suggested in part by William Lazonick, *Competitive Advantage on the Shop Floor* (Cambridge: Harvard University Press, 1990), especially 264–69; John R. Harris and Michael P. Todaro, "Migration, Unemployment and Development: A Two-Sector Analysis," *American Economic Review* 61:1 (March 1979), 126–42; Karl Ove Moene, "A Reformulation of the Harris-Todaro Mechanism with Endogenous Wages," *Economics Letters* 27:4 (1988), 387–90.

9. The union was even able to negotiate agreement to a host of uniform work and apprenticeship rules that helped level the competitive playing field by standardizing costs. Russell S. Bauder, "National Collective Bargaining in the Foundry Industry," *American Economic Review* 24:3 (September 1934), 467–68; Thomas A. Klug, *The Roots of the Open Shop: Employers, Trade Unions, and Craft Labor Markets in Detroit, 1859–1907*, dissertation, Wayne State University, 1993, 476, 483, 489–96, 508–9.

10. After deadlocks in 1910, 1914, and 1922, negotiation devolved to the district level. Waldo Fisher, "Bituminous Coal," in Harry A. Millis, ed., *How Collective Bargaining Works: A Survey of Experience in Leading American Industries* (New York: Twentieth Century Fund, 1942), 234–38; John R. Bowman, *Capitalist Collective Action: Competition, Cooperation and Conflict in the Coal Industry* (Cambridge: Cambridge University Press, 1989), 93–110.

11. Bruno Ramirez, *When Workers Fight: The Politics of Industrial Relations in the Progressive Era, 1898–1916* (Westport, CT: Grennwood Press, 1978), 17, 22, and 34.

12. Mitchell quotation from Ramirez, *When Workers Fight*, 49; *Black Diamond* quotation from Bowman, *Capitalist Collective Action*, 107.

13. Ramirez, *When Workers Fight*, 79–80; Melvyn Dubofsky and Warren Van Tine, *John L. Lewis: A Biography* (New York: Quadrangle/New York Times, 1977), 144–48.

14. Quoted in Bowman, *Capitalist Collective Action*, 119. West Virginian operators' competitive advantage, due to more accessible and thicker veins of coal, and a cheaper and more pliable labor force, would have been undermined by contract terms sought by Northern operators and miners. Philip Taft, *Organized Labor in American History* (New York: Harper & Row, 1964), 172.

15. The union did not challenge the use of piece work partly because so much was at stake for employers. For them, monitoring and enforcing output levels at the mineface was costly and impractical. John R. Commons, *Union Policies and Industrial Management* (Washington, DC: Brookings, 1941), 287.

16. U.S. Commissioner of Labor, *Regulation and Restriction of Output: Eleventh Special Report* (Washington, DC: Government Printing Office, 1904), 412–26; *Proceedings of the Joint Convention of the Illinois Coal Operators Association and the United Mine Workers of America* (Joliet, IL: 1901), 123–32; Ethelbert Stewart, "Equalizing Competitive Conditions," in Commons, ed., *Trade Unionism and Labor Problems, Second Series* (Boston: Ginn and Company, 1921), 525–33; Ramirez, *When Workers Fight*, 51–52; Victor Hicken, "The Virden and Pana Wars," *Journal of the Illinois State Historical Society* 51 (Spring 1959), 263–78. For more on these and other wage differentials, especially to compensate for varying railroad freight rates, see Bowman, *Capitalist Collective Action*, 108–10, and Isador Lubin, *Miners' Wages and the Cost of Coal* (New York: Macmillan, 1924).

17. Morton S. Baratz, *The Union and the Coal Industry* (New Haven: Yale University Press, 1955), 71–72; "Lewis Demands 30-Hour Mine Week and $5 Daily Wage," and "Lewis's Plea for Miners at Coal Code Hearing," *New York Times*, 11 August 1933, 1, 4.

18. Dubofsky and Van Tine, *John L. Lewis*, 197–200, 494–504, and 508–10; Saul Alinsky, *John L. Lewis: An Unauthorized Biography* (New York: G. P. Putnam's Sons, 1949), 60; Nat Caldwell and Gene S. Graham, "The Strange Romance between John L. Lewis and Cyrus Eaton," *Harper's Magazine* (December 1961), 25–32; Commons, *Union Policies and Industrial Management*, 271–72. Because Lewis's policies forced mechanization, the Joy Manufacturing Company, a leading producer of continuous mining machinery, regarded him as "the best salesman Joy ever had." "Continuous Coal Mining," *Fortune* (June 1950), 18. See also Ivana Krajcinovic, *From Company Doctors to Managed Care: The United Mine Workers' Noble Experiment* (Ithaca: ILR Press, 1997), 17–49.

19. Dubofsky and Van Tine, *John L. Lewis*, xiv–xv; 503–5.

20. Dubofsky and Van Tine, *John L. Lewis*, 95, 109, and 125–27; Caldwell and Graham, "The Strange Romance," 27.

21. Warren R. Van Tine, *The Making of the Labor Bureaucrat: Union Leadership in the United States, 1870–1920* (Amherst: The University of Massachusetts Press, 1973), 171–73; Croly, *Hanna*, 388; Ramirez, *When Workers Fight*, 55.

22. Marguerite Green, *The National Civic Federation and the American Labor Movement 1900–1925* (Washington, DC: Catholic University of America Press, 1956), esp. 1–132; James Weinstein, *The Corporate Ideal in the Liberal State 1900–1918* (Boston: Beacon Press, 1968), 3–39; Croly, *Hanna*, 386–410; Ramirez, *When Workers Fight*, 49–84.

23. Ramirez, *When Workers Fight*, 61; Baratz, *The Union and the Coal Industry*, 60; Hoover quotation cited in George H. Nash, *The Life of Herbert Hoover: The Engineer 1874–1914* (New York: Norton, 1983), 487; Dubofsky and Van Tine, *John L. Lewis*, 108; Frances Perkins, *The Roosevelt I Knew* (New York: Viking, 1946), 325.

24. Von Sydow quoted in "Arbetskraftsledning och arbetsintensitet, *Göteborgs Handels- och Sjöfartstidning*, 1 February 1911, 3. Wage and employment data are from Kungliga Socialstyrelsen, *Lönestatistisk årsbok för Sverige 1929* (Stockholm: Socialstyrelsen, 1931), 56–63.

25. Kungliga Socialstyrelsen, *Lönestatistisk årsbok för Sverige 1929*, 56–63.

26. Dwight Edward Robinson, *Collective Bargaining and Market Control in the New York Coat and Suit Industry* (New York: Columbia University Press, 1949), 58–59; "The Situation in the Women's Garment Trades," *Monthly Labor Review* 29:3 (September 1929), 30.

27. Cohen, *Law and Order in Industry: Five Years' Experience* (New York: Macmillan, 1916), 16. On competitive warfare, see Carpenter, *Competition and Collective Bargaining in the Needle Trades 1910–1967* (Ithaca, NY: New York State School of Industrial and Labor Relations, Cornell University, 1972), 11–24 and 41.

28. Robert J. Myers and Joseph W. Bloch, "Men's Clothing," in Millis, ed., *How Collective Bargaining Works*, 385–93 (quote on 392).

29. Cohen, *Law and Order*, 17–18; Carpenter, *Competition and Collective Bargaining*, 797, 803.

30. Philippa Strum, *Louis D. Brandeis: Justice for the People* (New York: Schocken Books, 1984), 173–79.

31. On impartial machinery, see Carpenter, *Competition and Collective Bargaining*, 139–72, 210–15, 440–50 and Joel Seidman, *The Needle Trades* (New York: Farrar & Rinehart, 1942), 259–62.

32. Carpenter, *Competition and Collective Bargaining*, 560–65, 616–17, 666–67, and 816–17.

33. Carpenter, *Competition and Collective Bargaining*, 610, 624, 648, and 814.

34. Carpenter, *Competition and Collective Bargaining*, 554–56; Myers and Bloch, "Men's Clothing," 409–10 and 435–43.

35. Carpenter, *Competition and Collective Bargaining*, 732–34 and 750; George W. Taylor, "Hosiery," in Millis, ed., *How Collective Bargaining Works*, 454–57.

36. Carpenter, *Competition and Collective Bargaining*, 61 (quotation) and 254; David Dubinsky and A. H. Raskin, *David Dubinsky: A Life With Labor* (New York: Simon & Schuster, 1977), 82.

37. Seidman, *The Needle Trades*, 249, and Carpenter, *Competition and Collective Bargaining*, 179–81, 203, and 501. On unions' and employers' organizations efforts to strengthen each other, see Carpenter, 206–8, 221–22, 427, 433–38, 515, 519, 528, 541, and 567–68.

38. Seidman, *The Needle Trades*, 262–24; Carpenter, *Competition and Collective Bargaining*, 8, 40–44, 83, 87, 188–93, 227, 399, 466–78, 507, 515–16, and 570.

39. Carpenter, *Competition and Collective Bargaining*, 233–45, 478–80, 492–93, and 525.

40. Carpenter, *Competition and Collective Bargaining*, 74–76, 204–5, 333, and 447.

41. Carpenter, *Competition and Collective Bargaining*, 70–72, 117, 126–34, 330–41, 351–361, 551, 807–9, and 831 (quotation from page 352). See also Myers and Bloch, "Men's Clothing," 417 and 421.

42. Carpenter, *Competition and Collective Bargaining*, 95, 164, 203, 461, and 669–70.

43. Carpenter, *Competition and Collective Bargaining*, 97, 101–3, 155–56, and 163–64; Myers and Bloch, 431.

44. Quotation from Myers and Bloch, "Men's Clothing," 425. On ACWA relations with the Taylor Society, see Steven Fraser, *Labor Will Rule: Sidney Hillman and the Rise of American Labor* (New York: Free Press, 1991), 132–33, 171–72, and 268–69.

45. Carpenter, *Competition and Collective Bargaining*, 184 and 364.

46. E. W. Paues, "Avskrift," Appendix 2 to Sveriges Konfektionsindustriförbund, Minutes, Styrelse, 11 December 1925.

47. Evidence from the low-pay textile industry in Sweden suggests why: wage pressures from other sectors, particularly engineering, were probably pulling workers out of the garment industry, and some garment manufacturers probably responded defensively with higher wages that threatened other garment producers' supply of labor.

48. Sveriges Konfektionsindustriförbund, Minutes, Styrelse, 25 August 1931; 8 September and 11 October 1932.

49. *Organiserad samverkan inom svenskt näringsliv—Betänkande avgivet av 1936 års näringsorganisationssakkunniga*, SOU 1940:35 (Stockholm, 1940), 209–11, 257–60, 291, 308, and 323–24.

50. To some extent, organized crime occasionally joined forces with unions to carry out the cartel function. Operating at the local level, this unholy alliance sometimes met with clean-up efforts by central labor and employer statesmen alike. John Hutchinson, *The Imperfect Union: A History of Corruption in American Trade Unions* (New York: E. P. Dutton, 1972), 74–92; Fraser, *Labor Will Rule*, 242–55. See also note 65.

51. Myers and Bloch, "Men's Clothing," 425; Carpenter, *Competition and Collective Bargaining*, 804–7.

52. Booth Mooney, *Builders for Progress: The Story of the Associated General Contractors of America* (New York: McGraw-Hill, 1965), 64–69. On the objectionable details, see "Contractors Score Wage Rates Bill," *New York Times*, 9 February 1931, 3. For the text of the 1935 revision, see John T. Dunlop and Arthur D. Hill, *The Wage Adjustment Board: Wartime Stabilization in the Building and Construction Industry* (Cambridge: Harvard University Press, 1950), 135–37.

53. For details on the legislation and debate, see *Congressional Record 71* (1931), 6504–21, 6893–94. Hoover's views about minimum wages are in his *Memoirs of Herbert Hoover: The Great Depression 1929–1941* (New York: Macmillan, 1952), 458, 461. Hoover had seemed somewhat less enthusiastic in 1937, favoring only temporary measures for industries "sick from destructive competition or devoid of effective collective bargaining." The minimum, he told businessmen assembled in the Chicago Economic Club in 1937, should be applied only "when they are sick" and would help unions, for "certainly employers would be quickened to collective bargaining as a relief from the restrictions." Hoover, "Economic Security and the Pre-

sent Situation," 16 December 1937, in *Addresses upon the American Road* (New York: Scribner, 1938), 297.

54. William Haber, "Building Construction," in Millis, ed., *How Collective Bargaining Works*, 206; Haber, *Industrial Relations in the Building Industry* (Cambridge: Harvard University Press, 1930), 517.

55. Robert A. Christie, *Empire in Wood: A History of the Carpenters' Union* (Ithaca, NY: Cornell University Press, 1956), 62.

56. Louis Stanley, "Prosperity, Politics and Policy," in J. B. S Hardman, ed., *American Labor Dynamics in the Light of Post-War Developments* (New York: Harcourt, Brace: 1928), 197.

57. Michael Kazin, *Barons of Labor: The San Francisco Building Trades and Union Power in the Progressive Era* (Urbana and Chicago: University of Illinois Press, 1989), especially 82–112. See also Haber, *Industrial Relations in the Building Industry*, 400–9; Ira B. Cross, "The San Francisco Building Trades," in John R. Commons, *Trade Unionism and Labor Problems, Second Series* (Boston: Ginn and Company, 1921), 477–88.

58. Haber, *Industrial Relations in the Building Industry*, 421–22, 434, 574; Walter Galenson, *The United Brotherhood of Carpenters: The First One Hundred Years* (Cambridge: Harvard University Press, 1983), 204–6.

59. Haber, *Industrial Relations in the Building Industry*, 420–21 and 558, note 24; Frederick Forbes, "San Francisco Sees Novel Wage Stand," *The New York Times*, 11 October 1931, III:5.

60. On Brandle, see Harold Seidman, *Labor Czars: A History of Labor Racketeering* (New York: Liveright, 1938), 149–56. On shared offices, see New York State Organized Crime Task Force, *Corruption and Racketeering in the New York City Construction Industry: An Interim Report* (Ithaca, NY: ILR Press, 1988), 51.

61. Seidman, *Labor Czars*, 261. Details and examples of corruption can be found in Philip Taft, *Corruption and Racketeering in the Labor Movement* (Ithaca, NY: Cornell School of Industrial and Labor Relations, 1958); Hutchinson, *The Imperfect Union*, and "The Anatomy of Corruption in Trade Unions," *Industrial Relations* 8:2 (February 1969), 135–50. For useful details on New York City over time, see the "Lockwood Commission" report, State of New York, *Intermediate Report of the Joint Legislative Committee on Housing* (Albany: J. B. Lyon, 1922) and New York State Organized Crime Task Force, *Corruption and Racketeering.*

62. On Brindell and New York, see Seidman, *Labor Czars*, 68–93; quote on employers from 268. On past and recent mafia control, see New York State Organized Crime Task Force, *Corruption and Racketeering*, 67–69; and Selwyn Raab, "Many New York Builders Accept the Mafia Willlingly, Report Says," *New York Times*, 9 September 1987, 1.

63. "The Anatomy of Corruption in Trade Unions," *Industrial Relations* 8:2 (February 1969). See also Paul A. Weinstein, "Racketeering and Labor: An Economic Analysis," *Industrial and Labor Relations Review* 19:3 (April 1966), 402–13. On the similar industry characteristics that favor unions, see Frank Pierson, "Cooperation Among Managements in Collective Bargaining," *Labor Law Journal* 11:7 (July 1960), 622–3,and "Recent Employer Alliances in Perspective," *Industrial Relations* 1:1 (October 1961), 41–43.

64. Marquis Childs, *This is Democracy: Collective Bargaining in Sweden* (New Haven: Yale University Press, 1938), 53.

65. Differences in anti-trust regulation suit Hutchinson's explanation. In the United States, as Seidman concludes, anti-trust laws prohibited contractors from legally regulating competition by joint action. For that reason, they "invited labor

racketeers to organize their industry." Seidman, *Labor Czars*, 264. In Sweden, by that logic, union officials would have had few services to offer, because unilateral cartelism could do the job unhindered by law.

66. On New York, see Christie, *Empire in Wood*, 61–62; on Chicago, see Richard Schneirov and Thomas J. Suhrbur, *Union Brotherhood, Union Town: The History of the Carpenters' Union of Chicago, 1863–1987* (Carbondale, IL: Southern Illinois University press, 1988), 49.

67. Haber, *Industrial Relations in the Building Industry*, 228; Solomon Blum, "Trade-Union Rules in the Building Trades," in Jacob H. Hollander and George E. Barnett, eds., *Studies in American Trade Unionism* (New York: Henry Holt, 1905), 302. See also Sumner Slichter, *Union Policies and Industrial Management* (Washington, DC: Brookings, 1941), 296. On Sweden, see Childs, *This is Democracy*, 51, and chapter 5 here. John Dunlop notes the unusually high level of piece-work usage in construction in places like Scandinavia and the Netherlands, attributing it in the Dutch case to labor scarcity under conditions of controlled hourly rates, and therefore workers' practice of "arranging piecework with their employers." Thus solidarism seemed to be at work in the Netherlands as well. Dunlop, *Industrial Relations Systems* (Boston: Harvard Business School Press, 1993), 220–23.

68. Haber, *Industrial Relations in the Building Industry*, 227–28, 440; Frederick L. Ryan, *Industrial Relations in the San Francisco Building Trades* (Norman: University of Oklahoma Press, 1936), 182–83, 189, and 195–98.

69. Unions played a restraining role on workers resorting to wildcat strikes to take advantage of temporary labor shortages in 1920 and 1946, for example. Carpenter, *Competition and Collective Bargaining*, 6–7, 254, 258–59, 266, 278, and 292–95. Richard A. Lester, in *The Economics of Labor* (New York: Macmillan, 1941), 138–39, cites an unusual case of unilateral solidarism, where shipowners and waterfront employers were able to impose ceilings on wages for longshoremen up and down the Pacific Coast in the 1920s and 1930s.

70. "The American Worker in the Progressive Age: A Comprehensive Analysis," in Brody, *Workers in Industrial America: Essays on the 20th Century Struggle* (New York: Oxford University Press, 1980), 31.

71. Carpenter, *Competition and Collective Bargaining*, 364 and 676; John Kenneth Galbraith, *American Capitalism: The Concept of Countervailing Power* (Boston: Houghton Mifflin, 1956), revised edition, 116.

8. World War and Class Politics

1. Alexander M. Bing, "The Work of the Wage-Adjustment Boards," *Journal of Political Economy* 27:6 (June 1919), 443; Michael E. Parrish, *Felix Frankfurter and His Times: The Reform Years* (New York: Free Press, 1982), 102–10.

2. Hugh S. Hanna and W. Jett Lauck, *Wages and the War: A Summary of Recent Wage Movements* (Cleveland: Doyle and Waltz, 1918), 3.

3. Frank Freidel, *Franklin D. Roosevelt: The Apprenticeship* (Boston: Little, Brown, 1952), 217, 327–31; George Barnett, "American Trade Unionism and the Standardization of Wages During the War," *Journal of Political Economy* 27:8 (October 1919), 687; Paul H. Douglas and F. E. Wolfe, "Labor Administration in the Shipbuilding Industry During War Time," in John R. Commons, ed., *Trade Unionism and Labor Problems* (Boston: Ginn and Company, 1921), 313–16.

4. On Brandeis, minimum wages, garments, and Frankfurter, see Philippa Strum, *Louis D. Brandeis: Justice for the People* (New York: Schocken, 1984), 126, 172–79, 373–75.

5. Sanford Jacoby discusses personnel and welfare practices in *Employing Bureaucracy: Managers, Unions, and the Transformation of Work in American Industry, 1900–1945* (New York: Columbia University Press, 1985) , 133–65 and 196. On the conditions leading to efforts at standardization, see "War Labor Policies Board Rushing Standardization of All Wages for War Labor," *U.S. Employment Service Bulletin* 1:22 (25 June 1918), 1.

6. "Organization and Functions of the War Labor Policies Board," *Monthly Labor Review* 7:1 (July 1918), 25–26.

7. W. A. Grieves, "Organize the Labor Market," *100%: The Efficiency Magazine* 10:4 (April 1918), 84–90.

8. Stearns, "Standardization of Occupations and Rates of Pay," *Proceedings of the Employment Managers' Conference*, Bureau of Labor Statistics Bulletin No. 247 (1918), 36–42.

9. Valerie Jean Conner, *The National War Labor Board: Stability, Social Justice, and the Voluntary State in World War I* (Chapel Hill: University of North Carolina Press, 1983), 32–33; "Organization and Functions of the War Labor Policies Board," *Monthly Labor Review* 7:1 (July 1918), 25. On Frankfurter and Taft, see Parrish, *Felix Frankfurter and His Times*, 40–41.

10. On the recruitment problem, see especially Charles T. Clayton of the U.S. Employment Service and William Blackman, Shipping Board's director of labor, on "Destructive Labor Recruiting," *Proceedings of the Employment Managers' Conference*, Bureau of Labor Statistics Bulletin No. 247 (1918), 51–62. On the municipal activities and ordinances, see Thomas Klug, "Employers' Strategies in the Detroit Labor Market, 1900–1929," in Nelson Lichtenstein and Stephen Meyer, eds., *On the Line: Essays in the History of Auto Work* (Urbana: University of Illinois Press, 1989), 51, 58–61, and 69; on Indianapolis see A. J. Hain, "Nation Swinging to Open Shop," *Iron Trade Review*, 23 September 1920, 851. It appears to have been normal policy even in peacetime for the Metal Manufacturers' Association of Philadelphia to encourage its members to hire exclusively through its "labor bureau" in part to prevent local poaching of skilled men, not just to blacklist union agitators. Howell John Harris, "Getting it Together: The Metal Manufacturers' Association of Philadelphia, c. 1900–1930," in Sanford Jacoby, ed., *Masters to Managers: Historical and Comparative Perspectives on American Employers* (New York: Columbia University Press, 1991), 124.

11. Parrish, *Felix Frankfurter and His Times*, 110. On union and worker radicalism during the war, see Jeffrey Haydu, *Between Craft and Class: Skilled Workers and Factory Politics in the United States and Britain, 1890–1922* (Berkeley: University of California Press, 1988), and Haydu, *Making America Safe for Democracy: Comparative Perspectives on the State and Employee Representation in the Era of World War I* (Chicago: University of Illinois Press, 1997).

12. Howell John Harris, *The Right to Manage: Industrial Relations Policies of American Business in the 1940s* (Madison: University of Wisconsin Press, 1982), 58; William H. McPherson, "Tripartitism," in *Problems and Policies of Dispute Settlement and Wage Stabilization During World War II* (Washington, DC: U.S. Department of Labor, Bureau of Labor Statistics, 1950), 266; "The Tripartite WLB," *New York Times* 22 March 1943, I:18; "NWLB Set-up Defended: Employer Members See Merit in Tripartite Organization," *New York Times*, 28 March 1943, IV:8. The employer group was dominated by friends of collective bargaining like Cyrus Ching of U.S. Rubber, George H. Mead of Mead Pulp and Paper, and Almon Roth of the Pacific American Shipowners' Association and the Pacific Coast Waterfront Employers' Association.

13. See especially Paul A. C. Koistinen, "Mobilizing the World War II Economy: Labor and the Industrial-Military Alliance," *Pacific Historical Review* 42:4 (November 1973), 443–78; Brian Waddell, "Economic Mobilization for World War II and the Transformation of the American State," *Politics and Society* 22:2 (June 1994), 165–94. On the chaos and lack of coordination, especially in procurement practices, see Donald M. Nelson, *Arsenal of Democracy: The Story of American War Production* (New York: Harcourt, Brace, 1946).

14. John T. Dunlop, "An Appraisal of Wage Stabilization Policies," in *Problems and Policies of Dispute Settlement and Wage Stabilization During World War II*, 157 and 163; John T. Dunlop and Arthur D. Hill, *The Wage Adjustment Board: Wartime Stabilization in the Building and Construction Industry* (Cambridge: Harvard University Press, 1950), 61; *The Termination Report of the National War Labor Board: Industrial Disputes and Wage Stabilization in Wartime, Vol. 1* (Washington, DC: NWLB, 1947), 226–59; John B. Parrish, "Relation of Wage Control to Manpower Problems," in *Problems and Policies of Dispute Settlement and Wage Stabilization During World War II* 195, 198–207.

15. James N. Baron, Frank R. Dobbin, and P. Devereaux Jennings, "War and Peace: The Evolution of Modern Personnel Administration in U.S. Industry," *American Journal of Sociology* 92:2 (September 1987), 360; Clark Kerr, *Labor Markets and Wage Determination: The Balkanization of Labor Markets and Other Essays* (Berkeley: University of California Press, 1977), 55–58; 78; Dunlop, "An Appraisal," 178. On steel, see Robert Tilove, "The Wage Rationalization Program in United States Steel," *Monthly Labor Review* 64 (1947), 967–82; Katherine Stone, "The Origins of Job Structures in the Steel Industry," *Review of Radical Political Economics* 6:2 (1974), 113–73.

16. Baron, Dobbin, and Jennings, "War and Peace," 370; Thomas M. Hills, *The War Manpower Commission and Its Problem, April 18, 1942–February 1, 1943*, master's thesis, Wharton School of Business Administration, University of Pennsylvania, Philadelphia, 1943.

17. Van Dusen Kennedy, *Union Policy and Incentive Wage Methods* (New York: AMS Press, 1968), 129; Harris, *The Right to Manage*, 63 and 132; Management Consultant Division, War Production Board, "Guiding Principles for Wage Incentive Plans," 20 September 1943 (NAM I/282/Industrial Relations, General, April 1946); Parrish, "Relation of Wage Control to Manpower Problems," 197, 210, 222, and 225. On the postwar decline of incentive pay, see Harry C. Katz, *Shifting Gears: Changing Labor Relations in the U.S. Automobile Industry* (Cambridge: MIT Press, 1985), 31; Sumner Slichter, James J. Healy, and E. Robert Livernash, *The Impact of Collective Bargaining on Management* (Washington, DC: Brookings Institution, 1960), 494–96; Ronald Schatz, *Electric Workers*, 140–49, 237–38. The aircraft comparison is from Joseph Sherman, "Incentive Pay in American Industry, 1945–46," *Monthly Labor Review* (November 1947), 535–38, and L. Earl Lewis, "Extent of Incentive Pay in Manufacturing," *Monthly Labor Review* 83:5 (May 1960), 460–63.

18. Claudia Goldin and Robert Margo, "The Great Compression: The Wage Structure in the U.S. at Midi-Century," *Quarterly Journal of Economics* 107 (1992), 1–34; Parrish, "Relation of Wage Control to Manpower Problems," 198 and 203.

19. Also, implementation of the Little Steel formula gave proportionate increases across firms. Within firms, however, the increases had an upward leveling effect. Parrish, "Relation of Wage Control to Manpower Problems," 195, 198, 203, 206–10, 213, 221, and 224.

20. In basketball, the first salary cap was negotiated in 1983. There was a summer-long lockout in 1995 and another 7-month lockout between July 1998 and

January 1999. In the second instance, the 29 National Basketball Association team owners locked out over 400 players organized in the National Basketball Players Association in order to maintain salary caps and postpone "free agency," or full labor mobility, for players until the lapse of five rather than three years. The players bargained for some upward leveling for "mid-level players" whose earnings potential was reduced by star players' ability as free agents to "eat up a team's salary cap room and force an unprecedented group of players to earn the minimum salary." See Patrick Ewing, Billy Hunter, and the NBPA Negotiating Committee, "Setting the Record Straight; Remember: This is not a Strike, It's a Lockout." *New York Times* 28 December 1998, A13. The first salary cap in baseball was imposed in 1994; lockouts as well as strikes disrupted the previous eight labor negotiations. Jim Bunning, "How Sporting a Business? Repeal That Antitrust Exemption," *New York Times*, 3 October 1994, A15.

21. Senate Committee on Education and Labor, *Violation of Free Speech and Rights of Labor—Labor Policies of Employers' Associations, Part II: The Associated Industries of Cleveland* 76th Cong., 1st sess., 1939, 9–10, 25–31, 39, 42–44, 88–96, 220–21, and 226.

22. Senate Committee on Education and Labor, *Violation of Free Speech and Rights of Labor, Part II*, 26.

23. Thomas A. Klug, *The Roots of the Open Shop: Employers, Trade Unions, and Craft Labor Markets in Detroit, 1959–1907*, dissertation, Wayne State University, 1993, 853. On the EAD's composition and its efforts in 1904, see 729–34, 851–60.

24. Robert Ozanne, *A Century of Labor-Management Relations at McCormick and International Harvester* (Madison: University of Wisconsin Press, 1967), 49–52; Clarence Bonnett, *Employers' Associations in the United States* (New York: Macmillan, 1922), 369.

25. Irving Bernstein, *The Lean Years: A History of the American Worker 1920–1933* (Boston: Houghton Mifflin, 1960), 154. See also Lewis L. Lorwin, *The American Federation of Labor: History, Policies, and Prospects* (Washington, DC: Brookings, 1933), 203. Sawmill owners in San Francisco, providing building materials, were prime movers. Robert A. Christie, *Empire in Wood: A History of the Carpenters' Union* (Ithaca, NY: Cornell University Press, 1956), 158–160.

26. Noel Sargent, "How Manufacturing Industries Operate," 29 April 1928 (NAM/I/520/Industrial Relations Department, Open Shop Department/Special Articles and Studies, 1920–1930).

27. Bonnett, *Employers' Associations in the United States*, 518, 521, 522, 539; A. J. Hain, "Nation Swinging to Open Shop," *Iron Trade Review*, 23 September 1920, 848–51; Senate Committee on Education and Labor, *Violation of Free Speech and Rights of Labor, Part II*, 25–31.

28. Senate Committee on Education and Labor, *Violation of Free Speech and Rights of Labor, Part II*, 9; Haber, *Industrial Relations in the Building Industry*, 387–99; Galenson, *United Brotherhood of Carpenters*, 202–3; Royal E. Montgomery, *Industrial Relations in the Chicago Building Trades* (Chicago: University of Chicago Press, 1927), 235. On the Impartial Wage Board, see chapter 7 here.

29. Originally called the National Association of Manufacturers and Erectors of Structural Steel and Iron Work in 1903. By the end of 1903, the word "Manufacturers" was dropped, and the new name, NEA, was adopted in 1906. Sidney Fine, *Without Blare of Trumpets: Walter Drew, the National Erectors' Association, and the Open Shop Movement, 1903–57* (Ann Arbor: University of Michigan Press, 1995), 24, 34, 49, 175, 213–14; "The American Bridge Company Perfected," *Iron Age*, 24 May 1900, 25.

30. Fine, *Without Blare of Trumpets*, 79, 237.

31. Fine, *Without Blare of Trumpets*, 132; see also 15, 213, and 237.

32. "Handbook of the Ninth Semi-Annual American Plan Open Shop Conference," May 1926, and "Excerpt from Proceedings of Eighth Semiannual American Plan Open Shop Conference," November 1925, in Senate Committee on Education and Labor, *Violation of Free Speech and Rights of Labor, Part II*, 211, 221.

33. NAM press release, "Says the Automobile Industry Is Threatened by Closed Shop Plan," for 26 May 1925 or 1926 (NAM/I/520/IR Department/Open Shop/1921–1930); Alfred P. Sloan, *My Years with General Motors* (New York: Doubleday, 1990), 405; Senate Committee on Education and Labor, *Violation of Free Speech and Rights of Labor, Part II*, 25.

34. "Excerpts from Proceedings and Conclusions of the Seventh Semi-Annual Session of the American Plan Open Shop Conference," and "Handbook of the Ninth Semi-Annual American Plan Open Shop Conference," May 1926 in Senate Committee on Education and Labor, *Violation of Free Speech and Rights of Labor, Part II*, 207, 209, and 219–21.

35. National Industrial Conference Board, *Wages in the United States, 1914–1927* (New York: NICB, 1928), 42 and 64; M. Ada Beney, *Wages, Hours, and Employment in the United States 1914–1936* (New York: NICB, 1936), 52–54, 196; Engineering News Record, *Construction Cost* (New York: McGraw-Hill, 1935), 11.

36. Noel Sargent, "Observations Presented before the President's Conference on Home Building and Home Ownership," December 3, 1931, reprinted as "Building Wage Rates Must Come Down" *Industrial Relations* 3:1 (January 1932), 59; "San Francisco Sees Novel Wage Stand; Employers in Building Trades Seek to Prove Reductions are Unwarranted," *New York Times* 11 October 1931, III:5; Rorty, "Is Collective Bargaining Compatible with a Free Price and Wage System?" *The American Management Review* 24:2 (February 1935), 35.

37. Sanford Jacoby, *Modern Manors: Welfare Capitalism Since the New Deal* (Princeton: Princeton University Press, 1997), 63; Ronald W. Schatz, *The Electrical Workers: A History of Labor at General Electric and Westinghouse 1923–1960* (Urbana: University of Illinois Press, 1983), 87; Herbert Feis, *Labor Relations: A Study Made in the Procter and Gamble Company* (New York: Adelphi, 1928), 128.

38. Samuel Hannaford, "The Present High Prices of Building and Why," *The Open Shop* 7 (1907), 113; NAM, "Open Shop Department," 6 June 1922 (NAM/520/Industrial Relations/Open Shop Department Meeting reports); Drew, "Building and the Public," Closed Shop pamphlet No. 51 (New York: NAM, 1922). This was also an address delivered at the annual meeting of the Associated Employers of Indianapolis in February 1922; "Handbook of the Ninth Semi-Annual American Plan Open Shop Conference," May 1926 in Senate Committee on Education and Labor, *Violation of Free Speech and Rights of Labor, Part II*, 205.

39. See the following NAM Press Releases: "Building Throughout Nation Greater in Open Shop Cities," 12 October 1923; "Rentals Increased in Cities Where Closed Shop Prevails," 18 April 1923; "Declares Closed Shop Building Raises Costs and Increases Rents," 25 April 1924; "Detroit's Remarkable Expansion Due to the Open Shop, He Says," 6 October 1926; "Says The Automobile Industry Is Threatened by Closed Shop Plan," 26 May 1925; "Says Religion Pays Tribute to the Closed Shop System," 15 May 1925; "School Building Costs Higher Under Closed Shop Conditions," 6 August 1927. For Eliot's account, see Charles William Eliot, "Closed Shop or Open," published in *The Harvard Alumni Bulletin*, 13 December 1923 (NAM/I/520/Industrial Relations Department; Open Shop Department/Special Articles and Studies, 1920–1933).

40. See especially James A. Gross, *The Reshaping of the National Labor Relations Board: National Labor Policy in Transition 1937–1947* (Albany: State University of New York Press, 1981), 61–84.

41. Walter Galenson, *The CIO Challenge to the AFL: A History of the American Labor Movement 1935–1941* (Cambridge: Harvard University Press, 1960), 521–26. The first and real punch in the jaw was delivered by Lewis on the floor of the 1935 AFL convention to the powerful boss of the United Brotherhood of Carpenters. "Fist Fight Puts A.F. of L. in Uproar: Lewis and Hutcheson, Labor Leaders, Trade Punches on Convention Floor," *New York Times*, 20 October 1935. The bloodied Hutcheson led the successful fight against resolutions supported by Lewis to authorize the formation of AFL unions to organize unskilled workers in mass production industries. Lewis then broke with the AFL to help set up the CIO.

42. On wartime control of the building trades, see John T. Dunlop, *The Wage Adjustment Board*, 36–37, and *The National Wage Stabilization Board, January 1, 1946-February 24, 1947* (Washington, DC: U.S. Department of Labor, 1948), 212–22.

43. David Loth, *Swope of General Electric: The Story of Gerard Swope and General Electric in American Business* (New York: Simon and Schuster, 1958), 167–72; Alice Hamilton, *Exploring the Dangerous Trades* (Boston: Little, Brown & Co., 1943), 291; Josephine Young Chase and Everett Needham Chase, *Owen D. Young and American Enterprise* (Boston: David R. Godine, 1982), 379, and 847, note 38, Frances Perkins, *The Roosevelt I Knew* (New York: Viking, 1946), 309.

44. A. B. Gates, "Discussion," in Almon E. Roth, Ivan L. Willis, and A. B. Gates, *Employer Associations in Collective Bargaining* (New York: American Management Association, 1939), 27. On the backlash to restore management rights, see Harris, *The Right to Manage*, 168–70. For a list of the wartime encroachments and their costs for output, see George Romney's testimony before a Senator committee chaired by James Mead of New York, released as "Automotive Industry Charges Misuse of CIO Power: Romney Documents Charges for Senate War Investigating Committee," Press Release, Automotive Council for War Production, 9 March 1945 (NAM/Industrial Relations Department, Collective Bargaining, 1922–1945).

45. Baron, Dobbin, and Jennings, "War and Peace," 372; Kerr, *Labor Markets and Wage Determination*, 76. On the hybrid mix of segmentalism within local labor markets and cartelism across industries, see chapter 2.

46. *The Termination Report of the National War Labor Board: Industrial Disputes and Wage Stabilization in Wartime, Vol. 1* (Washington, DC: NWLB, 1947), 306–402; Allan R. Richards, *War Labor Boards in the Field* (Chapel Hill: University of North Carolina Press, 1953), 143–57; Donna Allen, *Fringe Benefits: Wages or Social Obligation? An Analysis with Historical Perspectives from Paid Vacations* (Ithaca, NY: Cornell University Press, 1969), xv; Beth Stevens, "Labor Unions and the Privatization of Welfare: The Turning Point in the 1940s," in Michael Shalev, ed., *The Privatization of Social Policy? Occupational Welfare and the Welfare State in America, Scandinavia and Japan* (London: Macmillan, 1996), 73–103.

47. For statistics, see Jacoby, *Employing Bureaucracy*, 266; Alfred Skolnick, "Private Pension Plans, 1950–1974," *Social Security Bulletin* 39:6 (June 1976), 4; Louis Reed, "Private Health Insurance: Coverage and Financial Experience," *Social Security Bulletin* 30:11 (November 1967), 12. On wartime regulation of benefits, see Dunlop, "An Appraisal of Wage Stabilization Policies," 178.

48. Allen, *Fringe Benefits*, 33–35, 53–57, 59–66, 70–79, 90–96, 241–43, and 251.

49. On Wilson, see Peter Drucker, *Adventures of a Bystander* (New York: Harper and Row, 1978), 274, and chapter 1. On employers' interests, see Allen, *Fringe Benefits*, 172, 236, 241–44, and 254.

50. Jacoby analyzes the non-union cases in *Modern Manors*. On GE, see Schatz, *Electrical Workers*, 153. On the auto industry and benefits of pattern bargaining, see Robert M. MacDonald, *Collective Bargaining in the Automobile Industry* (New Haven: Yale University Press, 1963), 391–401; Harry C. Katz, *Shifting Gears: Changing Labor Relations in the U.S. Automobile Industry* (Cambridge: MIT, 1985), 30–36; Michael Piore and Charles Sabel, *The Second Industrial Divide: Possibilities for Prosperity* (New York: Basic, 1984), 79–83; and James R. Zetka, *Militancy, Market Dynamics, and Workplace Authority: The Struggle over Labor Process Outcomes in the U.S. Automobile Industry, 1946-1973* (New York: State University of New York Press, 1995), 27–46.

51. Jacoby, *Modern Manors*, 195–205; Jack Barbash, "Unions and Rights in the Space Age," in Howard B. Morris, ed., *The American Worker* (Washington, DC: U.S. Department of Labor, 1977), 251; Jesse Freidin, *The Taft-Hartley Act and Multi-Employer Bargaining* (Philadelphia: University of Pennsylvania Press, 1948).

52. *Report of the Commission on Industrial Relations in Sweden* (Washington, DC: U.S. Department of Labor, 1938), vii. On the debate following the FDR commission reports, see Edwin E. Witte, "Economic Aspects of Industry-Wide Collective Bargaining: An Institutional Approach," in Colston E. Warne, *Industry-wide Collective Bargaining: Promise or Menace?* (Boston: D.C. Heath, 1950), 55. NAM Commissioner Homer Sayre parted company with Hook in his "The Price of Industry-wide Bargaining," August 1939 (NAM 512/Industrial Relations, Industry-Wide Collective Bargaining). On Romney, see "Automotive Industry Charges Misuse of CIO Power." On pulp and paper, see Clark Kerr and Roger Randall, *Crown Zellerbach and the Pacific Coast Pulp and Paper Industry* (Washington, DC: National Planning Association, 1948). On glass, see E. H. Van Delden (director of industrial relations, Libbey-Owens-Ford), "Problems of Industry-Wide Collective Bargaining," in *Trends in Union Demands* (New York: American Management Association, 1945), 14–23. On San Francisco, see "Statement by Almon E. Roth, President San Francisco Employers Council on the Subject of Multi-Employer Bargaining," (NAM I/512/Industrial Relations Department, Industry-wide Bargaining 1948–1952).

53. On working days lost, see "Collective Bargaining Held Destroyed by Industry-wide Practices," *NAM News*, 1 February 1947, 4. On the UMW Welfare and Retirement Fund, see Edward Berkowitz, "Growth the U.S. Social Welfare System in the Post-World War II Era: The UMW, Rehabilitation, and the Federal Government," *Research in Economic History* 5 (1980), 233–36. For typical NAM positions, see NAM, "Industry's View on the Lewis Coal Royalty," March 1945 (NAM I/282/Committee on Industrial Relations/Labor Legislation 1945); "Labor Monopoly: Threat to Nation's Prosperity and Security," *NAM News*, 18 January 1947, 10; NAM, "Labor Monopoly and Industry-Wide Bargaining: Text of Statement filed with the Senate Banking and Currency Committee," 8 August 1949 (NAM I/200/U.S. Government, Labor, General). Federal mediation to end a nationwide steel strike also brought undesirably generous results in 1949. See Robert W. Stoddard (NAM board member), "Significance and Aftermath of the Steel Fact-Finding Panel," NAM Press Release, 9 December 1949 (NAM I/202/Bargaining, Coal-Steel Fact-Finding).

54. C. Dickerman Williams and Charles E. Wilson in Warne, ed., *Industry-wide Collective Bargaining*, 99 and 96. They neglected to note, or were not aware, that national bargaining for elevator manufacturing allowed for local differentiation. See "Collective Bargaining with Employers' Associations," *Monthly Labor Review* 49:2 (August 1939), 305.

55. Ford had long been one company that chose to pay uniformly even prior to union organization in the 1930s. Richard A. Lester, "Reflections on the 'Labor Mo-

nopoly' Issue," in Warne, *Industry-wide Collective Bargaining*, 33; Bunting to Jack W. Schroeder (General Director, Associated Industries of Minneapolis), 19 April 1950 (NAM I/202, "Bargaining/Collective/General").

56. "Study Group on Monopolistic Aspects of Unions 1955" (NAM I, Box 281). For the group's final report, and other NAM arguments leading to the 1959 legislation, see United Business Committee of the NAM, *A Problem for Every Businessman: Monopoly Power as Exercised by Labor Unions* (New York: NAM, 1957) and the pamphlet by Cola G. Parker, NAM's Chairman of the Board, *Union Monopoly Power: Challenge to Freedom* (New York: NAM, 1957). For the employer defense of multi-employer bargaining, see the 1947 statement to Congress by Almon E. Roth of the National Federation of American Shipping, reprinted in George W. Taylor et al., "Industrial Experiences with Industry-Wide Bargaining," reprinted in Warne, *Industry-wide Collective Bargaining*, 91–94. On labor racketeering, see chapter 7 here.

57. Stanley Vittoz, "World War I and the Political Accommodation of Transitional Market Forces: The Case of Immigration Restriction," *Politics and Society* 8:1 (1978), 67–73. Hoover's view is from *The Memoirs of Herbert Hoover: The Cabinet and Presidency 1920–1933* (New York: Macmillan, 1952), 108; Harding's is reported in "A Look Ahead for the Immigrant," *Nation's Business*, 5 June 1923, 58. To be sure, American businessmen were critical of the overly rigid legislation of the day, which was not well designed for adjusting immigration to the business cycle, growth trends, specific skill shortages, and regionally differentiated needs. If there was a consensus view, it was for restrictive but flexible policy. "We condemn unrestricted immigration as we do its prohibition," according to a committee of the NAM. As Magnus Alexander, director of the NICB, put it, "cheap labor maintained in continuous streams was not a boon . . . but rather a menace." The United States, he maintained, was rapidly approaching the saturation point in immigration. In short, just as business suffered from overly rigid as well as chaotic fluctuations in money creation, so it suffered from badly regulated labor flux. See "Recommendations of Immigration Committee of National Association of Manufacturers," *American Industries*, April 1924, 31–32; "The Problems of Our Immigration," *American Industries*, February 1923, 5–6; and "Selective Immigration Favored," *Iron Trade Review*, 20 December 1923, 1653 (Alexander).

58. L.W. Moffett, "Little Opposition to Immigration Bill," *Iron Age*, April 24, 1924, 1233. Even the quotas in the 1924 law that discriminated against immigrants from places like southern and eastern Europe, in favor countries of origin of older immigrant stock like northern and western Europe, seem to have resonated with segmentalist interests. Segmentalists, after all, pursued their practices in part to reduce expensive labor turnover, and it was immigrants from places like Italy and Poland who often came only temporarily, saving their high wages perhaps to buy a farm or for other small ventures back home. In their case, it seems, high segmentalist wages could have a perverse rather than desired effect on turnover. See "More Immigration Bills," *Iron Age* March 6, 1924, 706.

59. *Congressional Record* 71 (1931), 6510–13, 6515.

9. The New Deal for Market Security

1. To reduce the fund, Fuller also advocated, like most in the business and insurance community, a shift to pay-as-you-go financing. Among other things, this change would, it was thought, prevent politicians from tapping into the fund in response to popular pressure for higher benefits. It was not a reflection of business opposition in principle to social insurance. NAM Press Service, "Proposed Amend-

ments to the Social Security Act: Statement by Walter D. Fuller before Finance Committee of the United States Senate, June 14, 1939" (NAM I/ Box 209), Hagley Museum and Library, Wilmington, Delaware; "Federal Social Security Amendments Proposed: Address by Walter D. Fuller before the State Associations Group" [no date, probably summer 1938], NAM I/Box 209, Hagley. Fuller was a member of the Social Security Advisory Council, appointed by the Senate and the Social Security Board.

2. "What Business Thinks," *Fortune* October 1939, 52, 90, 92.

3. "Current NAM Positions on Federal Program for Old Age and Survivors Insurance" (NAM I/Box 209). On the NAM's growing membership, see Richard W. Gable, "A Political Analysis of an Employers' Association: The National Association of Manufacturers," dissertation, University of Chicago, September, 1950, 190–92.

4. "A 'New' C. of C.," *Business Week* August 8, 1942, 19; "Interview with Marion Folsom," Social Security Project, Columbia University Oral History Collection (typescript, 1965), 75–76. In this interview and a later article, Folsom recalled incorrectly that the NAM did not come around until later in the 1940s or even 1950. Folsom, "Millions of Workers Still Lack Adequate Benefits," in Clarence C. Walton, ed., *Business and Social Progress: Views of Two Generations of Executives* (New York: Praeger, 1970), 98.

5. On the oppositional organizations, see Arthur Altmeyer, *The Formative Years of Social Security* (Madison: University of Wisconsin Press, 1966), 33; Sanford Jacoby, "Employers and the Welfare State: The Role of Marion B. Folsom," *Journal of American History* 80:2 (September 1993), 538.

6. Theron F. Schlabach, *Edwin E. Witte: Cautious Reformer* (Madison: State Historical Society of Wisconsin, 1969), 123; Witte, "The Government and Unemployment," *American Labor Legislation Review* 25:1 (March 1935), 8.

7. Joseph Huthmacher, *Senator Robert F. Wagner and the Rise of Urban Liberalism* (New York: Atheneum, 1968), 9. FDR quoted in Arthur M. Schlesinger Jr., *The Coming of the New Deal* (Boston: Houghton Mifflin, 1958), 308–9.

8. "Chamber Distorts Voice of Business," *New York Times*, 4 May 1935.

9. See, for example (on social security), Abraham Holtzman, *The Townsend Movement: A Political Study* (New York: Bookman, 1963), and David Harry Bennett, *Demagogues in the Depression: American Radicals and the Union Party 1932–1936* (New Brunswick: Rutgers University Press, 1969); (on unemployment insurance and labor law) Frances Fox Piven and Richard A. Cloward, *Poor People's Movements: Why They Succeed, How They Fail* (New York: Pantheon Books, 1977), 41–180; and (on labor law) Michael Goldfield, "Worker Insurgency, Radical Organization, and New Deal Labor Legislation," *American Political Science Review* 83:4 (December 1989), 1257–82.

10. Use of the term regulatory is borrowed from Colin Gordon, *New Deals: Business, Labor, and Politics in America 1920–1935* (Cambridge: Cambridge University Press, 1994), 35–165, who makes a related argument (with differences, discussed in chapter 10). The diverse literature attributing influence to capitalists in the making of Social Security, which this analysis both draws on and differs from, includes Kim McQuaid, *Big Business and Presidential Power: From FDR to Reagan* (New York: William Morrow, 1982), 18–61; Tom Ferguson, "From Normalcy to New Deal: Industrial Structure, Party Competition, and American Public Policy in the Great Depression," *International Organization* 38:1 (Winter 1984), 41–94; Jill Quadagno, "Welfare Capitalism and the Social Security Act of 1935," *American Sociological Review* 49:5 (October 1984), 632–47; Edward Berkowitz and Kim McQuaid, *Creating*

the Welfare State: The Political Economy of Twentieth-Century Reform (New York: Praeger, 1988); J. Craig Jenkins and Barbara G. Brents, "Social Protest, Hegemonic Competition, and Social Reform: A Political Struggle Interpretation of the Origins of the American Welfare State," *American Sociological Review* 54:6 (December 1989), 891–909; G. William Domhoff, *The Power Elite and the State: How Policy is Made in America* (New York: Aldine de Gruyter, 1990) and *State Autonomy or Class Dominance? Case Studies on Policy Making in America* (New York: Aldine de Gruyter, 1996); and Jacoby, "Employers and the Welfare State," 525–56 and "From Welfare Capitalism to the Welfare State: Marion B. Folsom and the Social Security Act of 1935," in Michael Shalev, ed., *The Privatization of Social Policy? Occupational Welfare and the Welfare State in America, Scandinavia, and Japan* (London: Macmillan, 1996), 44–72.

11. See especially Sanford Jacoby, *Modern Manors: Welfare Capitalism Since the New Deal* (Princeton: Princeton University Press, 1997), especially 26–56. On welfare cutbacks, see also Brandes, *American Welfare Capitalism* (Chicago: University of Chicago Press, 1970), 142; Brody, "The Rise and Decline of Welfare Capitalism" in his *Workers in Industrial America* (New York: Oxford University Press, 1980), 48–81; Lizabeth Cohen, *Making a New Deal Industrial Workers in Chicago, 1919–1939* (Cambridge: Cambridge University Press, 1990), chapter 4. For a discussion of the moral economy of pay and worker militancy in industrial societies, see Peter Swenson, *Fair Shares: Unions, Pay, and Politics in Sweden and West Germany* (Ithaca, NY: Cornell University Press, 1989), 11–108. On employers' current strong disinclination to cut pay to preserve worker "morale," see Truman F. Bewley, *Why Wages Don't Fall During a Recession* (Cambridge: Harvard University Press, 1999).

12. By 1938, eleven mostly midwestern states were covered for dry freight hauling. See David Previant, "Economic and Political Implications of the National Trucking Agreement of 1964," *Proceedings of New York University Seventeenth Annual Conference on Labor* (Washington, DC: BNA Incorporated, 1964), 281–82.

13. In a strictly limited way, the argument echoes the work of Gabriel Kolko, for whom progressive legislation before the New Deal was the result of instrumental "business control over politics" for the sake of regulating disruptive competition. It differs, however, from Kolko's in its explicit focus on the decisive agency of politicians who initiate and broker regulatory alliances, and who are jolted into action by political pressures coming, for the most part, from outside the business community. It differs also in that Kolko himself did not seem to detect a regulatory logic behind the New Deal's social legislation. *The Triumph of Conservatism: A Reinterpretation of American History, 1900–1916* (New York: Free Press, 1963), 3. See also *Railroads and Regulation* (Cambridge, MA: Harvard University Press, 1965). On social security, see his *Main Currents in American History* (New York: Harper & Row, 1976), 145–46.

14. U.S. Senate, Committee on Education and Labor, *To Create a National Labor Board*, Hearings on S. 2926 (Washington: 1934), 374–75.

15. On New York, see Robert F. Wesser, "Conflict and Compromise: The Workmen's Compensation Movement in New York, 1890s–1913," *Labor History* 12:3 (Summer 1971), 345–72; David A. Moss, *Socializing Security: Progressive-Era Economists and the Origins of American Social Policy* (Cambridge, MA: Harvard University Press, 1996), 128–31. In Washington, legislation apparently resulted from cross-class "cooperation between organized labor and employers in the lumber industry anxious to rid themselves of personal injury litigation." Joseph F. Tripp, "An Instance of Labor and Business Cooperation: Workmen's Compensation in Washington State (1911)," *Labor History* 17:4 (Fall 1976), 530–50. Employers also took ac-

tive initiative in Missouri, according to Shawn Everett Kantor and Price V. Fishback, "Coalition Formation and the Adoption of Workers' Compensation: The Case of Missouri, 1911–1926," in Claudia Goldin and Gary D. Libecap, eds., *The Regulated Economy: A Historical Approach to Political Economy* (Chicago: University of Chicago Press, 1994), especially 274–76. George M. Gillette discusses fellow employers' widespread inactivity and even occasional opposition in "Employers' Liability," in *Employers' Liability and Industrial Insurance*, Proceedings of the Two Hundred and Twelfth Regular Meeting of the Commercial Club of Chicago, 19 February 1910, 6, 11. Thus James Weinstein, *The Corporate Ideal in the Liberal State 1900–1918* (Boston: Beacon Press, 1968), 47–48, and Roy Lubove, *The Struggle for Social Security 1900–1935* (Pittsburgh: University of Pittsburgh Press, 1986), 55, seem to overstate the strength and breadth of business support before state legislative action.

16. U.S. Senate, Committee on Education and Labor, *To Create a National Labor Board*, 375; Draper, "Industry Needs Unemployment Reserves," *American Labor Legislation Review* 22:1 (March 1932), 31; I. M. Rubinow, *The Quest for Security* (New York: Henry Holt & Co., 1934), 89 and 102.

17. John R. Commons, "Constructive Investigation and the Industrial Commission of Wisconsin," *Survey* 29:14 (4 January 1913), 445.

18. Theda Skocpol, *Protecting Soldiers and Mothers: The Political Origins of Social Policy in the United States* (Cambridge: Harvard University Press, 1992), 401, 411–12; 417; Felix Frankfurter, Mary Dewson, and John R. Commons, *State Minimum Wage Laws in Practice* (New York: National Consumers' League, 1924), 9, 60. According to a study of Washington state, organized employers were largely indifferent because agriculture and canning, the major employers of women, were exempted. Joseph F. Tripp, "Toward an Efficient and Moral Society: Washington State Minimum Wage Law, 1913–1925," *Pacific Northwest Quarterly* 67 (1976), 101.

19. Frankfurter et al., *State Minimum Wage Laws*, 50, 60, and generally 44–70.

20. Victor P. Morris, *Oregon's Experience with Minimum Wage Legislation* (New York: Columbia University Press, 1930), 213–22.

21. NAM quotes from Tripp, "Toward an Efficient and Moral Society," 100.

22. NAM, *Thirty-ninth Annual Convention*, Waldorf-Astoria, New York, 5–6 December 1934, 149–206 (Imprints collection, Hagley Library). See also "Text of New Parts of Recovery Platform Adopted by Manufacturers' Association," *New York Times*, 7 December 1934. Some employers around this time believed that minimum wage laws would be entirely unnecessary "if the Sherman Anti-Trust Law were amended to permit voluntary agreements on prices, production and allocation of territory between competitors," because "they would be able to eliminate 'destructive competition' and pay higher wages." "Are Minimum Wage Laws Needed?" *Information Service* 12:21 (27 May 1933).

23. Steven Fraser, *Labor Will Rule: Sidney Hillman and the Rise of American Labor* (New York: Free Press, 1991), 391–411; Edward Filene, "The Minimum Wage and Efficiency," *American Economic Review* 13 (September 1923), 411; Filene, "Good Business," *Survey* 50 (May 15, 1923), 219–20; Jacoby, *Modern Manors*, 289, note 21. On the purchasing power argument for the FLSA, see also Frances Perkins, *The Roosevelt I Knew* (New York: Viking Press, 1946), 259.

24. Many Southerners wanted regulation but feared that federal legislation would favor their New England competitors by fixing uniform instead of differential standards for all states, thus undermining their low-wage advantage. Louis Galambos, *Competition and Cooperation: The Emergence of a National Trade Association* (Baltimore: Johns Hopkins Press, 1966), 173–202; Perkins, *The Roosevelt I*

Knew, 257; James A. Hodges, *New Deal Labor Policy and the Southern Cotton Textile Industry 1933–1941* (Knoxville: University of Tennessee Press, 1986), 181; Stanley Vittoz, *New Deal Labor Policy and the American Industrial Economy* (Chapel Hill: University of North Carolina Press, 1987), 21–33 and 119–34.

25. All in all, it is hard to argue that labor was more enthusiastic than capital. For example, Secretary of Labor Frances Perkins recounts having to coach Thomas McMahon of the United Textile Workers of America not to ask for less in the way of hour reductions than she knew the employers were about to propose in public deliberations over the NRA textile code in 1933. Also, in Perkins's account, during deliberations the employers' Cotton Textile Industry Committee embarrassed the AFL's Green by taking the initiative in proposing the abolition of child labor in the industry. Perkins, *The Roosevelt I Knew,* 224 and 258–60; Hodges, *New Deal Labor Policy,* 50. On the content of the legislation, see Fraser, *Labor Will Rule,* 411.

26. Likewise, it should be added, the Guffey-Vinson Act of 1937 had been supported by a cross-class alliance of joint cartelists in bituminous coal mining desiring to impose competitive wage (and price) standards on shared enemies, low-wage mines and miners, principally in West Virginia and Kentucky. John Bowman, *Capitalist Collective Action: Competition, Cooperation, and Conflict in the Coal Industry* (Cambridge: Cambridge University Press, 1989), 203–10.

27. "Operation of Unemployment-Benefit Plans in the United States up to 1934," *Monthly Labor Review* 38:6 (June 1934), 1315–16; Daniel Nelson, *Unemployment Insurance: The American Experience 1915–1935* (Madison: University of Wisconsin Press, 1969), 88–90. Coal mining, apparently, according to historian Colin Gordon, was another sector where the idea of unemployment insurance was contemplated by some employers as a "means of shaking out marginal competition," and therefore as a complement to collective bargaining as a regulatory instrument in ruinous product market competition. In any event, no collectively bargained system emerged; legislation would prove necessary. Gordon, *New Deals,* 252.

28. Huthmacher, *Wagner and the Rise of Urban Liberalism,* 47–48, 341.

29. The trustees of the fund were to direct a new Labor Employment Bureau to supervise placements of workers. Lehman also served temporarily as an "impartial chairman" for the industry (as did New Dealer Harry Hopkins, many years later in 1945), which testifies to the esteem in which he was held by clothing manufacturers, not just the unions. Robinson, *Collective Bargaining and Market Control,* 4, 52, 59–61, 71, 98, 148; Raymond Munts and Mary Louise Munts, "Welfare History of the I.L.G.W.U.," *Labor History* 9, Special Supplement (Spring 1968), 86; Robert P. Ingalls, *Herbert H. Lehman and New York's Little New Deal* (New York: New York University Press, 1975), 7, 134–36; "Reminiscences of Herbert H. Lehman," Columbia University Oral History Collection (1972), 452.

30. Nelson, *Unemployment Insurance,* 125–27.

31. Nelson, *Unemployment Insurance,* 120, 124, and 128.

32. Elizabeth Brandeis, "Wisconsin Tackles Job Security," *The Survey,* 15 December 1931, 295–96, and "Employment Reserves vs. Insurance," *The New Republic,* 27 September 1933, 177–79. For similar speculation about "experience rating" in earlier workmen's compensation legislation, see Shawn Everett Kantor and Price V. Fishback, "Coalition Formation and the Adoption of Workers' Compensation: The Case of Missouri, 1911–1926," in Claudia Goldin and Gary D. Libecap, *The Regulated Economy: A Historical Approach to Political Economy* (Chicago: University of Chicago Press, 1994), 267. Ann P. Bartel and Lacy Glenn Thomas speculate about the political implication of job safety regulations with "asymmetric" costs

favoring big employers. "Direct and Indirect Effects of Regulation: A New Look at OSHA's Impact," *Journal of Law and Economics* 28:1 (April 1985), 1–25.

33. Nelson, *Unemployment Insurance*, 122 and 128; United States Senate, Committee on Finance, *Economic Security Act* (Washington, DC: 1935), 516–22.

34. "Operation of Unemployment-Benefit Plans," 1289. On Wrigley, see Edwin Witte, *The Development of the Social Security Act* (Madison: University of Wisconsin Press, 1962), 50; Berkowitz and McQuaid, *Creating the Welfare State*, 118; Nelson, *Unemployment Insurance*, 63.

35. Jacoby, "Employers and the Welfare State," 537, and "From Welfare Capitalism to the Welfare State," 54.

36. Gerard Swope, *The Swope Plan: Details, Criticisms, Analysis* (New York: The Business Bourse, 1931), 25–27, 43–45, and "Stabilization of Industry," in Charles A. Beard, ed., *America Faces the Future* (Boston: Houghton Mifflin, 1932), 184. See also David Loth, *Swope of G.E.: The Story of Gerard Swope and General Electric in American Business* (New York: Simon & Schuster, 1958), 201–15; Kim McQuaid, "Young, Swope and General Electric's 'New Capitalism': A Study in Corporate Liberalism, 1920–33," *American Journal of Economics and Sociology* 36:3 (July 1977), 323–35; and McQuaid, "Competition, Cartelization and the Corporate Ethic: General Electric's Leadership During the New Deal Era, 1933–40," *American Journal of Economics and Sociology* 36:4 (October 1977), 417–28.

37. Irving Bernstein, *The Lean Years: A History of the American Worker 1920–1933* (Boston: Houghton Mifflin, 1960), 351; Loth, *Swope of G.E.*, 233–39; Perkins, *The Roosevelt I Knew*, 278–301; Witte, *The Development of the Social Security Act*, 19 and 47–76; Schlabach, *Edwin E. Witte*, 99–131; Daniel C. Roper, *Fifty Years of Public Life* (Durham: Duke University Press, 1941), 404–7. On Leeds, see Walter Licht, *Getting Work: Philadelphia, 1840–1950* (Cambridge: Harvard University Press, 1992), 189–93.

38. Gordon, *New Deals*, 155; "Annual Report of the Special Conference Committee, 1934" (Harrington Papers/19, Hagley). On the SCC, see chapter 3.

39. See Draper, "Industry Needs Unemployment Reserves"; Litchfield, "Paying the Bills for Social Insurance," *Today*, 9 February 1935, 3–4. (*Today*, which merged with *Newsweek* in 1937, was edited by FDR advisor and speechwriter Raymond Moley, who was also a member of the CES advisory committee.) Arthur Altmeyer, "Reminiscences," Social Security Project, Columbia University Oral History Collection (1966), 149.

40. G. William Domhoff, *The Power Elite and the State: How Policy Is Made in America* (New York: Aldine de Gruyter, 1990), 57, and *State Autonomy or Class Dominance? Case Studies on Policy Making in America* (New York: Aldine de Gruyter, 1996), especially 129–30, and 138–40. According to Fosdick's letter, in 1932 to 1933, the IRC received $100,000 from Rockefeller, and only about $14,000 from "service revenue" and retainers from firms. Among other things Fosdick praised was Murray Latimer's work on pensions (see 208 here). Cf. Ann Orloff and Eric Parker, who claim that "by the early 1930s, IRC was a self-supporting industrial relations consulting firm." "Business and Social Policy in Canada and the United States, 1920–1940," *Comparative Social Research* 12 (1990), 306.

41. Witte, *The Development of the Social Security Act*, 29; Domhoff, *State Autonomy or Class Dominance?* 133 and 157. Before working for the ACWU, Stewart had been director of Canada's National Employment Service from 1914 to 1922. Earlier connections between the IRC and Roosevelt's circle were established in New York when in 1928 his advisor Frances Perkins appointed Arthur H. Young, IRC's exec-

utive director since 1925, and former International Harvester and Colorado Fuel and Iron executive, to chair an Advisory Committee on Employment Problems. Domhoff, *State Autonomy or Class Dominance*, 135.

42. Jordan A. Schwartz, *The New Dealers: Power Politics in the Age of Roosevelt* (New York: Vintage, 1994), 183–87; Robert M. Collins, *The Business Response to Keynes, 1929–1964* (New York: Columbia University Press, 1981), 68–69; Domhoff, *State Autonomy or Class Dominance*, 60, 120, 123–24, and 137; Ferguson, "From Normalcy to New Deal," 83–84.

43. Testimony of Samuel W. Reyburn and Albert D. Hutzler, U.S. Senate, Hearings Before the Committee on Finance, Economic Security Act, 702–13, 802; Joseph M. Becker, *Shared Government in Employment Security: A Study of Advisory Councils* (New York: Columbia University Press, 1959), 205, 247, and 349; "State Study Asked on Job Insurance," *New York Times*, 10 December 1934, 2.

44. On businessmen and macro-economic stabilization, see Collins, *The Business Response to Keynes*. On the GMAC plan, see Robert G. Elbert, *Unemployment and Relief* (New York: Farrar & Rinehart, 1934), 127–30. See also Michael J. Piore and Charles F. Sabel, *The Second Industrial Divide: The Possibilities for Prosperity* (New York: Basic, 1984), 73–104, who suggest that Keynesian macro-economic regulation was a solution more or less accepted after the fact, rather than politically engineered by, mass production industry.

45. Domhoff, *State Autonomy or Class Dominance*, 131–32. See also Raymond B. Fosdick to John D. Rockefeller Jr., 22 March 1934, in which Fosdick expresses his hope that the IRC, with "friends on both sides of the fence" on union issues, would appear neutral to the detractors of company unionism who were gearing up for a legislative attack. Perhaps the fear was that its sometime association with employee representation plans, and therefore union-busting, would undermine its influence in other spheres. Rockefeller Family Archives, RG2, Box 16, Folder 127 (made available to me by Bill Domhoff).

46. Folsom, "Millions of Workers Still Lack Adequate Benefits," 99; Jacoby, "From Welfare Capitalism to the Welfare State," 46, 50, and 67.

47. Brown, *An American Philosophy of Social Security: Evolution and Issues* (Princeton: Princeton University Press, 1972), 21–22; Domhoff, *State Autonomy or Class Dominance?*, 151–56 and 166.

48. Brown, *An American Philosophy of Social Security*, 90–91; Domhoff, *State Autonomy or Class Dominance?* 133, 155; William Graebner, *A History of Retirement* (New Haven: Yale University Press, 1980), 184–89. On Folsom, see Jacoby, "From Welfare Capitalism to the Welfare State," 51. Latimer's pension study was *Industrial Pension Systems in the United States and Canada* (New York: Industrial Relations Counselors, 1932).

49. Brown in U.S. Senate, Committee on Finance, *Economic Security Act*, 284. See also Brown, "The Basic Philosophy of the Federal Old-Age Security Program,"in *Practical Aspects of Unemployment Insurance and Old-Age Security* (American Management Association Personnel Series, No. 23, 1935), 41. On segmentalists' precarious absence of pension funding and insurance, see, in addition to Latimer, *Industrial Pension Systems*, Folsom, "Discussion," in *Practical Aspects of Unemployment Insurance and Old-Age Security* (American Management Association Personnel Series, No. 23, 1935), 45; Rainard B. Robbins, "The Effect of Social Security Legislation on Private Pension Plans, *Journal of the American Association of University Teachers of Insurance* 5 (1938), 49–50, and 54; Stephen Sass, *The Promise of Private Pensions: The First Hundred Years* (Cambridge: Harvard University Press, 1997), 76–95.

50. Graebner, *History of Retirement*, 186.

51. On department stores, see Michael J. Carter and Susan B. Carter, "Internal Labor Markets in Retailing: The Early Years," *Industrial and Labor Relations Review* 38:4 (July 1985), 586–98, and Frank R. Dobbin, "The Origins of Private Social Insurance: Public Policy and Fringe Benefits in America, 1920–1950," *American Journal of Sociology* 97:5 (March 1992), 1425. On Folsom, see Jacoby, "From Welfare Capitalism to the Welfare State," 55 and 67. On International Harvester, see Robert Ozanne, *A Century of Labor-Management Relations at McCormick and International Harvester* (Madison: University of Wisconsin, 1967), 85–86. Harvester revised its plan downward, as did most other welfare capitalists. See Jennifer Klein, "Welfare Capitalism in the Era of the Welfare State: Insurers, Employers, and the Politics of Security, 1933–1939," paper presented at the Social Science History Association Annual Conference, 19 November 1998, 28.

52. Joseph Frazier Wall, *Alfred I. du Pont: The Man and His Family* (New York: Oxford University Press, 1990), 290–92, 515, 523–33, 542–43, and 547–49. Pierre du Pont was a key figure behind the American Liberty League, about the most shrill and alarmist organ of business opposition to the New Deal. See Robert F. Burk, *The Corporate State and the Broker State: The Du Ponts and American National Politics 1925–1940* (Cambridge: Harvard University Press, 1990), especially 20 and 143–277.

53. On the purchasing power argument for old age insurance, see William Graebner, *A History of Retirement*, 190–92.

54. Telegrams and letters to Malcolm Muir, President of McGraw Hill Publishing Co., New York, submitted with statement of L. C. Morrow of McGraw-Hill, editor of *Factory Management and Maintenance*, and representing the National Publishers' Association, U.S. Senate, Committee on Finance, *Economic Security Act: Hearings*, 796. Not surprisingly, then, some major oil firms—Standard Oil of New Jersey, Phillips Petroleum, Signal Oil, and Ohio Oil—were important Democratic contributors in the 1936 election. Thomas Ferguson, *Golden Rule: The Investment Theory of Party Competition and the Logic of Money-Driven Political Systems* (Chicago: University of Chicago Press, 1995), 210. But Republicans also received large amounts, indicating only that oil was divided, ideology still mattered, and oil industrialists hedged their bets. Cf. Michael J. Webber, "Business, The Democratic Party, and the New Deal: An Empirical Critique of Thomas Ferguson's 'Investment Theory of Politics,'" *Sociological Perspectives* 34:4 (1991), 486–87.

55. Telegrams and letters to Malcolm Muir, U.S. Senate, Committee on Finance, *Economic Security Act: Hearings*, 795 and 801.

56. Telegrams and letters to Malcolm Muir, U.S. Senate, Committee on Finance, *Economic Security Act: Hearings*, 791–815.

57. Telegrams and letters to Malcolm Muir, U.S. Senate, Committee on Finance, *Economic Security Act: Hearings*, 793 and 862–71; "Statement of L.C. Morrow," U.S. Senate, Committee on Finance, *Economic Security Act: Hearings*, 787–88, and telegrams and letters, 791–99.

58. Telegrams and letters to Malcolm Muir, U.S. Senate, Committee on Finance, *Economic Security Act: Hearings*, 791–801.

59. Telegrams and letters to Malcolm Muir, U.S. Senate, Committee on Finance, *Economic Security Act: Hearings*, 796–801, 918–19; Edgerton quoted in Swope, *The Swope Plan*, 53.

60. On Towers Perrin, see Witte, *The Development of the Social Security Act*, 105–6 and Schlabach, *Edwin E. Witte*, 150–51. On big employers' assessment of the Clark option, see Domhoff, *State Autonomy or Class Dominance?* 167–69. The letter

writers were probably middling-size firms for whom the only economical way of providing pensions was to contract out the business to life insurance companies. Metropolitan failed miserably in landing lucrative contracts with major segmentalists like American Rolling Mill, Bethlehem Steel, Du Pont, GE, R. H. Macy, Otis Elevator, Sears, Roebuck, Standard Oil of New Jersey, Union Carbide, U.S. Rubber, U. S. Steel, Western Electric, and many others. Funding their pension commitments properly in an insurance arrangement would have tied up a lot of capital, and they were big enough to take advantage of their own economies of scale. And AT&T, for one, considered its financial solvency as good as that of any insurance company. Sass, *The Promise of Private Pensions*, 70–78, 86–87, and 275–76 (note 26).

61. Folsom quote in Rainard B. Robbins, "The Status of Industrial Pension Plans as Affected by Old Age Benefits Sections of the Social Security Act" (no date). This was a preliminary report to the Committee on Social Security of the Social Science Research Council (SSRC Collection/261/Record Group 1.1, Rockefeller Archive Center), graciously made available to me by Bill Domhoff. On OAI as a bargain, see Marion Folsom, "Company Annuity Plans and the Federal Old Age Benefit Plan," *Harvard Business Review* 14:4 (Summer 1936), 420. Folsom's and Brown's 1935 views are in Folsom, "Discussion," 45, and Brown, "The Basic Philosophy of the Federal Old-Age Security Program," 41 (quote), both in *Practical Aspects of Unemployment Insurance.* By 1938, it was "widely recognized that the government is offering more for [Social Security] taxes than private industry can provide." Rainard B. Robbins, "The Effect of Social Security Legislation," 51.

62. Folsom, "Company Annuity Plans," 420–21; Paul Douglas, *Social Security in the United States: An Analysis and Appraisal of the Federal Social Security Act* (New York: McGraw-Hill, 1936), 283–89; Sass, *The Promise of Private Pensions*, 96; and Sanford Jacoby, "From Welfare Capitalism to the Welfare State," 63–64.

63. Marion Folsom, "Company Annuity Plans," 420; Folsom, "Coordination of Pension Plans with Social Security Provisions," *Personnel* 16 (1939), 41–42. On the spread of company plans, see Dobbin, "The Origins of Private Social Insurance," 1416–50, especially 1432–34. On the insurance industry, see Klein, "Welfare Capitalism in the Era of the Welfare State," especially 27.

64. Thomas Ferguson concludes on the basis of unspecified archival documents that Edward Filene, George Mead of Mead Paper, "probably Swope, and perhaps Teagle" endorsed the bill. "From Normalcy to New Deal," 88. On Swope's total silence, and the tidal wave of opposition from the business community as a whole, see Daniel Sipe, *A Moment of the State: The Enactment of the National Labor Relations Act, 1935,* unpublished doctoral dissertation, University of Pennsylvania, 1981, 176–90.

65. Uniform standards meant, in the American context, minimum standards or floors. Wagner, "Industrial Democracy and Industrial Peace," *Congressional Record* (Washington, DC: United States Government Printing Office, 1937), 7567–68. On Keynesian motives, see Kenneth H. Casebeer, "Holder of the Pen: An Interview with Leon Keyserling on Drafting the Wagner Act," *University of Miami Law Review* 42:3 (November 1987), 290–91, 295–96, 299, and 308–9.

66. The preamble to the act blamed labor's organizational weakness for, among other things, "preventing the stabilization of competitive wage rates and working conditions within and between industries." Casebeer, "Holder of the Pen," 291. Wagner quote from *The Congressional Record* 79 (1935), 7567–68; Drew quote from "Proceedings of the National Industrial Council" (April 22, 1937), 13, Imprints collection, Hagley Museum; Drew, however, was far from enthusiastic, of

course. Sidney Fine, *Without Blare of Trumpets: Walter Drew, the National Erectors' Association, and the Open Shop Movement, 1903–57* (Ann Arbor: University of Michigan Press, 1995), 269–70.

67. On the AFL's passivity, see Casebeer, "Holder of the Pen," 323 and 348. On the railroad unions, see Sipe, *A Moment of the State*, 90–92 and 174–75; and Casebeer, 328. In 1936, after passage of the Wagner Act, the garment industry was about the single most important source of business endorsements for Roosevelt and financing for the Democratic National Committee (DNC). On the garment industry, see Herman E. Kroos, *Executive Opinion: What Business Leaders Said and Thought on Economic Issues 1920s–1960s* (New York: Doubleday, 1970), 185, and Louise Overacker, "Campaign Funds in the Presidential Election of 1936," *American Political Science Review* 31:3 (June 1937), 485–87.

68. Some coal operators contributed to the Republicans. Overacker, "Campaign Funds," 488–90. On Lewis in 1932, see Sipe, *A Moment of the State*, 111. Wagner also planned to get testimony from tobacco producers. A cannery owner was sought because, according to a Wagner aide, "He wants to have his men organize, in the hope that this will force organization . . . among his competitors." Only two tobacco producers testified in support, while the other groups were absent. Gordon, *New Deals*, 216; U.S. Senate, Committee on Education and Labor, *National Labor Relations Board* (Washington, DC, 1935), 212–18. See also Sipe, 178, who notes that an association of 17 New York shoe manufacturers submitted a supportive petition.

69. Testimony of R. G. Wagenet, U.S. Senate, Committee on Education and Labor, *To Create a National Labor Board* (Washington, DC, 1934), Part 1, 283; "Brief Presented in Behalf of the Associated General Contractors of America," U.S. Senate, Committee on Education and Labor, *National Labor Relations Board* (Washington, 1935), 743–45; Booth Mooney, *Builders for Progress: The Story of the Associated General Contractors of America* (New York: McGraw-Hill, 1965), 85.

70. Cheney letter quoted in Gordon, *New Deals*, 215. Roosevelt addresses in U.S. Senate, Committee on Education and Labor, *To Create a National Labor Board* (Washington, DC, 1934), Part 2, 624, and Russell D. Buhite and David W. Levy, *FDR's Fireside Chats* (Norman: University of Oklahoma Press, 1992), 33.

71. U.S. Senate, Committee on Education and Labor, *To Create a National Labor Board* (Washington, DC, 1934), Part 1, 267, 278, and 283. On Walsh, see J. Joseph Huthmacher, *Massachusetts People and Politics 1919–1933* (Cambridge: Harvard University Press, 1959), 126–134, 146.

72. See Hillman's appeal in "Why Textile Unionization Means Profits" in *Barron's*, the financial weekly, September 20, 1937. On Amoskeag, see U.S. Senate, Committee on Education and Labor, *To Create a National Labor Board* (Washington, DC, 1934), 278. Support or sympathy, according to Fraser, was also anticipated from executives of Avondale, Riverside, Dan River, Burlington, Stillwater Worsted, Whitman, and Chase mills, mostly, but not exclusively, in the North. Kendall Mills was another (Henry Kendall was a BAC member in 1935). Fraser, *Labor Will Rule*, 388–89, 396.

73. Ching quote in Monthly Meeting, National Industry Conference Board, April 14, 1934, 90. (NICB 1057/Box 7/Folder 35, Hagley Museum and Library); Weyerhauser in Gordon, *New Deals*, 234. On the paper firms, see Ferguson, "From Normalcy to New Deal," 87, and Jacoby, *Modern Manors*, 33–34. On the workings of post–Wagner Act collective bargaining in paper, see Clark Kerr and Roger Randall, *Crown Zellerbach and the Pacific Coast Pulp and Paper Industry* (Washington, DC: National Planning Association, 1948).

74. Loth, *Swope of G.E.*, 270; Filene in U.S. Senate, Committee on Finance, *Investigation of the National Recovery Administration* (Washington, DC, 1935), 1431. On Filene and his foundation, see Ferguson, "From Normalcy to New Deal," 88.

75. M. C. Rorty, "Is Collective Bargaining Compatible with a Free Price and Wage System," *The Management Review* 24:2 (February 1935), 36–37; Gordon, *New Deals*, 238.

76. On cartelist regulation of management in garments, see chapter 3. On the open-ended inclusiveness of the clause requiring employers to bargain in good faith about "wages, hours, and conditions of employment," see Casebeer, "Holder of the Pen," 330–31.

77. On Wagner, see Mark Barenberg, "The Political Economy of the Wagner Act: Power, Symbol, and Workplace Cooperation," *Harvard Law Review* 106:7 (May 1993), 1381–1496. For Brandeis's views, see his *Scientific Management and the Railroads* (New York: The Engineering Magazine, 1911), especially 55–61. On the Taylor Society, see Fraser, *Labor Will Rule*, 131–33, 171–74, and 266–73. Quotes from Fred J. Miller, "Management and Production" and Morris Cooke, "Preface," in Cooke, Samuel Gompers, and Miller, eds., *Labor, Management and Production, Annals of the American Academy of Political and Social Science* 91:180 (September 1920). H. S. Person, the Taylor Society's managing director in 1931, favored obligatory unemployment insurance with experience rating. Person, "Unemployment Compensation—A Positive Force for Regularization," *American Labor Legislation Review* 21:2 (June 1931), 216.

78. On the NAM/AFL alliance, see especially James Gross, *The Reshaping of the National Labor Relations Board: National Labor Policy in Transition 1937–1947* (Albany, NY: SUNY Press, 1981). See Harry A. Millis and Emily Clark Brown on Taft-Hartley in *From the Wagner Act to Taft-Hartley: A Study of National Labor Policy and Labor Relations* (Chicago: University of Chicago Press, 1950), 289, 378–79.

79. "Without Benefit of NRA," *Wall Street Journal*, 10 June 1935. During the economic upturn early in 1937, U.S. Steel wanted to avoid an interruption in production and loss of markets. Two days before the agreement the company joined an international steel cartel agreement, which promised to protect it from foreign competition that might take advantage of its increased wages and prices. Also, Taylor possibly hoped that by signing with Lewis, the free-trading Roosevelt administration would look the other way. See Vittoz, *New Deal Labor Policy*, 158–64, and Richard A. Lauderbaugh, "Business, Labor, and Foreign Policy: U.S. Steel, the International Steel Cartel, and Recognition of the Steel Workers Organizing Committee," *Politics and Society* 6:4 (1976), 451. Lamont's letter quoted in Gordon, *New Deals*, 227. For Lamont on Roosevelt, see Arthur M. Schlesinger, *The Coming of the New Deal* (Boston: Houghton Mifflin, 1958), 498.

80. On the regulatory role of unionism in steel, see Lloyd Ulman, "Influences of the Economic Environment on the Structure of the Steel Workers' Union," *Proceedings of the Industral Relations Research Association* (December 1961), 232–33.

81. Robert M. MacDonald discusses the effects of unionism on competition in automobiles in *Collective Bargaining in the Automobile Industry: A Study of Wage Structure and Competitive Relations* (New Haven: Yale University Press, 1963), 391–401. See also Harry Katz, *Shifting Gears: Changing Labor Relations in the U.S. Automobile Industry* (Cambridge: MIT Press, 1985), 30–36.

82. Jacoby was referring in particular to the National Industrial Conference Board's opposition in "Employers and the Welfare State," 544. See also Domhoff, *The Power Elite and the State*, 56–57.

10. Whose Business Were the New Dealers Minding?

1. Raymond Moley, *After Seven Years* (New York: Harper & Brothers, 1939), 305–16.

2. Moley thought the Wagner Act too one-sided, but remediable, probably along the lines of the Taft-Hartley Act of 1947. Moley, *After Seven Years*, 292, 304, and 372–73. See also Arthur Schlesinger, Jr., *The Coming of the New Deal* (Boston: Houghton Mifflin, 1959), 497. Agreeing that the SSA was not the problem, Domhoff focuses instead on the Wagner Act as the reason for business disaffection: *The Power Elite and the State: How Policy Is Made in America* (New York: Aldine de Gruyter, 1990), 56–57, and *State Autonomy or Class Dominance? Case Studies on Policy Making in America* (New York: Aldine de Gruyter, 1996), 120 and 163.

3. William Leuchtenberg, *Franklin D. Roosevelt and the New Deal* (New York: Harper & Row, 1963), 165, 176–77, 183–84, and 339; Arthur M. Schlesinger, Jr., *The Coming of the New Deal*, esp. 301–13. For a useful though one-sided and therefore misleading discussion of the hostile climate, see Herman E. Kroos, *Executive Opinion: What Business Leaders Said and Thought on Economic Issues 1920s–1960s* (New York: Doubleday, 1970), 182–209. On this consensus about pervasive hostility, and a perspective on an underlying "pattern of accommodation," see Randall Collins, *The Business Response to Keynes, 1929–1964* (New York: Columbia University Press, 1981), chapter 3, especially 53 and note 1.

4. See Theda Skocpol and Kenneth Finegold, "State Capacity and Economic Intervention in the Early New Deal," *Political Science Quarterly* 97:2 (Summer 1982), 255–78; Skocpol and John Ikenberry, "The Political Formation of the American Welfare State in Historical and Comparative Perspective," *Comparative Social Research* 6 (JAI Press, 1983), 87–148; Margaret Weir and Skocpol, "State Structures and the Possibilities for 'Keynesian' Responses to the Great Depression in Sweden, Britain, and the United States," in Peter Evans et al., eds., *Bringing the State Back In* (Cambridge: Cambridge University Press, 1985), 107–63; Skocpol and Edwin Amenta, "Did Capitalists Shape Social Security?" *American Sociological Review* 50:4 (August 1985), 572–75; Skocpol, "A Brief Reply," *Politics and Society* 15:3 (1986–87), 331–32; Edwin Amenta, Elisabeth Clemens, Jefren Olsen, Sunita Parikh, and Theda Skocpol, "The Political Origins of Unemployment Insurance in Five American States," *Studies in American Political Development* 2 (1987), 137–82; Ann Orloff and Eric Parker, "Business and Social Policy in Canada and the United States," *Comparative Social Research* 12 (1990), 295–339; Edwin Amenta and Sunita Parikh, "Capitalists Did Not Want the Social Security Act: A Critique of the 'Capitalist Dominance' Thesis," *American Sociological Review* 56:1 (February 1991), 124–32; Skocpol, "State Formation and Social Policy in the United States," *American Behavioral Scientist* 35:4/5 (March/June 1992), 559–84; and Ann Orloff, *The Politics of Pensions* (Madison: University of Wisconsin Press, 1993).

5. Skocpol, "State Formation and Social Policy," 566.

6. James MacGregor Burns, *Roosevelt: The Lion and the Fox* (New York: Harcourt, Brace, 1956), 264–88. Noteworthy political scientists writing in this vein are Walter Dean Burnham, in *Critical Elections and the Mainsprings of American Politics* (New York: W. W. Norton, 1970), 55–58, and Ronald Rogowski, in *Commerce and Coalitions: How Trade Affects Domestic Political Alignments* (Princeton: Princeton University Press, 1989), 71–72. Skocpol, "State Formation and Social Policy," 567.

7. To be sure, this is not a fundamental critique of all "institutionalisms," but only of the practice of one particular school of thought in historical explanation of the New Deal. See chapter 1.

8. "President Rebuffs Business Leaders; Open Break Looms," *New York Times*, 2 May 1935. Much of the hostility, apparently, arose from divisive experiences with the NRA and Roosevelt's endorsement of the Wagner Act.

9. "Chamber Denounces Plans of New Deal" (Sibley quote), and "Van Horn Says 'Minority' Uses Chamber as 'Catspaw'," *New York Times*, 3 May 1935. See also "The Big Fight," *Business Week*, 11 May 1935, 8–9 and "Chamber of Commerce," *Newsweek*, May 11, 1935, 5–6.

10. "A 'New' C. of C.," *Business Week*, 8 August 1942, 19. For a discussion, see Collins, *The Business Response to Keynes*, 31–42 and 53–56.

11. United States Senate, Committee on Finance, *Economic Security Act* (Washington, DC: 1935), 797; Raymond Moley, "Misrepresenting American Business," *Today*, 11 May 1935, 12–13.

12. "TVA Friends Bolt Chamber Session," *New York Times*, 6 November 1935, and "Two Trade Groups Balk," *New York Times*, 15 November 1935. On Draper, see James M. Smallwood, *Urban Builder: The Life and Times of Stanley Draper* (Oklahoma City: University of Oklahoma Press, 1977), 81–83. On the chamber survey and its aftermath, see "Business Is Voting Against the New Deal," *New York Times*, 11 November 1935 and "Two Trade Groups Balk." Amenta and Parikh, in "Capitalists Did Not Want the Social Security Act," 126, rely on Kroos's problematic analysis of the survey in *Executive Opinion*, 183–85. On the later Chamber of Commerce survey, sponsored by Folsom, see chapter 9.

13. "Interview with Marion Folsom," Social Security Project, Columbia University Oral History Collection (typescript 1965) 11. In addition to the IRC support before passage of the SSA in 1935, the Rockefeller-controlled Chase National Bank and Manufacturers' Trust each loaned the Democratic National Committee $100,000 for the 1936 national election. Thomas P. Ferguson, *Golden Rule: The Investment Theory of Party Competition and the Logic of Money-Driven Political Systems* (Chicago: University of Chicago Press, 1995), 204; Isaac M. Rubinow, "The Movement Toward Unemployment Insurance in Ohio," *Social Service Review* 7:2 (June 1933), 213. Roosevelt's invitation to Wrigley, who had installed a company unemployment insurance plan, brought a curt and off-putting letter from his secretary. Nevertheless, Wrigley contributed to the Democratic party in 1936. Edwin Witte, *The Development of the Social Security Act* (Madison: University of Wisconsin Press, 1962), 50; Overacker, "Campaign Funds in the Presidential Election of 1936," *American Political Science Review* 31:3 (June 1937), 473–98; Edward Berkowitz and Kim McQuaid, *Creating the Welfare State: The Political Economy of Twentieth-Century Reform* (New York: Praeger, 1988), 118; Daniel Nelson, *Unemployment Insurance: The American Experience 1915–1935* (Madison: University of Wisconsin Press, 1969), 63.

14. "Chamber Distorts Voice of Business," *New York Times*, 4 May 1935. Filene's views are in David C. D. Jacobs, *Business Lobbies and the Power Structure in America* (Westport, Conn.: Quorum, 1999), 81–92. Progressive businessmen in America tend to be treated as "deviants" by their peers, according to David Vogel, "Why Businessmen Distrust Their State: The Political Consciousness of American Corporate Executives," *British Journal of Political Science* 8:1 (January 1978), 53.

15. Skocpol and Amenta, "Did Capitalists Shape Social Security," 572–73. See also Orloff and Parker, "Business and Social Policy," 306–7.

16. Nelson, *Unemployment Insurance*, 214–15.

17. "Supplemental Statement by M. A. Folsom, Assistant Treasurer Eastman Kodak Co.," and "Statement of Lincoln Filene," U.S. Senate, Committee on Finance, *Economic Security Act*, 585 and 823. Filene had served on the interstate

commission on unemployment insurance appointed by FDR when he was governor of New York and had been in close contact with the studies made by the King commission on stabilization of employment in Massachusetts.

18. Skocpol and Ikenberry, "The Political Formation of the American Welfare State," 128–29 and 143, note 15; Ikenberry and Skocpol, "Expanding Social Benefits: The Role of Social Security," *Political Science Quarterly* 102:3 (Fall 1987), 408–9. Orloff and Parker, in "Business and Social Policy," 306, also argue that the "pro-public social insurance capitalists" wanted a plan with "more uniformity."

19. Arthur Altmeyer, *The Formative Years of Social Security* (Madison: University of Wisconsin Press, 1966), 24; Nelson, *Unemployment Insurance*, 208; Folsom, Leeds, Lewisohn, Moley, Swope, and Teagle to Perkins, 15 December 1934. U.S. Senate, Committee on Finance, *Economic Security Act*, 324–25.

20. Folsom, Leeds, Lewisohn, Moley, Swope, and Teagle to Perkins, December 15, 1934. U.S. Senate, Committee on Finance, *Economic Security Act*, 324–25. See also "Job Insurance by States, With a Federal Subsidy, Roosevelt Council's Plan," *New York Times*, 15 December 1934.

21. "Supplemental Statement by M. A. Folsom," 582. On the vote in the advisory committee, see Witte, *The Development of the Social Security Act*, 58, note 33. Unlike the businessmen, the labor representatives were uncertain and divided on the committee. Two labor representatives were absent and failed to register a vote later, and the labor representative from Wisconsin voted for the Wagner-Lewis tax-offset option.

22. "Supplemental Statement by M. A. Folsom," 561–68; Theron F. Schlabach, *Edwin E. Witte: Cautious Reformer* (Madison: State Historical Society of Wisconsin, 1969), 144. On cross-class collusion in the use of pooled unemployment insurance funds in the needle trades, see "Interview with Folsom," 105–6.

23. Philippa Strum, *Louis D. Brandeis: Justice for the People* (New York: Schocken Books, 1984), 386. Cohen quote is from Quadagno's interview, as reported in her "Welfare Capitalism and the Social Security Act," 642. On Folsom, see Witte, *The Development of the Social Security Act*, 123–24, and "Supplemental Statement by M. A. Folsom," 582; and Sanford Jacoby, "From Welfare Capitalism to the Welfare State: Marion B. Folsom and the Social Security Act of 1935," in Michael Shalev, ed., *The Privatization of Social Policy? Occupational Welfare and the Welfare State in America, Scandinavia, and Japan* (London: Macmillan, 1996), 60–61.

24. "Statement of Senator Robert F. Wagner (January 22 1935)," U.S. Senate, Committee on Finance, *Economic Security Act*, 2–4.

25. Witte, *Development of the Social Security Act*, 130 and 141. In general, according to Murray Latimer (from Rockefeller's IRC outfit), Folsom was profoundly influential in getting legislators to believe "that a social insurance program was practicable." Schlabach, *Edwin E. Witte*, 144 and 150.

26. "Statement of Robert G. Elbert," U.S. Senate, Committee on Finance, *Economic Security Act*, 825. Paul Douglas, *Social Security in the United States: An Analysis and Appraisal of the Federal Social Security Act* (New York: McGraw-Hill, 1939), 104–5, 112–13, and 138–39. Whereas Folsom and other corporate liberals offered constructive criticism as well as support to move the legislation through, the AFL's Green "gave little assistance during the Congressional struggle." Nelson, *Unemployment Insurance*, 214–15.

27. According to the IRC's Murray Latimer, in 1935, the Southerners feared that the federal government would "require southern states to pay Negroes a benefit which would be regarded locally as excessive." Quoted in Domhoff, *State Autonomy or Class Dominance?* 160. (See also 170–74.) On the influence of Southern

planters on the Democratic party, and how they influenced the details of the New Deal, including old age assistance, in such a way as to make it palatable, see Lee J. Alston and Joseph P. Ferrie, *Southern Paternalism and the Rise of the American Welfare State: Economics, Politics, and Institutions in the South, 1865–1965* (Cambridge: Cambridge University Press, 1999) and Jill Quadagno, "From Old-Age Assistance to Supplemental Security Income: The Political Economy of Relife in the South, 1935–1972," in Margaret Weir et al., eds, *The Politics of Social Policy in the United States* (Princeton: Princeton University Press, 1988), 235–63. See also Domhoff, *The Power Elite and the State*, 97–98.

28. Altmeyer, *The Formative Years of Social Security*, 25 and 258; Witte, *Development of the Social Security Act*, 118–19. Ironically, Epstein, who is usually associated with fervent advocacy of strict pooling systems, drew up the federal subsidy plan around which the cross-class alliance formed. On Epstein, see Schlabach, *Edwin Witte*, 140; Nelson, *Unemployment Insurance*, 196; and Roy Lubove, *The Struggle for Social Security* (Pittsburgh: University of Pittsburgh Press, 1986), 174–78.

29. Jacoby, "From Welfare Capitalism to the Welfare State," 64–66; Edward D. Berkowitz, "The First Advisory Council and the 1939 Amendments," in Berkowitz, ed., *Social Security after Fifty: Successes and Failures* (Westport, CT: Greenwood, 1987), 55–78; Jennifer Klein, "Welfare Capitalism in the Era of the Welfare State: Insurers, Employers, and the Politics of Security, 1933–1939," paper presented at the Social Science History Association Annual Conference, 19 November 1998, 41–46; Domhoff, *State Autonomy or Class Dominance*, 169.

30. Jacoby, "From Welfare Capitalism to the Welfare State,"65, and *Modern Manors*, 265; Klein, "Welfare Capitalism in the Era of the Welfare State," 45.

31. Ikenberry and Skocpol, "Expanding Social Benefits," 410, 408; Skocpol, "A Brief Response," *Politics and Society* 15:3 (1986–1987), 332.

32. Witte, "The Government and Unemployment," 8; Witte, *Development of the Social Security Act*, 141; Schlabach, *Edwin Witte*, 92, 123, 150, 194; Altmeyer, *The Formative Years*, 24; Nelson, *Unemployment Insurance*, 207.

33. Theda Skocpol, *Protecting Soldiers and Mothers* (Cambridge: Harvard University Press, 1992), 300–1; Skocpol, "A Brief Response," 332.

34. Commons, *Myself* (New York: Macmillan, 1934), 153–54.

35. Commons, "Unemployment Compensation and Prevention," *The Survey*, 1 October 1921, 8.

36. Commons, "Constructive Investigation and the Industrial Commission of Wisconsin," *Survey*, 4 January 1913, 441, 443–44, 448.

37. Commons, *Myself*, 123–24, 143, 198–200; *Institutional Economics: Its Place in Political Economy* (Madison: University of Wisconsin, 1959 [1934]), 3, 852–53. "It was, indeed, through the aid of these ten-year discussions [about unemployment insurance legislation in Wisconsin] and my participation in them that I finally reached the formulation of the more abstract theory of 'institutional economics' which I now learned to define as collective action in control, liberation, and expansion of individual action," 841–42. For a short statement of the abstract theory, see Commons, "Institutional Economics," *American Economic Review* 21:4 (December 1931). Disregarding businessmen's noncompensated work for the WIC, Amenta and Parikh claim it "received no financial support from capitalists." "Capitalists Did Not Want the Social Security Act," 127.

38. Commons, *Myself*, 110–11, 133, 145, 164–65. See also Domhoff, *The Power Elite and the State*, 48–51.

39. Schlabach, *Edwin Witte*, 194 and 206.

40. Joseph M. Becker, *Shared Government in Employment Security: A Study of Advisory Councils* (New York: Columbia University Press, 1959), 363–64 (my emphasis in Altmeyer quotation); NAM, *National Conference on Unemployment Compensation*, 15. Cf. Robert H. Salisbury, "Why No Corporatism in America?" in Phillipe Schmitter and Gerhard Lehmbruch, eds., *Trends Toward Corporatist Intermediation* (London: Sage, 1979), 213–30, and Graham Wilson, "Why Is There No Corporatism in the United States?" in Lehmbruch and Schmitter, eds., *Patterns of Corporatist Policy-Making* (London: Sage, 1982), 219–36.

41. On the IRC in Wisconsin, see Domhoff, *State Autonomy or Class Dominance?*, 138. On OAI administration, see SSRC, "Planned Protection Against Unemployment and Dependency: Report on a Tentative Plan for a Proposed Investigation," November 1934, 1–2 (SSRC Collection, Subseries 28, Box 262, Folder 1530, Rockefeller Archive Center, graciously made availably by Bill Domhoff); Donald Fisher, *Fundamental Development of the Social Sciences: Rockefeller Philanthropy and the United States Social Science Research Council* (Ann Arbor: University of Michigan Press, 1993), 144–56; Domhoff, *State Autonomy or Class Dominance?* 60 and 124–25; Charles McKinley and Robert W. Fraser, *Launching Social Security: A Capture and Record Account* (Madison: University of Wisconsin Press, 1970), 348–49. For another critique of the argument about preexisting state programs and institutional constraints on the shape of federal old age insurance, see Quadagno, "Welfare Capitalism," 635–36.

42. Amenta et al., "The Political Origins of Unemployment Insurance in Five American States," especially 158–61. On the retailers, see Becker, *Shared Government*, 205, 247, and 349, and "State Study Asked on Job Insurance," *New York Times*, December 10, 1934, 2.

43. Becker, *Shared Government*, 429–30; Paul Litchfield, "Paying the Bills for Social Insurance," *Today*, February 9, 1935, 3–4. By the 1950s, Litchfield's liberalism of the 1930s appears to have given way over time to crabby anti-government and anti-union sentiments, though he never brings up Social Security for criticism. See P.W. Litchfield, *The Industrial Republic: Reflections of an Industrial Lieutenant* (Cleveland: Corday & Gross, 1946, revised edition), and *Industrial Voyage: My Life as an Industrial Lieutenant* (New York: Doubleday, 1954).

44. Katherine Baicker, Claudia Goldin and Lawrence F. Katz, "A Distinctive System: Origins and Impact of U.S. Unemployment Compensation," in Michael D. Bordo, Claudia Goldin, and Eugene N. White, *The Defining Moment: The Great Depression and the American Economy in the Twentieth Century* (Chicago: University of Chicago Press, 1998), 250 and 254. Becker, *Shared Government*, 246. Quadagno suggests a similar, yet distinct, argument in which "monopoly capitalists" do better in dealing with "national state managers," while "companies in the competitive sector of the economy" do better in Congress. Quadagno, "Welfare Capitalism," 633 and 643. See also Becker, *Shared Government*, especially 430, note 10.

45. Becker, *Shared Government*, 85–86, 110–11, 120, 124–25, 279–301, 310–11, 353, and 429–31.

46. Becker, *Shared Government*, 187–205; Robinson, *Collective Bargaining and Market Control*, 100; Loth, *Swope of G.E.*, 270; "Reminiscences of Herbert H. Lehman," Columbia University Oral History Collection (1972), 452.

47. Jesse T. Carpenter, *Competition and Collective Bargaining in the Needle Trades 1910–1967* (Ithaca, NY: New York State School of Industrial and Labor Relations, Cornell University, 1972), 236–45, 478–80, 492–94, 525.

48. U.S. Department of Labor, Bureau of Employment Security, *Comparison of State Unemployment Insurance Laws as of August 1954* (Washington, DC, 1954), 17.

Folsom had more success at the federal level, successfully persuading the Eisenhower administration to pass a provision through Congress extending experience rating to new employers. "Interview with Folsom," 105; Jacoby, "From Welfare Capitalism to the Welfare State," 71, note 21.

49. The NAM's earlier hesitation seems to have stemmed from divisions between industries with stable and unstable employment. See the 14 May 1936, statement by NAM Secretary Noel Sargent before a committee of the Ohio State Senate, "Should States Enact Unemployment Insurance Legislation Conforming to the Federal Social Security Act?" 19 (NAM I/Box 209). In 1939, NAM's social security committee "decided that the Association's activity with respect to the promotion of Experience Rating should be intensified." Meeting of the Advisory Committee on Economic Security, 18 December 1939 (NAM I/Box 274/Committee on Economic Security). On Meany, see Becker, *Shared Government*, 186–88, 203–4.

50. Fred Block, "The Ruling Class Does Not Rule: Notes on the Marxist Theory of the State," *Socialist Revolution* 33 (May–June 1977). Skocpol challenges Block on the issue of class struggle in "Political Response to Capitalist Crisis: Neo-Marxist Theories of the State and the Case of the New Deal," *Politics and Society* 10:2 (1980), 155–201. See also Michael Goldfield's enlightening responses in "Worker Insurgency, Radical Organization, and New Deal Labor Legislation," *American Political Science Review* 83: 4 (December 1989), 1257–82, and the Skocpol-Goldfield debate in "Explaining New Deal Labor Policy," *American Political Science Review* 84:4 (December 1990), 1297–1315.

51. Block, "The Ruling Class Does Not Rule," 25–26.

52. Harry A. Millis and Emily Clark Brown, *From the Wagner Act to Taft-Hartley: A Study of National Labor Policy and Labor Relations* (Chicago: University of Chicago Press, 1950), 655–64.

53. See, for example, J. Craig Jenkins and Barbara G. Brents, "Social Protest, Hegemonic Competition, and Social Reform," *American Sociological Review* 54:6 (1989).

54. Ferguson, "From Normalcy to New Deal: Industrial Structure, Party Competition, and American Public Policy in the Great Depression," *International Organization* 38:1 (Winter 1984), 52, note 26. The critique here is somewhat revised from an earlier one in Peter Swenson, "Arranged Alliance: Business Interests in the New Deal," *Politics and Society* (1997), 100–2. There I unfairly overstate the "instrumentalism" in Ferguson's argument.

55. Peter Gourevitch embraces Ferguson's depiction of the New Deal cross-class alliance in *Politics in Hard Times: Comparative Responses to International Economic Crises* (Ithaca, NY: Cornell University Press, 1986), 151. Domhoff, in *The Power Elite and the State*, on 38, 86, 98–99, similarly identifies internationalism as a factor apparently motivating capitalists' progressive political behavior. Later he attaches more importance, as this book does, to the motive of "shaping labor markets" through legislation. in *State Autonomy or Class Dominance?* 155–56.

56. On GE, see Michael J. Piore and Charles F. Sabel, *The Second Industrial Divide: Possibilities for Prosperity* (New York: Basic, 1984), 57. On big oil, see Telegrams and Letters to Malcolm Muir, U.S. Senate, Committee on Finance, *Economic Security Act: Hearings*, 796. Information on Kodak from Sanford Jacoby, personal communication. On Goodyear, see Litchfield, *The Industrial Republic*, 98.

57. The AGC sided, of course, with Harold Ickes, head of the Public Works Administration (PWA), who wanted to work through private contractors, against the Works Progress Administration (WPA), whose officials "seemed determined to push the general contractor completely out of the public works picture." Booth

Mooney, *Builders for Progress: The Story of the Associated General Contractors of America* (New York: McGraw-Hill, 1965), 82. See also Jordan A. Schwartz, *The New Dealers: Power Politics in the Age of Roosevelt* (New York: Vintage, 1994), 297–324.

58. Ferguson, "From Normalcy to New Deal," 69, note 53; H. S. Person, "Unemployment Compensation—A Positive Force for Regularization," *American Labor Legislation Review* 21:2 (June 1931), 216. Ferguson does mention once, though only in passing, that some textile and shoe firms supported the Wagner Act, "hoping to stop the flow of jobs to the South." "From Normalcy to New Deal," 88.

59. Gordon, *New Deals*, 2, 4, 31, 241, and 287–88.

60. Gordon, *New Deals*, 2, 4, 215, and over a dozen times on 257–281. It should be noted that these formulations clash with Gordon's one isolated assertion that although Social Security was "in essence a business bill," the legislation was "spurred in large part by reform and class pressures in the trough of a general depression" (278–79).

61. Gordon, *New Deals*, 278. In 1965, Medicare was on the agenda, and Folsom expected the same to happen after passage. "Interview with Folsom," 73, 77; Schlabach, *Edwin E. Witte*, 180.

62. Michael Katz, *In the Shadow of the Poorhouse: A Social History of Welfare in America* (New York: Basic, 1986), 36, 43, 52–53, and 55–56; Commons, *Institutional Economics*, 854. NAM leader Robert L. Lund, executive vice-president of Lambert Pharmacals, interpreted the support for unemployment legislation of practically all liberal businessmen on the Commerce Department's BAC this way. "Monthly Meeting, National Industrial Conference Board, October 25, 1934," 54–55 (NICB Transcripts/Series 1057/Box 7, Hagley).

63. Commons, "Social Insurance and the Medical Profession," *Wisconsin Medical Journal* (January 1915), 302–3; Rubinow, "Public and Private Interests in Social Insurance," *American Labor Legislation Review* 21:2 (June 1931), 184, 191.

64. "Roosevelt on Unemployment Insurance," *American Labor Legislation Review* 21:2 (June 1931), 219.

65. On policy legacies or policy feedback, see Margaret Weir and Theda Skocpol, "State Structures and the Possibilities for 'Keynesian' Responses to the Great Depression," 118–19, and Paul Pierson, "When Effect Becomes Cause: Policy Feedback and Political Change," *World Politics* 45 (1993), 595–628. On political entrepreneurship in the creation of regulatory alliances, see James Q. Wilson, "The Politics of Regulation," in Thomas Ferguson and Joel Rogers, eds., *The Political Economy* (Armonk, NY: M. E. Sharpe, 1984). On the role of presidents in particular in mobilizing alliances with business, see Cathie Jo Martin, *Shifting the Burden: The Struggle over Growth and Corporate Taxation* (Chicago: University of Chicago Press, 1991), and "Business and the New Economic Activism: The Growth of Corporate Lobbies in the Sixties," *Polity* 27:1 (Fall 1994).

66. Skocpol and Ikenberry, "Political Formation of the American Welfare State," 90.

11. From Solidarism to Social Democracy

1. K. A. Bratt, *J. Sigfrid Edström—En levnadsteckning* (Stockholm: Norstedt, 1953), 2:76–77. This is an authorized biography based largely on diaries Edström made available to its author. Edström raised the issue of industry representation in the Directors' Club in April 1934. Direktörsklubben, Minutes, Nr. 9, 24 April 1934.

2. On the IUI, see Rolf Henriksson, *Som Edström ville—hur IUI blev till* (Stocholm: IUI, 1990).

3. Bertil Kugelberg, "Minnesanteckningar från samtal på Bofors," 20 October 1957; Kugelberg, *Upp i vind* (Stockholm: Norstedt, 1985), 160 and 252.

4. Bratt, J. *Sigfrid Edström*, 2:77.

5. Per Gunnar Edebalk, *Arbetslöshetsförsäkringsdebatten—-En studie i svensk socialpolitik 1892–1934* (Lund: Ekonomisk-historiska Föreningen, 1975), 182.

6. Bernt Erici and Nils Roth, *Arbetslöshetsförsäkring i Sverige, 1935–1980* (Stockholm: Arbetslöshetskassornas Samorganisation, 1981), 35–36; Norman Ginsburg, "Sweden: The Social-Democratic Case," in Allan Cochrane and John Clarke, *Comparing Welfare States: Britain in International Context* (London: Sage, 1993), 183. By his measurement of decommodification, Esping-Andersen even finds that, as late as 1980, Swedish unemployment insurance ranked exactly at the mean among 18 affluent countries. *The Three Worlds of Welfare Capitalism* (Princeton: Princeton University Press, 1990), 50.

7. Von Sydow, *Om förslaget till lag angående försäkring för olycksfall i arbete* (Stockholm: Victor Petterson, 1915), 1–3. On international poaching, see Verkstadsföreningen, Öfverstyrelse, 20 November 1915; John Ekelöf, Söderhamns Nya Verkstads AB to Sveriges Verkstadsförening, 23 September 1915 (Appendix 7 to Verkstadsföreningen, Arbetsutskott, 30 September 1915). The recent peak in emigration occurred from 1902 to 1907.

8. *Yttrande och förslag angående införande af en planmässig lönestatistik inom Svenska Arbetsgifvareföreningen* (Stockholm: Victor Petterson, 1911), 6–7 (report prepared by a SAF committee chaired by von Sydow). On his memories of scarcity before 1911, see the interview with von Sydow, "Arbetsledning och arbetsintensitet," in *Göteborgs Handels- och Sjöfartstidning*, 1 February 1911.

9. Von Sydow, *Om förslaget till lag angående försäkring för olycksfall i arbete*, 4; Aktiebolaget L.M. Ericsson to Sveriges Verkstadsförening, 18 November 1916; and Aktiebolaget Pump-Separator to Sveriges Verkstadsföreningen, 2 June 1916 (VF/F 71100 1920/Arbetskraftsbrist/Utländsk värvning av arbetskraft); "Arbetarevärvning till utlandet," *Sydsvenska Dagbladet*, 19 September 1916; "Arbetarevärvning till Frankrike," *Göteborgs Handels- och Sjöfartstidning*, 3 November 1916.

10. SAF, *Verksamhetsberättelse för år 1916*, 24. Per Gunnar Edebalk characterizes the law as "the most modern of its time in the world." See his *Välfärdsstaten träder fram—Svensk socialförsäkring 1884–1955* (Lund: Arkiv, 1996), 77, and "Från 1891 års sjukkasselag till Gustav Möllers nederlag 1951," *Arbetarhistoria* 23:1 (1999), 20. That employers regarded accident insurance as a benefit that should not be privately provided is clear from the steel industry negotiations of 1908. Herman Sundholm, *Järnbruksförbundet 1906–1931* (Stockholm: Järnbruksförbundet, 1931), 50.

11. On American employers and the immigration laws of the 1920s, see chapter 8. On Swedish family policy in the 1930s, see Lisbet Rausing, "The Population Question: The Debate of Family Welfare Reforms in Sweden, 1930–38," *European Journal of Political Economy* 2:4 (1986), 536, 540, 544–47.

12. See Karl-Ove Moene and Michael Wallerstein, "Pay Inequality," in *Journal of Labor Economics* 15 (1997), 403–30 and chapter 6 here.

13. SAF, Minutes, Ombudsmannakonferens, 27 February 1935; Minutes, Styrelse, 22 March, 26 April, and 31 May, 1945.

14. For employer discussion of tight labor market conditions in this period, see, for example, SAF, *Styrelse- och revisionsberättelser för år 1947*, 49–50; SAF, Minutes, Styrelse, 27 February, 28 August, and 30 October 1947; 26 August, 21 October, and 11 November 1948; 17 February and 15 September 1949; 23 May and 19 October 1950; 15 November 1951; 22–23 April, 16 September, 21–22 October, and 18

November 1954; 15 September 1955; 18 October 1956; 17 October and 25 April 1957. See also SAF, Minutes, Ombudsmannakonferens, 13–14 September 1954; 11–12 November 1957; and 15 September 1958; SAF, Minutes, Arbetsutskott, 13 July 1955.

15. SAF, Minutes, Styrelse, 25 January and 6 September 1945; Minutes, Ombudsmannakonferens, 26 September 1945.

16. SAF, Minutes, Styrelse, 29 August 1946; Minutes, Ombudsmannakonferens, 18 November 1946.

17. SAF, *Styrelse- och revisionsberättelser för år 1946*, 35; SAF, Minutes, Styrelse, 29 August and 24 October 1946. One entertaining poster depicted a half-grasshopper, half-man jumping across the landscape from one factory to another.

18. SAF, Minutes, Styrelse, 24 October and 16 December 1946; "Anteckningar vid ett sammanträde i Göteborg ang. situationen på arbetsmarknaden," 27 May 1946 (Edström 29 [E3i/överstyrelsen]).

19. SAF, Styrelse, 27 November 1946; Ombudsmannakonferens, 18 November and 16 December 1946.

20. SAF, Arbetsutskott, 25 June 1946 and appendixes (F. Andersson, Nässjö Bryggeri AB to Bryggeriarbetsgivareförbundet, 14 June 1946 and Felix Brandel, Tranås Bryggeri AB to Bryggeriarbetsgivareförbundet, 15 June 1946); SAF, "Cirkulär till Svenska Arbetsgivareföreningens delägare," Appendix A to Minutes, Styrelse, 28 March 1946.

21. The 1952 survey covered firms with at least 50 workers, 86 percent of which responded. Vacation pay was excluded to make them roughly comparable with the 1948 survey. SAF, Utrednings- och Upplysningsbyrå, "Utredning rörande sociala åtgärder inom industrin," October 1948 (SAF A1/27ec); SAF, "Företagens indirekta personalkostnader år 1952—Preliminär redogörelse," SAF, Minutes, Styrelse, Appendix 6, April 1954. Pension and health benefits remained modest, between 0.7 for engineering and 2.1 percent of labor costs for the forest product industries. Given the great heterogeneity of the membership, the averages hide larger companies' higher figures. Also, some major welfare capitalist companies (especially in the paper industry), remained outside SAF. Finally, the 1946 pension reform probably vented off pressure from below in that area. Quote from Hydén, "Arbetsgivarna och socialpolitiken," *Sociala meddelanden* 5 (1953), 271.

22. De Geer, *SAF i förhandlingar*, 108, and *The Rise and Fall of the Swedish Model: The Swedish Employers' Confederation over Ten Decades* (Chichester, UK: Carden, 1992), 94. After SAF openly toyed with expulsion, negotiations with TIF generated a compromise: a fine of 200,000 crowns to be paid as a "symbolic measure." SAF, Minutes, Styrelse, 27 February 1947, 27 March 1947, and 29 May 1947.

23. SAF, Minutes, Styrelse, 27 March and 29 May 1947.

24. SAF, Minutes, Styrelse, 11 November 1948. VF had originally only prohibited advertising for skilled workers; now the prohibition extended to apply to all kinds of labor. See SAF, Minutes, Ombudsmannakonferens, 16 September 1947.

25. SAF, Minutes, Ombudsmannakonferens, 17 September 1948.

26. SAF, Minutes, Styrelse, 10 and 11 November 1948. Despite its threat to end prohibitions on advertising if other sectors would not regulate it, VF was not to suspend its prohibition until the early 1970s.

27. SAF, Minutes, Styrelse, 25 January and 22 March 1945; 27 March and 28 August, 1947. See also Tom Söderberg, "Pappersmasseförbundets första halvsekel," in *Pappersmasseförbundet 1907–1957* (Stockholm: PMF, 1957), 121–25; Bo Gustafsson, "Sågverksindustrins arbetare 1890–1945," and Torsten Thornander, "Arbetarlönernas utveckling 1950–1957," in *Sågverksförbundet 1907–1957* (Stock-

holm: SVF, 1957), 186–91 and 402–5. In 1951 LO even opposed a tenant association's campaign against company housing leases attached to employment, expressing "great appreciation" for industry's provision of "good housing at low rents" in a scarce housing market. Employer abuse was not a concern, for companies hoarded labor instead of dismissing it lightly. Inequalities in costs and standards were not a problem. By contrast, Hjalmar Åselius of the steel industry called for rent increases in company housing for "it would be repugnant from the standpoint of fairness" to favor a relatively small group of employees in company housing with abnormally low rents. SAF, Minutes, Styrelse, 20 September 1951.

28. Quarrying was truly exceptional in its joint cartelist tendencies. In this marginal rural sector, ruinous "overproduction and uninhibited price competition" moved employers to enlist the union to obstruct production in so-called "free hills" belonging to farmers willing to sell quarry rights "for a penny farthing" (*för en spottstyver*). When demand slumped, workers laid off by association operators took to the hills to quarry and sell stones on their own, further depressing prices. In exchange for union cooperation, the operators were to put money in a union-controlled fund to give unemployed members an alternative income source and keep them out of the free hills. SAF, Minutes, Styrelse, 22 June 1929. See also Jörgen Westerståhl, *Svensk fackföreningsrörelse—Organisationsproblem, verksamhetsformer, förhållande till staten* (Stockholm: Tiden, 1946), 197.

29. Edebalk, *Arbetslöshetsförsäkringsdebatten*, 182; "Den frivilliga arbetslöshetsförsäkringen i Sverige," *Industria* 12 (1934), 300.

30. Gustaf Söderlund, SAF, Yttrande . . . angående frivillig arbetslöshetsförsäkring, 14 February 1933 (SAFA71115/1e), 8–9. (Reprinted as "Svenska arbetsgivareföreningen om 'frivillig arbetslöshetsförsäkring," *Industria* 5 [1933]), 123. See also Sveriges Industriförbund, "Yttrande angående arbetslöshetsförsäkring," 17 February 1933 (SAF A711141/1d/1933), 9. Both of these statements pointed out a moral hazard problem: unemployment insurance could strengthen unions' and workers' tendency to choose unemployment over work or even cause it by forcing higher wages on employers.

31. Söderlund, "Yttrande . . . angående frivillig arbetslöshetsförsäkring," 6. See also Axel Brunius, "Tomhänt socialpolitik—Gentsystemet i Sverige," *Industria* 5 (1933), 131; Sveriges Industriförbund, "Yttrande angående arbetslöshetsförsäkring," 8; and Jernkontoret till Kungl. Kommerskollegium, (no date) (SAF A71115/1e), 4.

32. A. Ahlin, T. Andersson, and G. Hultman to SAF, 4 February 1933 (SAF A711150/1e).

33. Edebalk, *Arbetslöshetsförsäkringsdebatten*, 118 and 128; Nils Unga, *Socialdemokratin och arbetslöshetsfrågan 1912–1934* (Stockholm: Arkiv, 1976), 100; Georg Styrman, Verkstadsföreningen, to SAF, 8 February 1933 (SAF A711150/1e), 7.

34. On Möller, see Bo Rothstein, *Den korporativa staten—Intresseorganisationerna och statsförvaltning i svensk politik* (Stockholm: Norstedts, 1992), 323–24. For SAF on LO, see SAF, *Styrelse- och revisionsberättelse för år 1930*, 61.

35. On the tensions between Edström and Styrman, and Edström's desire to oust him, see Edström to Gustaf Tham, 18 May, 1929; Tham to Edström, 21 May 1929; Edström to Styrman, 2 March, 1929 and 15 December, 1930 (Edström 26 [A3f/styrelse m.m.]); Edström to Hugo Hammar, 18 August, 1933 (Edström 28 [A3h/styrelsen m.m.]); Edström to Styrman, 3 July, 1934 (Edström 29 [A3i/4.överstyrelse]); Edström to Styrman, 2 June 1938 (Edström 30 [A3j/3.Korrespondens]); and Direktörsklubben, Minutes, 4 October 1945. On Edström versus Styrman and

small firms, see Edström to Hugo Hammar, 18 August 1933 (Edström 28 [A3h/styrelsen m.m.]).

36. "P. M. angående organisationsväsendets reglering," 15 November 1935, 3 (Direktörsklubben 3/5). On Österberg's corporatist views, see also Sven Anders Söderpalm, "Industrin och samlingsregeringen," *Scandia* I (1973), 104.

37. Edebalk, *Arbetslöshetsförsäkringsdebatten,* 138–39, 181–82, and 197. SAF's strikebreaking activities, which LO fell silent about by the late 1930s, were directed largely at Syndicalists and Communists (especially in construction). Strikebreakers helped clear the way for LO unions to organize (see chapter 5). According to SAF's assistant executive director Ivar Larson, "We through our actions against Syndicalists are fighting LO's battle." SAF, Minutes, Ombudsmannakonferens, 11 April 1933, and Appendix A to Minutes, Ombudsmannakonferens, 6 December 1933.

38. Edebalk, *Arbetslöshetsförsäkringsdebatten,* 195; Edebalk, *Välfärdsstaten träder fram,* 130.

39. SAF, Minutes, Styrelse, 19 November 1953; Minutes, Ombudsmannakonferens, 13 February 1950. Though very tough in negotiations, Bratt was popular among union people, according to LO's Arne Geijer. Bertil Kugelberg, "Minnesanteckningar från lunchsammanträde på SAF med A. Geijer," 3 October 1963.

40. SAF, Minutes, Förbundsdirektörskonferens, 15 April 1957, 18 October 1965, 15–16 November 1965, and 11–12 November 1968; Minutes, Styrelse, 17 April 1959 and 17 October 1968; "Överenskommelse angående utländsk arbetskraft," 19 January 1966, in SAF, *Utländsk arbetskraft—Rapport från SAF:s arbetskraftskommitté* (SAF A71/8d).

41. SAF, Minutes, Styrelse, 14 January and 19 February 1970; and Minutes, Förbundsdirektörskonferens, 12 January 1970; Erici and Roth, *Arbetslöshetsförsäkringen,* 33.

42. Erici and Roth, *Arbetslöshetsförsäkringen,* 30.

43. SAF, Minutes, Styrelse, 25 January 1935.

44. Brunius, "Tomhänt socialpolitik—Gentsystemet i Sverige," 131; "Den frivilliga arbetslöshetsförsäkringen i Sverige," 302.

45. On the unions' and the party's division and ambivalence, see Edebalk, *Arbetslöshetsförsäkringsdebatten,* 151–52, 162, 180–82, 196–200, and especially 211–12.

46. Edebalk, *Arbetslöshetsförsäkringsdebatten,* 192–93, 204–5, 212, and 271; Erici and Roth, *Arbetslöshetsförsäkringen,* 35–36. See the relevant details of the law in "Den frivilliga arbetslöshetsförsäkringen i Sverige," 302–3, and SAF, *Styrelse- och verksamhetsberättelse* (1934), 40.

47. See the lengthy discussion in SAF, Minutes, Ombudsmannakonferens, 27 February 1935 and "P. M. angående ackordsreglering under löpande avtalstid," Appendix J to SAF, Minutes, Styrelse, 21 April 1937.

48. SAF, Minutes, Styrelse, 26 September 1939; Minutes, Ombudsmannakonferens, 20 February 1939 (and Appendix A, "Arbetsgivarna och yrkesutbildningen").

49. SAF, Minutes, Styrelse, 24 February 1944 and 25 January 1945.

50. Erici and Roth, *Arbetslöshetsförsäkring,* 36; Edebalk, *Välfärdsstaten träder fram,* 136.

51. Unga, *Socialdemokratin och arbetslöshetsfrågan,* 120; Edebalk, *Arbetslöshetsförsäkringsdebatten,* 157.

52. "Svenska Arbetsgivareföreningen om 'frivillig arbetslöshetsförsäkring,'" 126; SAF, *Styrelse- och verksamhetsberättelser för år 1935,* 36–37.

53. Edebalk, *Välfärdsstaten träder fram,* 150.

54. SAF, Minutes, Styrelse, 26 April 1935.

55. A pay-as-you-go system spends current tax revenues on current retirees instead of placing them in funds reserved for later pension payments to those paying into the funds.

56. Ivar O. Larsson, "Yttrande över . . . förslag rörande revision av den allmänna pensionsförsäkringen," 12 October 1934 (SAF A150/18b), 3. For the details, see *Pensionsförsäkringsreformen—Kortfattad framställning av 1928 års pensionsförsäkringskommittés förslag rörande revision av den allmänna pensionsförsäkringen* (SOU 1934:19), 21–22. The exemption extended an identical one already allowed for pensions arranged voluntarily by only 15 (mostly public and nonindustrial) employers, benefitting mostly women, through a government scheme introduced in 1918. Virtually no SAF employer, it seems, chose to participate, perhaps because the "faithful servant" incentive was lacking. Helen Fisher Hohman, *Old Age in Sweden: A Program of Social Security* (Washington, DC: Social Security Board, 1940), 127–29.

57. Rausing, "The Population Question"; Hohman, *Old Age in Sweden,* 15–17; Allan Carlson, *The Swedish Experiment in Family Politics: The Myrdals and the Interwar Population Crisis* (New Brunswick, NJ: Transaction, 1990), 172–74; Alva and Gunnar Myrdal, *Kris i befolkningsfrågan* (Stockholm: Bonnier, 1935). For the government report on the measures, see *Betänkande i sexualfrågan* (Stockholm: SOU 1936:59).

58. Åke Elmér, *Folkpensioneringen i Sverige* (Lund: CWK Gleerup, 1960), 69–75; 147–51. See also Hohman, *Old Age in Sweden,* 29–30.

59. See Lee J. Alston and Joseph P. Ferrie, *Southern Paternalism and the Rise of the American Welfare State: Economics, Politics, and Institutions in the South, 1865–1965* (Cambridge: Cambridge University Press, 1999).

60. Elmér, *Folkpensioneringen,* 85, 90, and 140; Edebalk, *Välfärdsstaten träder fram,* 157.

61. *Dagens Nyheter,* 9 February 1946.

62. Fritiof Söderbäck, "Till Konungen," 23 January 1946 (SAF A150/18x). See also *Socialvårdskommitténs Betänkande XI—-Utredning och förslag angående lag om folkpensionering* (SOU 1945:46), 134–35. SAF accepted incomes-tested supplementary housing benefits for those in high-rent areas only because universalistic benefits would put too much strain on government finances. The 1934 deductibility rules for company pensions were preserved, as employers wanted.

63. Biltrafikens Arbetsgivareförbund to SAF, 5 January 1946 (SAF A150/18x/Lag om folkpensionering/yttranden från förbund). In Stockholm, unorganized transport firms agreed to provide pension benefits. Stockholm members of the association felt compelled by competition over labor to follow suit, even at the risk of fines and expulsion. Unwilling to punish the Stockholm members harshly, the association granted them "permission" to keep their membership bonds if they resigned voluntarily. SAF, Minutes, Styrelse, 30 May 1947.

64. SAF, Minutes, Styrelse, 30 May 1947.

65. SAF, Minutes, Styrelse, 27 November 1947. Reductions downward to these levels would bring increases in incomes-tested housing and spouse benefits attached to legislated pensions. Even though the net effect of employer reductions and government increases would be mildly negative for workers, Nilsson thought the figure justified by the large savings to employers.

66. Anders Kjellström, *Normbildning och konfliktlösning—-En studie om SAFs roll i växelspelet mellan lag och avtal* (Stockholm: SAF, 1987), 76.

67. Edström regarded the NIRA as a dangerous precedent for the rest of the world. Edström to Söderlund, 9 August 1933 (Edström 28 [A3h/styrelsen m.m.]). For his views on the Fordist "theory of high wages," see chapter 5.

68. Peter T. Kilborn, "End to Social Security Penalty Welcomed by Companies and Their Workers," *New York Times*, March 5, 2000.

12. Expanding the Solidaristic Welfare State

1. Geijer quoted in Bertil Kugelberg, "Minnesanteckningar från samtal med Arne Geijer," 16 June 1958; Heckscher quoted in minutes taken by Tore Browaldh for a memo to Bertil Kugelberg and Curt-Steffan Giesecke, "Ärende: Högerpartiet," 20 December 1960 (Kugelberg P6:12/Diverse handlingar berörande högerpolitiken).

2. See discussion later in this chapter for sources on the health and labor market policy debate.

3. John B. Williamson and Fred C. Pampel, *Old Age Security in Comparative Perspective* (New York: Oxford University Press, 1993), 81. On solidaristic wage policy, see chapter 6.

4. SAF, Minutes, Styrelse, 12 November 1931.

5. Per Gunnar Edebalk, "Från 1891 års sjukkasselag till Gustav Möllers nederlag 1951," *Arbetarhistoria* 23:1 (1999), 22; Torsten Svensson, *Socialdemokratins dominans—En studie av den svenska socialdemokratins partistrategi* (Uppsala: Almqvist & Wiksell, 1994), 200–1.

6. "Den nya sjukkasselagen," (no date) (SAF A1350/22å-I/Diverse PM och diskussionsanteckningar); "Högerledaren: Ogenomförbar reform är propagandareform," *Svenska Dagbladet*, 17 March 1946.

7. Fritiof Söderbäck, "Remissyttrande över en inom socialdepartementet upprättad promemoria angående . . . allmän sjukförsäkring," 27 June 1945 (SAF A 1350/22m/Yttrande 1945).

8. Von Sydow, *Om förslaget till lag angående försäkring för olycksfall i arbete*, 18–19.

9. Olof Ruin, *Tage Erlander: Serving the Welfare State, 1946–1969* (Pittsburgh: University of Pittsburgh Press, 1990), 141–45; Per Gunnar Edebalk, *Välfärdsstaten träder fram*, 161.

10. Erlander, *Tage Erlander 1949–1954* (Stockholm: Tiden, 1974), 289.

11. Sven Hydén, "PM angående sjukförsäkring," 17 October 1952 (SAF 1350/22å/Svar från styrelseledamöter).

12. On the experience rating issue, see Matts Larsson, VF, to SAF, 29 December 1952; "Förbundens synpunkter på förslaget till samordnad sjuk- och yrkesskadeförsäkring," 3 January, 1953 (SAF A1350/22å-II); Kaj Åberg, for Sveriges Textilindustriförbund and Sveriges Konfektionsindustriförbund, to SAF, 2 January 1953 (SAF A1350/22å-II). A number of employer representatives disliked the precedent of using a payroll tax to help finance health care and sick pay, even though coordination with workmen's compensation strongly spoke for it. Others disliked the fact that people could now more freely choose their own doctors, who would compete for business by declaring workers ill. Some thought the three-day waiting period for benefits was too short to discourage absenteeism for minor ailments. "Förbundens synpunkter på förslaget till samordnad sjuk- och yrkesskadeförsäkring," 3 January, 1953; "Anteckningar från diskussion av SAF:s förslag till yttrande över socialförsäkringsutredningens betänkande om sjukförsäkring och yrkesskadeförsäkring," 10 January 1953; Tore Browaldh, "Remissyttrande över socialförsäkringsutredningens betänkande," 17 January 1953 (SAF A1350/22å-II).

13. Also, employer contributions to the health insurance system would be tax deductible. Sven Hydén, "PM angående sjukförsäkring," 17 October 1952 (SAF A1350/22å/Svar från styrelseledamöter); Träindustriförbundet, "Yttrande över förslaget till yrkesskadeförsäkring," (TIF Yrkesskadeförsäkring 1950–51 [filed in yellow box with miscellaneous documents, Träindustriförbundet's archive]).

14. Verkstadsföreningen to SAF, "Socialförsäkringsutredningens betänkande," 29 December 1952 (SAF A1350/22å-II); "Anteckningar från diskussion av SAF:s förslag till yttrande över socialförsäkringsutredningens betänkande om sjukförsäkring och yrkesskadeförsäkring," 10 January 1953 (SAF A1350/22å-II).

15. "Anteckningar från diskussion av SAF:s förslag till yttrande över socialförsäkringsutredningens betänkande," 10 January 1953.

16. "Remissvar," 17 January 1953 (SAF A1350/22å-II/yttrande).

17. "Anteckningar från diskussion av SAF:s förslag till yttrande över socialförsäkringsutredningens betänkande," 10 January 1953.

18. "Anteckningar från diskussion av SAF:s förslag till yttrande över socialförsäkringsutredningens betänkande," 10 January 1953.

19. Tom Söderberg, "Pappersmasseförbundets första halvsekel," in *Pappersmasseförbundet 1907–1957*, 121.

20. SAF, Utrednings- och Upplysningsbyrå, "P.M. rörande avlösning av sjukförmåner i avtalen" (by Sven Hydén), September 1949.

21. "Memorial, fört vid överläggning angående arbetarnas sjukförmåner," 2 June 1954. (Träindustriförbundet, "Arbetarnas sjukförmåner, 1954" [filed in yellow box with miscellaneous documents]); Sven Hydén, "PM angående sjukförsäkring," 17 October 1952 (SAF A1350/22å/Svar från styrelseledamöter).

22. Svensson, *Socialdemokratins dominans*, 201, 205, 225–27, and 236; Per Gunnar Edebalk, *Välfärdsstaten träder fram—Svensk socialförsäkring 1884–1955* (Lund: Arkiv, 1996), 143.

23. On Möller's distinctiveness, and the limits of his influence, see Bo Rothstein, "Managing the Welfare State: Lessons from Gustav Möller," *Scandinavian Political Studies* 8:3 (September 1985), 151–70; Edebalk, *Välfärdsstaten träder fram*, 152–77.

24. Rudolf Meidner, "Limits of Active Labour Market Policy, especially with Respect to the Case of Sweden," SAMF-Conference on "Public Policy to Combat Unemployment," (Nürnberg, Germany, 1983), 3.

25. Gösta Rehn, "Swedish Active Labor Market Policy: Retrospect and Prospect," *Industrial Relations* 24:1 (Winter 1985), 73.

26. Rehn, "Nyare tendenser i arbetsmarknadspolitik [1970]," 214 in Rehn, *Full sysselsättning utan inflation—Skrifter i urval* (Stockholm: Tiden, 1988).

37. *Fackföreningsrörelsen och den fulla sysselsättningen* (Stockholm: LO, 1951), translated as *Trade Unions and Full Employment* (London: Allen & Unwin, 1953). For useful discussions and descriptions in English, see Andrew Martin, "The Dynamics of Change in a Keynesian Political Economy: The Swedish Case and Its Implications," in Colin Crouch, ed., *State and Economy in Contemporary Capitalism* (New York: St. Martin's Press, 1979), 88–121; Lennart Erixon, "A Swedish Economic Policy: A Revindication of the Rehn-Meidner Model," Department of Economics, Stockholm University, November 1994.

28. See Giesecke's essays collected in *Stann-Anders och likheten: Inlägg i arbetsmarknadsfrågor* (Stockholm: Albert Bonnier, 1968), especially 89–92, 100, and 103.

29. Rehn, "Finansministrarna, LO-ekonomerna och arbetsmarknadspolitiken," in Rehn, *Full sysselsättning utan inflation—Skrifter i urval* (Stockholm: Tiden, 1988),

246; Rehn, "Den nya arbetsmarknadspolitiken," *Svensk sparbankstidskrift* 43:4 (1959), 221.

30. Sköld also dismissed the gang as "playful kittens" (*lekfulla kattungar*). "Finansministrarna, LO-ekonomerna och arbetsmarknadspolitiken, 234–37.

31. On the gang of querulants, see also Erlander, *Tage Erlander 1949–1954*, 234–39.

32. "The wage drift that nevertheless came about, half voluntarily and half involuntarily on the part of employers, rendered the steady wage policy which is usually posed as the principal goal—wage increases in step with productivity increases—impossible." Rehn, "Den nya arbetsmarknadspolitiken," 219.

33. "Primarily with fiscal policy as the demand suppressing instrument would such tight gross profit margins be maintained that employers would not release larger nominal wage increases than fundamental economic conditions allowed so as to prevent inflation. Since private enterprise then could no longer be expected to provide full employment everywhere, the state had to ensure it by fostering occupational and geographic transition to companies still expanding or through direct local job creation, though financed in a non-inflationary way. Only in such an economic climate could the trade union movement 'fulfill the requirements of self-discipline in wage policy that the stabilization of full employment imposes.'" Rehn, "Finansministrarna," 233.

34. Erlander, *Tage Erlander 1949–1954*, 240; Rehn, "Den nya arbetsmarknadspolitiken," 215; Rehn, "Finansministrarna, LO-ekonomerna och arbetsmarknadspolitiken," 239 and 243.

35. Rudolf Meidner, "Arbetsmarknadspolitikens målsättningar[1967]," in *I arbetets tjänst* (Stockholm: Tiden, 1984), 277. See also Rehn, "Finansministrarna, LO-ekonomerna och arbetsmarknadspolitiken," 243.

36. "Yttrande," 8 February 1951 (SAF A7100(2u)/Betr. den offentliga arbetsförmedlingens organisation).

37. *Rationaliseringsutredningens betänkande I. Motiv och förslag* (SOU 1939:13), 98–109. This commission's recommendations were close to those of another commission consisting of Gustav Möller, future prime minister Tage Erlander, and Arthur Tomsson, chief architect of the war years' labor market machinery. Interrupted by the wartime emergency, it worked "in close collaboration" with the one enlisting Söderlund's participation, according to Bo Rothstein, *The Social Democratic State: The Swedish Model and the Bureaucratic Problem of Social Reforms* (Pittsburgh: University of Pittsburgh Press, 1996), 92–93.

38. *Rationaliseringsutredningens betänkande I*, 105.

39. Gustaf Söderlund, "Remissvar över . . . lag om tjänsteplikt m.m.," 31 January 1939, 7–8 (SAF A75/28c/yttrande).

40. *Betänkande rörande ett centralt arbetsmarknadsorgan avgivet av inom socialdepartementet tillkallade sakkuniga* (SOU 1947:24), III.3; Bertil Kugelberg, "Minnesanteckningar fran Harpsund," 23 November 1961.

41. Rothstein, *The Social Democratic State*, 93; *Betänkande rörande ett centralt arbetsmarknadsorgan*, II and IV. A. Kugelberg objected to giving the proposed authority shared responsibility with the unemployment funds for overseeing the unemployment insurance system, taking away that role from the social affairs bureaucracy (*Socialstyrelsen*).

42. *Betänkande rörande ett centralt arbetsmarknadsorgan*, IV.A.

43. "Yttrande," 11 February 1947 (SAF A7700(29m)/Betr. ett centralt arbetsmarknadsorgan 1947).

44. "Yttrande över . . . lag om tjänsteplikt," 31 January 1939 (SAF 75/28c).

45. Betänkande rörande ett centralt arbetsmarknadsorgan, IV.C; Bo Rothstein, The Social Democratic State, 116–22; "Yttrande," 8 February 1951 (SAF A7100(2u)/Betr. den offentliga arbetsförmedlingens organisation).

46. Holmström and Wehtje in SAF, Minutes, Styrelse, 21–22 October and 18 November 1954; Kugelberg, "Minnesanteckningar från diskussion på Hotell Tunneln i Malmö," 8 November 1954. For wage drift statistics, see Rudolf Meidner, Samordning och solidarisk lnepolitik (Stockholm: Prisma/LO, 1974), 46–47.

47. Faxén, "Grundvalarna för en arbetsgivareorganisations lönepolitik" (Lönekommittén P.M. 9), 25 July 1956 (SAF AO/Lönekommittén), 27.

48. SAF, Minutes, Förbundsdirektörskonferens, 8 December 1969.

49. Giesecke, Stann-Anders och likheten, 103; Albåge, "Arbetsmarknadspolitiken bör ses som arbetsgivarnas bundsförvant," Arbetsgivaren 8 March 1968, 5. Albåge quotes SAF official Lars Wirström on active labor market policy as "an insurance premium to help firms and employees manage the second industrial revolution with increased international competition and reduced importance for our traditional raw materials and types of employment."

50. Quote from archival sources in Magnus Jerneck, SAFs Framtidssyn: Förutsägelser, målsättningar och dilemman (Stockholm: SAF, 1986), 116–17.

51. Stig Hadenius, Björn Molin, and Hans Wieslander, Sverige efter 1900 (Stockholm: Aldus/Bonniers, 1974), 230.

52. Bertil Kugelberg, "Minnesanteckningar," 3–4 February and 4 April 1960; "Minnesanteckningar från sammanträde och lunch på SAF angående bidragsgivningen till högern," 22 February 1961.

53. Bertil Kugelberg, "Minnesanteckningar," 3–4 February 1960.

54. Tore Browaldh to Bertil Kugelberg and C. S. Giesecke ("Ärende: Högerpartiet"), 20 December 1960 (SAF Kugelberg/P6:12, Diverse handlingar berörande högerpolitiken); Browaldh, Gesällvandring (Stockholm: Norstedt, 1976), 190 and 226.

55. On the dissatisfaction, see Ernfrid Browaldh (probable author), "Ang. högerpolitiken," confidential memorandum to directors Tore Browaldh, Höglund, and Wirström, 5 November 1960 (Kugelberg P6:12, Diverse handlingar berörande högerpolitiken). On the white-collar agreements, see SAF, Minutes, Styrelse, 21–22 April 1960; Kugelberg, "Minnesanteckningar från styrelsesammanträdet den 21 och 22 april 1960." For the Heckscher quote, see Tore Browaldh to Kugelberg and Giesecke, "Ärende: Högerpartiet," 20 December 1960 (Kugelberg P6:12, Diverse handlingar berörande högerpolitiken).

56. Stig Hadenius, Björn Molin, and Hans Wieslander, Sverige efter 1900—en modern politisk historia (Stockholm: Aldus, 1974), 213–26.

57. See especially recent work by Svensson, Socialdemokratins dominans, 274–81; 310–11; Gøsta Esping-Andersen, Politics Against Markets: The Social Democratic Road to Power (Princeton: Princeton University Press, 1985), 161–65; and John D. Stephens, The Transition from Capitalism to Socialism (Chicago: University of Illinois Press, 1979), 177–79. On employers' perceptions of the Social Democrats' political payoff, see Kugelberg, "Minnesanteckningar från lunchsamtal (på SAF)," 26 September 1960.

58. Employers worried a bit that that better pensions might reduce the supply of older manpower, a matter that only once, it seems, came up for discussion. Realism about the need for pensions was complete. Svenska Arbetsgivareföreningen and Sveriges Industriförbund (Sven Schwartz et al.), "Yttrande om Pensionsutredningens principbetänkande (SOU 1950:33)," 24 April 1951, 9–10, Appendix 2 to SAF, Minutes, Ombudsmannakonferens, 16 April 1951.

59. Sven Dahlberg, SAF, Minutes, Styrelse, 17 October 1957.

60. Uncle Bertil says: "Yes, I actually think he seems *Kugel*—I mean *kul* [fun]—in a way." The cartoon is reprinted in Tage Erlander, *Tage Erlander 1955–1960* (Stockholm: Tiden, 1976), 259.

61. Kugelberg, "Minnesanteckningar från lunchsamtal (på SAF)," 26 September 1960; Kugelberg to the author, 12 June 1991, and "Minnesanteckningar angående vissa politiska resonemang i mars 1961"; "Ärende: Högerpartiet," 20 December 1960. On Edström and Kugelberg, see Kugelberg, "Minnesanteckningar från lunch med Dodde [Marcus Wallenberg] på Enskilda Banken," 8 January 1966; Heckscher, *The Welfare State and Beyond: Success and Problems in Scandinavia* (Minneapolis: University of Minnesota Press, 1984).

62. SAF, Pensionskommitté, "Arbetarepensioner–Principbetänkande" 1953 (SAF A15120/18ak/1953), 12–18; Anders Kjellström, *Normbildning och konfliktlösning—En studie om SAFs roll i växelspelet mellan lag och avtal* (Stockholm: SAF, 1987), 73–74.

63. Edström to Styrman 2 June 1938 (Edström 30 [A3j/3.Korrespondens]); SAF, Utrednings- och Upplysningsbyrå, "P.M. angående arbetstagarpensionering," May 1948 (SAF A15120/18m, 1948), 6. Liberal politician Bertil Ohlin saw the connection between the People's Pension legislation and the freezing of company pensions. See Kugelberg, "Minnesanteckningar från samtal med Professor Bertil Ohlin," 28 February 1957. The "stalemate" point was made by Erik Kempe of MoDo, the welfare capitalist company still outside of SAF, who was invited to the meeting to represent the Swedish Federation of Industries. SAF, Minutes, Styrelse, 19 April 1951.

64. Kugelberg, "Minnesanteckningar från samtal med Arne Geijer," 23 September 1957.

65. Kassman, *Arne Geijer och hans tid*, 80–81. Geijer was possibly thinking of employers' solidaristic disinclination to provide pension benefits in saying, "When it comes to wages we have found bargaining to be the most successful means. When it comes to social reforms, bargaining has not been a successful means. The employers have not wanted to concede social reforms." Frederic Fleisher, *The New Sweden: The Challenge of a Disciplined Democracy* (New York: David McKay, 1967), 88.

66. Strand's efforts were recounted by Ohlin according to Kugelberg, "Minnesanteckningar från söndagen" (från samtal med Bertil Ohlin och Sven Schwartz), 24 November 1957. Hydén, "Arbetsgivarna och socialpolitiken," *Sociala meddelanden* 5 (1953), 269.

67. Sven Hydén, "Konfidentiell promemoria angående pensionsfrågans läge," 25 May 1951 (SAF A150/1950 års folkpensionering), 2.

68. Kjellström, *Normbildning och konfliktlösning*, 77.

69. SAF, Minutes, Styrelse, 24 April 1953.

70. On LO and the cost-of-living issue, see SAF, Minutes, Styrelse, 23 April 1954. Björn Molin argues that SAF acted three to five years too late. *Tjänstepensionsfrågan—En studie i svensk partipolitik* (Göteborg, Elanders, 1965), 131. In an analysis sponsored by SAF, Kjellström agrees, adding the point about SAF's tentativeness when it did act. Kjellström, *Normbildning och konfliktlösning*, 81–85. On Geijer, see Erlander, *Tage Erlander 1955–1960*, 132; SAF, Minutes, Ombudsmannakonferens, 17 May 1954, and Kjellström, 87.

71. Kugelberg, "Minnesanteckningar från samtal med Arne Geijer," 14 October 1957; "Minnesanteckningar från middag på Sällskapet," 22 November 1957. See also SAF, Minutes, Styrelse, 18 September 1958. On the blockage of a deal between SAF and the government, see Tore Browaldh to Bertil Kugelberg and Curt-

Steffan Giesecke, "Ärende: Högerpartiet," 20 December 1960 (Kugelberg P6:12/Diverse handlingar berörande högerpolitiken).

72. Danielsen in SAF, Minutes, Styrelse, 19 April 1951. Erik Brodén, SAF's member of the 1951 commission to draft principles for an obligatory system, advocated "a secure livelihood in old age for all occupational groups." His reasoning for uniformity may not have been entirely egalitarian. Anders Kjellström, *Normbildning och konfliktlösning*, 77.

73. Sven Hydén, "Promemoria angående taktiken i samband med framläggandet av det Åkenssonska förslaget," 17 May 1955 (SAF A150/18l), 2. Interest in the collective bargaining solution was mixed, with VF's apparently the strongest for some move away from company pensions. "PM angående förbundens svar på remiss av pensionskommitténs betänkande," Appendix 11 to SAF, Minutes, Styrelse, 24 April 1953.

74. Both organized employers and, interestingly enough, LO objected to this evasive practice, but the big shipbuilding firms relied heavily on the subcontractors to acquire labor indirectly and so evade solidaristic wage control. Expansion of output to take advantage of demand for Swedish ships was otherwise impossible in the short term. Tommy Svensson, *Från ackord till månadslön—En studie av lönepolitiken, fackföreningarna och rationaliseringarna inom svensk varvsindustri under 1900-talet* (Göteborg: Svenska Varv, 1983), 344–45.

75. Kugelberg, *Från en central utsiktspunkt* (Stockholm: Norstedt, 1986), 116; "Avskrifter av förbundens yttranden över pensionskommitténs betänkande om arbetarpensionering," in Appendix 1 to SAF, Minutes, Ombudsmannakonferens, 17 May 1954, 7–8.

76. Kugelberg, "Minnesanteckningar från samtal med LO:s ordförande Arne Geijer," 23 September 1957; "Minnesanteckningar från samtal med Arne Geijer," 14 October 1957. See also "Minnesanteckningar från samtal med Arne Geijer," 16 June 1958; *Från en central utsiktspunkt*, 118.

77. Tore Browaldh to B. Kugelberg and C. S. Giesecke, "Högerpartiet" (Kugelberg P6:12/Diverse handlingar berörande högerpolitiken), 7; "Minnesanteckningar från samtal med Arne Geijer," 14 October 1957.

78. Kugelberg, "Minnesanteckningar från middag på Sällskapet," 22 November 1957. Ohlin's proposals made LO and the Social Democrats "treat the Liberal Party and not the Conservative Party as their main opponent," according to Geijer's biographer. Kassman, *Arne Geijer och hans tid*, 81.

79. Erlander, *Tage Erlander 1955–1960*, 219–22, 229, and 248. See chapter 9 for a discussion of related, but fundamentally different regulatory reasons why corporate liberals in the United States rejected an opt-out provision (the "Clark amendment").

80. "Avskrifter av förbundens yttranden över pensionskommitténs betänkande om arbetarpensionering," 26; Sven Hydén, "P.M. till ombudsmannkonferens," 4 in Appendices 1 and 2 to Minutes, Ombudsmannakonferens, 17 May 1954.

81. SAF, Utrednings- och Upplysningsbyrå, "P.M. angående arbetstagarpensionering," 8.

82. Tage Erlander, *Tage Erlander 1955–1960*, 134. On labor mobility, see also 185.

83. Söderbäck, Appendix 6 to SAF/LO, Arbetsmarknadskommittén, 31 May–1 June 1944; SAF, Minutes, Styrelse, 27 April 1944 and 19 March 1953.

84. "Arbetarepensioner"Appendix 10, and "PM angående förbundens svar på remiss av pensionskommitténs betänkande," Appendix 11 to SAF, Minutes, Styrelse, 24 April 1953.

85. Sven Hydén, "Pensionsfrågan," 13 October 1958 (Kugelberg P6–11: Diverse handlingar berörande pensionsfrågan). See also the concerns expressed by Sven Schwartz et al. in "Yttrande om Pensionsutredningens principbetänkande," 24 April 1951, 9, 12–13.

86. Credit policy, supported by a broad-based political consensus for massive housing construction, privileged the sector with access to loans at low interest rates. Private banking interests were never happy with the use of rationed credit ceilings instead of interest rates to control the money supply, but they benefitted from attendant restrictions on competitive entry into finance. On credit and housing policies, see Lars Jonung, "Riksbankens politik 1945—En krönika," in Lars Werin, ed., *Från räntereglering till inflationsnorm—Det finansiella systemet och riksbankens politik 1945–1990* (Stockholm: SNS, 1993), 317–18, 329, 343–44, 361–64, and 370–71; Per-Martin Meyerson, Ingemar Ståhl, and Kurt Wickman, *Makten över bostaden* (Stockholm: SNS, 1990), 16.

87. Kugelberg, "Minnesanteckningar från samtal med Tor och Jytte Bonnier," 4 August 1958; SAF, Minutes, Styrelse, 24 April 1953.

88. Kugelberg, "Minnesanteckningar från samtal med Arne Geijer," 23 September 1957 and 14 October 1957.

89. "Direktör Ernfrid Browaldhs anförande på Arosmässan 1955," (SAF A150/18l/Betr. Pensionsutredningen). On Ohlin, see Kugelberg,"Minnesanteckningar från samtal med Professor Bertil Ohlin," 4 February 1959, and "Minnesanteckningar från samtal med Professor Bertil Ohlin," 28 February 1957.

90. Kugelberg, *Från en central utsiktspunkt* 35, 73, 144, 185–86, 213, 216, 243, 252, 279, 292; *Upp i vind* (Stockholm: Norstedt, 1985), 301–3, 310.

91. Kugelberg, "Minnesanteckningar från samtal med Arne Geijer," 8 January 1958. The report produced was *Promemoria med förslag om fondförvaltning m.m. i samband med utbyggd pensionering* (SOU 1958:4).

92. Ingvar Ohlsson, a high government civil servant, had, however, pushed for three, though apparently without pressure from Finance Minister Sträng. Kugelberg, "Minnesanteckningar från samtal med Arne Geijer," 16 June 1958.

93. Kugelberg, "Minnesanteckningar från samtal med Arne Geijer," 16 October 1959. Browaldh did not go uncriticized for participation on the commission, he recalls in his memoirs. His effusive praise of labor leaders exceeds that of Kugelberg's. Browaldh, *Gesällvandring*, 224; 184–92,

94. Erlander, *Tage Erlander 1955–1960*, 188; Jonas Pontusson, *The Limits of Social Democracy: Investment Politics in Sweden* (Ithaca: Cornell University Press, 1992), 81.

95. Kugelberg, "Minnesanteckningar från samtal med Direktör Jarl Hjalmarsson," 13 January 1959, and Kugelberg, "Minnesanteckningar från middag på socialdepartementet," 29 September 1960.

96. Quote from "Högerpartiet" (minutes recorded by banker Tore Browaldh), 5 January 1961 (SAF, Kugelberg P6:12: Diverse handlingar berörande högerpolitiken). The others present were Jarl Hjalmarsson, Curt Ewerlöf, Gunnar Heckscher, Lars Thunholm, Boy [Marc] Wallenberg, Sven Dahlberg, Nils Danielsen, Ernfrid Browaldh, Carl Jacobsson, Axel Iveroth, Hjalmar Åselius, Curt-Steffan Giesecke, and Harald Nordenson. See also Kugelberg, "Minnesanteckningar från lunch på SAF," 4 January 1961; "Minnesanteckningar från samtal med Jarl Hjalmarsson," 4 January 1961.

97. Browaldh, *Företagaren och samhället* (Stockholm: Bonniers, 1961), 116; Heckscher, *The Welfare State and Beyond*, 60.

98. Pontusson, *The Limits of Social Democracy*, 81–87.

99. This is the conclusion reached by Pontusson, who argues that the highly restrictive legal-institutional framework imposed by the Social Democratic government on the administration of the large pension funds "effectively precluded the politicization of investment decisions that business had feared." *The Limits of Social Democracy,* 94.

100. Kugelberg, "Minnesanteckningar från samtal med kommerserådet Österberg och direktör Lindenkrona," 16 March 1959.

101. Kugelberg, "Minnesanteckningar från telefonsamtal med regeringsrådet Strömberg i Bankföreningen," 9 March 1957; "Minnesanteckningar från samtal med Arne Geijer," 23 September 1957.

102. From Åke Elmstedt, "Hur avtalsparter och lagstiftare reglerat arbetsvillkoren—några erfarenheter och tankar," in Kugelberg et al., *Fred eller fejd—Personliga minnen och anteckningar* (Stockholm: SAF, 1985), 207. See also SAF, Minutes, Styrelse 18 September 1958; Kugelberg, *Från en central utsiktspunkt,* 124; Kjellström, *Normbilding eller konfliktlösning,* 90.

103. For other analyses, all of which are useful and informative, but overlook the essential consensus around the final result, see Björn Molin, *Tjänstepensionsfrågan;* Sven Anders Söderpalm, *Arbetsgivarna och Saltsjöbadspolitiken—En historisk studie i samarbetet på svensk arbetsmarknad* (Stockholm: SAF, 1980), 82–92; Elmstedt, "Hur avtalsparter och lagstiftare reglerat arbetsvillkoren," 195–207; and Anders Kjellström, *Normbildning och konfliktlösning,* 73–91.

104. Esping-Andersen, *Politics against Markets: The Social Democratic Road to Power* (Princeton: Princeton University Press, 1985), 162.

105. Esping-Andersen, "Class Coalitions in the Making of West European Economies," in *Political Power and Social Theory* 3 (1982), 17, 19, and 47.

106. Bo Rothstein, "State and Capital in Sweden: The Importance of Corporatist Arrangements," *Scandinavian Political Studies* 11:3 (1988), 255–56.

107. Hugh Heclo, *Modern Social Politics in Britain and Sweden: From Relief to Income Maintenance* (New Haven: Yale University Press, 1974), 299.

108. Heclo, *Modern Social Politics,* 84.

109. To the extent that an interest group plays a strong contributory role in initiating and shaping social policy, in Heclo's view, it depends on their organized "capacity . . . to recognize its interests . . . at stake and to define what that stake is." By this token, SAF should have been prominent in his analysis. Heclo, *Modern Social Politics,* 221, 226, 229–31, and 300.

110. An exception is Margaret Weir and Theda Skocpol, "State Structures and the Possibilities for 'Keynesian' Responses tot he Great Depression in Sweden, Britain, and the United States," in Peter Evans et al., eds., *Bringing the State Back In* (Cambridge: Cambrdige University Press, 1985), especially 120–32. They argue that the deficit-financed crisis program in Sweden was a result of state structures and policy legacies that (1) channeled policy thinking in the direction of jobs creation rather than unemployment insurance, and that (2) facilitated the breakthrough of Keynesianism in the design of the jobs program—union wages and deficit financing. However, as Per Gunnar Edebalk shows, in *Arbetslöshetsförsäkringsdebatten—En studie i svensk socialpolitik 1892–1934* (Lund: Ekonomisk-historiska Föreningen, 1975), unemployment insurance, a major preoccupation of the labor movement throughout the 1920s and 1930s, was blocked by bourgeois opposition, not institutionally conditioned disinclination. Nils Unga, in *Socialdemokratin och arbetslöshetsfrågan 1912–1934* (Stockholm: Arkiv, 1976), shows that Social Democratic as well as conservative economists were ambivalent about demand stimulation through wage increases and borrowing, favoring monetary stimulus

instead. There were other reasons for insisting on union wages, and the deficit spending was rather small.

111. *Den demokratiska klasskampen—Svensk politik i jämförande perspektiv* (Stockholm: Tiden, 1981), 27. For a thorough list of works by Korpi and Esping-Andersen with similar formulations and conclusions, see Baldwin, *The Politics of Social Solidarity: Class Bases of the European Welfare State 1875–1975* (Cambridge: Cambridge University Press, 1990), 62.

112. *The Working Class and Welfare Capitalism: Work, Unions and Politics in Sweden* (London: Routledge & Kegan Paul, 1978), 47–48, 317–19. According to Korpi, "power resources influence distribution processes . . . indirectly, via [social] politics, in that the extent and direction of state intervention in the distributional processes depend on differentials in power resources in society." *Den demokratiska klasskampen*, 196. On the decline of industrial conflict, see Peter Swenson, "Bringing Capital Back In, or Social Democracy Reconsidered: Employer Power, Cross-Class Alliances, and Centralization of Industrial Relations in Denmark and Sweden," *World Politics* 43:4 (July 1991), 479–512.

113. Korpi, *The Working Class and Welfare Capitalism*, 86; *Den demokratiska klasskampen*, 25; and "Den svenska arbetarrörelsens förutsättningar och strategier," in Per Thullberg and Kjell Östberg, eds., *Den svenska modellen* (Lund: Studentlitteratur, 1994), 20.

114. See Sven Anders Söderpalm's *Direktörsklubben—Storindustrin i svensk politik under 1930- och 1940-talen* (Stockholm: Prisma, 1978), especially 19. Also relying on Söderpalm for this now widespread misconception are Göran Therborn, *Borgarklass och byråkrati i Sverige—Anteckningar om en solskenshistoria* (Lund: Arkiv, 1989), 159; James Fulcher, *Labour Movements, Employers, and the State: Conflict and Cooperation in Britain and Sweden* (Oxford: Clarendon, 1991), 146–49; Gregg Olsen, "Labour Mobilization and the Strength of Capital: The Rise and Stall of Economic Democracy in Sweden," *Studies in Political Economy* 34 (Spring 1991), 130. For another critique, see Niklas Stenlås, *Den inre kretsen—Den svenska ekonomiska elitens inflytande över partipolitik och opinionsbildning 1940–1949* (Lund: Arkiv, 1998), 14–17. Söderpalm, it should be added, corrects himself, though not explicitly, in his *Arbetsgivarna och Saltsjöbadspolitiken*, especially 27–37, where he presents Edström and export interests generally as central participants in highly consensual labor relations.

115. There was indeed concern among leading industrialists and financiers, for example, Marcus Wallenberg, about taxes, but it was shared by SAF's Söderlund and the Directors' Club. Also Edström's ASEA (in the Wallenberg "sphere") benefitted famously from the public works activities of the time—railroad electrification, for example. See Söderlund to Axel Palmgren, 22 December 1933 and 11 January 1935, Palmgren papers, Åbo Akademins Bibliotek; Rolf Henriksson, *Som Edström ville—hur IUI blev till* (Stockholm: IUI, 1990). For Lindberg's view on Edström, see "Utdrag av tal vid direktör J.S. Edströms middag å Riche," 7 March 1939 (SAF P6/Edström, J.S.), 2–3.

116. In response to one newspaper's cry for help, Edström wrote, "I must say I am despondent about these badly managed Conservative newspapers that we are always supposed to assist. In my own company we have ceased with this. If the conservative press cannot run on its own steam then may it die." Edström to Fritiof Söderback, 11 June 1941 (Edström 35[A14e]). Nevertheless, Edström was busy organizing the secret channeling of SAF money to Näringslivets Fond, the purpose being to consolidate and rationalize the Conservative press, which all in all was still needed as a bulwark against the radical impulses that remained in the Social De-

mocratic labor movement. On the planning and socialization debate, see Pontusson, *The Limits of Social Democracy*, 50–53.

117. "But the power of one agent cannot simply be indicated by its own resources: it will depend on the resources of the contending forces, on the historical durability of its mobilization, and on patterns of power alliances." Esping-Andersen, *The Three Worlds of Welfare Capitalism*, 16.

118. *The Three Worlds of Welfare Capitalism*, 18. See also Esping-Andersen and Korpi, "Social Policy as Class Politics in Postwar Capitalism," in J. Goldthorpe, ed., *Order and Conflict in Contemporary Capitalism* (Oxford: Oxford University Press, 1984).

119. Francis G. Castles, *The Social Democratic Image of Society: A Study of the Achievements and Origins of Scandinavian Social Democracy in Comparative Perspective* (London: Routledge & Kegan Paul, 1978), especially 73–78.

120. As one SAF official noted, Hansson's successor, Tage Erlander, appreciated the division, which allowed Social Democrats to rule and therefore take credit for "rather self-evident social reforms that without much difficulty are carried out in other countries run by bourgeois parties." Lars Wirström, "Minnesanteckningar," 28 November 1960 (Kugelberg P6:12/Diverse handlingar berörande högerpolitiken), 5.

121. Rothstein, "State Structure and Variations in Corporatism: The Swedish Case," *Scandinavian Political Studies* 14:2 (1991), especially 159.

122. See *Den korporativa staten—Intresseorganisationer och statsförvaltning i svensk politik* (Stockholm: Norstedts, 1992), especially 126–32.

123. Per Thullberg, *Bönder går samman—En studie i Riksförbundet Landsbygdens Folk under världskrisen 1929–1933* (Stockholm: LTs förlag, 1977), 259–64. For farmers' organizations, the agreement included only a tax on the sale of animals for slaughter, which, among other things, was to be spent on "fostering organization" in that sector. It is unlikely that this component was the pivotal one. Olle Nyman, *Krisuppgörelsen mellan Socialdemokraterna och Bondeförbundet 1933* (Uppsala: Almqvist & Wiksell, 1944), 102–4.

124. Edebalk, *Välfärdsstaten träder fram*, 149; Rothstein, *Den korporativa staten*, 130; Olle Nyman, *Svensk parlamentarism 1932–1936—Från minoritetsparlamentarism till majoritetskoalition* (Uppsala: Almqvist & Wiksell, 1947), 544–45.

125. In the 1926 Stripa case, it only affected LO because its miners' union sided, unusually, with a Syndicalist-led miners' strike. Had that union acted in a strictly corporatist (i.e., monopolistic) fashion, the strikebreaking rule would not have affected it. Nils Unga, *Socialdemokratin och arbetslöshetsfrågan 1912–1934* (Stockholm: Arkiv, 1976), 95–97; Ragnar Casparsson, *LO under fem årtionden 1924–1947* (Stockholm: LO, 1948), 2:45–67. LO remained fully opposed, like SAF, to the monopolistic (closed shop) practices of some of its own building trade unions. See Gustaf Söderlund, "Yttrande angående Arbetslöshetsutredningens betänkande II," 31 January 1936 (SAF A/71114/1m), 2.

126. Unga, *Socialdemokratin och arbetslöshetsfrågan*, especially 142–43.

127. Rothstein, "Labor Market Institutions and Working Class Strength," in Sven Steinmo, Kathleen Thelen, and Frank Longstreth, *Structuring Politics: Historical Institutionalism in Comparative Analysis* (Cambridge: Cambridge University Press, 1992), 34–37, and 48–50. See also Rothstein, *Den korporativa staten*, 305–31.

128. SAF, Minutes, Styrelsesammanträde 22 January 1920; "P.M. rörande oorganiserad arbetares förhållande under arbetskonflikt," December 1934 (SAF A555/20b); Rothstein, "Labor Market Institutions and Working Class Strength," 33.

129. SAF, Minutes, Ombudsmannakonferens, 13 February 1950.

130. Bo Rothstein, *The Social Democratic State*, 116–22. See also Rothstein, "AMS som socialdemokratisk reformbyråkrati," *Arkiv för studier i arbetarrörelsens historia* 18 (1982), 56–76; and Rothstein, *Den korporativa staten*, 175.

13. Legacies and Transformations

1. Michael Goldfield, *The Decline of Organized Labor in the United States* (Chicago: University of Chicago Press, 1987), 3–25; Garth Mangum and R. Scott McNabb, *The Rise, Fall, and Replacement of Industrywide Bargaining in the Basic Steel Industry* (Armonk, NY: M. E. Sharpe, 1997), 13–46; Charles R. Perry, *Collective Bargaining and the Decline of the United Mine Workers* (Philadelphia: The Wharton School, University of Pennsylvania, 1984), 78–79; David Previant, "Economic and Political Implications of the National Trucking Agreement of 1964," *Proceedings of New York University Seventeenth Annual Conference on Labor* (Washington, DC: BNA Incorporated, 1964), 285–86.

2. On American employers' begrudging accommodation of unions and surviving unilateral segmentalism during this period, see Howell Harris, *The Right to Manage* (Madison: University of Wisconsin Press, 1982), 129–39 and 198–99; Thomas Kochan, Harry C. Katz, and Robert B. McKersie, *The Transformation of American Industrial Relations* (New York: Basic, 1986), 13–15; Sanford Jacoby, *Modern Manors: Welfare Capitalism Since the New Deal* (Princeton: Princeton University Press), chapter 7.

3. Union membership and immigration in Sweden are discussed in chapter 11.

4. On wage drift from the mid-1950s into the 1980s, see Rudolf Meidner *Samordning och solidarisk lönepolitik* (Stockholm: Prisma, 1974), 45–46; Robert J. Flanagan, "Efficiency and Equality in Swedish Labor Markets," in Barry P. Bosworth and Alice M. Rivlin, eds., *The Swedish Economy* (Washington, DC: Brookings, 1987), 166–69.

5. Tommy Svensson, *Från ackord till månadslön— En studie av lönepolitiken, fackföreningarna och rationaliseringarna inom svensk varvsindustri under 1900-talet* (Stockholm: Svenska Varv, 1983), 344–45, discusses defection from solidarism in shipbuilding. On company level collusion, and LO complaints to SAF, see SAF, Minutes, Styrelse, 21 January 1971. For a report of a union leader's request that employers control wage drift—to illustrate a hysterical right-wing view of social democracy's oppressiveness—see Roland Huntford, *The New Totalitarians: A Terrifying Portrait of an "Ideal" Society That Has Destroyed Democracy* (New York: Stein and Day, 1972), 98–99. On Volvo and SAAB, see VF, Minutes, Överstyrelse, 21 September 1978.

6. Sanford Jacoby, "Employers and the Welfare State: The Role of Marion B. Folsom," *Journal of American History* 80:2 (September 1993), 525–27, 538, 551 (Folsom quote), and 554. The NAM quote is from *National Conference on Unemployment Compensation: Proceedings* (New York: National Association of Manufacturers, 1965), 15.

7. C. E. Wilson, "Pensions in Our Society: Excerpt from 'Economic Factors of Collective Bargaining,' a talk before the Chicago Executives Club, January 6, 1950," in Neil W. Chamberlain, ed., *Sourcebook on Labor* (New York: McGraw-Hill, 1958), 1001; Edwin E. Witte, "Organized Labor and Social Security," in Milton Derber and Edwin Young, eds., *Labor and the New Deal* (Madison: University of Wisconsin Press, 1957), 271; Nelson Lichtenstein, "From Corporatism to Collective Bargaining: Organized Labor and the Eclipse of Social Democracy in the Postwar Era," in Steve Fraser and Gary Gerstle, eds., *The Rise and Fall of the New Deal Order, 1930–*

1980 (Princeton: Princeton University Press, 1989), 122–52; Alan Derickson, "Health Security for All? Social Unionism and Universal Health Insurance 1935–1958," *Journal of American History* 80 (March 1994); Michael K. Brown, "Bargaining for Social Rights: Unions and the Reemergence of Welfare Capitalism, 1948–1952," *Political Science Quarterly* 112:4 (Winter 1997–1998). Also, employers saw fringe benefits as a way of forestalling social legislation. Donna Allen, *Fringe Benefits: Wages or Social Obligation? An Analysis with Historical Perspectives from Paid Vacations* (Ithaca, NY: Cornell University Press, 1969), 251–57.

8. Witte, "Organized Labor and Social Security," 264; Wilson, "Pensions in Our Society,"1001–2. The usual reason cited for broader business support was that OAI, being "contributory," made visible for workers a direct tradeoff between higher wages and higher federal benefits, thus slowing its growth in the long term. OAA, depending on general revenues from the federal government, lacked that feature. Businessmen were not, I believe, just being miserly toward retirees. They probably recognized that the faster OAA grew, the more irrational it became for them to provide company pensions. Another reason often given for big employer support is that steel and auto workers had just signed recent contracts in 1950 for company pensions guaranteeing the difference between OAI benefits and $100.00. This created a strong incentive for these industries to advocate increases in OAI taxes and benefits, and thus reductions in their contractual obligations. Well before this happened, however, Folsom had begun advocating increases. Also, corporate liberals in the Committee for Economic Development, the Chamber of Commerce, and a large part of the NAM's Social Security Committee were backing Folsom's early call for increases. The auto and steel makers' support was just icing on the cake. See Jill Quadagno, *The Transformation of Old Age Security: Class and Politics in the American Welfare State* (Chicago: University of Chicago, 1988), 162–68; Jacoby, "Employers and the Welfare State," 550–51; Frank Dobbin and Terry Boychuck, "Public Policy and the Rise of Private Pensions: The US Experience since 1930," in Michael Shalev, ed., *The Privatization of Social Policy? Occupational Welfare and the Welfare State in America, Scandinavia and Japan* (London: Macmillan, 1996), 120–21.

9. Jacoby, "Employers and the Welfare State," 548; Folsom, "Millions of Workers Still Lack Adequate Benefits," in Clarence C. Walton, ed., *Business and Social Progress: Views of Two Generations of Executives* (New York: Praeger, 1970), 98–99; Interview with Marion B. Folsom, June 1965 (New York: Columbia University Oral History Project, 1970), 76–77; Cathie Jo Martin, *Stuck in Neutral: Business and the Politics of Human Capital Formation* (Princeton: Princeton University Press, 2000), 228–31. John Myles makes a conventional "changing balance of power" argument about these increases, saying that it was business's loss of power in the 1960s and 1970s that opened the door to expansion of Social Security benefits. Here he assumes invariantly oppositional business interests, using as evidence the 1980s attacks on Social Security from business-financed right-wing think tanks. "Postwar Capitalism and the Extension of Social Security into a Retirement Wage," in Margaret Weir, Ann Shola Orloff, and Theda Skocpol, eds., *The Politics of Social Policy in the United States* (Princeton: Princeton University Press, 1988), 274–76.

10. Gøsta Esping-Andersen, *The Three Worlds of Welfare Capitalism* (Princeton: Princeton University Press, 1990), 157–58 and *Social Foundations of Postindustrial Economies* (Oxford: Oxford University Press, 1999), 78–81; Torben Iversen, "The Choices for Scandinavian Social Democracy in Comparative Perspective," *Oxford Review of Economic Policy* 14:1 (1998), 64; Sherwin Rosen, "Public Employment, Taxes, and the Welfare State in Sweden," in Richard B. Freeman, Robert Topel, and

Birgitta Swedenborg, eds., *The Welfare State in Transition: Reforming the Swedish Model* (Chicago: University of Chicago Press, 1997), 84–85.

11. Lars Svensson, "Politics for Gender Equality? The Impact of Welfare State Policies on the Position of Women in the Swedish Labour Market," *Lund Papers in Economic History* 49 (1995), 7–8, and *Closing the Gender Gap: Determinants of Change in the Female-to-Male Blue Collar Wage Ratio in Swedish Manufacturing 1913–1990* (Lund: Ekonomisk-historiska föreningen,1995), 141, 151–52; Jon Pierre, "Organized Capital and Local Politics: Local Business Organizations, Public-Private Committees, and Local Government in Sweden," *Urban Affairs Quarterly* 28:2 (December 1992), 248. For SAF's early views, overlapping with LO's, see SAF and LO, "Betänkande avgivet av arbetsmarknadskommitténs kvinnoutredning," (1951), Appendix to Arbetsmarknadskommittén, Minutes, 7–8 February 1951; Arbetsmarknadens Yrkesråd, *Kvinnorna som arbetskraftsresurs—En konferens i Saltsjöbaden den 17 December 1964* (Stockholm: SAF and LO, 1965).

12. Apparently, employer-supported economizing measures of the 1990s, discussed later, forced daughters of the elderly, especially poorer ones, to do more domestic caring work than had been done ten years earlier. This did not conform to the preferences of the elderly and often put stress on family budgets and relations. Sune Sunesson, Staffan Blomberg, Per Gunnar Edebalk, Lars Harrysson, Jan Magnusson, Anna Meeuwisee, Jan Petersson, and Tapio Saonen, "The Flight from Universalism," *European Journal of Social Work* 1:1 (1998), 25.

13. Feminist analyses disagree on the role of the women's movements, agree on the importance of the Swedish labor movement and its power for child care and related policies, and routinely ignore employer interests. See Jane Lewis, "Gender and the Development of Welfare Regimes," *Journal of European Social Policy* 2:3 (1992), 159–73; Rianne Mahon, "Child Care in Canada and Sweden: Policy and Politics," *Social Politics* 4:3 (Fall 1997), 382–415; Evelyne Huber and John D. Stephens, "Partisan Governance, Women's Employment, and the Social Democratic Welfare State," *American Sociological Review* 65:3 (June 2000), 323–42. On employers versus physicians, see Mark Carder and Bendix Klingeberg, "Toward a Salaried Medical Profession: How 'Swedish' Was the Seven Crowns Reform?" in Arnold J. Heidenheimer and Nils Elvander, eds., *The Shaping of the Swedish Health System* (London: Croom Helm, 1980), 163.

14. Fritz W. Scharpf, "The Viability of Advanced Welfare States in the International Economy: Vulnerabilities and Options," *Journal of European Public Policy* 7:2 (June 2000), 202; Siv Gustafsson, "Separate Taxation and Married Women's Labour Supply," *Journal of Population Economics* 5 (1992), 61–85; Lewis, "Gender and the Development of Welfare Regimes," 169; Svensson, *Closing the Gender Gap,* 115; Rosen, "Public Employment," 90.

15. For some economists' views on Sweden's "workfare state," see Richard B. Freeman, Robert Topel, and Birgitta Swedenborg, "Introduction," 23 (quote), and Anders Björklund and Richard B. Freeman, "Generating Equality and Eliminating Poverty, the Swedish Way," in Freeman, Topel, and Swedenborg, eds., *The Welfare State,* 48–49; Jonas Agell, "Why Sweden's Welfare State Needed Reform," *Economic Journal* 106 (November 1996), 1767.

16. Rothstein exclusively attributes employer representatives' budgetary largesse, which he discovered, only to the socializing effect, or mental entrapment, resulting from participation in corporatist administration, not to employer interests and their own socializing effects over time. Both may have been at work. Bo Rothstein, "State and Capital in Sweden: The Importance of Corporatist Arrangements," *Scandinavian Political Studies* 11:3 (1988), 235–60.

17. Perry, *Collective Bargaining*, 263; B. Drummond Ayres, "Though Coal Strike Spreads, Time Blunts the Weapon," *New York Times*, 22 June 1989; Michael H. Belzer, "The Motor Carrier Industry: Truckers and Teamsters Under Siege," in Paula B. Voos, ed., *Contemporary Collective Bargaining in the Private Sector* (Madison, WI: Industrial Relations Research Association, 1994), 259–302.

18. Charles Craypo, "Meatpacking: Industry Restructuring and Union Decline," 63–96; Harry Katz and John Paul MacDuffie, "Collective Bargaining in the U.S. Auto Assembly Sector," 181–224; Joel Cutcher-Gershenfeld and Patrick P. McHugh, "Collective Bargaining in the North American Auto Supply Industry," in Voos, ed., *Contemporary Collective Bargaining*, 225–48.

19. James Gross, *Broken Promise: The Subversion of U.S. Labor Relations Policy, 1947–1994* (Philadelphia: Temple University Press, 1995), especially 172–74. For the management view, see Guy Farmer, *Management Rights and Union Bargaining Power—An Assessment of Supreme Court and NLRB Decisions* (New York: Industrial Relations Counselors, 1965).

20. Guy Farmer, *Coalition Bargaining and Union Power* (New York: Industrial Relations Counselors, 1967).

21. Mangum and McNabb, *The Rise, Fall, and Replacement of Industrywide Bargaining*, 77–108; Katz and MacDuffie, "Collective Bargaining in the U.S. Auto Sector," in Voos, ed., *Contemporary Collective Bargaining*, 185–208.

22. Belzer, "The Motor Carrier Industry," in Voos, ed., *Contemporary Collective Bargaining*, 266–67, 279–86, and 92–94; Richard Hannah and Garth Mangum, *The Coal Industry and Its Industrial Relations* (Salt Lake City, UT: Olympus, 1985), 42–44.

23. Kim McQuaid, *Uneasy Partners: Big Business in American Politics 1945–1990* (Baltimore: Johns Hopkins University Press, 1994), 149.

24. Construction of GM's huge Vega and small truck plant in Lordstown caused construction wages in Ohio to peak at about 175 percent of engineering wages in 1972. On the CUAR, see Gross, *Broken Promise*, 234–36; Goldfield, *The Decline of Organized Labor*, 109–10, 191–92; McQuaid, *Uneasy Partners*, 149–50; *The Bargaining Structure in Construction: Problems and Prospects* (Washington, DC: U.S. Department of Labor, 1980), especially 20; Mangum and McNabb, *The Rise, Fall, and Replacement of Industrywide Bargaining*, 56, 63.

25. Quotes from Goldfield, *The Decline of Organized Labor*, 110, and Steven Allen, "Developments in Collective Bargaining in Construction in the 1980s and 1990s," in Voos, *Contemporary Collective Bargaining*, especially 425 and 430. See also McQuaid, *Uneasy Partners*, 149–50; *Bargaining Structure in Construction*, especially 20.

26. Paul Osterman, *Securing Prosperity: The American Labor Market, How It Has Changed, and What to Do about It* (Princeton: Princeton University Press, 1999), chapter 2; Peter Cappelli, *The New Deal at Work: Managing the Market-Driven Workforce* (Boston: Harvard Business School Press, 1999), 75–85.

27. David E. Bloom and Richard B. Freeman, "The Fall in Private Pension Coverage in the United States," *American Economic Review Papers and Proceedings* 82:2 (May 1992), 539–45; Ellen E. Schultz, "How a Single Sentence by IRS Paved the Way to Cash-Balance Plans," *Wall Street Journal*, 28 December 1999; David Cay Johnson, "Pension Funds Reverse Decade of Deterioration," *New York Times*, 30 November 1995.

28. Mark V. Pauly, *Health Benefits at Work: An Economic and Political Analysis of Employment-Based Health Insurance* (Ann Arbor: University of Michigan Press, 1997), 78–9; Mary Williams Walsh, "Factory Workers Fight the Squeeze on Health Benefits," *New York Times*, 25 October 2000; Milt Freudenheim, "Cuts in

Health Benefits Squeeze Retirees' Nest Eggs," *New York Times*, 31 December 2000; Mary Williams Walsh, "Reversing Decades-Long Trend, Americans Retiring Later in Life," *New York Times*, 26 February 2001. On the decline of "private welfare" generally, see also Michael B. Katz, *In the Shadow of the Poorhouse: A Social History of Welfare in America* (New York: Basic Books, 1996, revised edition), 317–21.

29. On the wage structure, see Douglas A. Hibbs, Jr., And Håkan Locking, *Wage Dispersion and Productive Efficiency: Evidence For Sweden*, Working Paper No. 128 (Stockholm: Trade Union Institute for Economic Research, 1996); Peter Swenson and Jonas Pontusson, "The Swedish Employer Offensive against Centralized Bargaining," in Torben Iversen, Jonas Pontusson, and David Soskice, eds., *Unions, Employers, and Central Banks: Macroeconomic Coordination and Institutional Change in Social Market Economies* (Cambridge: Cambridge University Press, 2000), 77–106.

30. For early reactions to wage compression within firms, the "most repugnant" of Metall's demands, see SAF, Minutes, Förbundsdirektörskonferens, 15 September, 13 October, and 17–18 November 1969, 30 April 1971, 20 June 1972, 12–13 November 1973, and 14 January, 22 April, and 14 October 1974; SAF, Minutes, Styrelse, 18 September 1969, 12 April and 15–16 November 1973, and 17 October 1974.

31. Initially at least, the SAF leadership disputed VF's views on the strong causal connection between interoccupational wage compression and disturbing levels of wage drift. SAF, Minutes, Styrelse, 16 January 1975 and 18 November 1976; Förbundsdirekörskonferens, 15 September, 20 October, and 17–18 November 1975; Arbetsutskott, 9 February 1976. The weak "power of resistance" displayed by the retail sector association (Handelns Arbetsgivareorganisationen), a problem since even before it joined SAF for extra strength, was particularly disturbing. SAF, Minutes, Styrelse, 11 February 1955.

32. SAF, Minutes, Förbundsdirekörskonferens, 20 June 1972, 18–19 November 1974, 20 October 1975, 17 October, 14–15 November, 15 August, and 12 December 1977; SAF, Minutes, Styrelse, 12 April 1973 and 15 December 1977; "Minnesanteckningar från sammanträde av SAFs och VFs styrelsers arbetsutskott," 2 June 1976; VF, Överstyrelsens grupp för förhandlingsfrågor, "Förhandlingsformerna," 3 December 1975, and VF, Minutes, Överstyrelse, 24 November 1977. See also Nils Elvander, *Den svenska modellen—Löneförhandlingar och inkomstpolitik, 1982–1986* (Stockholm: Almänna Förlaget, 1988), 94–98; Kristina Ahlén, "Swedish Collective Bargaining Under Pressure: Inter-union Rivalry and Incomes Policies," *British Journal of Industrial Relations* 27:3 (November 1989), 330–46; Andrew Martin, "Wage Bargaining and Swedish Politics: The Political Implications of the End of Central Negotiations," Working Paper No. 36 (Cambridge: Center for European Studies, Harvard University, 1991), 84–87.

33. For more detail on decentralization in the 1980s and 1990s, see Peter Swenson and Jonas Pontusson, "The Swedish Employer Offensive against Centralized Bargaining," in Iversen, et al., eds., *Unions, Employers, and Central Banks*, 77–106; Hans De Geer, *I vänstervind och högervåg—SAF under 1970-talet* (Stockholm: Almänna Förlaget, 1989); Nils Elvander and Bertil Holmlund, *The Swedish Bargaining System in the Melting Pot: Institutions, Norms and Outcomes in the 1990s* (Stockholm: Arbetslivsinstitutet, 1997); Anders Kjellberg, "Sweden: Restoring the Model?" in Anthony Ferner and Richard Hyman, *Changing Industrial Relations in Europe* (London: Blackwell, 1998), 84–92.

34. Hibbs and Locking, *Wage Dispersion and Productive Efficiency*. On negotiated pensions, see "New Scheme Enables Employees to Choose How Their Pension Contributions are Invested," www.eiro.eurofund.ie/1998/11/features (November 1998); "Pensionerna—Uppgörelse inom räckhåll," *SAF-tidningen*, 21 January 2000.

35. See especially Bernt Schiller, *"Det förödande 70-talet"—SAF och medbestämmandet 1965–1982* (Stockholm: Allmänna Förlaget, 1988).

36. On this aspect of the wage earner funds idea, see Peter Swenson, *Fair Shares: Unions, Pay, and Politics in Sweden and West Germany* (Ithaca, NY: Cornell University Press, 1989), 156–73. SAF's Per Martin Meyerson saw LO's motivation as "primarily motivated by the difficulty of pursuing solidaristic wage policy if excess profits arise." SAF, Minutes, Styrelse, 21–22 November 1974.

37. For more on SAF's retooling for political and ideological battle, see Sven Ove Hansson, *SAF i politiken—En dokumentation av näringslivsorganisationernas opinionsbildning* (Stockholm: Tiden, 1984).

38. For varying views, see Martin, "Wage Bargaining and Swedish Politics," 82–99; Michael Wallerstein and Miriam Golden, "Postwar Wage Setting in the Nordic Countries," in Iversen et al., eds., *Unions, Employers, and Central Banks*, 131–35; Bo Rothstein, "Trust, Social Dilemmas and Collective Memories: On the Rise and Decline of the Swedish Model," paper presented at the Twelfth International Conference of Europeanists, 30 March–1 April 2000; John Stephens, "Is Swedish Corporatism Dead? Thoughts on its Supposed Demise in the Light of the Abortive 'Alliance for Growth' in 1998," paper presented at the Twelfth International Conference of Europeanists, 30 March–1 April 2000.

39. SAF, Minutes, Styrelse, 20 March 1969, 18 September 1969, 18–19 November and 16 December 1971, and 17 February 1972; SAF, Minutes, Förbundsdirektörskonferens, 20–21 November 1969, 13 December 1971, and 17 January 1972. See also Schiller, *"Det förödande 70-talet,"* 30.

40. Willis J. Nordlund, *The Quest for a Living Wage: The History of the Federal Minimum Wage Program* (Westport, CT: Greenwood, 1997), 238; Christopher Howard, *The Hidden Welfare State: Tax Expenditures and Social Policy in the United States* (Princeton: Princeton University Press, 1997), 184.

41. Sar Levitan, Garth L. Mangum, and Stephen L. Mangum, *Programs in Aid of the Poor,* 7th ed. (Baltimore: Johns Hopkins, 1998), 94–95; Paul Pierson, *Dismantling the Welfare State: Reagan, Thatcher, and the Politics of Retrenchment* (Cambridge: Cambridge University Press, 1994), 66–67; R. Kent Weaver, "Ending Welfare As We Knew It," in Margaret Weir, ed., *The Social Divide: Political Parties and the Future of Activist Government* (Washington, DC: Brookings, 1998), 361–416.

42. On the EBRI and the growth and political robustness of tax expenditures for the "private" or "hidden" welfare state, see Howard, *The Hidden Welfare State,* 9–10, 133, and 175–88. On Democrats, see Adam Clymer, "Clinton Cool to Democrats' Ideas on Workers," *New York Times,* 29 February 1996.

43. The NLCHCR proposed a European-style tripartite rate- setting board composed of representatives from business, labor, and the government. The board was to have the power to set health care billing rates with the force of law and set a cap on overall expenditures. On the NLCHCR, see Frank Swoboda, "Major Firms, Unions Join in National Health Insurance Bid," *Washington Post,* 14 March 1990; Robert Pear, "Corporations and Unions Propose Tax to Pay for Health Insurance," *New York Times,* 13 November 1991; "Comprehensive Health Care Reform and Managed Competition," *New England Journal of Medicine* 327 (1992), 1525–28. On the benefits managers and other evidence for business support, see Cathie Jo Martin, "Together Again: Business, Government, and the Quest for Cost Control," *Journal of Health Politics, Policy, and Law* 18:2 (Summer 1993), 360–92, and *Stuck in Neutral,* 94–105.

44. An excellent account is David Broder and Haynes Johnson, *The System: The American Way of Politics at the Breaking Point* (Boston: Little, Brown, 1997).

45. For a full presentation of this argument, see Peter Swenson and Scott Greer, "Foul Weather Friends: Big Business and Health Care Reform in the 1990s in Historical Perspective," *Journal of Health Politics, Policy and Law* 27:4 (August 2002), 605–38. See also Broder and Johnson, *The System*, 325–26; James K. Glassman, "Is the Government's Health Care Cure Really Needed?" *Washington Post*, 7 January 1994; David Hilzenrath, "Trends Cost Health Plan Some Political Punch," *Washington Post*, 24 January 1994; Steven Pearlstein, "Big Business Has Gone to Sidelines in Health Care Debate," *Washington Post*, 3 August 1994.

46. Evelyne Huber and John D. Stephens, "Internationalization and the Social Democratic Model: Crisis and Future Prospects," *Comparative Political Studies* 31:3 (June 1998), 378–84; Scharpf, "The Viability of Advanced Welfare States," 199.

47. For various details, see John D. Stephens, "The Scandinavian Welfare States: Achievements, Crisis, and Prospects," in Gøsta Esping-Andersen, *Welfare States in Transition: National Adaptations in Global Economies* (London: Sage, 1996), 45–48; Sunesson et al., "The Flight from Universalism," 23–24; Mats Benner and Torben Bundgaard Vad, "Sweden and Denmark: Defending the Welfare State," in Fritz W. Scharpf and Vivien A. Schmidt, eds., *Welfare and Work in the Open Economy, Volume II: Diverse Responses to Common Challenges* (Oxford: Oxford University Press, 2000).

48. *Pensionsreformen—Slutrapport juni 1998* (Stockholm: Socialdepartementet, 1998).

49. On common pressures for austerity, see Paul Pierson, "Coping with Permanent Austerity: Welfare State Restructuring in Affluent Democracies," in Pierson, ed., *The New Politics of the Welfare State* (Oxford: Oxford University Press, 2001), 410–56. For data on public sector employment, see Iversen, "Choices for Scandinavian Social Democracy," 64, and Scharpf, "The Viability of Advanced Welfare States," 216.

50. On the new cross-class alliance, see Peter Swenson, "Labor and the Limits of the Welfare State: The Politics of Intraclass Conflict and Cross-Class Alliances in Sweden and West Germany," *Comparative Politics* 23:4 (July 1991), 379–99; Herman Schwartz, "Small States in Big Trouble: State Reorganization in Australia, Denmark, New Zealand, and Sweden in the 1980s," *World Politics* 46:4 (July 1994), 525–55. For the view that the class politics of welfare state development are profoundly different from the politics of retrenchment, and a critique, see Paul Pierson, "The New Politics of the Welfare State," *World Politics* 48:2 (1996), 143–79; Richard Clayton and Jonas Pontusson, "Welfare-State Retrenchment Revisited: Entitlement Cuts, Public Sector Restructuring, and Inegalitarian Trends in Advanced Capitalist Societies," *World Politics* 51:1 (October 1998), 67–98.

51. Karl Polanyi, *The Great Transformation: The Political and Economic Origins of Our Time* (Boston: Beacon Press, 1957 [1944]), 152–55; Jon Elster, *The Cement of Society: A Study of Social Order* (Cambridge: Cambridge University Press, 1989).

52. Polanyi, *The Great Transformation*, 146–56, 235–37, 251–57.

53. Polanyi, *The Great Transformation*, 162.

54. Comparative analyses of capitalist interests in social policy are just now beginning to appear. See, for example, Isabela Mares, "Strategic Alliances and Social Policy Reform: Unemployment Insurance in Comparative Perspective," *Politics and Society* 28:2 (June 2000), 223–44, and "Firms and the Welfare State: When, Why, and How Does Social Policy Matter to Employers?" in Peter Hall and David Soskice, eds., *Varieties of Capitalism: Institutional Foundations of Comparative Advantage* (New York: Cambridge University Press, 2001); Duane Swank and Cathie Jo Martin, "Employers and the Welfare State: The Political Economic Organization of Employ-

ers and Social Policy in Contemporary Capitalist Democracies," *Comparative Political Studies* 34:8 (October 2001), 889–923; Philip Manow, "Business Coordination, Wage Bargaining and the Welfare State: Germany and Japan in Comparative Historical Perspective," in Bernhard Ebbinghaus and Philip Manow, eds., *The Varieties of Welfare Capitalism: Social Policy and Political Economy in Europe* (London: Routledge, 2001), 27–51; Manow, "When Labour and Capital Collude: The Political Economy of Early Retirement in Europe, Japan, and the USA," in Ebbinghaus and Manow, eds., *Varieties of Welfare Capitalism*, 76–101. Excellent analyses of the role of employer interests in the shaping of vocational training systems are Margarita Estevez-Abe, Torben Iversen, and David Soskice, "Social Protection and the Formation of Skills: A Reinterpretation of the Welfare State," in Hall and Soskice, eds., *Varieties of Capitalism*, 145–83; Kathleen Thelen and Ikuo Kume, "The Rise of Nonmarket Training Regimes: Germany and Japan Compared," *Journal of Japanese Studies* 25:1 (1999), 33–64; Thelen, *How Institutions Evolve: The Political Economy of Skills in Comparative-Historical Perspective*, manuscript, Northwestern University, 2001.

INDEX

Boston, 154, 178, 235
Boulware, Lemuel, 48, 332–33n6
Bowman, John, 328n19
boycotts, 75, 103, 114, 258
Boytons Arbetsbyrå, 115
Brains Trust, 221
Brandeis, Elizabeth, 202, 232–33
Brandeis, Louis, 154, 167, 200, 202, 229
Brandes, Stuart, 68
Brandle, Theodore, 162
Bratt, Lennart, 124, 132, 256, 391n39
breweries. *See* beverage industry
Bridge and Structural Iron Workers' Union, 162
Brindell, Robert, 163
Brodén, Erik, 273, 285, 398n72
Brody, David, 50, 68, 165, 166
Brotherhood of Carpenters, 164
Browaldh, Ernfrid, 290, 399n96
Browaldh, Tore, 273, 281, 283, 290–91, 399n93
Brown, J. Douglas, 207–08, 212
Brunius, Axel, 76, 126
Bryce, James, 4
Buffalo, 178
Builders' Association of Detroit, 176
Building and Construction Trades Department, AFL, 182
building and construction, 101–02, 181, 310; in-house, 103, 180, 347n11; in Sweden, 15, 73, 76, 86, 91, 93, 99–120, 122, 124, 126, 130–33, 137, 139–40, 142, 175, 250–51, 254–55, 258–59, 278, 282, 286, 298, 342n34, 346n4, 347n12, 402n125; in the United States, 15, 22, 42, 61, 73, 144–45, 153, 168–72, 175–76, 180, 185–86, 215, 228, 235–36, 299, 308, 310, 406n24
Building Industry Employers'Association (BIF), Swedish, 110–11, 119
Building Masters' Association (BMF), Swedish, 86, 104–05, 107
Building Materials Association, Swedish, 92
building materials industry, 86, 107, 128, 278, 342n48, 366n25
Bunting, Earl, 186

Burns, James MacGregor, 223
Business Advisory Council (BAC), 200, 204–05, 227, 235
business confidence, 238
business cycle. *See* macro-economic conditions
Business Roundtable, 310
Business Week, 224
busing. *See* transportation industry
buyers' cartel. *See* monopsony

California, 198, 206, 235
California Metal and Mineral Producers' Association, 210
Canada, 205, 318
canning industry, 198, 379n68
capital mobility, 238–39
career mobility, interclass, 132, 149–50, 152, 155, 162
Carnegie, Andrew, 188
Carnegie Steel, 50
Carpenter, Jesse, 153–54, 156–58, 166
cartelism, 14–15, 21–24; negotiated, 21–24, 28, 36–37, 39–40, 42, 168, 201, 237; segmentalist opposition to, 187; in Sweden, 159, 254, 390n29; unilateral, 24, 49, 53, 65, 159, 162, 165; in the United States, 43, 49, 53, 63, 217–18, 142–66, 168, 187, 217–18, 303, 308; vulnerabilities of, 187–88, 194, 220
cash balance plans, 311
Casparsson, Ragnar, 80–81, 115
Castles, Francis, 296
CCF. *See* Central Competitive Field
Center Party, Swedish. *See* Agrarian Party
central bank, Swedish, 289
Central Competitive Field (CCF), 147, 148
Central Employers' Association, Swedish, 91
centralized collective bargaining, 4, 15, 19–20, 23, 28–29, 32, 35, 39–40; legal prohibition of, 185–86; multi-industry, 120–21, 123–33; in Sweden, 42, 72, 78, 82, 84–88, 140, 186–87, 304, 313–14; in the United States, 49, 51–54, 143–47, 151, 172, 185, 218–19, 303, 308, 324n10

immigration, 77, 146, 153, 160, 187, 250, 257, 304; restriction of, 187–88, 248, 370n57, 370n58
Immigration Act of 1924, 188
impartial machinery, 154–57
Impartial Wage Board, San Francisco, 162
implicit contracts, 27, 330n37
IMU. *See* International Molders' Union
incentive pay. *See* performance pay
income taxation, 307
income testing. *See* means testing
independents, steel industry, 51
Indiana, 146–47
Indianapolis, 62
Industrial Association of San Francisco, 176
Industrial Bureau of Philadelphia, 235
Industrial Relations Counselors (IRC), 57, 68, 205–08, 222, 234, 375n41, 376n45
industrial unionism, 181–83
industry-wide bargaining. *See* centralized collective bargaining
Inland Steel, 318
Inland Steel case, 184
inside manufacturers, 157, 202
Institute for Industrial Research, Swedish (IUI), 245
institutional equilibrium, 35, 37, 141
institutionalism, 8–9, 14, 16, 127, 130, 222–37, 238, 240, 244, 293–94, 381n7, 400n110
institutions, 4–5, 7, 14, 22, 321
instrumentalism, 240, 242–43
insurance industry, 208, 213, 230, 272, 318
internal labor markets, 26, 48
International Association of Bridge and Structural Iron Workers (IABSIW), 177–78
International Association of Machinists (IAM), 53, 79
International Brotherhood of Teamsters, 186, 303
international cartels, 94, 380n79
international competition. *See* product market competition, international
international forces, 16, 77, 84, 277, 309–12, 322

International Harvester, 56, 58, 66–68, 171, 176, 180, 205, 209, 376n41, 377n51
internationalists, 240
International Ladies' Garment Workers' Union (ILGWU), 154–55
International Molders' Union (IMU), 51–53, 79, 146
International Paper, 318
intersectoral conflict, 90, 101–06, 162, 175–82, 253, 310
investment control, 289–92, 309, 315
Iowa, 146
IRC. *See* Industrial Relations Counselors
Iron Age, 66, 188, 210
Iron and Steel Industry Employers' Association, Swedish (JBF), 83, 95
iron industry, 49, 50, 73, 252
iron ore mining, 92–94, 100, 104, 120, 151
Irving National Bank, 56
Isacson, Mats, 136
Italy, 77
IUI. *See* Institute for Industrial Research
Iveroth, Axel, 399n96
Iversen, Torben, 324n5, 410n54

Jacksonville Agreement, 150
Jacobsson, Carl, 399n96
Jacobsson, Gunnar, 88
Jacoby, Sanford, 48, 55–56, 59, 68–69, 192, 204, 209, 220, 231
James River, 318
Japan, 36, 310
JBF. *See* Iron and Steel Industry Employers' Association, Swedish
Jeffrey Manufacturing, 170
jewelry industry, 236
J. I. Case Company, 203
job control unionism, 48
job creation measures, 76, 109–12, 160–61, 349n39
job evaluation, 124, 170, 172–73, 183
job hopping, 80, 170, 250, 259, 288
Johansson, Albin, 358n3
Johansson, Edvard, 97
Johnson & Johnson, 200, 216
Johnson, Lyndon B., 309

Johnson, Robert Wood, 200, 216
Johnston, Eric A., 224
jurisdictional disputes, 181–82, 239

Kansas City, 178–79
Katz, Michael, 243
Kellgren, Nils, 139
Kempe, Carl, 71–72, 74
Kempe, Erik, 397n63
Kennedy, John F., 309, 328n12
Kentucky, 148
Kerr, Clark, 173
Keynes, John Maynard, 38
Keynesian policy, 26, 206, 230, 295, 376n44, 400n110
Kirstein, Louis, 200
Klug, Thomas, 176
Knights of Labor, 146–47
Kockums, 95, 128
Kodak, 19, 48, 59, 69, 180, 183–84, 203–04, 213, 237, 241–42, 254, 303–04, 311
Kohler, 59
Kolko, Gabriel, 372n13
Korean War, 128, 277
Korpi, Walter, 294–96, 401n112
Krueger, Alan, 330n35
Kugelberg, Bertil, 123, 125, 128, 131–36, 139, 246, 252, 268, 275, 278, 281, 283–84, 286–87, 290–92, 315, 328n12, 395n41
Kull, George, 203
Kume, Ikuo, 410n54

Labor Court, Swedish, 106, 138, 347n11
labor exchanges, 33, 80, 89, 156, 259–60, 277, 280, 296–97, 341n22
labor hoarding, 137
Labor Law Study Group (LLSG), 310
Labor Market Board, Swedish (AMS), 275, 279–80
labor market competition, 21, 25, 29–35, 40–41; in Sweden, 86, 90–91, 103, 133, 135, 140, 158, 250, 286–87, 392n63; in the United States, 169, 172
labor militancy. See strikes
labor mobility, 31, 34; effects of social insurance on, 254, 259–60; 288–89; frictional versus structural,

288; international, 77, 146; intersectoral, 131, 146, 355n26, 361n47; promotion of, 259–60, 274–76; in Sweden, 85, 91, 111, 135, 250, 252, 260, 278, 288; in the United States, 160–61, 169–70, 173–74, 179; wartime restriction of, 171, 173
labor productivity, 28, 33, 39, 42, 54, 56, 77–79, 134, 136, 158, 284, 336n43, 355n27
labor rationing, 31, 33, 279–80
labor scarcity, 29, 33–34, 37; in Sweden, 77, 80, 85, 88, 104, 120, 125, 128, 137, 139, 141, 164, 184, 248–50, 253, 256–58, 261, 263–64, 266–67, 270–71, 280, 286, 304; in the United States, 42, 52, 168, 171–74, 179
labor supply, 22, 26, 28, 33–34, 36, 40–41, 58, 98, 170, 298, 308, 316, 276
labor surplus, 38, 146; in the United States, 62, 137, 151, 164, 187, 248
LaFollette, Philip F., 202
LaFollette, Robert M. Jr., 64, 175, 179, 231
Lamont, Thomas, 219
Landrum-Griffin Act, 187
Larson, Ivar, 99, 107, 116, 118
Larsson, Gunnar, 128–29, 135, 252
Larsson, Matts Bergom, 135, 279–80, 285
Latimer, Murray, 58, 68, 208, 336n43, 375n40, 383n25, 383n27
laundries, 174, 198, 211
layoff notice, 113
Lazear, Edward, 356n43
leather industry, 73, 76, 129, 246
Leeds, Morris, 204, 227
Leeds & Northrup, 55, 204
legitimate manufacturers. See inside manufacturers
Lehman, Herbert H., 152, 202, 236, 243, 374n29
Leiserson, William, 158
Leuchtenberg, William, 222
Lewis, John L., 149–50, 181, 186, 215, 218–19, 359n18, 368n41
Lewis, Tom, 149–50
Lewis, William, 150

political class struggle. *See* power

political initiative taking, 21, 37, 41, 193–94, 223, 243, 293, 300, 321–22, 372n13, 387n65

Pontusson, Jonas, 326n29, 400n99, 409n50

popular mobilization, 12, 37–40, 193–94, 219, 238, 306, 321–22

post facto support, 191–94, 196–202, 243

power, 24, 35, 123, 145, 165, 282, 293–300, 326n28, 354n16, 405n13; balance of, 16, 18, 269, 293, 296, 316, 326–27n33, 404n9; measurement of, 10, 13, 76; resources, 4, 65, 76, 295, 298, 323n3, 323n4, 401n112; short-term, 24, 312; sectoral, 238; structural, 238; theorization about, 4, 7–10, 269, 316

prevailing wage law, 188. *See also* Davis-Bacon Act

prevention idea, 226, 228

Princeton University, 207

printing industry, 76, 150, 177, 341n20

Procter and Gamble, 48, 59, 68, 303, 336n52

productivity, 28, 33, 39, 54, 56, 77–79, 134, 136, 158, 284, 336n43, 355n27

product market competition, 21–24, 36–40, 239–42, 249; international, 77, 94, 98, 101–02, 104, 111, 120, 151, 204, 241, 248–49, 254, 280, 309–13, 316–20, 354n21; in Sweden, 158, 249, 266, 342n36; in the United States, 42–43, 49–50, 52, 60, 147–49, 153, 163–65, 195–97, 199, 203–05, 208, 211–12, 216, 233, 239–42, 267, 317, 333n11

profit sharing, 27, 55, 69, 134

progressive era, 12, 198, 201, 372n13

protectionism, 110–13, 151

Protocol of Peace, 154, 157

public sector, 96, 102, 264–65, 298, 307, 312, 320

public works, 241

Public Works Administration, 386n57

purchasing power, 66–67, 70, 106, 118, 200, 206–07, 214, 239, 266, 338n91, 339n3, 348n21

Pure Milk Products Cooperative, Wisconsin, 202

Quadagno, Jill, 19, 385n41, 385n43

Quaker Oats, 318

quarrying, 73, 246, 254, 390n28

race. *See* blacks

racketeering. *See* corruption

railroads, 96, 112, 169, 214

Railway Labor Act of 1926, 214

Rand, James, 206

Raskob, John, 204

rationing of credit, 289, 399n86

rationing of labor, 26, 31, 33–34, 41, 173, 278–80, 300

Raushenbush, Paul, 202, 232–33

Reagan, Ronald, 317

recession. *See* macro-economic conditions

recruitment of labor, 38, 80, 89, 168, 171

Reed, David A, 188

regularization of employment, 55–56, 203, 229. *See also* experience rating

regulation, 12, 14, 21–22, 320–22, 372n13; business interests in, 12, 14, 21–24, 30–34, 39, 196, 239–40; social insurance as, 39, 188, 194, 201–13, 226–27, 234, 240, 242–43, 317, 322, 326n31, 374n27; unions' role in, 34–35, 39–40, 51, 73, 152, 155, 166, 196, 219; Wagner Act's function in, 219, 378n66

Rehn, Gösta, 123–25, 275–76, 278–90, 355–56n38

Rehn-Meidner model, 11, 123, 275, 277

relationship-specific investments, 39, 332n57

relief jobs. *See* job creation measures

Remington Rand, 206

rent sharing, 27

Republican Party, 143–44, 150–53, 160–61, 188, 199, 242, 318, 377n54

reserve jobs. *See* job creation measures

retail industry, 22, 159, 198, 206, 209, 217, 235–36, 239, 241, 246

retirement insurance. *See* old age insurance

sick pay, 9, 11, 19–20, 270–73, 319
Skandinaviska Banken, 106, 281
Skånska Cement, 82, 119, 128
SKF, 102, 133, 136
skilled labor, 22, 27, 31, 34, 41, 52,
    78–79, 102
Skocpol, Theda, 8, 9, 11, 16, 198,
    222–23, 244, 294, 386n50,
    400n110
Sköld, Per-Edvin, 126, 132, 276–77,
    287
Skromberga conflict, 108
Slichter, Sumner, 56, 67, 329n28,
    330n37, 336n44
Sloan, Alfred, 17, 48, 66
Smith, Adam, 25, 328n23
Smith, Alfred E., 202
social democracy, 43, 100, 133, 246,
    262,
Social Democratic government,
    Swedish, 161, 245, 249–50, 255,
    259–60, 262, 270, 274, 277,
    292–93, 297, 315, 319; fiscal
    conservatism of, 270–71; legislation
    of, 15, 110, 246, 253–54, 259–63,
    266–67, 270–71, 273–74, 281–82,
    285, 287, 307; relations with
    Conservatives, 281; view on
    solidaristic wage policy, 126; wage
    bargaining interventions of, 107,
    117–18, 131
Social Democratic labor movement, 4,
    16, 20, 73, 78, 110, 121, 182, 267,
    280, 293, 299
Social Democratic Party, Swedish, 6, 9,
    11–12, 16, 73, 112, 131, 142–43,
    246, 260, 269–70, 281, 286–89,
    291, 294, 296, 298, 300, 315, 319;
    rise to power of, 98, 100, 262, 269
social democratic welfare regimes, 267,
    306, 320
Socialdemokraten, 109
Social Science Research Council
    (SSRC), 206, 212, 234–35
Social Security. *See* old age insurance,
    in the United States
Social Security Act (SSA), 5, 13,
    191–92, 196, 219, 221, 226, 230,
    232, 246, 317; business views on,
    206–13, 220–21; institutionalist

explanation of, 222–37; NAM on
    191–92;
Social Security Administration, 235
Social Security reserve fund, 191, 230
Söderbäck, Fritiof, 120, 251, 253, 264,
    272, 288
Söderlund, Gustaf, 21, 41–42,
    72, 97, 106–10, 112, 116–18,
    120, 134, 255–57, 261, 269–70,
    277–78, 281, 283, 288, 295, 315,
    395n37
Söderlund, Hans, 20–21, 41–42,
    124–25, 127, 130
Söderpalm, Sven Anders, 87, 295,
    401n114
soldiering, 137
solidarism, 14, 21, 29–37, 40–41, 71;
    and market disequilibrium, 129;
    negotiated, 34–35, 43, 87; and
    performance pay, 138; repudiation
    of, 312, 314; in Sweden, 42, 72,
    79–80, 85, 87, 90, 98, 115, 248,
    288, 304, 312; unilateral, 34,
    88–89, 251–53, 283, 363n69; in the
    United States, 165, 167–75; violation
    of, 92, 249, 398n74; vulnerability of,
    71, 77; and welfare state, 40–41,
    140–41, 260, 274
solidaristic wage policy, 10, 19, 32, 118,
    120, 140, 280; excess profits
    resulting from, 314; origins of, 121,
    123–27, 352n61, 353n2; postwar
    development of, 121–27; radicalized,
    121, 312, 315; wage restraint in
    exchange for, 121, 127, 269
Solow, Robert, 38, 329n23
Soskice, David, 332n57, 410n54
Southern California Edison, 318
Southern states, 308, 229–30, 241,
    263, 308–09, 373n24, 383–84n27
Soviet Union, 345n91
Special Conference Committee (SCC),
    56, 66, 205
SPIAF. *See* Swedish Paper Industry
    Workers' Union
spies, 54, 64
sports, 174–75
SSA. *See* Social Security Act
SSRC. *See* Social Science Research
    Council